# I CHRONICLES
# 10–29

VOLUME 12A

THE ANCHOR BIBLE is a fresh approach to the world's greatest classic. Its object is to make the Bible accessible to the modern reader; its method is to arrive at the meaning of biblical literature through exact translation and extended exposition, and to reconstruct the ancient setting of the biblical story, as well as the circumstances of its transcription and the characteristics of its transcribers.

THE ANCHOR BIBLE is a project of international and interfaith scope: Protestant, Catholic, and Jewish scholars from many countries contribute individual volumes. The project is not sponsored by any ecclesiastical organization and is not intended to reflect any particular theological doctrine. Prepared under our joint supervision, THE ANCHOR BIBLE is an effort to make available all the significant historical and linguistic knowledge which bears on the interpretation of the biblical record.

THE ANCHOR BIBLE is aimed at the general reader with no special formal training in biblical studies; yet it is written with the most exacting standards of scholarship, reflecting the highest technical accomplishment.

This project marks the beginning of a new era of cooperation among scholars in biblical research, thus forming a common body of knowledge to be shared by all.

*William Foxwell Albright*
*David Noel Freedman*
GENERAL EDITORS

THE ANCHOR BIBLE

# I CHRONICLES 10–29

A New Translation
with Introduction and Commentary

GARY N. KNOPPERS

THE ANCHOR BIBLE
Doubleday
New York London Toronto Sydney Auckland

THE ANCHOR BIBLE
PUBLISHED BY DOUBLEDAY
a division of Random House, Inc.
1745 Broadway, New York, New York 10019



LIBRARY OF CONGRESS CATALOGING-IN-PUBLICATION DATA
Bible. O.T. Chronicles X–XXIX, 1st. English. Knoppers. 2004.
I Chronicles 10–29: a new translation with introduction and commentary /
Gary Knoppers.—1st ed.
p. cm. (The Anchor Bible; v. 12A)
Includes bibliographical references and indexes.
1. Bible. O.T. Chronicles, 1st—Commentaries. I. Title: 1 Chronicles.
II. Title: First Chronicles. III. Knoppers, Gary N., 1956– . IV. Title.
V. Bible. English. Anchor Bible. 1964; v. 12A.
BS192.2.A1 1964 .G3 vol. 12A
[BS1345.53]
222'.63077—dc22 2003055813

ISBN 0-385-51288-0


Printed in the United States of America
July 2004

First Edition

10 9 8 7 6 5 4 3 2 1

*To my daughter Theresa and*
*my son David* (Prov 17:1)

# CONTENTS

# PREFACE

◆

In writing a commentary on Chronicles at the end of the twentieth century and at the beginning of the twenty-first century C.E., I stand in a very privileged position. The scholarly world has devoted much closer attention to the Persian era (538–332 B.C.E.) in the past three decades than in any other modern period that I am aware of. The bibliography in this volume attests to the keen interest contemporary scholars have exhibited in the Neo-Babylonian, Achaemenid, and Hellenistic eras. Scholars have come to view these periods, rightly in my judgment, to be more formative in the composition and editing of many biblical works than previous generations recognized. The careful attention devoted to the Persian period also holds true for the book of Chronicles. Long neglected by commentators, this work is finally being given its due. I would like to acknowledge the work of several influential scholars in particular. Sara Japhet, Thomas Willi, and Hugh Williamson have provided the scholarly community with insightful and stimulating treatments of the Chronicler's distinctive compositional technique. It is not too much of an exaggeration to say that these scholars have changed the way that we perceive the nature and theological relevance of the Chronicler's work. Pat Graham and Kai Peltonen have performed a real service in providing the scholarly community with detailed histories of Chronicles' interpretation and its relevance to the interpretation of the Pentateuch and the Former Prophets. Isaac Kalimi has compiled a comprehensive bibliography and provided an incisive analysis of the Chronicler's literary craft. The Chronicles-Ezra-Nehemiah section of the Society of Biblical Literature has always proved to be an exciting and supportive context to try out new ideas. John Wright, Steven McKenzie, and Tyler Williams kindly read earlier versions of my introduction and excursus on the genealogies. Ehud Ben Zvi and Bernie Levinson have always been willing to critique anything I write. Francis Andersen drew up a convenient computer-generated Hebrew concordance of Chronicles for my work, while Dean Forbes furnished me with a detailed word count for every chapter in the book.

Other scholars have directly and indirectly contributed to the preparation of this volume. Ray Dillard first piqued my interest in the Chronicler's writing during an end session course he taught at Gordon-Conwell Seminary in the early 1980s. Frank Cross, Tom Lambdin, Bill Moran, Paul Hanson, Michael Coogan, and James Kugel were excellent teachers and mentors during my graduate training at Harvard. I am especially indebted to Frank Cross for his invaluable guidance during the course of writing my dissertation. My current colleagues at Penn

State have been very helpful in aiding my research. John Betlyon, Baruch Halpern, and Paul Harvey supplied me with helpful critiques of my introduction. Ann Killebrew has been a valuable resource for my work with material remains. Don Redford has proved to be a handy consultant on all matters Egyptological, while Phil Baldi, Deborah Beck, David Engel, Garrett Fagan, Stephen Wheeler, and Mark Munn have been handy consultants on all matters Classical. For help in the New Testament and the Patristics, I always turn to my colleagues Bill Petersen and Paul Harvey. Three graduate students, Eugene Shaw Colyer, Deirdre Fulton, and Jeffrey Veenstra, proofread parts of the manuscript.

The completion of the first installment of a two-volume set on 1 and 2 Chronicles is an appropriate time to express one's sincere gratitude to those institutes and libraries that have made the research for this book possible. The Institute for the Arts and Humanities and the Research and Graduate Studies Office of the College of the Liberal Arts (both at Penn State) awarded me with timely travel to collection grants to aid my studies. The Oxford Centre for Hebrew and Jewish Studies graciously bestowed upon me a fellowship during my sabbatical year of 1995–96. The kind support of the staff and faculty of the Centre were of enormous help to me as I conducted the research for this commentary. At Penn State, Roberta Astroff and Daniel Mack have made tremendous strides in improving the quality of the library's collections. At Anchor Doubleday, Andrew Corbin has enthusiastically pushed this project to publication. I am also appreciative of the work of Siobhan Dunn, John Kohlenberger, and Leslie Phillips on this project. The general editor of the Anchor Bible, David Noel Freedman, represents an extraordinary combination of creativity and sensitivity to detail. I have never worked with an editor of his caliber, and I doubt that I shall ever again. Over the course of writing this volume, Noel provided me with over three hundred pages of commentary on my commentary. For this studious attention to matters both large and small in my work, I am truly grateful.

Finally, I would like to express my thanks to family members for their positive influence upon my work. During the course of my upbringing, my parents, Ms. Barthie Maria Boon Knoppers and Rev. Nicolaas Bastiaan Knoppers, communicated a profound love for the Old Testament within the larger context of the Dutch Reformed tradition. My wife, Laura, and our children, Theresa and David, have always encouraged my studies. When I began writing this commentary over nine years ago, I could scarcely imagine how much time and labor would be needed to complete the project. My family's patience, understanding, and unfailing support were invaluable as I slowly worked my way through the genealogies as well as the rest of my work on one of the longest books in the Hebrew Bible.

Gary Knoppers
*University Park, Pa.*

# ABBREVIATIONS

◆

REFERENCE WORKS in biblical and ancient Near Eastern studies dealing with grammar, lexicon, and primary sources. In the text citations, most are organized by paragraph or section, rather than by page number.

| | |
|---|---|
| Aharoni | Yohanan Aharoni, *Arad Inscriptions*. JDS. Jerusalem: Israel Exploration Society, 1981. |
| AP | A. Cowley, *Aramaic Papyri of the Fifth Century B.C.* Oxford: Clarendon Press, 1923. Repr. Osnabrück: Otto Zeller, 1967. |
| *ARAB, I (II)* | Daniel David Luckenbill, *Ancient Records of Assyria and Babylonia*. Vol. 1: *Historical Records of Assyria from the Earliest Times to Sargon. Ancient Records of Assyria and Babylonia*. Vol. 2: *Historical Records of Assyria from Sargon to the End*. Chicago: Chicago University Press, 1926–1927. |
| *ARI* | A. K. Grayson, *Assyrian Royal Inscriptions*. 2 vols. Records of the Ancient Near East 2. Wiesbaden: Otto Harrassowitz, 1972–1976. |
| ARM(T) | *Archives royales de Mari (Textes)*, Paris, 1946– . |
| BBSt | L. W. King, *Babylonian Boundary-Stones and Memorial Tablets in the British Museum*. London: Oxford University Press, 1912. |
| Beckman | Gary M. Beckman, *Hittite Diplomatic Texts*. Writings from the Ancient World 7. Atlanta: Scholars Press, 1996. |
| BP | E. G. Kraeling, *The Brooklyn Museum Aramaic Papyri: New Documents of the Fifth Century B.C. from the Jewish Colony at Elephantine*. New Haven: Yale University Press, 1953. |
| Cole and Machinist | Stephen Cole and Peter Machinist, *Letters from Priests to the Kings Esarhaddon and Assurbanipal*. SAA 13. Helsinki: Helsinki University Press, 1998. |
| *CTA* | A. Herdner, *Corpus des tablettes en cunéiformes alphabétique découvertes à Ras Shamra-Ugarit de 1929 à 1939*. Mission de Ras Shamra 10, 2 vols. Paris: Imprimerie Nationale, 1963. |
| *CTU* | Manfred O. Dietrich, O. Loretz, and J. Sanmartín, *The Cuneiform Alphabetic Texts from Ugarit, Ras Ibn Hani and Other Places*. 2nd ed. Münster: Ugarit-Verlag, 1995. |
| Davies | G. I. Davies, *Ancient Hebrew Inscriptions: Corpus and Concordance*. Cambridge: Cambridge University Press, 1991. |
| DNWSI | J. Hoftijzer and K. Jongeling, *Dictionary of the Northwest Semitic Inscriptions*. 2 vols. Leiden: Brill, 1995. |
| EA | J. A. Knudtzon, *Die El-Amarna Tafeln mit Einleitung und Erläuterungen*. Leipzig: Hinrichs, 1908–15. Reprint, Aalen, 1964. Continued in A. F. Rainey, *El-Amarna Tablets*, 359–79. 2nd revised ed. Kevelaer, 1978. |

*EDSS* Lawrence S. Schiffman and J. VanderKam, (eds.), *Encyclopedia of the Dead Sea Scrolls*. New York: Oxford University Press, 2000.

*FGrH* Felix Jacoby, ed., *Die Fragmente der griechischen Historiker*, vols. 1–3. Leiden: Brill, 1954–1964.

Frame Grant Frame, *Rulers of Babylonia: From the Second Dynasty of Isin to the End of Assyrian Domination (1157–612 B.C.)*. RIMB 2. Toronto: University of Toronto Press, 1995.

Friedrich Johannes Friedrich, *Staatsverträge des Ḫatti-Reiches in hethitischer Sprache*, Vol. 1: MVAeG 31 (1926). Vol. 2: MVAeG 34 (1930).

Grayson Albert Kirk Grayson, *Assyrian Rulers of the Early First Millennium B.C., 1 (858–745 B.C.)*. RIMA 3. Toronto: University of Toronto Press, 1996.

HAE Johannes Renz and Wolfgang Röllig, *Handbuch der althebräischen Epigraphik*. Darmstadt: Wissenschaftlishe Buchgesellschaft, 1995– .

Hinke W. J. Hinke, *Selected Babylonian Kudurru Inscriptions*. Semitic Study Series 14. Leiden: Brill, 1911.

Horbury and Noy William Horbury and David Noy, (eds.), *Jewish Inscriptions of Graeco-Roman Egypt*. Cambridge: Cambridge University Press, 1992.

*IBoT* Istanbul Arkeoloji Müzelerinde Bulunan Boğazköy Tableteri(nden Seçme Metinler). Istanbul, 1944, 1947, 1954; Ankara, 1988.

Jastrow Morris Jastrow, A *Dictionary of the Targumim, the Talmud Babli and Yerushalmi, and the Midrashic Literature*. Brooklyn: Traditional, 1903.

Joüon Paul Joüon, *Grammaire de l'hébreu biblique*. Rev. ed. Rome: Pontifical Biblical Institute, 1923.

*KAI* Herbert R. Donner and W. Röllig, *Kanaanäische und aramäische Inschriften*. 3 vols. Wiesbaden: Otto Harrassowitz, 1964–1968.

KBo *Keilschrifttexte aus Boghazköi*. Leipzig/Berlin: Gebr. Mann Verlag, 1916– .

Kropat Arno Kropat, *Die Syntax des Autors der Chronik Vergleichen mit der seiner Quellen: Ein Beitrag zur historischen Syntax des Hebräischen*. BZAW 16. Giessen: Töpelmann, 1909.

*KTU* Manfred O. Dietrich, O. Loretz, and J. Sanmartín, *Die Keilalphabetischen Texte aus Ugarit*. AOAT 24/1. Neukirchen-Vluyn: Neukirchener Verlag, 1976.

KUB *Keilschrifturkunden aus Boghazköi*. Berlin: Akademie Verlag, 1912– .

Lambdin Thomas O. Lambdin, *An Introduction to Biblical Hebrew*. New York: Scribners, 1971.

*TAD* Bezalel Porten and Ada Yardeni, *Textbook of Aramaic Documents from Ancient Egypt. Newly Copied, Edited and Translated into Hebrew and English; Vol. 1: Letters* (1986). *Vol. 2: Contracts* (1989). *Vol. 3: Literature, Accounts, Lists* (1993). *Vol. 4: Ostraca and Assorted Inscriptions* (1999). Jerusalem: The Hebrew University, Department of the History of the Jewish People.

VTE Donald J. Wiseman, The Vassal Treaties of Esarhaddon. *Iraq* 20 (1958), 1–99.

Waltke and O'Connor Bruce K. Waltke and M. O'Connor, *An Introduction to Biblical Hebrew Syntax*. Winona Lake: Eisenbrauns, 1990.

WDSP Douglas M. Gropp, *Wadi Daliyeh II: The Samaria Papyri from Wadi Daliyeh*. DJD 28. Oxford: Oxford University Press, 2001.

Weidner E. F. Weidner, *Politische Dokumente aus Kleinasien: Die Staatsverträge in akkadischer Sprache aus dem Archiv von Boghazköi*. Boghazköi-Studien, 8–9. Leipzig: J. C. Hinrichs, 1923 [rpt. Hildesheim: Georg Olms, 1970].

| | |
|---|---|
| Williams | Ronald J. Williams, *Hebrew Syntax.* 2nd ed. Toronto: University of Toronto Press, 1976. |

SOURCE ABBREVIATIONS

| | |
|---|---|
| AASF | Annales Academiae scientiarum fennicae |
| AASOR | Annual of the American Schools of Oriental Research |
| AB | Anchor Bible |
| ABAW | Abhandlungen der Bayerischen Akademie der Wissenschaften |
| *ABD* | *Anchor Bible Dictionary.* Edited by D. N. Freedman. 6 vols. New York, 1992 |
| ABRL | Anchor Bible Reference Library |
| ADPV | Abhandlungen des Deutschen Palästinavereins |
| *AfO* | *Archiv für Orientforschung* |
| AGJU | Arbeiten zur Geschichte des antiken Judentums und des Urchristentums |
| *AHw* | *Akkadisches Handwörterbuch.* W. von Soden. 3 vols. |
| *AJBI* | *Annual of the Japanese Biblical Institute* |
| *AJSL* | *American Journal of Semitic Languages and Literature* |
| *AJT* | *American Journal of Theology* |
| ALBO | Analecta lovaniensia biblica et orientalia |
| AnBib | Analecta biblica |
| *ANET* | *Ancient Near Eastern Texts Relating to the Old Testament.* Edited by J. B. Pritchard. 3rd. ed. Princeton, 1969. |
| AnOr | Analecta orientalia |
| AOAT | Alter Orient und Altes Testament |
| AOS | American Oriental Series |
| *ARAB* | *Ancient Records of Assyria and Babylonia.* Daniel David Luckenbill. 2 vols. Chicago, 1926–1927. |
| ArBib | The Aramaic Bible |
| AS | Assyriological Studies |
| ASOR | American School of Oriental Research |
| *Asp* | *Asprenas: Rivista di scienze teologiche* |
| ATANT | Abhandlungen zur Theologie des Alten und Neuen Testaments |
| ATD | Das Alte Testament Deutsch |
| *Aug* | *Augustinianum* |
| *AUSS* | *Andrews University Seminary Studies* |
| *BA* | *Biblical Archaeologist* |
| *BAR* | *British Archaeological Reports* |
| *BARev* | *Biblical Archaeology Review* |
| BARIS | Biblical Archaeological Report International Series |
| *BASOR* | *Bulletin of the American Schools of Oriental Research* |
| BBB | Bonner biblische Beiträge |
| BBET | Beiträge zur biblischen Exegese und Theologie |
| *BBR* | *Bulletin for Biblical Research* |
| *BCH* | *Bulletin de correspondance hellénique* |
| BDB | Brown, F., S. R. Driver, and C. A. Briggs. *A Hebrew and English Lexicon of the Old Testament.* Oxford, 1907. |
| BEATAJ | Beiträge zur Erforschung des Alten Testaments und des antiken Judentum |
| *BeO* | *Bibbia e oriente* |

*Ber* — *Berytus*
BETL — Bibliotheca ephemeridum theologicarum lovaniensium
*BHAch* — Bulletin d'histoire achéménide
*BHK* — *Biblia Hebraica.* Edited by R. Kittel. Stuttgart, 1905–1906; 2nd ed., 1925; 3rd ed., 1937; 4th ed., 1951; 16th ed., 1973.
*BHS* — *Biblia Hebraica Stuttgartensia.* Edited by K. Elliger and W. Rudolph. Stuttgart, 1983.
BHT — Beiträge zur historischen Theologie
*Bib* — *Biblica*
*BibInt* — *Biblical Interpretation*
BibS(F) — Biblische Studien (Freiburg, 1895– ).
*BIOSCS* — *Bulletin of the International Organization for Septuagint and Cognate Studies*
*BJ* — *Bonner Jahrbücher*
*BJRL* — *Bulletin of the John Rylands University Library of Manchester*
BJS — Brown Judaic Studies
BKAT — Biblischer Kommentar, Altes Testament. Edited by M. Noth and H. W. Wolff.
*BLit* — *Bibliothèque liturgique*
*BN* — *Biblische Notizen*
BMes — Bibliotheca mesopotamica
*BR* — *Biblical Research*
*BTB* — *Biblical Theology Bulletin*
BWANT — Beiträge zur Wissenschaft vom Alten und Neuen Testament
*BZ* — *Biblische Zeitschrift*
BZAW — Beihefte zur Zeitschrift für die alttestamentliche Wissenschaft
CahRB — Cahiers de la Revue biblique
*CAD* — *The Assyrian Dictionary of the Oriental Institute of the University of Chicago.* Chicago, 1956– .
*CANE* — *Civilizations of the Ancient Near East.* Edited by J. Sasson. 4 vols. New York, 1995.
CAT — Commentaire de l'Ancien Testament
CBC — Cambridge Bible Commentary
CBET — Contributions to Biblical Exegesis and Theology
*CBQ* — *Catholic Biblical Quarterly*
CBQMS — Catholic Biblical Quarterly Monograph Series
*CHJ* — *Cambridge History of Judaism.* Edited by W. D. Davies and Louis Finkelstein. Cambridge, 1984– .
*CIS* — *Corpus inscriptionum semiticarum*
ConBOT — Coniectanea biblica: Old Testament Series
*COS* — *The Context of Scripture.* Edited by W. W. Hallo and K. L. Younger, Jr. 3 vols. Leiden, 1997–2002.
*CRBS* — *Critical Review: Biblical Studies*
CRINT — Compendia rerum iudaicarum ad Novum Testamentum
*CTM* — *Concordia Theological Monthly*
*CTU* — *The Cuneiform Alphabetic Texts from Ugarit, Ras Ibn Hani, and Other Places.* Edited by M. Dietrich, O. Loretz, and J. Sanmartín. Münster. 2nd ed., 1995.
DJD — Discoveries in the Judaean Desert
*DSD* — *Dead Sea Discoveries*
EB — Echter Bibel

| | |
|---|---|
| *EBib* | *Etudes bibliques* |
| EdF | Erträge der Forschung |
| *EI* | *Eretz Israel* |
| *EncJud* | *Encyclopaedia Judaica*. 16 vols. Jerusalem, 1972. |
| *ErIsr* | *Eretz-Israel* |
| *ETL* | *Ephemerides theologicae lovanienses* |
| *ETR* | *Etudes théologiques et religieuses* |
| *ExpT* | *Expository Times* |
| FAT | Forschungen zum Alten Testament |
| FB | Forschung zur Bibel |
| *FoiVie* | *Foi et vie* |
| FOTL | Forms of the Old Testament Literature |
| FRLANT | Forschungen zur Religion und Literatur des Alten und Neuen Testaments |
| GAT | Grundrisse zum Alten Testament |
| GBS | Guides to Biblical Scholarship |
| GCS | Die griechische christliche Schriftsteller der ersten Jahrhunderte |
| GKC | *Gesenius' Hebrew Grammar*. Edited by E. Kautzsch. Translated by A. E. Cowley. 2nd ed. Oxford, 1910. |
| GTA | Göttinger theologischer Arbeiten |
| *HALOT* | Koehler, L., W. Baumgartner, and J. J. Stamm. *The Hebrew and Aramaic Lexicon of the Old Testament*. Translated and edited under the supervision of M. E. J. Richardson. 4 vols. Leiden, 1994–1999. |
| *HAR* | *Hebrew Annual Review* |
| HAT | Handbuch zum Alten Testament |
| *HBT* | *Horizons in Biblical Theology* |
| *Hen* | *Henoch* |
| *HeyJ* | *Heythrop Journal* |
| *Hok* | *Hokhma* |
| *HS* | *Hebrew Studies* |
| HSAT | *Die Heilige Schrift des Alten Testaments*. Edited by E. Kautzsch and A. Bertholoet. 4th ed. Tübingen, 1922–1923. |
| HSM | Harvard Semitic Monographs |
| HSS | Harvard Semitic Studies |
| *HTR* | *Harvard Theological Review* |
| ICC | International Critical Commentary |
| *IDB* | *The Interpreter's Dictionary of the Bible*. Edited by G. A. Buttrick. 4 vols., Nashville, 1962. |
| *IDBSup* | *The Interpreter's Dictionary of the Bible: Supplementary Volume*. Edited by K. Crim. Nashville, 1976. |
| *IEJ* | *Israel Exploration Journal* |
| *Int* | *Interpretation* |
| IOSCS | International Organization for Septuagint and Cognate Studies |
| *Iraq* | *Iraq* |
| *JANES* | *Journal of the Ancient Near Eastern Society of Columbia University* |
| *JAOS* | *Journal of the American Oriental Society* |
| JAOSSup | Journal of the American Oriental Society: Supplement Series |
| JB | Jerusalem Bible |
| *JBL* | *Journal of Biblical Literature* |
| *JCS* | *Journal of Cuneiform Studies* |

| | |
|---|---|
| JDS | Judean Desert Studies |
| *JESHO* | *Journal of the Economic and Social History of the Orient* |
| *JET* | *Jahrbuch für Evangelische Theologie* |
| *JETS* | *Journal of the Evangelical Theological Society* |
| *JJS* | *Journal of Jewish Studies* |
| *JNES* | *Journal of Near Eastern Studies* |
| *JNSL* | *Journal of Northwest Semitic Languages* |
| *JPOS* | *Journal of the Palestine Oriental Society* |
| JPS | Jewish Publication Society |
| *JQR* | *Jewish Quarterly Review* |
| *JR* | *Journal of Religion* |
| *JRAS* | *Journal of the Royal Asiatic Society* |
| *JSJ* | *Journal for the Study of Judaism in the Persian, Hellenistic, and Roman Periods* |
| JSNTSup | Journal for the Study of the New Testament: Supplement Series |
| *JSOT* | *Journal for the Study of the Old Testament* |
| JSOTSup | Journal for the Study of the Old Testament: Supplement Series |
| *JSP* | *Journal for the Study of the Pseudepigrapha* |
| *JSS* | *Journal of Semitic Studies* |
| *JTS* | *Journal of Theological Studies* |
| *Judaica* | *Judaica: Beiträge zum Verständnis des jüdischen Schicksals in Vergangenheit und Gegenwart* |
| *Judaism* | *Judaism* |
| KAT | Kommentar zum Alten Testament |
| KBL | Koehler, L., and W. Baumgartner. *Lexicon in Veteris Testamenti libros.* 2nd ed. Leiden, 1958. |
| KJV | King James Version |
| LD | Lectio divina |
| LEC | Library of Early Christianity |
| *LS* | *Louvain Studies* |
| *LTQ* | *Lexington Theological Quarterly* |
| LUÅ | Lunds universitets årsskrift |
| *MdB* | *Le Monde de la Bible* |
| MDOG | Mitteilungen der Deutschen Orient-Gesellschaft |
| *MIOF* | *Mitteilungen des Instituts für Orientforschung* |
| *MGWJ* | *Monatschrift für Geschichte und Wissenschaft des Judentums* |
| MVAeG | Mitteilungen der Vorderasiatisch-ägyptischen Gesellschaft, vols. 1–44, 1896–1939. |
| NAB | New American Bible |
| NCB | New Century Bible |
| *NEAEHL* | *The New Encyclopedia of Archaeological Excavations in the Holy Land.* Edited by E. Stern. 4 vols. Jerusalem, 1993. |
| NEchtB | Neue Echter Bibel |
| NIV | New International Version |
| NJB | New Jerusalem Bible |
| *NJBC* | *The New Jerome Biblical Commentary.* Edited by R. E. Brown et al. Englewood Cliffs, 1990. |
| NJPS | New Jewish Publication Society |
| *NovT* | *Novum Testamentum* |

| | |
|---|---|
| NRSV | New Revised Standard Version |
| OBO | Orbis biblicus et orientalis |
| ÖBS | Österreichische biblische Studien |
| OBT | Overtures to Biblical Theology |
| *OCD* | *Oxford Classical Dictionary*. Edited by S. Hornblower and A. Spawforth. 3rd ed. Oxford, 1996. |
| *OEANE* | *The Oxford Encyclopedia of Archaeology in the Near East*. Edited by E. M. Meyers. New York, 1997. |
| OLA | Orientalia lovaniensia analecta |
| OLP | Orientalia lovaniensia periodica |
| *Or* | *Orientalia* (NS) |
| OTG | Old Testament Guides |
| OTL | Old Testament Library |
| *OTP* | *Old Testament Pseudepigrapha*. Edited by J. H. Charlesworth. 2 vols. New York, 1983. |
| *OTS* | *Oudtestamentische Studiën* |
| OTS | Old Testament Studies |
| PEFQS | Palestine Exploration Fund Quarterly Statement |
| *PEQ* | *Palestine Exploration Quarterly* |
| PIBA | Proceedings of the Irish Biblical Association |
| *PJ* | *Palästina-Jahrbuch* |
| *PRU* | *Le palais royal d'Ugarit* |
| RANE | Records of the Ancient Near East |
| *RB* | *Revue biblique* |
| REB | Revised English Bible |
| *REJ* | *Revue des études juives* |
| *RelSoc* | *Religion and Society* |
| *ResQ* | *Restoration Quarterly* |
| *RevQ* | *Revue de Qumran* |
| RIMA | The Royal Inscriptions of Mesopotamia, Assyrian Periods |
| RIMB | The Royal Inscriptions of Mesopotamia, Babylonian Periods |
| *RivB* | *Rivista biblica italiana* |
| RS | Ras Shamra |
| RSV | Revised Standard Version |
| *RTP* | *Revue de théologie et de philosophie* |
| SAA | State Archives of Assyria |
| SBB | Stuttgarter biblische Beiträge |
| SBLABS | Society of Biblical Literature Archaeology and Biblical Studies |
| SBLDS | Society of Biblical Literature Dissertation Series |
| SBLEJL | Society of Biblical Literature Early Judaism and Its Literature |
| SBLMS | Society of Biblical Literature Monograph Series |
| SBLSCS | Society of Biblical Literature Septuagint and Cognate Studies |
| SBLSymS | Society of Biblical Literature Symposium Series |
| SBLTT | Society of Biblical Literature Texts and Translations |
| SBLWAW | Society of Biblical Literature Writings from the Ancient World |
| SBT | Studies in Biblical Theology |
| SBTS | Sources for Biblical and Theological Study, Eisenbrauns. |
| *Schol* | *Scholastik* |
| ScrHier | Scripta hierosolymitana |

| | |
|---|---|
| SE | *Studia evangelica I, II, III* (= TU 73 [1959], 87 [1964], 88 [1964], etc.) |
| *Sem* | *Semitica* |
| SFSHJ | University of Southern Florida Studies in the History of Judaism |
| SHANE | Studies in the History of the Ancient Near East |
| SHCANE | Studies in the History and Cultures of the Ancient Near East |
| SJLA | Studies in Judaism in Late Antiquity |
| *SJOT* | *Scandinavian Journal of the Old Testament* |
| SNTSMS | Society for New Testament Studies Monograph Series |
| SP | Sacra pagina |
| *SR* | *Studies in Religion* |
| SSN | Studia semitica neerlandica |
| SSS | Semitic Study Series |
| *ST* | *Studia theologica* |
| STDJ | *Studies on the Text of the Desert of Judah* |
| *TA* | *Tel Aviv* |
| *Tarbiz* | *Tarbiz* |
| TBC | Torch Bible Commentaries |
| TCS | Texts from Cuneiform Sources |
| *TDOT* | *Theological Dictionary of the Old Testament.* Edited by G. Kittel and G. Friedrich. Translated by G. W. Bromiley. Grand Rapids, 1974– . |
| *Text* | *Textus* |
| *Them* | *Themelios* |
| *TLOT* | *Theological Lexicon of the Old Testament.* Edited by E. Jenni, with assistance from C. Westermann. Translated by M. E. Biddle. 3 vols. Peabody, Mass., 1997. |
| *TLZ* | *Theologische Literaturzeitung* |
| TOTC | Tyndale Old Testament Commentaries |
| *TQ* | *Theologische Quartalschrift* |
| *Transeu* | *Transeuphratène* |
| *TRE* | *Theologische Realenzyklopädie.* Edited by G. Krause and G. Müller. Berlin. 1977– . |
| *TRu* | *Theologische Rundschau* |
| *TSK* | *Theologische Studien und Kritiken* |
| TU | Texte und Untersuchungen |
| *TynBul* | *Tyndale Bulletin* |
| *TZ* | *Theologische Zeitschrift* |
| *UF* | *Ugarit-Forschungen* |
| *USQR* | *Union Seminary Quarterly Review* |
| VAB | Vorderasiatische Bibliothek |
| *VT* | *Vetus Testamentum* |
| VTSup | Vetus Testamentum Supplements |
| WBC | Word Biblical Commentary |
| *WO* | *Die Welt des Orients* |
| *WTJ* | *Westminster Theological Journal* |
| WUNT | Wissenschaftliche Untersuchungen zum Neuen Testament |
| WVDOG | Wissenschaftliche Veröffentlichungen der deutschen Orientgesellschaft |
| *ZAH* | *Zeitschrift für Althebräistik* |
| *ZAW* | *Zeitschrift für die alttestamentliche Wissenschaft* |
| *ZDPV* | *Zeitschrift des deutschen Palästina-Vereins* |

GENERAL ABBREVIATIONS

| | |
|---|---|
| abs. | absolute |
| acc. | accusative |
| Akk. | Akkadian |
| Ann. | Annal(s) |
| Arab. | Arabic |
| Aram. | Aramaic |
| Arm. | Armenian |
| Assyr. | Assyrian |
| BH | biblical Hebrew |
| Bibl. Aram. | biblical Aramaic |
| Boh. | Bohairic |
| CH | classical Hebrew |
| Chr$^{1,2,3,\mathrm{MPR}}$ | Chronicles editors |
| const. | construct |
| D | Deuteronomy or the old Deuteronomic law code |
| DN | divine name |
| E | the Elohist |
| Eg. | Egyptian |
| ET | English translation |
| Eth. | Ethiopic |
| f. | feminine |
| Gk. | Greek |
| gen. | genitive |
| GN | geopolitical or geographic name |
| H | the Holiness Code |
| HB | Hebrew Bible |
| Heb. | Hebrew |
| Hitt. | Hittite |
| inf. | infinitive |
| impv. | imperative |
| J | the Yahwist |
| Jer C | a series of texts in the Book of Jeremiah with affinities to Deuteronomy and the Deuteronomistic History |
| LBH | late biblical Hebrew |
| *Liv. Pro.* | *Lives of the Prophets* |
| LXX | Septuagint |
| LXX$^{\mathrm{A}}$ | Codex Alexandrinus of the Septuagint |
| LXX$^{\mathrm{B}}$ | Codex Vaticanus of the Septuagint |
| LXX$^{\mathrm{L}}$ | the Lucianic recension or the majority of the Lucianic manuscripts of the Septuagint |
| LXX$^{\mathrm{N}}$ | Codex Venetus of the Septuagint |
| LXX$^{\mathrm{S}}$ | Codex Sinaiticus of the Septuagint |
| masc. | masculine |
| ms(s) | manuscript, manuscripts |
| MT | the Masoretic Text of the Hebrew Bible |
| Nab. | Nabatean |
| NT | New Testament |

| | |
|---|---|
| Off. Aram. | official Aramaic |
| OL | Old Latin |
| OSA | Old South Arabic |
| OT | Old Testament |
| P | the Priestly writer(s) |
| pass. | passive |
| pers. | person |
| Phoen. | Phoenician |
| Pl. | plate |
| pl. | plural |
| PN | personal name |
| prep. | preposition |
| pres. | present |
| pron. | pronoun |
| ptc. | participle |
| Pun. | Punic |
| RH | Rabbinic Hebrew |
| RN | regal name |
| sg. | singular |
| SP | Samaritan Pentateuch |
| *sub ast.* | *sub asteriscus* |
| subj. | subject |
| suf. | suffix |
| Summ. | Summary |
| Syr. | Syrian/Syriac |
| T. | Tel or Tell |
| *Tg.* | *Targum* |
| *Tg. Ket.* | *Targum of the Writings* |
| *Tg. Neb.* | *Targum of the Prophets* |
| *Tg. Neof.* | *Targum Neofiti* |
| *Tg. Onq.* | *Targum Onqelos* |
| *Tg. Ps.-J.* | *Targum Pseudo-Jonathan* |
| Theodoret | *Quaestiones in Reges et Paralipomena* |
| Ug. | Ugaritic |
| Vg. | Vulgate |

# Translation, Notes, and Comments

# 2. The Reign of Israel's First King

◆

## XIII. The Fall of Benjaminite Saul (9:35–10:14)

*The Jeielite Genealogy*

35 The father of Gibeon, Jeiel, resided in Gibeon and the name of his wife was Maacah. 36 Her firstborn son: Abdon, Zur, Qish, Baal, Ner, Nadab, 37 Gedor, Aḥio, Zechariah, and Miqloth. 38 Miqloth sired Shimeah, and they also resided opposite their kinsmen in Jerusalem. 39 Ner sired Qish, and Qish sired Saul, and Saul sired Jonathan, Malchi-shua, Abinadab, and Eshbaal. 40 The son of Jonathan was Merib-baal, and Merib-baal sired Micah. 41 The sons of Micah were Pithon, Melech, Taḥarea, and Aḥaz. 42 Aḥaz sired Jadah, and Jadah sired Alemeth, Azmaveth, and Zimri. Zimri sired Moza, 43 and Moza sired Binea; Raphaiah his son, Eleasah his son, Azel his son. 44 Azel had six sons and these were their names: Azriqam his firstborn, Ishmael, Sheariah, Azariah, Obadiah, and Ḥanan. All of these were sons of Azel.

*Defeat and Death at the Hands of the Philistines*

10:1 Now the Philistines made war with Israel and the men of Israel fled from before the Philistines. The slain fell on Mount Gilboa. 2 The Philistines pursued Saul and his sons and the Philistines struck down Jonathan, Abinadab, and Malchi-shua, the sons of Saul. 3 The battle weighed upon Saul and the archers found him with the bow. He was wounded by the archers and 4 so Saul said to his arms bearer, "Unsheath your sword and run me through with it lest these uncircumcised come and abuse me." Nevertheless, his arms bearer was unwilling, because he was very frightened. Saul then took the sword and fell upon it. 5 When his arms bearer saw that Saul was dead, he also fell upon the sword and died. 6 So Saul died along with his three sons. All of his house died together. 7 When all the men of Israel who were in the valley saw that they fled and that Saul and his sons died, they abandoned their towns and fled. Then the Philistines came and occupied them. 8 When, on the next day, the Philistines came to strip the slain, they found Saul and his three sons, fallen on Mt. Gilboa. 9 They stripped him and carried off his head and his armor and sent them to the surrounding territory of the Philistines to herald the news to their idols and people. 10 They set his armor in the temple of their gods and his skull they impaled in the Temple of Dagon. 11 When all of the inhabitants of Jabesh-gilead heard all that the Philistines did to Saul and to Israel, [12]all of the warriors arose and carried off the corpse of Saul along with the corpses of his sons and brought them to Jabesh. They interred their bones under the oak in Jabesh and fasted for seven days.

*Evaluation*

[13]Saul died in his transgression by which he transgressed against Yhwh concerning the word of Yhwh, which he did not observe, even consulting a necromancer to seek (counsel). [14]He did not seek Yhwh and so he put him to death and turned the kingdom over to David, son of Jesse.

## TEXTUAL NOTES

9:35–44. For a more detailed analysis of this passage, see the TEXTUAL NOTES to the parallel text in 8:29–38.

9:35. "his wife." A few Heb. MSS "his sister."

9:37. "Zechariah" *(zkryh)*. 1 Chr 8:31 "Zecher" *(zkr)*. LXX$^{A}$ *Zachchour* (= *zakkûr*); LXX$^{L}$ *Zechrei*.

9:38. "Shimeah" *(šmʾh)*. So 8:32. See LXX* 9:38 *Samaa*, as well as LXX$^{B}$ *Semaa*, LXX$^{L}$ bgmnc$_2$ 1 Chr 8:32 *Samaa*. MT 1 Chr 9:38 "Shimeam" reflects a *hê/mêm* confusion.

"opposite their kinsmen." See the 2nd TEXTUAL NOTE to 8:32.

9:40. "Merib-baal." So MT 9:40 and MT 1 Chr 8:34 (bis). In the second instance, MT 1 Chr 9:40 reads "Meri-baal." Cf. LXX$^{B}$ 1 Chr 9:40 *Mareibaal* (bis); LXX$^{N}$ *Mephibaal*; LXX$^{L}$ *Memphibaal*. On the PN *mrbʿl*, which appears in the Samaria ostraca (Davies, §3.002.7), see Layton (1993).

9:41. "Taḥarea" *(tḥrʿ)*. So MT. 1 Chr 8:35 "Taarea" *(tʾrʿ)*.

"and Aḥaz." So MT 8:35. Lacking in MT 1 Chr 9:41, but present in Tg., some Vg. MSS, and perhaps the *Vorlagen* of LXX$^{L}$ *(kai Azaz)*, i *(kai Chaaz)* and Arm. The name was lost to MT by haplography (*homoioarkton* before *wĕʾāḥāz* at the beginning of v. 42).

9:42. "Jadah." So LXX$^{B}$ *Iada* (= *yʿdh*); cf. LXX$^{L}$ *Iō(a)da*. MT "Jarah" *(yʿrh)* reflects a *dālet/rêš* confusion. MT 1 Chr 8:36 "Jehoadah" (*yhwʿdh*; TEXTUAL NOTE).

9:44. "his firstborn" *(bkrw)*. So several Heb. MSS, Tg., and LXX (1st TEXTUAL NOTE to 8:38).

"Azariah." See the 2nd TEXTUAL NOTE to 8:38.

10:1–12. Paralleled by 1 Sam 31:1–13. Each of the differences between Chronicles and Samuel will be assessed individually. It should be noted, however, that when Chronicles and MT Samuel are compared, many of these differences amount to lacunae in Chronicles. Chronicles exhibits very few pluses. Even though Chronicles is a late text, it would be methodologically flawed to assume that such minuses necessarily result from the Chronicler's abridgment of Samuel. Quite the contrary, the version of Samuel used by the Chronicler was probably a shorter text than MT Samuel (McCarter 1980b; McKenzie 1985; Ho 1995).

10:1. "made war." Reading with MT, LXX *(epolemēsan)*, and LXX 1 Sam 31:1 *(epolemoun)*. MT 1 Sam 31:1 *nlḥmym*.

10:2. "Abinadab." So MT. LXX *Am(e)inadab*. The lists of Saul's sons (1 Sam 14:49; 1 Sam 31:2 [//1 Chr 10:2]; 1 Chr 8:33; 9:39) are not entirely consonant. In 1 Chr 8:33 and 9:39 Syr. has *yšwy* for MT *ʾšbʿl*. It has often been suggested that *yšwy* is shorthand (**ʾyšw)* or euphemistic (**ʾyš yhwh)* for *ʾyšbʿl*. See 1 Sam 14:49 *(yšwy)* and 2 Sam 2:8 (*ʾyšbwšt*; Noth 1928: 227–28). But McCarter (1980b: 254) points out with reference to the fragmentary evidence of 4QSam$^{a}$ 1 Sam 14:49 *(yhwntn wyš[_w]mlkyšʿ)* that one cannot be sure that *yšwy* represents Ishbaal. To this can be added the genealogical evidence of Chronicles. Both 1 Chr 8:33 and 9:39 list four sons of Saul: Jonathan, Malchishua, Abinadab, and Eshbaal.

10:3. "the battle weighed upon Saul" (ותכבד המלחמה על-שאול). So MT. MT 1 Sam 31:3 ותכבד המלחמה אל-שאול (the preps. *ʾel* and *ʿal* are often confused in Samuel; S. Driver 1912). I prefer a literal translation of *tkbd*, because most contemporary translations (e.g., NJPS: "the battle raged around Saul") do not accurately convey the sense of *kbd*. The point is not that Saul was in the midst of battle (this is obvious from vv. 1–2), but that events were closing in on Saul following the deaths of his three sons.

"the archers" *(hmwrym bqšt)*. So MT. MT and LXX 1 Sam 31:3 are probably expansionary, "the archers, men with the bow" *(hmwrym ʾnšym bqšt)*, although the possibility of haplography *(homoioteleuton)* should not be overlooked (from *hmwrym ʾnšym* to *hmwrym)*.

"found him with the bow." So MT *(lectio brevior)*. The phrase is ambiguous, suggesting either that Saul came into range of the Philistine archers or that they had actually succeeded in shooting him. LXX explicates, *kai heuron autous* [LXX$^{AN}$ *auton*] *hoi toxotai en toxois kai ponois*, "and the archers found them (him) with bows and toils."

"wounded by the archers." A conjecture. MT "trembled from the archers" *(wayyāḥel min-hayyôrîm)*. MT 1 Sam 31:3 *wayyāḥel mĕʾōd mēhammôrîm*. LXX$^{B}$ $c_2$ 1 Chr 10:3 *kai eponesan apo tōn toxōn* ("they inflicted pain by means of the bows"); LXX$^{ANS}$ *kai eponesen apo tōn toxōn* ("he inflicted pain by means of the bows"); LXX$^{L}$ *etropōthē apo tōn toxōn*. Rudolph (1955) thinks that LXX$^{A}$ reflects *wayyēḥol*, "he was made sick" *(hopʿal* of *ḥlh)*. Given the use of *ponein*, it is possible to reconstruct **wayyeḥōlal*, "he was wounded by the archers" (*ḥll*, "to pierce or wound"). Cf. LXX$^{B}$ 1 Sam 31:3 *kai etraumatisthē* (= *wayyēḥel* or *wayyeḥōlal?)*. See also the witnesses to 1 Kgs 22:34(//2 Chr 18:33) and 2 Chr 35:23.

10:4. "arms bearer" *(nōśēʾ kēlāyw)*. So also NJPS. Traditionally "armor bearer."

"lest these uncircumcised come." Thus MT and LXX. MT and LXX 1 Sam 31:4 add "and run me through" (ודקרני).

10:5. "died." So MT and LXX *(lectio brevior)*. MT and LXX 1 Sam 31:5 add "with him."

10:6. "along with his three sons." So MT *(lectio brevior)*. Alternatively, the absence of MT 1 Sam 31:6 "and his arms bearer" (ונשא כליו) from the Chronicler's *Vorlage* could have been triggered by haplography *(homoioteleuton)* after בניו.

"all of his house together" *(wkl bytw yḥdw)*. MT and LXX$^{B}$ 1 Sam 31:6 "even all of his men on that day together" *(gm kl-ʾnšyw bywm hhwʾ yḥdw)*. The phrase "all of his men" is missing from LXX$^{OL}$. Like 1 Sam 31:6 (MT and LXX$^{B}$), LXX 1 Chr 10:6 specifies "on that day."

10:7. "all the men of Israel" *(kl-ʾyš yśrʾl)*. So MT and LXX$^{B}$. MT 1 Sam 31:7 "men of Israel" *(ʾnšy-yśrʾl)*.

"who were in the valley." So MT and LXX. MT (and LXX) 1 Sam 31:7, "who were on the other side of the valley and on the other side of the Jordan."

"they fled" (נסו). So MT *(lectio difficilior)*. The subject is ambiguous. LXX "Israel fled" *(ephugen Israēl)*. Similarly, MT and LXX 1 Sam 31:7, "the men of Israel fled" (נסו אנשי ישׂראל). Mosis (1973: 23), Williamson (1982b: 93), and Japhet (1993a: 224) cite MT's accentuation to contend that the referent of "they" is the nearest antecedent: Saul and his sons (10:6). But the text never refers either to Saul or to his sons as fleeing from the Philistines. It seems more likely, given Israel's fleeing *(wyns)* from the Philistines (10:1), that the subject is Israel. Hence, the interpretation of LXX is sound. The first part of 10:7—"when all the men of Israel . . . saw that they fled and that Saul and his sons died"—summarizes the defeat and regicide to explain the subsequent Israelite withdrawal from the valley.

10:8. "Saul and his three sons." Reading with 1 Sam 31:8. MT and LXX 1 Chr 10:8, "Saul and his sons," have suffered haplography *(homoioteleuton)* from *wʾt-šlšt bnyw* to *wʾt bnyw*.

10:9. "stripped him *(wayyapšîṭuhû)* and carried off *(wayyiśʾû)* his head." Rudolph (1955) adds *wyrʾšwhw* ("and they beheaded him") on the basis of MT 1 Sam 31:9, *wykrtw ʾt rʾšw wypšṭw ʾt-klyw*. But the beheading is probably not original, given its absence from LXX$^{AB}$ 1 Sam 31:9 (καὶ ἀποστρέφουσιν αὐτον καὶ ἐξέδυσαν τὰ σκεύη αὐτοῦ). It is more likely that *1 Sam 31:9 and 1 Chr 10:9 preserve ancient variants.

"to herald the news to their idols" *(lbśr ʾt-ʿṣbyhm)*. So MT and LXX$^{AB}$ 1 Chr 10:9, and LXX 1 Sam 31:9. On the basis of cursives bdjmp-ze$_2$, Syr., Tg., and MT 1 Sam 31:9 *(lbśr byt ʿṣbyhm)*, some read, "to herald the news to the house of their idols" *(lbśr byt ʿṣbyhm)*. But the latter may assimilate toward *byt ʾlhyhm* in 10:10.

10:10. "temple of their gods" *(byt ʾlhyhm)*. So MT. The Heb. consonants can also be read as "the temple of their god" (so LXX). MT 1 Sam 31:10 "house of Ashtaroth" *(byt ʿštrwt)*; LXX 1 Sam 31:10 εἰς τὸ Ασταρτεῖον. The discrepancy has been the subject of much speculation, but the Samuel and Chronicles readings may simply be ancient variants.

"and his skull they impaled in the Temple of Dagon" *(wʾt-glgltw tqʿw byt dgwn)*. Thus MT followed by LXX. MT 1 Sam 31:10, "they impaled his corpse on the wall of Beth-shean" *(wʾt-gwytw tqʿw bḥwmt byt šn)*.

10:11. "all of the inhabitants of Jabesh-gilead" *(kl yšby ybyš glʿd)*. A reconstruction based on MT, "all of Jabesh-gilead," and LXX, "all of the inhabitants of Gilead" *(pantes hoi katoikountes Galaad = kl yšby glʿd)*. Both MT and LXX have suffered haplography. MT 1 Sam 31:11, "inhabitants of Jabesh-gilead" *(yšby ybyš glʿd)*.

"to Saul and to Israel" *(lšʾwl wlyśrʾl)*. So LXX. MT has lost "and to Israel" *(wlyśrʾl)* because of haplography.

10:12. "all of the warriors arose" *(wyqwmw kl-ʾyš ḥyl)*. Reading tentatively with MT and LXX *(lectio brevior)*. It may be that the plus of 1 Sam 31:12, "and traveled the whole night" *(wylkw kl-hlylh)*, was lost to the *Vorlage* of Chronicles by haplography *(homoioteleuton)*.

"and carried off the corpse of Saul along with the corpses of his sons" *(wyśʾw ʾt-gwpt šʾwl wʾt gwpt bnyw)*. The terminology for corpse(s), *gwpt*, is a *hapax legomenon*. First Sam 31:12 has the more familiar *gwyt*, "body" or "corpse," perhaps due to the influence of 1 Sam 31:10. First Sam 31:12 adds "from the wall of Beth-shean" (2nd TEXTUAL NOTE to 10:10).

"brought them to Jabesh" *(wybyʾwm ybyšh)*. The text, as witnessed by the use of the *hipʿil*, the direct object, and the locative *hê*, is unambiguous (cf. MT 1 Sam 31:12 *wybʾw ybšh)*. Syr. assimilates toward 1 Sam 31:12, which adds "and they burned them there."

"interred their bones" *(wyqbrw ʾt-ʿṣmwtyhm)*. Reading with MT and LXX. MT (and LXX) 1 Sam 31:13 are more expansive, "and they took their bones and buried (them)" *(wyqḥw ʾt-ʿṣmtyhm wyqbrw)*.

"under the oak" *(tḥt hʾlh)*. Similarly, LXX *hypo tēn dryn*. MT 1 Sam 31:13 "under the tamarisk" *(hʾšl)*.

10:13–14. These verses, unparalleled in Samuel, are filled with typical Chronistic expressions, but the syntax is rough.

10:13. "even consulting a necromancer" *(wgm-lšʾwl bʾwb)*. On the substitution of the infinitive for a finite verb, see GKC, §114p. LXX *hoti epērōtēsen Saoul en tō engastrimythō*, "because Saul inquired of a trance-speaker."

"to seek (counsel)" *(ldrwš)*. So MT and LXX. Lacking in Syr. Some (e.g., R. Braun 1986: 148) delete as a gloss on or a variant of *lšʾwl*. In an allusion to 1 Sam 28:15–19, LXX adds *kai apekrinato autō Samouēl ho prophētēs*, "and the prophet Samuel answered him."

## NOTES

9:35–44. These verses, marking the Benjaminite Jeielite genealogy, duplicate the material in 1 Chr 8:29–38. In the context of 1 Chr 8, the Jeielite lineage extends two additional generations (8:39–40) through a collateral line (see also the NOTE to 8:29–40). The Jeielite lineage is well situated in this literary context in that it prefaces the tenure of its most famous member: Saul. The genealogy extends some fifteen generations and exhibits a combination of linear and segmented forms (vv. 36–37, 39, 41, 44). In one case, the segmentation extends to the offspring of a collateral line (v. 38; cf. 8:39–40). The lineage of Jeiel may be compared with the royal Davidic genealogy of 1 Chr 3, the priestly genealogy of 5:27–41, and the Ephraimite genealogy of 7:20–21, 25–27. Like these other lineages, the Jeielite lineage is extensive and covers not only ancient and recent times but also the intermediate past. Assigning Saul to the eleventh century and assuming twenty years per generation, the genealogy would not be long enough to reach the Babylonian Exile. Yet if the genealogy is telescopic in some portions, the genealogy might extend to the writer's own time. Because there are no temporal synchronisms in the latter part of the lineage, it is impossible to tell in which particular century the sons of Azel lived.

9:35. "Gibeon." In some texts Saul is associated with Gibeah (1 Sam 11:4; 15:34; Isa 10:29). The Jeielite genealogy does not preclude this possibility; it simply associates Jeiel himself with Gibeon. The case for some clear associations between Gibeon and Saul has also been argued (2 Sam 2:12–3:1; 21:1–14; Edelman 1996). On the identification of the site with el-Ǧîb, see the 2nd NOTE to 8:29.

"Maacah." Within the genealogies, there are multiple occurrences of Maacah as the wife, concubine, or sister of different individuals among Israel's tribes (1 Chr 2:48; 3:2; 7:16; 9:35; cf. 27:16). Given Maacah's Syrian associations (2 Sam 10:6, 8; 1 Chr 19:6, 7), it is not necessary to label some or most of these relationships as contradictory and therefore as later additions or glosses (3rd NOTE to 4:19). Genealogists may employ the same name to posit multiple or overlapping connections between different tribes and peoples (Flanagan 1983). If this is the case with Maacah, then Judah, Manasseh, and Benjamin all have links to the Aramaean east.

9:39. "Ner sired Qish." According to 1 Sam 9:1, Abiel *(ʾăbîʾēl)* was the father of Qish. Targum 1 Chr 8:33 harmonizes 1 Sam 9:1 with 1 Chr 8:33 by claiming that Abiel was another name for Ner. Aside from Qish and Saul, there is virtually no overlap between the two lineages. The references in 1 Sam 14:50–51 to Saul's relatives provide further information.

| *8:29–33//9:35–38* | *1 Sam 9:1* | *1 Sam 14:50–51* |
|---|---|---|
| | Apiaḥ | |
| | Becorath | |
| Jeiel | Zeror | |
| Ner | Abiel | Abiel |
| Qish | Qish | Ner |
| Saul | Saul | Abiner |

In 1 Sam 14:51 Ner appears as the father of Ab(i)ner and hence Qish's brother, not his father (cf. Josephus, *Ant.* 6.130). But 1 Sam 14:50 is more ambiguous. Some construe *ʾăbînēr ben-nēr dôd šāʾûl*, "Abiner son of Ner uncle of Saul," to mean that Ab(i)ner was Saul's cousin, while others see Ab(i)ner as Saul's uncle. Unfortunately, the text is not clear. Does the appositional phrase *dôd šāʾûl* refer to Abiner or to Ner? To complicate matters, neither Abiel nor Ab(i)ner appear in the Chronicler's genealogy of Saul. It is possible that 1 Sam 9 or 1 Chr 8(//9) telescopes Saul's genealogy, but it is more likely that 1 Sam 9 and 1 Chr 8 (//9) bear witness to different traditions, the reconciliation of which may be impossible.

"Saul." The reign of Israel's first king is summarily depicted and evaluated in 10:1–14. Only the last event of Saul's life (his death) is included in Chronicles. On Saul's Benjaminite roots, see 1 Sam 9:1, 4, 16, 21; 10:2, 20–21; 22:7; 2 Sam 21:14; Acts 13:21. The coverage of his reign in 1 Samuel is richly detailed and varied (1 Sam 9:2–2 Sam 22:1; Jobling 1978; V. Long 1989; Edelman 1991; Dietrich and Naumann 1995), although the Chronicler's depiction has its own nuances (COMMENT).

"Abinadab" is mentioned in 1 Sam 31:2(//1 Chr 10:2), along with Jonathan and Malchi-shua, as one of Saul's slain sons. His absence from 1 Sam 14:49 may be due to a text-critical error.

"Eshbaal" *(ʾešbāʿal)*, or "Ishbaal" ("man of Baal"), succeeded his father Saul and was king over the northern tribes for a few years before David united both Judah and Israel under his command (2 Sam 2:8–4:12). In Samuel his other name, "Ishbosheth" (2 Sam 2:8, 10, 12, 15; 3:8, 14, 15; 4:5, 8), has usually been interpreted as dysphemistic: "man of shame." But recent research into Akk. and Amorite PNs with the element **bāšt-* suggests "man of the protective spirit" as an alternative meaning (Hamilton 1998).

9:40. "Merib-baal" *(mĕrîb baʿal)*, so vocalized, means "one contending with Baal" (1 Chr 8:34; 9:40; cf. Judg 6:32) and is to be contrasted with "Meri-baal" *(mĕrî baʿal)*, meaning "rebelliousness of Baal" (later in MT 1 Chr 9:40). The name could have originally meant "the lord contends" *(mērîb baʿal)* or "the lord is my master" *(mĕrî baʿal*; cf. Aram. *mar)*. In other words, the element "Baal" could have originally referred to Yhwh (McCarter 1984: 82). The same son of Saul is also called "Mephibosheth" (2 Sam 4:4; 9:6). The narratives in Samuel mention a series of incidents through which Saul and his line suffer tremendous losses (2 Sam 3:1; 4:5–8; 5:2; 21:1–14). The story of Saul's suicide and loss of progeny at Mount Gilboa (1 Chr 10:1–14) is thus only one of a number of catastrophes to devastate the house of Saul. The genealogist traces the continuation of Saul's line through his physically disabled son.

9:41. "sons of Micah." Samuel mentions the survival of Mephibosheth and his son Micah (2 Sam 9:3–13; 2nd TEXTUAL NOTE to 8:34), but no family of Micah appears in Samuel. By tracing the continuation and floruit of the Jeielite line through this son of Merib-baal (9:41–44), Chronicles keeps the lineages of Saul and David completely separate and distinct. In Samuel the situation is much more complicated (see COMMENT).

9:44. "Azel." The verse is arranged chiastically:

a Azel had six sons
    b and these were their names . . .
a′ All of these were sons of Azel.

For a full discussion of chiasm in Chronicles, see Kalimi (1995a: 191–234). First Chronicles 8:39–40 adds further information about a collateral line, "the sons of Esheq his brother."

10:1. "the men of Israel fled from before the Philistines." Of the many and varied incidents in Saul's career depicted in 1 Samuel, the Chronicler presents only the last—the story of Saul's death. The transition from the genealogy in 1 Chr 9 is abrupt, but not entirely unique (Ezra 7:1; Neh 1:1; Willi 1972: 10; Mosis 1973: 17–18).

"Mount Gilboa" was the site of the camp for the Israelite army (1 Sam 28:4).

10:4. "lest these uncircumcised come and abuse (*htʿllw*) me." The *hitpaʿel* of *ʿll* means to deal with someone arbitrarily, usually with connotations of ruthlessness or brutality (e.g., Judg 19:25; 1 Sam 6:6). Saul is not so much afraid of death as he is of torture and humiliation by the enemy.

"took the sword and fell upon it." In spite of medieval and modern pronouncements about suicide being dishonorable or sinful, there is no clear indication that such views were widely held in the ancient Near East. In Chronicles, Saul's problem is not suicide. Saul's rebellion against Yhwh led to his demise, and hence to the termination of his rule (10:6, 13–14).

10:6. "all of his house died together." This summarizing statement, unique to Chronicles, bears dynastic connotations (Willi 1972: 160; Mosis 1973: 22). There is a tension between the claim made here and the genealogy of 9:40–44 that Saul's line continued on for many generations. In speaking of Saul's "house," the Chronicler may have Jonathan, Abinadab, and Malchi-shua (10:2) in mind. These sons may have represented (to the Chronicler) the legitimate or obvious claimants to the Saulide throne. The genealogy of 9:35–44 traces continuity in Saul's line through Jonathan's disabled son, Merib-baal (9:40). The presentation of 10:1–14 makes no mention of Merib-baal (Mephibosheth). In any case, the author's larger point is clear. Saul's royal regime is finished. Cf. 1 Sam 28:15–19.

10:7. "abandoned their towns and fled." The Israelite defeat, coupled with the death of Saul and his sons, lead to a state of panic for those Israelites remaining in the valley.

10:9. "to herald the news to their idols and the people." The verb *bśr* "to spread news" often has positive overtones (2 Sam 1:20; 4:10; Isa 40:9; Jer 20:15; Ps 68:12 [ET 68:11]), as it does here. In the ideology of Canaanite kingship, the king enjoys a degree of kinship with the divine realm. The king, although human and vulnerable, is mythologically paired with the gods. In the Kirta legend, King Kirta plays a "divine" role as a nexus between heaven and earth. This role raises questions as to how Kirta, "the son of El," the "beloved of El," can become ill and die.

Shall you also die, O father, as mortals,
or (shall) your court pass over to mourning,
to the control of women, O Father of the Heights?
Or shall gods die,
shall the offspring of the Kind One not live? (*KTU* 1.16.II.40–44)

Like the king of Ḫubur in the Kirta legend, Saul enjoys a critical position in divine-human affairs. The health of the king's body is linked to the health of the body politic. By treating Saul's head and armor as trophies of war, the Philistines vaunt the triumph of their deities over Israel's deity. This victory, publicly disseminated by spreading the triumphal news, is commemorated by displaying Saul's head and armor in the Philistine sanctuaries.

10:10. "his armor in the temple of their gods." A ritual dedication on the part of the Philistines and a humiliation for the Israelites (cf. 1 Sam 21:9–10 [ET 21:8–9]). Ackroyd (1977: 6) calls attention to the story of David and Goliath (1 Sam 17). After beheading Goliath, the Philistines flee and David brings the head of Goliath to Jerusalem (1 Sam 17:54). See also the NOTES to 18:8, 11.

"his skull they impaled." Saul's earlier fears were well-founded: "The Philistines, failing to take Saul alive, took vengeance on his body" (Japhet 1993a: 224).

"Dagon" (Akk. "Dagan") is one of the earliest and most widely-attested deities of the western Semitic world. Dagan was the chief god of Ebla (third millennium B.C.E.) and the Lord of Terqa and other cities of the Middle Euphrates in the Old

Babylonian period (Dion 1995: 1291). Some scholars think that Dagan was primarily an agricultural deity, but texts from Mari and Emar point to his martial responsibilities as well. Texts from Emar, for instance, speak of Dagan as both "lord of the seeds" and "lord of the military camp" (van der Toorn 1995: 2045). At Ugarit, Dagan had a temple approximately the same size as that constructed for Baal. Though Ugaritic texts sometimes refer to Dagan as the father of Baal, Dagan does not play any significant role in the Ugaritic myths (*KTU* 1.24:14; cf. 6.13, 14). Biblical writings portray Dagon as god of the Philistines (Judg 16:23) or, more specifically, as god of Ashdod (1 Sam 5:7). Temples of Dagon at Ashdod are attested in biblical (1 Sam 5:2, 5) and deuterocanonical literature (1 Macc 10:83; 11:4; Azotus = Ashdod).

10:11. "Jabesh-gilead" was one of the principal towns in the region of Gilead. Its location is uncertain. Some identify it as T. Abū al-Ḫaraz, located about 32 km southeast of the Sea of Kinnereth (Galilee), in the Transjordan, while others identify it as T. al-Maqlub. Traditions in Judges and Samuel speak of a special relationship with the Benjaminites in general and with the house of Saul in particular (Judg 21:8–14; 1 Sam 10:27–11:15 [4 QSam[a]; Josephus, *Ant* 6.68–71]; 31:11–12; 2 Sam 21:12).

"did to Saul." Near the beginning of Saul's career, Saul heroically delivered the residents of Jabesh-gilead from oppression (1 Sam 10:27–11:15). See the discussions of 4QSam[a] and Josephus *Ant.* 6.68–71 in McCarter (1980b: 198–207) and Cross (1983a). Now the town's residents return the favor.

10:12. "fasted (*wyṣwmw*) for seven days." Fasting is often associated with impending death (2 Sam 12:16; Joel 1:14; 2:15; cf. 12:21–23) or a crisis (1 Sam 7:5; 2 Chr 20:3; Ezra 8:21; Neh 1:4; Jdt 4:13; 1 Macc 3:47). But fasting after defeat and death is also attested (Judg 20:26; Bar 1:5).

10:13. "in his transgression (*bmʿlw*) by which he transgressed (*mʿl*) against Yhwh." The negative evaluation of Saul plays on the root *mʿl*, one of the Chronicler's choice terms for profound infidelity and disobedience (Curtis and Madsen 1910: 31 [#68]; Mosis 1973: 29–33; Milgrom 1976: 16–35; Johnstone 1996: 243–48). In this respect, the debate about whether *mʿl* is purely cultic or theological (Knierim 1997: 680–82) poses a false dichotomy. Cultic infractions can presuppose certain beliefs about the divine. By the same token, certain conceptions of the divine may be tied to orthopraxis. In Chronicles acts of *mʿl* involve the deity, whether directly or indirectly. Some instances of *mʿl* explictly involve trespass upon the *sancta* (Milgrom 1976: 17). These include Uzziah's offering incense inside the Temple (2 Chr 26:16–18), Aḥaz's plundering of the Temple and his desecration of the sacred furnishings (2 Chr 28:18–19, 22–25; 29:19), and the officers', priests', and people's pollution of the Temple (2 Chr 36:14). Other acts of *mʿl* can directly involve the deity. These include defrauding Yhwh (1 Chr 2:7; cf. Josh 7:1; 22:16, 20, 22) and worshiping other gods (1 Chr 5:25; 2 Chr 28:19). Whether the act of *mʿl* involves a cultic property or a direct infraction against the deity, the consequences are severe. Uzziah is struck with leprosy (2 Chr 26:19–21), while Aḥaz is punished with foreign domination (2 Chr 28:20). The worship of other gods by the Transjordanian tribes leads to their Assyrian exile (1 Chr 5:26), while the pollution of the Temple contributes to Judah's Babylonian exile (2 Chr 36:17–21; cf. 1 Chr 9:1). In the case of Saul, the divine punishment involves death and the transfer of the kingdom to David (10:14).

"concerning the word of Yhwh, which he did not observe" *(ʿl-dbr yhwh ʾšr lʾ-šmr).* The language is reminiscent of that employed in the Deuteronomistic History (Weinfeld 1972a: 335 [#14], 336 [#16–17]). But is this, as some scholars suggest, a specific reference to a prophetic command of Samuel (e.g., 1 Sam 13:13–14 with *šmr*; 15:22–23 with *šmʿ*) disregarded by Saul? Or is it a reference to Saul's violation of the legal injunctions against necromancy? The use of *dbr yhwh* would seem to point to the former, but it is impossible to identify the exact source with any more precision (1 Sam 15:22–23 *mʾst ʾt-dbr yhwh*; cf. 1 Sam 13:13–14 *lʾ šmrt ʾt-mṣwt yhwh).* Both the laws of Moses and the words of the prophets carry prestige in Chronicles (e.g., 2 Chr 20:20).

"even consulting a necromancer" *(wgm-lšʾwl bʾwb).* Playing on Saul's name (*šāʾûl—lišʾôl*; Kalimi 1995b: 37) and referring to the prelude to Saul's disastrous last battle (1 Sam 28:3, 7–25). Consultation with soothsayers to obtain contact with the dead is forbidden in legal texts (Lev 19:31; 20:6, 27; Deut 18:10–11), but is conceded to have occurred in Judahite history (2 Kgs 21:6; 23:24). The practice is also condemned in Isa 8:19–20 (Lewis 1989: 128–32).

"to seek (counsel)" *(ldrwš).* The verb *drš* is one of the Chronicler's favorites to express divine inquiry and veneration (Curtis and Madsen 1910: 29 [#23]; Mosis 1973: 39–41; Duke 1990: 149; Graham 1999). Begg (1982) argues that the concept lies at the heart of Chronistic theology. The elliptical use of the verb requires some discussion. One employs a necromancer to gain access to the deceased. The necromancer becomes the medium through which the spirit speaks and delivers advice. For the Chronicler, reverencing a spirit, or another deity for that matter (2 Chr 17:3; 25:14–15), is the opposite of seeking Yhwh (1 Chr 10:14).

10:14. "did not seek *(drš)* Yhwh." This statement contrasts with the assertions in 1 Sam 14:37; 15:31; 28:6. In 1 Sam 28:6 Saul inquires *(šʾl)* of Yhwh, but Yhwh does not answer him by dreams, lots, or prophets (Cogan 1995). In the Chronicler's work, Yhwh responds to those who call out to him (2 Chr 15:4). According to the Chronicler, Saul's infraction, like that of Israel in Jeremiah, had two dimensions. In the judgment oracle of Jer 2:10–13, the prophet faults Israel both for abandoning its deity, the fount of living waters, and for turning to "no-gods," broken cisterns that cannot hold water. Similarly, the Chronicler faults Saul both for not seeking God and for conferring with a necromancer.

"put him to death" (וימיתהו). In Samuel this claim is not made. In Chronicles it is not enough for an upheaval in the kingdom to take place, because that would involve simply a communal, and not a personal, punishment. Given that Saul committed the transgression (NOTE to v. 13), Saul himself must suffer the consequences. A similar interpretive strategy is evident in the Chronicler's handling of Jeroboam, the first king of the rebellious northern kingdom. Having chosen not to narrate the independent history of the northern realm, the Chronicler alludes to Jeroboam's sins in the context of his treatment of Reḥoboam (2 Chr 11:13–17) and Abijah (2 Chr 13:4–12; Knoppers 1993a). In the aftermath of

Abijah's victory in holy war against Jeroboam, "Yhwh struck him [Jeroboam] and he died" (ויגפהו יהוה וימת; 2 Chr 13:20). No such claim is made in Kings. There the downfall of the northern kingdom is tied to the foundation and perpetuation of Jeroboam's countercultus (1 Kgs 14:7–18; 2 Kgs 17:21–23; Knoppers 1994e), but Jeroboam himself reigned for "twenty-two years and slept with his fathers" (1 Kgs 14:20).

"and turned (*wysb*) the kingdom over to David." As elsewhere in Chronicles, the kingdom does not belong to the king, but to God (e.g., 1 Chr 17:14; 28:2–5; 29:10–12). The use of *sbb* in this context is significant. Machinist (1995b) points to other unexpected transitions in biblical literature, including the change from the United Monarchy to the dual monarchies, in which *nsbh* (2 Chr 10:15; *sbh* in the parallel of 1 Kgs 12:15) occurs, "But the king would not listen, because it was a turning point from God." To this can be added the Chronicler's judgment on the death of King Aḥaziah: "the downfall (*tbwst*) of Aḥaziah was from God" (2 Chr 22:7). In each case, divine power is confirmed, despite an unexpected turn of events. That the Chronicler views all three transitions as divine judgments does not entail, however, that he sanctions the activities of the Philistines (1 Chr 10:1–10), the (northern) Israelites under Jeroboam (2 Chr 10:1–19), or Jehu (2 Chr 22:7–9).

## Sources and Composition

The question of sources for the Jeielite genealogy (9:35–44) is dealt with in our discussion of 1 Chr 8:1–9:1 (see SOURCES). At first glance, the composition of 10:1–14 would seem to be fairly easy to explain. The first twelve verses are drawn from a version of 1 Sam 31:1–13. Because of the language, style, and theology evident in 10:13–14 (see NOTES), these final verses may safely be attributed to the Chronicler. The Chronicler's direct dependence on Samuel, a widely shared assumption among critical scholars since the time of de Wette, has been challenged recently by Ho (1995: 82–106), who favors the common-source hypothesis and thinks that the material in 1 Chr 10 is closer to the original source than 1 Sam 31 is. In Ho's view, the edited story of 1 Sam 31 was added by the same redactor of Samuel who added other material designed to exonerate David of responsibility for the fall of Saul and his house. Ho's work rightly challenges the all-too-common supposition that the Chronicler abbreviated and changed his *Vorlage*, a text presumed for all intents and purposes to be MT Samuel. Such a supposition cannot be sustained (see TEXTUAL NOTES). One can further agree that some (but not all) of the pluses in 1 Sam 31 fall into a pattern, involving a wider Philistine presence (e.g., Beth-shean) than is presupposed in Chronicles, and that these pluses have literary connections to 2 Sam 21:1–14. Nevertheless, it is a gigantic leap in argumentation to assert that the Chronicler only had access to a largely truncated story of Saul (1 Sam 1–18*; 28). The shared pluses that MT and LXX 1 Sam 31:1–13 have over against MT and LXX 1 Chr 10:1–12 offer no clear evidence that shows that the version of Saul's story held by the Chronicler lacked both the stories of David's rivalry with Saul (1 Sam 18:1–27:4) and the stories dealing with the final fate of the Saulide remnants (e.g., 2 Sam 21:1–14; 1 Kgs 2:46). Indeed, given the Chronicler's learned allusions to David's early rise in the narration of David's reign (COMMENT on 1 Chr 12), it seems quite likely that the Chronicler knew of Samuel's stories about the rivalry between Saul and David. The writer chose to formulate his own distinctive presentation of the early monarchy, rather than to follow his source slavishly. The most one can say, given the limited amount of textual evidence available, is that the Chronicler's source was slightly shorter than MT Samuel. The Chronicler's *Vorlage* represents a briefer, typologically more primitive text of Samuel than MT 1 Sam 31. If either Samuel or Chronicles clearly exonerates David vis-à-vis the demise of Saul, it is Chronicles (see COMMENT).

## COMMENT

The chapter dealing with Saul's final battle has itself become the scene of considerable scholarly conflict. Although the Chronicler's treatment of Saul is extremely brief in comparison to the attention he devotes to David and Solomon, the interpretive issues are important. It may be useful to survey the major interpretive options as a prelude to the present discussion (Knoppers forthcoming [b]). Each of the four major theories offers helpful insight into the placement and meaning of this story, but fails to provide, in my judgment, a complete explanation. Many scholars think that the Chronicler included a chapter on ill-fated Saul as a foil to David's glories (e.g., Kittel 1902: 56; Rothstein and Hänel 1927: 199; von Rad 1930: 79; Galling 1954: 41; Rudolph 1955: 96). This view highlights the stark contrast the Chronicler draws between Saul and David, but it does not explain the appearance of other more temperate comments about the tribe of Benjamin and the age of Saul (e.g., 5:10; 8:33//9:39; 26:28). Moreover, the inclusion of the long Jeielite genealogy points to the importance of Saul's ancestral house. To sustain the stark contrast between Saul and David, some of these scholars attribute the temperate references to the work of later editors. But this position has another shortcoming. If the Chronicler wished to establish a comparison between David and a period of rank anarchy, why did he not begin his narrative with the period of the Judges? Surely the chaos attending this era (esp. Judg 17–21), when coupled with other failures of Saul (e.g., 1 Sam 13:1–14; 15:1–31), would contrast tremendously with the triumphs of David. Yet Chronicles begins with the last episode in Saul's life.

Mosis (1973: 17–43) and Ackroyd (1977: 3–9) offer a second hypothesis, stressing that the story of Saul is an important narrative in its own right that should be interpreted primarily in the context of Chronicles and not in the context of Samuel. The Chronicler dramatically recasts a specific defeat of Saul as a paradigm of failure, defeat, divine judgment, and exile. This second view commendably calls attention to the theological nuances inherent within the Chronicler's work and his propensity to draw connections between the various events he depicts. In this respect, Saul's demise illustrates the Chronicler's understanding of divine justice. Yet one wonders how archetypal the presentation is. As Zalewski (1989: 450–52) points out, the Chronicler's depiction of Judahite kings makes no mention of Saul whatsoever. Nor is there a substantial change in Israel's general geographical situation (Japhet 1993a: 225–30). There is a local, but not a widespread dislocation of people (10:7). Finally, the references to "the word of Yhwh" (דבר יהוה) and to necromancy (לשאול באוב) point the reader back to Samuel (NOTES to 10:13–14). It is no assault against the literary integrity of the Chronicler's narrative to acknowledge that he has made some learned allusions to Samuel. Indeed, as Mitchell (1999: 326) has commented, the reader of Chronicles who "knows Samuel-Kings can appreciate the dialogue between the two, as well as the little ironies and playfulness that Chronicles has built into its text."

Japhet (1989: 405–10; 1993a: 225–30) presents a third theory, in some respects the converse of the first theory and a repudiation of the second. Over against Ackroyd and Mosis, she argues that the Chronicler rewrites Saul's final battle to play down its severity for the Israelite people. In her judgment, the Chronicler portrays the loss to the Philistines as primarily affecting Saul and his family. Instead of presenting Saul's downfall as an exilic situation, the Chronicler purportedly stresses the continuity from Saul's regime to that of David. There is something to be said for Japhet's view, because it highlights the manner in which the Chronicler's depiction of Saul provides a context for David's rise. The careers of the two kings are not contemporaneous, but consecutive. Nevertheless, the kingdom does change hands. The attempt to downplay the disaster is not entirely convincing, because it is predicated on the faulty assumption that the minuses in Chronicles represent the Chronicler's deliberate abridgment and reworking of MT Samuel (see TEXTUAL NOTES). Moreover, while it is true that the Chronicler draws attention to the annihilation of Saul's house (10:6), his portrayals of the Philistine victory (10:1–6), the Israelite abandonment of the valley (10:7), the stripping of Saul's corpse, and the dedication of Saul's head and armor in the Philistine temple (10:9–10) clearly have national implications.

Zalewski (1989: 455–66; 1997) offers a fourth view, stressing that the treatment of Saul is intimately tied to the narratives in Samuel and should be interpreted accordingly. The Chronicler's presentation of Saul presents his death as the fulfillment of Samuel's prophecies (1 Sam 13:13–15; 15:26–28; 28:16–19). Because the oracles of Samuel not only authorize Saul's demise but also hint at the ascent of David, the Chronicler's allusions to them legitimate the rise of David. Zalewski commendably draws attention to the importance of intertextuality for the interpretation of Saul's reign in Chronicles. Especially with respect to the Chronicler's judgment against Saul in 1 Chr 10:13, Zalewski's theory is well-founded. This is a specific, not a general, reference to an act of necromancy mentioned elsewhere only in Samuel. But as Mosis points out, the Chronicler's references to Saul's transgression *(mʿl)* against the word of Yhwh (10:13) and his failure to seek *(drš)* Yhwh (10:14) are couched in typical Chronistic idiom. Efforts to tie these general judgments to any one specific event in Samuel flounder for want of direct evidence (2nd NOTE to 10:13).

With the theory of Zalewski, one sees the interpretation of the Saul story coming full circle. Like Rothstein, Hänel, von Rad, and Rudolph, Zalewski sees a tremendous contrast between the ignominious fall of Saul and the rise of an ideal David. Nevertheless, along with Ackroyd, Mosis, and Japhet, one must pursue the issues of context and coverage. The interpretative issue may not be a question of either continuity or discontinuity, but of both continuity and discontinuity. The Chronicler's narrative draws a sharp line between the careers of Saul and David, but also avers that these monarchs are consecutive rulers of the same kingdom.

What, then, is the role and function of the Saul narrative in Chronicles? In my judgment, this question is best addressed by pursuing two considerations. The first has to do with the Chronicler's historiography, while the second has to do with the Chronicler's circumstances in Persian period Judah. One may begin by recognizing the importance of a particular feature of the Chronicler's allocation of coverage—his focus upon the monarchy. He begins his narrative with Israel's first king (1 Chr 10), and he ends it with Judah's last (2 Chr 36). As many have observed (e.g., Japhet 1989: 395–44), the writer views the monarchy as the authoritative polity for Israel. The Davidic-Solomonic monarchy is the era in which Israel's national institutions achieve their definitive form. In view of the Chronicler's concern with the story of the monarchy, he has to devote at least some attention to its first king. The question is, therefore, not why the author begins his narrative with Saul, but what he says about him. One should examine not only how the authors of Samuel have configured the relationship between Saul and David but also how these authors have portrayed the inception of the monarchy itself. Second, to understand the depiction of Saul in Chronicles, one has to acknowledge, to a much higher degree than commentators have in the past, the Chronicler's own geopolitical context. The author lived during an age in which kinship relations and the question of lineage were of great consequence for determining status and self-identity. Given the prominence of the tribe of Benjamin in the Chronicler's own day, a prominence the author affirms (COMMENT on 8:1–9:1), Samuel's stories about Benjaminite Saul's demise and Judahite David's rise were likely sensitive issues.

In Samuel the beginnings of the monarchy are steeped in controversy. Israel's last pre-monarchic leader, Samuel, is both successful and well-respected. Nevertheless, when Samuel grows old, the elders of Israel demand a king to replace him because Samuel's sons are corrupt (1 Sam 8:1–3). Samuel considers the people's request to be a step backward and voices sharp opposition to what he considers to be the inherently abusive nature of royal rule (1 Sam 8:11–18). Yhwh's evaluation of the request for kingship is also illuminating. He considers the people's request as, not a rebuke of Samuel, but a rejection of his own divine kingship (1 Sam 8:7; cf. Judg 8:22–23). Nevertheless, Yhwh counsels Samuel to accede to the people's demand. In deference to Yhwh's wishes, Samuel oversees the institution of the monarchy and personally anoints Saul (1 Sam 9:1–10:1). In his final speech to "all Israel," however, Samuel reminds Israel of their past infidelity and sternly warns both them and their future king to be faithful (1 Sam 12:1–25). Should Israel stubbornly persist in its wrongdoing, both Israel and its monarch will be swept away (1 Sam 12:25). Both the warnings about and the begrudging acceptance of kingship are significant. The book of Samuel associates the inauguration of kingship with conflict.

Compared to the profound suspicions about kingship in 1 Samuel, the Chronicler's condensed version of the Saul story is extraordinary. For the Chronicler, the institution of monarchy is not the issue. When Saul fails, a change of polity is not entertained (Riley 1993: 39–53). The defeat of Saul's forces, his beheading, and the Philistine ritual display of his skull represent a humiliation of Israel. Because writers in the ancient world often associated the health and well-being of a monarch with the well-being of his people, the sickness, failure, or death of a king could reflect negatively on the nation the monarch served. Nevertheless, when Saul's rule ends in ignominy and three of his male heirs perish, the kingdom endures (1 Chr 10:14). As in the legend of Kirta (*KTU* 1.16.VI.41–54; Knoppers 1994a), the adverse effects of one king's problems do not lead to a debate about exchanging kingship for another polity. Rather, Prince Yaṣṣub cites the ill health and negligence of royal duties by Kirta as an argument for his father's abdication and transfer of power to Yaṣṣub (*KTU* 1.16.VI.41–54). Similarly, the deaths of Saul and his three sons do not result in a change of polity. After Saul's failure, God turns the kingdom over to David (1 Chr 10:14).

The Chronicler's unique treatment of Saul is important for a related reason. By omitting all the material in Samuel that casts doubts upon the viability of the monarchy, the Chronicler's treatment of the early monarchy shifts the focus from the institution of the monarchy to the conduct of individual kings. Here too the Chronicler's presentation differs considerably from that of Samuel. In Samuel, Saul begins with promise and never himself engages in the kinds of royal abuses Samuel criticizes. Both Saul and his son Jonathan enjoy military success (1 Sam 10:27–11:13; 13:1–3; 14:1–23). Nevertheless, Saul disappoints and is repeatedly denounced by the very prophet who anointed him. To complicate matters further, Saul's eventual replacement is a younger contemporary who happens to be his son-in-law. As the narrators depict the conjunction between Saul's slow demise and David's inexorable rise, the fate of Saul's family (e.g., Jonathan, Michal, Mephibosheth) and David's family become closely intertwined (Edelman 1991). On more than one occasion Saul even speaks of "my son David" (בני דוד; 1 Sam 24:17 [ET 24:16]; 26:17, 21, 25). Because David marries into the family of Saul, he provides himself with a chance, should all of Saul's sons perish, to inherit through his wife Michal part or all of his father-in-law's estate and kingdom (1 Sam 18–19). In a kinship-based society this is one example of the practice of optative affiliation, the attempt to improve one's potential future claims through marriage (Flanagan 1983). When one after another of Saul's sons die, David's potential to gain (through Michal) from his father-in-law's death increases.

The tensions between the house of Saul and the house of David do not end with Saul's tragic death. When David becomes king over Judah, Ishbosheth (Ishbaal), Saul's son, is king over Israel (2 Sam 2:1–11). Given his earlier relationship with the house of Saul, it comes as no great surprise that David sets Michal's return to his household as a condition in the negotiations with Abner for Ishbosheth's crown (2 Sam 3:12–16). That the only surviving male member of Saul's house, Mephibosheth (Merib-baal) the son of slain Jonathan, is crippled further complicates the matter of the Saulide succession (2 Sam 4:4; 9:1–13; 21:7). Later, when David himself encounters many political troubles and his very future is in jeopardy, Mephibosheth expresses the hope that the throne would return to the house of Saul (2 Sam 16:3). David's throne survives, of course, but his relations to Saul's house are clouded by David's inconstancy to Mephibosheth, a trait that bothered the early interpreters (e.g., Tg. 1 Chr 9:40; *b. Yoma* 22b). Subsequently, David surrenders seven more of Saul's descendants, who are put to death by the Gibeonites (2 Sam 21:1–9). David is thus very much involved in Saul's life, kingdom, and family affairs, even though the authors of Samuel defend David against the charge that he was complicit in the tragic demise of Saul and his sons (Halpern 2001). In short, the authors of Samuel concede not only that David's ascent to power was a protracted and difficult affair but also that negative relations between the house of Saul and the house of David continued throughout most of David's reign.

There is much in Samuel that would be problematic for the Chronicler. Indeed, there was a great advantage to be had by simply ignoring most of this material. Omitting all of the stories about David's relationships with Saul, Jonathan, and the members of Saul's house gives the writer a free hand to dissociate David from Saul. The manner in which the Chronicler fashions a lengthy genealogy, ignores most Samuel narratives about Saul, recasts the story of Saul's death, and alludes to a few other events in Saul's career creates a distinctively new portrait of Saul and his relationship to David. To be sure, the Chronicler knows of Michal (1 Chr 15:29), but he chooses not to tell her story. Similarly, by posting two completely different genealogies in two different tribes, the Chronicler distances the house of David from the house of Saul. The lengthy Jeielite genealogy testifies to the prominence and perdurability of the family to which Saul belonged (Oeming 1990: 173–79). The Chronicler settles the matter of David having any chance to profit personally from his father-in-law's ruin historically by showing that the Jeielite lineage continued well beyond the United Monarchy. In this context, the author can freely acknowledge that the tribe of Benjamin furnished Israel with its first king. The Chronicler can also stress the contributions that the Benjaminites made to the establishment of David's kingdom (1 Chr 11:31; 12:2, 17–19, 30; 27:12, 21). The lineage and tribe of Israel's first monarch are given their due.

By focusing on the last battle of King Saul's life and ignoring, for the moment, Saul's and Jonathan's positive accomplishments, the author casts Saul's royal legacy in a negative light. The actions of one member of one Benjaminite line, not the tribe of Benjamin, are at issue. The careers of Saul and David are sequential and essentially do not overlap. Because the Chronicler makes no mention of David in his depiction of Saul's demise, David is not associated in any way with Saul's downfall. To be sure, the later references to Saul indicate that the Chronicler knew otherwise (1 Chr 11:2; 12:1, 2, 20, 24; 13:3). But consistent with the author's understanding of divine justice, Saul is judged according to his own actions. The cause of his demise is straightforward: Saul "did not observe" the word of Yhwh and so Yhwh "put him to death." David does not appear as part of the story line until Saul and his royal house are gone. Remarkably, many of Saul's own relatives recognize and endorse the new order. The Jeielite line continues, even though the Saulide monarchy is history. Among those who join David in Ḥebron "to turn (*lĕhāsēb*) the kingdom of Saul over to him, according the word of Yhwh" (1 Chr 12:24), are 3,000 Benjaminites, kin to Saul, who had earlier maintained allegiance to Saul's house (1 Chr 12:30). In Chronicles, the fact that David succeeds Saul has nothing to do with lineage, marriage, inheritance, or political machination. David comes to the kingdom because of divine choice and human acclamation.

In discussing Saul's death in the context of Saul's complicated relationship to David, McCarter (1980b: 443) comments that "the report of Saul's death is remarkable for its lack of finality." Given the way in which the destinies of Saul and David overlap in Samuel, there is much validity to this observation. But there is a sense of finality in the Chronicler's depiction of Saul's demise. The circumstances and results of Saul's death are unambiguous. His transgression (מעל) means that his life is ended and his royal regime is terminated. Saul's ruin does not mark, however, the end of his family or of the Israelite kingdom itself. Indeed, the history of "the kingdom of Yhwh in the hands of the sons of David" (2 Chr 13:8) is just beginning. But Saul's death definitively ends the first chapter in the Israelite monarchy.

# 3. The Rise and Reign of David

◆

## *XIV. David Is Acclaimed King by All Israel and Endorsed by the Armed Forces (11:1–47)*

*The Acclamation of David as King*

1 And all Israel gathered to David at Ḥebron, saying, "We are your bone and
your flesh. 2 Even formerly, when Saul was king, you were the one who led Israel
out and led Israel in. And Yhwh said to you, 'As for you, you will shepherd my people Israel and you, you will become ruler over Israel.' " 3 When all the elders of Israel came to the king at Ḥebron, David cut a covenant with them before Yhwh.
And they anointed David as king over Israel, according to the word of Yhwh
through the hand of Samuel.

*The Capture of Jerusalem*

4 And David and all Israel went to Jerusalem—that is, Jebus, where the Jebusites
were the inhabitants of the land. 5 And they told David, "You will not enter here,"
but David captured the fortress of Zion, that is, the City of David. 6 David
said, "Whoever strikes a Jebusite first will become commander in chief." When
Joab son of Zeruiah was the first to go up, he became commander. 7 David resided
in the fortress; hence, they called it "the City of David." 8 And he built up the city
on all sides, from the millo to the surrounding area, while Joab restored the rest
of the city. 9 David grew more and more important and Yhwh Sebaoth was
with him.

*Introduction to David's Forces*

10 These are the commanders of David's warriors, who continually strengthened him in his kingship, along with all Israel, to make him king, according to the
word of Yhwh concerning Israel.

*Jashobeam, Eleazar, and David*

11 And this is the muster of David's warriors: Jashobeam son of Ḥachmon, commander of the Three. He brandished his spear over three hundred slain on one occasion. 12 And after him, Eleazar son of Dodai the Aḥoḥite. He was among the
three warriors. 13 He was with David at Pas Dammim. The Philistines were gathered there for battle and there was a section of the field full of barley. When the

people fled from before the Philistines, [14]they took their stand in the middle of the
section, held it, and routed the Philistines. Thus, Yhwh achieved a great victory.

*The Exploits of Three Commanders*

[15]Three of the thirty commanders went down by the rock to David, to the cave
of Adullam, the force of the Philistines being encamped in the Valley of Rephaim.
[16]At that time David was in the fortress, while at the same time a garrison of the
Philistines was in Bethleḥem. [17]And David said wishfully, "Who would give me a
drink of water from the cistern at Bethleḥem that is inside the gate?" [18]The Three
broke through the Philistine camp and drew water from the cistern at Bethleḥem
that is inside the gate. They carried it and brought it to David, but he was unwilling to drink it. He poured it to Yhwh, [19]saying, "Far be it from me before my God
that I should do this! Shall I drink the blood of these men with their lives? For by
(risk of) their lives they have brought it." Hence, he was unwilling to drink it.
Such were the deeds of the three warriors.

*Abshai and Benaiah*

[20]As for Abshai the brother of Joab, he became commander of the Thirty. He
brandished his spear over three hundred slain. He did not attain a name among
the Three. [21]Of the Thirty, he was the most honored and functioned as their
leader. But he did not attain to the Three. [22]Benaiah son of Jehoiada from Qabzeel
was a valiant man who accomplished many deeds. He struck down the two sons of
Ariel of Moab. He went down and struck a lion in the midst of a pit on a snowy day.
[23]He also struck down the Egyptian man, a giant five cubits tall. In the hand of the
Egyptian was a spear like a weavers' beam. Yet he went down to him with a staff,
wrenched the spear out of the Egyptian's hand, and killed him with his spear.
[24]Such were the deeds of Benaiah son of Jehoiada. He did not attain a name
among the three warriors. [25]He was honored among the Thirty, though he did not
attain to the Three, and David appointed him over his bodyguard.

*David's Valiant Warriors*

[26]The valiant warriors:

Asah-el brother of Joab;
Elḥanan son of Dodai from Bethleḥem;
[27]Shammoth the Ḥarodite;
Eliqa the Ḥarodite;
Ḥelez the Pelonite;
[28]Ira son of Iqqesh the Teqoaite;
Abiezer the Anathothite;
[29]Sibbekai the Ḥushathite;
Ilai the Aḥoḥite;
[30]Mahrai the Neṭophathite;
Ḥeled son of Benaiah;
[31]Ittai son of Ribai from Gibeah of the Benjaminites;
Benaiah the Pirathonite;
[32]Ḥurai from the wadis of Gaash;
Abiel the Arbathite;
[33]Azmaveth the Baḥarumite;

Eliaḥba the Shaalbonite;
34 Jashen the Gunite;
Jonathan son of Shageh the Hararite;
35 Aḥiam son of Sakar the Hararite;
Eliphal son of Ur;
36 Ḥepher the Mecherathite;
Aḥijah the Pelonite;
37 Ḥezro the Carmelite;
Naarai son of Ezbai;
38 Joel brother of Nathan;
Mibḥar son of Hagri;
39 Zeleq the Ammonite;
Naḥrai the Berothite, the arms bearer for Joab son of Zeruiah;
40 Ira the Ithrite;
Gareb the Ithrite;
41 Uriah the Hittite;
Zabad son of Aḥlai;
42 Adina son of Shiza the Reubenite, a commander among the Reubenites, and thirty with him;
43 Ḥanan son of Maacah;
Jehoshaphaṭ the Mithnite;
44 Uzziah the Ashterothite;
Shama and Jeiel the sons of Ḥotam the Aroerite;
45 Jedaiel son of Shimri;
Joḥa his brother the Tizite;
46 Eliel the Maḥavite;
Jiribai and Joshaviah the sons of Elnaam;
Ithmah the Moabite;
47 Eliel;
Obed;
and Jaasiel the Mezobite.

## Textual Notes

11:1. "all Israel." So MT and LXX[AB]. LXX[L] *pas anēr Israēl* (= *kl ʾyš yśrʾl*). MT 2 Sam 5:1 "all the staff bearers *(šbṭy)* of Israel."

"gathered *(wyqbṣw)* to David." So MT and LXX[L]. LXX[AB] follow MT 2 Sam 5:1 "came (*wybʾ*) to David."

"Ḥebron." MT and Tg. 2 Sam 5:1 add "and they said." Lacking in 4QSam[a] and OL.

11:2. "when (Saul) was" (גם בהיות). The shorter lemma of MT 2 Sam 5:2 (בהיות) may be earlier, but one cannot rule out the possibility of haplography *(homoioteleuton)* from שלשום גם בהיות to שלשום בהיות.

"who led" (המוציא). So MT 11:2, Qere 2 Sam 5:2, and fragmentary 4QSam[a]. Kethib MT 2 Sam 5:2 evinces a misdivision of words, הייתה מוציא.

"Yhwh." Reading with LXX[B], Syr. and 2 Sam 5:2 *(lectio brevior)*. MT, LXX[L], and Arm. *(Dominus Deus tuus)* expand to "Yhwh your God."

"ruler over Israel." Reading with LXX[AB] and 2 Sam 5:2 *(lectio brevior)*. MT, LXX[L], Arm. "ruler over my people Israel" assimilates toward the expression "my people Israel" earlier in the verse.

11:3. "David." So MT. LXX[BL], Arm., Syr., and MT 2 Sam 5:3 add "the king."

"according to the word of Yhwh through the hand of Samuel." So MT and LXX. Josephus (*Ant.* 7.53) is similar, but the phrase is lacking in 2 Sam 5:3. MT and LXX 2 Sam 5:4–5 add regnal formulae for David (cf. 1 Kgs 2:11; 1 Chr 29:27). But these data are missing both from the OL of Samuel and evidently from 4QSam[a] (Ulrich 1978: 60–62). Given the text-critical evidence, it is likely that the *Vorlage* of Chronicles did not contain this information.

11:4. "David and all Israel." So MT, LXX[L], Syr. LXX[AB] and MT 2 Sam 5:6 "the king and his men."

"that is, Jebus." A parenthetical explanation lacking in 2 Sam 5:6.

"where the Jebusites" *(wšm hybwsy)*. So MT and LXX. MT 2 Sam 5:6 "to the Jebusites" *(ʾl hybwsy)*.

"the land." So MT, LXX[AN], and Arm. LXX[B] "Jebus." On the expression "the Jebusites (were) inhabitants of the land," see Kropat, §17.

11:5. "they told David" *(wyʾmrw ldwyd)*. So LXX[B] $c_2$ *(lectio brevior)*. MT and LXX[L] explicate to "the inhabitants of Jebus told David." MT (and LXX) 2 Sam 5:6 read the sg. and add a citation formula, *wyʾmr ldwd lʾmr*. OL, Syr., and Tg. (of Samuel) have the pl. *(wyʾmrw)*.

"You will not enter here." 2 Sam 5:6 adds a saying about the blind and the lame (the textual witnesses, including 4QSam[a], vary; see Ulrich 1978: 128–29; McCarter 1984: 135–37; Olyan 1998). The reference may be an addition, however, inserted by repetitive resumption from *lʾ tbwʾ hnh* to *lʾ ybwʾ dwd hnh*. See also 2nd TEXTUAL NOTE to (v. 6).

11.6. "David said." MT 2 Sam 5:8 adds "on that day."

"whoever strikes a Jebusite." The texts of Samuel and Chronicles offer two completely different apodoses for this protasis. 2 Sam 5:8 begins, "whoever strikes a Jebusite and strikes at (or through) the *ṣnwr*" (translations differ: "windpipe," "channel," "shaft," etc.). There follows in Samuel another extended reference to the blind and the lame (the textual witnesses vary; see McCarter 1984: 136–37; Caquot and de Robert 1994: 401–4), followed by an explanatory comment as to why the blind and lame may not enter the Temple. Textual reconstructions and interpretations of this passage in Samuel vary widely (Olyan 1998: 219–27). The difference between the two texts baffled the early interpreters, such as Pseudo-Jerome (Saltman 1975: 114–15), who basically harmonized the two readings or combined them. The witness of Josephus (*Ant.* 8.63–64) is complex in that he seems to have supplemented his Samuel text with material from his version of the Greek Chronicles (Ulrich 1978: 188–89). Many have assumed that the Chronicler rewrote the Samuel text, but one cannot rule out the possibility that at least part of the Samuel text is a later addition (Hertzberg 1964: 268–69; McCarter 1984: 137–40; Trebolle Barrera 1989a: 96–97). This makes reconstructing the most primitive reading difficult. It is interesting to note that Chronicles, like Samuel, contains an explanatory comment—the bestowal of the title "commander" (ראש) to Joab after he attacked the Jebusites. In Chronicles the remark informs the reader that title of "commander" was bestowed upon Joab for his assault against the Jebusites. Hence, the structure of the Samuel and Chronicles texts bears some resemblances—protasis (introduced by a ptc.; GKC, §116w), apodosis, explanatory comment—even though their content is dissimilar. The texts of Samuel and Chronicles both preserve material (in the shared protasis) that has been developed in very different ways.

"commander in chief." Taking *lr'š wlśr* as a hendiadys.

11:7. "in the fortress; hence, they called it" *(bmṣd ʿl kn qr'w lw)*. So MT. LXX* has the sg. "he called it." MT 2 Sam 5:9 *bmṣdh wqr' lh*, "the fortress and (re)named it."

11:8. "and built up the city on all sides" *(wybn hʿyr msbyb)*. So MT and LXX[ABN] 11:8 and LXX[L] 2 Sam 5:9. LXX[AB] 2 Sam 5:9 and 4QSam[a] 2 Sam 5:9 evince a different word division, but essentially agree with MT 1 Chr 11:8: *w[y]bnh ʿyr*[__]. See also Josephus (*Ant.* 7.65). MT 2 Sam 5:9 *wybn dwd sbyb*, "and David built up (the) surrounding (area)," is deficient.

"from the millo to the surrounding area" *(mn hmlw' wʿd hsbyb)*. So MT and LXX[L]. The phrase is lacking in LXX*, perhaps due to haplography by *homoioteleuton* (from *msbyb* to *hsbyb*). MT 2 Sam 5:9 is somewhat different, *mn hmlw' wbyth* ("from the millo to the palace"). On the use of *sbyb* as a substantive in LBH, see Qoh 1:6; Num 22:4; Ezek 16:57; 28:24; Dan 9:16.

"while Joab restored the rest of the city" *(wywʾb yḥyh ʾt šʾr hʿyr)*. LXX[AB] construe David as the subject of *kai epolemēsen kai elaben tēn polin* ("and he waged war and took the city"). Galling (1954: 40) suggests a slight emendation, "while Joab restored the gates of the city" *(šʿry hʿyr)*. The entire expression is lacking in Samuel, but its presence here is consistent with the Chronicler's earlier narrative (v. 6b). On the meaning "restore" for *ḥyh* in the *piʿel*, compare Neh 3:34 [ET 4:2] (BDB 311). Note as well the meaning of *ḥwy* "to restore" in Phoen. (*KAI* 4.2 [Byblos] and perhaps 26.A.I.3–4 [Karatepe]) and Pun. (*KAI* 153.3/5; Krahmalkov 2000: 179).

11:9. "(and) David grew more and more important" *(wylk dwyd hlwk wgdwl)*. So MT and LXX[AN]. On the idiomatic use of *hlk* with the inf. abs. of the same root, see Lambdin, §170. LXX[B] lacks *wgdwl* due to haplography *(homoioarkton)* before *wyhwh*.

"Yhwh Sebaoth was with him" (יהוה צבאות עמו). So MT and LXX, as well as LXX[B] and 4QSam[a] 2 Sam 5:10. MT 2 Sam 5:10 expands to "Yhwh the God of hosts was with him" (יהוה אלהי צבאות עמו).

11:10. "who continually strengthened him" (המתחזקים עמו). Understanding the *hitpaʿel* of *ḥzq* as iterative (Lambdin, §177).

11:11. "and this is the muster of David's warriors" *(w'lh mspr hgbrym ʾšr ldwyd)*. So MT *(lectio difficilior)*. LXX* has the expected sg. *houtos*. The use of the pl.

demonstrative pron. *ʾlh* is not impossible (cf. Esth 1:9; contra Kittel 1902: 58). 2 Sam 23:8 "These are the names *(ʾlh šmwt)* of David's warriors." Tg. adds a lengthy panegyric to David and attributes to him the slaying of three hundred on one occasion.

"Jashobeam" *(yšbʿm)*. See also 12:7; 27:2. LXX$^{B}$ $c_2$ *Iesebada*; bb′ *Iessebaal*; iny *Isbaal* (= *ʾyšbʿl*, "Ishbaal"). LXX$^{L}$ 1 Chr 27:2 *Iesboam*. MT 2 Sam 23:8 *yšb bšbt*; LXX$^{B}$ *Iebosthe*; LXX$^{L}$ *Iesbaal*. The name is lacking in Tg., hence Tg. attributes his accomplishments to David (see previous TEXTUAL NOTE). The original Samuel reading was most probably "Ishbaal" (Budde 1902: 319), but Chronicles evinces, in this case, a different or later stage of textual development.

"son of Ḥachmon." The textual witnesses differ about Jashobeam's patronymic (cf. 1 Chr 27:2). MT 11:11 *bn hḥkmny*; MT 2 Sam 23:8 *tḥkmny* (corrupt). Chronicles may conflate two variants: "son of Ḥachmon" *(bn ḥkmn)* and "the Ḥachmonite" (*hḥkmny*; McCarter 1984: 489). Cf. OL and LXX$^{L}$ 2 Sam 23:8.

"commander of the Three" *(hšlwšh)*. So LXX$^{L}$ 11:11 and LXX$^{L}$ 2 Sam 23:8. Qere 11:11 (and LXX$^{B}$ 2 Sam 23:8) "commander of the officers" *(hšlyšym)*. MT 2 Sam 23:8 is similar, *hšlyšy*. Kethib 11:11 (and LXX$^{B}$) "commander of the Thirty" *(hšlwšym)*.

"he brandished his spear" *(hwʾ ʿwrr ʾt ḥnytw)*. So MT. LXX is similar. MT 2 Sam 23:8 *hwʾ ʿdynw hʾṣnw* is problematic (Budde 1902: 319).

"three hundred." So MT and LXX$^{B}$ *(lectio difficilior)*. Josephus (*Ant.* 7.308); LXX$^{L}$ "nine hundred;" 2 Sam 23:8 "eight hundred." Since Jashobeam has pride of place among the Three, the impetus would be to inflate his figure.

11:12. "Dodai" *(dwdy)*. So LXX$^{BL}$ *Dōdai*. LXX$^{S}$ *Dōde*. MT 11:12 and Qere 2 Sam 23:9 "Dodo" *(dwdw)* is also possible (Tallqvist 1914: 71). The variants reflect a *wāw/yôd* confusion. Cf. Kethib 2 Sam 23:9 *ddy*.

11:13. "at Pas Dammim" *(bps dmym)*. Some LXX cursives *bʾps dmym* (cf. 1 Sam 17:1). LXX$^{L}$ *en* (bb′ *tois*) *Serran*. 2 Sam 23:9 *bḥrpm*.

"the Philistines were gathered there for battle." 2 Sam 23:10–11a add information, detailing the exploits of Eleazar and introducing Shammah son of Age. The absence of this material, which was lost in the *Vorlage* of Chronicles due to haplography (from *bplštym nʾspw šm lmlḥmh* in 2 Sam 23:9 to *wyʾspw plštym lḥyh* in 2 Sam 23:11), has important consequences for the Chronicler's presentation. First, the text contains the names and deeds of two, not three, warriors. Second, as Chronicles lacks both the accomplishments of Eleazar and the name of Shammah, Chronicles attributes the latter's deeds (2 Sam 23:12) to David and Eleazar (v. 14).

"there was" *(wthy)*. Some restore "there" *(šm)* on the basis of 2 Sam 23:11, but given the context in Chronicles, this is unnecessary.

"full of barley" *(śʿwrym)*. So MT and LXX$^{AB}$ *(krithōn)*. LXX$^{L}$ *(phakou)*, OL *(lenticulae)*, Arm. *(Lente)*, and 2 Sam 23:11 read "full of lentils" *(ʿdšym)*. Tg. combines both readings.

11:14. "they took their stand" *(wytyṣbw)*. So MT. LXX and 2 Sam 23:12 have the sg.

"held it" *(wyṣylwh)*. Again, LXX, Syr., and 2 Sam 23:12 have the sg.

"and routed" *(wykw)*. LXX, Syr., and 2 Sam 23:12 have the sg. *wyk*.

"thus, Yhwh achieved a great victory." Reading with LXX, Syr., and 2 Sam 23:12 *wyʿś* (cf. Rothstein and Hänel 1927: 211). MT's "and he delivered" *(wywšʿ)* evinces metathesis. On the expression, *ʿśh yšwʿh/tšwʿh*, see Exod 15:2; 1 Sam 14:45; Isa 12:2; 26:18; Hab 3:8; Pss 20:6 [ET 20:5]; 21:2, 6 [ET 21:1, 5]; 44:5 [ET 44:4]; 68:20 [ET 68:19]; 118:14, 15, 21.

11:15. "three." So MT and LXX. MT 2 Sam 23:13 "thirty."

"the thirty commanders" *(hšlwšym rʾš)*. For MT and LXX$^{L}$ *rʾš*, LXX* has the pl. *archontōn*. It is possible that *rʾš*, occurring both here and in MT 2 Sam 23:13, should be deleted as a gloss designed to distinguish between these warriors and the earlier three (vv. 11–14; cf. 2 Sam 23:9).

"by the rock" *(ʿl hṣwr)*. Thus MT and LXX. MT 2 Sam 23:13 *ʾl qṣyr* ("to harvest" or "at harvest time;" McCarter 1984: 490–91).

to the cave of Adullam." So MT and LXX *(eis to spēlaion Odollam)*, as well as 2 Sam 23:13. Many follow Wellhausen in emending MT *mʿrt* ("cave") to *mṣdt* ("fortress"), which assimilates the lemma of v. 15 toward the formulation of v. 16. But vv. 15 and 16 are not synonymous. Both provide information about the whereabouts of David and the Philistines, but in neither case are the locations for David ("cave of Adullam," "the fortress") and the Philistines ("the Valley of Rephaim," "Bethleḥem") identical. The discrepancy may reflect larger source-critical and redactional issues in the composition of Samuel, but such issues should not be resolved artifically by text-critical emendation.

11:16. "a garrison" *(nṣyb)*. MT 2 Sam 23:14 *mṣb*, "station" or "outpost."

11:17. "and David said wishfully" *(wytʾw)*. 2 Sam 23:15 *wytʾwh* (GKC, §75bb).

"cistern" *(bwr)*. Some translate "well" (e.g., NRSV), but *bwr* (or *bʾr* in Samuel) almost always means "cistern" (*HALOT* 116).

11:18. "the Three" *(hšlwšh)*. So MT and LXX *(lectio brevior)*. 2 Sam 23:16 *šlwšt hgbrym*, "the three warriors."

"and brought it" (וַיָּבִאוּ). Lacking in LXX*, but see v. 19 (הביאום). Some Heb. MSS, LXX$^{ABaLNS}$, and Tg., "and they came" (וַיָּבֹאוּ).

11:19. "before my God that I should do this" *(mʾlhy mʿśwt zʾt)*. So MT. The prep. *min* conveys relationship (Williams, §323). LXX *ho theos tou poiēsai to rhēma touto*. MT 2 Sam 23:17, "O Yhwh, that I should do this" *(yhwh mʿśty zʾt)*. But a few Samuel MSS and some of the versions, like Chronicles, have an inf. construction.

"with their lives" *(bnpšwtm)*. On the *b*- of accompaniment, see GKC, §119n. MT 2 Sam 23:17 "they went by (risk of) their lives" *(hhlkym bnpštm)*. Some (e.g., Rothstein and Hänel 1927: 213; Rudolph 1955: 98) delete this first occurrence of *bnpšwtm* in Chronicles as a dittography of the second (see next TEXTUAL NOTE). But it seems more likely that this phrase, attested in all witnesses, was added (perhaps already in the *Vorlage*) to create a deliberate wordplay (see NOTE).

"for by (risk of) their lives they have brought it" *(ky bnpšwtm hbyʾwm)*. Thus MT and LXX. Lacking in 2 Sam 23:17 because of haplography from *bnpšwtm ky bnpšwtm* to *bnpšwtm*.

11:20. "Abshai" (אבשי). Thus MT. LXX$^{BS}$ mc$_{2}$ *Abeisa*, LXX$^{AN}$ *Abessa*, and 2 Sam 23:18 reflect "Abishai" (אבישי). Similar variants appear in 2:16 (2nd TEXTUAL NOTE).

"of the Thirty." Cf. Syr. *(lectio facilior)*. MT and LXX 11:20, as well as Qere 2 Sam 23:18, read "the Three." Kethib 2 Sam 23:18 *šlyšy*. In reading with MT, NJPS is forced to translate "of another Three." On the originality of the lemma "the Thirty," see further Samuel Driver (1913: 367–68).

"over three hundred slain." I read with MT *(lectio brevior)*. The addition of LXX *(en kairō heni = bpʿm ʾḥt)* assimilates toward the formulation of v. 11.

"he did not attain a name" *(wlʾ šm)*. So MT. LXX, Vg., Syr., Tg., and 2 Sam 23:18, "he attained a name" *(wlw šm)*, is followed by many commentators. Others (e.g., Budde 1902: 321–22) would read *wlw šm kšlwš*, "and he had a name like that of the Three" (but he did not actually belong to them). In either case, the authors of Samuel and Chronicles seem to distinguish among the Three (vv. 11–14), the three commanders (vv. 15–19), Abshai and Benaiah (vv. 20–25), and (other) warriors or members of the Thirty (vv. 26–47).

"among the Three." So MT and LXX, as well as MT and LXX 2 Sam 23:18. Some emend to "among the Thirty" (cf. Syr.).

11:21. "of the Thirty." Cf. Syr. MT and LXX, as well as MT and LXX 2 Sam 23:19 "of the Three" *(mn hšlwšh)*.

"he was the most honored." MT *bšnym nkbd* is problematic. LXX *hyper* (b′ *epi*) *tous duo*. I follow Rudolph (1955: 98) and others in deleting MT's *bšnym*, which Syr. lacks. MT 2 Sam 23:19 is corrupt *hky (nkbd)*. LXX$^{B}$ 2 Sam 23:19 *ekeinos* (= *hwʾ*). LXX$^{L}$ 2 Sam 23:19 reflects *mšnym*, which may correct *mn šlwšh*, "above the Three," to "above the Two" (McCarter 1984: 491). Some (e.g., Curtis and Madsen 1910: 190) emend to *hnw* because of the parallel in v. 25.

11:22. "Benaiah *(bnyh)* son of Jehoiada *(yhwydʿ)*." LXX$^{ABN}$ *Iōdae*; LXX$^{L}$ *Iōad*; Arm. *Youad*. Syr. reflects *ywdʿ*.

"a valiant man" *(ʾyš ḥyl)*. I read with Syr. and LXX$^{AB}$ 2 Sam 23:20 *(lectio brevior)*. MT and LXX$^{L}$ 11:22 "son of a valiant man" *(bn ʾyš ḥyl)*. MT 2 Sam 23:20 contains a double reading: *bn ʾyš ḥyl* (Qere) and *bn ʾyš ḥy* (Kethib; Talmon 1960a: 165–66).

"he struck down the two sons of Ariel of Moab" *(hwʾ hkh ʾt šny bny ʾryʾl mwʾb)*. Reading with LXX$^{L}$ 11:22 and LXX$^{ABLN}$ 2 Sam 23:20. MT 11:22 *(hwʾ hkh ʾt šny ʾryʾl mwʾb)* and MT 2 Sam 23:20 have lost *bny* by haplography *(homoioteleuton)*. The import of *ʾryʾl* (literally, "lioness of El") is uncertain (*DNWSI* 100–101). In Ezek 43:15 and in the Mesha inscription, אראל (*KAI* 181:12) seems to designate an altar hearth (*HALOT* 87), but some (e.g., Albright 1968b: 151, 218) construe the term as referring to a hero or champion and understand *ʾrʾl* to mean "underworld, denizen of the underworld" (cf. *KAI* 30.5 אראלם).

11:23. "a giant" *(ʾyš mdh)*. So MT. The lemmata of LXX$^{AB}$ and MT (Qere) 2 Sam 23:21, "a man of appearance" *(ʾyš mrʾh)* and MT 2 Sam 23:21 (Kethib) *ʾšr mrʾh*, evince a *dālet/rêš* confusion.

"five cubits tall" *(ḥmš bʾmh)*. So MT and LXX. Lacking in MT and LXX 2 Sam 23:21.

"like a weavers' beam" *(kmnwr ʾrgym)*. So MT and LXX. Wanting in MT 2 Sam 23:21, but see the different LXX witnesses.

11:24. "Benaiah *(bnyhw)* son of Jehoiada *(yhwydʿ)*." So MT. LXX$^{BL}$ *Banaias huios Iōad* (1st TEXTUAL NOTE to v. 22).

"did not attain a name among the three warriors." Reading *wlʾ šm*, as in v. 20 (4th TEXTUAL NOTE). Cf. LXX^L *kai toutō onoma en tois trisi dynatois*; MT *wlw šm bšlwšh gbwrym.*

11:25. "he was honored among the Thirty *(mn hšlwšym hnw nkbd hwʾ)*, though he did not attain to the Three." So MT. LXX lacks the demonstrative particle with the suf. *(hnw)*. LXX^L "he was honored above the Two, but he did not attain to the Three." Cf. OL *De triginta in duobus praeclarus et ed tres non venit.*

"over his bodyguard" *(ʿl mšmʿtw)*. So MT. LXX *epi tēn patrian autou* (= *ʿl mšpḥtw*, "over his family," or *ʿl byt ʾbwtyw*, "over his ancestral house"). On the meaning of *mšmʿt* as "bodyguard," see Budde (1902: 323).

11:26. "valiant warriors" *(wgbwry hḥylym)*. So MT (GKC, §124q). LXX is similar, *kai* (LXX^ALN add *hoi*) *dynatoi tōn dynameōn*. The phrase is lacking in MT 2 Sam 23:24, but see the various LXX witnesses.

"brother of Joab." 2 Sam 23:24 adds "among the Thirty" *(bšlwšym)*.

"Dodai" *(dwdy)*. Cf. LXX^B *Dōdōe*; LXX^L *Dōdei* (TEXTUAL NOTE to v. 12). MT "Dodo" *(dwdw)*.

"from Bethleḥem." So MT and LXX^L. LXX^B reads with MT 2 Sam 23:24 "Bethleḥem."

11:27. "Shammoth" *(šmwt)*. Thus MT. LXX^BS $c_2$ *Samaōth*; Arm. *Samoutʿ* (= *šmhwt*?). Cf. MT 27:8 "Shamhuth" *(šmhwt)*. MT 2 Sam 23:25 *šmh* (cf. 2 Sam 23:11).

"the Ḥarodite." So MT 2 Sam 23:25. A *dālet/rêš* and a *hê/ḥet* confusion have affected MT and LXX "the Harorite" (cf. vv. 34, 35).

"Eliqa the Ḥarodite" *(ʾlyqʾ hḥrdy)*. So MT 2 Sam 23:25. Lost from 11:27 and LXX^B 2 Sam 23:25 by haplography *(homoioteleuton)*.

"Ḥelez the Pelonite." So MT and LXX, as well as LXX^ALMN 2 Sam 23:26. MT 2 Sam 23:26 "the Palṭite."

11:28. "Ira son of Iqqesh the Teqoaite." So MT. LXX^B *Ōrai huios Ektēs ho Thekō.*

11:29. "Ilai *(ʾyly)* the Aḥoḥite." So MT. MT 2 Sam 23:28 "Zalmon *(ṣlmwn)* the Aḥoḥite." Rudolph (1955: 100) thinks that *ʿyly* reflects **ṣyly*, a hypocoristicon of *ṣlmwn*. But it is more likely that "Ilai" is a hypocoristicon from *ʿwl*, "to give suck."

11:30. "Mahrai the Neṭophathite." So MT. LXX^BS *Neere* may reflect *nhry*.

"Ḥeled son of Benaiah." 1 Chr 27:15 "Ḥeldai." MT 2 Sam 23:29 reads erroneously *ḥlb* (McCarter 1984: 492).

11:32. "Ḥurai." So MT and LXX. MT 2 Sam 23:30 "Hiddai" *(hdy)*.

"Abiel" *(ʾbyʾl)*. So MT and LXX. The witnesses to Samuel lead some (e.g., Wellhausen) to reconstruct "Abibaal" *(ʾbybʿl)*. In the Persian period, PNs with the theophoric ʾĒl were quite popular.

11:33. "the Baḥarumite" *(hbḥrwmy)*. LXX^B *ho Beermein*; LXX^AN (and Arm.) *ho Barsami*. MT 2 Sam 23:31 *hbrḥmy*. Some conjecture *habbaḥūrîmî.*

11:34. "Jashen *(yšn)* the Gunite." Both MT (*bny hšm*, "sons of the name") and LXX (LXX^B *Bennaias ho Somologennounein*; LXX^L *huioi Asom* [bʹ *Asōm*] *tou Senn*[*e*]*i*, etc.) are corrupt. My reconstruction is partially based on MT 2 Sam 23:32 "sons of Jashen." Following Elliger (1935: 31), I understand *bny* to have resulted from a dittography after *šʿlbny* at the end of v. 33. McCarter (1984: 492–93) defends the lemma "the Gizonite," but see LXX$^{AN}$ 11:34 *ho Gōuni* (= *hgwny*). Guni was the name of a Naphtalite family (Gen 46:24; Num 26:48).

"Shageh *(šgh)* the Hararite." The witnesses vary. LXX$^{B}$ $c_2$ *Sōla* (cf. *b*b′ *Samaias*; $e_2$ *Samaia*; Arm. *Samea*). MT 2 Sam 23:33 *šmh* (cf. 2 Sam 23:11).

11:35. "Sakar *(śkr)* the Hararite." So MT and LXX$^{AN}$. LXX$^{BS}$ *Achar* (cf. LXX$^{AN}$ *Sachar*; LXX$^{L}$ *Issachar*). MT 2 Sam 23:33 "Sharar" *(šrr)*.

"Eliphal" *(ʾlypl)*. So MT and LXX$^{AN}$ (cf. LXX *Eliphael*). LXX$^{BS}$ *Elphat.* MT 2 Sam 23:34 "Eliphelet" *(ʾlyplṭ)*.

11:36. "Ḥepher." MT 2 Sam 23:34 "son of Ahasbai" *(bn ʾḥsby)*.

"the Mecherathite" *(hmkrty)*. So MT. LXX$^{B}$ $c_2$ *Mochor.* LXX$^{L}$ ($e_2$) *ho Mechōrathei.* MT 2 Sam 23:34 "son of the Maacathite" (cf. 1 Chr 2:48; 4:19).

"Aḥijah the Pelonite." The lemma of MT 2 Sam 23:34, "Aḥithophel the Gilonite" *(ʾḥytpl hglny)* may be original (McCarter 1984: 493).

11:37. "Ḥezro the Carmelite." So MT and Kethib 2 Sam 23:35. LXX$^{L}$ *Hesrei* follows Qere 2 Sam 23:35 "Heṣrai" *(hṣry)*.

"Naarai son of Ezbai" *(nʿry bn ʾzby)*. MT 2 Sam 23:35 "Paarai the Arbite" *(pʿry hʾrby)*.

11:38. "Joel brother of." So MT and LXX$^{AN}$. LXX$^{B}$ "Joel son of." MT 2 Sam 23:36 "Yigal son of," but LXX$^{L}$ "Joel brother of," as here.

"Mibḥar." LXX$^{BS}$ $c_2$ *Mebaal*; LXX$^{AN}$ b$e_2$ *Ma(a)bar.* MT 2 Sam 23:36 "Mizzobah" or "from Zobah" (מצבה).

"son of Hagri" *(bn hgry)*. So MT and LXX *(huios Hagarei)*. MT 2 Sam 23:36 "Bani the Gadite" *(bny hgdy)* is probably corrupt. LXX$^{LMN}$ 2 Sam 23:36 agree with 11:38.

11:40. "the Ithrite" *(hayyitrî)*. So MT 11:40 and MT 2 Sam 23:38. Some favor LXX$^{B}$ *ho Ēthērei*, reconstructing *hayyattirî*, "the Jattirite" (cf. 1 Sam 30:27; 1 Chr 2:53).

11:41. "Zabad." LXX$^{B}$ *Zabet*; Syr. "Zabdi" *(zbdy)*.

11:42. "and thirty with him" *(wʿlyw šlwšym)*. LXX *kai epʾ autō* (fin$e_2$ *autōn*) *triakonta.* The prep. *ʿl* conveys accompaniment (Williams, §293). Syr. reflects "over the thirty" *(ʿl hšlwšym*; cf. Arm. *super triginta)*, a reading favored *(ʿl šlwšym)* by Bertheau (1873) and Benzinger (1901).

11:43. "the Mithnite." So MT. Cf. LXX$^{L}$ *ho Matthan(e)i.* LXX$^{B}$ $c_2$ *ho Baithanei*; LXX$^{A}$ *ho Maththani.*

11:44. "the Ashterothite." So LXX$^{ABN}$ *(ho Astarōthei)*. MT "the Ashterathite." On the divine pl., see also "Anathothite" in v. 28.

"Jeiel." So Qere, LXX$^{ALN}$, Vg., and Tg. *yʿyʾl.* Kethib *yʿwʾl.* Syr. *ʿmyʾl.*

11:45. "Joḥa" *(yḥʾ)*. So MT. LXX$^{AB}$ *Iōazae*; LXX$^{L}$ *Ēla.*

"the Tizite" *(htyṣy)*. So MT. LXX$^{BS}$ $c_2$ *ho Ieasei.* LXX$^{AL}$ *ho (A)thōs(e)i*; Arm. *Tousi* (= *htwṣy*?).

11:46. "the Maḥavite" *(hmḥwym)*. So MT (maximum variation). LXX$^{BS}$ $c_2$ *ho Miei*; LXX$^{L}$ *ho Maōth(e)i*; LXX$^{A}$ *ho Maōein*; Vg. *Maumites.* Possible emendations include *hammaḥănî* ("the Maḥanite"), *hammĕʿônî* ("the Maonite"), and *hammaḥănaymî* ("the Maḥanaimite").

"Joshaviah" *(ywšwyh)*. LXX$^{ABS}$ $c_2$ *Iōseia.*

"the sons of." So MT and LXX^L^. LXX^AB^ *huios autou*, "his son."

11:47. "the Mezobite" *(hmṣbyh)*. So MT. LXX^BS^ $c_2$ *ho Meinabeia*; LXX^A^ *ho Mesōbia*; LXX^L^ *ho Mas*(b′ + s)*abia*. Rothstein and Hänel (1927: 221) propose *mṣbh* ("from Zobah") or *hṣbty* ("the Zobite").

# Notes

11:1–3. These verses are drawn from the author's *Vorlage* of 2 Sam 5:1–3, which contextualizes the coronation of David by Israel (= northern Israel) very differently. There David is finally accepted as king by the representatives of the northern tribes following a divisive and bloody seven-year civil war between the northern tribes, represented by the house of Saul, and Judah, represented by King David. Following a series of losses and the homicide of Saul's son and successor Ishbaal (Ishbosheth), the northern tribes accede to Davidic rule over their domain by sending representatives to Ḥebron to meet with victorious David and anoint him king. By omitting all of this material from Samuel (2 Sam 1–4), except for the final coronation of David by the northern tribes (2 Sam 5:1–3), the Chronicler ingeniously creates a literary proximity between the demise of Saul (1 Chr 10:1–14) and the acceptance of David as king by the northern representatives (Kalimi 1993c: 318–22). The reproduction (with some rewriting; see the following NOTES) of older material in a new literary context generates strikingly new meanings. Whereas the "Israel" of 2 Sam 5:1–3 clearly designates the northern tribes, in the context of Chronicles it designates both the northern and the southern tribes. One gains the impression that immediately after the death of Saul, all of the Israelites embraced David as their new king. Subsequent material in the portrayal of David's early career (11:10–12:39a) makes it clear that the author recognizes that things were not quite this simple. Yet even this alternate picture of David's rise to power radically contests the depiction of David's arduous and controversial ascent found in Samuel.

11:1. "all Israel gathered (קבץ) to David." This initial statement introduces a major theme for the entire section (1 Chr 11–12). Various Israelites from various quarters at various times and in various circumstances rally to David to strengthen his position as leader. As opposed to 2 Sam 5:1 in which "all of the staff bearers" *(šbṭy)* of the northern tribes approach David, the entire population welcomes David in Chronicles (Romerowski 1986: 5). Pan-Israelite assemblies are regular occurrences in Chronicles, and the Chronicler often uses the verb *qbṣ* ("to assemble") in such official contexts (1 Chr 13:2; 2 Chr 15:9; 20:4; 23:2; 24:5; 25:5; 32:4, 6; Wright 1991). The parallel (2 Sam 5:1) uses the verb *bw'* ("came"). The Chronicler's presentation of such representative gatherings may be compared with the portrayal of urban assemblies *(puḫru)* in Assyrian, neo-Babylonian, and Achaemenid sources. The members of these assemblies were mainly composed of elders *(šībūtu)* and free citizens (*mār banê*; Dandamaev 1995a: 26–29). The powers of such councils would vary depending on the time and place. Traditionally, such assemblies sought to preserve the sacred privileges of their cities (e.g., exemptions from certain taxes, forced labor, and military service). During the Achaemenid era, in which the role of the Babylonian assemblies was significantly reduced, such assemblies could still adjudicate property litigations, Temple cases, and local crimes (Dandamaev 1995a: 26–27). Hence, even in despotic monarchical political systems there was some gain to be had by allowing traditional authorities, such as the "elders of Israel" (זקני ישׂראל; 1 Chr 11:3), to exercise a certain role in society. In the Deuteronomistic and Chronistic portrayals of the monarchy, traditional forms of leadership often reappear during times of crisis (H. Tadmor 1971; 1982). In this particular case, the author plays on such power relationships by portraying traditional authorities as occasioning the advent of a new regime. The people gather to David; he does not assemble them. Most national gatherings in Chronicles occur at the instigation of a king.

"your bone and your flesh." In the portrayal of the meeting between David and the northern representatives in the Chronicler's source (2 Sam 5:1–3), the declaration of a relationship of blood kinship (cf. Gen 2:23; 29:14) becomes the means to ratify a formal covenant. The assertion of kinship is the device or legal mechanism whereby the two separate parties are brought together into one larger group (Cross 1998: 3–21). The literary context, however, differs here. Because the Israel of Chronicles represents all of the tribes (see vv. NOTE to vv. 1–3), the affirmation of kinship between the tribal sodalitics and David means that an old bond is simply being given a new political expression. The promise of loyalty is predicated on this underlying kinship (cf. Judg 9:1–2).

11:2. "even formerly, when Saul was king." The Chronicler will develop the implications of this claim in the sections that follow (esp. 12:1–2, 20–22, 24, 30). In his narration of Saul's demise (10:1–14), the Chronicler made the case that David's kingship was both consequent to that of Saul and divinely ordained. In 1 Chr 11–12, the writer additionally claims that David was attracting troops and loyal adherents from all sectors of the country, even while Saul was king. The cumulative effect of this steady stream of volunteers bolsters David's cause and fulfills Yhwh's will for Israel.

"you were the one." The repetition of the second-person singular pronoun (אתה) three times in this verse underscores that David's critical leadership role in the recent past makes him the most suited to succeed Saul in the present.

"who led Israel out and led Israel in." The idiom refers to the activity of a soldier (Josh 14:11; 18:13; 1 Sam 29:6; cf. 2 Sam 5:24; van der Lingen 1992). In the *hipʿil* the expression designates military leadership (e.g., Num 27:11). Hence, in this context, the idiom alludes to David's service as an Israelite military leader during the reign of Saul (1 Sam 18:13), a service David handled quite adeptly (1 Sam 18:14–16).

"Yhwh said to you." The use of the divine citation formula adds gravity to the declaration. No such oracle is attested within the earlier material in Chronicles. The claim has been made that it refers to 1 Sam 23:10 (Eissfeldt 1931: 27), but another possibility seems more likely (see next NOTE).

"you will shepherd my people Israel, and you, you will become ruler over Israel" (על ישׂראל ואתה תהיה נגיד). The message is drawn from Nathan's dynastic oracle (2 Sam 7:7). In Chronicles these words are first proclaimed by the tribal representatives as a prophecy that should be realized. The words are then later echoed in Nathan's dynastic oracle. There David is asked the rhetorical question of whether Yhwh ever requested one of Israel's judges, who "shepherded (רעה) my people," to build him a house of cedars (1 Chr 17:6//2 Sam 7:7). In the same oracle Yhwh continues the shepherding analogy by declaring to David, "I took you from the pasture, from behind the flock, to be ruler over my people Israel" (להיות נגיד על עמי ישׂראל; 1 Chr 17:7//2 Sam 7:8). Hence, the prophecy of Nathan marks the fulfillment of the declarations made here and employs them as the basis for formulating new promises to David (1 Chr 17:9–14).

"ruler *(nāgîd)* over Israel." The term *nāgîd* has been much debated: charismatic ruler (Hertzberg 1964: 267), tribal leader (Yeivin 1971: 165), military commander (Cross 1973: 220–21), crown prince (Lipiński 1974b: 497–99), king-designate (Mettinger 1976: 151–84; Ishida 1977b: 35–51; McCarter 1980b: 178–79). Suffice it to say, the term has different nuances in different contexts (1 Sam 9:16; 10:1; 13:14; 25:30; 2 Sam 7:8; 1 Kgs 1:35; 14:7; 16:2; 2 Kgs 20:5). In the material peculiar to Chronicles, *nāgîd* is often used in administrative contexts. The term appears, in fact, twice as often in Chronicles as it does in any other biblical book (Knoppers 1994b: 75–76). Context dictates that *nāgîd* carries connotations of "king-designate" here.

11:3. "all the elders." The presence of Israel's traditional leaders confirms David's kingship (see the 1st NOTE to v. 1).

"cut a covenant." That is, David entered a formal agreement with the Israelites. Enacted "before Yhwh," the pact was most probably mutually binding (Kalluveettil 1982: 18–19, 60; Mettinger 1976: 114–41, 228ff.). The narrator portrays David in a privileged position. The elders come to him, and he ratifies a covenant with them (not vice versa).

"anointed David." As McCarter (1980b: 178) points out, the "rubbing or smearing with a sweet-smelling substance . . . involved a symbolic transfer of sanctity from the deity to an object or person and thus was essentially a sacramental act." Priests could also be anointed (Exod 40:10–15; Lev 4:3, 5; 6:15). There is also one instance of an instruction that a prophet (Elisha) should be anointed (1 Kgs 19:16), but there is no record of this having been done. The person receiving such unction could be called the "anointed one" or "messiah" *(māšîaḥ)* of Yhwh. Campbell (1986: 18–47) points to a pattern in Samuel-Kings relating to how Saul, David, and Solomon become king through a series of steps, one of which is anointing (1 Sam 9:16; 10:1; 15:1, 17; 16:1–13; 2 Sam 2:4; 5:3; 12:7; 1 Kgs 1:34, 39, 45; cf. 1 Kgs 19:15, 16; 2 Kgs 9:6; 11:12; 23:30). The Chronicler, consistent with his royal interests, largely reserves the title *māšîaḥ* and exclusively the verb *mšḥ*, "to anoint," to refer to the Davidic monarchs (1 Chr 11:3; 14:8; 29:22; 2 Chr 6:42[//Ps 132:10]; 22:7; 23:11; cf. 1 Chr 16:22[//Ps 105:15]).

"according to the word of Yhwh through the hand of Samuel." This phrase, absent from the text of the Chronicler's *Vorlage*, alludes to the prophecies of Samuel (1 Sam 15:28; 16:1–13). It does not seem to refer directly to v. 2b ("you will shepherd my people Israel") because that prophecy is attributed directly to Yhwh. The notation presumes, therefore, that readers have some knowledge of the events presented in Samuel. As with the prophecy referred to in v. 2b, this prophetic citation underscores the divine election of David by presenting the path to David's kingship over all Israel as following a divinely authorized plan. For other examples of the Chronicler's creation of prophecy-fulfillment schemas to unite his work, see Kalimi (1995a: 143–48).

11:4–9. In Chronicles David captures Jerusalem as his first public act upon being made king. This material, drawn from the author's version of 2 Sam 5:6–10, has been cited to argue that David subjugated Jerusalem fairly early in his reign (B. Mazar 1963a: 241–43). But there are severe problems in employing the Chronicles account in this way: "Jerusalem could not have been conquered and built during the very event of the enthronement" (Japhet 1993a: 234). Elsewhere, the Chronicler makes it quite clear that David ruled in Ḥebron for seven years (e.g., 1 Chr 3:4; 29:27) before he came to reign in Jerusalem. Rather than rewrite the chronology of David's reign, it would be better to recognize that the author is applying to the figure of David an epic-heroic topos long established in Ancient Near Eastern historiography. Assyrian kings claim to have taken some of their most significant actions at the very outset of their reigns or to have achieved their greatest victories during the first year *(ina šurru šarrūtiya)* or term *(palû)* of their reign (H. Tadmor 1981). In his annals Ashurnasirpal II announces, "In my accession year in my first term . . . I mustered my chariotry and troops, I passed through difficult paths and rugged mountains" (*ARI* 2 §544; H. Tadmor 1981: 19). As if the point about timing was not clear enough, Tukulti Ninurta I claims, "At the beginning of my reign, upon my accession to the throne, in my first term" (*ina šurru kussê šarrūtiya ina maḫrê palêya*; H. Tadmor 1981: 15). The studied use of this heroic topos in royal Assyrian historiography illumines puzzling features in the sequence of David's royal career. The placement of the conquest of Jerusalem at the very beginning of David's reign is an excellent example of achronological historiography. This technique, sometimes also called chronological displacement, involves deliberately narrating events out of chronological order to make a larger point (H. Tadmor 1958: 22–40, 77–100; 1965: 351–63; Martin 1969: 179–86; Halpern 1990: 81–141; Glatt 1993: 10–54). Foregrounding critical accomplishments early in a monarch's reign glorifies the timing and impact of those actions. The Chronicler, by situating the capture of Jerusalem at this earliest point in the narrative, underscores the fundamental importance of Jerusalem both to David and to Israel. The conquest of Jerusalem thus contributes to a heroic picture of David's reign (Scippa 1989; Oeming 1994: 415–20). Indeed, the connection between David and Jerusalem figures already in the Davidic genealogy (3:4).

11:4. "went to Jerusalem." In Samuel, David captures Jerusalem with his own forces (אנשיו), not with the armies of Israel or Judah (2 Sam 5:6). But consistent with his pan-Israel theme, the Chronicler attributes the conquest of Jerusalem to David and all the people. In this manner, the author makes the case that Jerusalem was the patrimony of all Israelites from the day it first was captured.

"Jebus, where the Jebusites were the inhabitants of the land." Already in the second millennium B.C.E., as attested in the El Amarna letters (EA 285–90; Moran 1992: 325–34), Jerusalem was called Uru-salim, "the foundation of (the deity) Shalim" (*šalim*; cf. Josh 10:5). The author of Ezek 48:35 may be alluding to Jerusalem's pre-Israelite status when he forecasts a change in Jerusalem's name to *yhwh šmh*, "Yhwh is there." There is, however, another tradition (Josh 15:63; Judg 1:21; 19:10–11; 2 Sam 5:6), reflected here, that names Jerusalem Jebus and the pre-Israelite inhabitants of Jerusalem as Jebusites. The Jebusites were, according to this tradition, Canaanites (Gen 10:16; 1 Chr 1:14; Josephus, *Ant.* 7.61).

11:5. "You will not enter here." A taunt by the inhabitants of Jebus, reflecting their confidence in being able to defend their fortress against any would-be conquerers. The reference to "the blind and the lame" in the final text of Samuel (2nd TEXTUAL NOTE to v. 5) intensifies the ridicule, but the challenge is already inherent in this Jebusite declaration to David.

11:6. "Joab." Chronicles does not evince sustained interest in Joab's career. Nevertheless, the Chronicler's coverage is more uniformly positive than that of Samuel-Kings. There Joab appears as one of David's generals (e.g., 2 Sam 18:16; 19:14 [ET 19:13]; 20:23), who runs afoul of David after he assassinates Abner (2 Sam 3:22–39). In David's "testament" (1 Kgs 2:5–6), David calls on his successor Solomon to rectify the bloodguilt Joab brought upon David. Hence, the Deuteronomistic version of David's final speech to his successor justifies Joab's ignominious end at the hands of Solomon (1 Kgs 2:33; Knoppers 1993c: 71–74). In Chronicles, Joab receives better press and appears as the second in command of David's kingdom. Joab contributes to the refortification of the City of David, becomes David's commander in chief, and is treated more sympathetically in the story of the census than he is in Samuel (1 Chr 11:6, 8, 26, 39; 18:15; 19:8–14; 21:2–6; 27:34; cf. 2 Sam 3:29, 39; 16:10; 24:2–4). There is no mention in Chronicles of Joab's demise. See also the NOTE to 19:12 and the 3rd NOTE to 20:1.

"son of Zeruiah" (*ṣĕrûyâ*). Zeruiah ("the one fragrant with mastic") was David's sister (2:16). It is standard procedure for biblical authors to identify someone by their patronymic. It may well be that Joab, Abshai (v. 20), and Asah-el (v. 26) are all identified by a matronymic because of their mother's status. The claim of Josephus (*Ant.* 7.11) that Joab's father was named Souri is probably based on the assumption that the Joab appearing in the Judahite genealogy ("Seraiah [*śĕrāyâ*] sired Joab") refers to this same Joab (4:14; 2nd NOTE).

11:7. "resided in the fortress." The pre-Israelite town was situated on the top of a hill overlooking the Qidron Valley and the Gihon spring (at the southeast corner of the site). Archaeological excavations have revealed that the town was fortified before David occupied it (see NOTE to v. 8).

"the City of David." Originally, this would refer to the area atop the hill in the southeast. When the town grew in later centuries to include the Temple mount to the north and the so-called suburbs in the west, the titles "Zion" (v. 5) and the "City of David" came to be used more broadly.

11:8. "built up the city." David's building projects consisted essentially of a palace and fortifications in Jerusalem (2 Sam 5:9, 11; 7:2; cf. 1 Chr 15:1; 17:1; 2 Chr 2:2 [ET 2:3]). But as this verse indicates, the Chronicler attributes more building activity to David than the authors of Samuel-Kings do. To take another example, only in Chronicles does David, not Solomon (1 Kgs 9:15), rebuild the millo. The impression of substantial restoration is consistent with the portrait of David as the one who meticulously plans for his chosen son to rule and construct the promised Temple (1 Chr 17). Some comment on the archaeological remains is necessary. British excavations in Jerusalem revealed a large stepped-stone structure, constructed perhaps to undergird a platform, on the northern section of the City of David (Kenyon 1974: 100–103). This terraced structure was dated to the tenth century and associated with the much-discussed *millōʾ* rebuilt by David and Solomon (1 Kgs 9:15). For discussions, see Shiloh (1981) and Mare (1987: 59–88). But more recent analysis has challenged this older thesis in a variety ways. The large stepped-stone structure, earlier thought to be the *millōʾ* of the Davidic-Solomonic era, is now thought to be part of a single architectural complex (along with its terraced foundations). Whether this complex was constructed in a single phase or in multiple phases and what dates one should assign to such a phase or phases are matters of avid debate. Some opt for the late Bronze Age, some defend the tenth-century date, some (following a low chronology) opt for a ninth-century date, and some opt for some combination of the above. See the discussions of Steiner (1989; 1994); Ariel (1990); Cahill and Tarler (1994: 32–36); Wightman (1993: 29–38); E. Mazar (1994: 64–72); Bahat and Hurvitz (1996); Niemann (1997: 252–95); Knauf (2000: 75–90); Finkelstein (2001: 105–15); de Groot (2001), and the articles edited by Vaughn and Killebrew (forthcoming). The proposals to redate the stepped stone structure leave few undisputed finds from the tenth century.

11:9. "grew more and more important." Construction of public works is typically associated with times of obedience, divine support, and prosperity (e.g., 2 Chr 11:5–12; 17:1–5; 26:9–10). Hence, the inclusion of this material from 2 Sam 5:10 dovetails nicely with the Chronicler's own theology.

"Yhwh Sebaoth was with him." In Chronicles the story of the consolidation of David's kingship manifests complementary concerns. David is elect of God (28:4) and succeeds Saul because God wills it (10:14). Yet this divinely ordained act is also taken for Israel's benefit. Israel rallies to David to accomplish God's will for David (11:2–3, 10, 12:23–24), and Israel rejoices in the aftermath of his initial success (12:39–41). The new king, in turn, is blessed with God's presence.

11:10. "commanders of David's warriors." This verse, an introductory rubric to the Chronicler's version of the list of warriors that follows in vv. 11–47, has been added to his *Vorlage* by the technique of repetitive resumption from ואלה ראשי הגברים אשר לדויד in v. 10 to ואלה מספר הגברים אשר לדויד at the beginning of v. 11. The new material is likely the Chronicler's own addition (Willi 1972: 224). Hence, the author has supplemented his source (2 Sam 23:8) to provide a distinctively Chronistic perspective on the identities, functions, and actions of these soldiers. In Samuel, the list of soldiers appears near the end of David's reign, but here the soldiers appear near the very beginning. Given the Chronicler's claim that these warriors strengthened David "in his kingship, along with all Israel, to make him king," he presents these soldiers not as a group of military personnel whom

David gathered over the course of his career, but as a group of military personnel who presented themselves to David early in his royal career. Hence, the scene seems to have shifted back to Ḥebron. The text does not return to the subject of Jerusalem (vv. 4–9) until David makes his first attempt to transfer the Ark (13:1–11).

"continually strengthened him." Israel's call to David to serve as king is followed by a visible demonstration of military support. The voluntary endorsement by troops from various tribes, "along with all Israel," progressively strengthens David and establishes his kingship (11:10; 12:1, 23, 24, 39). The catalogue of heroic warriors may be compared, in some respects, to the much longer catalogue of the Argonauts presented by the Hellenistic poet Apollonius of Rhodes (*Argon.* 1.23–233). There the greatest heroes of the time rally to Jason (the heir of King Pelias of Iolcus) to accompany him on his journey to recover the fleece of a golden ram.

"according to the word of Yhwh concerning Israel." Another allusion to prophecy (cf. 1 Sam 15:28; 16:1–13). Unlike the citation in 1 Chr 11:2, there is no reference to Samuel.

11:11–41a. These verses are drawn from an earlier version of 2 Sam 23:8–39 (TEXTUAL NOTES). The first section (1 Chr 11:11–14) deals with the exploits of a select group—"the three warriors" (//2 Sam 23:8–12).

11:11. "Jashobeam son of Ḥachmon." According to 1 Chr 27:2, Jashobeam's father was Zabdiel, one of the descendants of Perez (1 Chr 2:4–15; Ruth 4:18–22) and, therefore, a distant relation of David. In the Chronistic version of David's administration, Jashobeam is put in charge of the first of the twelve (monthly) divisions of David's army (1 Chr 27:2).

11:12. "Eleazar son of Dodai." Eleazar, like Jashobeam, was in charge of one of the twelve divisions of David's army (LXX 27:4; TEXTUAL NOTE).

"the Aḥoḥite." Aḥoaḥ, or in alternate form, Aḥiah (8:7; Fowler 1988: 151), is listed as a son of Benjamin's firstborn Bela (3rd TEXTUAL NOTE to 8:4).

"three warriors." In Samuel "the Three" are Ishbaal or Yeshbaal (McCarter 1984: 489), Eleazar, and Shammah son of Agee (2 Sam 23:8–11). Due to haplography in 1 Chr 11:13 (TEXTUAL NOTE), Chronicles only lists two of the Three: Jashobeam (= Ishbaal) and Eleazar.

11:13. "Pas Dammim." Perhaps to be associated with modern Damun, some 7 km northeast of Socoh. Pas Dammim (= Ephes-dammim) was the site of the battle with the Philistine giant (1 Sam 17:1; Stoebe 1973: 316).

"gathered there for battle." This statement points to an earlier time in David's career, either before he served as a Philistine mercenary (1 Sam 27) or while he reigned in Ḥebron. For David's victories against the Philistines, see 1 Chr 14:8–16 (//2 Sam 5:17–25).

11:14. "they took their stand." That is, David and Eleazar. In Samuel the feat is attributed to Eleazar alone, but in Chronicles (TEXTUAL NOTES) the heroic rout of the Philistines is attributed to both David and Eleazar. Note the earlier comment that "he [Eleazar] was with David at Pas Dammim."

"Yhwh achieved a great victory." In the Chronicler's ideology of war, Israel battles against its enemies, but ultimate credit for its victories and defeats lies with

Yhwh, who works through, alongside, and even independently of Israel's forces (Knoppers 1999c). In this respect, the inclusion of material from the Chronicler's *Vorlage* comports well with his own theology.

11:15–19. The material dealing with the exploits of three commanders at Bethleḥem is drawn from the author's version of 2 Sam 23:13–17. The three anonymous figures are associated with the warriors who follow in 1 Chr 11:26–47.

11:15. "three of the thirty commanders." Not to be confused with the Three alluded to in v. 12, who comprise a special elite (vv. 20–21, 24). In the view of Elliger (1935: 29–75) and Benjamin Mazar (1986: 99–103), the "thirty" were a select military institution, a cadre of David's most loyal men. Many scholars follow Elliger and Mazar, but Na'aman (1988b), contending that *šlyšym* ("officers") be read in 2 Sam 23:8 and consistently elsewhere (2 Sam 23:13, 19a, 23, 24), argues that there was no such institution. Na'aman thinks that 2 Sam 23 (and 1 Chr 11) opens with David's highest-ranking commander, followed by "the Three," the commander of the king's bodyguard, and a list of the rest of the officers. This approach helpfully calls attention to the overall structure of the lists in Samuel and Chronicles. Nevertheless, sustaining this line of interpretation entails dismissing many of the variants from Samuel and especially from Chronicles as corruptions of an original text. The text-critical evidence is more complex (see above). One cannot discount the possibility that by the time of the composition of 2 Sam 23:8–39, "the Thirty" was already a traditional number for the collection of warriors associated with David. Chronicles takes this development a stage further. The warriors, who flock to David total forty-seven or more (1 Chr 11:42, 44). There is no clear evidence, moreover, that the Chronicler emphasized the Thirty as an institution any more than his *Vorlage* did (11:20, 21, 25; cf. 12:4, 19; 27:6).

"Valley of Rephaim." Most scholars identify this valley or lowland (*ʿmq*) with the ridge opposite the old city of Jerusalem to the southwest (*el-Baqaʿa*). According to Josephus (*Ant.* 7.12.4), this valley began twenty stadia south of Jerusalem and reached Bethleḥem (cf. 1 Chr 14:9; Josh 15:8; 18:16; 2 Sam 5:17–25; 23:13; Isa 17:5; Aharoni 1982: 255).

11:16. "at that time." The Chronicler, like the authors of Samuel, does not explain the apparent discrepancies between the two locations of David and the two locations of the Philistines (vv. 15–16). Scholars have suggested that v. 15 (//2 Sam 23:13) represents a fragment of a larger narrative that has been associated with the story that begins in v. 16 (//2 Sam 23:14). In short, the Samuel text reflects more than one stage of composition. This is a plausible explanation for the tension in the Samuel text, but the Chronicler's incorporation of this tension into his own narrative requires additional comment. The Chronicler is fully capable of authoring harmonistic explanations (Kalimi 1995a: 113–48), but in this instance he makes no attempt to reconcile the incongruity found in his *Vorlage*. The Chronicler sometimes quotes his biblical sources verbatim and in succession. He occasionally juxtaposes citations with little or no intervening material or with only slight editing. Such a compositional technique plays havoc, however, with the notion that an ancient author's writing (*Grundschrift*) is ipso facto an internally consistent, flowing, seamless whole. Clearly, the writer draws from unrelated sources and allows differences in vocabulary, style, and even theme to stand. In brief, the Chronicler's compositional technique does not fit the traditional literary-critical model. Given that at least some of the (biblical) sources are known to scholars, the Chronicler's historiography should prove to be helpful in revising older constructions of source and redaction criticism.

11:17. "wishfully." Thirst, drought, or hunger are not the principal issues. David is goading his troops. David yearns specifically for water "from the cistern at Bethleḥem that is inside the gate." David is "idly wishing for water from his hometown" (McCarter 1984: 496). In neither Chronicles ("cistern," *bwr*; see the TEXTUAL NOTE) nor Samuel ("cistern," *b'r*) does the water seem to be fresh water (*pace* Stoebe 1994).

11:18. "drew water . . . inside the gate." By using the same vocabulary that David uses in v. 17, the narrator emphasizes the warriors' exact compliance with David's wishes.

"unwilling to drink it." David realizes that his earlier request was ill-considered. He had needlessly risked the lives of his warriors. For a similar sequence of events—David regretting an earlier, ill-considered decree—see 1 Chr 21 (the story of the census). The Chronicler does not include most of the unsavory details about David's personal life found in Samuel, but his David is still a fallible human being.

"poured it to Yhwh." That is, as a libation. Cf. 1 Sam 7:6; Jer 44:16–18 (libations to the Queen of Heaven; Blenkinsopp 1995: 80–81). On water libations in classical Judaism, see *t. Sukkah.* 3.3; *b. Sukkah* 50a; *m. Sukkah.* 5.1–4. For libations in classical literature, most often consisting of wine, oil, milk, honey, or water, see Hesiod, *Op.* 724–26; Euripides, *Bacch.* 284–85; Appollonius of Rhodes, *Argon.* 2.1271–75.

11:19. "drink the blood of these men." Because of the risk involved in obtaining this water, David likens it to his men's blood (cf. Gen 9:4; Lev 17:11). In Deuteronomic law Israelites are not to eat the blood of animals, but to pour it on the ground like water (Deut 12:16, 23–25; 15:23).

11:20–25. The exploits of Abshai and Benaiah (//2 Sam 23:18–23). Scholars generally agree that this duo is distinct from the initial triad (1 Chr 11:11–14), but disagree whether they are also distinct from the Thirty (e.g., S. Driver 1913: 367–68) or to be reckoned among the Thirty (e.g., Myers 1965a: 89). Given the assertion in v. 21 (TEXTUAL NOTE) that "of the Thirty" Abshai "was the most honored," the latter opinion holds sway.

11:20. "Abshai," Joab's older brother and the oldest of Zeruiah's three sons (2:16), becomes a prominent figure in David's entourage, known both for his prowess in battle and for his fierce loyalty (1 Chr 18:12; 1 Sam 26:6–12; 2 Sam 2:18; 16:9–12; 18:2; 19:21–23; 21:16–17).

11:22. "Benaiah." Captain of the Cherethites and Pelethites, David's royal bodyguard (2 Sam 8:18; 20:23; 1 Chr 11:25; 18:17). According to 1 Chr 27:5–6, Benaiah, or his son Ammizabad, was put in charge of the third military division for the third month. Zeron (1978: 25–26) calls attention to Canaanite and Egyptian stories of heroic exploits that form broad parallels to Benaiah's feat. See, for instance, the tale of Sinuhe's single combat and victory over a Syrian warrior (Lichtheim 1997: 77–82). In the context of biblical literature, see 2 Sam 21:15–22; 23:8–23.

"Qabzeel" (*qbṣʾl*). Judging by biblical references, Qabzeel was a town in the deep south of Judah, near Arad and Beersheba (Josh 15:21; Neh 11:25).

11:23. "spear like a weavers' beam." A detail similar to that found in the story of Goliath (1 Sam 17:7; Willi 1972: 155).

"killed him with his spear." As in the David and Goliath story, the antagonist's own weapon is wielded against him (1 Sam 17:51).

11:25. "he was honored among the Thirty." That is, among the warriors listed in vv. 26–47.

"though he did not attain to the Three." That is, to those mentioned in vv. 11–14.

11:26. "valiant warriors" (גבורי החילים). A brief introduction to the following list that has been borrowed from the end of the book of Samuel (2 Sam 23:24–39). Many scholars, most recently Naʾaman (1988b: 77), contend that the list in the context of Samuel refers to David's professional troops. There is no reference either in this verse (cf. 2 Sam 23:19) or in v. 41 to "the Thirty" (cf. MT and LXX 2 Sam 23:39). Given the inclusion of vv. 41b–47 (lacking in Samuel), the roster far exceeds thirty in number. In the context of Chronicles, the warriors listed in vv. 26–47 are but an important component of those "who continually strengthened" David in his early kingship (v. 10; NOTE).

"Asah-el brother of Joab." The youngest of Zeruiah's sons (1 Chr 2:16; 2 Sam 2:18). According to 1 Chr 27:7, Asah-el was placed in command of the fourth military division to serve during the fourth month of every year. In Samuel, the battle between Abner and the forces of Ishbaal at Gibeon includes a description of Asah-el's death (2 Sam 2:12–32).

"Elḥanan son of Dodai from Bethleḥem." Elḥanan is the name of Goliath's killer in 2 Sam 21:19, but Chronicles provides a more involved (harmonistic) explanation (1 Chr 20:5).

11:27. "Shammoth" (שמות). Probably the same figure as the Zeraḥite (27:8; TEXTUAL NOTE) placed in charge of the fifth military division on station during the fifth month.

"the Ḥarodite." The origin of the name is uncertain. ʿĒn Ḥarod ("Spring of Ḥarod") or ʿAin Jālūd was located near Mount Gilboa (Judg 7:1), but Elliger (1935: 39–40) favors Khirbet el-Ḥarēḏān, a few km southeast of Jerusalem.

"Ḥelez the Pelonite" was later put in charge of David's military division for the seventh month (27:10).

11:28. "Ira son of Iqqesh the Teqoaite." In charge of the division serving the king in the sixth month (27:9). On Teqoa, see the last NOTE to 2:24.

"Abiezer the Anathothite." He later serves as commander of the ninth division for the ninth month (27:12). The priestly town of Anathoth (Anâta) in Benjamin was located some 5 km northeast of Jerusalem (1 Chr 6:45; Naʾaman 1986a: 232–33). Anathoth was the birthplace of Jeremiah (Jer 1:1).

11:29. "Sibbekai the Ḥushathite." Also mentioned in 2 Sam 21:18 (cf. 2 Sam

23:27) and 1 Chr 20:4. Descended from Zeraḥ, Sibbekai was responsible for David's military division during the eighth month (27:11). On Ḥushah, southwest of Bethleḥem, see the 3rd NOTE to 4:4.

"Ilai the Aḥoḥite." First Chronicle 27:4 mentions another Aḥoḥite. See also the 2nd NOTE to v. 12.

11:30. "Mahrai the Neṭophathite." Like Sibbekai, Mahrai descended from Zeraḥ. He was responsible for the division on guard during the tenth month (27:13). The PN Mahrai *(mhry)* is attested on a seventh-century-B.C.E. Phoenician funerary stele (Lemaire 2001: 8). On Neṭophah, see the NOTE to 2:54.

"Ḥeled son of Benaiah." To be identified with Ḥeldai and Ḥeleb (in 2 Sam 23:29; 2nd TEXTUAL NOTE to v. 30). He was in charge of the military division for the twelfth month (27:15).

11:31. "Benaiah the Pirathonite." Not to be confused with the Benaiah of vv. 22–25. Benaiah the Pirathonite was to serve as commander of the 24,000-troop division during the eleventh month (27:14). Pirathon (פרעתון) was a town in Ephraim (Judg 12:15; 1 Macc 9:50), perhaps Farʿâtā, about 8 km southwest of Shechem.

11:32. "wadis of Gaash" (נחלי געש). Mount Gaash was in the hill country of Ephraim southwest of Shechem (Josh 24:30; Judg 2:9).

"Abiel the Arbathite." From Beth-arabah (בית הערבה), a town in Judah or Benjamin near the Dead Sea (Josh 15:6, 61; 18:18, 22; Elliger 1935: 48).

11:33. "Azmaveth" (עזמות). The name means "(the god) Death is strong." Azmaveth, or Beth-azmaveth, was a Benjaminite site near Jerusalem (Ezra 2:24//Neh 7:28; 12:29; cf. 1 Chr 8:36//9:42). According to 1 Chr 27:25, a certain "Azmaveth son of Adiel," perhaps this same Azmaveth, was responsible for David's treasuries. Azmaveth's sons are mentioned in 12:3.

"the Baḥarumite." From Baḥurim, modern Râs eṭ-Ṭmîm, east of Mount Scopus, a Benjaminite town (2 Sam 3:16; 16:5; 17:18; 19:17 [ET 19:16]; 1 Kgs 2:8).

"Eliaḥba the Shaalbonite." Shaalbim was a town of Dan and is mentioned in association with Ayyalon and Beth-shemesh (Josh 19:41–42; $LXX^B$ Judg 1:35). Some would identify it as Selbît T. Šaʿalʾwīm), some 13 km north of Beth-shemesh and 4.5 km northwest of Ayyalon, but the location is uncertain (Elliger 1935: 50–53; Noth 1953: 121; 1968: 68).

11:34. "Jonathan son of Shageh." Cf. 2 Sam 23:32–33.

11:35. "Aḥiam." On the PN, compare Phoen. *ʾḥʾm* (Krahmalkov 2000: 42) and *ʾmyʾḥ* (Lemaire 2001: 8–9).

11:37. "Ḥezro the Carmelite." Not the famous Carmel of Elijah (1 Kgs 18), but Carmel, T. el-Kirmil, a town located about 12 km south of Ḥebron (Josh 15:55; 1 Sam 15:12; 25:2–3).

11:38. "Mibḥar son of Hagri." On the Hagrites, one of the peoples in the Transjordan, see the 1st NOTE to 5:10.

11:39. "Naḥrai the Berothite." Beeroth (בארות) was a town in Benjamin (Josh 9:17; 18:25; 2 Sam 4:2–3, 5, 9; 23:37; Ezra 2:25//Neh 7:29), whose location is uncertain. Suggestions include Khirbet ʾel-Burǧ, a little more than 7 km northwest of Jerusalem (Yeivin 1971: 142–44); ʾel-Bīre, south of Bethel; and ʾen-Nabi Ṣamwīl (Kallai 1986a: 402–4).

"arms bearer for Joab son of Zeruiah." See the NOTES to v. 6.

11:40. "Ithrite." The Ithrites were one of the native families of Qiriath-jearim (1 Chr 2:53).

11:41. "Uriah the Hittite." One of David's generals, the ill-fated husband of Bathsheba (2 Sam 11:1–12:14).

11:41b–47. These verses are unparalleled in 2 Sam 23:8–39. In Chronicles the tally of warriors, who flock to David numbers forty-seven or more (vv. 42, 44). Most of the warriors in vv. 26–41a stem from Judah, Benjamin, Simeon, Ephraim, and (old) Dan, while only a few hail from the Transjordan. Given David's place of origin, this might be expected. But the picture changes with the addition of vv. 41b–47. Many of the warriors listed in these verses stem from the Transjordan. Such a broad show of support is consistent with the Chronicler's pan-Israel interests. David attracts troops from a variety of geographical locations (see the SOURCES AND COMPOSITION). David's connections to Moab are underscored in the book of Ruth (4:13–22).

11:42. "commander among the Reubenites." A Transjordanian representation among David's early supporters is not unique to this literary setting (12:38).

"thirty with him" (ועליו שלושים). This thirty (without the article) evidently refers to a different entity from "the Thirty" referred to earlier (vv. 15, 20, 21, 25).

11:43. "Ḥanan son of Maacah." On the different referents for Maacah, see the 3rd NOTE to 4:19.

11:44. "the Ashterothite." Ashtaroth appears as a town in Bashan in Deut 1:4; Josh 9:10 (cf. *aštartu*; EA 197.10; 256.21; Moran 1992: 275, 309; Aḥituv 1984: 72–73) and as part of Manasseh's eastern inheritance in Josh 13:31 (see the 1st NOTE to 6:56).

"the Aroerite." An Aroer is attested in both Moab (Num 32:34; 1 Chr 5:8 [NOTE]) and southern Judah (MT 1 Sam 30:28, but see McCarter 1980b: 434).

11:46. "Eliel the Maḥavite." Scholars have argued that this clause be emended in various ways (see TEXTUAL NOTE). One option is to reconstruct "the Maḥanite," that is, from Maḥanaim east of the Jordan (Josh 13:26, 30; Na'aman 1986a: 110). Alternatively, one could reconstruct "the Maonite," that is, from Beth-maon in Reuben (Josh 13:17).

"Ithmah the Moabite." Again, the Transjordanian provenance is obvious.

11:47. "Jaasiel the Mezobite." If "the Mezobite" (המצביה) is to be emended to "from Zobah," or "the Zobite" (see TEXTUAL NOTE), this does not in itself solve the problem of Zobah's location. One option is that Zobah refers to a territory in the Lebanese Beqaʿ (Aram-zobah) between Ḥamath and Damascus (Pitard 1987: 88–97). The same area may be referred to as Ṣūbat, an Assyrian province (of Aram-damascus), in the inscriptions of Tiglath-pileser III and Esarhaddon (Parpola 1970: 325). A somewhat neglected option is a site within Judah. LXX$^{A}$ Josh 15:59a lists *Sōbēs* (LXX$^{B}$ *Sōrēs*) as a town in the so-called Bethleḥem district of Judah. If *Sōbēs* represents Ṣobah, this site may be Ṣuba, about 5 km southeast of Qiriath-jearim.

## Sources and Composition

Most of 1 Chr 11 is drawn from two different chapters in Samuel. The parallels between Chronicles and Samuel may be summarized as follows:

| | *Chronicles 11* | *Source* |
|---|---|---|
| David enthroned at Ḥebron | 1–3 | 2 Sam 5:1–3 |
| Conquest of Jerusalem | 4–9 | 2 Sam 5:6–10 |
| Introduction to David's Commanders | 10 | |
| The Three | 11–14 | 2 Sam 23:8–12 |
| Three Commanders | 15–19 | 2 Sam 23:13–17 |
| Abshai and Benaiah | 20–25 | 2 Sam 23:18–23 |
| David's Valiant Warriorsy | 26–41a | 2 Sam 23:24–39 |
| Additional Valiant Warriors | 41b–47 | |

As the chart suggests and our earlier discussion demonstrates, the Chronicler has repositioned material from his *Vorlage*, recontextualized it, and slightly overwritten certain parts. He has furnished an introductory rubric and added warriors. The additional tabulation of troops (41b–47) has been the subject of much discussion. There are essentially three points of view. First, some scholars, (e.g., Rothstein and Hänel 1927: 241) argue that vv. 41b–47 forms an integral section of the list unavailable to or lost by the authors of Samuel. Budde (1902: 318–26), followed by Curtis and Madsen (1910: 194), argues for a modified form of this theory. Noting that the place-names reflected in vv. 42–47 mostly represent locations east of the Jordan, these commentators propose that the original placement of vv. 41b–47 would be between 1 Chr 12:7 and 1 Chr 12:8. A second group of scholars (e.g., B. Mazar 1986: 101–2; Myers 1965a: 90–91) argues that vv. 41b–47 are a later, but pre-Chronistic, expansion of the Samuel list. Similarly, Williamson (1982b: 104) and Japhet (1993a: 235–36) think that the Chronicler had access to an additional source, which he incorporated, at least in part, into the Samuel list available to him. Elliger (1935: 36) and Noth (1987: 136) espouse a third position, namely, that the additional names are a postexilic creation.

Resolving the issue of composition is difficult. In favor of a disjunction between this list and the preceding list are several stylistic differences and the reference to thirty accompanying Adina son of Shiza in v. 42, which seems to indicate an additional thirty to the Thirty mentioned earlier. These differences suggest that vv. 41b–47 are not an original part of the list in Samuel. In favor of the second position is the makeup of the addition itself. The Transjordanian and non-Israelite provenance of several names (Myers 1965a: 90–91; Williamson 1982b: 104; Japhet 1993a: 235–36) is said to conflict with the mood and tenor of the Persian era. The supposition of a source has some merit, but one may question some of the reasoning given for it. To begin with, the Transjordanian provenance of several warriors in vv. 41b–47 dovetails with the detailed attention given to the Transjordanian tribes in the genealogies (5:1–26). The inclusion of Transjordanian soldiers also comports with the author's concern to demonstrate support for David from all quarters of Israel.

The non-Israelite origin of some warriors is not a problem. Foreigners are found, for example, in the Chronicler's genealogy of Judah (2:1–4:23). In this context, one should resist one-sided depictions of life in the Persian period. As Japhet and Williamson have themselves repeatedly argued, the negative attitude toward the incorporation of other peoples is more a feature of Ezra-Nehemiah than it is of Chronicles. In my judgment, a stronger argument that the material in vv. 41b–47 stems from a source is the obscurity of several names in vv. 41b–47, for instance, "Jehoshaphaṭ the Mithnite" (v. 43), "Joḥa . . . the Tizite" (v. 45), "Eliel the Maḥavite" (v. 46), and "Jaasiel the Mezobite" (v. 47). If these verses stemmed from the Chronicler's own hand, one would expect them to be more straightforward than they are and to reflect something of the Chronicler's distinctive style and vocabulary. This suggests that the Chronicler has included, but not overwritten, traditional, probably extrabiblical material. But one cannot eliminate the possibility that the Chronicler found the extra material in his version of Samuel. Such additional material need not conform precisely to the form of registration found in 2 Sam 23:8–39. Compare, for instance, the additions to 2 Sam 24 reflected in 4QSam[a] that do not appear in MT Samuel. (For discussion with references, see the TEXTUAL NOTES to 1 Chr 21.)

One could argue a fourth position, that the verses are a post-Chronistic supplement to the text, but this seems unlikely. First, there are no telltale signs of late insertion, such as repetitive resumption (Kuhl 1952) or an inverted quotation (Seidel 1955–56). Second, most late additions to the biblical text are designed to clarify issues, not obscure them (Tov 1992b: 58–63; 1994). Hence, it is unlikely that the abstruse roster of names in vv. 41b–47 stems from a post-Chronistic glossator.

## COMMENT

Since 1 Chr 11 is part of a larger unity that includes 1 Chr 12, these chapters are discussed together in the COMMENT to 1 Chr 12.

# *XV. The Israelite Tribes Mobilize to Support David (12:1–41)*

*Benjaminites*

1 The following came to David at Ziqlag while he was still a refugee from Saul
the son of Qish. They were among the warriors who lent support in battle. 2 Armed
with the bow, capable of using either the right hand or the left hand to sling stones
and to shoot arrows with the bow, they were kinsmen of Saul from Benjamin. 3 At
the head were Aḥiezer and Joash the son of Shimeah the Gibeathite, Jeziel and

Peleṭ the sons of Azmaveth, Berechiah and Jehu the Anathothite, 4 Ishmaiah the
Gibeonite, a warrior among the Thirty and in charge of the Thirty, 5 Jeremiah,
Jaḥaziel, Joḥanan, and Jozabad the Gederathite, 6 Eluzai, Jerimoth, Baaliah,
Shemariah, and Shephaṭiah the Ḥariphite, 7 Elqanah, Isshiah, Azarel, Joezer, and
Jashobeam the Qoraḥites, 8 Joelah and Zebadiah the sons of Jeroḥam.

*Gadites*

9 Some of the Gadites withdrew to David at the wilderness fortress, valiant warriors, men of the army (trained) for battle, armed with shield and lance. Their face
was the face of a lion and they were swift as gazelles upon the hills: 10 Ezer the
commander, Obadiah the second, Eliab the third, 11 Mishmanah the fourth, Jeremiah the fifth, 12 Attai the sixth, Eliel the seventh, 13 Joḥanan the eighth, Elzabad
the ninth, 14 Jeremiah the tenth, Machbannai the eleventh. 15 These were from
the descendants of Gad, commanders of the army. One to a hundred the least
and the greatest to a thousand. 16 They were the ones who crossed over the Jordan
in the first month, when it was flooding all of its banks, rendering the lowlands impassable to the east and to the west.

*Benjaminites and Judahites*

17 Some of the Benjaminites and Judahites came up to the fortress, to David.
18 When David went out before them, he answered and said to them, "If you have
come in peace to me to help me, then my heart shall be one with yours, but if (you
have come) to betray me to my enemies, even though there is no violence in my
hands, may the God of our fathers see and judge." 19 Then a spirit enveloped Amasai, commander of the officers :

"We are yours, O David,
We are with you, O Son of Jesse.
Peace, peace be to you,
and peace to the one who supports you,
for your God supports you."

So David received them and appointed them as commanders of the brigade.

*Manasseh*

20 Some of the people of Manasseh defected to David when he came with the
Philistines against Saul for battle. But he did not help them, because upon taking
counsel the Philistine lords sent him away saying, "At the cost of our heads, he will
defect to his master Saul." 21 When he went to Ziqlag, the following defected to
him from Manasseh: Adnaḥ, Jozabad, Jediael, Michael, Elihu, and Zillethai,
commanders of the thousands of Manasseh. 22 It was they who supported David
against the raid, for they were valiant warriors, all of them, and they became officers in the army. 23 Indeed, from day to day they came to David to support him so
that his camp became immense, like the camp of God.

*The Tribal Musters*

24 These are the musters of the commanders of those equipped for military service who came to David at Ḥebron to turn the kingdom of Saul over to him, according to the word of Yhwh:

25 the descendants of Judah, carrying shield and lance, 6,800 equipped for military service;

26 from the descendants of Simeon, valiant warriors of the army, 7,100;

27 from the descendants of Levi, 4,600; 28 also Jehoiada the leader of Aaron and with him 3,700; 29 Zadoq, a valiant young warrior, along with his ancestral house, 22 officers;

30 from the descendants of Benjamin, kinsmen of Saul, 3,000; hitherto, their great number were keeping the watch of the house of Saul;

31 from the descendants of Ephraim, 20,800 valiant warriors, men of repute by their ancestral houses;

32 from the half-tribe of Manasseh, 18,000 who were enlisted by name to come and make David king;

33 from the descendants of Issachar, those understanding the times, knowing what Israel should do, 200 of their commanders and all of their kinsmen, according to their word;

34 from Zebulun, those going out on the campaign, in battle formation with all kinds of weapons, 50,000, to assist David with single-mindedness;

35 from Naphtali, 1,000 officers accompanied by 37,000 with shields and lances;

36 from the Danites, 28,600 in battle formation;

37 from Asher, those going out on the campaign in battle formation, 40,000;

38 from across the Jordan—from the Reubenites, the Gadites, and the half-tribe of Manasseh—with all kinds of military weapons, 120,000.

39 All these men of war—helping with the battle line, wholly dedicated—came to Ḥebron to make David king over all Israel.

*Celebratory Feast*

Even all the rest of Israel was of one heart to make David king. 40 They were there with David three days, eating and drinking, because their kinsmen provided for them. 41 Even those near to them (and) as far away as Issachar, Zebulun, and Naphtali were bringing food by asses, by camels, by mules, and by oxen—provisions of flour, cakes of figs, raisin cakes, wine, oil, cattle, and sheep in abundance, because there was joy in Israel.

## TEXTUAL NOTES

12:1. "a refugee from Saul" (*ʿṣwr mpny šʾwl*). So MT and LXX. It is also possible to translate, "a refugee because of Saul." To insert "from Israel" (Rudolph 1955: 104) is unnecessary. Syr. adds material narrating how David's warriors could have killed Saul, had David desired them to do so (Weitzman 1999: 112–13).

"who lent support" (*ʿzry*). On the attributive acc. of state with a ptc., see Joüon (§127a).

12:2. "armed with the bow" (*nšqy qšt*). LXX* lacks *nšqy* and prefaces *sphendonētai* ("slingers" = *qlʿy*?) before *bʾbnym*, "with stones." The expression *nšqy qšt* also occurs in 2 Chr 17:17 and Ps 78:9.

12:3. "son." So some Heb. MSS and LXX$^{AB}$. MT and LXX$^{L}$ "sons."

"Shimeah" *(šmʿh)*. Cf. LXX$^{AN}$ *(Samaa)*; Vg. *Sammaa*; Tg. *šm*" (cf. Syr. *šmʿyh*). MT *hšmʿh* ("the Shemaah") is corrupt and may reflect **y(h)wšmʿ*. LXX$^{B}$ $c_2$ *Ama*; LXX$^{L}$ *Asma*.

"(and) Jeziel." So Qere (and LXX$^{A}$, Vg., Tg.) *wyzyʾl*. Kethib *wyzwʾl* ("Jezoel" or "Jezuel"). A few Heb. MSS, LXX$^{B}$ *(kai Iōēl)*, and Syr. *ywʾl*, "and Joel."

"and Peleṭ" *(wplṭ)*. LXX$^{B}$ includes the theophoric *kai Iōphalēt*.

"Berechiah" *(brkyh)*. So LXX$^{B}$ *(Bercheia)*. Cf. LXX$^{ALN}$ *Barachia*. MT "Beracah" *(brkh)*.

12:4–5. In many English translations, these verses appear as one verse (12:4).

12:4. "the Thirty." So MT and LXX. Begrich *(BHK)*, citing the 1524/5 C.E. edition of Jacob ben Ḥayyim *(Bombergiana)*, thinks that MT is in error (cf. Tg. "warriors").

12:6–41. In many English translations, these verses appear as 12:5–40.

12:6. "Eluzai" *(ʾlʿwzy)*. LXX$^{B}$ *Azai*; LXX$^{L}$ *Eliezer*; LXX$^{AN}$ *Eliōzi*.

"Baaliah" *(bʿlyh)*. So MT. Syr. adds *ʿz(r)y*.

"the Ḥariphite." So Kethib *haḥărîpî*. Cf. LXX$^{BL}$ *ho Chara(i)phei*. Qere *haḥarûpî*, "the Ḥaruphite" (cf. Tg. *dmn ḥrwp*, "from Ḥaruph").

12:7. "Isshiah" *(yšyhw)*. LXX$^{L}$ *Iessoue* (= *yšwy*?).

"Azarel" *(ʿzrʾel)*. Some Heb. MSS and LXX$^{B}$ *(Ozreiēl)* *ʿzryʾl*; LXX$^{AN}$ *Eliēl*.

"Jashobeam" *(yšbʿm)*. So MT. Cf. LXX$^{B}$ *Sobokam*; LXX$^{S}$ *Soboam*. LXX$^{ALN}$ and Vg. *Iesbaam* (= *yišbĕʿām*?).

"the Qoraḥites" *(hqrḥym)*. So MT and Vg. *(de Careim)*. LXX prefaces the copula.

12:8. "Joelah" *(ywʿʾlh)*. So MT and LXX$^{ALN}$. LXX$^{BS}$ $c_2$ *Elia*; Syr. *ywʾḥ*. Kittel (1895: 65) proposes reading *yʾlh* with some Heb. MSS.

"Zebadiah" *(zbdyh)*. So MT and LXX. Syr. *zkryh*.

"the sons of Jeroḥam." MT adds "from Gedor" *(mn hgdwr*; cf. LXX$^{L}$ *tou Geddōr)*; some Heb. MSS *gdwd* (cf. Syr. *gdd*). LXX$^{ANS}$ "sons" (= *bny*). Begrich *(BHK)* proposes deleting the prep. and reading "the Gederite" *(haggĕdērî)* or "the Gedorite" *(haggĕdōri)*. But Arnold Ehrlich (1914: 335) is probably right in deleting the entire phrase as a dittography of *min hgdy* at the start of v. 9.

12:9. "withdrew *(nbdlw)* to David." Some contend that the *nipʿal* has to be translated "separated themselves" (e.g., Curtis and Madsen 1910: 197). But as other usage of the *nipʿal* of *bdl* with the prep. *ʾl* indicates (Ezra 6:21; 10:29; cf. LXX 2 Sam 1:23), withdrawal inherently involves separation.

"fortress" *(mṣd)*.. So MT. The lacuna in LXX means that the Gadites come to David from the wilderness.

"and lance" *(wrmḥ)*. Some Heb. MSS "and shield" (*wmgn*; Jer 46:3). But see vv. 25, 35.

"as gazelles" *(wkṣbʾym)*. So MT and LXX$^{BL}$ *(hōs dorkades)*. LXX$^{A}$ *hōs dorkados*.

12:10. "Ezer" *(ʿzr)*. So MT and LXX$^{L}$. LXX$^{B}$ *Aza*; Syr. *ʿzryh*.

"Obadiah" *(ʿbdyh)*. LXX$^{ABL}$ *Abd(e)ia* (see also 1 Chr 7:3).

12:12. "Attai" *(ʿty)*. LXX$^{AB}$ *Ethoi*; LXX$^{L}$ *Ethei*; bb' *Eththi*; Syr. *ʿtr*.

"Eliel" *(ʾlyʾl)*. A few Heb. MSS and LXX$^{B}$ *Eliab*.

12:13. "Elzabad" *(ʾlzbd)*. LXX$^{B}$ *Eliazar*.

12:14. "Jeremiah" *(yrmyhw)*. Syr. *mkwn*

"Machbannai" *(mkbny)*. LXX$^{B}$ *Melchabannai*. Syr. *šptyʾ*.

12:16. "all of its banks." Thus Qere *gĕdôtāyw*. Kethib *gidyōtāyw*.

"rendering the lowlands impassable." The MT is problematic: "and they caused all of the lowlands to flee" *(wybryḥw 'ṯ kl h'mqym)*. How could "the commanders of the army" (v. 15), the nearest antecedent, cause the lowlands to flee? NJPS translates *h'mqym* as "the lowlanders," but this meaning of *'mq* is not otherwise attested. Begrich *(BHK)* reconstructs *wy'brw mymyw*, but I favor a slighter emendation advocated by Rudolph (1955: 105): the sg. *wybrḥ* (of the denominative *brḥ*, "to bar").

12:17. "to the fortress, to David" *(lmṣd ldwyd)*. I read with MT. LXX has "to the assistance" or "to the rescue" (of David) *(eis boētheian = l'zr)*.

12:18. "he answered and said to them." So MT and and LXX$^{L}$. LXX$^{AB}$ lacks "and he answered" because of haplography *(homoioarkton* from *wy'n wy'mr* to *wy'mr)*.

"to help me" *(l'zrny)*. So MT and LXX$^{L}$. Missing from LXX$^{AB}$ due to haplography *(homoioteleuton* from *'ly l'zrny* to *'ly)*.

"my heart shall be one *(lyḥd)* with yours." This is only one of a few uses of *yḥd* as a subst. in the HB (Deut 33:5; Joüon, §102d), but such usage becomes common in the Dead Sea Scrolls (Talmon 1953: 136).

"with no violence on my hands" *(bl' ḥms bkpy)*. LXX$^{AB}$ *ouk alētheia cheiros*, but LXX may be corrupt (Rudolph 1955: 105).

12:19. "a spirit" (רוח). If the author wished to speak of "the spirit" (so many translations), he could have added the article (Joüon 1932: 87).

"Amasai" *('mśy)*. So MT. That Kittel (1895: 65), Benzinger (1901: 47), and others associate "Amasai" with "Ab(i)shai," *'b(y)šy*—the warrior who figures prominently in 11:20—is understandable, but none of the root consonants are the same.

"the officers." So Qere *hšlyšym*. Kethib (and LXX, Syr., Vg.) "the Thirty" *(hšlwšym)*. LXX *(kai eipen)* and Vg. *(et ait)* explicate by adding the citation formula *(wy'mr)*, "and said."

"yours" *(lk)*. LXX reflects a different interpretation of the same consonants, "go" *(poreuou = lēk)*. To preface *klnw* on the basis of Vg. (Rudolph 1955: 106; Myers 1965a: 93) is unnecessary. One of the characteristics of Chronistic style is the occasional omission of subjects (e.g., 1 Chr 9:33; 15:13; 2 Chr 10:11, 14; 11:22; Kropat, §24).

"David." The versions reflect a different word order. "David" is lacking in LXX$^{B}$, while LXX$^{L}$ reads "to you David son of Jesse, you and your people." See the following TEXTUAL NOTES.

"and with you" *(w'mk)*. LXX interprets the same consonants differently, "and your people."

"son of Jesse." So MT. LXX$^{B}$ explicates to "David son of Jesse."

"to the one who supports you." LXX$^{B}$ reflects the pl. "to those who support you."

"as commanders" (בראשי). Reading the prep. *b-* as a *bêt essentiae*.

12:20. "defected to David." For other instances of the verb *npl* ("to fall") with this sense, see 2 Chr 15:9; 2 Kgs 25:11; Jer 21:9; 37:14; 39:9.

"he did not help them" *('zrm)*. So LXX$^{AL}$ (= *'ăzārām*). The vocalization of MT (and LXX$^{B}$) reflects the third-per. pl. of the verb.

"at the cost of our heads" *(br'šynw)*. The trans. follows NJPS. LXX* "with the heads of these men" *(en tais kephalais tōn andrōn ekeinōn)*. LXX[L] is closer to MT *(en tais kephalais hēmōn)*. The location plays on the conflict of interest created by someone becoming a "commander" (ראש) of the Philistines who already has a "master" (אדון) among the enemy. The Philistines are afraid that David will prove unreliable because he will be encumbered by divided loyalties.

12:21. "Adnaḥ" *(ʿdnḥ)*. A few Heb. MSS "Adnah" (cf. LXX *Edna*).

"Jozabad" *(ywzbd)*. So MT and LXX[AN]. LXX[B] *Iōzabath*. Rothstein and Hänel (1927: 230), followed by Rudolph (1955: 106), reconstruct *ywzkr*.

"Elihu" *(ʾlyhwʾ)*. So MT and LXX[LN]. LXX[B] $c_2$ *Elimouth*. LXX[A] *Elioud* (= *ʾlyhwd*).

"the thousands" *(hʾlpym)*. The alternate translation, "divisions" or "clans" (e.g., NJPS), is also possible (*HALOT* 59–60). In 1 Sam 10:19, 21 אלף parallels משפחה. The language is reminiscent of the martial segmentation of Manasseh as depicted by the Priestly writers (Num 31:14, 48, 52, 54). See further the NOTE to v. 38.

12:22. "against the raid" *(ʿal-haggĕdûd)*. Thus MT. LXX presents a transliteration *epi ton geddour*. Similarly, see LXX 1 Sam 30:8, 15, 23 and the discussion of Brock (1996: 157).

12:23. "to David." Thus LXX, although MT *(ʿl dwyd)* is also possible, given that *ʿl* can mean "to, towards" in Chronicles (Kropat, §15).

"to support him." So MT and LXX[L]. Lacking in LXX[AB]. Syr. reads quite differently.

"musters" *(mspry)*. LXX[AB] "names" (= *šmwt*). Similar variants occur in 11:11.

12:24. "commanders of those equipped for military service" *(rʾšy hḥlwṣ lṣbʾ)*. Thus MT. The shorter reading of LXX *(tōn archontōn tēs stratias = rʾšy hṣbʾ)*, lacking "the equipped" *(hḥlwṣ)* after *rʾšy*, is not impossible as one could translate *rʾšy* as "divisions" (cf. *rʾš* in Judg 7:16, 20; 9:34, 37, 43, 44 [bis]; 1 Sam 11:11; 13:17 [bis], 18 [bis]; Job 1:17; *HALOT* 1166). But LXX seems to have suffered haplography *(homoioarkton* from *rʾšy hḥlwṣ lṣbʾ* to *rʾšy hṣbʾ)*.

"who came" *(bʾw)*. Some (e.g., Kittel 1895: 65; Benzinger 1901: 48; Rothstein and Hänel 1927: 233) preface *ʾšr*, which one would normally expect to introduce a relative clause following a determinate noun *(lṣbʾ)*, but *ʾšr* is sometimes omitted after a determinate noun in Chronicles (e.g., 9:22; 29:3; 2 Chr 15:11; 18:23; 30:17; 31:19; GKC §155d).

"to David" *(ʿl dwyd)*. See the 1st TEXTUAL NOTE to v. 23.

"Yhwh." LXX[L] adds "and this is the muster."

12:31. "men of repute" *(ʾnšy šmwt)*. The pl. of both nouns is a common construction in Chronicles (Kropat, §2; Joüon, §136o).

12:32. "who." LXX[B] adds the copula.

12:33. "Issachar." See the 2nd TEXTUAL NOTE to 2:1.

"times." One Heb. MS and Syr. "their time."

"knowing" (לדעת). The inf. continues a preceding verb (יודעי; Joüon, §124p).

"according to their word" *(ʿl pyhm)*. So MT. LXX *metʾ autōn*.

12:34. "to assist" *(lʿdr)*. So MT *(lectio difficilior)*, but omitting the connective *wāw* with LXX. Some Heb. MSS read *lʿzwr*, "to help support," a common verb in this ch. (e.g., vv. 18, 22, 23). Cf. LXX *boēthēsai*; Vg. *venerunt in auxilium*. There are only two occurrences in Chronicles of the rare verb *ʿdr*. The other appears as a pl. construct in v. 39 *ʿdry mʿrkh*, which some (e.g., BDB 727) emend to *ʿrky mʿrkh* (see the TEXTUAL NOTE). In Off. Aram. *ʿdr* can mean (1) "to strip, weed, clean" or (2) "to help, assist" (= Heb. *ʿzr*; *DNWSI* 830–31). In OSA, *ʿḏr* means "to help" (Biella 1982: 355). The meaning commonly attributed to Heb. *ʿdr*—"to arrange" (BDB 727) or "to gather" (*HALOT* 793)—is surprising, given the comparative Semitic data.

"David" *(ldwyd)*. So LXX. The PN has dropped out of MT by haplography, from *lʿdr ldwyd* to *lʿdr*.

"with single-mindedness" *(blʾ lb wlb)*. I read with MT *(lectio difficilior)*. Some ten MSS have *bkl lb wlb*. The impetus would be, however, to change an uncommon idiom into a more common one. LXX$^{B}$ has *ou cherokenōs*, a *hapax legomenon*. On the Heb. locution, compare Ps 12:3 [ET 12:2] and see Waltke and O'Connor (§7.2.3c).

12:36. "28,600." So MT and LXX$^{L}$. Instead of "six," LXX$^{B}$ has "eight."

12:37. "in battle formation." Literally, "to line up for battle" *(lʿrk mlḥmh)*. Thus MT *(lectio difficilior)*. As in v. 34, LXX has *boēthēsai* (= *lʿzwr*).

12:38. "military weapons" *(kly mlḥmh)*. So LXX *(lectio brevior)*. MT adds *ṣbʾ* ("army") after *kly*. Cf. 1 Chr 7:4 (see the NOTE), 40.

12:39. "helping with the battle line" *(ʿdry mʿrkh)*. So MT *(lectio difficilior)*. A few Heb. MSS and LXX$^{AB}$ (παραταξάμενοι ἐν παρατάξει) have *ʿrky mʿrkh* (see the 1st TEXTUAL NOTE to v. 34). On the noun *mʿrkh*, compare 1 Sam 4:2, 12, 16; 17:8, 20–22, 45, 48; 23:3 (Nab. *ʿrkwtʾ*; Arab. *maʿra/ukat*, "battle, battlefield;" *HALOT* 616).

"rest." So Qere (LXX, Vg.) *šĕʾērît*. Kethib *šērît*.

12:41. "even those near to them [and] as far away as" *(wgm hqrwbym ʾlyhm ʿd)*. LXX *kai hoi homo(r)rountes autois heōs* lacks the particle *gm*.

"Issachar." See the 2nd TEXTUAL NOTE to 2:1.

"food" *(lḥm)*. LXX "for them" (= *lhm*). Tg. conflates the two variants *lhwn lḥmʾ*.

# NOTES

12:1–23. The first section of 1 Chr 12 narrates how warriors from Benjamin (vv. 1–8), Gad (vv. 9–16), Benjamin and Judah (vv. 17–19), and Manasseh (vv. 20–23) all rally to David. The material is not chronologically arranged. Quite the contrary, if one wished to arrange vv. 1–23 in terms of the historical progression suggested by the book of Samuel, the order would probably be: vv. 9–16 and 17–19, vv. 1–8, and 20–23. This achronological order of presentation represents deliberate literary artifice on the part of the author, who, having sketched Israel's coronation of David (11:1–3) and David's immediate conquest of Jerusalem (11:4–9), presents snapshots of earlier phases in David's rise to power. The latter sections of the chapter (vv. 24–29a, 39b–41) are also part of this larger schema (see SOURCES AND COMPOSITION).

12:1. "Ziqlag." According to 1 Sam 27:5–28:2, David spent sixteen months at Ziqlag, while he was hiding from Saul (R. Klein 1983b: 260–66; Caquot and de Robert 1994: 326–29).

"they were among the warriors who lent support (*ʿzr*) in battle." The use of the root *ʿzr*, "to help," is a leitmotiv in the Chronicler's depiction of David's earliest reign. Of the eighty-two occurrences of the verbal root *ʿzr* in the HB, twenty-five appear in Chronicles. Of these, eight appear clustered in 1 Chr 12 (vv. 1, 18, 19 [bis], 20, 21, 22, 23). Elsewhere the author employs the verb *ʿzr* in a number of different ways (Williamson 1981: 166–67), but here he uses *ʿzr* to underscore both human (vv. 1, 19, 22, 23) and divine (v. 19) support of David.

12:2. "either the right hand or the left hand" (מימינים ומשׂמאלים). The statement comports with the reputation of the Benjaminites as left-handed slingers and dexterous marksmen in earlier sources (Judg 3:15; 20:16; Halpern 1988). In emphasizing their dexterity, the Chronicler puns on the meaning of "Benjamin" (בנימין, "son of the right hand").

"kinsmen of Saul from Benjamin." According to 2 Sam 2:12–32, Benjaminites remained loyal to Saul's house, even after Saul's death (McCarter 1980b: 91–99). But the authors of Samuel present later fissures in this loyalty (2 Sam 3:6–39; A. Anderson 1989: 51–64; Caquot and de Robert 1994: 389–92). In any case, the Chronicler presents his own account of Benjaminite activities. Benjaminites defect to David while Saul is still alive (1st NOTE to 11:2).

12:3. "the head . . . Aḥiezer." The name Aḥiezer appears elsewhere as a chieftain of the Danites (Num 1:12; 2:25; 7:66, 71; 10:25).

"Joash the son of Shimeah the Gibeathite." The patronymic refers to Gibeah of Benjamin (2nd NOTE to 8:6).

"Jeziel and Peleṭ the sons of Azmaveth." On Azmaveth, see the 1st NOTE to 11:33.

"Jehu the Anathothite." On Anathoth, see the 2nd NOTE to 11:28.

12:4. "Ishmaiah the Gibeonite." The relations between the Gibeonites and the Saulides were not always amicable (2 Sam 21:1–9). On the site of Gibeon (el-Ǧîb), see the 1st NOTE to 9:35.

"a warrior among the Thirty and in charge of the Thirty." Referring to the elite unit mentioned in 11:15, 20, 21, 25. Ishmaiah does not appear, however, in the lists there.

12:5. "Jozabad the Gederathite." Perhaps from Geder (or Gederah), a town in southern Judah (Josh 15:36; 2nd NOTE to 4:23).

12:6. "Baaliah" (בעליה) means "Yhwh is (my) lord." If *bʿl* was to be read as a theophoric, we would translate literally, "Yhwh is Baal." The *bʿl* element is not uncommon in PNs in Chronicles (e.g., 1:49; 5:5; 8:1, 30, 33; 9:36, 39 (NOTE), 40 (NOTE); 11:11 [LXX]; 12:6; 14:7; 27:28).

"Ḥariphite." First Chronicles 2:51 mentions a certain Ḥareph, a descendant of Caleb, and associated with Beth-gader. A number of the descendants of Ḥariph are said to have returned from exile with Zerubbabel (Neh 7:24 [cf. Ezra 2:12]; 10:20 [ET 10:19]).

12:7. "Qoraḥites." Likely stemming from the town of Qoraḥ in Judah (2:43). On the Levitical Qoraḥ and the Qoraḥites, see the 1st NOTE to 9:19.

12:9. "withdrew to David." These particular Gadites withdrew from other Gadites, who were supporters of Saul, to lend their support to David.

"at the wilderness fortress" (למצד מדברה). The Chronicler does not identify the stronghold. David lived in Adullam (1 Sam 22:1–5; 23:14//1 Chr 11:15; R. Klein 1983b: 219–22) and elsewhere in the Judean wilderness (1 Sam 23:14 [//1 Chr 11:15], 15–18; 24:1) before he journeyed to Ziqlag (1 Sam 27:5–28:2). It would seem, then, that chronologically the events of 1 Chr 12:9–16 precede those narrated in 12:1–8, because the Gadites defected to David during his wilderness period (Elliger 1935; Williamson 1981).

"valiant warriors, men of the army (trained) for battle" (גברי החיל אנשי צבא למלחמה). As in some of the genealogies (e.g., 1 Chr 7:5, 11, 40), the military prowess and heroic qualities of Israel's tribal leadership are stressed. The mention of such valiantry is part of a larger attempt to portray the Davidic-Solomonic monarchy as a classical age.

"face of a lion." The metaphor refers to their fierce visage in battle, hence the translation of NJPS, "they had the appearance of a lion." Cf. Gen 49:24; Exod 15:15; 2 Sam 1:23. Animal names could also be used in the ancient Near East as titles of officers, leaders, and deities to heighten their heroic character (P. Miller 1970: 177–86).

"as gazelles upon the hills." Cf. 2 Sam 2:18.

12:10–14. A register of the eleven Gadite army commanders. On the use of names followed by ordinals, see also 2:13–15 and 3:1–3.

12:15. "These were from the descendants of Gad." The summary notation corresponds to the earlier introduction (v. 9). Cf. 1 Chr 26:32.

"commanders of the army" (ראשי הצבא). See the 3rd NOTE to v. 9 (cf. v. 24).

"hundred . . . thousand." An excellent example of chiasm in the Heb.

a one to a hundred
    b the least
    b′ and the greatest
a′ to a thousand.

The author is referring to the warriors' prowess in battle rather than to an administrative arrangement (contra Kittel 1902: 61). The least was a match for a hundred, the greatest a match for a thousand. Similar expressions occur in Lev 26:8 and Isa 30:17.

12:16. "in the first month." That is, Nisan (April), the time of the barley harvest, when the spring runoff increased the flow of the Jordan.

12:17–19. "Benjaminites and Judahites." The pairing of Judah and Benjamin is occasionally found in the Deuteronomistic work (e.g., 1 Kgs 12:21). The close attachment between the two probably dates to at least the late preexilic age, when the kingdom of Judah contained parts of Benjamin. In Chronicles, one often finds Judah and Benjamin leagued together (2 Chr 11:12, 23; 14:7 [ET 14:8]; 15:2, 8–9; 17:17; 31:1; 34:9). This reflects a Persian period reality in which three tribes dominated Yehud: Benjamin, Judah, and Levi (see "Excursus: The Genealogies").

12:17. "came up to the fortress, to David" (ויבאו . . . עד למצד לדויד). As a refugee from Saul, David lived in the Judean wilderness before he stayed in Ziqlag (2nd NOTE to v. 9). In the Chronicler's depiction of this early period in David's career, David attracts the allegiance of only some Benjaminites and Judahites. One might think that the warriors from Judah would be David's natural allies and would turn to him en masse, but only an unspecified portion of these warriors rally to David and David accords them no special favors. The warriors come up to, but do not actually enter, the fortress in which David is staying. David is wary of these visitors and does not invite them in. Instead, "David went out before them" (ויצא דויד לפניהם). In fact, it is only these soldiers from Benjamin and Judah from whom David exacts an oath of loyalty. See further the COMMENT.

12:18. "if you have come in peace." The words reflect the implicit threat posed by the approaching forces. That this is so is confirmed by his subsequent warning, "if [you have come] to betray me to my enemies."

"my heart shall be one *(lyḥd)* with yours." David's declaration has covenantal overtones (Talmon 1953: 133–40; Kalluveettil 1982: 53–56). A covenant establishes, structures, or ratifies a relationship between two or more parties (Pedersen 1940: 279–96; Knoppers 1996a; 1996c).

"no violence in my hands." The declaration reflects tensions between the house of Saul and David. Given David's status as a fugitive from Saul, Benjaminite suspicions of David would be understandable. The authors of Chronicles assert Davidic innocence in the relationship between his kingdom and that of Saul (10:13–14). What is particularly interesting is the fact that David has to assert his innocence to troops from both Benjamin and Judah. It may be, as Myers (1965a: 97) maintains, that the repeated betrayals of David by people such as Doeg the Edomite (1 Sam 21–22), the community of Qeilah (1 Sam 23), and the Ziphites (1 Sam 26) explain David's hesitation in dealing with this Benjaminite and Judahite force. But if this is so, the picture presented of David's acceptance by the various tribes is more complex than many have imagined it to be (see COMMENT).

"God of our fathers" (אלהי אבותינו). The expression is a favorite of the Chronicler, occurring some twenty-seven times in his work compared with a total of nineteen times in the rest of the Bible (Japhet 1989: 14–19; Römer 1990: 344–52). Inasmuch as the Ancestral age represents the formative beginning of Israel (1 Chr 2:1–2) and the starting point for each of the tribal genealogies, it is a very important marker in the Chronicler's understanding of the past. His use of the idiom "the God of our fathers" underscores continuity in divine-human relations from the age of the Matriarchs and Patriarchs to the time of the United Monarchy and beyond.

"see and judge" *(wykḥ)*. To judge in the sense of reprove. In betraying David, the Judahites and Benjaminites would be subjecting themselves to the specter of divine retribution.

12:19. "Then a spirit enveloped" (ורוח לבשה). The language is reminiscent of the period of the Judges (Judg 6:34; 11:29), but similar phraseology is also found elsewhere in Chronicles (2 Chr 15:1; 20:14; 24:20; 36:22). The application of the possession formula to introduce Amasai's words accords to them a kind of prophetic status (Schniedewind 1995: 70–74; cf. Petersen 1977).

"Amasai *(ʿmśy)*, commander of the officers." Amasai (with the hypocoristic ending *-ay*) is probably to be identified with Amasa *(ʿmśʾ < ʿmśyh)*, a commander under both Absalom and David (2 Sam 17:25; 19:14; 20:10; 1 Chr 2:17; Noth 1928: 253; Fowler 1988: 356).

"peace to the one who supports you *(lʿzrk)*, for your God supports you *(ʿzrk)*." The text plays on the possibilities of congruence in divine and human actions. In the portrayal of the latter portion of David's reign, the authors of Samuel document anti-David sentiment on the part of some Benjaminites, represented by Sheba: "We have no inheritance in David, no share in the son of Jesse" (2 Sam 20:1). Similarly, in their portrayal of Reḥoboam's early reign, the authors of Kings and Chronicles have the northern tribes echo Sheba's declamation as they separate from the house of David (1 Kgs 12:16//2 Chr 10:16; Ackroyd 1973a: 55; Williamson 1981: 172–76). In the context of David's early reign, however, the Chronicler plays on the theme of assistance for David (cf. 1 Sam 25:6). Amasai acknowledges that David has divine sustenance and, precisely because of this divine support, that those who support David will also be blessed. The language is reminiscent of the blessing bestowed upon Abram (Gen 12:3), except that there is no curse. The poem accentuates the positive.

"commanders of the brigade" (ראשי הגדוד). In Samuel הגדוד refers to David's company of four or six hundred men (1 Sam 22:2; 27:2; 30:8–31; 2 Sam 3:22). The term גדוד can also carry the sense of "brigade" or "detachment" in the Chronicler's work, although the size of such units is depicted as much larger (1 Chr 7:4; 2 Chr 25:9, 10, 13; 26:11). In this case, those "Benjaminites and Judahites" who rallied to David (1 Chr 12:17), along with "Amasai, commander of the officers" (ראש השלישים; v. 19), are made commanders of David's detachment.

12:20. "with the Philistines against Saul." See 1 Sam 28:1–3; 29:1–2. The writer is pinpointing the time in which these men from Manasseh deserted to David—when David went to Ziqlag (1 Chr 12:21). Hence, these warriors from Manasseh were able to assist David in his attack against the Amaleqites (v. 22). But the Chronicler's explanation is interrupted by a digression in defense of David's conduct while he sojourned among the Philistines. The manner in which the continuation of the explanation in v. 21 is worded ("when he went to Ziqlag, the following defected to him from Manasseh") leads one to suspect that the digression is a later addition, inserted into the text by inverted quotation, a compositional technique also known as Seidel's Law (Seidel 1955–56; Beentjes 1982):

v. 20 ממנשה נפלו על דויד

v. 21 נפלו עליו ממנשה

The interpolation draws upon 1 Sam 29:4–11 to insist that David did not fight against his fellow Israelites while he was allied with the Philistines.

"Philistine lords" (סרני פלשתים). The language is traditional in referring to the governors of the five major Philistine cities (Josh 13:3; Judg 3:3; 16:5–30; 1 Sam 5:8, 11; 7:7; 29:2–6).

12:22. "against the raid" (על-הגדוד). The reference is abstruse, alluding apparently to the band (גדוד) of Amaleqite raiders who set Ziqlag aflame in David's absence (1 Sam 30:1–25).

12:23. "from day to day." With the martial aid David receives from the various

Israelite tribes, David gradually acquires extraordinary power. A similar comment occurs in 11:9.

"like the camp of God" (כמחנה אלהים). On the use of the superlative, compare 1 Sam 14:15; Pss 36:7 [ET 36:6]; 80:11 [ET 80:10]; Jonah 3:3. While it is true that the Chronicler sometimes draws close connections between Israelite armies and heavenly armies in descriptions of battles (e.g., 2 Chr 13:13–20; 14:7–14; 20:21–23), he uses a simile here to underscore the army's might and not to identify this army with Yhwh's heavenly host (*pace* R. Braun 1986: 166).

12:24–39a. The beginning of v. 24, "These are the musters," introduces a long stylized list (vv. 25–38). This rubric is similar to the one, in 11:11 prefacing the list of David's warriors. The divisions of the army are organized according to a tribal format. Each tribe—in conjunction with its size, internal makeup, and abilities—mobilizes its own militia in the effort to turn the kingdom over to David. Individual tribes might specialize in particular weapons (e.g., vv. 25, 35) or dispatch both troops and officers (vv. 29, 33, 35). In some respects, the musters recorded at the beginning of David's reign recall the pan-tribal censuses that punctuate the book of Numbers (1; 26). Like the earlier censuses of the Israelites, these musters accentuate the extraordinary size of the various tribal contingents and promote their military prowess. Unlike the censuses conducted in the wilderness of Sinai, these censuses only occasionally make reference to subunits within each tribe (1 Chr 12:28–29). By drawing an implicit parallel between the Israel encamped in the Sinai and the Israel that mobilizes in support of its new king, the author promotes the Davidic monarchy as a highly important new beginning in Israelite history. As in the censuses of Numbers, a summary notation (1 Chr 12:39a; NOTE) closes the roster (Num 1:44–46; 26:63–65).

12:24. "equipped for military service" *(ḥḥlwṣ lṣbʾ)*.The expression used recalls the tribal musters of ages past; compare *ḥlwṣ ṣbʾ*, "equipped for war" (Num 32:27) and *ḥlwṣy (h)ṣbʾ*, "equipped for military service" (Num 31:5; Josh 4:13; 1 Chr 12:25; 2 Chr 17:18; cf. Num 32:21, 29, 30, 32; Deut 3:18; Josh 6:7, 9, 13; 2 Chr 20:21; 28:14).

"came to David at Ḥebron." The text refers, chronologically speaking, to the time in which David's rule was established in Ḥebron (NOTE to vv. 1–23).

"turn the kingdom of Saul over to him, according to the word of Yhwh." The statement echos a recurrent theme in 1 Chr 11–12—the active allegiance shown by Israelite military officials to David accords with divine will and results in a smooth transfer of power (10:14; 11:3, 10; 12:24, 32, 39 [bis]).

12:25–38. This tribal muster totals thirteen, unless one counts the two halves of Manasseh—one grouped with the northern tribes (v. 32) and the other an integral part of the Transjordanian tribes (v. 38)—as one tribe. It is occasionally claimed that in the HB this list claims the largest numbers of Israelite tribes (Gen 29:31–30:24; 35:16–20, 22b–26; 46:8–27; 49:1–27; Num 1:5–15, 20–43; 2:3–31; 7:12–83; 10:14–28; 13:4–15; 26:4–50; Deut 33:1–24; Judg 5:14–18; 1 Chr 2:1–2; 27:16–22; R. Wilson 1977: 183–84; R. Braun 1986: 9–10, 169). But the total number of groups within the tribes' genealogies is even longer (2:3; 4:24; 5:1, 11, 23, 27; 7:1, 6, 12 [TEXTUAL NOTE], 13, 14, 20, 30; 8:1). The writer seems to be more fixated on providing a full complement of tribes than he is on arriving at the precise number twelve. This list basically moves from south to north and concludes with the Transjordanian tribes. The roster is not simply a tally of raw numbers, however. Military statistics are embellished by anecdotal comments about the preparations of individual tribes. Ackroyd (1973a: 55–56) compares the "odd pieces of tradition" found in these verses with "the blessings on the tribes found in Gen. 49 and Deut. 33." One should also compare the tribal responses to David with different tribal responses to the summonses of various judges, such as Deborah (Judg 5:1–31) and Gideon (Judg 6:34–35). In the Song of Deborah, as well as in the Blessing of Jacob and the Blessing of Moses, tribes have identifiable traits. The manner in which tribes respond to Deborah's challenge reveals something of their distinctive character (Judg 5:14–18). The summonses in the Song of Deborah achieve mixed results, reflecting divided loyalties, the difficulties of distance, and diverse circumstances. Some of the other tribal musters in Judges reflect outright dissension or occur in the context of civil war (Judg 8:1–3; 12:1–6; 19:29; 20:48). The Chronicler's portrayal of the Israelite tribes projects, however, a pattern of intertribal solidarity. A comparison may be made with the long catalogue appearing in Homer's *Iliad* (introduced in 2.484–93), which details the various contingents—"the chiefs and rulers of the Danaans . . . the leaders of the ships and all of the ships together"—constituting the Greek forces at Troy. The list includes information about the geographical origins of the contingents, the names and heroic feats of the commanders, various anecdotal comments, and the number of ships associated with each group (*Il.* 2.494–762). Within Chronicles, the heroic description of large tribal militias contrasts with the description of fickle tribal allegiances in Judges. In this, one can see the author portraying not only David in a very positive light, but also Israel.

12:25. "6,800." The number for Judah is small when compared with two other benchmarks: (1) the contingents supplied by most of the other tribes and (2) the tallies of Judahites in the wilderness of Sinai (74,600 in Num 1:27; 76,500 in Num 26:22).

12:26. "descendants of Simeon." The Simeonites follow the Judahites (v. 25), just as in the genealogies (2:3–4:23; 4:24–43). Again, the numbers are comparatively small (59,300 in Num 1:22; 22, 200 in Num 26:14).

12:27. "the descendants of Levi" are of sustained interest in the presentations of Israelite identity (5:27–41; 6:1–66) and the return (9:2, 10–34). But the notion in 1 Chr 12 that a priestly tribe furnishes warriors for the benefit of David's kingship has troubled scholars. Because of the apparent incongruity, some regard v. 26, vv. 27–28 (e.g., Williamson 1982b: 111), or all of vv. 26–28 (e.g., Rudolph 1955: 109–110; R. Braun 1986: 170) as later additions. Benzinger's judgment (1901: 48) that the depiction of the Levites as soldiers is intended to reflect a prepriestly phase of the tribe's existence assumes the same political-cultic dichotomy. One wonders whether the rigid demarcation of secular and religious interests is true to most ancient historiography. The overlap among military, political, and cultic matters reflected in 1 Chr 12 is consistent with other contexts in the book. The gatekeepers (9:19, 23–27; 26:1–19 [COMMENT]), for instance, have martial responsibilities (Wright 1990: 69–81). Priests and Levites sometimes play significant roles in war (e.g., 2 Chr 13:12; 20:14–19, 21–22) and occasionally take on military functions (e.g., 2 Chr 23:4). Temple staff in ancient Mesopotamia could also have military responsibilities, such as guarding a temple (Ahlström 1982: 44–74; Postgate 1994a: 124–28). In any case, the reason for the inclusion of the Levites is clear. Israel's priestly tribe, no less than the other twelve tribes, actively endorses the nation's new king.

12:28. "Jehoiada." The father of Benaiah (1 Chr 11:22, 24; 2 Sam 8:18; 1 Kgs 2:28–35). The Chronicler's determination that Benaiah was of priestly descent may well be based on his reading of 1 Kgs 2:28–35 in which Benaiah killed Joab in the Tent of Yhwh (אהל יהוה). Only someone of Levitical pedigree, the writer may have reasoned, could have had access to the sanctuary.

"the leader of Aaron" (הנגיד אהרן). The tribe of Levi dispatches its own contingent of 4,600 to David (NOTE to vv. 24–39a), as well as contributions from two important tribal subunits—3,700 from the house of Aaron (2nd NOTE to 5:29) headed by Jehoiada (v. 28), and twenty-two officers headed by Zadoq, along with his ancestral house (v. 29). Aaron and Zadoq figure prominently in the Chronicler's conception of Israel's priestly tribe, but both are subsumed within a larger Levitical genealogy (COMMENT on 5:27–41). So also here, the martial contingents associated with Aaron and Zadoq fall under the larger rubric of Levi (מן-בני הלוי; v. 27).

12:29. "Zadoq, a valiant young warrior" (נער גבור חיל). This may refer to the priest who served with Abiathar at the court of David (2 Sam 8:17) and who subsequently enjoyed exclusive patronage in the Jerusalem court (1 Kgs 2:35; cf. 1 Chr 29:22). An important caveat: Jehoiada (and not Zadoq) is presented as "the leader of Aaron" (v. 28). Zadoq's ancestral house is mentioned here, but not named. On Zadoq's genealogy and role within the presentation of the United Monarchy, see the 1st NOTE to 5:34 and the NOTES to 18:16.

"with his ancestral house, 22 officers." Twenty-two (or more usually twenty-four) priestly courses appear in the Persian period (1 Chr 24:7–18; Neh 12:1–7, 12–21; Benzinger 1901: 48, 72–73; Williamson 1979a; 1985: 341–64). Understanding this system of rotating watches is critical to understanding the calendar maintained by the Qumran covenanters (4Q317; 4Q319; 4Q320; 4Q321; 4Q327; VanderKam 1998: 71–90).

12:30. "were keeping *(šmrym)* the watch *(mšmrt)* of the house of Saul." The term *mšmrt* is used often in Chronicles and in the Priestly source with the sense of guard duty (NOTE to 9:27).

12:31. "ancestral houses" *(bêt ʾăbôt)*. On these major social units in the Persian period, see the 1st NOTE to 15:12.

12:32. "half-tribe of Manasseh." It is customary for the Chronicler to separate the two halves of Manasseh and discuss them in different literary contexts (5:23–24; 7:14–19). The Transjordanian portion of Manasseh appears in 12:38. Of the northern tribes, Manasseh figures regularly in the depiction of the Passovers of Ḥezeqiah (2 Chr 30:1, 10, 11, 18; 31:1) and Josiah (34:6, 9).

"enlisted by name" (נקבו בשמות). For this particular tribe the Chronicler envisions a registry from which no less than 18,000 were selected to enthrone David. The designation by name (cf. 16:41[MT]; 2 Chr 28:15; 31:19; cf. Num 1:17; Ezra 8:20) may be compared with the written registration in the census of Simeon (1 Chr 4:38, 41) and with earlier censuses by head (גלגלת) count (Exod 16:16; 38:26; Num 1:2, 18, 20, 22; 3:47; 1 Chr 23:3, 24). A similar locution *(ypqdw klm bšmwtyhm)* appears in the *Damascus Document*[a] with reference to a census of priests, Levites, Israelites, and proselytes (14:3–6 [4Q266]; Japhet 1993a: 124). On the large numbers involved, see the NOTE to v. 38.

12:33. "understanding the times, knowing what Israel should do." Wisdom appears as one of Issachar's attributes. In the writing of Qoheleth, the times (for sowing, weeping, dying, etc.) are also deemed important (Qoh 3:1–8), but Qoheleth despairs because these times cannot be predicted and lie ultimately beyond human control (3:9–15). The Chronicler's comment about Issachar reflects a more optimistic assessment of the relationship among experience, analysis, and action (cf. 2 Sam 20:18; Esth 1:13).

"commanders and all of their kinsmen." In this particular case, the Chronicler portrays a large turnout but does not specify a number.

12:34. "those going out on the campaign" *(yṣ'y ṣb')*. On the idiom, see the 5th TEXTUAL NOTE to 5:18 (cf. Num 1:3; 26:2; Deut 20:1; 1 Chr 12:37).

"battle formation" (ערכי מלחמה). The Chronicler is envisioning a mass scene in which the members of this tribe are regimented as a fighting force. On the technical expression, see also Gen 14:8; Judg 20:20, 22; 1 Sam 17:2, 8; 2 Sam 10:8; 2 Chr 13:3; 1QM 2:9.

"50,000." A northern tribe, Zebulun, fields the largest contingent of all the Israelite groups. These troops are not inexperienced conscripts, but battle ready and equipped "with all kinds of weapons." Zebulun is missing from the genealogical introduction (2:3–8:40). See further the COMMENT.

12:36. "Danites." On the possible appearance of Dan in the genealogies, see the 1st TEXTUAL NOTE to 7:12. Like Zebulun, Dan contributes a huge contingent to bolster David's embryonic rule.

12:38. "120,000." The figure probably reflects a round number of 40,000 for each of the three tribes. The high count requires some discussion because some of the Chronicler's numbers here and elsewhere are stupendous (e.g., 1 Chr 5:18; 23:3–5; 27:1–15; 2 Chr 13:3–17; 14:8–9; 17:14–18; 25:5–6; 26:12–13; 28:6–8). The problem is complicated by the fact that in certain cases, for instance, in some synoptic passages, the Chronicler's numbers cause no special problem (e.g., 1 Chr 12:29; Payne 1978: 7–28). But this apparent inconsistency only exacerbates the issue: why are most, but not all, of the numbers incredible? The force of the issue can be seen from another angle. Consideration of the evidence provided by archaeology renders the fantastic numbers in Chronicles highly problematic. Recent surface surveys provide significantly lower population estimates for Iron Age Israel and Judah than scholars previously assumed. Archaeological surveys indicate that the entire population of western Palestine in the tenth century was approximately 150,000 (Broshi and Finkelstein 1992: 50–53). Given this estimate, the figure of 120,000 for the Transjordanian tribes and 340,822 for the total muster cannot be taken at face value. There are four theories about how best to deal with the issue:

1. The term *ʾelep*, "thousand," should be understood as a subtribal division or a military unit; hence, 1 Chr 12:38 would be construed as referring to 120 divisions or 120 clans (e.g., Mendenhall 1958: 52–66; Myers 1965a: 97–99; Gottwald 1979: 270–84; Boling 1982; Milgrom 1990: 336–39; Humphreys 1998).
2. The term *ʾelep*, "thousand," is a traditional term; the actual numbers involved would be far less (e.g., de Vaux 1965: 216).
3. The term *ʾelep*, "thousand," was originally vocalized *ʾallûp* and meant "chief;" hence, v. 38 would be translated as "120 chiefs" (e.g., J. Wenham 1967: 19–53; Payne 1978: 5–58).
4. The incredible numbers are a literary convention or a scribal embellishment (e.g., R. Braun 1986: 170; Levine 1993: 139–40; Fouts 1994; 1997; Skolnic 1995: 24–65; R. Klein 1997; Heinzerling 1999).

First, in evaluating these four theories, it may be helpful to begin by observing that none takes the inflated numbers literally. Each attempts to make sense of impossible figures. Second, many of the Chronicler's fantastic numbers are also round numbers, whether to the nearest thousand (e.g., vv. 30, 32, 34, 35, 37, 38) or hundred (e.g., vv. 25, 26, 27, 28, 31, 36). The kind of specificity sometimes found in Assyrian royal inscriptions—Tiglath-pileser III claims that he settled 1,223 people of the province of Ulluba (H. Tadmor 1994: 63 [Ann. 19.12])—is highly unusual in the Chronicler's work (e.g., 1 Chr 7:7). Third, the employment of high numbers cannot be isolated entirely from the Chronicler's predilection for favorite numbers, such as three, six, seven, twelve, and forty (and multiples thereof). To be sure, inflated numbers and so-called holy numbers represent two different issues, but given the Chronicler's well-known preference for the latter (e.g., Johnson 1988: 24ff.), one cannot rule out the related possibility that he also employed large numbers for stylistic purposes.

Fourth, it is possible for theory 1 to be at least partially true and still fail as a comprehensive solution to the problem. The term *ʾelep* may occasionally designate "division" instead of "thousand" as v. 21 might attest (see TEXTUAL NOTES). But the proposed solution cannot be applied universally because some of the figures (Ephraim's twenty units would comprise 800 men, while Levi's four units would total 600) do not match up well. Similar problems bedevil the census figures for Num 1 and 26 (Heinzerling 1999; 2000). Moreover, the problem with large numbers does not pertain only to martial or tribal matters. Chronicles also supplies instances of colossal amounts of bullion (e.g., 1 Chr 22:14; 29:4) and extraordinary quantities of animals (e.g., 1 Chr 5:21; 2 Chr 30:24; 35:7–9; R. Klein 1997: 275–76). In other words, interpreting *ʾelep* as "unit" or "division" can work in certain martial or tribal contexts, but can be of little or no help in other contexts. To apply the theory generally would lead to the unappealing and dubious conclusion that the Chronicler comprehended neither his sources nor his subject matter.

Fifth, theory 3, however ingenious, also has its shortcomings. It does not seem likely that the text of Chronicles was so corrupted that virtually every instance of

*ʾallûp* was mistakenly later read as *ʾelep* and that this shift somehow left no trace in any of the versions. Moreover, if the original connotations of *ʾallûp* were no longer evident to the Chronicler (or to later editors), it is unclear why he repeatedly reproduces *ʾallûp* from Gen 36:15–43 in his own genealogy of 1:51–54 with the normal meaning "chieftain" (TEXTUAL NOTES to 1:51–54). Sixth, theories 2 and 4 are actually not that different, at least as far as Chronicles is concerned. Whether the incredible numbers are early legendary lore or a later scribal convention, the numbers are hyperbolic. Moreover, the Chronicler does not stand at the beginning of tradition. Since he is heir to a variety of earlier biblical writings, one may entertain the distinct possibility that he took note of the use of high numbers in his sources and extended the trope (see below).

Seventh, one distinct advantage of theory 4 is ancient Near Eastern precedent. The Kirta legend from Ugarit (*KTU* 1.14.II.35–40; IV.15–18) and Assyrian royal inscriptions (Millard 1991; Fouts 1994) contain examples of numbers used in an exaggerated way. Indeed, Grayson (1981: 45) considers hyperbole to be a regular literary device in enumerations of booty taken and enemy slain in Assyrian royal inscriptions. But the case for exaggeration in the Assyrian texts should not be pressed too far (De Odorico 1995). Within the HB, the use of large numbers as a literary convention is attested within the Deuteronomistic History (e.g., 2 Sam 8:13; 24:15; 1 Kgs 8:5, 62–64; Knoppers 1995b: 251; R. Klein 1997: 274). Similarly, in the Priestly work, the census numbers are clearly inflated or symbolic (Num 1; 26). Of the four positions, then, some combination of theories 2 and 4 would seem to have the most merit. Large numbers are one means by which the Chronicler configures what is for him a heroic past. In writing about the so-called Catalogue of Ships in the *Iliad* (2.484ff.), Bowra (1961: 245) comments that "big numbers mean big events." Incredible quantities of people, troops, bullion, and sacrifices contribute to a highly stylized presentation of Israel's past. The Chronicler expands the use of a trope found in the Deuteronomistic and the Priestly works. In this case, the 120,000 volunteers from the eastern tribes underscore a larger point, that elite warriors from Israel's remote tribes turned out en masse to support David.

12:39. "all these men of war." A summary notation corresponding to the introductory rubric of v. 24. Other such rubrics are found scattered throughout chapters 11 and 12 (11:10, 11, 26; 12:1).

"king over all Israel." The circumstances by which David becomes king in Chronicles are remarkable. In the ancient Near East, the manifestation of kingship is often bound up with victory over one's enemies. The six main tablets relating to the god Baal from ancient Ugarit, for example, center on Baal's battles with Yamm (Sea) and Mot (Death) and his concommitant rise to kingship over the gods. By defeating Yamm, Baal achieves a great victory (*KTU* 2.4.18–30; 4.4.20–62; 4.5.63–81). Yhwh's defeat of the Egyptians at the sea means that he "reigns forever and ever" (ימלך לעלם ועד; Exod 15:18). On a human plane, the celebration of Saul's kingship (1 Sam 11:14–15) occurs after he routed the Ammonites (11:1–13). But in Chronicles David is enthroned and his kingdom is won without a battle. David himself is a relatively passive figure.

"all the rest of Israel was of one heart to make David king." The general populace endorses the coronation of David. This stylized summary forms an *inclusio* with the Chronicler's earlier declaration that all Israel gathered at Ḥebron to offer David the kingship (11:1).

12:40. "eating and drinking." The elaborate feast celebrated by David and representatives from the various Israelite tribes is reminiscent of earlier feasts, most notably those at Mount Sinai (Exod 24:1–11) and Jerusalem (celebrating the anointing of Solomon; 1 Kgs 1:38–40, 43–48). Within Chronicles such feasts punctuate high points in Israelite and Judean history (1 Chr 15:25–16:3; 29:20–22; 2 Chr 7:8–10; 20:27–28; 29:30–36; 30:21–27). The celebration brings the movement of 11:4–12:39 to its culmination. From a literary standpoint, the celebration at Ḥebron corresponds to the earlier assembly at the same site (11:1–3). To be sure, the festivities at Ḥebron do not complete the story, because there are battles to be fought, a national administration to be organized, and a temple to be planned. Yet the feast hosted by David for his newly acquired forces comprises the natural conclusion to what precedes rather than the penultimate act to what follows (13:1–5; *pace* Willi 1972: 224; Mosis 1973: 43–50). The martial, political, and social aspects of David's rise are all related and cannot be reduced simply to a cultic agenda.

## Sources and Composition

The composition of 1 Chr 11–12 is much contested. How scholars view the genesis of chapter 12 is closely related to how they understand the relationship of the two major sections within it (vv. 1–23 and vv. 24–41) and how they construe the relationship between these two sections and the material found in 1 Chr 11. Rudolph (1955: 103–7) and Mosis (1973: 49) regard 12:1–23 as a later addition to the text because they think that it disrupts the continuity between 11:10–47 and 12:24–41. Noth (1987: 34) and Myers (1965a: 95) postulate a two-stage process in the writing of 1 Chr 12. They view 12:24–41 as a late addition because they believe that this material duplicates 11:10–47. The addition of 12:24–41 was followed by an even later supplement, 12:1–23 (Noth 1987: 34–35; Myers 1965a: 95), depicting a gradual rise to power purportedly at odds with the Chronicler's view of David's early regnal years, which focuses on David's reign over all Israel (11:1–47; 13:2). Rothstein and Hänel (1927: 222–36) consider 1 Chr 12 to be more unified than Noth, Rudolph, Myers, and Mosis do, but postulate a number of later additions to what they reconstruct as the basic text.

These scholars insightfully call attention to the distinctive features of the various sections within 1 Chr 11–12 and the overlap among them. One wonders, however, whether attributing either part or all of 1 Chr 12 to later redactors or glossators is the best way to explain the repetition. To begin with, it is methodologically hazardous to ascertain the Chronicler's position on anything by excising most of the texts that pertain to the issue as later insertions. It is true that the

Chronicler, in contrast to the authors of Samuel, does not devote major narrative sections either to David's sojourn in the wilderness of Judah or to his stay at Ziqlag. The Chronicler dwells on David's career as king and more specifically on his tenure in Jerusalem, but this does not mean that he denies earlier phases in David's career or that he takes no interest in them whatsoever. Even if one excludes, for the sake of argument, all of the material in 1 Chr 12 as later material, other texts make it clear that the writer acknowledged earlier periods in David's career (11:2; 17:7; 29:27).

Second, assuming, for the sake of argument, that repetition justifies excising texts as later additions, repetition would not validate removing all of 12:24–41 from the original composition of Chronicles. The pan-Israelite feast narrated in 12:39b–41, for example, is unparalleled by anything in 11:10–12:39a. Third, if one were to push the force of traditional source-critical and redaction-critical arguments, one might be compelled to excise not only 1 Chr 12 but also much of 1 Chr 11 (vv. 11–47) as extraneous to the presentation. That 11:11–41a stem from 2 Sam 23:8–39 is no argument against such a move. These verses could have been borrowed from Samuel some time after the Chronicler wrote his work. Considering that subsequent to David's anointing (11:1–3), "David and all Israel" capture Jerusalem (11:4–9), it is possible to move from the capture of Jerusalem straightaway to David's summons to "the entire assembly of Israel" (13:2) to bring the Ark to Jerusalem. After David has seized Jerusalem, it only remains to bring the Ark to its new home. This is, after all, the force of the Deuteronomistic presentation in 2 Sam 5–6. On this basis, one could maintain that all of 11:10–12:39a comprise later additions, because all of this material retards the narrative development.

Review of the arguments for disunity raises, therefore, fundamental questions about the nature of the Chronicler's work. Did he write a tightly organized, fast-paced narrative work with only a minimum of lists and genealogies? Regarding the Chronicler's narration of David's early kingly career, how indebted was he not only to the content of Samuel but also to Samuel's sequence of pericopes? Need the literary progression of the Chronicler's work match the chronological order of David's career in Samuel? How does one explain the relationship between the texts mentioning David's reign over Israel as consequent to Saul's reign (10:14; 11:1–9) and the texts depicting David's gradual rise to power, beginning already during Saul's reign? Finally, how does one explain the multiple appearance of certain tribes within the Chronicler's lists? The Benjaminites, for example, appear within the roster of David's warriors (11:10–47), the list of those who came to David at Ziqlag (12:1–8), the register of those who came to David at the stronghold (12:17–19), and the muster of tribal militias (12:30) associated with David's reign at Ḥebron (12:24–39a). Is this evidence of composite authorship or of a deliberate literary strategy?

The issues can be addressed in turn, beginning with the last. A good case can be made that the multiple references to the same tribe represent deliberate literary artifice. The repeated mention of Benjamin, for example, alludes to different times within David's public life. In Chronicles, members of Saul's tribe rally or defect to David at every stage of David's rise. The very repetition drives home a larger point. This explanation is the most economical explanation of the data and does not involve reconstructing hypothetical stages in the history of the text. This explanation also does justice to the brief chronological and topographical notes interspersed throughout 1 Chr 11–12. Finally, it comports with other features of the Chronicler's distinctive portrayal of David's career (see below). In adopting this position, one has to acknowledge that the author composed a literary work that included a series of lists and lineages, some of which, demographically at least, overlapped with others. But to string together a series of pericopes of varied length with only brief connectives is a characteristic feature of the Chronicler's compositional technique. Parataxis works not only with stories but also with lists and genealogies embedded within a larger narrative structure (Knoppers 1991).

There is, therefore, much to be said for those scholars who have stressed the overall unity of 1 Chr 11–12 and their integrity to the Chronicler's work (e.g., Curtis and Madsen 1910; Williamson 1981; R. Braun 1986; De Vries 1989; Japhet 1993a). These writers have seen redundancy within the lists as reinforcing the claim that all Israel supported David at various stages in his early career. The argument that the Chronicler ignores David's life in the wilderness, at Ziqlag, and at Ḥebron can be, in fact, turned on its head. First Chronicles 11–12, with the exception of Jerusalem's capture, which for theological reasons is introduced early to underscore the importance of Jerusalem to David and Israel (NOTE to 11:4–9), *is* the Chronicler's stylized version of David's tenure in the wilderness, at Ziqlag, and at Ḥebron. Having narrated the beginning of David's kingship (10:14; 11:1–3) and the conquest of Jerusalem (11:4–9), the Chronicler explains how David came to be king. The partial dependence on Samuel has made it difficult for some scholars to recognize how the author has forged an independent presentation of David's ascent to power.

Rather than presenting a strictly linear development, the Chronicler follows his description of David's anointing (11:1–3) and conquest of Jerusalem (11:4–9) with a series of flashbacks (R. Braun 1986: 167), which recapitulate earlier stages of David's career. These flashbacks complement the narration of Saul's demise (10:1–14) by elucidating how David came to be unanimously acclaimed by Israelites and anointed by Israel's elders following Saul's death. Each of the different pericopes, alluding to different stages in David's early public life, depicts how Israelites from various quarters strengthened David's position. The cumulative effect of these defections secures David's kingship.

As for the literary structure of 1 Chr 11–12, the work of Williamson (1981: 164–76) has been rightfully influential. He argues that the Chronicler had access to sources beyond Samuel, but that he reordered this material, adding rubrics and comments to unify the whole. In this view, 1 Chr 11–12 evinces an elaborate, essentially achronological, chiastic structure. Slightly modifying his reconstruction, one can discern the following pattern.

a All-Israel Coronation of David (11:1–3)
  b Warriors Strengthen David's Position (11:10–47)
    c Benjaminites Assemble to David at Ziqlag (12:1–8)
      d Gadites Rally to David at His Fortress (12:9–16)

d′ Judah and Benjamin Come to the Fortress (12:17–19)
c′ Manasseh Assembles to David at Ziqlag (12:20–23)
b′ Tribal Militias Congregate to David at Ḥebron (12:24–39a)
a′ All-Israel Celebration of David's Kingship (12:39b–41)

The middle sections refer, therefore, to the earliest part of David's career narrated in Chronicles: the sojourn at his stronghold. The other sections, characterized by lists and vignettes, fill out the picture by depicting steadily growing support for David from various individuals and tribes. "The centre of the pattern goes back to the earliest time at which David began to attract support" (Williamson 1982b: 105–6). From this midpoint the pattern moves out until it involves representatives from the entire nation in the coronation and pan-Israel feast at Ḥebron.

## COMMENT

In his discussion of royal ideology in early Mesopotamia, Postgate (1994a: 268–70) identifies two traditional justifications for royal rule: divine election and popular demand. The first rhetorical strategy involves asserting that a given king had been singled out by a deity for future rule while that king was but a young child or a youth. The second involves asserting that a monarch became king due to popular acclamation. Both tropes could be employed to explain the ascent of a king who was a usurper or who came to rule in unusual circumstances. If the new monarch was not tied dynastically to the previous monarch, the usurper might also justify his rise to power by characterizing the previous king or dynasty as corrupt or inept (Ishida 1985; 1991). In his portrayal of David's rise, the Chronicler employs all of these strategies to justify David's kingship. He characterizes Saul's rule as degenerate and Saul as rejected by Yhwh (10:1–14). The gravity of Saul's transgression justifies the deity's decision to turn the kingdom over to David (10:14). In the later report about the deity's dynastic promises to David and his line, Yhwh declares that he provided for David from the time David was a shepherd (17:7–14). The presentation in 1 Chr 11–12 contributes to this picture by recounting Israel's enthusiastic endorsement of David (Zeron 1974). Dissociating David from the demise of Saul, the Chronicler presents Israelites from a wide variety of tribes as acting deliberately to strengthen David's position and eventually to make him king (Knoppers, forthcoming [b]). Popular and divine election coalesce in establishing David's rule.

The Chronicler's presentation of David's rise to power is perhaps best appreciated by comparing it with the presentation in Samuel of David's rise to kingship. There David begins his long and arduous rise in the service of Saul (e.g., 1 Sam 18:5–7, 14–16, 30; 19:7) only to become a refugee from Saul. David gathers a band of followers to himself, but is repeatedly betrayed by others (1 Sam 22:9–23; 23:19–20; 24:1–2). Despite such setbacks, David successfully evades capture. For a time David escapes from Saul's troops by allying himself to the Philistines (1 Sam 27:1–12; 29:1–11). Eventually the threat dissipates as Saul's rule deteriorates, and following Saul's death, David becomes king of Judah (2 Sam 2:1–4). During this period Israel is riven by rivalries and internal disputes. Some seven years ensue in which an Israelite kingdom, headed by Saul's son Ishbaal, and a Judahite kingdom, headed by David, coexist (2 Sam 2:8–4:12.). In the war between the two royal houses David gradually gains the upper hand. But David wins the support of the northern tribes only after Ishbaal's kingdom disintegrates and Ishbaal's own troops assassinate him (2 Sam 4:1–8). Only in the aftermath of this divisive struggle does David become king of all Israel (2 Sam 5:1–3). Given the complexity of the presentation in Samuel, scholars have debated the very nature of Israel—its early history, constitution, and *raison d'être*. Alt (1967: 171–237) influentially spoke of a "personal union," an artificial unity imposed upon the fractious Israelite tribes by the force of David's charismatic leadership.

When seen against the background of the tumult depicted by Samuel, the Chronicler's alternative picture of David's rise is a tour de force. In Chronicles one should speak not so much of a united kingdom constituted by a Davidic personal union, but of an Israelite union that establishes a Davidic monarchy. David does not woo the Israelite tribes; they unanimously woo him. In this schema, the Davidic king becomes a unifying figure for all Israel (Abadie 1994). To be sure, the Chronicler does not deny that David's ascent to power was a protracted process. The would-be king attracts an extensive group of retainers who strengthen his position (11:10–47). The text alludes to David's sojourn among the Philistines (12:20), his battles against the Philistines (11:11–13, 15–19), his early conflicts against various foes (11:20–23; 12:1, 22), a tenure at his stronghold (11:16; 12:9, 17), a stay at Ziqlag (12:1, 21), and a rule at Ḥebron (11:1, 3; 12:24, 39). The lineaments of a long historical process are still visible in the Chronicler's highly stylized presentation.

Nevertheless, the author selectively employs these stages to generate a comprehensive picture of widespread and steadily growing support for David from all quarters. By beginning and ending with David's reign at Ḥebron, the author acknowledges a long rise to power without portraying this rise as either bloody or divisive. Quite the contrary, David's rise is a picture of an orderly and ever-expanding intertribal consensus. The Chronicler deconstructs Samuel even as he draws heavily from it to construct his own story. Instead of depicting a movement from David and his followers to Judah and then to Israel, he narrates a movement from Israel to David. When "all Israel gathered to David at Ḥebron, saying, 'We are your bone and your flesh' " (11:1), the people claim a fundamental kinship affinity with David, not vice versa. The body politic is instrumental. Following the elders' anointing of David (11:3), a variety of individuals and groups rally to David with the express purpose of consolidating his position (11:10; 12:24, 32, 39). Militarily speaking, Israel may be organized according to a system of tribal militias (Yadin 1963: 275–77), but these tribal militias all rally to the new monarch. In this context, it is no accident that Benjamin, the tribe of Saul, sends troops David's way at virtually every stage of David's ascent to power (11:10–47; 12:1–7, 17–19, 24–39a).

The body politic enthusiastically endorses David, but it does not act entirely on its own initiative. David's rise is divinely ordained. When the people approach David to make him king, they appeal to the force of prophecy, "Yhwh said to you, 'As for you, you shall shepherd my people Israel and you, you shall become ruler over Israel' " (11:2). The narrator also cites prophecy to validate David's anointing (11:3) and to elucidate the function of David's brigade: they "continually strengthened him in his kingship, along with all Israel, to make him king, according to the word of Yhwh concerning Israel" (11:10). If Saul transgresses Yhwh's word to his demerit (10:13), Israel follows Yhwh's word to its merit (11:3, 10; Abadie 1999: 166). The author not only ties the presence of David's retainers (2 Sam 23:8–39) to the broader pattern of popular support for David, but he also subordinates their allegiance to the implementation of Yhwh's desire for Israel. Similarly, the author explains the unanimous decision of the tribal militias "to turn the kingdom of Saul over" to David as consonant with "the word of Yhwh" (12:24; cf. 10:14). Popular election simultaneously acknowledges and implements divine election.

The desire to portray unanimity of support for David is evident in virtually every feature of the Chronicler's presentation, but perhaps most notably in the additions he makes to the material he borrows from Samuel. The expansion of the list of David's warriors to include commanders from the Transjordanian tribes and non-Israelites broadens the base of David's support (11:41b–47). By portraying the arrival of Gadites (12:9–16) and Benjaminites (along with Judahites) at David's stronghold (12:17–19), and subsequently the arrival of Benjaminites (12:1–7) and soldiers from Manasseh at Ziqlag (12:20–23), the author narrates early support for David from a variety of tribes outside of his own. In the Chronicler's presentation, northerners do not acquiesce to David's kingship only after the house of Saul comes to a humiliating end (2 Sam 2:10). Northerners are already supporting David in tremendous numbers while Saul is king.

Perhaps the most stunning example of far-flung support can be found in the roster of tribal militias (12:25–38). The distribution of troops varies considerably, but the northern sodalities contribute by far the largest contingents of warriors. The differences may be sketched as follows:

| | |
|---|---|
| Judah | 6,800 |
| Simeon | 7,100 |
| Levi | 8,322 |
| Benjamin | 3,000 |
| Ephraim | 20,800 |
| Half-Manasseh | 18,000 |
| Issachar | 200 chiefs and all of their kinsmen |
| Zebulun | 50,000 |
| Naphtali | 38,000 |
| Dan | 28,600 |
| Asher | 40,000 |
| Transjordan (Reuben, Gad, and East Manasseh) | 120,000 |

As the chart indicates, David draws some of his greatest support from those tribes that are the furthest distance from his own. Of the total of 340,822 troops drawn from the sundry Israelite tribes, only 9,800 stem from Judah and Benjamin. Indeed, the grand total for Judah, Simeon, Levi, and Benjamin does not match the single contribution of Dan! It could be argued that since Saul stemmed from Benjamin, his tribe was not inclined to give much assistance to David. But as we have seen, Benjaminites figure prominently elsewhere in supporting David's claim to the throne. That Judah's number is comparatively small has confounded commentators. Keil, for instance, contends that because David was already in Ḥebron, Judahites needed to manifest only token support. But one would think the contrary would be true: because their very future was at stake the Judahites would be most enthusiastic and forthcoming of all in supporting their native monarch.

Another explanation seems likely. The writer goes to great lengths to promote David as a king for all Israelites. David stems from Judah, but it is the tremendous support he receives from areas outside his own natural power base that consolidates his kingship so impressively. The new king draws modest support from Judah, Levi, Simeon, and Benjamin and good support from Ephraim and East Manasseh. But he draws his strongest support from the far-distant tribes of Zebulun, Asher, Dan, and Napthali and from the Transjordanian tribes of Reuben, Gad, and Half-Manasseh. In this typology, one can see a related feature of a larger literary design. Aside from the capture of Jerusalem in which David is clearly in command, all of the other military actions are taken by individuals and militias who rally to David to draft him as king. David himself is relatively passive. David does not make Israel; God and Israel make David.

The unusual symmetry between divine and human wills that renders David king and consolidates the kingdom elucidates the presentation of a joyful pan-Israel banquet as one of the high points in Israelite history (12:39b–41; NOTE). For three days David and Israel feast together. In comparison with Samuel's presentation, in which David's rise is punctuated by divisive conflicts and outright civil war, in Chronicles David's rise is characterized by a growing national consensus. While it is true that the solidarity shown by the various tribes reflects well on David, it also reflects well on the people. Popular action accords with and accomplishes God's will for Israel.

# *XVI. Israel's Aborted Attempt to Retrieve the Ark (13:1–14)*

*The Agreement to Transfer the Ark*

1 And David took counsel with the officers of the thousands and of the hundreds—with every commander. 2 Then David said to the entire assembly of Israel, "If it seems good to you and if it is from Yhwh our God, let us send out far and wide to our kin, to those remaining in all the regions of Israel, and with them the priests

and the Levites in the towns of their open lands that they may gather themselves to us. [3] Let us bring back the Ark of our God to us, for we did not seek it in the days of Saul." [4] And all (the members) of the assembly said to do so, because the word was right in the eyes of all of the people.

*The First Attempt to Transfer the Ark*

[5] Then David assembled all Israel, from Shiḥor of Egypt to Lebo-ḥamath, to bring the Ark of God from Qiriath-jearim. [6] Then David and all Israel went up to Baalah, to Qiriath-jearim, which belongs to Judah, to bring back from there the Ark of God, which is invoked by the name "Yhwh enthroned upon the cherubim." [7] They transported the Ark of God upon a new cart from the house of Abinadab. Uzza and Aḥio were guiding the cart [8] while David and all Israel were performing before God with all their strength—with songs, lyres, harps, drums, cymbals, and trumpets. [9] When they came by the threshing floor of Kidon, Uzza extended his hand to steady the Ark because the oxen had let it slip. [10] The anger of Yhwh was kindled against Uzza and he struck him down, because he set his hand upon the Ark. And he died there before God. [11] Then David became angry, because Yhwh had created a breach against Uzza—and that place is called Perez-uzza to this day.

*The Attempt Abandoned*

[12] And David became fearful of God on that day, saying, "How can I bring the Ark of God (home) to me?" [13] So David did not take the Ark away with him to the City of David, but redirected it to the house of Obed-edom the Gittite. [14] The Ark of God remained with the house of Obed-edom for three months and Yhwh blessed the house of Obed-edom and all that he had.

## Textual Notes

13:1–14. These verses should be compared with 2 Sam 6:1–11. Of the material in Samuel, 4QSam[a] is available (in fragmentary form) for 2 Sam 6:2–9.

13:1. "officers" (שָׂרֵי). So MT and LXX[AB]. LXX[L] expands by prefacing *tōn presbyterōn kai*, "the elders and" (= *hzqnym w-*).

"the officers of the thousands and of the hundreds" (שָׂרֵי האלפים והמאות). The construct chain with a single construct and two absolutes is unusual (see the 1st TEXTUAL NOTE to 28:13).

"with every commander" *(lkl ngyd)*. So MT. Cf. LXX[AB] *panti hēgoumenō*; LXX[L] (and Vg.) *kai meta pantos hēgoumenou* (= *wʿm kl-*). In LBH the prep. *l-* can be translated as "with" when it is prefixed to nouns in enumeration or apposition (Kropat, §18; Waltke and O'Connor, §10.4b). Joüon (§125l) proposes to interpret the prep. *l-* as analogous to the direct object marker *ʾt*. On *ngyd*, see 3rd TEXTUAL NOTE to 11:2.

13:2. "if it seems good to you" (אם-עליכם טוב). In LBH, the prep. *ʿl* occasionally governs an indirect object that would be governed by the prep. *l-* in CH (Waltke and O'Connor, §11.2.13g). The phrase "if it seems good to you" is common in

LBH (Neh 2:5, 7; Esth 1:19; 3:9; 5:4, 8; 7:3; 8:5; 9:13 [BDB 758]). A similar locution occurs in Bibl. Aram. (Ezra 5:17; 7:18).

"let us send out far and wide" *(nprṣh nšlḥ)*. Thus MT *(lectio difficilior)*. The first verb *(nprṣh)* can be read with what precedes (so LXX) or with what follows (MT). LXX[B] *euōdōthē*; LXX[ANS] *euodōthē* ("prospered" or "put in the right way") is the *lectio facilior*. That MT is difficult does not justify deleting *nprṣh* altogether (*pace* Rudolph 1955: 110). Begrich *(BHK)* proposes reconstructing *nrṣth*, while some others (e.g., BDB 829) favor reconstructing *nḥrṣh*. But emendation may be unnecessary. The verb *prṣ* is used quite often in Chronicles—thirteen of fifty-one OT occurrences (1 Chr 4:38; 13:2, 11; 14:11 [bis]; 15:13; 2 Chr 11:23; 20:37; 24:7; 25:23; 31:5; 32:5). In most cases *prṣ* designates "to breach" or "to break up/out," but in some cases *prṣ* must be rendered more idiomatically as "to spread" or "to increase" (e.g., 1 Chr 4:38; 13:2; 2 Chr 11:23; 31:5). It seems best to read *nprṣh* asyndetically, as a *qal* cohortative with the following verb "let us send out" (*nšlḥ*; GKC §120h; cf. Gen 24:50).

"to our kin" *(ʿl-ʾḥynw)*. On the interchange between the preps. *ʿl* and *ʾl* in Chronicles, see the 1st TEXTUAL NOTE to 12:23. Waltke and O'Connor (§11.2.13b) argue that with some verbs of motion both *ʾl* and *ʿl* have a terminative sense ("on, to, onto").

"lands." So MT *(lectio difficilior)*. LXX has the sg.

"they may gather themselves to us." The *nipʿal* is used reflexively (Lambdin, §140).

13:3. "we did not seek it" *(lʾ dršnhw)*. So MT and LXX[L]. LXX[AB] "they did not seek it" (= *lʾ dršwhw)*. Cf. 1 Chr 15:13.

13:4. "said to do so." On the use of the inf. after *ʾmr*, see also 1 Chr 27:23; 2 Chr 21:7; Ps 106:23; Esth 4:7.

13:5. "Shiḥor." So MT. LXX *horiōn*, "boundaries."

"God." A few Heb. MSS and Syr. "Yhwh."

13:6. "(and) David and all Israel went up." So MT. LXX[L] is similar, *kai anebē Daueid kai pas anēr Israēl*, "and David and all of the men of Israel went up." LXX[ABN] *kai anēgagen autēn Daueid*, "and David brought it up." That LXX[ABN] continue with *kai pas Israēl anebē eis polin Daueid* may indicate this tradition has experienced a dittography. MT 2 Sam 6:2 reads somewhat differently, *wyqm wylk dwd wkl hʿm ʾšr ʾtw*, "and David and all of the people with him arose."

"to Baalah, to Qiriath-jearim, which belongs to Judah" *(bʿlth ʾl qryt yʿrym ʾšr lyhwdh)*. So MT. MT 2 Sam 6:2 is corrupt, *mbʿly yhwdh* (Benzinger 1901: 49; Ulrich 1978: 194, 198–99). Some claim that the identification of Baalah with "Qiriath-jearim, which belongs to Judah" is an early addition to Samuel (cf. Josh 15:9); nevertheless, 4QSam[a] *bʿlh hyʾ qr[yt yʿrym ʾšr] lyhwdh*, "Baalah, that is Qiriath-jearim, which belongs to Judah," indicates that the clause is pre-Chronistic in nature.

"to bring back from there the Ark of God, which is invoked by the name 'Yhwh enthroned upon the cherubim' " *(lhʿlwt mšm ʾt ʾrwn hʾlhym ʾšr nqrʾ šm yhwh ywšb hkrwbym)*. A reconstruction. MT *lhʿlwt mšm ʾt ʾrwn hʾlhym yhwh ywšb hkrwbym ʾšr nqrʾ šm*. LXX is similar, *tou anagagein ekeithen tēn kibōton tou theou Kyriou kathēmenou epi Cheroubein[-im] hou epeklēthē (to) onoma autou*. 2 Sam 6:2 "to bring back from there the Ark of God, whose name upon it is invoked 'Yhwh Sebaoth enthroned upon the cherubim' " (*lhʿlwt mšm ʾt ʾrwn hʾlhym ʾšr nqrʾ šm šm* [the second *šm* is lacking in LXX and 4QSam[a]] *yhwh ṣbʾwt* [*ṣbʾwt* is apparently lacking in 4QSam[a]] *ywšb hkrbym ʿlyw*). Comparison of MT 2 Sam 6:2, 4QSam[a], and MT 1 Chr 13:6 reveals that 4QSam[a] and Chronicles are less verbose than MT 2 Sam 6:2 and that Chronicles, *yhwh ywšb hkrwbym ʾšr nqrʾ šm*, has experienced a transposition (Ulrich 1978: 197). Note, in this respect, Begrich's proposal (*BHK*) to read *šmw šm* and to insert *ʾsr nqrʾ šm* after "God" (cf. 2 Sam 6:2).

13:7. "Ark of God." So MT, LXX, and MT 2 Sam 6:3. 4QSam[a] and LXX 2 Sam 6:3 "Ark of Yhwh."

"Aḥio." MT 13:7 and MT 2 Sam 6:3 *ʾaḥyô*; some Heb. MSS *ʾaḥîô*. LXX *ho adelphoi autou* (= *ʾḥyw*), "his brothers." The name אחיו is common at Elephantine (*TAD* A4.4.7; B2.1.15; 2.18; 6.38; 10.19; 11.18; B3.1.22; 2.2, 12; 3.6.17). 2 Sam 6:3 continues with "sons of Abinadab."

"were guiding the cart" (*nhgym bʿglh*). MT 2 Sam 6:3 "were guiding the new cart" (*nhgym ʾt hʿglh ḥdšh*). Not present in Chronicles is the lemma of MT 2 Sam 6:4, "and they carried it (*wyśʾhw*) from the house of Abinadab, which is on the hill, with the Ark of God, and Aḥio was walking before the Ark." This plus is partly lacking in 4QSam[a]: "[with the Ark of God. Aḥio was walking before the Ar]k." A comparison of 1 Chr 13:7, 4QSam[a], MT 2 Sam 6:4, and (shorter) LXX 2 Sam 6:4 suggests that MT 2 Sam 6:4 results from a double reading.

13:8. "David and all Israel." MT 2 Sam 6:5 "David and all the house of Israel;" 4QSam[a] and LXX* 2 Sam 6:5 "David and [all] the sons of Israel."

"performing" (*mśḥqym*). The common trans. "making merry" is possible, but the argument has been made (Sasson 1973: 152) that the verbs *śḥq* and *zḥq* designate performance (e.g., dancing, sports, miming, and singing). To the case based on comparative evidence from ancient Mesopotamia and Greece, one can add a contextual consideration from Chronicles. It is more likely that David and the Israelites would be performing "with all their strength" than making merry "with all their strength." See also 1 Chr 15:29 and *HALOT* 1315–16.

"with all their strength and with songs" (*bkl ʿz wbšyrym*). MT 2 Sam 6:5 is problematic: "with all (kinds) of cypress wood (instruments?)" (*bkl ʿṣy brwšym*; Soggin 1964). Fragmentary 4QSam[a] agrees with Chronicles.

"drums" (*tuppîm*). Cf. Ugaritic *tp*. "drum." The term could also be translated as "tambourines," because ancient drums resembled tambourines or timbrels. Nevertheless, the *tōp* did not have any jingles attached to its sides.

"cymbals and trumpets" (*bmṣltym wbḥṣṣrwt*). MT 2 Sam 6:5 "sistrums (or rattles) and cymbals" (*bmnʿnʿym wbṣlṣlym*). On the terminology in 2 Sam 6:5, see J. Braun (1999).

13:9. "Kidon" (*kydwn*). Reading tentatively with MT and Vg. (*Chidon*). Lacking in LXX[B], probably due to haplography (*homoioteleuton* from *grn kydwn* to *grn*). LXX[AN] and some codices of Josephus *Cheilōn* (*Ant*. 7.81); $gme_2$ *Chelōn*; bb′ *Chailōn*. MT 2 Sam 6:6 *nkwn* "does not satisfy the requirements of sense" (S. Driver 1912: 266). 4QSam[a] reads either *nwrn* or *nyrn*.

"Uzza extended his hand to steady the Ark" (*wyšlḥ ʿzʾ ʾt ydw lʾḥz ʾt hʾrwn*). So

MT and LXX. MT 2 Sam 6:6 "Uzza sent to the Ark of God and took hold of it" *(wyšlḥ ʿzʾ ʾl ʾrwn hʾlhym wyʾḥz bw)*. 4QSam[a] *wyšlḥ ʿzʾ* [*ʾt*] *ydw ʾl ʾrwn h*[*ʾ*]*l*[*whym*] *lʾḥz* (Ulrich 1978: 195–99) supports the suspicion of older commentators (e.g., S. Driver) that MT 2 Sam 6:6 has suffered parablepsis *(homoioarkton* from *ʾt ydw ʾl ʾrwn* to *ʾl ʾrwn)*.

"had let it slip." Many translate "stumbled," but there is no clear evidence that the verb *šmṭ* has a transitive meaning in the *qal*. MT 13:9 and MT 2 Sam 6:6 read the pl. *šmṭw*, "they let it fall." I follow Budde (1902: 229), who reads *šĕmāṭô* on the basis of *periespasen autēn* (LXX 2 Sam 6:6). Cf. *exeklinen autēn* (LXX 13:9); *bos quippe lasciviens paululum inclinaverat eam* (Vg. 13:9); and *declinaverunt eam* (the Clementine text of Vg. 2 Sam 6:6).

13:10. "he struck him down" (ויכהו). So MT *(lectio brevior)*. LXX *kai epataxen auton ekei*. MT and 4QSam[a] 2 Sam 6:7 explicate "God struck him down there" (ויכהו שם האלהים).

"because he set his hand upon the Ark" *(ʿl ʾšr šlḥ ydw ʿl hʾrwn)*. MT 2 Sam 6:7 "on account of the error[?]" *(ʿl hšl)*. LXX[B] 2 Sam 6:7 lacks *ʿl hšl*. The root *šlh*, from which apocopated *šl* is sometimes derived, is quite rare (2 Kgs 4:28; Jer 12:1; Job 12:6; 2 Chr 29:11; *HALOT* 1503). Cf. *šlw* (Job 3:26; Ezra 4:22; 6:9; Dan 6:5). 4QSam[a] 2 Sam 6:7 basically comports with MT 13:10 [*ʿl ʾšr šlḥ ydw*] *ʾl* [*h*]*ʾrwn*.

"before God" *(lpny ʾlhym)*. So MT 13:10 and 4QSam[a] 2 Sam 6:7 *l*[*pny hʾ*]*l*[*w*]*h*[*ym*]). LXX *apenanti tou theou*, "over against God." MT 2 Sam 6:7 "with the Ark of God" *(ʿm ʾrwn hʾlhym)*.

13:11. "then David became angry" *(wyḥr ldwyd)*. So MT 13:11 and MT 2 Sam 6:8, as well as 4QSam[a] ([*w*]*yḥr ld*[*wd*]). On the basis of LXX *kai ēthymēsēn Daueid* and Vg. *contristatusque David*, Begrich *(BHK)* proposes "and he trembled" *(wyḥrd)* or "and he was distressed" *(wyṣr)*. Cf. Jonah 4:9. But LXX and Vg. are, in all likelihood, euphemistic versions of the Heb., which is the *lectio difficilior*.

13:12. "how" *(hyk)*. 2 Sam 6:9 *ʾyk*.

13:13. "so David did not take the Ark away with him" (ולא-הסיר דויד את-הארון אליו). MT 2 Sam 6:10 "so David was unwilling to take the Ark of Yhwh with him" (ולא-אבה דוד להסיר אליו את-ארון יהוה).

"the Gittite." So 13:13 and 2 Sam 6:10. Josephus (*Ant.* 7:83) "a Levite."

13:14. "with the house" *(ʿm-byt)*. LXX *en oikō*; Vg. *in domo*. Lacking in Tg. due to haplography *(homoioarkton* from *ʿm-byt ʿbd* to *ʿbd)*. MT 2 Sam 6:11 *byt*. There is no need to emend "house" to "tent" because of the Chronicler's supposed inability to accept that the Ark could reside in a "house" (contra Kittel; Curtis and Madsen). MT and LXX suggest otherwise.

"Obed-edom." Reading with LXX[ABN] and Vg. *(lectio brevior)*. MT adds "in his house" *(bbytw)*. 2 Sam 6:11 adds "the Gittite" *(hgty)*.

"and Yhwh blessed the house of Obed-edom and all that he had." So MT and LXX 1 Chr 13:14 and LXX[L] 2 Sam 6:11. MT and LXX[A] 2 Sam 6:11, "Yhwh blessed Obed-edom and all his house." The continuation of 2 Sam 6:12 is lacking in 1 Chr 13: "and it was reported to King David, saying, "Yhwh has blessed the house of Obed-edom and all that he had, because of the Ark of God." This addition may have been interpolated into Samuel by repetitive resumption from ויברך יהוה את־עבד אדם ואת־כל־ביתו in 2 Sam 6:11 to ברך יהוה את־בית עבד אדם ואת־כל־אשׁר־לו בעבור ארון האלהים in 2 Sam 6:12. It seems unlikely that all of this additional material was in the Chronicler's *Vorlage*.

# NOTES

13:1–5. The Chronicler has prefaced his own introduction to the material he borrows from Samuel (13:6–14//2 Sam 6:2–11). His pan-Israel emphasis puts a new slant on the material that he draws from his source. The narrative of 2 Sam 6:1–19 also begins with David convoking an assembly to bring the Ark to Jerusalem, but there the gathering consists of David's elite troops (כל־בחור בישׂראל שׁלשׁים אלף; 2 Sam 6:1). Over against this brief notice of a martial summons, the Chronicler substitutes a detailed description of a conference among David, Israel's leadership, and the people as a whole. The king makes an appeal to those scattered far and wide and invites the participation of the priests and Levites (1 Chr 13:2). The juxtaposition of pericopes in Chronicles is striking. The enormous troop strength at David's disposal (11:10–12:39a) contrasts with David's conscious choice to involve the entire assembly of Israel (כל קהל ישׂראל) in the decision to retrieve the Ark. One mark of the stature of the Chronicler's David is that he exercises due restraint in the use of royal power. He involves the populace at large, not just their military leadership, in transferring this national cultic symbol to Jerusalem.

13:1. "took counsel." David confers with his military commanders, who previously figured so prominently in consolidating his kingship (11:10–12:39a). The setting for this convocation is, however, evidently not Ḥebron, but Jerusalem. One possible explanation is that an interval must be assumed between the events that conclude the pan-Israel banquet at Ḥebron (12:39b–41) and the Jerusalem assembly convoked by David (13:1; Japhet 1993a: 272). But another explanation seems preferable. All of the material in 11:10–12:41 consists of a series of flashbacks relating to David's inexorable rise to power prior to his capture of Jerusalem, the signal event at the beginning of his kingly career (11:4–9). In other words, the temporal narrative ended in 11:9 resumes again in 13:1. Having seized Jerusalem, David consults with Israel's leaders about bringing the ancient palladium into the newly won capital. That this line of interpretation has merit can be seen in the Chronicler's reuse of 2 Sam 5:17 to introduce the next major event in David's reign (1 Chr 14:8). There the Philistines, having learned of David's anointing "as king over all Israel" (cf. 11:1–3), decide to pursue David. The sequence of events, as narrated in Chronicles, presumes that the Philistine attack came about not long after David became king, presumably when his new regime was still vulnerable.

"officers of the thousands and of the hundreds" (שׂרי האלפים והמאות). Referring to military leaders (Num 31:14, 54; 1 Sam 22:7; 2 Sam 18:1; 2 Kgs 11:4, 9, 10, 15) rather than to judicial officials (Exod 18:21, 25; Deut 1:15). If the term "thousands" is figurative for small companies of five to fourteen men, as some scholars believe, it is unclear what the significance of "the hundreds" is (NOTE to 12:38).

13:2. "to those remaining" (הנשארים). David wants those people who have not yet rallied to the capital to do so (cf. 12:39b–41). The narrative, like the story describing David's early conquest of Jebus (11:4–9), demonstrates Jerusalem's centrality to Israel. It should be observed that the Chronicler's Israel is broadly defined, containing members of all its tribes, whether living at home or far away (Japhet 1989; Williamson 1977b; COMMENT on 5:1–26). Hence, there is some validity to the argument that the Chronicler's audience, living in the context of the Persian period, would interpret David's words as an unequivocal affirmation of Jerusalem's pivotal role within Judaism in spite of the diaspora (Mosis 1973: 51; Willi 1999: 83–89).

"regions." The use of the pl. of "land" *(ʾrṣ)* is common in Chronicles (and LBH), occurring some twenty-two times. In the pl., the term can refer to regions within the territorial state (2 Chr 11:23; 15:5; 34:33) or to regions abutting it (1 Chr 14:17; 22:5; 29:30).

"the priests and the Levites." The Chronicler envisions the Levites as living at various sites within Israel's tribal territories (COMMENT on 6:39–66). Because this priestly tribe is an essential component of Israel and any attempt to transfer Israel's most sacred symbol to Jerusalem must be handled properly, the participation of the priests and Levites is necessary to implement David's plan successfully.

"open lands." See the 3rd NOTE to 5:16.

13:3. "let us bring back" *(nsbh)*. Having won the support of all Israel (11:1–3, 10–47; 12:1–41) and captured Jerusalem (11:4–9), David immediately turns his attention to cultic issues (see COMMENT).

"Ark of our God." In the Chronicler's biblical sources the Ark appears as a portable box carried about by the Israelites along their sundry early travels. See further the COMMENT.

"we did not seek it *(lʾ dršnhw)* in the days of Saul." The context for David's attempt to bring the Ark to Jerusalem differs from that of Samuel. There, the Ark stays in Qiriath-jearim for some twenty years (1 Sam 7:1) after the Philistines no longer wished to have anything to do with it (1 Sam 4:1–6:21). But in Chronicles the need to retrieve the Ark is explicitly linked to the decline of Israel during Saul's tenure. The same catchword "seek" *(drš)* is used both to describe Saul's failure to venerate Yhwh (10:13–14) and to explain the neglect of the Ark during Saul's reign. This evaluation is in keeping with the depiction of Saul's rule as the nadir of the United Monarchy (COMMENT on 9:35–10:14).

13:4. "all (the members) of the assembly said to do so." See the NOTE to vv. 1–5.

"the word" *(haddābār)*. Referring to the public proposal put forward by the king (v. 3).

13:5. "from Shiḥor of Egypt to Lebo-ḥamath." Shiḥor (Josh 13:3; Isa 23:3; Jer 2:18) is usually associated with Pʾ-š-Ḥr, "Lagoon of Horus," a body of water in northeastern Egypt, perhaps at the lower reaches of the Bubastite or Pelusiac Nile (Lambdin 1962: 328). Lebo-ḥamath (לבוא חמת), understood by many of the versions as "the entrance of/to Ḥamath" has been construed by modern scholars (e.g., B. Mazar 1986: 189–202; Dion 1997: 166–67; Na'aman 1999: 421) as T. Qaṣr Lebwe or Lab'u, a site on the upper reaches of the Orontes mentioned in Egyptian sources and in one of the inscriptions of Tiglath-pileser III (Summ. 5 II.25; H. Tadmor 1994: 149). In biblical texts, Lebo (ḥamath) is often associated with the northeastern border of Canaan (Num 13:21; 34:8; Josh 13:5; Judg 3:3; 2 Kgs 14:25; Amos 6:14; Ezek 47:15; 48:1). The use of the clause "from Shiḥor of Egypt to Lebo-ḥamath" in this particular context is, therefore, important and requires some discussion. In Japhet's opinion (1979: 208–9; 1993a: 277–78), the use of the expression correlates to the most extensive description of the promised land (Josh 13:1–7; cf. Num 34:3–12; Ezek 47:13–20). According to this theory, the Israelite state under Saul and David occupied all of the land from the Nile to Lab'u. The territory covered by the expression is wide-ranging, but there are a number of complications that make the reconstruction difficult to sustain. First, more extensive descriptions of Israel's promised land than that which appears in Josh 13:1–7 occur in other texts (Gen 15:18; Exod 23:31; Deut 1:7; 11:24; Josh 1:3–4; Na'aman 1986a: 60–73, 244–49). In these texts the border extends all the way from the Euphrates (not Lebo-ḥamath on the Orontes) in the northeast to the eastern Nile Delta and to the Gulf of Elath in the south. Some have argued that these comprehensive land claims were influenced by the Assyrian definition of the province "Beyond the River" *(eber nāri)*, that is, Syria west of the Euphrates (Na'aman 1980b: 98; Anbar 1982; Veijola 1983: 22–29). Indeed, the Deuteronomist, followed by the Chronicler, seems to have applied such an expansive concept to the reach of the United Monarchy (1 Kgs 5:1, 4; 2 Chr 9:26). In the pan-Israel assembly celebrating the dedication of the Temple the participants stem "from Lebo-ḥamath to the wadi of Egypt" (1 Kgs 8:65//2 Chr 7:8). Hence, if the Chronicler wished to depict the greatest possible extent of the land attributed to Israel, he would not have used the expression "from Shiḥor of Egypt to Lebo-ḥamath." Second, it is unclear how much one can make out of the claim that David gathered Israelites "from Shiḥor of Egypt to Lebo-ḥamath." The comment relates to an ingathering of Israelites and not to national borders. There is no prior comment in the book about the territorial extent of the kingdom of Saul and David and the anecdotes about the tribal territories in the genealogies of 2:3–9:1 relate to a variety of periods in Israelite and Judahite history. They do not amount to a systematic description of Israel's borders along the lines of the surveys in Num 34, Josh 13, and Ezek 47. In the narrative portions of the Chronicler's work, the expression for the extent of Israel's land is sometimes "from Beer-sheba to Dan" (1 Chr 21:2; 2 Chr 30:5) or "from Beer-sheba to the hill country of Ephraim" (2 Chr 19:4). Third, in the depiction of David's reign, the time of David's great territorial conquests lies still in the future. David does not defeat the Moabites, the Aramaeans, the Ammonites, and the Edomites, some of whom become his clients (1 Chr 18:1–13; 19:1–19; 20:1–8), until after the ancient palladium is already secure in the City of David (17:1). But if the advent of the Davidic "empire" is still to be narrated, how should one interpret the expression here? One possibility is that the assembly reflects an idealistic portrait of broad support for David. A related possibility involves distinguishing state from people. The geographical description of participants in David's national assembly may not be congruent with the geographical extent of his territorial state. The Chronicler lives at a time in which religions could and often did transcend state and provincial boundaries. The convocations he depicts could attract, therefore, people from beyond Israel's borders. In either case, one must ask what role the geographical allusion plays in the context of the author's larger presentation. The allusion seems to have three functions. First, participation from such a wide geographical area honors David's leadership. Second, such broad support constitutes a wide public endorsement of his plan to transfer the Ark to Jerusalem. Third, the attempt to reach out to Israelites far and wide establishes a model for the Chronicler's own time in which Judaism had already become an international religion.

13:6–14. At this point the Chronicler joins the narrative of Samuel (2 Sam 6:2–11), depicting the ascent of the Ark to Jerusalem.

13:6. "Qiriath-jearim, which belongs to Judah." This town is also called Baalah in the depiction of Judah's tribal allotment (Josh 15:9, 10). The Chronicler is presupposing some knowledge of the book of Samuel on the part of his readers. In one of the psalms celebrating the deity's devotion to David and Zion, the search for the Ark also begins with "Jaar" (יער; Ps 132:6), that is, Qiriath-jearim (קרית יערים). On the site, see the NOTE to 1 Chr 2:50b–51.

"all Israel went up." In 2 Sam 6:1 David is accompanied by "thirty thousand," but the Chronicler, consistent with his pan-Israelite interest, has David accompanied by all Israel.

"invoked by the name" (נקרא שם). In the ancient Semitic world, a name was associated with a person's identity (e.g., Gen 2:19–20; 17:5–6, 15–16; Exod 3:13–14; 6:3; Westermann 1984: 227–29). In Deuteronomic theology there is a tendency toward the hypostatization of the divine name (Mettinger 1982: 130). In mandating a central sanctuary, Yhwh announces that he will "place his name there" (Deut 12:5, 11). Similarly, Solomon "builds a temple for the name of Yhwh" (Weinfeld 1972a: 193–209, 325). The epithet "Yhwh enthroned upon the cherubim" links the divine presence to these mythological creatures and the cultic symbol they adorn (cf. 2 Kgs 19:15//Isa 37:16; Pss 80:2 [ET 80:1]; 99:1; Keel 1978: 166–69). Given the association between a name and someone's identity, the Ark was an appropriate location for Yhwh to be invoked.

"the cherubim" (הכרובים). These were sphinxlike creatures, often depicted as attending a king's throne (Haran 1978). In the Yahwist's narrative (J), cherubs guard the garden of Eden (Gen 3:24). Israelite poets portrayed Yhwh as flying in a chariot among the clouds or as riding on the cherubs (2 Sam 22:11//Ps 18:11 [ET 18:10]). The Chronicler also associates the cherubim with the chariot of Yhwh in his description of David's plan for the Temple (1 Chr 28:18; cf. Ezek 1:5–28; 9:3; 10:1–22; 11:22). Two massive cherubs stand in the דביר, "shrine," of the Temple (1 Kgs 6:23–28; 8:6–7; 2 Chr 3:10–13; 5:7–8). Hence, the title "Yhwh enthroned upon the cherubim" speaks of Israel's God as being invisibly present to his subjects above these mythological figures.

13:7. "they transported" (וירכיבו). The text does not identify the subject. David earlier called the priests and Levites to be part of the proceedings, but the text never mentions them again. Given the following narrative (NOTE to v. 8) and David's later analysis (15:13), it is unlilkely that the priests and Levites were directly involved in the transfer.

"the house of Abinadab." The Ark was deposited here by the residents of Qiriath-jearim after the Philistines returned the Ark to the Israelites (1 Sam 7:1). The issue is, therefore, not that the ancient palladium is in enemy hands (e.g., 1 Sam 4:1–11), but that the Ark should be brought to Israel's new capital.

"Uzza and Aḥio." Abinadab was the father of Eleazar, who was consecrated to take care of the Ark (1 Sam 7:1; 2 Sam 6:3–4). In neither Samuel nor Chronicles is there any claim made for an official priestly connection for Uzza, Abinadab, or Eleazar (McCarter 1980b: 137). The names are, however, common in Levitical contexts. Some have intimated that Uzza and Aḥio may have been brothers of Eleazar (1 Chr 8:7, 14, 31; 9:37), but this is also uncertain (McCarter 1984: 169). The Chronicler's later comment upon the failure of the first attempt to bring the Ark into the City of David suggests that he did not regard either Uzza or Aḥio as of Levitical descent (15:13).

13:8. "songs, lyres, harps, drums, cymbals, and trumpets." The parallel in 2 Sam 6:5 speaks of "cypress wood [4QSam[a] songs], lyres, harps, drums, sistrums, and cymbals" (see TEXTUAL NOTES). The discrepancy is significant, because the Chronicler regards sacred songs to be a Levitical responsibility (Kleinig 1993) and lyres, harps, and cymbals to be Levitical instruments (15:19–21; 16:5). Similarly, he regards the playing of trumpets to be a priestly responsibility (15:24; 16:6, 42). The Chronicler evidently viewed his version of Samuel as indicating a lack of intimate Levitical and priestly involvement. In the Chronicler's retelling of his source, the failure of the first ark procession becomes a lesson about the need for the priests and Levites to play a central role in cultic affairs.

13:9. "threshing floor of Kidon." Not otherwise known (see TEXTUAL NOTE).

13:10. "the anger of Yhwh was kindled against Uzza" (ויחר-אף יהוה בעזא). The story is reminiscent of two incidents in Samuel: the disease and death associated with the Ark's sojourn among the Philistines (1 Sam 5) and the slaughter of many residents of Beth-shemesh on account of their treatment of the Ark (1 Sam 6:19–21). All of these episodes, despite the different circumstances they reflect, contribute to the Ark's reputation as a sacred and potentially lethal object. Desecration of the *sancta*, whatever the reasons and the circumstances, elicits absolute and immediate divine punishment (Milgrom 1976: 43).

13:11. "became angry" (ויחר). David's immediate response to the display of divine anger is to become angry himself. Uzza's unintentional mistake results in his dying at the hands of the very deity whom he worshiped and whose cultic symbol he attempted to safeguard. From David's perspective, the deity has become (momentarily) inscrutable.

"because Yhwh had created a breach against Uzza" *(ky prṣ yhwh prṣ bʿzʾ)*. The Chronicler plays on the different connotations of the root *prṣ* (v. 2; Kalimi 1995b: 40). As Mosis (1973: 60–61) and Allen (1988: 27–28) point out, *prṣ* is employed as a keyword in 1 Chr 13–15 (13:2, 11; 14:11; 15:13). According to the narratives of Samuel and Chronicles, the toponym Perez-uzza ("Uzza's Breach") derives its name from the interruption of Uzza's family line caused by his untimely death. But the Chronicler's literary strategy is, in my judgment, more complex than simply a paronomasia on the different nuances of *prṣ*. He employs *prṣ* in these chapters in conjunction with another keyword—*drš*, "to seek." Saul dies in his transgression, because of his "consulting a necromancer to seek *(drš)* counsel." This sin of commission is coupled with a sin of omission: "He did not seek *(drš)* Yhwh" (10:13–14). Saul's dual infidelity leads to the end of his kingdom: Yhwh "put him to death and turned the kingdom over to David" (10:14). After providing his readers with a series of flashbacks to narrate how the Israelites deserted Saul and flocked to David, consolidating his rise and establishing his early kingship in Ḥebron (11:10–12:41), the writer broaches the topic of Saul's rebellion again to explain David's plan to retrieve the Ark: "for we did not seek *(drš)* it in the days of Saul" (13:3). The plan to undo the damage done during Saul's reign is suddenly halted, however, by the outbreak of divine anger against Uzza. Yhwh's rage, largely unexplained in this context, is explained in the later account of David's subsequent attempt to bring the Ark to the City of David. In this later context, the Chronicler ties the two recurring motifs of "seeking" and "breaching" together and, in so doing, elucidates the divine action against Uzza: "Indeed, when at first you did not carry it, Yhwh our God created a breach against us *(prṣ yhwh ʾlhynw bnw)* because we did not seek *(drš)* it according to the convention *(kmšpṭ)*" (TEXTUAL NOTES to 15:13). Hence, the problem was not David's intention to move the Ark, but the manner in which the move was handled. The Chronicler's double paronomasia, highlighting the ritual care with which Israel's ancient palladium must be treated, underscores the pivotal role the priests and Levites play in Jerusalem's worship.

13:12. "became fearful of God on that day" (ויירא דויד את-האלהים ביום). David's anger gives way to anxiety. Up to this point in the story, David has not suffered any setbacks. His meteoric rise to power was uniformly endorsed by warriors from Israel's tribes and blessed by God. From the time Benjaminite, Judahite, and Gadite warriors journeyed to his wilderness fortress (12:9–19) until the all-Israelite banquet celebrating his coronation (12:39b–41), events were congruent with the deity's will. But the divine will now becomes mysterious. The sensational death of Uzza forces David to suspend his plans for any further conveyance of the Ark. He is left to ponder, "How can I bring the Ark of God (home) to me?"

13:13. "the City of David." That is, Mount Zion, the section of Jerusalem fortified by David and renamed in his honor (2nd NOTE to 11:7). The detainment of the Ark at "the house of Obed-edom" means that the Ark resided not in the City of David, but in another part of Jerusalem.

"the house (בית) of Obed-edom the Gittite." The earlier evidence in Samuel suggests that Obed-edom was a foreigner from Gath, most probably the Gath of the Philistines (Albright 1968b: 140; C. Ehrlich 1996). David served in the army of Gath's king when he was a refugee from Saul (1 Sam 27). In Chronicles, the name Obed-edom seems to be associated with two figures (2nd NOTE to 15:24). One appears as a Levitical gatekeeper (15:18, 24), while another Obed-edom appears as a Levitical musician (15:21; 16:5). Given the broader cultural context in which the Chronicler lived, it is understandable why he and Josephus (*Ant.* 7.83) after him came to the conclusion that the Obed-edom of this story had to be a Levite. When temporarily storing highly important sacred symbols, such as divine images, the temporary quarters for such artifacts function as alternate dwellings for the displaced gods associated with the artifacts (Hurowitz 1993). On the basis of ancient Near Eastern precedent, the "house" of Obed-edom would be regarded as a sanctuary, albeit perhaps a temporary one, and Obed-edom as a sacerdotal official or priest. Such a time of transition, when the divine image was in transport, was a delicate time for the cult because the deity was in between dwellings. If the artifact is associated with divine power and is potentially quite lethal (see COMMENT), the personnel entrusted to guard the holy symbol have to be properly sanctified.

13:14. "three months." In Chronicles this period takes on new relevance. Because the Chronicler has David fighting against the Philistines (1 Chr 14:8–17) after the first attempt to bring up the ark, the Chronicler is able to account for David's activities in between the two attempts to bring back the ark (see SOURCES AND COMPOSITION). During the three-month interlude, David leads Israel in fighting against their enemies (Japhet 1993a: 272).

"blessed." According to 1 Chr 26:4–8, Obed-edom sired eight sons "because Yhwh blessed him." The Targum introduces some of this material at the end of v. 14. That the theme of blessing on Obed-edom also appears here provides a hint that the setback suffered by David and Israel is only temporary.

## SOURCES AND COMPOSITION

In writing his narrative about the attempts to move the Ark, the Philistine wars, and related issues, the Chronicler is heavily dependent upon the version of Samuel available to him (see TEXTUAL NOTES). There are, however, a number of interesting and important variants between the two accounts. The parallels and differences may be summarized as follows.

| | *1 Chronicles* | *2 Samuel* |
|---|---|---|
| Assembly | 13:1–5 | 6:1 |
| First Attempt to Move the Ark | 13:6–14 | 6:2–11 |
| Support from Ḥuram of Tyre | 14:1–2 | 5:11–12 |
| David's Family | 14:3–7 | 5:13–16 |
| Wars against the Philistines | 14:7–17 | 5:17–25 |
| David's Domiciles and the Ark's Tent | 15:1–2 | — — |
| New Preparations to Move the Ark | 15:3–24 | — — |
| Second Attempt to Move the Ark | 15:25–16:3 | 6:12–19 |

As the outline indicates, the Chronicler has repositioned material from his *Vorlage* of Samuel, recontextualized it, overwritten certain parts, furnished rubrics, introduced selections from a variety of biblical psalms, and added new material. The Chronicler's discussion of priestly preparations will be addressed in the commentary to 1 Chr 15, while his selective citation of the Psalms will be discussed in the commentary to 1 Chr 16. The main issue that needs to be addressed in this context is the Chronicler's rearrangement of material from Samuel. Why does the writer take Samuel as a base, but alter its sequence of pericopes? Two instances of this literary strategy are particularly prominent and call for discussion. First, why does the Chronicler delay providing his readers the tale about Ḥuram and the information about David's family until after David makes his first attempt to retrieve the Ark? Second, why does the author reposition the wars against the Philistines after the first failed attempt to transfer the Ark?

The answers to both questions are generally recognized to involve dischronological displacement (e.g., Glatt 1993; NOTE to 11:4–9). The Chronicler pushes everything pertaining to Jerusalem, the Ark, and the House of God to the very beginning of David's rule. In this manner, the author shows his high regard for the Yahwistic cultus in Jerusalem. To be sure, the sequence of events in Samuel is also very much open to debate. A number of scholars (e.g., Hertzberg 1964: 272–75) have argued that the order in Samuel is fundamentally achronological, determined by the narrator's desire to have David address cultic issues only after he has successfully pacified the very Philistines who had earlier captured the Ark (1 Sam 4:1–11). The Chronicler alters this inherited order to demonstrate David's love for Jerusalem. The point seems unassailable, but one might inquire as to the source of the Chronicler's idea. From what does he derive the notion that David placed such a high priority on retrieving the Ark and bringing it to Jerusalem? To return to the first question above, why does he delay providing information about David's family and his construction of houses until David has made an attempt to move the Ark?

In my judgment, the order of the Chronicler's presentation may have been affected by the presentation of events in Ps 132. We can be confident that the Chronicler knew this psalm well, because he quotes it directly in his narrative of the ascent of the Ark into the Temple (2 Chr 6:41–42//Ps 132:8–10). There also seems to be an indirect reference to Ps 132 in one of David's speeches to the assembled dignitaries. In preparing these Israelite leaders for the transition to his son's rule, David explains that he "had it in mind to build a house of rest (בית מנוחה) for the Ark of the covenant of Yhwh and for the footstool of the feet of our God (הדם רגלי אלהינו) (1 Chr 28:2). The term "footstool" (הדם) is relatively rare, especially when applied to the Ark (Pss 99:5; 132:7; 1 Chr 28:2). Psalm 132 contains a summons to worship at "the footstool of his feet" (הדם רגליו; v. 7) and implores Yhwh and the Ark to go to "your resting place" (מנוחתך; v. 8). Aside from the direct quotation and indirect citation of Ps 132 in the Chronicler's work, one should also mention that there are some strong connections between the Zion-centered perspective of this poem (Mettinger 1976; Kruse 1983; Seow 1989; Veijola 1990; Laato 1992b; Patton 1995) and the Chronicler's own theology (Knoppers 1998).

Psalm 132 begins with a supplication to Yhwh (v. 1) that recalls all of David's self-denial (כל-ענותו) and his desire to find a "place (מקום) for Yhwh" (vv. 2–5; Knoppers 1998). The psalmist's summons to Yhwh to remember David (v. 1) is associated with David's oath to Yhwh that he would find him an appropriate sanctuary (vv. 2–5). David avoids his house and abstains from sleep until he finds a domicile for "the Mighty One of Jacob" (vv. 3–5). The comparison with Chronicles is intriguing. The material dealing with the supplies David received for his palace from Ḥuram of Tyre (1 Chr 14:1–2), David's family (14:3–7), his wars against the Philistines (14:8–17), and his construction of buildings for himself (15:1) is all postponed until David has made a full attempt to bring the Ark into Jerusalem. In Chronicles David's concern for the Ark is explictly set against the neglect of the ancient palladium by Saul (13:3). David's first public action following his conquest of Jerusalem is to convoke a national assembly and begin immediate plans to "bring back the Ark of our God" (13:3). The king then leads all Israel to Qiriath-jearim (קרית־יערים) "to bring back from there the Ark of God" (13:6). Similarly, the attempt to retrieve the Ark in the psalm begins with the summons, "Lo, we have heard it in Ephrathah; we found it in the fields of Jaar" (שׂדי־יער; Ps 132:6). Against this backdrop, it is interesting to observe that the Chronicler sees the culmination of this movement of the Ark into Jerusalem as the ascent of the Ark into the Temple (2 Chr 6:41–42//Ps 132:8–10). He does not associate the palladium's ascent into the tent David pitched for it (1 Chr 16:1–3) as representing Yhwh rising up to take his "resting place." In narrating David's attempts to deliver the Ark into the City of David, the Chronicler has the construction of the Temple already in view.

## Comment

The influence that Ps 132 may have exerted on the sequence of events in the presentation of David's early monarchy raises the larger issue of the Chronicler's interest in the Ark of the covenant. Why does the author, living in the late Persian or early Hellenistic period, show such a concern for a relatively small artifact that presumably either disappeared or was destroyed centuries earlier in the Babylonian exiles of 597 (2 Kgs 24:10–16) and 586 B.C.E. (2 Kgs 25:13–17; Jer 52:17–23). At the time in which the author wrote, the Jerusalem Temple, not the Ark or the Tabernacle, was the dominant cultic institution. It is surely relevant in this context that the blueprint for the reconstructed Temple in Ezek 40–48 does not mention the Ark at all. Nor is there any evidence that a new ark was made when the Second Temple was built (Jer 3:16; Ezra 3:1–10; 5:2–17; 6:1–18; Josephus, *Ant.* 14.71–72; *J.W.* 1.152–53; 5.5; Tacitus, *Hist.* V.9; *m. Yoma* 5:2). Given the writer's historical context, he might be excused for skipping over the matter of the ancient palladium entirely. So, what is the nature of the Chronicler's interest in the Ark? How does his treatment of this cultic symbol compare with those of earlier writers?

Some of the references in Priestly law and in Joshua show a tremendous reverence for the Ark. Its construction, ordained by God, implemented by Moses, and constructed by Bezalel, is described in considerable detail in Exodus (25:10–21; 37:1–15). The portable box carried by the Israelites along their sundry travels is also a unifying cultic symbol in the larger Deuteronomistic presentation of the premonarchic period. Carried by the Levitical priests, the Ark leads the Israelites on a miraculous journey through the temporarily blocked Jordan River (Josh 3:1–4:18). One can find more complicated attitudes toward the Ark within Deuteronomy and the narratives of Samuel (1 Sam 4:1–7:1). The construction of the Ark is not described in Deuteronomy. It is simply described as "the Ark of the covenant" (Deut 10:1–9), the repository of the tablets of the covenant, to be carried by the Levitical priests (Fretheim 1968a). In the view of some scholars (von Rad 1966b: 103–24; Noth 1957; Weinfeld 1991; Seow 1992), the authors of Deuteronomy demythologize the Ark, neglect its martial value, and lessen its cultic significance. In Samuel's time, the Ark resided for a while in Shiloh (1 Sam 1:3), but subsequently was sent on a variety of travels. It was undoubtedly the association between the Ark and Yhwh's presence that led the Israelites to bring the Ark into battle with them against the Philistines (1 Sam 4:3; cf. Num 10:35; 14:44). Thinking that the ancient palladium's power would ensure victory, the Israelites promptly lost the Ark to the Philistines (1 Sam 4:10–11). The capture of the sacred artifact by a foreign power tells against the assumption that an ineluctable link exists between Yhwh's presence and the Ark (1 Sam 4:17–22; Miller and Roberts 1977). In this respect, the Ark narrative demystifies the Ark. But the stories in Samuel also tell against the assumption that the Ark had no relevance whatsoever. While in captivity the cultic artifact wreaked havoc on the residents of Ashdod because Yhwh afflicted them with a plague of hemorrhoids and mice (1 Sam 5:1–7). After the Philistines dealt unsuccessfully with their medical and rodent problems for about seven months by transferring the Ark from town to town, they finally concluded that the Ark was more trouble than it was worth (1 Sam 5:8–6:2). When the Philistines returned the Ark, along with reparation offerings consisting of golden hemorrhoids and golden mice, the Ark came to reside in Qiriath-jearim (1 Sam 6:3–7:1).

That both the Deuteronomist (1 Kgs 8:1–11, 21) and the Chronicler (1 Chr 6:31–32; 15:1–29; 16:1–3, 37–38; 17:1–2; 2 Chr 5:2–14; 6:41–42; 35:3) devote significant attention to the ancient palladium and to its later incorporation into the Temple testifies to its symbolic importance for these writers (Knoppers 1995c). To be sure, Chronicles does not contain a continuous ark narrative analogous to the Ark narrative reconstructed in Samuel (Wright 1998). The Chronicler's coverage of David's early reign deals with a number of matters, such as the Philistine wars, that have little to do with the Ark. Nevertheless, given the many references to the Ark during the reign of David, it is appropriate to inquire as to the nature of the coverage the Chronicler does devote to the sacred artifact. The references both to Israel's ancient palladium and to the Tabernacle, for that matter, are reverential in character (Eskenazi 1995). As in Samuel the Ark is associated with lethal power and in Chronicles the Ark's neglect is deemed to be one of the great deficiencies of Saul's regime (13:3). By arguing that David gave the ancient palladium highest priority, the Chronicler can present him as a reliable and devoted patron of a venerable institution.

In the context of the late Persian or early Hellenistic age, this presentation would have a number of related benefits. First, the author is able to tie the Second

Temple of his own day to the institutions of Israel's ancient past. Not only is the Second Temple linked to the First Temple, but the First Temple is itself linked to the Sinaitic age. The prestige and importance of the Jerusalem Temple are enhanced by such ties to Israel's distant past. By bringing the Ark into Jerusalem, David links the old to the new, the authority of this antique artifact to his recently acquired capital. In this way, the Jerusalem cultus of the Chronicler's day could claim continuity with the original cultic community instituted under Moses.

Second, the writer can argue (by implication) that the Yahwistic cultus is no longer inherently portable, but tied to one centralized, permanent sanctuary. The Chronicler lives in an age in which Yahwists inhabit a variety of lands. In many different contexts, Yahwists could point to evidence in the Pentateuch to support the notion that Yhwh traveled with his people. While the Chronicler does not deny the historical existence of other Yahwistic sanctuaries (e.g., 1 Chr 16:39–42; 21:29; 2 Chr 1:3, 13), he affirms centralization and the preeminence of the Jerusalem Temple. In this manner, he can present the time of the Ark and the Tabernacle as a central, even necessary, part of Israel's past. But by the same token, this past was only temporary, designed to be fulfilled in a later Jerusalem-centered age. Because the Ark and Tabernacle find their final home in Jerusalem, Yahwists may honor these Sinaitic institutions by honoring the Temple that incorporated them. In other words, for Judeans living in the late Persian and early Hellenistic periods, the Ark and Tabernacle are no longer necessary. The author's account of the early monarchy and of David's attempts to retrieve the Ark ultimately ratify the historical primacy, central status, and continuing privileges of the Jerusalem Temple.

# *XVII. The Newly Established Kingdom Flourishes and is Attacked (14:1–17)*

*Ḥuram Builds David a Palace*

1 Ḥuram king of Tyre sent messengers to David with cedar timber, masons, and
carpenters to construct a palace for him. 2 Then David knew that Yhwh had established him as king over Israel (and) that his kingship was highly exalted for the
sake of his people Israel.

*David's Family Expands*

3 David took more wives and concubines in Jerusalem and David sired more
sons and daughters. 4 And these are the names of those who were born to him in
Jerusalem: Shammua, Shobab, Nathan, Solomon, 5 Ibḥar, Elishua, Elpaleṭ,
6 Nogah, Nepheg, Japhia, 7 Elishama, Beeliada, and Eliphaleṭ.

*David Routs the Philistines*

8 When the Philistines heard that David had been anointed as king over all Israel, all the Philistines went up to seek David. When David heard, he went out before them. 9 And the Philistines came and raided the Valley of Rephaim. 10 Then

David inquired of God saying, "Shall I go up against the Philistines? Will you deliver them into my hand?" And Yhwh said to him, "Go up, for I shall deliver them
into your hand." [11]When they went up at Baal-perazim, David defeated them
there. And David said, "God has broken through my enemies by my hands, like a
breakthrough of waters." Therefore they called the name of that place Baal-
perazim. [12]And they abandoned their gods there. Then David gave the word and
they were consigned to fire.

*David Routs the Philistines Again*

[13]But the Philistines again raided the valley [14]and David again inquired of
God. And God told him, "Do not go up after them. Encircle them and engage
them in front of the Bacas. [15]When you hear the sound of the marching in the
tops of the Bacas, then you will go out into battle because God will go out before
you to defeat the Philistine forces."

[16]When David did as God commanded him, they defeated the Philistine forces
from Gibeon to Gezer. [17]And the reputation of David spread throughout all of the
lands and Yhwh brought the fear of him on all of the nations.

## Textual Notes

14:1–16. These verses are largely paralleled by 2 Sam 5:11–25. 4QSam$^{a}$ is available for parts of 2 Sam 5:11–16.

14:1. "Ḥuram." I read with Qere and Tg. *ḥwrm*. Kethib, followed by LXX, Syr., and Vg., reads "Ḥiram" *(ḥyrm)* along with MT and 4QSam$^{a}$ 2 Sam 5:11.

"masons" *(ḥršy qyr)*. Literally, "craftsmen of wall(s)." LXX$^{BS}$ (and $c_2$) *oikodomous*; LXX$^{L}$ *tektonas toichou*. MT 2 Sam 5:11 reads "stone masons" *(ḥršy ʾbn qyr)*, but the lemma *ḥršy qyr* is found in 4QSam$^{a}$, LXX$^{L}$, and OL 2 Sam 5:11 (cf. Josephus, *Ant.* 7.66). LXX$^{BMN}$ 2 Sam 5:11 read *lithōn*, that is, *ʾbn(ym)*. On the diverse Samuel readings, see further Ulrich (1978: 99–100) and McKenzie (1985: 45–46).

"to construct a palace for him" *(lbnwt lw byt)*. MT and 4QSam$^{a}$ 2 Sam 5:11 "and they built a palace for David."

14:2. "David knew that" *(wydʿ dwyd ky)*. Tg. and 2 Sam 5:12 preface "that" *(ky)* with connective *wāw*.

"his kingship was highly exalted" *(nśʾt lmʿlh mlkwtw)*. MT 2 Sam 5:12 reads simply, "that Yhwh exalted his kingship *(nśʾ mmlktw)*." Space considerations suggest that 4QSam$^{a}$ was similar. Some of the versions of 2 Sam 5:12 share the lemma *nśʾt* of MT 1 Chr 14:2. The adv. *lmʿlh* may be the Chronicler's own addition.

14:3. "wives and concubines" (נשים ופלגשים). So LXX$^{B}$ 2 Sam 5:13. MT and LXX 14:3 simply read "wives." MT and 4QSam$^{a}$ 2 Sam 5:13 פיל[ג]שים ו[נשים], "concubines and wives." Ulrich (1978: 182) argues that the Samuel reading is the earliest on the grounds that the Chronicler omitted "concubines" to ensure the sons' pedigree. But the Chronicler elsewhere shows no aversion to concubines, and in any case, David's concubines are mentioned in 1 Chr 3:9. It seems more likely that the reading was lost to the Chronicler's *Vorlage* by haplography (*homoioteleuton* after נשים).

"in Jerusalem." Preferable to MT 2 Sam 5:13, "from Jerusalem." 2 Sam 5:13 continues with "after they came from Ḥebron." This phrase was likely omitted by the Chronicler because it did not fit the context of his own presentation.

"and David sired more" *(wywld dwyd ʿwd).* MT 2 Sam 5:13 "and there were more born to David" *(wywldw ʿwd ldwd).* 4QSam[a] seems to follow MT Samuel [*wywld*]*w ldwd ʿwd.*

14:4. "those who were born to him" *(hylwdym ʾšr hyw lw).* MT 2 Sam 5:14 "those born to him" *(hayyillōdîm lô).* There are two lists of David's Jerusalem sons in Chronicles and one in MT Samuel. LXX 2 Sam 5:14–16 contains two lists, one that contains eleven names (like MT Samuel) and another (2 Sam 5:16a) that contains thirteen names (like Chronicles). Unfortunately, only a few of the names have been preserved in fragmentary 4QSam[a]. Variations occur among the textual witnesses (see table below). The double occurence of Elishama in 1 Chr 3:5–8 is an obvious mistake (the first should read Elishua; TEXTUAL NOTE to 3:6). In distinction from MT 2 Sam 5:15, 1 Chr 3:7 and 1 Chr 14:6 both read "Eliphelet/ Elpaleṭ" and "Nogah" before "Nepheg." These names are also attested, albeit in variant forms, in LXX 2 Sam 5:16a. Whether there was space enough for these names in 4QSam[a] is unclear. Many have followed Wellhausen (1871: 165) in thinking that MT 2 Sam 5:15 is the most primitive reading, both because of the repetition of *ʾl(y)plṭ* in all the lists and the obscurity of the name "Nogah." McCarter (1984: 148) argues, however, for a haplography in the tradition represented by MT Samuel. In any case, the longer text was already reflected in the Chronicler's *Vorlage.* This is evident from the numerical summaries in 1 Chr 3:5, 8, totalling thirteen sons. The following NOTES detail comments on the variants supplied by the versions.

"Shammua" *(šmwʿ).* So MT. LXX[BL] *Samaa*; LXX[A] *Sammaou.* The parallel list

| *1 Chr 3:5–8* | *1 Chr 14:4–7* | *2 Sam 5:14–16* | *LXX 2 Sam 5:16a* |
|---|---|---|---|
| 1. Shimei | Shammua | Shammua | Samae |
| 2. Shobab | Shobab | Shobab | Iesseibath |
| 3. Nathan | Nathan | Nathan | Nathan |
| 4. Solomon | Solomon | Solomon | Salamaan |
| 5. Ibḥar | Ibḥar | Ibḥar | Iebaar |
| 6. Elishama | Elishua | Elishua | Theēsous |
| 7. Elipheleṭ | Elpaleṭ | — | Elphalat |
| 8. Nogah | Nogah | — | Naged |
| 9. Nepheg | Nepheg | Nepheg | Naphek |
| 10. Japhia | Japhia | Japhia | Ianatha |
| 11. Elishama | Elishama | Elishama | Leasamus |
| 12. Beeliada | Beeliada | Eliada | Baaleimath |
| 13. Elipheleṭ | Eliphaleṭ | Elipheleṭ | Eleiphalath |

in 1 Chr 3:5 has "Shimea" *(šmʿʾ)*. Cf. LXX 2 Sam 5:14 *Sammous*. See also the 2nd TEXTUAL NOTE to 3:5.

"Shobab" *(šwbb)*. So MT 14:4 and MT 2 Sam 5:14, as well as 4QSam[a]. LXX[B] $c_2$ *Isoboam*; dp *Susōbath* may be compared with LXX 2 Sam 5:16a *Iesseibath*.

14:5. "Ibḥar." LXX[B] *Baar*; LXX[AL] *Iebaar*.

"Elishua" (So MT) also appears in 2 Sam 5:15b. LXX[B] 1 Chr 14:5 *Ektae*; LXX 2 Sam 5:15 *Elisous*. MT 1 Chr 3:6 "Elishama" (see TEXTUAL NOTE).

"Elpaleṭ." Thus MT. 1 Chr 3:6, many of the versions, and 2 Sam 5:16 have "Elipheleṭ" or "Eliphaleṭ." See also "Eliphaleṭ" in v. 7.

14:7. "Beeliada" *(bʿlydʿ)*. So MT and LXX[L] *(Baaliada)*. Cf. LXX 2 Sam 5:16a *Baaleimath*. MT 1 Chr 3:8 "Eliada" *(ʾlydʿ*; see TEXTUAL NOTE). Cf. cursive c 2 Sam 5:16 *Eliadaei*. Beeliada is most probably the earliest form of the name. It is more likely that the theophoric "Baal" was changed to "El" than vice versa.

14:8. "had been anointed" *(nmšḥ)*. So MT and LXX 1 Chr 14:8 and LXX 2 Sam 5:17. MT 2 Sam 5:17 "they had anointed" *(mšḥw)*.

"all of Israel." The lemma of MT 2 Sam 5:17 "Israel" may reflect haplography (*homoioteleuton* from *ʿl-kl-yśrʾl* to *ʿl-yśrʾl*).

"went out before them" *(wyṣʾ lpnyhm)*. So MT. LXX "went out to meet them" *(exēlthen eis apantēsin autois)*. Cf. Syr. and Vg. MT 2 Sam 5:17 "went down to the stronghold" *(wyrd ʾl-hmṣdh)*.

14:9. "and raided" *(wypšṭw)*. So MT and LXX[L] *exechythēsan*. See also v. 13. 2 Sam 5:18 "and they spread out" *(wynṭšw)*. LXX[AB] 1 Chr 14:9 and 2 Sam 5:18 are similar, "assembled" *(synepeson/an)*. The use of the expression *pšṭ b-* is found elsewhere in Chronicles (2 Chr 25:13; 28:18). The variants may have originally arisen because of a graphic confusion of *nûn* and *pê* and the transposition of *šîn* and *ṭêt* (McCarter 1984: 151).

14:10. "Philistines." So Qere. Kethib *plštyym*.

"him." MT 2 Sam 5:19 reads "David."

"go up, for I shall deliver them into your hand" *(ʿlh wnttym bydk)*. I am interpreting the *wāw* after the impv. "go up" as introducing a subordinate clause (Joüon, §170c; Waltke and O'Connor, §38.1h). The subordination is explicit in the more expansive version of MT 2 Sam 5:19, "because I shall indeed deliver the Philistines into your hand" *(ky ntn ʾtn ʾt hplštym bydk)*.

14:11. "they went up" *(wyʿlw)*. A few LXX cursives and Syr. have the sg. 2 Sam 5:20 "and David entered" *(wybʾ dwd)*.

"and David said." 2 Sam 5:20 "and he said."

"by my hands." Syr. reads with 2 Sam 5:20 "before me."

"Baal-perazim" *(bʿl-prṣym)*. So MT and LXX[L] *Baelpharas(e)in*. LXX[AB] *Diakopē(n)*. *Pharis(e)in* (= *prṣ prṣym*?, "Breach of Breaches").

14:12. "they abandoned." So MT and LXX[AB] *(lectio brevior)*, but the specification of LXX[L] (be$_2$) *hoi allophyloi*, "the Philistines," may have been lost by haplography (*homoioteleuton* from *wyʿzbw-šm hplštym* to *wyʿzbw-šm*).

"their gods" *(ʾlhyhm)*. So MT, as well as LXX 2 Sam 5:21 and LXX 1 Chr 14:12 *(tous theous autōn)*. Tg. 14:12 reads along with MT 2 Sam 5:21 "their idols" *(ʿṣbyhm)*.

"then David gave the word and they were consigned to fire" *(wyʾmr dwyd wyśrpw bʾš)*. MT 2 Sam 5:21 reads "and David and his men carried them away." LXX^LM^, Arm., and Eth. 2 Sam 5:21 add lemmata, resembling the text of Chronicles.

14:13. "the Philistines again." MT 2 Sam 5:22 adds the inf. "to go up" *(lʿlwt)*.

"raided." See the TEXTUAL NOTE to v. 9.

"the valley" *(bʿmq)*. Reading with MT *(lectio brevior)*. One Heb. MS, LXX *(tōn gigantōn)*, Syr., and 2 Sam 5:22 add "Rephaim," as in v. 9.

14:14. "inquired of God." So MT and LXX. MT 2 Sam 5:23, "inquired of Yhwh."

"and God told him." So MT and LXX. MT 2 Sam 5:23 "and he told him."

"do not go up after them" *(lʾ tʿlh ʾḥryhm)*. So MT. LXX is similar, *Ou poreusē opisō autōn*. MT 2 Sam 5:23 reads "do not go up" *(lʾ tʿlh)*, but LXX 2 Sam 5:23 adds *eis synantēsin autōn*. Assuming a haplography, some add *ʿl/lpnyhm ʿlh* after *lʾ tʿlh*.

"encircle" *(hsb)*. Begrich *(BHK)* proposes reading *sōb*.

"them" *(mʿlyhm)*. MT 2 Sam 5:23 *ʾl ʾḥryhm*

"in front of" *(mmwl)*. Literally, "from the front" or "off the front." On the use of the prep. *mn* with *mwl*, see also Lev 5:8; Num 22:5; 1 Kgs 7:39; 2 Chr 4:10.

"the Bacas" *(hbkʾym)*. So MT. MT 2 Sam 5:23 lacks the article *(bkʾym)*. The precise reference is obscure: BDB (557) "the mulberry trees"; *HALOT* (129) "shrubs." Whether *hbkʾym* relate to "the valley of Baca" *(ʿmq hbkʾ)* located in the vicinity of Jerusalem (Ps 84:7 [ET 84:6]) is another issue. The testimony of the versions is of limited help: LXX^A^ "the pear trees" *(tōn apiōn)*; LXX^B*S^ "the causes" *(tōn aitiōn)*; *b*b′ "the lamentings" *(tōn kleontōn)*. The translation of LXX^A^, followed in large part by Josephus (*Ant.* 7.76–77), is consonant with the meaning of *bĕkāy* ("pear") in RH (Jastrow 1903, 169). McCarter (1984: 155–56) provides another interpretive option, construing *(h)bkʾym* as a place-name. See also v. 15.

14:15. "the marching" *(hṣʿdh)*. So MT 14:15 and MT 2 Sam 5:24. LXX^LMN^ 2 Sam 5:24 and LXX 1 Chr 14:15 *tou (syn)seismou*, "the shaking."

"in the tops" *(brʾšy)*. So MT and LXX. On the basis of witnesses to OL 2 Sam 5:24, McCarter (1984: 152) contends for an original "in the asherahs" *(bʾšry)*. But there is no evidence for such a reading in Chronicles.

"go out into battle" *(tṣʾ bmlḥmh)*. So MT and LXX. 2 Sam 5:24 "act decisively" *(tḥrṣ)*.

14:16. "they defeated." I read the pl. with MT (maximum variation). LXX and Syr. follow 2 Sam 5:25 in reading the sg. "he defeated." As opposed to the Samuel account, which consistently reads the sg., Chronicles fluctuates between the sg. and the pl. (2nd NOTE to v. 16).

"Gibeon" *(gbʿwn)*. So MT and LXX 2. Sam 5:25 "Geba" *(gbʿ)*.

"to Gezer" *(ʿd gzrh)*. I read with MT and LXX *(lectio brevior)*. MT 2 Sam 5:25 reads "as far as the approach to Gezer" *(ʿd bʾk gzr)*.

14:17. "(and) spread" *(wyṣʾ)*. So MT and LXX^L^. LXX^AB^ "was" *(kai egeneto)*.

## NOTES

14:1. "Ḥuram." The name (cf. "Ḥiram" in Samuel-Kings) is likely an abbreviated form of a more original *ʾaḥuram*, "the (divine) brother is exalted," the "u" being a remnant of an old nominative case ending without the pronominal suf. The aphaeresis of the initial *ʾālep* is especially characteristic of Phoen. PNs (Benz 1972: 263; Garr 1985: 50). Hence, the PN is essentially the same as the patronymic *ʾḥrm* that appears on the sarcophagus of the eleventh to tenth-century king of Byblos (*KAI* 1.1). Most of our knowledge about Ḥuram and the other Tyrian monarchs stems from biblical and Assyrian sources. Late references to the kings of Tyre occur in the citations of Menander of Ephesus found in Josephus (*Ag. Ap.* 1.116–26; *Ant.* 8.166). According to 1 Kgs 5:15–26 [ET 5:1–12] (cf. 2 Chr 2:2–15 [ET 2:3–16]) Ḥiram (Ḥiram in Chronicles) had very good relations with David. The Tyrian king provided materials and craftsmen for the construction of Solomon's temple. Solomon, in turn, sent Ḥiram assorted foodstuffs annually. This amicable relationship led Ḥiram to enter into a formal treaty relationship with Solomon (1 Kgs 5:21–26). Although this arrangement had to be renegotiated later (1 Kgs 9:11–14; Knoppers 1993c: 124–32), the Tyrian and Israelite kings continued to cooperate in joint trading ventures (1 Kgs 9:26–28; 10:11, 22). On the history of Tyre (*ṣûr*) a major Phoenician city in both preexilic and postexilic times, see Elayi (1980; 1987).

"cedar timber." Cedar was a durable and sought-after wood, used for panels, pillars, and roofs. Cedar logs would be taken from the mountains of Lebanon, transported in rafts to Joppa, and then sent inland to Jerusalem (2 Chr 2:16).

14:2. "Yhwh had established him as king over Israel" (הכינו יהוה למלך על-ישׂראל). The phraseology in this verse anticipates the dynastic language of Nathan's oracle (2 Sam 7:8–16//1 Chr 17:7–14). The exaltation of David's kingship and line is a major theme in the Davidic promises. The tie between blessings for David and blessings for Israel is found both in Nathan's dynastic oracle (17:7–14) and in David's prayer (17:16–27). Indeed, the reciprocal relationship between Davidic and Israelite success is a prominent theme throughout 1 Chr 11–29. The latter is sometimes derived from the former, hence the assertion that God exalted David's kingship "for the sake of his people Israel." In this context, the theme of divine blessing is important because it removes any doubt that the failure of the first attempt to bring up the Ark (13:5–14) reflected a negative divine judgment on David's actions (Mosis 1973: 61). On the contrary, that David experiences God's blessings (see the next NOTE) suggests that the problem with the transport of the Ark lies elsewhere.

14:3. "more wives and concubines in Jerusalem." Accumulating wives and progeny is consistently a positive sign of stature in Chronicles (e.g., 1 Chr 14:3–7; 25:5; 26:4–5; 2 Chr 11:18–23; 13:21; 14:3–7). The position of this notice plays, therefore, a critical role in the larger presentation. It underscores the motif announced in v. 2, namely, Yhwh's beneficence to David in Israel's new capital.

14:4. "Shammua, Shobab, Nathan, Solomon." According to 3:5, these four were sons of Bathshua, the daughter of Ammiel. On the particular names of these and the other sons in vv. 6–8, see the NOTES to 3:5–8.

14:6–7. In 1 Chr 3:6–8 the nine sons listed in these verses appear as a separate group from the four listed in v. 4. Although all thirteen sons are said to have been born in Jerusalem, as opposed to those born in Ḥebron (1 Chr 3:5; cf. 2 Sam 3:2–5), these nine were likely born of mothers other than Bathshua. On the possible meanings of each name, see the survey of opinion in A.A. Anderson (1989: 87–88).

14:8. "Philistines heard." David's anointing is mentioned at the beginning of the Chronicler's narration of David's royal career (1 Chr 11:1–3). This raises the issue of the chronology of events in David's reign. Whatever chronological displacement has occurred in Samuel (SOURCES AND COMPOSITION to 1 Chr 13), the Chronicler has repositioned these materials (again). By omitting Samuel's reference to the "stronghold" (המצודה; 2 Sam 5:17), which recalls events much earlier in David's career, the writer has more firmly placed the accounts of David's victories in the context of his newly established reign in Jerusalem. All of the material in 1 Chr 11:10–12:41, as we have seen, relates to earlier points in David's ascent to power, prior to his capture of Jerusalem. Hence, the Philistines mount a challenge to David at a time when his new regime might still be vulnerable. Having heard of his anointing, they quickly press the attack. The Philistines are, of course, the same opponents who were instrumental in the demise of Saul and his sons (10:1–12). From a literary standpoint, it can be no accident that the Chronicler has just finished recounting David's many sons (14:3–5). Will David and his progeny share a fate similar to that of Saul and his progeny at the hands of the Philistines? The Chronicler's rearrangement of and additions to his sources show considerable subtlety and sophistication. If the mishandling of the Ark represented an internal challenge to David's establishment of Jerusalem's cult, the Philistine aggression represents an external threat to the viability of David's rule.

"went up to seek David." The campaign of the Philistines against David is one of a number of cases that militate against a narrow view of the Chronicler's understanding of divine justice, sometimes mechanically labeled "immediate retribution." The Philistine campaign does not fit the definition because David has not done anything to warrant the punishment of a foreign invasion. The Chronicler's view of international affairs and of divine-human dealings is more open-ended and nuanced (B. Kelly 1996).

14:9. "Valley of Rephaim." By launching their assault against David to the southwest of Jerusalem, the Philistines threaten to drive a wedge between David's southern and northern territories. On the location, see the 2nd NOTE to 11:15.

14:10. "then David inquired of God" (וישאל דויד באלהים). The two narratives detailing the king's exploits against the Philistines are replete with sacral-war phraseology. Consistent with proper martial etiquette, David consults with the deity before undertaking any campaign (Judg 20:13, 18; 1 Sam 7:9; 14:37, 41–42; 23:2, 4, 9–12; 28:6; 30:7–8; 2 Sam 2:1). Again, there is an implicit comparison to be made with Saul (שאול), who preceded David. In the Chronicler's play on Saul's name (שאול), Saul failed and was condemned because he transgressed against God and inquired of a necromancer (לשאול באוב; 1 Chr 10:13–14).

"Shall I go up . . . ? Will you deliver them . . . ? " Since formulating questions to be answered in oracular form with yes or no answers was standard procedure in the ancient Near East (Van Dam 1997), it was all the more important to ask the right questions.

"I shall deliver them into your hand." The phraseology is a ubiquitous but critical component of many sacral-war narratives (e.g., Exod 14:4, 18; Josh 2:24; 6:2, 16; 8:1, 18; 10:8, 19; Judg 3:28; 4:7, 14; 7:9, 15; 18:10; 20:28; 1 Sam 14:12, 23; 23:4), reflecting the notion that Yhwh fights on behalf of his people and secures victory for them (von Rad 1991: 44–47; Kang 1989). Indeed, the assurance treats the outcome of the battle as tantamount to an accomplished fact. Because divine action is considered to be decisive, oracular promises bolster the confidence of the combatants (Pedersen 1940: 15).

14:11. "Baal-perazim." Literally, "lord of breaches" or "Baal of the breaches" (Heb. *bʿl* can mean "Baal," "lord," or "husband"). Some have thought that Baal-perazim refers to a sanctuary associated with Mount Perazim (Isa 28:21). If so, the sanctuary could be dedicated to either the god Baal (Haddu) or to Yhwh (as *bʿl*). The exact location of Baal-perazim is unknown.

"God has broken through *(pāraṣ)* my enemies by my hands, like the breakthrough *(pereṣ)* of waters." In Samuel the play on the root *prṣ*, "to break out" or to "break through," represents a "parenthesis" (McCarter 1984: 154) in the context of a larger story, but in Chronicles it represents a key to the whole sequence of events begun when David first attempted to bring the Ark into the City of David. David compares the divine rout of the Philistines to waters breaking through whatever obstacles may lie in their path. In a play on David's pronouncement, the people (re)name the site Baal-perazim, thereby proclaiming that Yhwh is "lord of the breaches." In the larger context of the narrative, Yhwh's "breakthrough" on behalf of Israel is significant. During the ark procession Yhwh "broke through" to doom Uzza, thereby halting Israel's hopes of stationing its national shrine in Jerusalem. The triumph in sacral war signifies a clear shift from a state of divine disfavor to a state of divine favor.

14:12. "abandoned their gods." The text satirically plays on the relationship between icons and the metaphysical realities they communicated. Not only do two human armies do battle in war, but also their deities (Exod 15:4–10; Josh 5:13–15; Judg 5:20). The sacred images brought into battle by competing armies symbolized divine presence and power. Because of the close ties perceived between images and gods (e.g., 1 Sam 4:3–4; 5:4), the term "gods" could be used for images. In the Ancient Near East victorious armies sometimes carried off the "gods" of their defeated enemies to underscore the superior power of their deities (Miller and Roberts 1977: 9–16). To celebrate their victory over Saul and his forces, the Philistines carried off the head and armor of Israels slain king and sent them around to surrounding territories. In this way, they could "herald the news to their idols and people" (10:9). The Philistines placed Saul's armor in the temple of their gods and "his skull they impaled in the Temple of Dagon" (10:10) In this case, however, the subdued Philistines seem to concede their deities' impotence. After the gods fail to secure victory for the Philistines, the Philistines give them up.

"gave the word and they were consigned to fire" *(wyʾmr dwyd wyśrpw bʾš)*. In Samuel David's troops carry the Philistine images away, presumably as war booty

(3rd TEXTUAL NOTE to v. 12). Such actions are consistent with ancient Near Eastern war protocol in which the enemy's gods would be captured in war and brought home for display (Cogan 1974). Eventually, such captured images might be returned home. But the Chronicler has David act in accordance with Deuteronomic law in which Israel is commanded: "consign their asherahs to the fire *(wʾšryhm tśrpwn bʾš)*, cut down the images of their gods *(psly ʾlhyhm)* and destroy their name from that place" (Deut 12:3). Similarly, in Deut 7:25 Israel is told, "As for the images of their gods, you will consign them to fire *(psyly ʾlhyhm tśrpwn bʾš)*" (cf. Deut 7:5). Chronicles does not dwell on David's cultic reforms, but the divergence from Samuel is nonetheless important. By ordering the disposal and incineration of the Philistine gods, David becomes the first of a long list of reformers—Asa, Jehoshaphaṭ, Jehoiada, Ḥezeqiah, and Josiah—whom the author commends to his readers. In these and other matters David is a model for others to follow.

14:13. "But the Philistines again raided the valley" *(wysypw ʿwd plštym wypšṭw bʿmq)*. Because of the resemblances between this battle narrative (vv. 13–16) and the previous one (vv. 8–12), some scholars have thought that this narrative is a duplicate of the first. Others (e.g., Hertzberg 1964: 274–75) believe that the second account reflects different geographical and historical circumstances from the first Philistine encounter. Whatever the case, one should also probe the force of juxtaposing the two tales. Both the similarities and the differences are important to the larger literary design. Undeterred by their earlier defeat, the Philistines test David's mettle by renewing their challenge.

14:14. "and David again inquired of God" *(wyšʾl ʿwd dwyd bʾlhym)*. In his piety, David again appears as a counterpoint to Saul (1st NOTE to v. 10), who is condemned both for "consulting a necromancer to seek [counsel]" and "for not seeking Yhwh" (10:13–14). In contrast, David consults the deity before taking any major action.

"do not go up after them." The threat posed by the Philistine attack is nearly identical to the first, and David responds exactly as he had in the first instance, by keeping to the protocol of holy-war preparation and seeking oracular advice. Yet the advice he receives is the opposite of the advice he received earlier. Will David question, ignore, or follow the new instructions?

"encircle them." The plan is to subvert enemy expectations and take them by surprise. Instead of a direct engagement, David is to attack the Philistines from the rear.

14:15. "God will go out before you." A similar assurance to the one David received earlier (v. 10). In the context of sacral warfare, Yhwh is depicted as going forth before the people (Deut 1:30; 20:4; Judg 4:14; cf. 2 Chr 20:21; 1QM 11:1, 4–5, 13–14).

14:16. "as God commanded him." In the aftermath of the aborted attempt to bring up the Ark to Jerusalem, David is careful to comply with divine directives. See also the last NOTE to v. 12.

"they defeated." In many holy-war accounts Yhwh fights against "the enemies of Israel" (2 Chr 20:29; cf. Josh 10:14, 42; Judg 20:35). In this account, the subj.

fluctuates between the sg. David (vv. 8, 10, 11, 12, 14, 16) and the pl. Israel (vv. 11, 12, 16). Given that the authors of Samuel stress the actions of David (2 Sam 5:17, 19, 20, 23, 25) or of David and his men (2 Sam 5:21), the Chronicler's slightly different version makes the victory one for both David and Israel.

"from Gibeon to Gezer." Gibeon was located about 12 km northwest of Jerusalem, while Gezer was situated some 24 km southeast of Gibeon. Hence, David succeeds in securing Israel's western flank.

14:17. "the reputation of David spread." In Chronicles there is a correlation between divine pleasure and national and international respect (e.g., 2 Chr 9:5–8, 23; 17:12; 26:8, 15; 32:23).

"Yhwh brought the fear of him on all of the nations." In standard holy-war ideology "the fear of Yhwh" descends upon neighboring kingdoms (Josh 2:9, 11; 9:1–3; 2 Chr 17:10; 20:29). In this case, God makes the nations fear David, thereby accentuating the theme announced in v. 1—David gains respect from his neighbors (Wright 1998). Israel, by implication, is afforded security and peace.

## Sources and Composition

For the sources and composition of 14:1–17, see the section devoted to SOURCES AND COMPOSITION in the commentary on 1 Chr 13.

## Comment

In the context of the Chronicler's larger narration, it is certainly significant that this particular account begins with international recognition of David's rule. In Chronistic ideology, commendations, tribute, and gifts from other leaders and nations denote divine blessing. Hence, when Ḥuram of Tyre dispatches men and materials to build David a palace, there can be no doubt that David stands in good stead with his patron deity. The first attempt to bring up the Ark (13:5–14) may have failed, but this failure does not reflect an unfavorable divine judgment on David's individual performance (1st NOTE to v. 2). But why does David only come to realize that "Yhwh had established him as king over Israel" after Ḥuram builds him a palace? Throughout his earlier account of David's rise (11:10; 12:24, 32, 39) and early kingship (10:14; 11:1–3), the author has been consistent in stressing the legitimacy of David's rule. Why is it that David only recognizes as much when the Tyrian king builds him a palace?

The Chronicler's presentation of David's being blessed, borrowed from Samuel, participates in a long-standing Near Eastern tradition. It was common among the societies of the ancient Mediterranean world for victorious and successful monarchs to commemorate the establishment of their rule and the victories they had won over their enemies by building a palace (Oppenheim 1977; Postgate

1994a). Conversely, rulers—whether human or divine—might not regard themselves as truly having achieved the status of king unless they enjoyed the comforts of their own domiciles. In one of the Ugaritic myths, the god Baal defeats his rival Yamm and achieves a great victory. Baal is, however, unable to consolidate his rule because he, unlike the other gods, does not have a house. Nor can he exercise his royal office unless he acquires one. The manifestation of kingship is closely bound up with the construction of a "house," a temple or royal palace. Having none, Baal maneuvers to convince the high god El to grant him permission to have one built (*KTU* 4.1.4–19). When Athirat, El's consort, finally convinces El to act on Baal's behalf (*KTU* 4.4.20–62), she proclaims a series of transformations in the world of nature that are expected to follow the construction of Baal's palace (*KTU* 4.5.63–81). Although not all Israelite writers would associate the construction of a royal palace or temple with new life and fertility, the general typology still holds in the Persian period (e.g., Hag 1:9–11; 2:6–9, 14–19). David comes to comprehend that "his kingship was highly exalted" (1 Chr 14:2). Nor does it seem accidental, in this context, that the narrator mentions David's marrying more women and siring many offspring (14:3–5).

Following these indications of divine blessing, there is no doubt that David knows how to enjoy success. The question is, How will he handle adversity? Until this point in the story, David has benefited enormously from the enthusiastic support he received throughout his royal career from his anointing (11:1–3) and conquest of Jerusalem (11:4–9) to his attempt to retrieve the Ark (13:1–14). Earlier, the unstinting military support he received from each of the tribes was instrumental in his rise and coronation (11:10–12:41). But this picture of consolidation and internal tranquility is interrupted as Philistine invasions test David's ability to handle external affairs. How will he respond to a crisis created by the same people who were so successful in routing Israel under Saul?

David's responses to the foreign interventions contrast markedly with those of Saul (see NOTES). The monarch acts deliberately in conformity with the deity's wishes. Yhwh, in turn, decisively defeats one of Israel's major enemies. Designed to challenge the strength of David's kingdom, the Philistine campaigns have the opposite effect. Instead of exploiting the weaknesses of a new king, the Philistines unwittingly contribute to his growing reputation: "Yhwh brought the fear of him on all of the nations" (14:17). David's fame now extends "throughout all of the lands" (v. 17). With his nation's external affairs firmly under control, at least for the moment, the king can turn his attention back to domestic affairs. The way is now open for David to resume his earlier quest to bring the Ark into the City of David.

# *XVIII. The Procession of the Ark to the Tent of David (15:1–16:3)*

*A Tent for the Ark*

1 When he [David] constructed dwellings for himself in the City of David, he established a place for the Ark of God and pitched a tent for it.
2 Then David said, "No one is to carry the Ark of God except the Levites, because Yhwh chose them to carry the Ark of Yhwh and to minister to him forever."

*David Convokes a National Assembly*

3 David assembled all Israel to Jerusalem to carry the Ark of Yhwh to the place that he established for it.
4 And David gathered the sons of Aaron and the Levites:

5 the descendants of Qohath, Uriel the officer and his kinsmen—120;
6 the descendants of Merari, Asaiah the officer and his kinsmen—220;
7 the descendants of Gershon, Joel the officer and his kinsmen—130;
8 the descendants of Elizaphan, Shemaiah the officer and his kinsmen—200;
9 the descendants of Ḥebron, Eliel the officer and his kinsmen—80;
10 the descendants of Uzziel, Amminadab the officer and his kinsmen—112.

*David's Charge to the Priests and the Levites*

11 David called for Zadoq and Abiathar, the priests, and for the Levites—Uriel, Asaiah, Joel, Shemaiah, Eliel, and Amminadab,
12 saying to them, "You are the heads of the Levitical houses. Consecrate yourselves, you and your kinsmen, and you will carry the Ark of Yhwh, the God of Israel, to (the place) I have established for it.
13 Indeed, when at first you did not carry (it), Yhwh our God created a breach against us, because we did not seek it according to the convention."

*Priestly and Levitical Compliance*

14 Then the priests and the Levites consecrated themselves to carry the Ark of Yhwh, the God of Israel.
15 And the Levites carried the Ark of God as Moses commanded in accordance with the word of Yhwh, by means of poles upon their shoulders.

*David's Liturgical Instructions to the Levites*

16 And David told the Levitical officers to appoint their kinsmen, the singers, with musical instruments—harps, lyres, and cymbals—making themselves heard by raising a joyful sound.

*Levitical Compliance*

17 So the Levites appointed:

Heman son of Joel;
from his kinsmen: Asaph son of Berechiah;
from the descendants of Merari their kinsmen: Ethan son of Qishaiah;
18 with them their kinsmen of the second rank: Zechariah, Uzziel,
Shemiramoth, Jeḥiel, Unni, Eliab, Benaiah, Maaseiah, Mattithiah,
Eliphalah, Miqneiah, Obed-edom, Jeiel, and Azaziah—the gatekeepers;

[19] the singers—Heman, Asaph, Ethan to sound the bronze cymbals;
[20] Zechariah, Uzziel, Shemiramoth, Jeḥiel, Unni, Eliab, Maaseiah,
Benaiah with harps set to (the voice of) young women;
[21] Mattithiah, Eliphalah, Miqneiah, Obed-edom, Jeiel, and Azaziah
to lead with lyres, set to the *šĕmînît*;
[22] Chenaniah, officer of the Levites, to wield authority in the porterage,
because he was an expert in it;
[23] Berechiah and Elqnanah—gatekeepers for the Ark;
[24] Shebaniah, Joshaphaṭ, Nethanel, Amasai, Zechariah, Benaiah, and
Eliezer the priests—sounding the trumpets before the Ark of God;
Obed-edom and and Jeḥiah—gatekeepers for the Ark.

*The Joyful Procession of the Ark*

[25] Then David, together with the elders of Israel and the officers of the thousands, went forth joyfully to carry the Ark of the Covenant from the house of
Obed-edom. [26] And God helped the Levites, those carrying the Ark of the Covenant of Yhwh. They sacrificed seven bulls and seven rams. [27] David was clothed in
a robe of fine linen as were all the Levites, those carrying the Ark, and those
singing. David also wore a linen ephod. [28] Thus David and all Israel were carrying
the Ark of the Covenant of Yhwh with acclaim, with the blast of the horn, with trumpets, with cymbals sounding, with harps, and with lyres.

*Michal's Displeasure with David's Conduct*

[29] As the Ark of the Covenant of Yhwh entered the City of David, Michal daughter of Saul gazed through the window and saw King David, dancing and performing, and she despised him in her heart.

*National Celebration for the Ark*

[16:1] When they brought up the Ark of God, they stationed it in the midst of the tent that David had pitched for it. Then they brought near burnt offerings and
offerings of well-being before God. [2] When David finished sacrificing the burnt offerings and the offerings of well-being, he blessed the people in the name of
Yhwh. [3] He also apportioned to every Israelite person—male and female alike—a loaf of bread, a roll, and a raisin cake.

## TEXTUAL NOTES

15:1. "dwellings" *(btym)*. So MT and LXX. In spite of the use of the pl., there is no need to declare the text corrupt (contra A. Ehrlich 1914: 338–39).

"established" *(wykn)*. So MT and LXX *(hētoimasen)*. Many Heb. MSS, Syr., and Vg. read the expected "built" *(wybn)*.

15:2. "no one is to carry the Ark." The inf. (of *nś*ʾ) is used to express obligation (GKC §114l). On the use of the negative *l*ʾ with an inf. const. to render a negative absolute, see Joüon (§160j).

"to carry the Ark of Yhwh." So MT. Lacking in LXX$^{BS}$ due to haplography *(homoioteleuton* from *yhwh* to *yhwh)*. Cf. LXX$^{AN}$.

"to minister to him" (לשרתו). The suf. can also be translated "it," hence "to minister to it" (the Ark).

15:3. "to the place." So LXX. MT "to its place" *(ʾl mqwmw)*.

15:4. "and the Levites." LXX[B] omits the copula, hence ("the Levitical sons of Aaron").

15:5. "120." So MT. LXX[BS], $c_2$ "110."

15:6. "220." So MT. LXX[B] "250."

15:7. "Gershon." MT, LXX[BS], and $c_2$ read "Gershom." I am following LXX[N] *(Gērsōn)* and LXX[L] *Gedsōn* (*dālet*/*rêš* confusion) by reading "Gershon," a spelling which appears elsewhere in Chronicles (as a son of Levi; 1 Chr 5:27; 23:6). The gentilic גרשוני, also appears (1 Chr 23:7; 26:21; 2 Chr 29:12). MT 1 Chr 6:1, 2, 5, 28, 47, 56 "Gershom" (TEXTUAL NOTE to 6:1).

"130." So MT. A few Heb. MSS "230"; LXX[B] "150." If the original document employed numerals (e.g., Aharoni, §47.1; 49.1–3, 5–7, 10–11, 13–16; 65.2; 67.1–5; 72.1–5) rather than spelled out the numbers, the loss or misreading of one stroke would change the reading.

15:8. "200." So MT and LXX. One Heb. MS "80."

15:12. "the heads of the Levitical houses" (ראשי האבות ללוים). Literally, "heads of the fathers of the Levites." The expression is an elision of ראשי בית האבות ללוים (Exod 6:14; 12:3; Num 1:2, 18; Josh 22:14; 1 Chr 5:13, 15, 24; 7:7, 9, 40; BDB 3). On the elided form, see Exod 6:25; Josh 14:1; 19:51; 21:1; 1 Chr 7:11; 8:6, 10, 13, 28; 9:9, 33, 34; 15:12; 23:9, 24; 24:6, 31; 26:21, 26, 32; 27:1; 2 Chr 1:2; 19:8; 23:2; 26:12.

"to (the place) I have established for it" *(ʾl hkynwty lw)*. So MT and LXX *(hou hētoimasa autē)*. Syr., Tg., Vg., explicate by adding *mqwm ʾšr* after *ʾl*. In so doing they assimilate the lemma to the expression occurring in MT Exod 23:20. Rudolph (1955: 116), followed by Williamson (1982b: 124), proposes instead to insert *hʾhl h(hkynwty)*, hence "to the tent that I have established for it." This is possible, as parablepsis may have occurred. But positing a haplography may also be unnecessary. In some contexts the relative is omitted (Kropat, §29). In a few cases, the article is employed in Chronicles as a relative (GKC §155n; Joüon, §158d). For constructions in Chronicles in which the prep. precedes the verb, see 1 Chr 29:2; 2 Chr 1:4; 16:9; 30:18.

15:13. "when at first." My translation largely follows LXX[B] *(lectio brevior)*. No satisfactory explanation has been given for MT's *lĕmabbāriʾšônāh*, which seems to reflect the combination of the interrogative "why" *(lmh)* and "at the first" *(brʾšwnh)*. Rudolph (1955: 116) favors reading *lĕmibbāriʾšônāh*, along with a few Heb. MSS, reflecting a combination of *lmn* and "at the first" *(brʾšwnh)*. Japhet (1993a: 301) advocates disregarding both the initial *lāmed* and the following *bêt* as corruptions and reading simply "at the first" *(brʾšwnh)*. This suggestion would bring MT more in line with LXX[B], which reads, "because you were not at the former occasion" *(hoti ouk en tō proteron hymas einai)*. Benzinger (1901: 52) follows LXX[L], "because you were not prepared at the former occasion," *hoti ouk en tō proteron hymas einai hetoimous* (= *ky lʾ ʿtm nkwnym brʾšwnh*). But LXX[B] probably represents an earlier reading than the more expansive LXX[L].

"you did not carry (it)" (לא אתם נשׂאתם). MT *(lōʾ ʾattem)* and LXX$^{B}$ "you were not" are cryptic. LXX$^{L}$ adds *hetoimous* (previous TEXTUAL NOTE). I follow the suggestion of a haplography by Hanson (1992) and Dirksen (1995a: 271). The verb was lost by haplography after לא אתם *(homoioarkton)*. Also supposing a haplography, Rudolph (1955: 116; *BHS*) emends to "you were not with us" (לא אתם אתנו). But the problem was not the absence of the Levites, but their lack of involvement in carrying the Ark (1 Chr 13:2; 15:2, 25).

15:15. "in accordance with the word of Yhwh" *(kdbr yhwh)*. So MT. LXX, reflecting *bdbr yhwh*, is followed by Arnold Ehrlich (1914: 340).

"by means of poles upon their shoulders" *(bktpm bmṭwt ʿlyhm)*. So MT. LXX$^{AB}$ lack *bktpm*, perhaps due to haplography (*homoioarkton* of *bktpm* before *bmṭwt*). The assertion by Begrich *(BHK)* that LXX$^{L}$ lacks *ʿlyhm* is simplistic, *en anaphoreusin en ōmois autōn*. Cf. Theodoret *en ōmois autōn* (= *bktpm*). Some (e.g., Benzinger 1901: 52) think that MT's *bktpm* is a gloss modeled on Num 7:9, *ʿlyhm bktp yśʾw* ("they will carry [it] upon themselves by shoulder"). But the testimony of LXX is more complex. LXX$^{AB}$ lack *bktpm* (see above), but LXX$^{AB}$ add *kata tēn graphēn* (= *kktwb*, "as it is written"). In other words, it seems likely that the *Vorlage* of LXX included a citation of an older text (see NOTE).

15:16. "by raising up" *(lhrym)*. The inf. expresses means (GKC §119q). The syntax is difficult in the second part of 15:16 (see the following TEXTUAL NOTES).

"a sound" *(bqwl)*. Joüon (§125m) argues that when the object is an instrument, especially in poetry, the construction with the prep. *b*—is used instead of the acc.

"joyful" *(lśmḥh)*. The prep. *l*—can express mode or manner (Williams, §274). Many commentators (e.g., Kittel 1895: 66; Benzinger 1901: 52; Curtis and Madsen 1910: 217; Rudolph 1955: 116) delete the *lāmed* as a dittography after *bqwl*.

15:17. "Qishaiah" *(qyšyhw)*. On the basis of LXX$^{B}$ *Keisaiou*, bb′ *Kisaiou*, and MT 6:29 (*qyšy*, a shorter form of *qyšyhw* [Gottheil 1898: 199; Kittel 1895: 66]), it is possible to reconstruct *qyšyhw*. See also LXX Esth 2:5 *Keisaiou* (MT *qyš*). On the PN, "Yhwh has given" or "gift of Yhwh," cf. Akk. *qiāšu*, "to give." MT reads *qwšyhw* (cf. $ye_2$ *Kousaiou*).

15:18. "of the second rank" *(hmšnym)*. So MT and LXX. Cf. MT 1 Sam 15:9; Ezra 1:10. Some (e.g., Curtis and Madsen 1910: 215) emend to "their twelve kinsmen."

"Zechariah." So a few Heb. MSS and LXX *(lectio brevior)*. MT and LXX$^{L}$ add "*ben*." Some would emend MT to "Bani" (*bny*; cf. 1 Chr 6:31; Neh 11:22), but see Bertheau (1873: 142–43) and Rudolph (1955: 116).

"Uzziel" *(ʿzyʾl)*. Reading with LXX$^{BSh}$ *Oz(e)iēl*. MT *yʿzyʾl*, "Jaaziel" (cf. LXX$^{L}$ *Ieiēl*), has suffered a dittography after the conjunction (*wāw* and *yôd* confusion). Given the variants in 15:20 (see the 1st TEXTUAL NOTE to 15:20), this is a more likely explanation than haplography (*pace* Allen 1974b: 43).

"Unni" *(ʿny)*. So MT (cf. LXX$^{A}$ *Ani*). LXX$^{B}$ *Eliōēl* and LXX$^{S,}$ $c_2$ *Iōēl* reflect a different *Vorlage*.

"Eliab." LXX and Syr. preface the copula.

"Eliphalah" *(ʾĕlîpālâ)*. I read basically with LXX$^{AN}$ *kai Eliphala*. LXX$^{B}$

*Eleiphena*; LXX[L] *Eliphal*. As Rothstein and Hänel (1927: 277) point out, MT "Elipheleiah" *(ʾĕlîpĕlēhû)* reflects a dittography of a *wāw*.

"Azaziah." The reconstruction *ʿăzazyāh(û)* is partially based on LXX's *kai Oz(e)ias*. MT's list ends with Jeiel. See the parallel list in 15:21 and the comments of Rothstein and Hänel (1927: 277–78) and Allen (1974b: 137–38).

"the gatekeepers." Some (e.g., Rothstein and Hänel 1927: 277; Rudolph 1955: 116) think that this term is a gloss from 15:24.

15:19. "bronze cymbals" *(mṣltym nḥšt)*. On the apposition, see Driver (1892: §188), GKC (§131d), and Joüon (§131d). Cf. 1 Chr 28:15, 18.

15:20. "Uzziel" *(ʾzyʾl)*. So LXX *(Oziēl)* and Tg. (see 15:18). MT has the same consonants, *ʿzyʾl*, but vocalizes "Aziel." The suggestion to emend to "Jeiel" *(yʿyʾl*; so Curtis and Madsen 1910: 215) is ill advised, because "Jeiel" reappears in 15:21 and the double appearance of "Jeiel" in 16:5 is probably a mistake (see TEXTUAL NOTE).

"set to (the voice of) young women" *(ʿal ʿălāmôt)*. Deriving *ʿălāmôt* from *ʿlmh*, "young woman" (Song 1:3; 6:8; Ps 68:25; BDB 761; Dahood 1965: 277), seems to be the best understanding of this obscure and contested phrase (see NOTE). LXX transliterates *epi alaimōt*. The translators of LXX[L] interpreted the term as the pl. of *ʿlm* ("secret") and rendered *peri tōn kryphiōn* (*Spottorno 2001: 72). The collocation* ʿal ʿălāmôt also appears in the superscription of Ps 46:1 (cf. 9:1; 48:15 [ET 48:14] *ʿalmût*; Mowinckel 1962.2: 215–16). A second (related) interpretation renders *ʿălāmôt* as the key in which the psalm was to be sung or accompanied (Weiser 1962: 23). Begrich *(BHK)*, followed by Rudolph (1955: 118), changes *ʿal ʿălāmôt* to *ʿal ʿēlāmît*, "in the Elamite way," but this emendation creates more problems than it solves. The JB represents *ʿălāmôt* as "the keyed harp," but the translators unfortunately provide no evidence or justification for this rendering.

15:21. "(and) Eliphalah." See the 6th TEXTUAL NOTE to 15:18. LXX[Aal] *kai Eliphalaias*; LXX[L] *Eliphal*.

"Azaziah" *(ʿăzazyāhû)*. So MT. Two Heb. MSS *ʿuzzîyāhû*; LXX *Oz(e)ias*. Kittel (1902: 68), followed by Curtis and Madsen (1910: 216), doubts that the term is original because it is wanting in both 15:18 and 16:5. But one can make the opposite argument, that Azaziah has been lost from 15:18 (7th TEXTUAL NOTE to 15:18).

"to lead" *(lnṣh)*. The *piʿel* inf. with the prep. *l*—designates directing, supervising, or leading (Ezra 3:8; 1 Chr 23:4; 2 Chr 34:12; BDB 663–64). For a somewhat different view, see Kraus (1988: 29), who translates *lnṣh* as "for the musical performance."

"set to the *šĕmînît*" *(ʿal-haššĕmînît)*. Like *ʿal ʿălāmôt* in 15:20 (2nd TEXTUAL NOTE), the meaning of this technical locution is uncertain. The most common translation is based on a derivation from *šmnh*, "eight" (BDB 1033). The Syr. "every day at the third, sixth, and ninth hours" elaborates on the ordinal line of interpretation (Weitzman 1994: 154). Cf. Lev 25:22; 1 Chr 24:10. Gunkel (1926: 21) translates "upon the eighth," probably to a deep octave or in the bass. Cf. LXX[L] *peri tēs ogdoes*, "with the octave." An eight-stringed instrument has also been suggested (e.g., Oesterly 1959: 16; Kraus 1988: 31). Note, in this regard, the translation of JB, "the octave lyre." According to Josephus (*Ant.* 7.306), the *nebel* (15:16, 20) had twelve notes, while the *kinnôr* (15:16, 21) had ten strings. Ancient Near Eastern lyres could have eight strings, but lyres with twelve, eleven, and nine strings are also attested (King 1999). Like *ʿal ʿălāmôt,* the expression *ʿal-haššĕmînît* appears within a couple of psalm superscriptions (Pss 6; 12). Hence, it seems likely that the phrase involves musical directions. Unfortunately, the precise nuance of the expression eludes us. Begrich *(BHK)* suggests a somewhat different approach, emending to the gentilic *ʿal-haššimrōnît* "in the Shimronite way" (Josh 11:1; 19:15) or *ʿal-haššimyōnît,* "in the Simeonite way." This proposal has little explanatory force.

15:22. "Chenaniah" *(knnyhw).* See also 15:27 (MT) and 26:29. A few Heb. MSS "Benaniah." LXX$^{BS}$ *(Kōnenia),* LXX$^{A}$ *(Chōnenia),* and Vg. *(Chonenias)* probably reflect **kwnnyhw,* "Conaniah," a name that also appears in 2 Chr 31:12. LXX$^{L}$ *Iechonias,* "Jechoniah."

"officer of the Levites" (שׂר-הלוים). Reading with LXX$^{AB}$ *(lectio brevior).* MT adds *bmśʾ*, a dittography of *bmśʾ* later in the verse, rendered by Vg. as *ad praecinendam melodiam,* "[Chenaniah] had the duty to chant the melody."

"to wield authority." I read with many Heb. MSS, which have *yśr* (from the root *śrr,* "to rule, govern"). Tg. and Vg. are similar. MT reads the inf. abs. of *ysr,* "to discipline, chastise, admonish" (BDB 415–16). LXX *archōn,* "officer (of the odes)," reflects either *śr* (Kittel 1895: 66–67; Benzinger 1901: 53) or less likely *yśr* (Bertheau 1873: 144–45).

"in the porterage" *(bmśʾ).* The Heb. can be translated in different ways. Some of the interpretive options date to antiquity. The translation "in the porterage," supported by Tg., comports with the duties laid down for the Levites in Num 1:51; 4:15–20; Deut 10:8, and reaffirmed in Chronicles (1 Chr 15:2, 3, 12, 14–15, 22, 25, 26–28; 2 Chr 35:3). A second translation, "with the oracle" (JB), supported by the allusion to prophecy in Vg. *prophetiae (praeerat),* is based on the rendering of *mśʾ* in 2 Chr 24:27 and elsewhere (e.g., 2 Kgs 9:25; Isa 14:28; Ezek 12:10) as an "oracle." As Freedman (personal communication) points out, Jer 23:33–38 plays on the double meaning of *mśʾ* as "burden" or "pronouncement." A third translation, "in music," may be supported by LXX *tōn ōdōn,* "the odes." The immediate context of 15:16–24, most of which deals with music and singing, lends some credence to the third translation, but it ignores the larger context (15:1–15, 25–28) and presents a false choice of Levitical duties as either being singers or porters. Clearly, the situation is both/and, not either/or. The whole purpose of David's appointing the Levites is, among other things, to transport the Ark. In Chronicles the Levitical duties include carrying the Ark, gatekeeping, and music.

"because he was an expert in it" *(kî mēbîn hûʾ).* So MT. LXX is similar, *hoti synetos ēn.*

15:24. "sounding." I read with Kethib *maḥăṣōṣĕrîm (lectio difficilior).* See further, GKC §53o. Qere *maḥṣĕrîm.* Other suggestions include *maḥṣaṣrîm* or *maḥăṣarṣĕrîm.* On the verb, see also 2 Chr 5:12; 7:6; 13:14; 29:28 (all *hipʿil* ptcs.); 2 Chr 5:13 *(piʿel).* This use of the verb describes movements of quick succession (GKC §55e).

"Jeḥiah" *(yḥyh)*. So MT and perhaps the *Vorlage* of LXX[B] *(Ieia)*. Curtis and Madsen (1910: 217) add "Jeiel" based on LXX[L] *Ieiēl* and the pattern of 15:18, but this only harmonizes 15:18 with 15:24.

15:25. "together with the elders of Israel and the officers of the thousands." So MT and LXX. The phrase is lacking in 2 Sam 6:12. The addition is likely from the Chronicler's own hand (NOTES to 15:25).

"went forth" *(hhlkym)*. So MT and LXX[BL] *(hoi poreuomenoi)*. The article *(hoi)* is missing from some LXX miniscules by parablepsis (after *chilarchoi*). Vg. *ierunt.*

"the Ark of the Covenant." So LXX[BS], $c_2$. MT expands to "the Ark of the Covenant of Yhwh" (as in 15:26). MT 2 Sam 6:12 "the Ark of God." That the Chronicler deliberately changed Samuel's terminology (Curtis and Madsen 1910: 218) is doubtful, because he does not show any consistent preference for this locution elsewhere.

"from the house of Obed-edom." So MT and LXX. MT 2 Sam 6:12 adds "to the City of David."

15:26. "and God helped the Levites" *(wyhy bʿzr hʾlhym ʾt hlwym)*. So MT and LXX. MT 2 Sam 6:13 reads a different and less expansive subordinate clause, "and when they moved forward" *(wyhy ky ṣʿdw)*. The lemma in Chronicles likely stems from the author's own hand. In some cases, the Chronicler substitutes a synonym or a more common term for a rare and obscure term in his *Vorlage* (Weiss 1968; Japhet 1987; 1st NOTE to 15:26).

"Ark of the Covenant of Yhwh" (ארון ברית-יהוה). So MT and LXX. MT 2 Sam 6:13 "Ark of Yhwh six steps" (ארון יהוה ששה צעדים).

"and they sacrificed seven bulls and seven rams." So MT and LXX. MT 2 Sam 6:13 "and he sacrificed an ox and a fatling." But fragmentary 4QSam[a] reads *šb*[*ʿh*] *prym wšbʿ*[*h ʾylym*], "sev[en] bulls and seven [rams]." Josephus (*Ant* 7.85) expands by also mentioning seven choirs.

15:27. "David was clothed *(mkrbl)* in a robe of fine linen *(bmʿyl bwṣ)*." So MT and LXX. The quadriliteral verb *krbl* is on the analogy of the *piʿel* (Joüon, §60). Akk. *karballatu,* or less often *karballutu,* refers to a piece of linen headgear for soldiers (*CAD* K [8] 215). MT 2 Sam 6:14, "David was whirling *(mkrkr)* with all (his) might *(bkl ʿṣ)* before Yhwh."

"as were all the Levites, those carrying the Ark, and those singing" (וכל-הלוים הנשאים את-הארון והמשררים). MT (and LXX) is more expansive "as were all the Levites, those carrying the Ark, the singers, Chenaniah the officer in charge of the porterage, the singers" (וכל-הלוים הנשאים את-הארון והמשררים וכנניה השר המשא המשררים). The phraseology is entirely lacking in 2 Sam 6:14. The text of Chronicles seems to have suffered expansion at a pre-LXX stage of transmission. Through the technique of repetitive resumption (from "those singing" to "those singing") new material was added to the text. Hence, the clause "Chenaniah the officer of the porterage, those singing" seems to be an early addition, designed to bring the description of 15:27 more in line with the preceding list of participants (esp. 15:22).

"and David wore a linen ephod" *(wʿl dwyd ʾpwd bd)*. So MT and LXX. MT 2 Sam 6:14 "and David was girded with a linen ephod" *(wdwd ḥgwr ʾpwd bd)*.

15:28. "thus David and all Israel." The reconstruction is based on the fuller reading of MT 2 Sam 6:15, "and David and all the house of Israel" (cf. Rothstein and Hänel 1927: 284; Rudolph 1955: 119). Part of the original Chronicles reading, ודויד וכל-ישׂראל, was lost to MT and LXX 15:28 ("and all Israel") because of haplography after אפוד בד and before וכל-ישׂראל. In other words, the trigger could have been either *homoioteleuton* or *homoioarkton*.

"the Ark of the Covenant of Yhwh." So MT and LXX. MT 2 Sam 6:15 "the Ark of Yhwh."

"with trumpets, with cymbals sounding, with harps, and with lyres." So MT (and LXX). 2 Sam 6:15 lacks this material. The instruments are replaced by "praise, voice, and mouth" in Syr.

"sounding" *(mšmʿym)*. So MT. LXX is similar, "calling aloud" *(anaphōnountes)*. Rudolph (1955: 119) proposes to preface *wāw*, but the connective is lacking in both Chronicles and Samuel. The ptc. "sounding" functions circumstantially (Joüon, §159a).

15:29. "the Ark of the Covenant of Yhwh." So MT and LXX. MT 2 Sam 6:16 "the Ark of Yhwh."

"to the City" *(ʿd ʿyr)*. So MT and LXX. The prep. *ʿd* is missing from many Heb. MSS and from MT 2 Sam 6:16 due to haplography before *ʿyr dwyd*.

"dancing and performing" *(mrqd wmśḥq)*. So MT and LXX. MT 2 Sam 6:13 "leaping and whirling before Yhwh" *(mpzz wmrkrkr lpny yhwh)*. On the translation of *mśḥq* as "performing," see the 2nd TEXTUAL NOTE to 13:8.

"and she despised" *(wattibez)*. Arnold Ehrlich (1914: 341), followed by Rudolph (1955: 119), proposes *wattāboz* (from *bwz*, instead of from *bzh*, but with essentially the same meaning). Cf. 2 Sam 6:16.

16:1. "in the midst of the tent." So MT and LXX 16:1 and Syr. 2 Sam 6:17. MT and LXX 2 Sam 6:17 add "in its place" (במקומו), which could have been lost by haplography before בתוך, "in the midst." 4QSam[a] is fragmentary.

"then they brought near" (ויקריבו). MT 2 Sam 6:17 "and David went up" (ויעל דוד).

16:2. "Yhwh." MT 2 Sam 6:18 adds "Sebaoth."

16:3. "to every Israelite person" *(lkl-ʾyš yśrʾl)*. On the expression, see Joüon (§147d). MT 2 Sam 6:19 reads more expansively, "to all the people, to the entire throng of Israel."

"a loaf of bread" *(kkr lḥm)*. See also Exod 29:23; 1 Sam 2:36; Jer 37:21; Prov 6:26. MT 2 Sam 6:19 reads "ring of bread" *(ḥlt lḥm)* and adds *ʾḥd* to each of the following terms. LXX 2 Sam 6:19 agrees with 1 Chr 16:3. But in the case of *kkr lḥm*, LXX[AB] 1 Chr 16:3 adds *hena* (= *ʾḥd*). Whichever is the most primitive reading, the basic meaning is not affected (Joüon, §137u).

"roll" *(ʾšpr)*. Until recently, the translation was conjectural (cf. Arab. *sufrat*, "victuals"). Perhaps perplexed by the term, the translators of Tg. divided it *(ʾš pr)* to read "a sixth of an ox." In the HB *ʾšpr* is a *hapax legomenon*, appearing only here and in the parallel (2 Sam 6:19). But the term *ʾšprm* with the meaning of "rolls" or "cakes" has recently appeared on a late-seventh- to early-sixth-century-B.C.E. Heb. ostracon listing a variety of foods, perhaps for a feast (Lemaire 1997b: 460–61).

"raisin cake" *(ʾšyšh)*. The translation of MT is largely according to context, but the term *ʾšyšh* is attested elsewhere (Isa 16:7; Hos 3:1; Song 2:5; Pope 1977b: 378–80). LXX$^{L}$ 16:3 reads *kollyritēn*, "bun" (cf. LXX$^{B}$ amoreitēn, "cake").

## Notes

15:1–24. This material, although broadly indebted to the work of a variety of earlier biblical writers (Brettler 1995), is unique to Chronicles. The Chronicler uses these preparations, instructions, and appointments as a preface to the material he borrows from Samuel depicting the triumphant procession of the Ark (15:25–16:3). The additions he makes to his *Vorlage* underscore the significance of this event to his audience.

15:1. "when he [David] constructed dwellings *(wyʿś btym)* for himself." This most likely refers to domiciles in addition to the palace *(byt)* built for David by Ḥuram, king of Tyre (14:1; Bertheau 1873: 140–41; Kittel 1902: 65). It is possible to construe "constructed" *(ʿśh)* as indicating preparation, hence, refurbishment and renovation of an already-existing palace (Keil 1873: 200; Curtis and Madsen 1910: 214). But this is less likely in view of the explicit reference to (literally) "houses" *(btym)* instead of a sg. "house" *(byt)*. The passage should be read in the context of other construction activity in Jerusalem: David's building up the city "on all sides, from the millo to the surrounding area" (11:8), Joab's restoration of the rest of the town (11:8), and Ḥuram's construction of a palace for David (14:1). The attention paid to public works is important in two respects. First, by documenting such building activity, the Chronicler establishes indelible ties between this particular king and Israel's capital city. Second, David's construction activity parallels the Chronicler's complimentary portraits of other kings whose reigns are characterized, at least in part, by building activity. The record of numerous public works in David's tenure establishes a standard for others to follow. Royal buildings and fortifications are always associated with times of divine blessing. In this respect, they constitute a literary topos in Chronicles (Welten 1973).

"a place for the Ark of God." The reference to David's preparation of "a place *(māqôm)* for the Ark" does not seem to be accidental (cf. 2 Sam 6:17). In certain contexts, the term *māqôm*, "place," can bear connotations of a sacred precinct or sanctuary (e.g., Deut 12:5, 11, 14, 18, 21, 26; 14:23, 24–25; 15:20; Josh 9:27; Cowley 1916). In the Chronicler's version of the negotiations between David and Ornan, for example, David repeatedly refers to the threshing floor (the future site of the Temple) as a *māqôm* (1 Chr 21:22, 25). Similarly, the Chronicler later avers that Solomon built the Temple on Mount Moriah, the place *(māqôm)* where Yhwh appeared to David at the threshing floor of Ornan the Jebusite (2 Chr 3:1). In Phoen., the term *mqm* can also refer to a sanctuary (Tomback 1978: 195–96). In speaking not merely of David's pitching a tent for the Ark (so 2 Sam 6:17) but also of his establishing a place for it, the Chronicler presents a very complimentary picture of David's piety. In the ancient Near East successful kings were expected to honor the deities who led them by supporting the cult (Frankfort 1948;

Kapelrud 1963: 56–62; Postgate 1994a: 260–64). Much of 1 Chr 15–16 elaborates on this very point. In explaining the Chronicler's presentation, one must also deal with the phenomenon of inner-biblical exegesis. In some respects, the preparations David makes for the Ark's ascent recall (and are perhaps indebted to) the arrangements Solomon makes for the Ark's entrance into the Temple within the Deuteronomistic History (1 Kgs 8; Brettler 1995: 26–34).

"a tent for it." In Chronicles, as opposed to Samuel, the need to pitch a tent for the Ark is overtly explained. The Chronicler consistently places the Tabernacle at Gibeon (1 Chr 16:39; 21:29; 2 Chr 1:3); hence, the Ark needs "curtains" (1 Chr 17:1). Only with the construction of a permanent, centralized temple does this bifurcation of Israel's cult between the Tabernacle at Gibeon and the Ark at Jerusalem come to an end (3rd NOTE to 16:39).

15:2. "then." Alluding either to the three months the Ark had spent in the house of Obed-edom (1 Chr 13:14//2 Sam 6:11; Bertheau 1873: 141; Benzinger 1901: 52) or to a time after the preparations mentioned in 1 Chr 15:1 (Curtis and Madsen 1910: 213).

"David said." The explanation of the earlier failure to retrieve the Ark is based on the interpretation and application of authoritative texts (see below). In this respect, the Chronicler presents King David as a shrewd expositor of earlier scriptures. In the so-called law of the king (Deut 17:14–20), the authors of Deuteronomy mandate that the monarch keep a copy of the Torah scroll close by and read it all the days of his life so that he might learn to fear Yhwh and "observe all the words of this Torah" (17:19). Only by fulfilling the terms of the instruction, straying "neither to the right nor to the left," will the king and his descendants experience a long reign in the midst of Israel (17:20). In this respect, the Chronicler's David is a model monarch. Nevertheless, the Chronicler's monarchs are more interventionist than Deuteronomy's authors anticipated. In Deuteronomy the king's only positive duty is to read the Torah daily; he has no authority either to teach the Torah or to interpret it (Deut 17:18–19). Teaching the Torah is a function of the priesthood, which has custody of the Torah (17:18). Speaking on behalf of God (18:1–8) is a prophetic function (18:15–22). But in Chronicles David's personal intervention is the decisive difference in the two attempts to bring up the Ark. His analysis of the previous failure, informed by an interpretation of older prestigious texts and pronounced before any assembly has been convened, is the basis for all of the changes that ensue.

"no one is to carry the Ark of God except the Levites." David utters this pronouncement in the aftermath of Uzza's unfortunate death (13:10), the implication being that the proper personnel had not been intimately involved in the first attempt to bring the Ark into the City of David. He subsequently mobilizes and instructs the priests and Levites to take a much more active and direct role in the liturgical proceedings. The following verses detail what personnel and actions David deems necessary to install the Ark successfully.

"Yhwh chose *(bḥr)* them." The Chronicler considers the Levites as elect of God (2 Chr 29:11). This is one of the clearest indications of the esteem in which the Levites are held (cf. Deut 33:8–10). Other divinely chosen persons, entities, and institutions are Judah (1 Chr 28:4; cf. Ps 78:68), David (1 Chr 28:4; cf. Ps 78:70), Solomon (1 Chr 28:5–6; 29:1), the Temple (2 Chr 6:5, 34, 38; 7:12, 16), and Jerusalem (2 Chr 6:5–6; 12:13).

"to carry the Ark *(lśʾt ʾt ʾrwn)* of Yhwh." David quotes from Deut 10:8, in which one of the duties of the Levites is "to carry the Ark" *(lśʾt ʾt ʾrwn)*. To be sure, the transport of the Ark is a concern in the Priestly work, as well. According to Num 1:50–53 and 3:5–9 (P), the tribe of Levi was supposed to tend and carry the Tabernacle and its furnishings, including the Ark. But the quote is from Deuteronomy.

"to minister to him *(lšrtw)* forever." Again, the Chronicler has David quote from Deuteronomy, in which the tribe of Levi is "to stand in attendance before Yhwh, to minister to him *(lšrtw)*, and to bless the name of Yhwh" (10:8; cf. Deut 17:12; 18:5, 7; 21:5; 31:25; Jer 33:21). In the Priestly source, the situation is different. There, the priests serve *(šrt)* Yhwh and the Levites are accountable to the priests (Exod 28:35; Num 3:6; 8:26; 18:2). Similarly, Ezekiel presents the Levites as servitors *(mšrtym)* appointed over the temple gates, guards who perform various temple chores (Ezek 44:11–27). Of the descendants of Levi, only the priests may approach Yhwh to serve *(šrt)* him (Ezek 40:46; 43:19; 44:15–16). The Chronicler presents a third view, in some respects a via media between the perspectives found in the Deuteronomic and Priestly sources. The priests and the Levites have their distinct responsibilities, but both minister to Yhwh (1 Chr 6:17; 16:4, 37; 23:13; 26:12; 2 Chr 5:14; 8:14; 13:10; 23:6; 29:11; 31:2). The Chronicler's view is only one of many in the Persian period (Ezra 8:15, 17; Neh 10:37, 40 [ET 10:36, 39]; Joel 1:9; 2:17; Mal 1:6–2:9; 3:1–5; MT Jer 33:21–22).

15:3. "assembled *(qhl)* all Israel to Jerusalem." The notice is consistent with the Chronicler's pan-Israel focus, evident in earlier sections of David's reign (11:1; 12:39). David also enjoyed broad bipartisan support in his first attempt to retrieve the Ark (13:2). By narrating the presence of all Israelites in Jerusalem, the author makes the people participants in and supporters of this momentous event. After expounding on the duties of various sacerdotal personnel, the Chronicler will return to this pan-Israel motif (15:25, 28; 16:1–3).

15:4. "sons of Aaron" (בני אהרן). In conjunction with a reference to the Levites, one expects a reference to the priests (הכהנים), rather than to Aaronides. But in Chronicles the priests are descendants of Aaron (2nd NOTE to 5:29).

15:5–10. "descendants." Given the pattern of the Levitical genealogy (5:27–41; 6:1–66 [ET 6:1–81]), the first three patronyms—Qohath, Merari, and Gershon—are expected (15:5–7). The second three—Elizaphan, Ḥebron, and Uzziel—represent a new development (NOTE to 15:8–10). The later administrative reorganization of David involves the three major phratries (23:6–23). But in the reform of Ḥezeqiah, there are additional phratries to the three named after Qohath, Merari, and Gershon (2 Chr 29:12–14). These additional phratries only partially overlap with those mentioned here: the sons of Elizaphan, the sons of Asaph, the sons of Heman, and the sons of Jeduthun (2 Chr 29:13–14).

15:5. "Qohath." In Num 3:27–31 (P) the clan headed by Qohath is charged with care for the Ark, the table, the lampstand, the altars, and the sacred furnishings. According to Curtis and Madsen (1910: 213), Qohath is mentioned first because the Qohathites had the duty of transporting sanctuary furnishings (Num 4:15). This is basically true, but the situation is more complex. The sons of Aaron—that is, the priests—were to prepare the Ark, the altar, and the sacred vessels both for setup and for transport (Milgrom 1990: 343–44). In P, only priests could do the actual work of dismantling and reassembling (Num 4:4–15) because only they were qualified to handle the Ark and the other sacred objects. These sacred objects ipso facto were potentially lethal (Num 4:15). Because the Levites did not have the same status as priests, their touch or sight of the *sancta* could be fatal (Num 4:15–20). The labor assigned to the Qohathite Levites was porterage of the *sancta*—including the Ark—upon their shoulders (Num 4:15, 17–20). Hence, no wagons were given to the Qohathite Levites. They had responsibility for the transport of the most sacred materials and their porterage had to be by shoulder (Num 7:9).

"Uriel the officer" *(ʾwryʾl hśr)*. The name Uriel also appears in the Qohathite genealogy of Elqanah (6:9).

15:6. "the descendants of Merari." The duties of the Merarites are outlined in Num 4:29–33. The Merarites, along with the Gershonites, were to transport tabernacle furnishings, such as the planks, posts, and sockets of the Tabernacle, by oxcart after the Tabernacle had been dismantled by the priests (Num 4:21–33; 10:17; Milgrom 1990: 30–31). Because they are involved in various kinds of work *(ʿbwdh)*, there is no need to deny that these responsibilities included porterage (*mśʾ*; Num 4:31). Such porterage involved the use of oxcarts and did not involve the transport of the *sancta*. As we have seen, porterage of the *sancta* is the specific responsibility of the Qohathite Levites (Num 4:15; 7:9; 1st NOTE to 15:5).

"Asaiah." A Merarite by this name is also mentioned in 6:15.

15:7. "the descendants of Gershon." The duties of the Gershonites are enumerated in Num 4:24–28. Like the Merarites, the Gershonites were to transport certain tabernacle furnishings by oxcart. For the Gershonites, these included the curtains and the Tent of Meeting.

"Joel." No Joel appears in the Gershonite genealogies, but a Gershonite by this name from the family of Ladan is mentioned in 23:8.

15:8–10. Each of the three ancestral clans mentioned in these verses stems from the Qohathite phratry of Levites. In this respect, the Qohathite phratry dominates (four out of six clans; 512, 59.4 percent out of 862) the sacerdotal representation in David's Jerusalem assembly. By contrast, the Merarite branch registers 25.5 percent (220) and the Gershonide branch only 15.1 percent (130) of the total. The Qohathite branch of Levi also plays a major role in the genealogies of Levi (5:27–41 [1st NOTE to 5:28]; 6:1–66).

15:8. "Elizaphan." In Num 3:30 Elizaphan, a son of Uzziel, appears as a chieftain *(nśyʾ)* of the ancestral house of the Qohathite families (Levine 1993: 160). This figure should not be confused with the chieftain *(nśyʾ)* Elizaphan, son of Parnach, who hails from a different tribe (Zebulun). In 2 Chr 29:13 an Elizaphan heads a group of Levites.

15:9. "Ḥebron." A son of Qohath in Exod 6:18; Num 3:19; 1 Chr 5:28; 6:3; 23:12; 26:23.

"Eliel" appears in the Qohathite Levitical singer genealogy (6:19) and as the name of a Levitical overseer (2 Chr 31:13). But the PN also appears in a variety of non-Levitical contexts (1 Chr 5:24; 8:20; 11:46; 12:12).

15.10. "Uzziel." Like Ḥebron, Uzziel appears as a son (or clan) of Qohath (Exod 6:18; Num 3:19; 1 Chr 5:28; 6:3; 23:12; 26:23).

"Amminadab." Mentioned as a son of Qohath in MT 6:7.

15:11. "Zadoq and Abiathar." These two priests appear during the reign of David (2 Sam 8:17; 15:29, 35; 19:11; 20:25). Under David each of these priests heads or represents major priestly houses (Cross 1973: 207–15; Olyan 1982). In the Deuteronomistic History, Solomon deposes Abiathar in the early part of his reign, leaving Zadoq with control of the Jerusalem Temple priesthood (1 Kgs 2:27, 35). In Chronicles Zadoq and Abiathar also function as David's priests, but the priestly succession proceeds along different lines (1 Chr 18:16 [2nd NOTE]; 24:6; 27:34). Aḥimelek seems to succeed his father Abiathar already during David's reign, but neither figure in the reign of the Chronicler's Solomon.

"Uriel, Asaiah, Joel, Shemaiah, Eliel, and Amminadab." The names of the Levitical officers correspond with those names mentioned in the earlier list (15:5–10).

15:12. "heads of the Levitical clans." The language is technical. The "heads of the clans," literally, the heads of the fathers" *(rāʾšê hāʾābôt)*, refers to a form of social organization that appears in the literature dealing with the Persian period: ancestral houses. The Chronicler lived during an age in which kinship relations and the question of lineage were of great consequence for determining status and self-identity. Ancestral houses were one major means through which one's identity might be defined. The terminology, *rʾšy (bty h)ʾbwt*, "heads of the ancestral houses," is quite common in Chronicles (1 Chr 12:31; 15:12; 27:1; 29:6; 2 Chr 1:2; 17:14; 19:8; 23:2; 25:5; 26:12; 31:17; 35:4, 5, 12), Ezra (1:5; 2:59, 68; 3:12; 4:2, 3; 8:1; 10:16), and Nehemiah (7:61, 69, 70; 8:13; 10:35 [ET 10:34]; 11:13; 12:12, 22, 23). Note, for example, how often the terminology recurs in the genealogies (1 Chr 5:13, 15, 24; 7:2, 4, 7, 9, 11, 40; 8:6, 10, 13, 28; 9:9, 13, 33, 34) and tribal lists (1 Chr 23:9, 24; 24:4, 6, 30, 31; 26:13, 26, 32). In contrast, the expression in the sg., "the house of the father" *(bêt ʾāb)*, appears much less often in Chronicles (1 Chr 12:29; 24:6; 28:4; 2 Chr 21:13; 35:5), only once in Nehemiah (1:6), and not at all in Ezra. The Priestly authors reference both the *bêt ʾāb* (Gen 20:13; 24:7, 23, 38, 40; 28:21; 34:19; 38:11; 41:51; 46:31; 47:12; 50:8, 22; Lev 22:13; Num 3:24, 30, 35; 17:18; 25:14, 15; 18:1; 25:14, 15; 30:4, 17) and the *bêt ʾābôt* (Exod 6:14; Num 1:4, 18–45; 2:2, 32, 34; 3:15, 20; 4:22, 29, 34, 38, 40, 42, 46; 7:2; 17:17, 18, 21; 26:2; 34:14; Josh 22:14). A straightforward use of the *bêt ʾāb/bêt ʾābôt* in the Priestly work to reconstruct social conditions of the Persian period should not be made because the Priestly writing seems to preserve some memories of preexilic social and material conditions (Vanderhooft 1999b). In the Persian period, ancestral houses *(bêt ʾābôt)* are thought to be large agnatic-kinship or quasi-kinship groups (Weinberg 1974: 400–414; Dion 1991: 285). In this context, one should not think of the ancestral house only in linear terms. The house of one's fathers might be defined by social and geographic considerations as well as by bloodlines. An ancestral house was larger than a family *(mšpḥh)*, but smaller than a tribe *(šbṭ; mṭh)*. The precise configuration of ancestral houses remains, however, to be clarified. In this context, note the important reservations of Williamson (1998).

"consecrate yourselves" (התקדשו אתם). Again, the expression is fairly common, especially in 2 Chronicles (5:11; 29:5, 15, 34; 30:3, 15, 24; 31:18; 35:6 [all *hitpaʿel*]). In all cases the reference is to preparation for a major cultic initiative. Consecration could involve washing one's body or one's clothes (Gen 35:2; Exod 19:14), anointing (Lev 8:12, 30), or abstention from certain activities that would render the person ritually impure (Gen 35:2; Exod 19:10, 14, 15; cf. Lev 8:12, 30; Num 11:18; 1 Sam 7:1). Williamson (1982b: 124) calls attention to the specific example of Moses warning the priests to remain consecrated (*hitpaʿel* of *qdš*) "lest Yhwh break out *(prṣ)* against them" (Exod 19:22). Given the repeated use of the keyword *prṣ* in the discussions of Uzza's death (13:2, 11; 14:11; 15:13), the author may have thought that this rite of preparation was especially important to the procession's success. He may also have thought of the example of Josh 3:5–6 in which Joshua tells the people to sanctify themselves before the Ark can be conveyed across the Jordan River (Brettler 1995: 30). Note the carefully worded comment that such consecration was later implemented (1 Chr 15:14). It is also important to observe that the consecration in Chronicles involves both priests and Levites. In this respect, the Chronicler shows his own perspective on sacerdotal affairs, both indebted to and independent of the works of the Deuteronomic, Deuteronomistic, and Priestly writers (Knoppers 1999a). The Chronicler stresses cooperation and complementarity, not competition and hierarchy, among the priests and Levites. Both the priests and the Levites are commanded to consecrate themselves. In Joshua the people are instructed to consecrate themselves. In P only the priests are holy, but in Chronicles both the Levites and the priests are holy (*qādôš*; 2 Chr 23:6). In the reforms of Josiah the Levites are referred to as "those holy to Yhwh" (*haqqĕdôšîm lyhwh*; 2 Chr 35:3). In the Priestly source and Ezekiel, the Levites are never called *qādôš*.

15:13. "when at first you did not carry (it)." David's comment sheds light on the Chronicler's interpretation of the first attempt to retrieve the Ark. The priests and the Levites were not directly involved. Evidently, the Chronicler did not regard Uzza and Aḥio as of either priestly or Levitical pedigree (13:7). There may be, as Japhet (1993a: 300–301) claims, a critique of priestly and Levitical behavior in David's remark. The force of David's observation is, therefore, to fix the role the priests and Levites are to play in this new attempt to bring the Ark into the City of David. It should come as no great surprise that much of David's attention in what follows is on making sure that proper personnel are present and that proper protocol is followed.

"Yhwh our God created a breach against us" *(prṣ yhwh ʾlhynw bnw)*. An allusion to the death of Uzza (2nd NOTE to 13:11). The Chronicler continues his plays on the roots *prṣ*, "to break out" (13:2, 11; 14:11; 15:13) and *drš*, "to seek." The earlier attempt to redress neglect of the Ark—"for we did not seek *(drš)* it in the days of Saul" (13:3)—was brought to a swift end by the divine outbreak against Uzza (*prṣ yhwh prṣ bʿzʾ*; 13:10–11). As later events made clear, the problem was not Israel's communal decision "to seek" the ark, but the manner in which the arrangements were handled. In the new attempt, David insists on the intimate involvement of the priests and Levites to rectify this deficiency.

"because we did not seek it" *(dĕrašnuhû)*. The phrase *dĕrašnuhû* can also be translated, "because we did not seek him," thereby taking Yhwh (and not the Ark) as the antecedent. Since this issue has divided commentators, it requires some discussion. The impulse to construe the deity as the object of the verb "seek" *(drš)* is understandable. First, the nearest antecedent is "Yhwh our God," earlier in the verse. Second, the verb, "to seek" *(drš)* in a cultic context usually has Yhwh (1 Chr 16:11[//Ps 105:4]; 28:9; 2 Chr 12:14; 14:3, 6 [ET 14:4, 7]; 15:2, 12; 16:12; 22:9; 26:5; 34:21) or God (2 Chr 17:4; 19:3; 26:5; 30:19) as object. Conversely, one is not supposed to "seek the Baals" (*drš lb ʿlym;* 2 Chr 17:3) or "seek the god(s) of Edom" (*dršw ʾt ʾlhy ʾdwm;* 2 Chr 25:20). The expression "to seek Yhwh" (or God) in the context of worship has, in fact, been long recognized as a standard Chronistic locution (e.g., S. Driver 1914: 503; Begg 1982). Nevertheless, a strong case can be made that the Ark is in view. To begin with, the Chronicler occasionally speaks of "seeking" objects. One example is David's reference to the disregard for the Ark during the tenure of his predecessor, "For we did not seek *(drš)* it in the days of Saul" (13:3). Another example occurs in the context of Solomon's reign, "As for the bronze altar that Bezalel made . . . Solomon and the assembly sought it" (*wydršhw;* 2 Chr 1:5). Mention should also be made of the Chronicler's play on Saul's infidelity. Saul *(šʾwl)* was rejected because of his consulting *(lšʾwl)* a necromancer to seek counsel (*ldrwš;* 1 Chr 10:13; cf. 2 Chr 24:6, 22; 25:15, 20). In Chronicles one can also seek the Torah. For instance, Solomon implores his subjects: "Keep *(šmrw)* and seek out *(drwšw)* the commandments of Yhwh" (1 Chr 28:8 [TEXTUAL NOTE]; cf. 2 Chr 32:3). Finally, the argument that *dĕrašnuhû* refers to the Ark can also be made on the basis of context. David is clearly not blaming the earlier debacle on a failure to seek God, but on improper care for this holy cultic symbol. In this respect, David's remark signals corporate responsibility for the earlier setback. In Chronicles one cannot make an absolute distinction between care for the *sancta* and care for God. Seeking Yhwh is a recurrent theme, but is bound up with proper worship (the Ark, the altar, the Tabernacle, the Temple, the involvement of the priests and Levites, etc.). One seeks God through recourse to these officially prescribed means.

"according to the convention" *(kammišpāṭ)*. Alluding to an established precedent or regulation. The locution *kmšpṭ* is found many times in Chronicles, almost always in a cultic context (1 Chr 6:17; 23:31; 24:19; 2 Chr 4:7, 20; 8:14; 30:16; 35:13; cf. Ezra 3:4; Neh 8:18). Similar adverbial references to legislation occur in the Priestly writing (e.g., Lev 5:10; 9:16), especially in Numbers (15:24; 29:6, 18, 21, 24, 27, 30, 33, 37). The expression *kmšpṭ* "is a mechanism for abbreviating the formulation of the law" (Levine 1993: 396–97). The writer, assuming that the reader knows the legal reference, does not repeat it. Hence, the use of this citation formula in 15:13 reinforces the notion that the previous disaster was caused by disregarding an authoritative ordinance. See further Spawn (2001: 181–83).

15:14. "consecrated themselves to carry the Ark of Yhwh, the God of Israel" (ויתקדשו הכהנים והלוים להעלות את-ארון יהוה אלהי ישׂראל). The verbiage underlines the exact compliance with David's earlier directive in 15:12: "Consecrate yourselves, you and your kinsmen, and you will carry the Ark of Yhwh, the God of Israel" (התקדשו אתם ואחיכם והעליתם את ארון יהוה אלהי ישׂראל).

15:15. "and the Levites carried the Ark of God" (וישׂאו בני-הלוים את ארון האלהים). Again, the narrative underscores that the instructions of David, "No one is to carry the Ark of God except the Levites" (לא לשׂאת את-ארון האלהים כי אם-הלוים; v. 2), were followed.

"as Moses commanded in accordance with the word of Yhwh" (כאשר צוה משה כדבר יהוה). The author acknowledges the nuances of his source (Num 7:1–9), recognizing Moses' role in formulating the details of the Tabernacle arrangements (Num 7:1, 6–9), all the while insisting that these arrangements accorded with a divine imperative (Num 7:4–5).

"by means of poles (*mṭwt*) upon their shoulders [*bktpm*]". The Chronicler asserts that Mosaic law was followed (Num 7:9). In Priestly lore, it was the specific duty of the Qohathites to carry the Ark upon their shoulders (Num 4:15–20). By this standard, the first advance of the Ark violated authoritative precedent because the Ark was carried upon a cart. According to the Priestly work, some of the Tabernacle paraphernalia were to be carried by the Merarites and the Gershonites via oxcarts, but not the most sacred objects, such as the Ark (NOTES to 15:6–7). Some may object to this use of Priestly law to explain the Chronicler's presentation because some of the Chronicler's terminology differs from that of the Priestly writers. It is true that the Priestly term for "poles" is always *bdym* (Exod 25:13–15; 35:12; 37:4, 5; 39:35; 40:20; Num 4:6) and never *mṭwt* (Curtis and Madsen 1910: 214). Yet not too much should be made of the difference in verbiage. The two terms are clearly synonymous. The Chronicler, in conformity with his source (1 Kgs 8:7, 8), also uses the term *bdym* to refer to the staves used to carry the Ark (2 Chr 5:8, 9).

15:16. "David told the Levitical officers." In earlier verses David prepared for the second advance of the Ark by making direct appointments. In this case (15:16–24), he delegates authority to the Levitical officers themselves.

"to appoint *(hʿmyd)* their kinsmen." The use of the *hipʿil* of *ʿmd*, in the sense of "to appoint" is characteristic of LBH (1 Chr 6:16; 15:16; 16:17[//Ps 105:10]; 17:14; 22:2; 2 Chr 8:14; 9:8; 11:15, 22; 19:5, 8; 20:21; 24:13; 25:5, 14; 30:5; 31:2; 33:8; 35:2; Ezra 3:8; Neh 4:3; 6:7; 7:3; 10:33; 12:31; 13:11, 30). See also Dan 11:11, 13, 14. In earlier sources, the *hipʿil* of *ʿmd* usually means "to station" (S. Driver 1914: 535 [#4]; Curtis and Madsen 1910: 32 [#89]).

"singers." The official appointment of singers and musicians is a case in which the Chronicler goes beyond Deuteronomic and Priestly precedent. There are stipulations governing priests, prophets, judges, and kings in Deuteronomy (16:18–18:22), but none governing singers and musicians. Singers and musicians, as a class, do not even appear in Deuteronomy. The Priestly code addresses a great variety of issues and covers many areas not found in Deuteronomy, but the roles to be played by cultic singers and musicians are not among them. With some justification, Kaufmann (1960) refers to the Priestly sanctuary as a sanctuary of silence.

As Levine (1993: 176) observes, the Priestly source hardly ever refers to ritual recitations. But singers and musicians play an integral role in the national administration established by David (see also the COMMENT on 1 Chr 25:1–31). In the reigns of subsequent kings, Levitical choirs are an essential part of the Chronicler's cult, appearing some thirty times in his work (e.g., 1 Chr 6:16, 17; 13:8; 16:7–36; 25:6–7; 2 Chr 23:18; 29:28; cf. Neh 12:27, 46). In highlighting the role of singers, the author's treatment may be compared with the Psalms (e.g., 28:7; 69:31 [ET 69:30]; 137:4).

It would be tempting to see the many references to singers in Chronicles as reflecting the author's own time. The Chronicler's description of David's cultic innovations resonates with and provides a historical precedent for the practice of worship at the Jerusalem Temple in the late Persian or early Hellenistic period. This is undoubtedly true, but the historical situation is surely more complex. The relative absence of singers and musicians from earlier legal and historiographic (biblical) texts is striking for two reasons.

First, musicians and singers were a constituent feature of temple worship in a variety of ancient Near Eastern societies. In urban temples musicians would normally belong to the temple staff and form a hierarchy. In ancient Egypt, as attested in papyri and on reliefs from Abydos, Edfu, Karnak, and other sites, the sacerdotal responsibility of conscrecating the divine image and of satisfying her/him with offerings was performed on a daily basis as a temple ritual (R. Anderson 1995). Although much of this evidence stems from the New Kingdom, scholars believe that such temple rituals had already become a regular daily occurrence in the Old Kingdom. An essential part of this daily service was not only to provide food and drink offerings to the deity but also to entertain him/her with music, songs, and poetry. Temples employed choirs of female and male singers to intone morning and evening hymns (Redford 1995). Singers were often among those involved in the cult of a dead king. In the third century B.C.E., some six hundred singers and three hundred harpists are said to have performed for Philadelphus II (R. Anderson 1995: 2567). Ancient Sumerian and Akkadian literary texts speak of a wide variety of singers, choirs, and orchestras. In ancient Babylon, temple orchestras and choral performances were directed by professional cult musicians *(nâru; kalû)*, and music became part of the "school curriculum" at least as early as the Old Babylonian period (ca. 1800 B.C.E.; Kilmer 1995: 2604). Mention should also be made of the appearance of "singers" *(šrm)* in one of the fifth-century Kition temple tariff inscriptions (*KAI* 37a.6). There the singers are associated with the town in which the holy Queen had her dwelling (Peckham 1968: 311–12).

Second, singers, whether male or female, do appear in some biblical texts (2 Sam 19:36 [ET 19:35]; 1 Kgs 10:12; Ezek 40:44; Qoh 2:8; Pss 68:26 [ET 68:25]; 87:7). Third, there is extra-biblical evidence that indicates that musicians existed in preexilic Jerusalem. Sennacherib's tribute list from Ḥezeqiah mentions both male and female musicians (Oppenheim 1969: 288). The complete absence of singers from the Pentateuch and from most of the Deuteronomistic work tells us more about the limitations of these sources than it does about the conditions at the Jerusalem Temple during the monarchy. Rather than viewing the Chronicler as inventing the tradition of song and music at the Temple, it may be the better part of wisdom to say that he took a special interest in Levitical singers (Kleinig 1993) and sought to advance their cause. His work provides an impeccable precedent for a certain kind of worship at the Jerusalem Temple. The central role given to the Levitical singers during the reign of David justifies an integral liturgical role for their descendants in the author's own time.

"musical instruments" *(kly šyr)*. These figure prominently in national cultic liturgies (1 Chr 16:42; 2 Chr 5:13; 7:6; 23:13; 34:12). Given the declaration that David inaugurates, or at least structures, the Levitical ministry of accompanied music, it is not surprising that in some texts the instruments are associated with David himself (2 Chr 29:25, 26, 27; Neh 12:36; cf. Amos 6:5).

"harps, lyres, and cymbals." That the three are regularly mentioned together in Chronicles (1 Chr 13:8; 15:28; 16:5; 2 Chr 5:12; 29:25) and once in Nehemiah (12:27) suggests that they were thought of as a kind of ensemble accompanying the Levitical singing.

"harps" *(nblym)*. These instruments appear often in the Chronicler's work, always in the context of public worship (1 Chr 16:5; 25:1, 6; 2 Chr 5:12; 9:11; 20:28; 29:25). The *nblym* also appear regularly in the Psalms (57:9 [ET 57:8]; 81:3 [ET 81:2]; 92:4 [ET 92:3]; 108:3 [ET 108:2]; 150:3). On the question of whether the *nēbel* was actually a kind of lyre, see J. Braun (1999).

"making themselves heard" (משמעים). Alternatively, some (e.g., Keil 1873; BDB 1034; Zöckler 1877) think that the *hip'il* of *šm'* is used in this context as a musical convention to mark the time.

15:17. "Heman . . . Asaph . . . Ethan." The same triumvirate of singers is assigned to sound the cymbals (15:19). All three also appear in the Levitical genealogy of 6:16–32, in which Ethan is a descendant of Merari (6:29). The genealogy of Judah also includes an Ethan, who is a son of Zeraḥ (2:6 [2nd NOTE], 8). Elsewhere Ethan (איתן) appears in the superscription to Ps 89 (as an Ezraḥite). But the text of Chronicles does not speak with one voice about the composition of this triumvirate. In 25:1–31 Jeduthun appears in place of Ethan. In this latter passage, David and the officers of the army set the sons of Asaph, Heman, and Jeduthun apart for service, "those prophesying to the accompaniment of lyres, harps, and cymbals" (25:1). The compositional issue affects the very presentation of David's initial rounds of sacerdotal appointments. First Chronicles 16:5, 7, 37 refer to Asaph, whom David appoints to serve in Jerusalem, while 1 Chr 16:41–42 refer to Heman and Jeduthun, whom David appoints to serve at the Tabernacle in Gibeon. As in 25:1, Heman and Jeduthun are accompanied by musical instruments (16:42).

15:18. "of the second rank." Many of the singers are mentioned again in 15:20–21 (see TEXTUAL NOTES). Some, but by no means all, of the names reappear in the list of Levites whom David appoints to serve before the Ark in Jerusalem (16:5–6).

"Zechariah." Perhaps to be compared with the Zechariah of 9:21; 26:2, 14. Zechariah also appears in the list of 16:5 as second in rank to Asaph. The name is Asaphite in 2 Chr 20:14, but priestly in Neh 12:35, 41.

"Uzziel." The name may be reconstructed in the list of 16:5 (see the 3rd TEXTUAL NOTE).

"Shemiramoth" appears again in 16:5. A Levite by this name serves in King Jehoshaphaṭ's judicial reform (2 Chr 17:8).

"Jeḥiel," like many others, reappears in the list of David's Jerusalem cultic appointments (16:5–6).

"Unni." A Levite by this name is mentioned in Qere Neh 12:9. The name is lacking in the list of 16:5–6.

"Eliab" reappears in the list of 16:5–6.

"Benaiah." The name reappears as the name of a priest (15:24). Both reappear as Davidic appointees in 16:5–6. An Asaphite by this name is mentioned in 2 Chr 20:14.

"Maaseiah" is lacking in 16:5.

"Mattithiah." The name, which reappears in 16:5, also appears in 9:31. A Mattithiah is mentioned as a son of Jeduthun in 25:3, 21.

"Eliphalah." Lacking in the account of 16:5.

"Miqneiah" *(miqnēyāhû)*. The PN *(mqnyhw)* appears on an eighth-century-B.C.E. Arad ostracon (Davies, §2.060.4), an eighth- to early-seventh-century seal (Deutsch and Heltzer 1999: 35–36), a seventh-century-B.C.E. seal (Davies, §100.162.1), and a seventh- to sixth-century bulla (Davies, §100.654.2). A related PN appears on the legend of a eighth-century-B.C.E. seal in the Harvard Semitic Museum, *lmqnyw ʿbd yhwh*, "belonging to Miqneyaw, servant of Yhwh" (Davies, §100.272.1, 3). Miqneyaw may have been a member of the cultic staff in the Temple (Cross 1983b) or a senior member of the Temple administration (Millard 1999). The name Miqneiah does not appear in the account of 1 Chr 16:5–6.

"Obed-edom." His status and pedigree in Chronicles differ from those in Samuel (2nd NOTE to 13:13).

"Jeiel." The name reappears in 15:21 and twice in MT 16:5 (see TEXTUAL NOTE).

"Azaziah." The name is not found in 16:5–6.

"gatekeepers" *(šʿrym)*. Gatekeepers play a meaningful role in the genealogies, lists, and narratives of Chronicles. "Gatekeeper" was not simply an honorific title, but denoted important duties. The main obligation of gatekeepers was to guard the sanctuary from possible encroachment. Young Samuel performed such a duty at Shiloh (1 Sam 3:1–3). A guard for the Ark was appointed immediately upon its return from its exile with the Philistines (1 Sam 7:1). One function implicit in the very mission of a gatekeeper was, therefore, military duty (Wright 1990: 69–81). In 9:17–32 gatekeepers serve multiple purposes, not only guard duty but also administration and even baking. Understanding that the Chronicler's gatekeepers can have more than one function sheds some light on the complex presentation of 1 Chr 15, in which there are no less than three lists of gatekeepers (vv. 18, 23, 24). In v. 18 fourteen individuals are appointed as gatekeepers. These should be understood, as the general description implies, simply as a class. The lists of vv. 23 and 24 are more specific. On the gatekeepers' functions, see further the COMMENT on 26:1–19.

15:19–21. “the singers.” The complete overlap between the names in these verses and those that appear earlier (15:17–18) reflects the division of the appointees (15:17–18) into three sections, according to their musical responsibilities.

15:20. “set to (the voice of) young women” *(ʿal ʿălāmôt)*. My assumption is that these “young women” were singers or musicians involved in the cult. Alternatively, the allusion may be to female musicians trained to play particular stringed instruments *(nblym)*. Among the personnel mentioned in the fifth-century Phoenician Kition tariff inscriptions, which list expenses incurred by a temple in two distinct months, are *ʿlmt*. The term *ʿlmt* appears, in fact, twice in one line, *lʿlmt wlʿlmt* 22 *bzbḥ* (*KAI* 37B.9). The second group of *ʿlmt* are involved in some capacity with sacrifice, but the identity and function of these two sets of young women are unclear. Because the term appears twice, some think that it has two different meanings, for example, “prostitutes” and “musicians,” hence, “for the prostitutes and the twenty-two musicians at the sacrifice” (Van den Branden 1966: 262; Peckham 1968: 323). Whatever the case, the former meaning is much less secure than the latter meaning. In describing processions into the sanctuary, the psalmist writes:

The singers (שרים) come after the musicians (נגנים),
in the midst of young women striking the drums (עלמות תופפות;
Ps 68:26 [ET 68:25]; cf. Exod 15:20; Judg 11:34; 21:21; 1 Sam 18:6; Jer 31:4, 13). Among the state records of Neo-Assyrian court staff are lists of a variety of female personnel, including palace heralds, weavers, chief cupbearers, cupbearers, bakers, scribes, temple stewardesses, smiths, stone borers, treasurers, and harem governesses (Fales and Postgate 1992: 32–35). Of particular relevance in this context is the mention of female chief musicians (§24.20), female musicians (§24.27), and female singers (§25.7). Finally, it should be recalled that ancient Egyptian temple choirs were made up mostly of women. The hymns offered by such groups were an important component of worship services.

15:19. “Heman, Asaph, Ethan.” This troika (see 15:17) is given the special responsibility of sounding the bronze cymbals mentioned in the description of David’s appointment (15:16).

15:21. “to lead” *(lnṣḥ)*. That is, to orchestrate and lead the service of praise. In the *piʿel*, the verbal root *nṣḥ* appears only in Chronicles (1 Chr 23:4; 2 Chr 2:1, 17; 34:13), Ezra (3:8, 9), Habakkuk (3:19), and fifty-five psalm titles. In the context of the Psalms, *lmnṣḥ* is usually translated as “for the music/choir director.”

15:22–24. “Chenaniah.” The agreement between the Levitical lists of 15:17–18 and 15:19–21 largely breaks down in these verses. Most of the figures, such as the Levitical officer Chenaniah and the seven priests (15:24), appear for the first time. There is, moreover a contrast between what these verses narrate and what the mandate of v. 16 stipulated, namely, that the Levitical officers *(śry hlwym)* were to appoint “their kinsmen the singers.” In vv. 22–24, one finds appointments pertaining to: Chenaniah, a Levitical officer *(śr hlwym)*, to oversee the Ark’s transport (v. 22), seven priests to sound the trumpets before the Ark’s advance (v. 23), and two gatekeepers to attend to the Ark (v. 24).

15:23. “Berechiah and Elqanah.” Lists of gatekeepers also occur in 15:18, and

24, but neither Berechiah nor Elqnanah appear in these other contexts. The only other Berechiah appears as the patronym of Asaph (15:17).

"gatekeepers." While the persons appointed earlier were simply assigned to the general office of gatekeeper (15:18), the individuals in 15:23, 24 are appointed to play a more precise role, as "gatekeepers for the Ark."

15:24. "Shebaniah, Joshaphaṭ, Nethanel, Amasai, Zechariah, Benaiah, and Eliezer." Benaiah will later be assigned to the Ark cultus in Jerusalem (16:6), while the rest of the priests are apparently assigned to the Gibeon cultus headed by Zadoq (16:39–43). The claim that seven priests performed as trumpeters (מחצצרים בחצצרות) before the advance of the Ark is striking, given the pattern of other biblical texts. A similar construction occurs in the depiction of the Israelite procession around Jericho. There seven priests march with seven horns (שופרות) for seven days around the town (Josh 6:4). Nine priests officiate at the dedication of Jerusalem's wall in the time of Nehemiah (Neh 12:35–36).

"Obed-edom and and Jeḥiah—gatekeepers for the Ark." The name Obed-edom also appears in 15:18, referring to a Levite assigned to play the lyre. The authors of Chronicles may hold to the existence of two individuals by the name of Obed-edom, both of whom are Levites (1 Chr 13:13; 15:18, 21, 24, 25; 16:5, 38; 26:4, 8, 15; 2 Chr 25:24; Dirksen 1996a). First Chronicles 16:38 distinguishes between Obed-edom and his sixty-eight kinsmen and Obed-edom son of Jeduthun. The former is a musician, while the latter is a gatekeeper. The later treatment of gatekeepers (26:1–19) situates Obed-edom's pedigree in the context of the phratry of Qohath through Qoraḥ (cf. Exod 6:21, 24; 1 Chr 6:7–9; 9:19). See further the NOTE to 26:4. Over against the multiple references to Obed-edom, the name Jeḥiah does not appear again.

"sounding the trumpets before the Ark." The "trumpet" (*ḥṣṣrh*; 15:24, 28) is to be distinguished from the "horn" (*šwpr*; 15:28). LXX Psalm 97:6 [MT 98:6] translates *ḥṣṣrwt* as *salpigxin elatais*, "metal trumpets," and *šwpr* as *salpinggos keratinēs*, "horn trumpet." The latter was a curved horn of a ram or cow, which was used in a variety of contexts: to signal a war (Judg 3:27; 6:34; 7:8; 1 Sam 13:3; Jer 4:5), to crown monarchs (2 Sam 15:10; 1 Kgs 1:34, 39, 41; 2 Kgs 9:13), to announce rebellion (2 Sam 20:1), and to scare an enemy (Judg 7:8, 16–22). Antecedents to such short horns may be found in Ḫatti (Duchesne-Guillemin 1981: 291; Plate 40). The horn was also employed in certain cultic contexts (Josh 6:4; Lev 25:9; 2 Sam 6:15; Joel 2:15; Pss 47:6 [ET 47:5]; 81:4 [ET 81:3]; 2 Chr 15:14). The *ḥṣṣrh* was a straight metal horn with a flaring mouth, usually employed in cultic contexts and almost always by priests (Num 10:2–10; Hos 5:8; 2 Kgs 12:14; 1 Chr 13:8; 15:24, 28; 16:6, 42; 2 Chr 5:12; 13:14; 15:14; 20:28; 29:26, 27; Ezra 3:10; Neh 12:35, 41; Sir 50:16; 1QM 2.15–3.11; 7.9; 9.9; Josephus, *Ant.* 3.291–294; Milgrom 1990: 372–73). But given the Chronicler's consistent presentation of Israel's wars as sacral wars, a hard and fast distinction between martial and cultic contexts cannot be maintained (contra Curtis and Madsen 1910: 216).

15:25–28. At this point in the narrative Chronicles rejoins its biblical source. The account of the Ark's successful procession is modified from that of 2 Sam 6:12–15.

15:25. "the elders." The involvement of this traditional institution is not found in Samuel. There David simply retrieves the Ark (2 Sam 6:12). The reference recalls the involvement of "all the elders of Israel" in David's anointing (11:3).

"the officers of the thousands" *(śry h'lpym)*. Like the reference to the participation of the elders, this reference is not found in Samuel. The depiction recalls David's taking counsel with "the officers of the thousands and the hundreds" *(hśry h'lpym whm'wt)* prior to his first attempt to retrieve the Ark (13:1). In this respect, the Chronicler, having introduced certain figures to his audience, likes to bring them back on stage at appropriate points in his presentation. By mentioning the involvement of both the elders (see previous NOTE) and the officers, the author underlines the broad support David enjoyed in his campaign to station the Ark in a new setting.

"went forth joyfully." Joy characterizes practically all of the major communal liturgies in Chronicles. The use of songs and musical instruments, perhaps a feature of temple worship in the author's own day, is emblematic of such celebrations (15:16).

15:26. "And God helped the Levites" *(wyhy bʿzr h'lhym 't hlwym)*. This statement, not found in Samuel (see TEXTUAL NOTE), is most likely from the Chronicler's own hand. The God who calls the Levites to perform a special and difficult task also helps them to accomplish it. "The God who had hindered (13:10–12) now helps" (Eskenazi 1995: 268). In analyzing the causes of the earlier failure to advance the Ark, the Chronicler's David points to the failure to observe proper protocol (15:13). In this view, Israel is to worship God through divinely prescribed channels. But as much as the writer emphasizes proper procedure, he also maintains that divine initiative is a source of the Levitical tribe's success. The comment is broadly consistent with a major theme in one of David's blessings: "Everything is from you, and from your hand have we given back to you" (29:14).

"seven bulls and seven rams." In Samuel, David sacrifices an ox and a fatling (or a fatted ox; Freedman, personal communication) every six paces (2 Sam 6:13), but in Chronicles a numerically balanced number of seven sacrifices is offered. For similar ratios, see Num 23:1; Job 42:8; and 2 Chr 29:21.

15:27. "clothed in a robe of fine linen." The Chronicler's depiction of festal apparel constitutes a tour de force when compared to the earlier depiction in Samuel. In Chronicles not only is David fully clothed, but so are "all the Levites, those carrying the Ark and those singing." In 2 Sam 6:14 David is simply clad in a linen ephod, but in Chronicles this linen ephod accompanies David's other clothing. The contrast between Samuel and Chronicles continues in the following verses. In 2 Sam 6:20 a scantily clad David is rebuked by an indignant Michal. But the Chronicler omits this rebuke and David's forbidding reaction (2 Sam 6:21–23). The combination of revisions and omissions transforms this entire subplot in the Samuel narrative. On sacerdotal vestments, see further Exod 28:39–43; Sir 45:8. On the priestly ephod, see Exod 28:6–14.

15:28. "all Israel." The Chronicler's concluding summary resonates with earlier parts of his narrative. "All Israel," earlier assembled by David for the precise purpose of carrying the Ark to the tent pitched for it (15:3), does so.

"with trumpets, with cymbals sounding, with harps, and with lyres." Referring to the participation of both the priests (15:24) and the Levites (15:16, 19–21).

15:29. "Michal daughter of Saul." The retention of this notice from 2 Sam 6:16 might, at first glance, seem odd. Why does the Chronicler, having omitted the narrative depicting Michal's scolding of David (2 Sam 6:20–23), include this short vignette? For some commentators the inclusion of this notice results from incomplete and inconsistent editing, "a mark of the unskillful art of the Chronicler" (Curtis and Madsen 1910: 219). But the text should be read in the context of Chronicles, which presents its own distinctive perspective on Saul, his household, and the tribe of Benjamin, from which Saul stems. The fall of Saul results from Saul's own apostasy (10:13–14; 13:3). The transfer of the kingdom to David results from a divine decision (10:14; 12:24). Recognizing the presence of Yhwh with David, members of Saul's own tribe defect to David (12:1–8, 17). The decision to retrieve the Ark stems from its neglect during the regime of Saul (13:3). Given the Chronicler's recontextualization and recasting of older material, a different perspective emerges from that found in Samuel. In Samuel, Michal has legitimate grounds for complaint. But in Chronicles, which depicts David as properly attired and well-behaved, Michal's contempt is baseless. Her reaction to David, however, is, consistent with her father's earlier posture toward the Ark (Japhet 1993a). In Chronicles, Michal's attitude reflects badly on her and the fallen Saulide house she represents.

"dancing and performing." The behavior of David and the other participants is consistent with the pattern of ancient Near Eastern festivals, which featured banquets, sports, miming, and singing to honor the gods (2nd TEXTUAL NOTE to 13:8).

16:1–3. This material, with some modifications, is drawn from the author's *Vorlage* of 2 Sam 6:17–19.

16:1. "when they brought up (ויביאו) . . . they stationed (ויציגו)." The subject is unclear. The nearest pl. antecedent is "all Israel" in 15:28, but "the Levites" mentioned in 15:26 are also a possibility. In the parallel (2 Sam 6:17–18), David is consistently the subject (see TEXTUAL NOTES). But 1 Chr 16:1 presents the pl. three times. To complicate matters further, 16:2 mentions that David "finished sacrificing the burnt offerings and the offerings of well-being." This may be a case in which the Chronicler is adapting material from his *Vorlage* to underscore the broad participation of king, priestly personnel, and people in a national festal occasion.

"the tent." David's establishment of a tent for the Ark (15:1) finally fulfills its purpose. That the Ark needed a shelter may be illumined by ancient Near Eastern precedent (Cross 1981; Weinfeld 1983: 95–129). Tents for deities are mentioned in Hittite texts (*KUB* 35.135; RS 20). In Ugaritic myths El lives in a tent (*ḏd*) located at the mouth of the two rivers (*KTU* 1.2.3.4–5; 3.5.5–8; 4.4.20–26; 6.1.32–36; 17.6.46–48). The textual evidence associating the residence or presence of a deity with a tent is complemented by archaeological evidence. The miniature house or shelter that housed a silver calf discovered at ancient Ashqelon (Stager 1991b: 24) provides a broad parallel to the notion of a tent shrine for the Ark. The Ashqelon model served as a house for the cultic symbol (the silver calf). As such, the shelter has also been usefully compared with clay receptacles for divine symbols from T. Munqaba, Kāmid el-Lōz, Ugarit, Deir ʿAlla, Cyprus, and Crete (Bretschneider 1993: 13–32). Temporary shrines for deities are attested in ancient Mesopotamian texts that deal with the destructive aftermath of an enemy invasion or the rebuilding of a sanctuary (Hurowitz 1993). During the reconstruction of a temple, a period of transition for the cult, the deity's statue would need to be housed elsewhere. In some cases, the divine image might simply be relocated to another shrine, but in other cases a short-term structure might be built for the deity. The terminology used for such buildings is itself revealing: "a small reed sanctuary," a "temporary sanctuary" *(bīt umakkal)*, a "secret place" *(puzru)*, a "second sanctuary" *(bīti šanimma)*. Whatever the differences between them, these structures are seen as provisional in nature. It may well be that the Chronicler thought of David's tent shrine along these lines. The question of the adequacy of a tent shrine for Yhwh will be raised later by David himself (2 Sam 7:2//1 Chr 17:1). In the context of the Chronicler's work, the antiquity of the association between Yhwh and a tent goes uncontested (17:5–6//2 Sam 7:6–7), but the tent provided by David is only a temporary shrine for Israel's God.

"burnt offerings." As the name suggests, these sacrifices would be completely incinerated on the altar (Lev 1:3–17). An *ʿōlâ*, which could only be an animal, had propitiatory and expiatory functions, covering a wide range of motives, such as devotion, appeasement, and thanksgiving.

"offerings of well-being" *(šĕlāmîm)*. Unlike burnt offerings, these sacrifices would be largely eaten by worshipers near the altar (Lev 3:1–17; Milgrom 1991: 202–25). If there is a common denominator to the offering of various *šĕlāmîm*, it is rejoicing (Deut 27:7).

16:2. "blessed the people." In the Sinatic era, Moses concludes the successful construction of the Tabernacle (Exod 39:42) by blessing the people (39:43). So also David blesses all the people after the Ark was successfully placed in its sacred precinct within the City of David. The parallel between Sinai and Zion undergirds royal Davidic authority and the notion that the Ark finds its rightful place in Jerusalem.

16:3. "apportioned to every Israelite person." The actions of king and people recall other corporate celebrations in the past, such as the ritual banquet at Sinai (Exod 24:1–11) and the earlier festive banquet at Ḥebron (1 Chr 12:40–41). The Chronicler is a believer in feasting and public festivals; they occur at certain highpoints in his work (1 Chr 29:20–22; 2 Chr 7:8–10; 20:27–28; 29:30–36; 30:21–27). This particular ceremony brings the movement begun in 13:1 to its culmination. The foodstuffs provide refreshment to the people. Yet the celebration hosted by David also forms a transition to what follows. David seizes upon this festive occasion to make the service of praise that characterized the ascent of the Ark (15:25–29) a constituent feature of public worship in Jerusalem.

## Sources and Composition

Since the composition of 1 Chr 15 is intimately tied to the composition of 1 Chr 16, the discussion of the sources and editing of this chapter will be taken up in the commentary on 1 Chr 16:4–43.

## Structure and Context

Scholars have expended considerable effort attempting to reconstruct the editorial history of 1 Chr 15, but they have devoted remarkably little attention to its organization and context. Like the authors of Samuel, the Chronicler depicts the successful ascent of the Ark as taking place after David has twice defeated the Philistines. Yet as we have seen, the Chronicler situates these wars immediately prior to the second effort to retrieve the ancient palladium (1 Chr 14:8–17; cf. 2 Sam 5:17–25). Like Samuel, Chronicles associates the successful ascent of the Ark with a national celebration (1 Chr 16:1–3; cf. 2 Sam 6:17–19). But the Chronicler, unlike the authors of Samuel, prefaces that ascent with material depicting David's public works, a national assembly, the appointment of Levites and priests, and definitions of their roles. The similarities and differences may be summarized in the table below. As the outline indicates, the many additions to Samuel transform the earlier account. Those lists and narratives that do not appear in Samuel communicate the solemnity and importance of this occasion for the authors of Chronicles (Eskenazi 1995). The chapter begins with David building domiciles for himself, preparing a sacred precinct for the Ark, and mandating that the Levites exercise exclusive control over the Ark's porterage. The attention then turns to the populace as a whole. The king assembles all Israel to convey the cultic symbol to its new home. The author later returns to this pan-Israel theme as David, the el-

| | *1 Chronicles* | *2 Samuel* |
|---|---|---|
| Wars against the Philistines | 14:8–17 | 5:17–25 |
| Houses for David and a Tent for the Ark | 15:1–2 | — |
| David Convokes a National Assembly | 15:3 | — |
| David Convenes the Aaronides and Levites | 15:4–10 | — |
| David's Charge to the Priests and Levites | 15:11–13 | — |
| Priestly and Levitical Compliance | 15:14–15 | — |
| David's Instructions to the Levites | 15:16 | — |
| Levitical Appointments | 15:17–24 | — |
| The Joyful Procession of the Ark | 15:25–28 | 6:12–15 |
| Michal's Displeasure with David's Conduct | 15:29 | 6:16 |
| National Celebration | 16:1–3 | 6:17–19 |
| Michal's Rebuke of David | — | 6:20–23 |

ders, and the officers retrieve the palladium from the house of Obed-edom. A broad social focus is maintained as "all Israel" carries the Ark into the City of David. Excepting Michal's displeasure, the ascent of the Ark is an occasion of national solidarity and great joy. The narrative in Samuel appends a description of the quarrel between Michal and David following the festivities for the Ark. Because the Chronicler omits this material, his narrative ends climactically with the communal banquet.

In between the all-Israel axis with which the text begins and ends, one finds David gathering priests and Levites, instructing them, and assigning them responsibilities. After making a general decree about the Ark's transport (15:2) and mobilizing the Aaronides and the Levites (v. 4), David orders the Aaronides and the Levites to consecrate themselves (vv. 11–13). In vv. 16–24 David attends to a second order of business, delegating to the Levitical leadership the task of making a series of subordinate appointments. In this manner, Chronicles depicts the king as playing a sustained role in ensuring that the second procession is successful. As the following table indicates, the author underlines royal authority by declaring that the priests and Levites obeyed each and every one of David's orders.

| *Davidic Order* | *Sacerdotal Obedience* |
|---|---|
| Levitic porterage (v. 2) | Levitic porterage (v. 15) |
| Consecration (vv. 11–13) | Consecration (v. 14) |
| Subappointments (v. 16) | Subappointments (vv. 17–24) |

To this emphasis on submission can be added another. The elders, officers, and people respond in a uniformly positive way to David's initiatives. The subject matter shifts often in 1 Chr 15, but David remains a constant. His words and work drive the action. To be sure, there is much material in the chapter dealing with Levitical and priestly appointees and assignments. But this is only part of the story. It is David who meticulously lays the groundwork for the Ark's parade into Zion by convening the Aaronides and Levites, defining their roles, ordering the priests and the Levites to consecrate themselves, and commanding the Levites to appoint singers and musicians. The question that must be addressed is, therefore, more basic than the question that has dominated most scholarly treatments, the question of sacerdotal matters. Given that the priestly and Levitical arrangements begin, proceed, and follow royal directives, why does the author evince such a fundamental preoccupation with Davidic leadership?

## COMMENT

In his discussion of Samuel's portrayal of the Ark's journey into Jerusalem, McCarter (1983; 1984: 180–82) calls attention to a ceremonial motif found in some ancient Near Eastern accounts narrating the introduction of a national god to a new royal city. These ceremonies consisted of a royal invitation of the gods and goddesses into the city, feasting, royal dedicatory gifts, royal sacrifices, and the participation of the populace in a large celebration. Such festivities were held following the (re)construction of the city in question and the erection of one or more royal palaces. The parallels lead McCarter (1984: 180) to conclude that 2 Sam 6:1–19 is "an account of the introduction of Yhwh, present in his holy ark, to the City of David." McCarter's arguments are insightful, but need to be modified, at least with respect to the situation in Chronicles. The connection with a royal city and a royal residence is not a problem. In Chronicles David enjoys the comfort of the town he fortified and Joab restored (11:7–9), the new palace built for him by Ḥuram of Tyre (14:1), and the dwellings he built for himself (15:1). Yet in Chronicles David invites the religious symbol to a specific "place" (*māqôm*), or sacred precinct, within his royal city. In other words, the destination of the Ark is neither the royal palace nor David's domiciles, but the tent specifically prepared for it. That the writer conceives of the place for the Ark as a sacred site is confirmed by the following narrative in which David appoints a full complement of cultic personnel to attend the Ark at its new Jerusalem home (16:4–6, 37–38). Hence, in observing the coordination between city construction and palace dedication, one should also attend to the coordination between city construction and cult-center (re)construction. Obviously, given the close links in the ancient Near East between palace and temple, king and cult, royal patronage and religious observance, the two situations are not mutually exclusive and one can find the same monarch claiming to have (re)built a city, a palace, and a cult center.

A few examples drawn from ancient Assyrian royal inscriptions will illumine specific features of the exposition. Upon the construction of his new royal city at Calah (Nineveh), various temples, and his palace in Calah, Ashurnasirpal II (883–859 B.C.E.) consecrated the palace and bid Ashur, as well as the other gods and goddesses of the land, to take up residence (*ARAB* I, §§467, 468, 511; Grayson 1976: §§A.O.101.3:132–36; 2:52–62; 17:v 1–24a; 29:9′–17′). Ashurnasirpal established festivals, offered the deities abundant sacrifices, and hosted an immense banquet, lasting ten days (Grayson 1976: §§A.O.101.30:74–140). To this incredible feast he claims to have invited 47,074 men and women from every part of his land, 5,000 dignitaries and foreign envoys, 16,000 people of Calah, and 1,500 *zarīqū* of his palace (Grayson 1976: §§ A.O.101.30:141–150). According to Ashurnasirpal, the mood was one of celebration and joy: "For ten days I gave them food, I gave them drink, I had them bathed, I had them anointed. (So) did I honor them (and) send them back to their lands in peace and joy" (Grayson 1976: §§A.O.30:151–54).

A number of inscriptions pertaining to the reign of Sargon II (721–705 B.C.E.) show a similar progression. The Display Inscription from the palace at Khorsabad relates how Sargon II built Dûr Šarrukîn ("Sargon City"), constructed a "palace without rival," invited the gods and goddesses to take up residence "in a favorable month on an auspicious day," established unceasing offerings, appointed priests, and "instituted a feast of music" (*ARAB* II, §§72, 73, 74). When the gods and goddesses entered their city "amid jubilation and feasting," princes, scribes, superintendents, nobles, officials, and elders were all in attendance (*ARAB* II, §74; cf. §§91–100, 138). The pattern of inviting deities to a reconstructed or new royal city, presenting them with sacrifices, and preparing a feast for the people of the land is also found in the memorial inscriptions of Sennacherib (704–681 B.C.E.).

This Assyrian ruler recounts how he rebuilt and enlarged Nineveh and constructed a new palace (*ARAB* II, §§363, 399). After completing his building campaign, Sennacherib invited Ashur, as well as the other gods and goddesses, into its midst, and offered them gifts and sacrifices. As with the celebration presided over by Sargon, the festivities hosted by Sennacherib had a corporate emphasis: "I drenched the foreheads of my people with wine and with mead; I sprinkled their hearts" (*ARAB* II, §§370, 403, 416).

Esarhaddon (680–669 B.C.E.) speaks of inviting Ashur, Ishtar of Nineveh, and all the deities of Assyria to Nineveh following Esarhaddon's restoration of the royal palace there (*ARAB* II, §§699, 700). Like Sargon and Sennacherib, Esarhaddon offered sacrifices and hosted festivities for nobles and people alike. In a different text, the so-called Akkadian inscription (Frame, §B.6.31.11), Esarhaddon reviews a number of his exploits, including his reconstruction of Babylon and Esagila. Esarhaddon claims that he reconfirmed a system of regular offerings, caused Marduk to reside in Esagila again, reconfirmed the income of the gods, established appropriate procedures at the great cult centers, and ensured that purification rites were performed correctly (Frame, §B.6.31.11.7–13; cf.§B.6.31.15.15–25). There is also, as McCarter (1984: 181–82) points out, an example of this ceremonial pattern in the eighth-century inscriptions of Azitawadda, the self-professed king of the Danunians. This ruler (re)built and dedicated a city he named Azitawaddiya (modern Karatepe in southern Turkey) and caused Ba'l-*krntryš* to take up residence there (*KAI* 26.A.II.9-III.2; Rosenthal 1969: 653–54). He also encouraged the offering of sacrifices for the images *(mskt)* there and, with the help of the gods Baal and Rešep, provided the town with plentiful food (*KAI* 26.A.II.12–13).

The congruence between specific features of these aforementioned inscriptions and the narratives in Samuel and Chronicles are intriguing. Since there are, as we have seen, some differences between the narrations of Samuel and Chronicles, my comments will focus on the parallels with Chronicles. Having rebuilt Jerusalem and constructed his houses within the city of David, the king sponsors the procession of the holy Ark, associated with Yhwh's presence, into his royal city. Like Ashurnasirpal, Sargon, Sennacherib, and Esarhaddon, David hosts a celebration characterized by rejoicing, music, and feasting. As in the Assyrian texts, the festivities are joined by various officials and the people at large. In each case a mood of joy pervades the ceremonies. Both the Assyrian kings and King David take a special interest in cult. Both Esarhaddon and David ensure that purification rites are performed. Both the Assyrian monarchs and King David offer sacrifices. Like David, Sargon appoints priests and institutes a "feast of music." Like Ashurnasirpal, David takes a personal interest in providing personnel for the new enterprise. David, Ashurnasirpal, and Esarhaddon establish proper procedures and rites in the royal cities they (re)establish.

Beyond noting parallels between the Assyrian and biblical texts, however, one should explore their significance. In the ancient Mediterranean world monarchs were expected to attend to infrastructure and to be efficient builders, beneficent rulers, and capable administrators. Monarchs were also expected to support the cult. The (re)construction of cities, palaces, and temples redounded to the credit of the rulers responsible for them. Aside from (re)building sanctuaries, monarchs were supposed to patronize and endow them. In this context, it is worth observing that many of the aforementioned Assyrian texts, as well as the inscriptions of Azitawadda, contain concluding invocations in which the king requests a blessing and conveys his hope that his good deeds will be remembered by deities and future rulers (e.g., *ARAB* II, §§75, 371, 404, 690, 700; *KAI* 26.A.III.2–11; C.III.16-IV.12). Conversely, in some cases, curses are directed toward those who would deface the royal inscription (e.g., *ARAB* II, §§90, 94; *KAI* 26.C.IV.13–20). The texts themselves commemorate royal accomplishments. In Chronicles there is no direct royal invocation of the deity's favor. But the Chronicler's own act of writing may be understood in a similar way. As the accomplishments of the Assyrian kings and Azitawadda reflect well on them, so the pious deeds performed by David reflect well on him and on his legacy. In Chronicles, the monarch's persistence and punctilious care for the Ark are a credit to him, to his administration, and to the city he founded.

There is an additional aspect to David's reputation. Unlike the Assyrian and Phoenician inscriptions, which *ipso facto* constitute discrete texts, the story of how David ushers the Ark to the tent he pitched for it in his royal city is part of a larger narrative complex that sheds light on this particular episode in David's life. Comparison of the two ark narratives reveals some interesting differences between their respective portrayals of David. In the first story David convenes all Israel, invites the priests and Levites, retrieves the Ark, and leads a joyful procession, but he does not personally attend to the care of the cultic symbol itself. When the first procession fails dramatically with Uzza's death, David suspends the operation, becomes angry, and is distraught. But he does not abandon the quest. As a resilient leader, he presses on. The Chronicler's David is also an astute expositor of the Torah. In conformity with an interpretation of Pentateuchal (Deuteronomic and Priestly) law (see NOTES), the king concludes that the reason for the first debacle was the noninvolvement of priests and Levites in carrying the Ark. In this manner, the Chronicler casts David as a devout and resourceful leader. The king accepts the divine verdict, adapts to the changed circumstances, and rectifies matters.

Analysis of the second ark procession sheds light on an important issue in the interpretation of the Chronicler's work. Some have viewed a separation of royal affairs from cultic affairs as a hallmark of the Chronicler's ideology, but such a distinction can be overdrawn. To be sure, the author holds to different spheres of royal and priestly sovereignty (e.g., 2 Chr 19:11; 26:16–21). David is perfectly capable of delegating responsibility to the priests and Levites. Since the author configures the time of David and Solomon as a golden age in Israel's past, the roles taken by the priests and Levites during the time of David establish a pattern for the author's own time. Yet this pattern also includes substantial royal involvement in the definition of sacerdotal roles. A comparison may be drawn with the law of the king found in the *Temple Scroll*, which rewrites and expands social and political legislation found in Deuteronomy (11Q19; 11Q20; Yadin 1983). One of the provisions limiting royal authority in the *Temple Scroll* states that the king is subject to a tripartite council, consisting of thirty-six members: twelve princes of his people (נשׂיי עמו), twelve members drawn from the priests, and twelve members drawn from the Levites (11Q1957.11–14). The large assembly greatly circumscribes the king's independence, because this council carries authority to set policy together with the king "so that his heart will not be exalted above them" (57:14; cf. Deut 17:20). The scope of this critical check on royal power is comprehensive; the monarch "shall do nothing without them with respect to anything" (57:14–15).

The author holds to mutual support between the royal and priestly spheres. The king consults with his military commanders and the assembly of Israel (קהל ישׂראל) prior to his first attempt to move the Ark (13:1–4). But there is also a major difference. Administratively speaking, kings are in charge. Monarchs are supposed to support the cult and cultic officials are normally supposed to obey their royal rulers. The presentation may shed some light on the Chronicler's own purposes and objectives. The writer lived at a time in which Davidides were not in charge of the political affairs of Yehud. The province of Judah had its own temple in Jerusalem, but was subject to the greater authority of the Persian crown. The Second Temple owed its construction in part to the efforts of the Davidide Zerubbabel and the high priest Jeshua, but the edifice was authorized and supported by a succession of Achaemenid kings (2 Chr 36:22–23; Ezra 1:1–4, 7–11; 5:13–16; 6:1–12; 7:11–24, 27–28; 8:36; 9:9; Neh 2:8–9, 18; 5:14; 11:23; 13:6). The author reclaims the Temple and its cultus for the Davidides. The priests and the Levites are not autonomous, but function as part of a national administration. Even in demarcating the respective duties of Levites and priests, the Chronicler's royalism shines through. It is after all in Chronicles, and not in Samuel, that David spearheads the efforts to establish a sacred precinct for the Ark and becomes intimately involved in directing the priests and Levites to bring the Ark to David's tent. The earlier failed attempt leads to considerably more, not less, direct royal involvement in religious affairs. To be sure, David allows the priests and Levites to play their respective roles in congruence with the Chronicler's interpretation and reapplication of biblical law. In one case, the king delegates authority to the Levites to make their own internal appointments (15:16–24). Nevertheless, in contrast with the constitution regulating officeholders in Deuteronomy (16:18–18:22) and its later rewrite in the *Temple Scroll*, the sacerdocy takes its orders from David. The Chronicler's king, much like the Mesopotamian kings discussed earlier, is in command. Precisely because David analyzes the root causes of the earlier disaster and directs the second procession, the second attempt is successful in bringing the Ark to its new home.

# *XIX. The Ark in Jerusalem and the Tabernacle in Gibeon (16:4–43)*

*The Establishment of a Cultus for the Ark in Jerusalem*

4 And he [David] stationed some of the Levites as ministers before the Ark of Yhwh to commemorate, to give thanks, and to give praise to Yhwh, the God of Israel: 5 Asaph the head; Zechariah his second in command; Jeiel, Shemiramoth,

Jeḥiel, Mattithiah, Eliab, Benaiah, Obed-edom, and Uzziel with harps and with
lyres; and Asaph sounding the cymbals; 6 and Benaiah and Jaḥaziel the priests
with trumpets regularly before the Ark of the Covenant of God.

*The Ministry of Song*

7 Then, on that day, David first put Asaph and his kinsmen in charge of giving thanks to Yhwh.

8 Give thanks to Yhwh;
call upon his name;
make known his deeds among the peoples.
9 Sing to him; laud him;
muse about all his wonderful deeds.
10 Boast in his holy name;
let the heart of those seeking Yhwh rejoice.
11 Seek Yhwh and his strength;
search out his presence regularly;
12 Remember his wonders that he has accomplished;
his signs and the judgments of his mouth.
13 O seed of Israel his servant,
O sons of Jacob, his elect ones,
14 he is Yhwh our God;
his judgments are throughout the land.
15 Remember his covenant forever,
the word he commanded to the thousandth generation,
16 that which he cut with Abraham,
his oath to Isaac,
17 he confirmed it as a statute to Jacob,
to Israel as an everlasting covenant,
18 saying, "To you I shall give the land of Canaan,
the territory of your inheritance."
19 When you were scant in number,
a few and sojourning in it,
20 wandering from nation to nation,
from one kingdom to another people,
21 he did not permit anyone to oppress them;
he disciplined kings on their account:
22 "Do not strike my anointed ones;
do not mistreat my prophets."
23 Sing to Yhwh all the earth;
proclaim his deliverance from day to day.
24 Recount his glory among the nations,
his wonders among all the peoples,
25 for great is Yhwh and greatly praised;
feared he is above all the gods.
26 Indeed, all the gods of the peoples are nonentities,
but Yhwh made the heavens.
27 Thanksgiving and majesty are before him;

strength and joy are in his place.
28 Ascribe to Yhwh, O families of the peoples,
ascribe to Yhwh honor and strength.
29 Ascribe to Yhwh the honor due his name;
carry tribute and come before him;
worship Yhwh, majestic in holiness.
30 Tremble, all the earth, before him;
the world is established; it cannot be shaken.
31 Let the heavens rejoice and the earth give cheer;
let them say among the nations, "Yhwh reigns!"
32 Let the sea and its fullness thunder;
let the fields and everything within them exult.
33 Then let the trees of the forest shout for joy
from before Yhwh,
because he comes to judge the earth.
34 Give thanks to Yhwh, for he is good,
for his loyalty endures forever.
35 Say, "Deliver us, O God of our deliverance;
gather us and liberate us from the nations,
to give thanks to your holy name,
to boast in your praise.
36 Blessed is Yhwh, the God of Israel,
from ages past to forevermore."
And all the people said, "Amen" and "Praise Yhwh!"

*Continuation of Jerusalem Appointments*

37 And he [David] left Asaph and his kinsmen there before the Ark of the Covenant of Yhwh to serve regularly before the Ark of Yhwh as each day required:
38 Obed-edom, Jeḥiel, and their kinsmen—68; Obed-edom son of Jeduthun and
Ḥosah—gatekeepers.

*The Investiture of the Tabernacle Cultus in Gibeon*

16:39 [He left] Zadoq the priest and his kinsmen the priests before the Tabernacle of Yhwh, at the high place that is in Gibeon, 40 to sacrifice burnt offerings to
Yhwh upon the altar, the regular morning and evening burnt offering according
to all that was written in the Torah of Yhwh, which he enjoined upon Israel;
41 with them were Heman and Jeduthun and the rest of the select who were designated by name to give thanks to Yhwh, for his loyalty endures forever; 42 with them
trumpets and cymbals for sounding, instruments of the song of God; the sons of Jeduthun to be at the gate. 43 Then all the people departed, each to his own house,
and David returned to bless his house.

## TEXTUAL NOTES

16:4. "stationed." On this meaning of the verb *ntn,* see *HALOT* 734a–b.

"the Ark of Yhwh." So MT *(lectio brevior)*. LXX "the Ark of the Covenant of Yhwh."

"some of the Levites." The prep. *min* carries a partitive sense (Williams, §324).

"ministers" *(mšrtym)*. So MT. LXX is similar *(leitourgountas)*. Tg. מְשַׁבְּחִיא, "those giving praise."

"to commemorate" *(lĕhazkîr)*. So MT. Consistent with its previous reading, LXX has "proclaimers" *(anaphōnountas)*.

"to give thanks, and to give praise to Yhwh" *(lĕhôdôt ûlĕhallēl lyhwh)*. So MT. LXX "and to confess and to praise the Lord" *(kai exomologeisthai kai ainein Kyrion)*.

16:5. "Jeiel" *(yʿyʾl)*. LXX$^{BS}$ *Eieiēl;* $c_2$ *Eisiēl.* The lemma of b′ *kai Ieēl* reflects a *wāw/yôd* confusion.

"Jeḥiel" *(yḥyʾl)*. LXX$^{BS}$ again have *Eieiēl;* LXX$^{L}$ *kai Ia(i)ēl;* LXX$^{N}$ *Iaeiēl.*

"Uzziel" *(ʿzyʾl)*. A reconstruction based partially on 15:18, 20. Cf. LXX$^{L}$ *Ozias;* Arm. *Osiay.* MT "Jeiel *(yʿyʾl);* LXX$^{AB}$ *Eieiēl.*

"with harps" *(bkly nblym)*. Literally, "with instruments of harps." LXX$^{BS}$ $c_2$ *en organois nablais,* "with instruments, harps;" jpqtz and Boh. *en organois kai nablais,* "with instruments and harps."

"and with lyres." Thus MT (ובכנרות). LXX *(kai kinyrais)* and Tg. וכנרין, "and lyres." Cf. 15:16.

16:6. "Jaḥaziel" *(yḥzyʾl)*. LXX$^{AB}$ *Ozeiēl;* $e_2$ *Ieziēl.*

"regularly" *(tāmîd)*. Not "continually" (RSV, NASB) or "eternally." See Exod 27:20; Num 28:6, 15; 2 Kgs 25:29–30; Ezek 39:14; Dan 8:11; 1 Chr 16:11, 37.

16:7. "then, on that day" *(bywm hhwʾ ʾz)*. LXX reads the clause "on that day" *(bywm hhwʾ)* with the end of the previous sentence, hence "the Ark of the Covenant of God on that day."

"David first put Asaph and his kinsmen in charge of giving thanks to Yhwh" (נתן דויד בראש להדות ליהוה ביד-אסף ואחיו). The Heb. can be rendered a number of different ways (cf. Rothstein and Hänel 1927: 289–91). On the construal of בראש as "for the first time," see Judg 7:19; Isa 40:21; 41:4, 26; 48:16; Ezek 40:1; Prov 8:26 (*HALOT* 1166).

16:8. "give thanks" *(hwdw)*. So MT. LXX prefaces "an ode" *(ōdē)*.

16:9. "his wonderful deeds." So MT *(lectio brevior)*. LXX adds "which the Lord did" by attraction to the locution of v. 12, "which he has accomplished" (אשׁר עשׂה).

16:10. "let the heart of those seeking Yhwh rejoice." LXX$^{AB}$ "let the heart seeking his favor *(zētousa tēn eudokian autou)* rejoice." Fragment E III (lines 10–11) of the *Psalms Scroll* (11Q5 Ps 105:3), [מבקשׁ] רצונו, "[seeking] rejoice," seems to agree with LXX$^{AB}$ 1 Chr 16:10 (Sanders 1967: 159, 164–65).

16:11. "his strength" *(ʿuzzô)*. LXX 16:11 "be strong" *(ischysate)* and LXX Ps 105:4 *krataiōthēte* reflect a different interpretation of the same consonants (= *ʿuzzû*).

16:13. "Israel." So MT and LXX$^{AB}$ (maximum differentiation). A few Heb. MSS, $c_2$, one version of Syr., Boh., and Arab. follow MT (and LXX) Ps 105:6 in reading "Abraham."

"his servant" (עבדו). So MT. LXX^AB "children" *(paides)*. LXX^L and Boh. "his servants" *(douloi autou)* agree with LXX^R Ps 105:6 and 11Q5 Ps 105:6 עבדיו, "his servants."

16:14. "he is Yhwh our God." Thus MT and LXX^AN. LXX* lacks the pron. 11Q5 Ps 105:7 prefaces כי ("for").

16:15. "remember" *(zkrw)*. LXX^B $mc_2$ "let us remember" *(mnēmoneuomen)*; LXX^AN (sg.) "remembering" *(mnēmoneuōn)*. MT, 11Q5, and LXX *(emnēsthē*, "remembered") Ps 105:8 also have the sg. *zkr*, but the pl. is found in a few Heb. MSS of Ps 105:8 and is a consistent feature in the Chronicler's medley (16:8, 9, 12, 23, 24).

"the word." So MT 16:15, MT Ps 105:8, and 11Q5 Ps 105:8. LXX "his word."

16:16. "(and) his oath." So MT and LXX 16:16 as well as MT and LXX Ps 105:9. 11Q5 Ps 105:9 lacks the connective *wāw*.

"Isaac" *(yṣḥq)*. MT Ps 105:9 and 11Q5 Ps 105:9 *yśḥq* (cf. Jer 33:26; Amos 7:9, 16).

16:18. "land of Canaan" *(ʾrṣ-knʿn)*. MT Ps 105:11 and 11Q5 Ps 105:9 preface the direct object marker *ʾt*. This may have been lost from the Chronicler's *Vorlage* because of haplography before *ʾrṣ*.

16:19. "when you were" *(bhywtkm)*. So MT 16:19, as well as many Heb. MSS and Tg. Ps 105:12. One Heb. MS, LXX^AB, Vg., and MT (and LXX) Ps 105:12 have "when they were" *(bhywtm)*. Although Curtis and Madsen (1910: 224) prefer the latter lemma, the former is more likely to be original to Chronicles (Wallace 1999: 270).

"Scant" *(mʿṭ)*. So MT 16:19, as well as MT and LXX *(oligostous)* Ps 105:12. LXX "they were of little account" *(esmikrynthēsan)*.

16:20. "nation." Reading with MT and Tg. LXX 16:20 and LXX Ps 105:13 "nations." Instead of MT's "wandering from nation to nation," Syr. reads "and you were led captive from nation to nation." There are a number of references to exile in the Peshiṭta that find no counterpart in MT or LXX (Weitzman 1999: 209–10).

"(and) from one kingdom" *(wmmmlkh)*. Thus MT and LXX. MT and LXX Ps 105:13 lack the *wāw* before this locution. Syr. adds to v. 20 "and you were led captive."

16:21. "anyone" *(lʾyš)*. A few Heb. MSS *ʾyš*; LXX *andra*. MT Ps 105:14 *ʾdm* ("a person"); LXX *anthrōpon*.

16:22. "(and) my prophets" *(wbnbyʾy)*. MT Ps 105:15 *wlnbyʾy*.

16:23–33. These verses are quoted from Ps 96:1–13. There is a fairly close match between the Chronicler's text and those parts of Ps 96 from which he quotes. In this respect, the author's *Vorlage* seems to resemble MT Ps 96. Yet there are certain clauses in his source that do not appear here. The portions of Ps 96 that do not appear in 1 Chr 16 are not of a different nature from the portions included (TEXTUAL NOTES to vv. 23–33). It is unclear why the author would omit poetic clauses paralleling other poetic clauses that he retains. Moreover, in citing Pss 105 and 106 he does not omit clauses within the lines he quotes. Given the existence of pluriform versions of biblical books in antiquity, as witnessed by the Dead Sea Scrolls, MT, and LXX (see "Introduction"), the possibility cannot be ruled out that the author had access to a shorter, less elaborate version of Ps 96. Alternatively, it is possible that the Chronicler was being selective in citing his sources. In this context, a comparison with the various collections of psalms found at Qumran is in order. The non-Masoretic psalms that appear in the *Psalms Scroll* from Qumran (11Q5) are mostly composed of quotations and paraphrases of earlier biblical literature (Sanders 1967; Flint 1997). Indeed, 1 Chr 16:8–36 is itself a pastiche made up of citations from earlier psalms. In this respect, the composition of 1 Chr 16:8–36 may anticipate the creative reuse of earlier biblical literature found in the Dead Sea Scrolls.

16:23. "sing to Yhwh all the earth." Boh. follows Ps 96:1 in prefacing "sing to Yhwh a new song." The LXX version of this psalm prefaces additional material (1st NOTE to v. 23).

"proclaim his deliverance from day to day." MT Ps 96:2 prefaces "sing to Yhwh, bless his name."

"to day" *(ʾl ywm)*. MT Ps 96:2 *lywm*.

16:24. "recount *(sprw)* his glory among the nations, his wonders among all the peoples." So MT. The entire verse is lacking in LXX$^{AB}$, although present in LXX$^{L}$ dfijp-z, Arm., and Boh. The material may have been lost through haplography (*homoioteleuton* from ישועתו in v. 23 to נפלאתיו in v. 24). The phrase "recount his glory among the nations" is also missing from LXX$^{AR}$ Ps 96:3.

"his glory" *(ʾt kbwdw)*. The direct object marker is wanting in MT Ps 96:3.

16:25. "(and) feared" *(wnwrʾ)*. The *wāw* is lacking in MT and LXX Ps 96:4, but present in Syr. and Tg. Ps 96:4.

16:26. "nonentities" *(ʾlylym)*. LXX$^{AB}$ *eidōla*, "idols." LXX$^{L}$ 16:26 and LXX Ps 96:5 *daimonia*, "divine beings."

"Yhwh." So MT. LXX$^{ABL}$ *ho theos hēmōn*, "our God."

16:27. "joy" *(ḥdwh)*. LXX$^{AB}$ "vaunt" *(kauchēma)*. Syr. and Arab. seem to read "splendor" with MT Ps 96:6 (*tpʾrt;* LXX *megaloprepeia*, "majesty, splendor"). Within the HB the term *ḥdwh*, an Aram. loanword, is quite rare, found elsewhere only in Neh 8:10. Four Heb. MSS of Ps 96:6 also read *ḥdwh*.

"in his place" *(bmqwmw)*. So MT and LXX$^{B}$ *(en topō autou)*. LXX$^{L}$, Syr., and Arab. read "in his sanctuary" *(bmqdšw)* with MT (and LXX) Ps 96:6. The Chronicler may have preferred the allusive *mqwm* over the more specific *mqdš* because the Temple had not yet been built.

16:29. "ascribe to Yhwh the honor due his name." So MT and LXX$^{L}$ 1 Chr 16:29, as well as Ps 96:8. The entire phrase is lacking in LXX$^{AB}$ 1 Chr 16:29.

"come" *(bʾw)*. So MT and $e_2$ (*eiselthate;* cf. Just. *eiselthete*). LXX$^{AB}$ and LXX Ps 96:8 *enegkate*, "bear." Following "come before him," Syr. adds "with the prayer of your mouths."

"before him" *(lpnyw)*. The lemma of Ps 96:8 *lḥṣrwtyw* ("to his courts") would be inappropriate in the context of Chronicles because the Temple had not yet been built.

"majestic in holiness" *(bĕhadrat-qōdeš)*. So MT. LXX "in his holy courts" (*en aylais hagiais autou* = *bĕḥazrôt-qodšô*). LXX Ps 96:9 is similar, *en aylē hagia autou* (= *bĕḥazrat-qodšô*), "in his holy court"). The context is difficult, but I translate *bĕhadrat-qōdeš* as "majestic in holiness" (so also NJPS) rather than "in beautiful apparel" or "in holy adornment" (e.g., Curtis and Madsen 1910: 224; Ackroyd 1966: 393–96; 1973a: 151; *HALOT* 240) because the phrase seems to refer to the deity himself and not to the appearance of his worshipers. Cross (1973: 152–53) observes that a passage in the Ugaritic legend of Kirta may be relevant to this discussion. Grieved by the loss of his progeny, King Kirta of Ḫubur performs an incubation rite (*CAT* 1.14.I.26–35) during which the supreme god El appears to him in a dream (*CAT* 1.14.I.35–37).

In his dream *(bḥlmh)* El came down,
in his vision *(bḏhdrth)*, the Father of Humanity.

The term in question designates apparition rather than human clothing. Whether Ugaritic *hdrt* is related etymologically to Heb. *hdr(h)* is, however, in question (C. Cohen 1999: 71–77). Aside from 1 Chr 16:29(//Ps 96:9), the expression *hadrat-qōdeš* occurs only in Ps 29:2 and 2 Chr 20:21. In the latter passage, a holy-war narrative, the use of *hadrat-qōdeš* in association with the deity is clear. Jehoshaphaṭ appoints "singers to Yhwh *(mšrrym lyhwh)* and those praising (the one) appearing in holiness *(lĕhadrat-qōdeš)* as they went forth before the vanguard of the army." In 2 Chr 20:21, the singers to Yhwh are parallel to those praising *lĕhadrat-qōdeš*, and both groups are governed by the verb "appoint" *(ʿmd)*. The prep. in the expression is, therefore, a *bêt essentiae* (C. Cohen 1999: 72–73).

16:30. "tremble before him" *(ḥylw mlpnyw)*. MT and LXX Ps 96:9 "tremble from his presence" *(ḥylw mpnyw)*.

"all the earth." MT Ps 96:10a adds *ʾmrw bgwym yhwh mlk*, "say among the nations, 'Yhwh reigns!' " The phrase is missing in some Heb. MSS of Ps 96:10, while in 1 Chr 16 it appears in v. 31 (see TEXTUAL NOTE).

"established" *(tkwn)*. So MT. LXX$^{AB}$ has the 3rd-per. aorist pass. impv. "be established" *(katorthōthētō)*. LXX$^{L}$ *katō/orthōsē*; $e_2$ *katorthōsai* (cf. LXX Ps 96:10 *katōrthōsen* = *tkn*) is adopted by the NEB.

"it cannot be shaken." Ps 96:10b adds "he judges the peoples with equity" *(ydyn ʿmym bmyšrym)*.

16:31. "let them say among the nations, 'Yhwh reigns!' " As we have seen (2nd TEXTUAL NOTE to v. 30), this phrase appears in Ps 96:10a. Why this clause was transposed immediately after v. 30a ("all the earth")—in other words, to its place in Ps 96 (Begrich in *BHK*; Rudolph 1955: 124; *BHS*)—is not at all clear. It is also unclear why NJPS omits the clause altogether. Within Chronicles, the phrase makes sense in its (new) context.

"let them say" *(yʾmrw)*. MT Ps 96:10 has the impv. "say" *(ʾmrw)*.

16:32. "let the fields and everything within them exult" *(yʿlṣ hśdh wkl-ʾšr-bw)*. So MT. MT Ps 96:12 is slightly different *(yʿlz śdy wkl ʾšr bw)*, but this does not affect the overall sense. The verb "exult" does not appear in LXX$^{AB}$ Chronicles. LXX$^{L}$ has the impv. sg. "rejoice exceedingly" *(agalliasthō)*.

16:33. "then let the trees of the forest shout for joy from before Yhwh" *(yrnnw ʿṣy hyʿr mlpny yhwh)*. MT Ps 96:12b–13a "then let all the trees of the forest shout for joy before Yhwh" *(ʾz yrnnw kl ʿṣy yʿr lpny yhwh)*.

"because he comes." This phrase is repeated in MT Ps 96:13. Either haplography or dittography is possible, but the latter is more likely because the second instance of the phrase is absent from many Heb. MSS and Syr.

"to judge the earth." Syr. and Arab. follow Ps 96:13 in adding "he judges the world in justice, and the peoples in his truth."

16:35. "(and) say" (ואמרו). So MT and LXX. Lacking in Ps 106:47.

"O God of our deliverance" (אלהי ישענו). MT (and LXX) Ps 106:47 "Yhwh our God" (יהוה אלהינו).

"gather us" *(qbṣnw)*. So MT. Lacking in LXX$^{AB}$, but appearing in Ps 106:47.

"and liberate us" (והצילנו). So MT and LXX. Lacking in MT and LXX Ps 106:47, perhaps due to haplography *(homoioteleuton)*.

16:36. "and all the people said *(wy'mrw)*." MT and LXX Ps 106:48 *(kai erei pas ho laos)* read the sg., "and let all the people say" *(w'mr)*.

"and praise" *(whll)*. So MT. LXX *kai ēnesan*, "and praised." MT Ps 106:48 has the pl. impv. "praise" *(hllw)*, while LXX Ps 106:48 repeats the earlier "Amen" (*Genoito, genoito* = אמן אמן).

"Yhwh." So MT and LXX *(tō Kyriō)*. MT Ps 106:48 יה ("Yah"). In LXX Psalms, the concluding sentiment of Ps 106:48 הללו-יה, "Praise Yah" appears at the very beginning of the next psalm *(Allēlouia)*.

16:37. "and he left Asaph and his kinsmen there before the Ark of the Covenant of Yhwh" *(wy'ṣb šm lpny 'rwn bryt yhwh l'sp wl'ḥyw)*. On the use of the prep. *l*— with a direct object, see GKC §117n.

16:38. "Jeḥiel, and their kinsmen" *(w'ḥyhm)*. Both MT and LXX *kai hoi adelphoi autou*, "and their kinsmen" (followed by Benzinger 1901: 54), are problematic because of the sg. antecedent (Obed-edom). A few commentators follow Syr., Vg., and Arab., which all have the expected sg., "and his kinsman." Another option is to transpose "and Ḥosah" to before "with their kinsmen" (Kittel 1902: 72). I prefer to make a third proposal to restore the PN *wyḥy'l* (15:18, 20; 16:5). "And Jeḥiel" *(wyḥy'l)* was lost by haplography (*homoioarkton* before "and their kinsmen" [*w'ḥyhm*]). This seems preferable to restoring "Jeḥiah" *(wyḥyh)* after the pattern of 15:24 (Rudolph 1955: 126; Williamson 1982b), because Jeḥiah was a gatekeeper (cf. v. 38b).

"Jeduthun" *(ydwtwn)*. So Qere and Tg. Kethib *ydytwn* (cf. Kethib Ps 77:[title]; Neh 11:17). LXX$^{B}$ $c_2$ *Ideithōn*. LXX$^{L}$ *Idithoum huios*, "Jedithun son of."

16:39. "[left] Zadoq" *(w't ṣdwq)*. Zadoq is the second direct object of the verb "he left" *(wy'ṣb)* in v. 37.

16:40. "which he enjoined upon Israel." So MT. LXX adds "by the hand of Moses the servant of God."

16:41. "Jeduthun" *(ydwtwn)*. LXX$^{B}$ $hc_2$ *Ideithōn;* LXX$^{S}$ m and Arm. *Idithōm;* LXX$^{N}$ *Ideithoun;* LXX$^{AL}$ and Eusebius *Idithoum.*

"the select" *(hbrwrym)*. The pass. ptc. of the root *brr* appears only in Chronicles and Nehemiah with this meaning (BDB 141; 1 Chr 7:40; 9:22; 16:41; Neh 5:18).

"who were designated" *('šr nqbw)*. So MT. The construction is wanting in LXX. It is possible that *hbrwrym* ("the select") and *'šr nqbw* ("who were designated") comprise a double reading. On this phenomenon, see Talmon (1960a).

16:42. "with them." So LXX$^{AB}$ *(lectio brevior)*. That MT and LXX$^{L}$ add "Heman and Jeduthun" results from a dittography (v. 41).

"trumpets and cymbals." Syr. replaces the references to musical instruments in this verse with references to "goodly mouth and pure and perfect prayer and righteousness and integrity" (Weitzman 1994: 156).

"for sounding" *(lmšmyʿym)*. So MT. LXX *tou anaphōnein*. Begrich *(BHK)* suggests emending either to *mšmyʿym* or to *lhšmyʿy* (cf. 1 Chr 15:28). The construction is viewed by some (e.g., Rudolph 1955: 128) as misplaced or as a later addition.

"the sons of Jeduthun *(ydwtwn)*." Variants include LXX$^{BS}$ *Ideithōn*; $c_2$ *Deithoun*; LXX$^{AN}$ and Arm. *Iditʿom*; LXX$^{L}$ and Eusebius, *Idithoum*. Cf. v. 41.

"the song of God" *(šyr h'lhym)*. LXX "the songs of God."

"at the gate" *(lšʿr)*. So MT and LXX$^{AB}$ *(eis tēn pylēn)*. Tg. על תרעייה, "in charge of the gates." LXX$^{L}$ ($be_2$) has the pl. "gatekeepers" *(to pylōrein)*.

16:43. "and David returned" *(wysb dwyd)*. MT 2 Sam 6:20 offers a different verb with the same meaning, *wyšb dwd*, "and David returned."

# NOTES

16:4–6. "some of the Levities." This material is unparalled in Samuel. Having successfully brought the Ark to the tent he pitched for it in the City of David (16:1–3), the king takes the next step of providing a cult to attend to the sacred symbol. In so doing, David draws on many of the personnel who were appointed to accompany the Ark on its journey from the house of Obed-edom (15:17–24). During this earlier procession, many of the Levitical personnel were assigned specific tasks (15:19–23, 24b). The priests were also assigned a role to play (15:24a). In this context, twelve officials, ten Levites (16:5) and two priests (v. 6), are mentioned by name. The new assignments made by David overlap with the previous responsibilities, but there are also some changes and new developments (NOTE to v. 7). As is evident by his allocation of coverage (vv. 4–38), the Chronicler's attention is very much focused on the establishment of the new cultus in Jerusalem. It should also be observed, however, that David reserves some of the appointees involved in the Ark's procession for service at the Tabernacle in Gibeon (NOTE to vv. 39–42).

16:4. "stationed." In this case, David appoints the Levites and priests directly. In the earlier instance, David delegated the authority to make appointments to the Levites themselves (15:16–24).

"ministers" (משרתים). On the choice of terminology, see the last NOTE to 15:2.

"to commemorate, to give thanks, and to give praise" (להזכיר ולהודות ולהלל). The instructions David gives to the Levites correspond in many respects to the sentiments expressed in the Chronicler's composite psalm (Watts 1992; Shipp 1993). In this context, the very choice of words sung by the Levites fulfills the mandate given to them by King David. The choral rite thus becomes an official and integral component of Israelite worship.

"to commemorate" (להזכיר). The significance of the use of the *hipʿil* of זכר in this context is disputed. In one line of interpretation, the *hipʿil* of זכר points to a specific sacrifice, either the אזכרה (Rothstein and Hänel 1927: 287; Mowinckel

1962.1:3), the meaning of which is debated (Lev 2:2, 9, 16; 24:7; Num 5:26; cf. Sir 38:11; 45:16; *HALOT* 27), or the לבנה (Kraus 1988: 29), "the offering of frankincense." While not denying the possibility that invocations could, in certain instances, be accompanied by sacrifices, one should begin with the literal meaning of the verb, "to cause to remember." One of the functions of the Asaphite Levites will be to bring Yhwh and his deeds to remembrance. The question is, Who is being called to participate in this act of remembrance? The text does not say. The common assumption that the people are in view is readily understandable. In this reading, the Levites are to "commemorate" or "invoke" the divine name, reminding the people of the deity they serve. Such an act is itself a kind of worship (Exod 23:13; Josh 23:7; Isa 26:13; 48:1; 62:6; Amos 6:10; Pss 38:[title]; 70:[title]). But the verb may also carry another sense. One of the duties of the Levites is to remind Yhwh of his relationship and promises to his people. Certainly, the accompanying verbs "to give thanks" (להודות) and "to praise" (להלל) take a divine object. Again, such an act is a form of worship (cf. Akk. *azkur šumuka,* "I call upon your name"). So also in speaking of his altars, Yhwh declares that they are the places "where I cause my name to be remembered" (אשר אזכיר את־שמי; Exod 20:24; cf. 2 Sam 18:18; Isa 12:4; Pss 45:18 [ET 45:17]; 71:16 [ET 71:15]; Tob 12:12). Indeed, to call Yhwh to remembrance invokes the presence of Yhwh himself (Eising 1980: 74).

"to give thanks" (להודות). That David's commission to the Levites, the specific commission to the Asaphites "to give thanks" (להודות; v. 7), and the first excerpt of what they are to sing, "Give thanks to Yhwh" (הודו יהוה; v. 8) all agree can be no accident. The Levites have a ministry of hymnody, thanksgiving, and praise (cf. Isa 12:1–5; Pss 33:2; 75:2 [ET 75:1]; 79:13; 92:2 [ET 92:1]; 100:4; 105:1; 136:1–26; 1 Chr 25:1–31; 29:13; 2 Chr 6:24, 26). This summary does not capture the sum total of their responsibilities, but it is an essential part of their duties (1 Chr 23:30–31; 25:3; 2 Chr 5:13; 7:6; 29:25–30; 30:21–22; 31:2; cf. Ezra 3:10–11; Neh 11:15–18; 12:23–25, 27–29, 45–46).

16:5. "Asaph" (אסף). As with the earlier arrangements in advancing the Ark to the tent in Zion, certain figures have both general positions and specific responsibilities (15:17–24). Asaph is both the administrative "head" (ראש) of the Levitical detachment in Jerusalem and responsible for "sounding the cymbals." Asaph also sounded the cymbals during the elevation of the Ark (15:19). The new commission given to Asaph and his kin carries, however, connotations of permanence. The passage functions as a charter for the rights of Asaph's guild to lead the ministry of praise to Yhwh. In this respect, there is an overlap between the attention devoted to the sons of Asaph in Chronicles (1 Chr 9:15; 16:37; 25:1–2; 2 Chr 20:14–23; 29:30), Ezra (2:41), and Nehemiah (7:44; 11:17 [MT]; 12:46) and the position Asaph enjoys in some of the superscriptions to the Psalms (50; 73–83). Clearly, the Asaphite guild was one of the leading families of singers in the Chronicler's own day, and his work bolsters its claims to a classical pedigree. The NOTE to 15:17 discusses Asaph's relationship to Heman and Ethan/Jeduthun. On his genealogy, see the 1st NOTE to 6:18.

"Zechariah," appointed by his fellow Levites prior to the Ark procession as a kinsman of "the second rank" (המשנים; 2nd NOTE to 15:18), is now selected by David as Asaph's "second in command" (משנהו).

"Shemiramoth" was part of the earlier Ark procession (4th NOTE to 15:18).

"Jeḥiel." Drawn from the earlier list of Levitical appointees (5th NOTE to 15:18).

"Mattithiah." Another appointee drawn from the earlier Levitical procession (10th NOTE to 15:18).

"Eliab." Also found in the lists of 15:18 (7th NOTE) and 20.

"Benaiah." Referring to the Levite (15:18, 20), as opposed to the priest with the same name (15:24; 16:6).

"Obed-edom." The musician (15:18, 21; 16:38a), as opposed to the gatekeeper (15:24 [2nd NOTE]; 16:38b; 26:4, 8, 15; 2 Chr 25:24). See also the 2nd NOTE to 13:13.

"Uzziel." Another appointee drawn from the earlier Levitical lists of officials accompanying the Ark (TEXTUAL NOTES to 15:18, 20; 16:5). One might have expected that the list of Levites in v. 5 would also include Unni (15:18, 20), Maaseiah (15:18, 20), Eliphalah (15:18, 21), Miqneiah (15:18, 21), and Azaziah (15:18, 21). But these Levites, in the Chronicler's presentation, are to become part of the Gibeonite cultus (re)organized by David (16:39–42). The text there (v. 41) alludes to "Heman and Jeduthun and the rest of the select who were designated by name to give thanks to Yhwh." Heman and Ethan (1st NOTE to 15:17) were part of the Ark procession (15:17, 19), but are not subsequently assigned to be part of the Ark cultus in Jerusalem (16:4–38). The "rest" of those "designated by name" refers to those Levites named in the earlier Ark procession who were not specifically assigned by David to serve as attendants to the Ark in Zion.

16:6. "Benaiah." One of the seven priests "sounding the trumpets" in the procession of the Ark (15:24).

"Jaḥaziel" is not mentioned among the seven priests (15:24) in the earlier round of Levitical appointments of 15:17–24. The name is Ḥebronite in 23:19 (Qohathite) and 24:23. Another "Jaḥaziel" appears as an Asaphite Levite in the reign of Jehoshaphaṭ (MT 2 Chr 20:14).

"priests with trumpets." As was the case in the earlier parade of the Ark (3rd NOTE to 15:24).

"regularly" (תמיד). The priests and Levites were to conduct a regular musical service. No regular sacrifices were being offered at the Ark in Jerusalem at this time (21:26). The use of the adv. תמיד, "regularly" (16:6 [TEXTUAL NOTE], 11, 37) drives home the point that psalms, singing, and praise are to be an integral part of Israel's worship (Kleinig 1993: 29–31). The attention given to music and song is consonant with the extensive coverage devoted to the Levitical singers in the genealogies (6:1–38) and to the Levitical singers (25:1–6) and courses in David's later reign (25:7–31). It is relevant to observe in this context that according to later Jewish tradition, as preserved in the Mishnah (*m. Tamid* 7.4), the Levites recited psalms each day in the Temple. A specific psalm was sung each day of the week including the sabbath. In MT only one such psalm (Ps 92:1) is so designated in the psalm superscriptions: "A psalm, a song for the day of the sabbath" (מזמור שיר ליום השבת), but six are so designated (including Ps 92 [LXX Ps 91]) in one or more witnesses to LXX Psalms.

| *LXX Psalm* | *Day* |
|---|---|
| 22 [= MT Ps 23] | First (so only one witness, MS 1219) |
| 23 [= MT Ps 24] | First (so LXX$^{AB}$) |
| 37 [= MT Ps 38] | Sabbath (so LXX$^{AB}$) |
| 47 [= MT Ps 48] | Second (so LXX$^{AB}$) |
| 80 [= MT Ps 81] | Fifth (so some witnesses, but not LXX$^{AB}$) |
| 91 [= MT Ps 92] | Sabbath (so LXX$^{ABL}$) |
| 92 [= MT Ps 93] | Day preceding the sabbath (so LXX$^{AB}$; MS 2110 Sabbath) |
| 93 [= MT Ps 94] | Fourth (so LXX$^{ABL}$) |

The available evidence from the Dead Sea Scrolls (4QPs$^{juid}$, MasP$^{auid}$, 11QPs$^{a}$, 4QPs$^{b}$) aligns itself with MT over against LXX (Flint 1997: 117–34). The psalms (and the days assigned to them) mentioned in the Mishnah (*m. Tamid* 7.4) only partially overlap with those in LXX.

| *Psalm* | *Day* |
|---|---|
| 24 | First |
| 48 | Second |
| 82 | Third |
| 94 | Fourth |
| 81 | Fifth |
| 93 | Sixth |
| 92 | Sabbath |

In the Mishnah, a different psalm is sung for each day of the week. The history of the superscriptions in LXX Psalms is a subject in and of itself (Pietersma 2001).

16:7. "put Asaph." The description, unparalleled in Samuel, is consistent with other contexts in the author's work (COMMENT on 1 Chr 25:1–31). In the realm of his nation's worship, David is many things: organizer, patron, leader, composer, and liturgist. But Chronicles does not stress the role of David as a singer himself.

"to give thanks (להדות) to Yhwh." On this responsibility of the Asaphite guild, see the 5th NOTE to v. 4.

16:8–36. The long thanksgiving offered by Asaph and his kin is actually a medley of selections taken from Pss 105; 96; and 106. Although each of these psalms exhibits its own themes and genre, the excerpts taken from these psalms, when placed together in a new literary context, take on additional significance. As recent studies (e.g., Butler 1978; Hill 1983; Watts 1992; Kleinig 1993; Shipp 1993; Auffret 1995; Eskenazi 1995) have shown, the poetry of vv. 8–36 is not a collage of disconnected pieces, but a skillful and artfully arranged composition. Inasmuch as it is a complex of selections taken from older psalms and placed in a new order, the Chronicler's medley is a new work. The significance of this psalm may be approached from at least five angles:

1. the author's selectivity in dealing with older materials
2. how the author has treated those portions of the psalms from which he quoted
3. the sequence created by placing the extracts in a distinctively new order
4. the placement of the piece in the context of the Chronicler's narrative,

namely, the ascent of the sacred Ark and the establishment of a cultus to attend the Ark in the City of David

5. the relevance of this material for the author's own time.

The NOTES and the COMMENT treat the third, fourth, and fifth considerations in greater detail. It will be useful to begin with the first two considerations. The author's preferences in quoting portions of certain psalms is revealing. The Chronicler has cited certain poems whose phraseology and content were deemed important for the occasion. Note, for example, the emphasis on remembrance, thanksgiving, singing, and praise throughout the psalm. In this respect, the psalm itself becomes paradigmatic for Israelite worship (Watts 1992: 161). By contrast, none of the three psalms selected is associated with either Asaph (cf. Pss 50; 73–83) or David in the psalm superscriptions (Auwers 1999: 209–21). The first section of hymnic material (1 Chr 16:8–22) has been drawn from Ps 105:1–15. With a few exceptions, the verses closely follow the text of MT Ps 105 (see TEXTUAL NOTES). In the second section (1 Chr 16:23–33), the author quotes from Ps 96:1–13. Again, among those portions of Ps 96 from which the author quotes, he follows his *Vorlage* closely. In the third section (1 Chr 16:34–36), the author quotes a small portion of Ps 106, its beginning (v. 1) and its final verses (vv. 47–48). He generally follows his *Vorlage* closely, but adapts its ending to his own purposes (see TEXTUAL NOTES and NOTE to v. 36).

16:8. "give thanks to Yhwh" *(hwdw lyhwh)*. The first psalm (105) the author quotes is one of the few so-called historical poems of the Psalter (cf. Pss 78; 106). The first five verses of the piece (Ps 105:1–5//1 Chr 16:8–12) provide an introduction to what follows: a long litany of Yhwh's great actions performed on behalf of his people (105:6–45). The psalmist begins by recounting Yhwh's covenant loyalty to the Patriarchs and Matriarchs during their peregrinations (Ps 105:6–15// 1 Chr 16:13–22). The other deeds celebrated are the journeys of Joseph (105:16–22), the Exodus (105:23–38), the miracles in the desert (105:39–41), and the successful settlement in the land (105:42–44). Of the mighty deeds the psalmist wishes to "make known," only the first, the journeys of the Ancestors (Ps 105:6–15//1 Chr 16:13–22), are rehearsed in Chronicles. That the references to Joseph, the Exodus, the miracles in the desert, and the settlement are excluded is not too surprising given that the Chronicler elsewhere displays no penchant for including narrative accounts of these events within his own work. The Chronicler's own narrative begins with the monarchy. That Abraham, Isaac, and Jacob appear (16:13, 16, 17) has occasioned some surprise because the Chronicler does not narrate the Ancestral age. Yet, this period is clearly of some importance to the author (1 Chr 1:27, 32, 34; 16:16; 29:18; 2 Chr 20:7; 30:6). As we have seen, the genealogies privilege the Ancestral age. Not only are the lineages of each of the tribes traced back to the era of the Matriarchs and the Patriarchs, but the lineages of David (2:3–5, 9–17; 3:1–24), the priests (5:27–41), and the Levites (6:1–38) are as well. Moreover, as the psalm reminds its readers, it is in the age of the Matriarchs and Patriarchs that the promise of land was first given. During the Persian and early Hellenistic periods the significance of the Abrahamic covenant should not be overlooked (Römer 1990; Fosse 1998). Those Judeans who had been able and willing to return to the land of their ancestors undoubtedly saw their restoration as a (re)confirmation of the validity of the Abrahamic promises (Isa 29:22; 41:8–16; 51:2; MT Jer 33:26; Mic 7:20; Neh 9:7; 1 Chr 16:18 [see NOTE]). The selective reuse of Ps 105 is, therefore, highly significant. In both Ps 105 and in Chronicles, the Ancestral age is formative to Israel's constitution.

16:9. "sing to him" *(šyrw lw)*. Given that one of the prime Levitical duties, in the view of the Chronicler, was praising Yhwh (15:19–21; 16:7), Ps 105:1 serves as an apt beginning for the Chronicler's citation of the Psalms. His initial citations of Ps 96:1(//1 Chr 16:23), "sing to Yhwh" *(šyrw lyhwh)*, and 106:1(//1 Chr 16:34), "give thanks to Yhwh" *(hwdw lyhwh)*, mirror the introduction to Ps 105:1–2 and hence to his own work (16:8–9). This creates a "broad connective structure" in the composition of vv. 8–36 (Hill 1983: 100).

6:11. "seek Yhwh (דרשו יהוה) and his strength (ועזו)." Probably an allusion to the Ark. In referring to the capture of the Ark by the Philistines (1 Sam 4:1–11), the author of Ps 78:61 declares, "He allowed his strength (עזו) to go into captivity, his splendor into the hands of the enemy." Similarly, in speaking of the ascent of the Ark into Jerusalem, the poet proclaims, "Arise, Yhwh, from your resting place, you and the Ark of your strength (עזך)" (Ps 132:8). Given both the Chronicler's own emphasis on "seeking" God (last NOTE to 10:13) and his narration of the Ark's ascent into Jerusalem, the Chronicler's audience would be led to associate the imperatives "seek Yhwh and his strength" and "search out his presence regularly" with journeying to Jerusalem to worship Yhwh there. In the context of the postexilic period, the text speaks to Yahwists who live both within the confines of Yehud and those who live much further away.

16:13. "sons of Jacob, his elect ones" (בחיריו). This is the only explicit reference in Chronicles to Israel's election. The Chronicler speaks of the divine election (בחר) of David, Solomon, Judah, Jerusalem, the Temple, and the Levites (4th NOTE to 15:2), but with the exception of this reference derived from Ps 105:6, he never broaches the subject of Yhwh's choice of Israel to be his people.

16:15. "Remember his covenant." The psalm is filled with summonses to the audience. As recent scholars (e.g., K. Nielsen 1999; Wallace 1999) have emphasized, such imperatives involve the Chronicler's own readers in the literary world created by the psalm. As the context makes clear, the particular covenant to which the poet is referring is the Abrahamic covenant (Gen 15:1–21; 17:1–27; 24:7; Luke 1:72–73). The version of the Abrahamic promises in Gen 15 is usually assigned to the J source, while the version of Gen 17 is usually ascribed to the P source (Westermann 1985: 209–31, 251–71). The oration in Neh 9 also refers to the Abrahamic promises as a covenant (ברית; Neh 9:8). That the ancestral covenant (ברית) remains in force is due to Yhwh's fidelity. This record of divine faithfulness becomes in and of itself the basis for the psalmist, and by implication the Chronicler's audience, to appeal to Yhwh to continue to show mercy to his people (1 Chr 16:35).

16:16. "oath to Isaac." See Gen 26:23–24.

16:17. "confirmed it as a statute to Jacob." See Gen 27:28–29; 28:3–4, 13–15; 31:13; 35:9–12.

16:18. "the land of Canaan." The content of the "everlasting covenant" with Abraham centers on the grant of land to Abraham. In Genesis the theme of land is a central element in the Abrahamic promises (Gen 15:7, 18–21; 17:8). The last section of Ps 105 celebrates the fulfillment of the divine pledge to Abraham by commemorating Israel's inheritance of the land (Ps 105:44–45). For the Chronicler's audience that promise had been renewed in the return(s) from exile. But in Genesis the Abrahamic promises also guarantee numerous progeny (Gen 15:4–5; 17:2–7, 16–21). Given the Chronicler's keen concern for the ties between the people of Israel and the land, the focus on "the territory of your inheritance" exhibited by Ps 105 suits the Chronicler's own interests well (Butler 1978: 144; R. Braun 1986: 191–92).

16:19. "scant in number" (מתי מספר). Given the few people in Yehud in the Persian period, the Chronicler's audience may have identified with the sentiments expressed in Ps 105. Yhwh's promises to and provisions for the Matriarchs and Patriarchs were probably a source of encouragement to a small community. Population estimates of Yehud have varied depending on the methods and assumptions of scholars. But recent archaeologically based estimates posit only a very small population for Yehud (Ofer 1993a; 1997; Carter 1994; 1999). Jerusalem itself likely housed only a few thousand people in the late fifth century B.C.E.

16:21. "disciplined kings on their account." This was especially true with reference to the dangers encountered by the Matriarchs (Gen 12:10–20; 20:1–18; 26:6–11).

16:22. "my anointed ones." The poem presents the Matriarchs and Patriarchs as a highly privileged and exalted group. Abraham is called a prophet (נביא) once in Genesis (20:7), but the title "anointed one" (משיח) is not an explicit part of the Genesis traditions.

16:23–33. These verses are drawn from Ps 96:1b–13, which has been described as "a cultic liturgy appointed for the celebration of the Enthronement of Yahweh" (Weiser 1962: 628; cf. Oesterly 1959: 422). Kraus (1993: 251) prefers to call it a "Yahweh as King hymn." Whatever the case, the form and content of Ps 96 are quite different from Pss 105 and 106, which focus their comments on events in Israel's past. If Pss 105 and 106 address the history of the relationship between Yhwh and the people of Israel, Ps 96 addresses the relationship between the universal (creation, divine sovereignty, the nations) and the worship of one particular deity at his sanctuary. Psalm 96 celebrates Yhwh's majesty and splendor in the heavens and beckons not only its Israelite audience but also the nations to give homage to Israel's creator God. In this respect, the themes of Ps 96 are especially appropriate to the Chronicler's use on this occasion, because the psalm describes how Israel, the land, and the nations are to respond to Yhwh's kingship, sovereignty, and glory by giving thanks and worshiping the one "majestic in holiness" (1 Chr 16:29). The very wording of the psalm presumes, therefore, that there is a harmonious relationship between the site of the people's worship on earth and the site of Yhwh's enthronement in the heavens. In Chronicles that harmony has been achieved by the Ark's safe and successful ascent into its tent in the City of David. Even the "families of the peoples" (משפחות עמים; v. 28) can now be summoned to Jerusalem to carry tribute before Yhwh and ascribe to him "the honor due his name" (v. 29).

16:23. "sing to Yhwh all the earth." Boh. follows Ps 96:1 in prefacing, "sing to Yhwh a new song." The version of Psalm 96 found in LXX (Ps 95) prefaces additional material. The title assigned to LXX Ps 95 (= MT Ps 96) is itself interesting, when compared with the setting in the time of David that the Chronicler has assigned the psalm. The superscription of LXX Psalm 95, *hote oikos ōkodomeito meta tēn aichmalōsian ōdē to Dauid* ("When the House was being rebuilt following the Exile. An Ode relating to David"), is not found in MT. Four brief observations may be made about this heading. First, given the postexilic setting assigned to the psalm, it is clear that *tō Dauid*, "relating to David," was not construed by the early Jewish scribes responsible for writing the superscription as indicating Davidic authorship. Second, it is unlikely that this title was found in the Chronicler's *Vorlage* of Ps 96. If the superscription had been part of the Chronicler's source, it is unlikely that he would have quoted this psalm in the context of his presentation of David's life. The psalm supercription most likely belongs to Greek exegetical tradition (Pietersma 2001: 111–13). Third, it seems likely that the early Jewish scribes responsible for writing the superscription of LXX Ps 95 (= MT Ps 96) were either unaware of the Chronicler's reuse of the psalm or forgot that he had done so. If they had been aware that the Chronicler situated the work in the time of David, it is improbable that they would have recontextualized this poem in the early Achaemenid era. Fourth, it is fascinating to see how the same psalm could be meaningfully employed by two different writers in two completely different historical settings. For the Chronicler, the work was appropriate to the Levites' singing on the occasion of the Ark's ascent into the City of David. But for the later scribes responsible for adding the superscription to LXX Psalm 95, the same work with its many references to renewal was appropriate to the construction of the Second Temple in the Persian period, centuries after the time of David. Thus, even within biblical tradition, one can see evidence of how adaptable the Psalms were to use in a variety of contexts. The TEXTUAL NOTES to vv. 23–34 document the selective use of Ps 96 in more detail.

"proclaim." Again, the author only quotes part of the verse (Ps 96:2b). Psalm 96:2a reads "sing to Yhwh, bless his name."

16:25. "feared he is (ונורא הוא) above all the gods (על-כל-אלהים)." In proclaiming Yhwh's superior relationship to other divine beings, the psalmist assumes a heavenly setting in which Yhwh heads the divine council. In this context, he is "greatly praised" and feared above "all" the other gods. Who are these divine beings within the heavenly assembly? In an ancient Near Eastern setting, the council would contain various male and female deities of different rank and responsibilities: major deities, minor deities, messenger deities, and divine attendants (Mullen 1980; Handy 1994). The structure and hierarchy embedded within the divine council was conceived differently by various ancient Near Eastern writers depending on their historical, social, and religious circumstances. The great Babylonian creation epic, *Enūma eliš* (Dalley 1989), for example, tells the story of how Marduk, the patron deity of Babylon, came to occupy the kingship among the gods. One of the Ugaritic myths describes Baal's struggles to establish his kingship (*CAT* 1.1–1.6; Parker et al. 1992: 81–176). As conceived by various Israelite writers, the divine council included a variety of divine beings with different characteristics and responsibilities (e.g., 4QDeut[j] 32:7–8; Ps 29:1–2; 82:1–8; 89:6–11; Isa 51:9–10; Job 1:6–12; 2:1–7). Biblical writers are wont to stress Yhwh's sovereignty within the divine world, but in so doing make comparisons between Yhwh and other gods (e.g., Ps 82). In the case of Ps 96, the author belittles the gods of other nations. Only Yhwh is a living, sentient divine being; they are not.

16:26. "all the gods of the peoples are nonentities." The psalmist creates a wordplay on the terms for "god" (אל) and "gods" (אלהים) by asserting that the gods of other peoples are "nonentities" (אלילים). The latter term can also be translated as "worthless ones" or as "worthlessness" (cf. Jer 14:14; Lev 19:4; 26:1; Isa 2:8, 18, 20; 10:10, 11; 19:1, 3; 31:7; Ezek 30:13; Hab 2:18; Ps 97:7; Sir 30:19). Such a view comports with the Chronicler's own form of monotheism, about which see Japhet (1989) and Frevel (1991).

16:27. "strength and joy are in his place" (עז וחדוה במקומו). The Chronicler alludes to the new site (מקום) of the Ark as its sanctuary (see TEXTUAL NOTE). In the poem there is a close relationship between Yhwh and the "place" (Chronicles) or "sanctuary" (מקדש; Ps 96) at which he is worshiped. On the use of the term "strength" (עז) to signify the Ark, see the NOTE to v. 11.

16:29. "carry tribute (שאו מנחה) and come before him." In the context of the Chronicler's day, such appeals would strengthen the position of the Jerusalem sanctuary. The words of the psalm invite a variety of peoples to join in the service of praise and thanksgiving.

16:30. "tremble, all the earth." The Chronicler's work normally does not exhibit the keen interest in the natural world shown by a number of other biblical authors (Hiebert 1996). In the context of the late Persian period, the incorporation of this text from the Psalms would serve as a source of comfort to the Chronicler's audience. They were only one small community in the context of a large and constantly changing ancient Mediterranean world, but they worshiped a sovereign deity before whom even nature was submissive. With Yhwh in control, the poet can exclaim, "let the heavens rejoice and the earth give cheer" (*yśmḥw hšmym wtgl h'rṣ*; v. 31). The God enthroned in the heavens and worshiped "in his place" (במקמו; v. 27) is coming to judge the earth (v. 33).

"earth." Psalm 96:10a adds *'mrw bgwym yhwh mlk*, "say among the nations, 'Yhwh reigns!' " In Chronicles, this phrase appears in v. 31 (see TEXTUAL NOTE).

"shaken." Psalm 96:10b adds another clause that does not appear in Chronicles, "he judges the peoples with equity" (*ydyn 'mym bmyšrym*).

16:33. "from before Yhwh . . . to judge the earth." The author follows Ps 96 through v. 13a. Psalm 96:13b adds, "he judges the world in justice, and the peoples in his truth."

16:34–36. The final portion of the author's selection from the Psalms is drawn from Ps 106:1, 47–48. Psalm 106, another one of the long, so-called salvation-history compositions (Gunkel 1926: 464), forms the conclusion to book 4 of the Psalms. The bulk of this psalm is a long historical review, lamenting Israelite behaviors during the Exodus (vv. 7–12), the wilderness journeys (vv. 13–15), the rebellion of Dathan and Abiram (vv. 16–18), the episode of the golden calf (vv. 19–23), the skeptical reaction to the report of the Israelite spies (vv. 24–27), the defection to Baal Peor (vv. 28–31), the rebellion at Meribah (vv. 32–33), and the conquest/settlement (vv. 34–46). Sections of author's negative rehearsal of the past have been compared with the Deuteronomic and Deuteronomistic works in their choice of events and themes, if not in their language (Kraus 1993: 318). But familiarity with some traditions found in the Priestly work (e.g., Num 11:1–34; 13:1–14:45; 16:1–35; 20:2–13; 25:1–9; 26:9–10) also seems to be presupposed. The end of the psalm (vv. 47–48) finds the people of Israel scattered throughout the lands imploring Yhwh to gather them "to glory in your praise" (v. 47b). Because of the poem's diasporic ending, commentators generally consider the work to be a Neo-Babylonian or Second Temple period composition. According to some (e.g., Kraus 1993: 317), Ps 106 was one of the penitential liturgies sung in the lamenting assemblies mentioned by Zech 7–8.

16:34. "give thanks to Yhwh, for he is good, for his loyalty endures forever." The summons to thanksgiving is taken from the Chronicler's *Vorlage* of Ps 106:1. This refrain or some variant of it is a favorite in Chronicles (last NOTE to v. 41).

16:35. "deliver us, O God." Whatever the original setting of Ps 106 (see NOTE to 34–36), it is highly relevant that the Chronicler has chosen not to cite any part of the historical litany, but only the beginning (Ps 106:1//1 Chr 16:34) and the concluding confession and appeal (Ps 106:47–48//1 Chr 16:35–36). One reason for the high degree of selectivity seems to parallel that for the selective citation of Ps 105, namely, the Chronicler's omission of the Exodus, Sinai experience, wilderness wanderings, and conquest from his own work (NOTE to v. 8). It is precisely because he excludes so much of Ps 106 from his own composition that his choice to include its final two verses becomes all the more interesting and relevant. Why conclude with a plaintive plea? In the context of natural harmony and communal joy, why does the author have Asaph and his kin appeal to God on behalf of Israel for a liberation from the nations? The repeated request can be taken on more than one level. The Israel David inherits had been defeated and to some extent dispersed following the failure and death of Saul (10:1–14). It is one of King David's main accomplishments to reunite and consolidate the people during the course of his long reign. By the time of the Ark's successful elevation, Israel has decisively rallied to David and he, for his part, had gone on to defeat the Philistines twice. Yet the bulk of David's many battles, both to the east and to the west, is still to come (18:1–20:8). His kingdom is still to be organized (1 Chr 23–27). In this respect, the plea in v. 35 does not so much result from the context of a long history of disobedience and rebellion (Ps 106:6–46) as it does from Israel's uncertain predicament in its larger geopolitical context (1 Chr 10:1–14:17). One is reminded of St. Augustine's repeated citation of Ps 106:47 in one of his sermons (*Serm.* #198) for New Year's Day (ca. 404 C.E.). Ostensibly, Christianity had emerged triumphant and had become the dominant and only legal religion in the Roman Empire. But one finds St. Augustine inveighing against the many continuing threats posed by paganism and repeatedly imploring God to "liberate us from the nations." On another level the appeal can be taken as a statement reflecting the author's own circumstances (Butler 1978; K. Nielsen 1999; Wallace 1999). The Judah of the Chronicler's time is not the Israel he projects in the time of David. In the Chronicler's day, early Judaism had become an international religion. Jews lived not only in Yehud but also in other places, such as Babylon and Egypt. Even those Jews who resided within their own homeland still lived under Achaemenid rule. The governors of the province of Yehud may have been able to exercise some autonomy in local affairs, but they were still accountable to the Persian crown (E. Stern 1984b; 2001; Dandamaev 1989; Berquist 1995; Frei 1996). The plea to "deliver us" and "gather us" is an appeal for Yhwh to reunite his people in Jerusalem. The plea to Yhwh to "liberate us from the nations" is an appeal for freedom from the tyranny of others.

16:36. "the people said, 'Amen' and 'Praise Yhwh.' " In the context of Chronicles, the psalmist's admonitions to "say, 'Amen' and 'Praise Yah!' " (Ps 106:48) are turned into a statement of historical fact.

16:37. "left Asaph and his kinsmen there." That is, with the Ark at the tent of David in Jerusalem. Verses 37–38 in summary fashion pick up the earlier material dealing with David's establishment of a cultus to attend to the Ark (vv. 4–6). Verses 37–38 are unparalled in Samuel.

16:38. "Obed-edom." Referring to Obed-edom the musician (v. 5; 2nd NOTE to 15:24). Counting Obed-edom and Ḥosah the gatekeepers (v. 38b), the total of the Levitical detachment assigned to the tent of David comes to seventy.

"Jeḥiel." One of the Levites taking part in the Ark procession (15:18, 20) and reassigned to Jerusalem by David (16:5). See the 1st TEXTUAL NOTE to v. 38.

"Obed-edom son of Jeduthun." This is the only case in which Obed-edom is given a patronymic, and the patronym is unexpected, given that Jeduthun is usually presented as a singer (1 Chr 25:1, 3, 6; 2 Chr 5:12; 29:14; 35:15). Indeed, Jeduthun functions as a singer at the Gibeon cultus (1 Chr 16:41). The superscriptions in Pss, 39; 62 (MT ידיתון); and 77:1, also seem to associate Jeduthun with song (Kraus 1988: 30), although some think that ידותון in each of these contexts refers to a liturgical or musical term (e.g., Gunkel and Begrich 1933: 458; Oesterly 1959: 15; Mowinckel 1962.2:95). Given the peculiar reference, it is not surprising that some (e.g., Curtis and Madsen 1910: 224; Rudolph 1955: 126; Dirksen 1996a: 88–90) delete this text as a gloss. There is, however, another association between Jeduthun and the gatekeepers. In staffing the cultus of the Tabernacle at Gibeon, the "sons of Jeduthun" serve at the gate (1 Chr 16:42). In some reconstructions (e.g., Dirksen 1996a), this later reference is also viewed as a gloss.

"Ḥosah" reappears among the divisions of gatekeepers appointed during the latter part of David's reign (26:10–11, 16). There he is said to belong to the sons of Merari.

16:39–42. These verses are unparalleled in Samuel. As the larger context makes clear, the Chronicler posits a temporary bifurcation in Israel's national cult. The assembly of the priests and Levites (15:3, 11) coupled with the successful elevation of the Ark (15:25–16:3) afford David the opportunity to reorganize Israel's national cultus. That David would need to do so was very likely occasioned by the author's knowledge and interpretation of older biblical texts. Drawing inferences from his sources dealing with the United Monarchy (Samuel-Kings), the Chronicler came to the conclusion that the Tabernacle and its altar were stationed at Gibeon (1 Kgs 3:4–14). If this was the case, it would be impious of David to neglect this sacred shrine. In Chronicles David honors both sites. Having brought the Ark into Zion (1 Chr 15:25–16:3) and having established its attendant cultus (16:4–6, 37–38), David proceeds to deal with the situation at Gibeon. Just as he designated certain Levites and priests to serve at Jerusalem (vv. 4–6, 37–38), he designates others to serve at Gibeon (see COMMENT).

16:39. "Zadoq the priest" (*ṣdwq hkhn*). Figures bearing the title "the priest" (הכהן) in Chronicles are also presented as high/chief priests: 1 Chr 16:39; 24:6; 29:22 (Zadoq); 2 Chr 22:11; 23:8, 9, 14; 24:2, 20, 25 (Jehoiada); 26:17 (Azariah); 34:14, 18 (Ḥilqiah). In contexts in which clarification is needed (e.g., the mention of other priests), the author adds further specification—הכהן הגדול or הכהן הראש (Koch 1992). See also the 1st NOTE to 15:11.

"his kinsmen the priests" (*'ḥyw hkhnym*). Referring to "Shebaniah, Joshaphaṭ, Nethanel, Amasai, Zechariah, and Eliezer" (1st NOTE to 15:24). "Benaiah," who was also part of the earlier priestly contingent assigned to help elevate the Ark, is not mentioned here because he was earlier assigned to the Ark cultus in Jerusalem (16:6).

"Gibeon." The Chronicler is drawing upon the notice of 1 Kgs 3:4 (cf. 2 Chr 1:3–6), in which the Deuteronomist explains Solomon's private journey to the "high place" (במה) at Gibeon (Knoppers 1993c: 77–82) by mentioning that the Temple had not yet been built. That Yhwh responded to Solomon's incubation rite (cf. *CAT* 1.14.I.26–35) with an impressive revelation signified to the Chronicler that this sacred precinct, "the great[est] high place" (הבמה הגדולה; 1 Kgs 3:4), was a legitimate and prominent, if not the most prominent, Yahwistic sanctuary. The Kings account does not mention that the Tabernacle was located at Gibeon. But given that (1) the Chronicler, following his reading of the sources contained within the Pentateuch, believed that both the Ark and the Tabernacle (or Tent) were essential features of the cultus bequeathed to Moses, (2) Solomon later installed "the Tent of Meeting" (אהל מועד) in the Temple (MT 1 Kgs 8:4; Knoppers 1993c: 98–99), (3) this tent was not mentioned in the account of the advance of the Ark into Zion (2 Sam 6:1–19), (4) Gibeon had an altar upon which Solomon sacrificed a thousand burnt offerings (1 Kgs 3:4), and (5) no other prominent Yahwistic sanctuaries are featured by specific location and name in the Deuteronomistic account of the reign of Solomon, the Chronicler apparently concluded that the Tabernacle must have resided at Gibeon. Hence, he can turn Solomon's later pilgrimage to Gibeon into a very public procession (2 Chr 1:2–3; cf. 1 Kgs 3:4). Indeed, the Chronicler justifies Solomon's pilgrimage in his own description of David's cultic innovations. At the dedication of the Temple, both the Ark and the Tent of Meeting ascend into the Temple (2 Chr 5:1–14). Much more so than his source (MT 1 Kgs 8:1–13), the Chronicler is careful to stress that David's Levitical and priestly arrangements (1 Chr 15–16; 25–26) were implemented (2 Chr 5:11–14).

16:40. "the regular morning and evening burnt offering." These are essential features of tabernacle worship in the Priestly source (e.g., Exod 29:38; Num 28:3, 6; Milgrom 1990: 237–40).

16:41. "with them." That is, with Zadoq and his fellow priests (v. 39). Given the textual evidence (1st TEXTUAL NOTE to v. 42), there is no clear reason for scholars to conclude that Heman and Jeduthun were considered to be priests as well.

"Heman and Jeduthun." Having earlier assigned Asaph to attend to the Ark in Jerusalem (v. 37), David assigns the rest of the triumvirate, Heman and Jeduthun, to the Tabernacle cult at Gibeon. On the appearance of Jeduthun, rather than Ethan, see the 1st NOTE to 15:17.

"the rest of the select, who were designated by name *(nqbw bšmwt)*." The language is formulaic (Num 1:47; Ezra 8:20; 1 Chr 12:32; 16:41; 2 Chr 28:15; 31:19). The phrase may be compared with Nabatean **נקובין בשמהן** (Starcky 1954: 165), which should be translated "designated by their names" (Rabinowitz 1955: 14). The author is referring to all of the remaining singers chosen when David prepared to have the Ark elevated to his Zion sanctuary. Presumably this would specify all those Levites appointed as singers (1 Chr 15:19–23), such as Unni, Maaseiah, Eliphalah, Miqneiah, and Azaziah, who were not chosen to serve the Ark in Jerusalem (16:4–6, 37–38). That this line of interpretation has validity is confirmed by the appearance of both Zadoq the priest (v. 39) and Heman the Levite (v. 41) among the Gibeonite contingent appointed by David. Neither figure appears among those selected to serve the Ark at Jerusalem (16:4–6, 37–38). Similarly, neither Obed-edom the musician (15:21; 16:38a) nor Obed-edom the gatekeeper (15:18, 24; 16:38b) appears among the Levites called to serve at Gibeon (16:41–42). In short, those priests and Levites singled out earlier to serve in the Ark procession (15:17–24) are subsequently elected to serve at one (but not both) of the cult sites affirmed by the crown: the Ark cultus in Jerusalem (16:4–38) and the Tabernacle cultus in Gibeon (16:39–42).

"to give thanks to Yhwh." In the Chronicler's conception, each of the sacred precincts at Jerusalem (vv. 4–38) and Gibeon has its own complement of Levitical singers. Each choir, in turn, is given similar musical instruments and charged with a service of thanksgiving (vv. 4, 7), "for his loyalty endures forever" (vv. 34, 41). The refrain is repeated at the dedication of the Temple (2 Chr 7:3, 6) and in the aftermath of an international crisis for Jerusalem and Judah (2 Chr 20:21; Shipp 1993). Cf. Ezra 3:11 and 1 Macc 4:24.

16:42. "with them." That is, with Zadoq and the priests (v. 39) and with Heman, Jeduthun, and the rest of the Levites (1st NOTE to v. 41).

"trumpets and cymbals." In Chronicles the former are normally priestly instruments (3rd NOTE to 15:24), while the latter are Levitical (6th NOTE to 15:16).

"instruments of the song of God" (**כלי שיר האלהים**). Referring to musical instruments employed to accompany sacred songs (cf. Ps 137:3; 2 Chr 29:27).

"the sons of Jeduthun to be at the gate." This phrase is regarded as a gloss by some commentators because Obed-edom is supposed to be the only son of Jeduthun in this role (v. 38b). But he cannot serve in this capacity at Gibeon because his assignment was to be a gatekeeper in Jerusalem. There are evidently two Obed-edoms in the present text of Chronicles (2nd NOTE to 15:24).

16:43. "all the people departed." The notice forms an *inclusio* with 15:3. With the elevation of the Ark and the Levites and priests appointed at both Jerusalem and at Gibeon, the assembled Israelites may return home.

"to bless his house" (לברך את־ביתו). Another allusion to the beginning of the larger literary unit of which the appointment of a Gibeonite cultus (vv. 39–42) is but one part. The narrative began with David's construction of buildings or houses (בתים) for himself and a tent for the Ark (15:1). Having succeeded both in stationing the Ark in the tent he pitched for it and in staffing the shrines in Jerusalem and Gibeon, David is now free to return home and bless his own house.

## SOURCES AND COMPOSITION

The relationship between the presentation in Chronicles and its relevant source material in Samuel and Psalms may be sketched as follows:

| | *1 Chronicles* | *Source* |
|---|---|---|
| Second Move of the Ark | 15:25–29 | 2 Sam 6:12–16 |
| Installation of the Ark | 16:1–3 | 2 Sam 6:17–19 |
| Ark Attendants and Liturgy | 16:4–6 | — |
| Commission to the Asaphites | 16:7 | — |
| Thanksgiving | 16:8–22 | Ps 105:1–15 |
| Communal Song | 16:23–33 | Ps 96:1b–13 |
| Thanksgiving | 16:34–36 | Ps 106:1, 47–48 |
| Ark Attendants | 16:37–38 | — |
| Tabernacle Attendants | 16:39–42 | — |
| Conclusion | 16:43 | 2 Sam 6:19–20 |

Almost all scholars agree that the author of 1 Chr 16:8–36 has drawn on a version of the book of Psalms. The alternative position, that the psalmists are indebted to Chronicles (Ackroyd 1973a: 64–65), has deservedly not become popular (see TEXTUAL NOTES). The recontextualization of and additions to the *Vorlagen* of Samuel and Psalms reveal the degree to which the material in Chronicles exhibits its own distinctive stamp and structure, despite its indebtedness to the works of earlier authors. Given the borrowing from older sources, one might not think that the composition of 1 Chr 15–16 would be highly contested. But it is. Despite their arcane nature, the lists, names, directives, and poetry of 1 Chr 15–16 are a controversial issue in the history of Chronicles criticism. Are these materials original, secondary accretions, random glosses, or the work of later editors?

There are four major issues at stake in the debate. First, many scholars (e.g., Büchler 1899; von Rad 1930; Noth 1943; Galling 1954; Rudolph 1955; Myers 1965a; R. Braun 1986; Hanson 1992) have deemed one or more of the lists (15:4–10, 17–24; 16:4–6, 37–38, 39–42) to be intrusive or repetitive, while others (e.g., Rothstein and Hänel 1927; Williamson 1982b; Japhet 1993a; Selman

1994a) have argued that the same lists stem from the Chronicler's sources. Second, some (e.g., Rothstein and Hänel 1927; Welch 1939; Williamson 1982b; Dirksen 1995a) have thought that at least one, and perhaps all, of the appearances of the priests (15:4, 11, 14, 24; 16:6, 39) result from the work of a later pro-Priestly editor. Third, many (e.g., Curtis and Madsen 1910; R. Braun 1986; Dirksen 1995a; 1996a) have thought that the repetition of names, most obviously Obed-edom (15:4–10, 11, 17–24; 16:4–6, 37–38, 39–42), is the result of later additions or glosses. Fourth, some (e.g., Noth 1943; Galling 1954; Rudolph 1955; Willi 1972) have thought that the psalms in 16:8–36 are later additions to the Chronicler's text. Because certain scholars employ more than one of these approaches simultaneously, the results affect more than a few odd verses. In Rudolph's reconstruction, for example, fifty-one verses (15:4–10, 16–21, 22–24; 16:5b–38, 42), or 71 percent, the total seventy-two verses in 1 Chr 15–16 are later additions. It is interesting to observe how closely such a resulting reconstruction of the Chronicler's original narrative mirrors its principal source (Samuel). In many respects, the debates about the composition of 1 Chr 15–16 resemble the debates about the composition of the genealogies in 1 Chr 1–9 and the lists in 1 Chr 23–27. Do the presence of these genealogies and lists reflect a series of redactions, a long process of textual growth, or the work of essentially one author? Are the genealogies and lists lengthy interruptions of an originally smooth narrative or are they an integral component of the Chronicler's literary craft? Do the appearance of both the priests and the Levites evince a sequence of two stages of composition, one pro-Levitical and the other pro-Priestly?

It may be best to address each of these major questions separately, even though some are related. I have argued, with reference to the work of ancient Mesopotamian and Greek writers, that genealogies and lists need not be seen as intrusive or secondary ("Excursus: The Genealogies"). In the ancient Mediterranean world, lists, poems, and lineages add depth, texture, and substance to surrounding narratives. In the Pentateuch, genealogies are a structuring device, and the details in lists provide an aura of credibility to the claims found in accompanying narratives (Van Seters 1983; Scolnic 1995). The book of Samuel contains both a long poetic piece associated with David (2 Sam 22) and a shorter composition (2 Sam 23:1–7). Some have even argued that the poem of 1 Chr 16:8–36 is an imitation and transformation of the former account (e.g., Plöger 1957: 41). Given that lists and poems may retard the flow of a narrative, one would expect the author/editor to make reference to or even repeat previous material when he rejoins his narrative (Welten 1973: 190–91). This does not exclude the possibility, of course, that later interpolators could have added some materials to the Chronicler's story. Both authors and interpolators may employ the technique of repetitive resumption. The critical question becomes whether the catalogue of names, whatever its origins, is intrusive or has some demonstrable relationship to the accompanying story. One wonders, for example, whether the list of 15:4–10 might be an addition, because it has little to do with the flow of the narrative aside from providing background information about the Levites mentioned in 15:11. Similarly, one wonders whether at least part of the list of 1 Chr 15:17–24 (specifically 15:22–24) may be a later addition, given the discrepancies between what the Davidic mandate calls for (v. 16) and what actually occurs. But, in any case, the comparative data place the onus on those scholars who advocate wholesale insertions and major redactions to argue why these are the most convincing ways to explain the present text. In the case of the selections from Psalms, there are many connections between the sentiments expressed in these extracts and the Chronicler's own concerns (NOTES to 16:8–36). Moreover, the selection of quotations from Psalms dovetails, as we have seen, with the Chronicler's own ideology. Even though these poetic pieces have been drawn from another source (the Chronicler's *Vorlage* of Psalms), they serve admirably in authorizing the Asaphite Levite ministry of praise and in setting the stage for the establishment of Jerusalem as the focal setting for Israelite worship. As for the repetition of names, not all of these can be shown to stem from a series of different hands. In some cases, as the NOTES have shown, the repetition is a deliberate literary device designed to enhance the flow of the story. In 15:17–18 a series of initial Levitical appointments is followed by a list of specific responsibilities (15:19–21). Following the Ark procession, when David makes his own assignments for the two cult sites of Jerusalem (16:4–6, 37–38) and Gibeon (16:39–42), he draws on many of the internal appointments the Levites and priests made earlier (15:16–24).

The question of the place of the priests and the Levites raises larger, complex issues about the composition of Chronicles (see "Introduction"). Rather than seeing the Chronicler as either pro-Levitical or pro-Priestly in orientation, the Chronicler may be seen as attempting to reconcile and mediate traditional points of view (Knoppers 1999a). The presentation in Chronicles has been undoubtedly influenced by Priestly law, but the influence of Deuteronomy (10:2–3; 31:9, 25–26) is also patent. Writing sometime in the late Persian or early Hellenistic period, the Chronicler was heir to a variety of traditions. The Chronicler's David follows directives pertaining to the Ark embodied in both his Deuteronomic and his Priestly sources (Brettler 1995). That both the priests and the Levites participate in the Ark procession and cooperate at the cultic sites of Jerusalem and Gibeon need cause no great alarm. In the Chronicler's view, the priests and the Levites have important and complementary functions to play in leading, protecting, and sanctifying Israelite worship.

The advocates of the pro-Priestly redaction do raise, however, some significant issues about how the roles and categorization of the Levitical singers, gatekeepers, and priests in Chronicles compare with those in the related literature of Ezra and Nehemiah. Given the appearance of all these groups in different configurations within 1 Chr 15–16, it will be useful to look at this involved question more closely. Whereas the gatekeepers here and elsewhere in Chronicles are Levites, the gatekeepers in the lists of Ezra and Nehemiah seem to belong to a largely separate category. Admittedly, the lists contained in Ezra and Nehemiah are not always as clear as one might like them to be on this difficult issue (Blenkinsopp 1988: 324–26). Moreover, as we have seen (1st NOTE to 15:17), the text of Chronicles does not speak with one voice about who precisely belongs to the troika of singers appointed by David. Some texts speak of Asaph, Heman, and Ethan, while others speak of Asaph, Heman, and Jeduthun. The standard way of dealing with this complex issue is to posit a historical progression in the categorization of singers (e.g., Büchler 1899; 1900; von Rad 1930; Nurmela 1998). That is, each of the major texts in Chronicles, Ezra, and Nehemiah reflects a different time in the postexilic period. The most influential recontruction has been that of Gese (1963). In his view there are multiple stages of development.

1. At the beginning of the Persian period (ca. 515 B.C.E.), the singers are "sons of Asaph" (Ezra 2:41//Neh 7:44), appear after the Levites and before the gatekeepers, and are not yet reckoned as Levites.
2. In Nehemiah's time (ca. 445 B.C.E.) the singers are regarded as Levites and are divided into two groups: the sons of Asaph and the sons of Jeduthun (Neh 11:3–19; 1 Chr 9:1–18).

3a. The Levitical singers appear divided into three groups: the sons of Asaph (the most prominent), the sons of Heman, and the sons of Jeduthun (1 Chr 16:4–6, 37–42; 2 Chr 5:12; 29:13–14; 35:15; Ezra 3:10).

3b. Ethan replaces Jeduthun and Heman becomes more prominent than Asaph (1 Chr 6:16–32; 15:16–24).

Given Gese's particular redaction criticism, indebted to that of Rothstein and Hänel (1927), Gese believes that the Chronicler stood at stage 3a in this schema (ca. 350–300 B.C.E.), whereas stage 3b represents a slightly later development. If one holds to the view that the materials in the Levitical genealogy and the list in 1 Chr 15:16–24 stem from either a source or the Chronicler's own hand (e.g., Williamson 1979a; 1982b; De Vries 1989), stage 3b represents the Chronicler's own time.

One can understand why Gese's theory has become popular, given the variegated testimony in Chronicles, Ezra, and Nehemiah. Nevertheless, the reconstruction is problematic. First, it presupposes that Chronicles, Ezra, and Nehemiah form a continuous work and that the lists reflect historical progress toward greater liberation. But this need not be so. Levine (1993: 176–77), for example, contends for the opposite position, that at least some of the lists in Chronicles antedate those in Ezra and Nehemiah. In this context, the evidence provided by other contexts in Ezra (3:10–12) and Nehemiah (12:8, 24) also complicates matters (a point Gese acknowledges).

Second, the evidence provided by textual criticism is relevant to the issue. Gese's reconstruction is based entirely on the testimony of MT. That he fails to deal with the LXX evidence is most unfortunate, because the LXX evidence from Nehemiah undermines one of the stages in his reconstruction (so also W. H. Barnes 1992). Both MT Neh 11:17 (Qere) and MT 1 Chr 9:16 mention the patronym "Jeduthun," but Jeduthun does not appear in LXX* Neh 11:17. Moreover, while MT Neh 11:17 links Mattaniah, one of the Levites to Asaph: "son of Zabdi son of Asaph, the head of the beginning [LXX$^{L}$ praise], who gave thanks in prayer, and Baqbuqiah, the second among his kinsmen" (בן-זבדי בן-אסף ראש התהלה יהודה לתפלה ובקבקיה משנה מאחיו), this material is lacking in LXX Nehemiah. This means that neither Jeduthun nor Asaph appear in the catalogue of LXX Neh 11. Given that LXX Neh 11–12 is generally considered to contain an older, more primitive version of the account than that of MT Neh 11 (Knoppers 2000c), one cannot assume that MT Neh 11–12 corresponds to a mid-fifth-century date in the postexiilic period. On the contrary, MT Neh 11:17 would seem to represent a later stage in the development of the text.

Third, the proposed stage 3b is rather curious, if not unconvincing. If an editor wished to supplant Jeduthun with Ethan, why would that editor insert the name Ethan only in the genealogies and in the early United Monarchy and never later? Would not such an approach amount to a faulty strategy? Even with the insertion of Ethan among the internal Levitical appointments for the Ark procession (15:16–17), it is Jeduthun who appears among the more permanent Davidic appointments (16:38, 41). Indeed, it is Jeduthun who remains the third member of the triumvirate in all of the material dealing with the later reign of David (25:1, 3, 6), the reign of Solomon, the time the Temple was actually built (2 Chr 5:12), and the kingdom of Judah (2 Chr 29:14; 35:15). Based on this literary evidence, one would think that Jeduthun replaced Ethan, not vice versa.

Fourth, and perhaps most important, the theory assumes what it needs to prove, namely, that there is a clear agreement between the lists in Chronicles, Ezra, and Nehemiah and the empirical realities of life in the Achaemenid era. Each major witness in the text is presumed to reflect a distinct epoch in the Persian and Hellenistic ages. One is sympathetic to the possibility that these passages reflect changing circumstances in changing times, but it also seems likely that the texts reflect in no small measure the perceptions, assumptions, and commitments of the authors. In this respect, the very classification of individuals and groups represents authorial values. Whether those values conflicted with or corresponded to the realities of the authors' times cannot always be determined. One could argue that the texts of Ezra, Nehemiah, and Chronicles diverge not so much (or simply) because they are written at various times, but (also) because they reflect different authorial judgments (COMMENT on 9:2–34). In this respect, one should acknowledge differences between the authors/editors of Chronicles and those of Nehemiah. To return to the lists in 1 Chr 9 and Neh 11 as an example, the different editors of this material seem to have handled and developed some common source material in strikingly different ways (Knoppers 2000c). The heading (1 Chr 9:2) and summary (9:34) in Chronicles make it clear that the editor of the list regards the gatekeepers as Levites. But the status of the gatekeepers in Neh 11 is much more ambiguous. The summary in MT Neh 11:18 (not found in LXX), which mentions "all of the Levites in the holy city" (כל-הלוים בעיר הקדש), does not include the gatekeepers who follow in Neh 11:19.

In short, the literary evidence provided by Chronicles, Ezra, and Nehemiah pertaining to the identity and classification of the singers is complex. Some of this evidence may reflect shifting circumstances relating to the status of the singers over the course of this long era. But the textual evidence probably also reflects ongoing disputes among different groups and individual authors over what the precise status and classification of the singers should be. Within this larger context, the authors of Chronicles stand very much in defense of the singers, classifying the singers, musicians, and gatekeepers as full-fledged Levites. Within the larger tribe, the singers stand alongside other Levites, including the priests, as participants in major cultic activities.

# COMMENT

The successful arrival of the Ark at the tent of David in Jerusalem marks a milestone in the narration of the United Monarchy. By bringing the Ark into the City of David, the king ties the authority of this ancient palladium to his recently acquired capital. The Chronicler's version of this important transition establishes the pedigree and prerogatives of religious functionaries in his own day. The mention of both the Ark and the Tabernacle is highly important because it creates vital links not only between the First Temple and the Second Temple but also between the First Temple and the Sinaitic institutions established many centuries before the Chronicler's own time. The long process is, however, incomplete until the proper personnel and services have been appointed for the Ark in its new ritual setting and for the Tabernacle in Gibeon (16:4–42). For the Chronicler's audience, the institution of a Jerusalemite shrine and the reorganization of the cultus, including the appointment of priestly and Levitical contingents (16:4–6, 37–42), mean that elements in the system of worship existing in their own day were not a new innovation, but honored the directives of their reverend king from long ago.

The successful installation of the Ark in Jerusalem creates, however, a dualism in the national cultus, an anomalous bifurcation in the practice of Israelite worship that remains unresolved until the Temple's dedication under Solomon (2 Chr 5:1–14). The much celebrated arrival of the Ark establishes the City of David as a national shrine (16:1), but it also leaves Israel with two major official sanctuaries, Jerusalem and Gibeon. While the Ark of Yhwh is attended by Levites and priests in Jerusalem (16:4–6, 37–38), the Tabernacle (משכן) of Yhwh resides in Gibeon, attended by Zadoq, his kin, and various Levites (16:39–42). Each of these religious centers is associated with its own complement of ritual trappings. Each sacred precinct has its own Levitical singers and each choir, in turn, is equipped with musical instruments and commissioned with a service of thanksgiving (16:4, 7), "for his loyalty endures forever" (16:34, 41). Each of the two authorized shrines has its own set of gatekeepers (16:38, 42).

There is, however, also a vital difference between the two sanctuaries. One features a regular litany of sacrifices, while the other does not. To be sure, when the Ark is first placed in the tent, burnt offerings and offerings of well-being are sacrificed before God (16:1–2). But the ministry at the Ark is basically one of commemoration, thanksgiving, and praise (16:4). After blessing the people, the king commissions some of the priests and Levites to serve regularly before the Ark (16:2–6). David appoints (נתן) Asaph and his kin to take the lead in praising Yhwh, and they oblige by singing a medley of excerpts (16:8–35) from the Psalms (105:1–15; 96:1b–13; 106:1, 47–48). As a later reference implies (21:26), the Ark shrine in Jerusalem is not associated with a regular regimen of sacrifices.

As for the sacred precinct at Gibeon, David (re)organizes the cultus there. Zadoq and his priests sacrifice burnt offerings to Yhwh there daily upon the altar (16:40). Like the newly dedicated ministry of praise associated with the Ark in Jerusalem, the Gibeon cult has its own coterie of singers and musicians authorized to praise Yhwh (16:42). The Chronicler does not deem the Gibeon shrine to be inherently illicit. Quite the contrary, he comments that the sacrifices performed there accorded with "all that was written in the Torah of Yhwh" (16:40). Contributing to the sacred aura of the proceedings is the use of "holy" numbers. There are consistently three main singers (15:17, 19; 16:5, 37, 41), seven priests in the procession (15:24), twelve named priests and Levites attending the Ark at its new location (16:5–6), a total contingent of seventy serving the Ark (16:37–38), and apparently seven priests stationed at Gibeon (2nd NOTE to v. 39).

In the Chronicler's theology of a unified national cult, which draws upon both Deuteronomic and Priestly materials, the Ark and the Tabernacle belong together in Jerusalem. Given the Deuteronomic mandate for one central sanctuary, the existence of two national shrines can only be temporary. All of the traditional cultic symbols of ancient Israel find their fulfillment in the Jerusalem Temple (Welten 1979). Both the Ark and the Tabernacle will eventually be (re)united in the shrine built by Solomon (2 Chr 5). In this respect, the elevation of the Ark and the reorganization of the Gibeon Tabernacle are penultimate events to the construction and dedication of the Temple.

But what is the upshot of the Chronicler's unique presentation? Or to put it somewhat differently, what does his unusual combination of Deuteronomic and Priestly motifs say about his priorities for Judean worship? What is striking, in my judgment, is that he associates ongoing sacrificial worship with the sacred precinct in Gibeon, not with the sacred precinct in Zion. The Chronicler, in conformity with the demands for the centralization of worship in Deut 12, holds to only one legitimate site for Yahwistic sacrifice. Hence, he can claim that the morning and evening burnt offerings were presented "according to all that was written in the Torah of Yhwh" (1 Chr 16:40). Yet his narrative, influenced by the presentation of Solomon's sacrifice at Gibeon in Kings (last NOTE to v. 39), associates that centralized sacrifice with Gibeon and not with Jerusalem!

This leads to a number of conclusions. First, the author does not take it for granted that centralized sacrifice, when it first occurred, had to occur in Jerusalem. Gibeon, for a few decades at least, qualifies as "the place that Yhwh your God shall choose . . . to bring your burnt offerings and other sacrifices" (Deut 12:5–6). In this respect, his work acknowledges the antiquity and status of one of the major towns found within Yehud during the author's own time. Second, sacrifice is not the sole function of the officiants assigned to this cultic site. The priests and the Levites have "trumpets and cymbals for sounding," instruments to be used for the "song of God" (1 Chr 16:42). Similarly, one of the functions of the priests Benaiah and Jaḥaziel, who serve in Jerusalem, is to play the trumpets before the Ark (16:6). Presumably, the priests might have some administrative functions as they do elsewhere, but these are not mentioned in this context. Third, in the Chronicler's understanding of Israelite law and lore, there can be multiple sites of Yahwistic worship, but only one legitimate place of (animal) sacrifice. One is reminded of the correspondence from Elephantine (Vincent 1937: 253–55; Porten 1968: 278–98) in which the authorities in Jerusalem and Samaria were petitioned to support the rebuilding of the Jewish Temple in Elephantine (AP 27, 30, 31, 32). The Jerusalem leaders seem to have given their blessing to the reconstruction of the Elephantine Temple with the proviso that it only present cereal offerings (מנחה), drink offerings ([נסך]), and incense (לבונה; AP 33.11; Grelot 1972: 417–19). Sheep, oxen, and goats were not to be offered there as burnt sacrifice (מקלו; AP 33.10). The issue posed by the possible reconstruction of the Elephantine sanctuary is resolved by recourse to the exclusive association between the central sanctuary and animal sacrifice (cf. Deut 12:5–6). If the problem is defined such that certain sacrifices may occur "only in the place that Yhwh will choose among your tribes" (כי אם-במקום אשר-יבחר יהוה באחד שבטיך; Deut 12:14), then the way is clear for other Yahwistic worship centers to exist, provided they not violate the exclusive prerogatives of the central sanctuary.

Fourth, Chronicles associates the establishment of worship in Jerusalem first of all with music and song, not with the sacrificial slaughter of animals. Animal sacrifice is essential to the services at the Jerusalem Temple. But not until that Temple is built during the reign of Solomon does centralized sacrifice come to Jerusalem. It is surely relevant to note that in the coverage of David's early reign, most of the attention is devoted to the establishment of the service of thanksgiving and praise in Jerusalem (16:4–38), whereas the reorganization of worship in Gibeon receives only brief attention (16:39–42). Even then, half of this coverage is given over to the establishment of singers, musicians, and gatekeepers at the Tabernacle (16:41–42). Both the allocation of coverage and the details of that coverage point toward the great importance of thanksgiving, music, and song in the Chronicler's vision of Yahwistic worship.

# *XX. The Divine Promises to David (17:1–15)*

*David's Plan to Build the Temple*

1 After David settled in his house, David said to Nathan the prophet, "Here
I am, living in the cedar house, but the Ark of the Covenant of Yhwh is under
curtains." 2 Nathan said to David, "Do all that is in your heart, because God is
with you."

*Nathan's Oracle of Rejection*

3 But during that very night the word of God came to Nathan, saying,
4 "Go and say to David my servant: 'Thus Yhwh said, As for you, you will not
build the House for me to reside (in). 5 Indeed, I have not resided in a house
from the day I brought up Israel until this very day, but have gone about from

tent to tent and from tabernacle to tabernacle. [6]In all of my traveling with all
Israel, did I ever speak to one of the chieftains of Israel whom I commanded
to shepherd my people, saying, "Why have you not built a house of cedars for
me?" '

*Nathan's Dynastic Oracle*

[7]"But now, thus will you say to my servant David, 'Thus said Yhwh
Sebaoth, I, I took you from the pasture, from behind the flock, to be ruler
over my people Israel. [8]I have been with you wherever you went and have cut
off all your enemies from before you. Moreover, I shall make a name for you
like the name of the greatest in the land. [9]I shall make a place for my people
Israel and I shall plant them so that they will reside in it and be disturbed no
longer. Evildoers will no longer wear them down as in the past, [10]ever since
the days I commanded chieftains over my people Israel. I shall humble all
your enemies and make you great. As for a house, Yhwh will build one for
you. [11]When your days are full (and you) go to be with your fathers, I shall establish your seed after you, one of your own sons, and I shall establish his
kingship. [12]As for him, he will build a house for me and I shall establish his
throne forever. [13]I, I shall be a father to him and he will be a son to me and I
shall not withdraw my loyalty from him as I withdrew it from your predecessor. [14]I shall appoint him in my house and in my kingship forever. His throne
will be established forever.' "

[15]According to all these words and according to all this vision did Nathan speak to
David.

## TEXTUAL NOTES

Textual analysis is critical to the interpretation of 1 Chr 17. 1 Chr 17:1–27 is paralleled by 2 Sam 7:1–29. Although Ps 89 contains another more elaborate version of the promises to David, the closest textual parallels are between the texts of Samuel and Chronicles. Even so, the Hebrew and Greek texts of Samuel and Chronicles contain numerous text-critical variants, as well as grammatical conundrums. Scholars disagree about how best to account for the variations between 1 Chr 17 and 2 Sam 7. In what follows, the impulse to correct the text of Chronicles by constant recourse to the text of Samuel will be resisted. Nor will it be assumed, as is common, that in those instances in which Chronicles is shorter than or differs from Samuel that the Chronicler omitted from or rewrote portions of Samuel. The text-critical evidence suggests that the Samuel text used by the Chronicler was a typologically more primitive text than either MT or LXX Samuel. This does not mean that the Chronicler never altered his *Vorlage*. The evidence suggests that he sometimes did. But one should look for distinctive Chronistic vocabulary, style, or themes to substantiate such a claim. In the textual criticism of 1 Chr 17, it is best to balance two aims: (1) to examine the witnesses to Samuel and Chronicles carefully to illumine the history of both texts and (2) to keep the integrity of the Chronicler's own text clearly in view. The primary goal of the textual criticism of Chronicles is to reconstruct, as closely as possible, the original text of Chronicles, not the original text of Samuel.

17:1. "David." MT 2 Sam 7:1 reads here (and in vv. 2–3) "the king" (Kalimi 1995a: 160–61).

"settled in his house." MT 2 Sam 7:1 adds "and Yhwh had given him rest from all of his surrounding enemies" *(wyhwh hnyḥ lw msbyb mkl ʾybyw)*. As McCarter (1984: 190–91) observes, LXX[B] 2 Sam 7:1 provides a different interpretation of the same consonants (= *hnyḥlw*). 1 Chr 17:1 lacks an equivalent to either MT or LXX Samuel for this part of the verse (see NOTE). It is possible, however, that the missing statement was lost by haplography (*homoioarkton* from *wyhwh* to *wyʾmr*, "and (David) said").

"here I am, living" *(hnh ʾnky ywšb)*. MT 2 Sam 7:2 "see I am living" *(rʾh nʾ ʾnky ywšb)*.

"in the cedar house." The Heb. should be read as definite *(bĕbêt hāʾărāzîm)*, not as indefinite, "in a house of cedar" (as in most modern translations).

"the Ark of the Covenant of Yhwh" *(ʾrwn bryt yhwh)*. So MT and LXX. MT 2 Sam 7:2 "the Ark of God" *(ʾrwn hʾlhym)*.

"under curtains" *(tḥt yryʿwt)*. MT 2 Sam 7:2 *btwk hyryʿh* "in the midst of the curtain." LXX[L] 2 Sam 7:2 expands to "curtains of Yhwh."

17:2. "do all that is in your heart" *(kl ʾšr blbbk ʿśh)*. MT and LXX 2 Sam 7:3 are more expansive "all that is in your heart, go [LXX and] do" (*kl ʾšr blbbk lk* [*w*]*ʿśh*).

17:3. "the word of God came to Nathan." So MT *(lectio brevior)*. Some Heb. MSS, Syr. 17:3 and LXX[L], Syr. 2 Sam 7:4 add "the prophet."

"saying." Reading with MT, LXX[ALN] Chr 17:3 and MT 2 Sam 7:4. LXX[BSf] lack *legōn*.

17:4. "to David my servant" *(ʾl dwyd ʿbdy)*. So MT 1 Chr 17:4 and LXX, Syr. 2 Sam 7:5 *(lectio brevior)*. MT 2 Sam 7:5 "to my servant, to David" (*ʾl-ʿbdy ʾl-dwd*; Kalimi 1995a: 221).

"you will not build" *(lʾ ʾth tbnh)*. So MT and LXX 1 Chr 17:4, LXX and Syr. 2 Sam 7:5. MT 2 Sam 7:5 *hʾth tbnh*, "will you build?"

"the House for me to reside (in)" *(ly hbyt lšbt)*. The text is elliptical. LXX "a house to reside in it" (*oikon tou katoikēsai me en autō* = *byt lšbt bw*). MT 2 Sam 7:5 "a house for my dwelling" *(byt lšbty)*. After "house" a few Samuel MSS add "for my name" (cf. 2 Sam 7:13).

17:5. "from the day I brought up Israel" *(mn-hywm ʾšr hʿlyty ʾt-yśrʾl)*. So MT (and LXX) *(lectio brevior)*. 2 Sam 7:6 "from the day I brought up the sons of Israel from Egypt" *(lmywm ʾšr hʿlyty ʾt-bny yśrʾl mmṣrym)*. Fragmentary 4QSam[a] is similar "[Egyp]t." Tg. 1 Chr 17:5 also adds "from Egypt."

"but have gone about" *(wʾhyh mthlk)*. So MT 2 Sam 7:7. MT and LXX 1 Chr 17:5 have lost the ptc. *mthlk* by haplography (*homoioarkton* before *mʾhl*).

"from tent to tent and from tabernacle to tabernacle" *(mʾhl ʾl-ʾhl wmškn ʾl mškn)*. MT 1 Chr 17:5 "from tent to tent and from tabernacle" *(mʾhl ʾl-ʾhl wmškn)*. LXX[B] "I have been in a tent and in a covering" *(kai ēmēn en skēnē kai en kalymmati)*. My reconstruction assumes a haplography (*homoioteleuton* from *wmškn* to *mškn*). Kittel (1895: 65) deems the reading of Chronicles a corruption of MT 2 Sam 7:6 "in a tent and in a tabernacle" *(bʾhl wbmškn)*, but MT 2 Sam 7:6 is itself corrupt and may reflect a combination of two lemmata (McCarter 1984: 192). This may be a case in which the Chronicler has slightly recast his *Vorlage* in accordance with his own narrative designs (see NOTES).

17:6. "did I ever speak." Reading an inf. abs. construction. See LXX 1 Chr 17:6 and LXX 2 Sam 7:7 *ei lalōn elalēsa* (= *hădabber dibbartî*). MT 1 Chr 17:6 and 2 Sam 7:7 *hădābār dibbertî* represent a different interpretation of the same consonants. Cf. Vg. *numquid loquens*.

"chieftains" *(špṭy)*. So MT. 4QSam[a] and MT 2 Sam 7:7 *šbṭy*. McCarter (1984: 192) and Caquot and de Robert (1994: 427–28) provide divergent perspectives on the Samuel reading. On the different roots *špṭ* and *šbṭ*, see Loewenstam (1980).

"my people." Thus MT and LXX *(lectio brevior)*. MT 2 Sam 7:7 adds "Israel."

17:7. "from the pasture, from behind the flock" *(mn-hnwh mn-ʾḥry hṣʾn)*. So MT (cf. MT 2 Sam 7:8 *mn-hnwh mn-ʾḥr hṣʾn*). Similarly, LXX 1 Chr 17:7 "from the fold, from behind the flocks" *(ek tēs mandras exopisthen tōn poimniōn)*. LXX[B] 2 Sam 7:8 *ek tēs mandras tōn probatōn* (= *mnwh hṣʾn*).

"ruler over my people Israel." So MT and LXX. 2 Sam 7:8 is more expansive, "ruler over my people, over Israel."

17:8. "cut off" *(ʾkryt)*. Thus MT. MT 2 Sam 7:9 *ʾkrth*.

"moreover, I shall make" *(wĕʿāśîtî)*. Reading MT as a converted perfect. It is also possible to take the *wāw* as merely conjunctive and to read the perfect as past tense (so Mosis [1973: 82–87] for all of vv. 8–10). See LXX (and Tg.) "I made" *(epoiēsa)*. On the switch in tenses in MT 2 Sam 7:9b(//1 Chr 17:8b), see Loretz (1961: 294–96), Gelston (1972: 92–94), Murray (1990), and most recently Vanderhooft (1999a).

"a name." Reading with MT and LXX. Some Heb. MSS and MT 2 Sam 7:9 expand to "a great name." But the expansion is missing from LXX[BAMN] 2 Sam 7:9.

17:9. "I shall plant them so that they will reside in it." Literally, "I shall plant him so that he will reside under it." The text may be referring to the people's residing under the deity's sacred mount or temple (*māqôm;* Vanderhooft 1999a).

"evildoers" *(bny ʿwlh)*. So MT 1 Chr 17:9, MT 2 Sam 7:10, and *Florilegium* (4Q174). But *bny* does not appear in LXX[AB] *(adikia tou tapeinōsai)*. LXX[L] *huios adikias*, "evil person" (= *bn ʿwlh*). Cf. LXX 2 Sam 7:10, *huios adikos*.

"will no longer" *(wlʾ-ywsypw)*. So MT. LXX has the sg. (= *ywsyp*).

"wear them down" *(lbltw)*. Literally, "to wear it out" (the *piʿel* of *blh*). I read with MT (maximum variation). Note the use of *blh* in Gen 18:12; Ps 32:3; and Dan 7:25. LXX 1 Chr 17:9 *tapeinōsai auton* follows MT 2 Sam 7:10 "to humble it" *(lʿnwtw)*. Cf. *lʾ yʿnnw* in MT Ps 89:23 [ET 89:22]. LXX Ps 89:23 *prosthēsei tou kakōsai auton* (= *ywsyp lʿnwtw*?) assimilates toward 2 Sam 7:10.

17:10. "ever since the days" *(lmymym)*. I read with a few Heb. MSS and Tg., which lack the connective *(wāw)* of MT and LXX. MT 2 Sam 7:11 "and from the day." But LXX[O], Syr., Vg., and some Tg. MSS lack "and."

"I shall humble all your enemies" *(whknʿty ʾt-kl-ʾwybyk)*. So MT. LXX has the aorist *kai etapeinōsa* (cf. Tg.). MT 2 Sam 7:11 reads "I shall give you rest from all your enemies" *(whnyḥty lk mkl ʾybyk)*. In this instance, the difference between 2 Sam 7 and 1 Chr 17 probably reflects slight rewording on the part of the Chronicler (see NOTES).

"and I shall make you great." Cf. LXX *kai auxēsō se* (= *wʾgdlk*). MT "and I reported to you" *(wʾgd lk)*. The lemma of 2 Sam 7:11 takes the corruption further, *whgyd lk*.

"as for a house, Yhwh will build one for you" *(wbyt ybnh lk yhwh)*. So MT and LXX. *Florilegium* (4Q174) is similar, *byt ybnh lkh*, but MT 2 Sam 7:11 differs, "that a house Yhwh will make for you" *(ky-byt yʿśh lk yhwh)*.

17:11. "when your days are full" *(whyh ky-mlʾw ymyk)*. So MT. McCarter (1984: 193–94) thinks that 1 Chr 17:11 combines the two readings reflected by MT 2 Sam 7:12 *ky ymlʾw ymyk* and LXX 2 Sam 7:12 *kai estai ean plērōthōsin hai hēmerai*. Freedman (personal communication) offers a different explanation, arguing that an original *whyh ky ymlʾw ymyk* has become corrupted in both texts.

"to go with your fathers" *(llkt ʿm-ʾbtyk)*. I read with MT *(lectio difficilior)*. LXX 1 Chr 17:11 and LXX 2 Sam 7:12 have *kai koimēthēsē meta tōn paterōn sou*. Similarly, 2 Sam 7:12 "and you sleep with your fathers" *(wškbt ʾt-ʾbtyk)*.

"one of your own sons" *(ʾšr yhyh mbnyk)*. So MT (maximum differentiation). LXX[AB] "who will be from your loins" *(hō estai ek tēs koilias sou)* is again closer to MT (and LXX) 2 Sam 7:12 "one from your own loins" *(ʾšr yṣʾ mmʿyk)*.

"I shall establish his kingship" *(whkynwty ʾt mlkwtw)*. So MT (maximum variation). LXX (1 Chr 17:11; 2 Sam 7:12) and MT 2 Sam 7:12 "I shall establish his kingdom" *(whkynty ʾt mmlktw)*.

17:12. "he will build a house for me." The lemma of 2 Sam 7:13, "he will build a house for my name," reflects Deuteronomistic phraseology.

"his throne." So MT and LXX. 2 Sam 7:13 is more expansive, "the throne of his kingship."

17:13. "son." MT 2 Sam 7:14 adds "when he commits iniquity, I shall chastise him with the rod of humans and with the stripes of the sons of man" *(ʾšr bhʿwtw whkḥtyw bšbṭ ʾnšym wbngʿy bny ʾdm*; cf. Ps 89:31–36 [ET 89:30–35]). If the Chronicler's *Vorlage* reflected the connective present in LXX 2 Sam 7:14 (= *wʾšr* . . . ), it is possible that the clause was lost by haplography (before *wḥsdy*). But it seems more likely that this is an instance in which the Chronicler, in the interests of his larger presentation, omitted some material from his *Vorlage* (NOTES).

"and I shall not withdraw my loyalty from him" *(wḥsdy lʾ-ʾsyr mʿmw)*. So MT and LXX. MT 2 Sam 7:15 has *yswr*, but a few Heb. MSS (and LXX, Syr., and Vg.) read *ʾswr*.

"from your predecessor." Literally, "from him who was before you" *(mʾšr hyh lpnyk)*. LXX reads the pl. "from those who were before you" *(apo tōn ontōn emprosthen sou)*. MT 2 Sam 7:15 both expands and specifies "from Saul, whom I removed from before you." On the variations among the witnesses to 2 Sam 7:15, see McCarter (1984: 194–95).

17:14. "I shall appoint him in my house" *(whʿmdtyhw bbyty)*. Similarly, LXX "I shall confirm him in my house" *(pistōsō auton en oikō mou)*. Here and later in this verse, the formulation differs from 2 Sam 7:16. MT 2 Sam 7:16 has "your house is enduring" *(n'mn bytk)*, but LXX 2 Sam 7:16 carries through with the 3rd per. *pistōthēsetai ho oikos autou*. While it is true that sufs., especially the easily confused *yôd* and *wāw*, are susceptible to scribal error (McKenzie 1985: 64), the other differences between Samuel and Chronicles do not easily submit to a simple text-critical explanation. One has to grant the possibility that the Chronicler has rewritten his *Vorlage* to conform to his own views (Brunet 1953: 505; Rudolph 1955: 135). A Chronistic rewriting becomes more probable when one recognizes the presence of Chronistic idiom in this verse. The use of the *hipʿil* of the verb *ʿmd* in the sense of "appoint" or "establish," for instance, occurs often in Chronicles, Ezra, and Nehemiah (Curtis and Madsen 1910: 32 [#89]).

"and in my kingship forever" *(wbmlkwty ʿd-hʿwlm)*. So MT. LXX "and in his kingdom forever" *(kai en basileia autou heōs aiōnos)*. LXX 2 Sam 7:16 is almost identical *(kai hē basileia autou heōs aiōnos)*. MT 2 Sam 7:16 "and your kingdom before you forever" *(wmmlktk ʿd-ʿwlm lpnyk)*. The 1st-per. formulation of MT is largely consistent with other related assertions in the book (1 Chr 28:5; 29:11; 2 Chr 13:8). See further the 2nd NOTE to v. 14.

"(and) his throne will be established forever" *(wks'w yhyh nkwn ʿd-ʿwlm)*. So also LXX, "and his throne will be established forever" *(kai thronos autou estai anōrthōmenos heōs aiōnos)*. The longer lemma of MT 2 Sam 7:16 retains the 2nd per., "your throne will be established forever before you" *(ks'k yhyh nkwn ʿd-ʿwlm lpnyk)*, while LXX retains the 3rd per., "and his throne." Whatever the most primitive reading in Samuel might be—McCarter (1984: 195) argues for an original Samuel lemma *lpny wks'k* (cf. LXX, Cyprian, and Syr.)—there is no textual problem in Chronicles.

## NOTES

17:1. "after David settled in his house." The reason for the nonappearance of MT 2 Sam 7:1 "and Yhwh had given him rest from all of his surrounding enemies" in Chronicles is uncertain. Many scholars view the omission as deliberate, but haplography cannot be ruled out (see TEXTUAL NOTE). Assuming, for the sake of argument, that the author intentially abbreviated his *Vorlage*, how does one explain the omission? In the standard view, the Chronicler associates the reign of Solomon, not the reign of David, with a time of rest for all Israel (1 Chr 22:8–9, 18–19; 23:25; 28:2–3; 2 Chr 6:41; Brunet 1953: 505–6). Some (e.g., Rudolph 1955: 129) think that the writer wanted to underscore the connection between the ascent of the Ark and the building of the Temple. While it is true that the author celebrates Solomon's tenure as an unprecedented era of peace, this is also true for the first period of Solomon's reign in the Deuteronomistic History (1 Kgs 5:17–19 [ET 5:3–4]; cf. 11:1–38; Knoppers 1993c). McKenzie (1985: 63; 1999b) argues a second position, that the clause was a late Deuteronomistic addition to Samuel and, as such, was missing from the Chronicler's *Vorlage*.

"the cedar house." From David's perspective, the completion of his palace

(14:1) has put him in an odd position. He lives in splendor, while the Ark, representing Yhwh's presence in Israel, resides in a tent (16:1–3; Kalimi 1995a: 170). Indeed, in the ancient Near East it was common for successful monarchs to give thanks to the deities who guided them by building or restoring temples (Postgate 1994a: 120–22, 260–64). Conversely, royal neglect of temples and their restoration could incur divine wrath (Frankfort 1948: 269). Seen in this context, it would be impious for successful David not to show gratitude to the deity who repeatedly supported him. Coming at the issue from a different (and later) perspective, Josephus (*Ant.* 7.342) also commends David's desire to build a temple. In the view of Josephus, the Israelites had been remiss in not constructing the sanctuary themselves. Given the mandate for a central sanctuary (Deut 12), the Israelites should have constructed such an edifice upon taking possession of the land.

"under curtains." That is, in the tent David pitched for the Ark (15:1; 16:1). The Tabernacle also had cloths or curtains (Exod 26:1–2, 7; Num 4:21–28), but it was located at Gibeon (1 Chr 16:39–42).

17:2. "do all that is in your heart." The prophet Nathan assures David of the deity's blessing, but Nathan does not use the citation formula, "thus said Yhwh." Given the subsequent nocturnal vision (vv. 3–4), Nathan is forced to countermand his own advice.

17:3. "the word of God came" (ויהי דבר-אלהים). The structure of Nathan's mission to David requires some discussion. In both Samuel and Chronicles, Nathan by divine command actually delivers two speeches (vv. 4b–6, 7b–14). The commissioning report ("the word of God came to Nathan, saying"; v. 3) governs both oracles because Nathan is told to deliver two oracles. Each oracle features its own commissioning formula, "go and say to David my servant" (v. 4) and "but now, thus you will say to my servant David" (v. 7) and each is introduced by its own citation formula, "Yhwh said" (v. 4) and "thus said Yhwh Sebaoth" (v. 7). A concluding summary, "according to all these words and according to all this vision did Nathan speak to David" (v. 15), closes the account and forms a transition to the prayer of David that follows (vv. 16–27). The organization of Nathan's words into two separate speeches calls attention to the distinctive characteristics of each. The first oracle (vv. 4b–6) is essentially negative, countermanding Nathan's initial positive response to David's inquiry (see the previous NOTE). The second oracle (vv. 7b–14) is positive, surprising David with its announcements of victory, temple construction, and dynasty building.

17:4. "as for you, you will not build the House for me" (לא אתה תבנה-לי הבית). Nathan's query in 2 Sam 7:5, "will you build a house for my dwelling?" proscribes temple construction, suggesting the improbability of Yhwh's dwelling in a humanly built domicile. But the emphasis in Chronicles is on timing (Schniedewind 1999b). Nathan's oracle prohibits David from building the Temple, but does not question temple construction itself. Indeed, Nathan's formulation assumes the future establishment of a sanctuary. That David "will not build the House" intimates that the author already has the construction of the Temple in view.

17:5. "not resided in a house." The text plays on David's earlier statement that he resides "in the cedar house" (*bĕbêt hāʾărāzîm*). The speech does not contest

David's point about the contrast between David's palace and the tent for the Ark, only the implication that the Ark needed a stationary sanctuary *(bayit)* to match "the cedar house." As mandated in the Sinaitic revelation concerning the Tabernacle and all of its furnishings (Exod 25:10–27:19), Israel's cult was designed to be mobile. The roving nature of Yhwh's presence was consistent with Israel's ambulatory existence since the Exodus.

"from tent to tent and from tabernacle to tabernacle" (מאהל אל-אהל ומשכן אל-משכן). The allusion to Yhwh's frequenting both tent and tabernacle may seem strange at first glance, but it is indebted to the varying terminology employed in the Pentateuch to describe Israel's sanctuary: "the [Tabernacle of the] Tent of Meeting" (אהל מעד; Exod 39:32; 40:2, 6, 29) and "the Tabernacle" (משכן; Exod 25:9; 26:1, 6; 27:9; Lev 17:4; Num 16:9; 17:28 [ET 17:13]; 19:13; 31:30, 47). Cf. 1 Chr 6:17, 33; 16:39; 21:29; 2 Chr 1:5; 29:6. In the context of Chronicles, the divine oracle covers both types of locutions.

17:6. "chieftains of Israel." Although the Judges period figures prominently in the Deuteronomistic History, this is only one of two explicit references to the Judges in Chronicles (cf. v. 10). It is quite possible, however, that the anarchy sketched in Azariah's prophecy (2 Chr 15:2–7) also alludes to the time of the Judges. In taking over this reference from his *Vorlage* (cf. 2 Sam 7:7), the author shows his willingness to acknowledge the existence of this particular era. The Chronicler's concern with upholding the United Monarchy as the formative epoch in Israel's past leads him to neglect the Judges, except in passing. For a different view, see Japhet (1979; 1989).

17:7. "from the pasture." Nathan underscores David's humble origins. The historical retrospect in Nathan's dynastic oracle stresses the divine election of and provisions for David (cf. 1 Chr 10:13–14; 11:1–2, 10; 14:2). Similar statements of divine election are found in the inscriptions of some Mesopotamian monarchs such as Adad-nirari III of Assyria, "a king whom Ashur, the king of the Igigi had chosen [already] when he was a youngster" (Oppenheim 1969: 281); Esarhaddon of Assyria, "whom Ashur, Shamash, Bel and Nebo, the Ishtar of Nineveh, [and] the Ishtar of Arbela have pronounced king of Assyria [ever] since he was a youngster" (Oppenheim 1969: 289); and Nabonidus of Babylon:

> They carried me into the palace and all prostrated themselves to my feet, they kissed my feet greeting me again and again as king. Thus I was elevated to rule the country by the order of my lord Marduk and [therefore] I shall obtain whatever I shall desire—there shall be no rival of mine! (Oppenheim 1969: 309)

The stress on the divine provision for these individuals while they were but babes or youths counters the charge that they were usurpers. Quite the contrary, the break in succession was divinely ordained, and the extraordinary nature of their paths to power confirms their divine patronage (Postgate 1994a: 268–69). These men could not have attained such high office, so the argument goes, unless the gods willed it. That these kings were raised in such obscurity and yet attained the highest office in the land proves their divine election. In the case of David, his divine election forms the first part of a larger pattern of divine support.

"ruler over my people Israel" (נגיד על עמי ישׂראל). In Chronicles, Nathan's statement confirms the declaration made by "all Israel" (11:1), when the tribes first asked David to become their king: "as for you, you will shepherd my people Israel and you, you will become ruler over Israel" (ואתה תהיה נגיד על ישׂראל; 11:2). The words are, of course, themselves drawn from Nathan's dynastic oracle in Samuel (5th NOTE to 11:2). Within Chronicles, the prophecy of Nathan takes the fulfillment of Israel's pronouncements for granted and employs them as the context for presenting David with a new set of promises.

17:8. "I have been with you wherever you went." "Yhwh is with you" is a stereotypical expression of divine support found in a variety of biblical traditions (Exod 3:12; Deut 31:8, 23; Judg 6:12, 16; 1 Sam 3:19; 16:18; 2 Sam 5:10; 2 Kgs 18:7; 1 Chr 17:2; 22:11, 16). The reference to Yhwh's presence with David in the past is complemented by a promise of continuing divine support (vv. 8b–10).

"the greatest." The establishment of outstanding renown is also a constituent element in the assurances provided to Abram (Gen 12:2). In fact, many scholars have seen parallels between the Abrahamic promises and the Davidic promises (e.g., Clements 1967). But there are also differences. The issue in the Davidic promises is not simply land (cf. Gen 15:7, 18–21; 17:8) but peace in the land. The author, like the Deuteronomist (1 Kgs 5:17–18 [ET 5:3–4]), associates such stability with the establishment of a permanent, centralized sanctuary.

17:9. "will reside in it and be disturbed no longer." In both the Deuteronomistic History and the Chronicler's history, this allusion applies to the reign of Solomon, which represents an unprecedented age of peace, prosperity, and international prestige (1 Kgs 4:20; 5:4; 8:66; 1 Chr 22:9, 18; 2 Chr 1:7–17; 8:1–9:31). The peace and security Israel enjoys during the time of Solomon fulfill this divine promise (Knoppers 1993c: 77–93). In *Florilegium* (4Q174) the divine pledge is reinterpreted to apply to an eschatological age (Brooke 1985).

17:10. "ever since the days." In this relatively rare allusion to the time of the Judges (NOTE to v. 6), the writer characterizes this period as a nadir in Israelite history, a time in which Israel was harassed by its enemies. Such upheaval contrasts with the repose to be created during the United Monarchy.

"I shall humble all your enemies." The wording of 2 Sam 7:11, "I shall give you rest from all your enemies," reflects Deuteronomistic editing (Weinfeld 1972a; Japhet 1987: 36). The use of *knʿ*, usually in the *nipʿal*, but also in the *hipʿil* (1 Chr 17:10; 18:1; 2 Chr 28:19; Neh 9:24), is typical of Chronistic usage (1 Chr 20:4; 2 Chr 7:14; 12:6, 12; 13:18; 30:11; 32:26; 33:12, 19, 23; 34:27; 36:12). With this allusion to David's future victories, the author prepares his audience for a major dimension of David's remaining career: his victories against the Philistines, Moabites, Aramaeans, Ammonites, and other foes (1 Chr 18–20).

"as for a house (*ûbayit*), Yhwh will build one for you." Nathan returns to the subject at hand. In addressing David's original query, the prophet develops a wordplay on the different connotations of Hebrew *bayit* ("house," "temple," "dynasty"). Earlier David had been told, "As for you, you will not build the House *(habbayit)* for me to reside (in)" (v. 4).

17:11. "one of your own sons." Construing Hebrew *bn* "son" as "descendant," some commentators see in this phraseology *(ʾšr yhyh mbnyk)* an indication of messianic expectation (e.g., von Rad 1930: 123–24; Noordtzij 1940: 163; Galling 1954: 54; Botterweck 1956: 422–23; Michaeli 1967: 101). But the slight difference between the text of Chronicles and that of Samuel *(ʾšr yṣʾ mmʿyk)* is a thin thread on which to hang a strong Chronistic messianic hope. The context (1 Chr 17:11–14) suggests that the reference is more immediate, referring to David's successor.

17:12. "his throne." The text in vv. 12b–14 exhibits a chiastic organization:

a I shall establish his throne forever
  b I shall be a father to him and he will be a son to me
    c I shall not withdraw my loyalty from him as I withdrew it from your predecessor
  b′ I shall appoint him in my house and in my kingship forever
a′ his throne will be established forever.

The chiastic structure underscores Yhwh's unwavering commitment to David's dynastic successor.

17:13. "I shall be a father to him and he will be a son to me." The text asserts a very close relationship between Yhwh and David's offspring (cf. 2 Sam 7:14; Ps 2:7–8; Isa 9:5 [MT]; cf. Ps 89:26). There are two theories that seek to elucidate the exalted father-son analogy. According to some scholars the language used reflects a Judahite coronation protocol patterned after a corresponding Egyptian coronation ritual (von Rad 1947; Roberts 1997). According to other scholars, the language used is that of adoption drawn from surrounding Near Eastern cultures (*KTU* 1.15.II.25–28; Jacobsen 1943: 119–21; Frankfort 1948: 297). Akkadian expressions for adoption include *ana māri epēšu*, "to make as a son;" *ana mārūti epēšu*, "to make into the status of sonship;" and *ana mārūti leqû*, "to take into the status of sonship" (Paul 1979–80: 180–85). Both of these theories are possible, but one wonders whether they are too narrowly construed. Similar father-son language occurs in the world of international diplomacy, for instance, in the Hittite bilingual testament of Ḫattušili I regarding the "young Labarna," not the real son of Ḫattušili, but a sister's son who is being designated for the throne: "I have appointed him my son, embraced him, and continually exerted myself with regard to him" (Sommer and Falkenstein 1938: 2–7, 12 [I.4–5; cf. I.37; III.24–25]). Regarding Ḫattušili himself, it is said of the sun goddess of Arinna that "she put him into her bosom, grasped his hand, and ran before him" *(ana šūnišu iškuššu u qāssu iṣbassu ina pānišu irṭup alākam;* Otten 1958: 79). The parallels in language are helpful because they establish a larger context in which to appreciate the expressions appearing in Samuel and Chronicles. In this context, one does not have to posit either an Egyptian coronation ritual or a set of official adoption procedures to explain the use of expressions relating to sonship in Nathan's dynastic oracle. The practice of adoption is poorly attested, if at all, in ancient Israel (Roberts 1997). In spite of von Rad's confidence about the existence of a standard coronation protocol in ancient Egypt, such an alleged ritual is but an abstraction culled from a variety of disparate sources from various locales dating to different times. The expressions relating to sonship may better be viewed as simply reflecting the high ideology of the royal court. The employment of metaphorical imagery accentuates the establishment of a close bond between a deity and his human client. The father-son parlance may be coupled, as it is in 2 Sam 7 and 1 Chr 17, with the granting of kingship or a dynasty (Weinfeld 1970: 190–91). In the Hittite treaty between Šuppiluliuma and Šattiwazza, for instance, Šattiwazza states,

> [The Great King] grasped me with [his ha]nd and took delight in me. . . . [And when] I defeat the land of Mittanni, I shall not cast you aside. I shall make you my son. I shall stand by for [your help], I shall make you sit on the throne of your father. And the Sun, Šuppiluliuma, the Great King, the king of the land of Ḫatti, the Hero, be[loved] of Tešup, the one whom the gods know, the word that comes out of his mouth will not return. (Weidner 2.22, 24–26)

Both the Deuteronomist and the Chronicler employ magisterial images to describe the relationship between Yhwh and David's successor. But there is also an important difference between the two biblical texts. The Chronicler, unlike the Deuteronomist, gives sustained expression to the father-son analogy to describe the relationship between Yhwh and Solomon (1 Chr 17:13; 22:10; 28:6). To be sure, the relationship between Yhwh and Israel remains. The oracle benefits Israel and David's prayer reaffirms Israel's unique status (1 Chr 17:21–23). But unlike some other writers (e.g., Exod 4:22; Jer 31:9; Hos 11:1; D. McCarthy 1965a: 144–47; Fensham 1971: 128–35; Kalluveettil 1982: 129–35), the Chronicler does not use the father-son analogy to describe the relationship between God and Israel. His use of the sonship metaphor is, therefore, significant. He highlights the intimate relationship between God and king as instrumental to implementing critical divine initiatives within Israelite history.

"I shall not withdraw my loyalty from him as I withdrew it from your predecessor." As we have seen (see TEXTUAL NOTES), Chronicles lacks the clause, "when he commits iniquity, I shall chastise him with the rod of humans and with the stripes of the sons of man" (2 Sam 7:14). Some scholars (e.g., Riley 1993: 29–36, 69–76) have argued that the omission implies a softening or conditionalizing of the promises to David. Close study of the so-called unconditional terminology in 2 Sam 7:13–14, 1 Chr 17:13, and other texts from the ancient Near East suggests otherwise. As de Vaux (1964: 125) and Calderone (1966: 56–57) point out, there is a parallel between the pledge to maintain a dynasty, even though its members might sin, in 2 Sam 7 (and Ps 89) and similar assurances Tudḫaliya IV of Ḫatti provides in his treaty with Ulmi-Tešup of Tarḫuntašša:

> If your son or [your] grands[on] should commit an offense, let the king of Ḫatti investigate him. And if an offense remains for him, let the king of Ḫatti do as he wishes. If he is worthy of death, let him die. But his house and country will not be taken and given to [one] from another's issue. Let only [one] of Ulmi-Tešup's descent take [them]. (KBo 4.10:obv. 9–13; Beckman 1986: 19–20)

Related to, but not identical to, this pledge is the commitment Muršili II makes in his treaty with Kupanta-Inara of Mirā-Kuwaliya. Muršili reinforces the claim of Kupanta-Inara to his father's house and land despite his father's transgressions (Friedrich 3.7.12–22; 24.8–21). Similarly, Muwatalli guarantees Alakšandu that his heir will occupy his throne even though his subjects may not want him (Friedrich 5.1.A.71–81; B.7–10 [cf. 5.4.37–46]). Indeed, the guarantee of succession to the throne for a vassal's issue is common in Hittite vassal treaties (Friedrich 1.8.23–28; 6.5.31–40; Weidner 6. rev. 13–16; 7.I.49–54; Korošec 1931: 89–91). The stability afforded by dynastic succession within the house of a loyal subject was advantageous to the suzerain (Goetze 1957: 98–101). The use of unconditional language appears in a variety of legal documents pertaining to property as well (Weinfeld 1970: 189–202).

The absolute promise of succession within a particular house clarifies the use of additional conditional phraseology in documents, such as the treaty of Tudḫaliya IV with Ulmi-Tešup and the presentations of the promises to David in 2 Sam 7 and Ps 89. In none of these texts are the recipients of the promises devoid of obligations. The Ulmi-Tešup pact stipulates that the inheritance of Ulmi-Tešup may not pass to the issue of one of his daughters. The treaty also contains a curse that Ulmi-Tešup along with his wife, family, property, and country will be decimated should he not fulfill the terms of the treaty (KBo 4.10.12–15, 33. rev. 5–7; Levenson 1979: 211–212; Halpern 1981a: 45–50). However much 2 Sam 7 and Ps 89 heighten the deity's obligation to David and his seed, they also contain a bilateral element (Knoppers 1996a; 1998). In both texts, David's descendants are not freed from their responsibility to obey Yhwh (2 Sam 7:14; Ps 89:31–33 [ET 89:30–32]). Their disobedience will bring divine chastisement (Eslinger 1994: 57–63). What is interesting in the above texts is that the guarantee of succession is not predicated upon the loyalty of the sons. One more often finds that the overlord's promise of dynastic succession is contingent upon continuing client loyalty, as in the version of the Davidic promises found in Ps 132:11–12.

Comparative analysis illumines the presentation of the promises to David in 1 Chr 17. If the author's intent were to conditionalize the dynastic promises, he would have reformulated the promises of 2 Sam 7 along the lines of Ps 132. Since the clause omitted from 2 Sam 7 represents a codicil pertaining to the chance that one of David's descendants might sin, the absence of the codicil does not affect the basic promise itself. In this respect, 1 Chr 17 is to be aligned with the formulations of the dynastic promises in 2 Sam 7 and Ps 89 rather than the conditional dynastic promises in Ps 132 (Knoppers 1998). Nevertheless, the Chronicler's conception of the promises to David differs in one important respect from the Ulmi-Tešup pact, 2 Sam 7, Ps 89, and Ps 132. The Chronicler consistently focuses attention on David's immediate successor (17:11–14). The absence of the clause referring to the sins of David's descendant(s) from the text of 1 Chr 17 is, therefore, consistent with the author's highly positive portrayal of Solomon's reign. In the Chronicler's portrayal of Solomon's tenure, Solomon is elect *(bḥr)* of God (e.g., 1 Chr 28:5–6), does not stumble, and fulfills his divinely allotted role admirably (2 Chr 1–9).

17:14. "appoint him in my house" *(wh'mdtyhw bbyty)*. The difference from MT 2 Sam 7:16, "your house is enduring," is important. In Samuel "your house" refers to David's dynasty, but in Chronicles Yhwh establishes David's offspring in Yhwh's House, that is, in Yhwh's Temple. Such a special tie between the House of

Yhwh and David's successor indicates that David's heir is to have an official role in the Temple. In this respect, the Chronicler's work follows the pattern of ancient Near Eastern royal ideology. In Canaan, Egypt, and Mesopotamia, kings had certain sacral privileges and responsibilities (Keel 1978: 278–79; Postgate 1994a: 265–66). Although the Chronicler places certain restrictions on the monarch's cultic role (2 Chr 26:16–20), he generally endorses a strong connection between king and temple (e.g., 1 Chr 21:26–22:1; 2 Chr 5:1–7:10).

"in my kingship forever." Yhwh manifests his kingship through the kingship of David and his heirs. Most extraordinary is that the Chronicler associates the kingdom or kingship of David with the kingdom or kingship of God on no fewer than four separate occasions (1 Chr 17:14; 28:5; 29:11; 2 Chr 13:8). Davidic monarchs represent Yhwh and administer his rule (Kuntzmann 1993). As Japhet (1989: 403) observes, the Chronicler "equates monarchy with theocracy—the Israelite mon-archy is Yhwh's kingship over Israel."

"his throne will be established forever." The author reaffirms the perdurability of the Solomonic throne (v. 12). Such usage underscores the close links the Chronicler draws between Yhwh and royal Davidic authority. On three occasions the author associates the throne of Yhwh with the Davidic-Solomonic throne (1 Chr 28:5; 29:23; 2 Chr 9:8). If the author wished to disavow the world of politics and confine the roles of David and his successor solely to cultic functions, that is, building the Temple (Rudolph 1955: xxiii–xxiv; Caquot 1966: 116; R. Braun 1973: 515; Riley 1993: 70–76, 180–85), it is doubtful that he would associate the Davidic-Solomonic throne with the throne of Yhwh and repeatedly underscore that the God of Israel promised to establish the throne of David's successor forever.

## Sources and Composition

Discussing the compositional history of 1 Chr 17:1–15 inevitably involves discussing two other texts depicting the promises to David: Ps 89:1–38 and 2 Sam 7:1–17. There are three major theories as to how these three texts relate to one another. First, according to some scholars, the poetic version of the Davidic promises in Ps 89 formed the basis for the later composition of both 2 Sam 7:1–17 and 1 Chr 17:1–15 (Mowinckel 1954: 100–101; Pfeiffer 1948: 368; Ahlström 1959: 182; Lipiński 1967: 91). According to a second theory, 1 Chr 17:1–15 has priority. In this view, the Chronicler's *Vorlage* was a proto-Samuel source, 2 Sam 7 being itself a secondary composition (Rothstein and Hänel 1927; van den Bussche 1948; Gese 1974: 124–25). By far the majority of commentators hold to a third position, that the Chronicler's *Vorlage* was practically identical to 2 Sam 7 (MT). Most also think that the dynastic oracle in 2 Sam 7 has been heavily edited, if not composed, by the Deuteronomist(s) (e.g., D. McCarthy 1965b; Cross 1973; Veijola 1975, 1990; Van Seters 1983; Dietrich 1992; McKenzie 1999b).

If the composition of 2 Sam 7 and Ps 89 are indeed related, the arguments of Sarna (1963) hold sway. He contends that Ps 89 represents an interpretation, extension, and reapplication of the Davidic promises in 2 Sam 7. As for the composition of 2 Sam 7 and 1 Chr 17, arguments for the priority of 2 Sam 7 (the third position) are generally convincing. Nevertheless, this position must be modified in one important respect. The text-critical evidence suggests that the Chronicler's *Vorlage* was an earlier, somewhat shorter version of 2 Sam 7 than that which survives in MT (Myers 1965a; Lemke 1963; 1965; McCarter 1984; McKenzie 1985). This view differs from the second position in that it acknowledges substantial Deuteronomistic editing in the author's *Vorlage*. But the Chronicler also seems to have edited and slightly rewritten this *Vorlage*. With respect to the older form of Samuel available to him, the Chronicler omitted certain words and clauses and rewrote a few others (see TEXTUAL NOTES). In this manner, he has left his own distinctive stamp on the text.

## COMMENT

In discussing Nathan's dynastic oracle in 2 Sam 7, most recent scholars have stressed that this passage plays a strategic role in the Deuternomistic narration of the monarchy. The surveys of recent scholarship by Jones (1990: 59–82) and Caquot and de Robert (1994: 421–33) provide helpful overviews. Nathan's oracle belongs to a series of Deuteronomistic speeches, summarizing reflections, and prayers by which the Deuteronomist unifies his story of Israel's life in the land. The promises to David in Samuel herald the reign of David's heir as a time of rest and integrate the Davidic monarchy into Israelite life. Upon consolidating his kingdom, David's successor Solomon capitalizes on his nation's peace and achievement of rest by building the Temple (Deut 12:10–11; 1 Kgs 5:17–19 [ET 5:3–5]). This construction of Israel's central sanctuary by the scion of David is both anticipated and justified by the dynastic oracle in 2 Sam 7. In the later presentation of disunion (1 Kgs 11:1–12:20) and Judahite history, the Deuteronomist repeatedly cites the promises to David to explain the survival of the Davidic dynasty (Knoppers 1993c: 167–223).

However important the role that Nathan's dynastic oracle plays in the Deuteronomistic construction of history, one can argue that the Chronicler has more systematically integrated this work into his account of the monarchy than the Deuteronomist has before him. Slightly recasting the dynastic oracle and David's prayer, the Chronicler employs these texts to tie David's career closely to that of his son (Mosis 1973; R. Braun 1973; 1976; Williamson 1976; 1983b; Schniedewind 1999b). The author also cites the promises to David to justify and shape his fascinating account of the divided monarchy (Knoppers 1989). It may be best to begin by discussing the distinctive features of the Chronicler's version of the dynastic oracle and then address how the Chronicler has integrated these promises into the larger structure of his work.

An important difference between the Deuteronomistic and Chronistic works can be seen already in the oracle of rejection (1 Chr 17:4b–6). What Nathan rejects in Chronicles is not the implausibility of building a permanent temple for Yhwh, but its timing. David's request to build a "temple" *(bayit)* was, of course, based on the incongruity between his settled condition "in his house" *(bĕbêtô)* and the austere, if not unsettled, condition of the Ark (v. 1). The divine response in Chronicles couches the matter differently from that in Samuel. The issue is not so much sanctuary construction itself, but rather whether David is the right person to erect "the house" (*habbayit;* v. 4). In both Samuel and Chronicles the first oracle rebuffs David. But the very wording of Nathan's rejection in Chronicles presumes that a temple will eventually be built.

Despite the initial rejection, the divine revelation is by no means complete. Nathan's second speech, the dynastic oracle (vv. 7b–14), continues to develop the elaborate play on the different meanings of *bayit* ("house," "palace," "dynasty," "temple"). Introduced by the citation formula "thus said Yhwh Sebaoth" (v. 7), Nathan's second oracle provides the appropriate context in which to understand the earlier rejection. As in Samuel, the second oracle begins with a historical retrospect recounting Yhwh's favor toward David (vv. 7b–8a). Taken together, Yhwh's choice of a shepherd to rule Israel, Yhwh's continuing presence with this person, and Yhwh's defeat of his enemies confirm the legitimacy of a king who did not himself rise to power through dynastic succession. Articulating events in this way heightens the following divine promises because these promises neither directly result from nor are tied to David's piety. Yhwh acts in accordance with his own freedom.

The commitments the prophet proffers to David are both incredible and wide-ranging, pertaining to David, the future peace of Israel, the construction of the Temple, and the establishment of an enduring royal throne. The fate of people, cult, and king are all closely linked. The Chronicler's version of these divine pledges exhibits its own distinctive features. First, Yhwh does not promise David rest from all of his enemies (2 Sam 7:11). Rather, Yhwh pledges to David that he will humble (*hipʿil* of *knʿ*) all of his enemies (1 Chr 17:10). The difference is important, because it signals that one of David's major tasks in the remaining part of his reign will be to defeat Israel's foes. The Chronicler's construction of the next period in David's reign (1 Chr 18–20) nicely comports with this picture. In the Chronicler's conception, the time of security, rest, and peace (שׁלום) is preeminently the time of Solomon (שׁלמה; 1 Chr 22:9).

Second, the version of Nathan's dynastic oracle in Chronicles ties the divine promises more closely to the work of David's son than Samuel does. The house *(bayit)* God will build for David is a dynasty (17:10b). Yhwh will provide David with a seed, "one of your own sons," whose kingship Yhwh will establish (v. 11). This offspring will build the house *(bayit)*, that is, the Temple, that David himself is not allowed to build (v. 12a). Yhwh will establish this successor's throne forever (v. 12b). Employing the mythological language of sonship, Nathan's oracle establishes a close tie between Yhwh and David's heir (v. 13a). This father-son relationship prefaces Yhwh's assurance that Yhwh will not withdraw his loyalty from David's successor as Yhwh withdrew his loyalty from David's predecessor (v. 13b). The contrast with Samuel is subtle, but important. Samuel speaks once of the seed's kingship (2 Sam 7:12), but Samuel also speaks of Yhwh establishing David's dynasty, throne, kingship, and kingdom (2 Sam 7:11, 16).

Third, the Chronicler posits remarkably close links between Yhwh's house, kingship, and throne and those of David's heir. Yhwh will appoint David's heir in Yhwh's house (v. 14a) and in Yhwh's kingship (v. 14b) forever. Where Samuel speaks of "your" (i.e., David's) house and "your" kingdom (2 Sam 7:16), Chronicles speaks of "my" (i.e., Yhwh's) house and "my" (i.e., Yhwh's) kingship. Hence, in Chronicles, as opposed to in Samuel, David's succesor is appointed in Yhwh's house (i.e., temple). That the Chronicler also posits intimate ties between the Davidic-Solomonic kingdom or kingship and God's kingdom or kingship (1 Chr 17:14; 28:5; 29:11; 2 Chr 13:8) is extraordinary. To be sure, the text speaks of the successor's throne (v. 14) and not that of Yhwh. But in three other nonsynoptic contexts, the author associates the throne of Yhwh with the Davidic-Solomonic throne (1 Chr 28:5; 29:23; 2 Chr 9:8).

The close links Nathan establishes among the fate of king, dynasty, temple, and people militate against a purely cultic interpretation of the promises to David. In Nathan's second oracle, social, martial, and political factors play no small role. Although occasioned by David's wish to build a temple, Nathan's oracle devotes most of its attention to the divine choice of David (vv. 7–8a), the security of Israel (vv. 9–10a), the institution of a royal dynasty (vv. 10b–11), the greatness of David (vv. 8b, 10b), the defeat of David's enemies (v. 10b), the divine choice of David's successor (v. 13), the perpetuity of the successor's throne (vv. 12b, 14b), and the establishment of David's heir in Yhwh's house and kingship forever (v. 14a). By contrast, Nathan explictly mentions the construction of the Temple only once (v. 12a). As opposed to the sempiternal guarantee granted to the throne of David's successor, the Temple is accorded no comparable divine pledge. This is not to say that the Temple is unimportant. On the contrary, some of the attention given to social and political issues provides the proper conditions for the construction of a central shrine. And David's successor enjoys the distinction of being appointed in Yhwh's house. But all of this only underscores how interrelated God, people, land, king, and temple are in the work.

Nathan's dynastic oracle and David's prayer (17:16–27) set the stage for the remainder of David's reign, the tenure of Solomon, and the portrayal of the divided monarchy in which the author insists that the promises to David still obtain for all of the Israelite tribes—both southern and northern (Knoppers 1989; 1990; 1993a). The Chronicler's stress on the pan-Israelite application of Nathan's pledge explains why the Chronicler, unlike the Deuteronomist, does not recount the independent history of the northern realm. In this respect, the importance of the dynastic oracle for the structure of the Chronicler's work can be scarcely underestimated (Knoppers forthcoming [e]). But if the promises to David set an agenda for David's successor and the divided monarchy, they also set an agenda for David. As divulged in v. 10, David has further battles to wage. His victories against Israel's neighbors consolidate Israel's position (18:1–20:8). The aftermath of the census (21:1–22:1) determines the site of the Temple altar. Most of David's remaining years are devoted to preparing his divinely chosen heir for his future duties. David assists Solomon by exhorting him (22:7–16; 28:9–10, 20–21), coordinating public and royal support for his successor (22:17–19; 28:1–8; 29:20–25), establishing a national administration (23:1–27:34), crafting a plan for the Temple (28:11–19), and endowing this future sanctuary with state resources and his own largess (22:2–6; 29:1–9). The Chronicler's version of the promises to David evinces careful formulation. The author, even more so than the Deuteronomist, ties the reigns of David and Solomon together as a unique era of Israelite consolidation, prosperity, and accomplishment.

# *XXI. The Davidic Prayer (17:16–27)*

*David Responds to Nathan's Dynastic Oracle*

16 When King David came in and took his seat before Yhwh, he said,
"Who am I, O Yhwh God, and what is my house that you have brought me so
far? 17 And if this were too little in your eyes, O God, you have spoken about
the house of your servant from a long time ago and you have caused me,
someone of human stature, to see into the future, O Yhwh God. 18 What
more can David add to you for honor? As for you, you have known your servant. 19 O Yhwh, for the sake of your servant and according to your heart, you
have done this entire great deed to make known all the great deeds. 20 O
Yhwh, there is no one like you and there is no God except for you, according
to everything that we have heard with our ears. 21 And who is like your people
Israel, a unique nation on the earth, whom God went forth to redeem as a
people for himself to make for himself a great and marvelous name, driving
out nations from before your people, whom you redeemed from Egypt.
22 And you appointed your people Israel as your own people forever. And you,
O Yhwh, you have become their God. 23 And now, O Yhwh, as for the word
that you have spoken about your servant and his house, may it be confirmed
forever. Do according to what you have promised. 24 May it be confirmed and
may your name be magnified forever, saying, 'Yhwh Sebaoth is God of Israel.' And may the house of David your servant be established before you.
25 Indeed, you are Yhwh my God; you have disclosed to your servant that you
will build for him a house. Therefore, your servant has found courage to pray
before you. 26 And now, O Yhwh, you are the God, and your words will come
true, and you have promised this good thing concerning your servant. 27 And
now you have been pleased to bless the house of your servant to abide forever
before you. Indeed, you, O Yhwh, you have blessed and are blessed forever."

## Textual Notes

17:16. "O Yhwh God" *(yhwh 'lhym)*. So MT. LXX *Kyrie ho theos*. MT 2 Sam 7:18 "Lord Yhwh" *('dny yhwh)*. Similar variants occur in 1 Chr 17:17 and 2 Sam 7:19.

"you have brought me" *(hby'tny)*. So MT 1 Chr 17:16 and 2 Sam 7:18. The reading of LXX 17:16 *hēgapēsas me*, "you have loved me," may reflect metathesis from *hb(y)'tny* to *'hbtny*.

"so far" *(ʿd-hlm)*. The lemma of LXX^B *heōs aiōnos*, "forever" (= *ʿd-ʿwlm*), assimilates toward a standard expression (vv. 12, 14 [*bis*], 22, 23, 24, 27 [*bis*]).

17:17. "too little." 2 Sam 7:19 adds *ʿwd*.

"God" *('lhym)*. So MT and LXX. MT 2 Sam 7:19 "Lord Yhwh" *('dny yhwh)*.

"from a long time ago" *(mlrḥwq)*. On the temporal use of *rāḥôq*, see also 2 Kgs 19:25 and Isa 37:26 (*HALOT* 1215).

"and you have caused me, someone of human stature, to see into the future" *(wattar'ēnî kĕtôr hā'ādām lĕmaʿlâ)*. Both MT and LXX are, as scholars have long acknowledged, difficult. LXX^B *kai epeides me hōs horasis anthrōpou*, "you have looked upon me as the vision of a man" (= *wtr'ny ktwr h'dm?*). MT reads literally "and you have seen me like the form of a man, the stair" *(ûrĕ'îtanî kĕtôr hā'ādām hammaʿălâ)*. MT 2 Sam 7:19 is even more corrupt, *wĕzō't tôrat hā'ādām*, "and this is the instruction of humanity." Proposed emendations of the Samuel and Chronicles texts include *wtr'ny dwrwt 'dm*, "you have shown me the generations of humanity" and *wtr'ny kmr'h 'dm*. My emendation of MT can best be explained by first discussing the individual terms in this clause.

*wattar'ēnî*. Along with Rothstein and Hänel (1927), I am reading the *hipʿil* of *r'h* in the sense of "to show," "to cause to experience" (*HALOT* 1161). The *hipʿil* of *r'h* is commonly used, as here, with the deity as subj. (Deut 1:33; Jer 24:1; Hab 1:3; Pss 50:23; 59:11 [ET 59:10]; 60:5 [ET 60:4]; 85:8 [ET 85:7]; 91:16). Alternatively, Willi (1972: 154) follows MT and construes the *qal* of *r'h* as "to choose."

*kĕtôr*. So MT *(lectio difficilior)*. A few Heb. MSS read *btwk*, "in the midst." One possible meaning for *tw'r* (McCarter 1984: 233) is a "turn (in a succession)," assuming that *twr* can be rendered as *tw'r* with a quiescent *'ālep*. Although this term appears in LBH (Esth 2:12, 15) and rabbinic Hebrew (Jastrow 1903: 1656; cf. Tg. 2 Sam 7:19), "turn" does not seem to fit the context here. The masc. noun *tw(')r* usually designates "appearance," "stature," or "form" (e.g., Gen 29:17; 39:6; 1 Sam 16:18; 28:14; 1 Kgs 1:6; Isa 52:14; 53:2; Lam 4:8; *HALOT* 1676–77; cf. Phoen. and Pun. *t'r*, "renown," "stature," "wealth;" *KAI* 14.11; 119.7; 138.5; *CIS* i 171.4; *DNWSI* 1201; Krahmalkov 2000: 487). In CH, the term usually, but not always (Isa 52:14; 53:2), has positive connotations. Note, for example, the description of David as "a man of stature" or "a man of distinction" *('yš t'r*; 1 Sam 16:18). Also of relevance for the use of *kt'r* in 1 Chr 17:17 is the use of *kt'r* in Judg 8:18. When asked by Gideon about the provenance of certain murdered men, Zebaḥ and Zalmunna reply that "they looked just like you *(kmwk kmwhm)*, like sons of the king [*kt'r bny hmlk*]." In the context of 1 Chr 17:17, the locution *kt'r* is used not so much to emphasize David's exalted status as to emphasize that the deity has communicated divine secrets about his involvement in history to someone of mortal status *(h'dm)*.

*lĕmaʿlâ*. MT *hmʿlh*, "the stair," "the ascent," or perhaps "the one who exalts (me)." LXX reads differently, "and you have exalted me" (*kai hypsōsas me* = *wtʿlny*). My reconstruction understands *mʿlh* as indicating direction in time "onwards" (1 Sam 16:13; 30:25; Hag 2:18). The expression can also indicate direction in time "backward" (Hag 2:15). In the context of 1 Chr 17:17, David is praising Yhwh for disclosing his involvement in the affairs of David's family from a distant time *(mrḥwq)* and for a long time to come *(lmʿlh)*.

17:18. "to you for honor" *(ʾlyk lkbwd)*. A reconstruction partially based on LXX *pros se tou doxasai*, "to you to express praise." MT's more expansive lemma, "to you for honor your servant" *(ʾlyk lkbwd ʾt-ʿbdk)*, may have been affected by the frequent appearance of the locution "your servant" elsewhere in David's prayer: vv. 17, 18, 19, 23, 24, 25 *(bis)*, 26, 27. On MT 2 Sam 7:20, "to speak to you" *(ldbr ʾlyk)*, compare the treatments of McCarter (1984: 233–34) and Caquot and de Robert (1994: 422–23).

17:19. "for the sake of your servant" *(bʿbwr ʿbdk)*. So MT and LXX$^{L}$. Lacking in LXX$^{AB}$. MT 2 Sam 7:21, "for the sake of your word" *(bʿbwr dbrk)*.

"you have done this entire great deed" *(ʿśyt ʾt kl-hgdwlh hzʾt)*. Thus MT 17:19, as well as MT and LXX 2 Sam 7:21. LXX 17:19 *epoiēsas tēn pasan megalōsynēn* lacks *tautēn* (= *hzʾt*, "this") because of a haplography (see next TEXTUAL NOTE).

"to make known all the great deeds" *(lhdyʿ kl-hgdlwt)*. Reading with MT and LXX$^{L}$. This clause is absent from LXX$^{AB}$ due to parablepsis (from *hgdwlh* [earlier in the verse] to *hgdlwt*). Although dittography is also a theoretical possibility, the reading of 2 Sam 7:21, "to make known your servant" *(lhwdyʿ ʾt-ʿbdk)*, makes this much less likely.

17:20. "O Yhwh, there is none like you" *(yhwh ʾyn kmwk)*. MT 2 Sam 7:22 expands to "therefore, you are great, O Yhwh God, because there is none like you" *(ʿl-kn gdlt yhwh ʾlhym ky-ʾyn kmwk)*.

"according to everything" *(kkl)*. Reading with many Heb. MSS, LXX (1 Chr 17:20 and 2 Sam 7:22), Syr., and Tg. MT 1 Chr 17:20 and 2 Sam 7:22 "in all" *(bkl)*.

17:21. "unique nation" *(gwy ʾḥd)*. The textual witnesses vary considerably in this verse. I read with MT 17:21 and MT 2 Sam 7:23. The lemma of LXX 17:21 and LXX 2 Sam 7:23 *ethnos allo* (= *gwy ʾḥr*, "other nation") reflects a *dālet/rêš* confusion, but is favored by some commentators and NAB.

"went forth" *(hlk)*. 2 Sam 7:23 has the pl.

"to make for himself a great and marvelous name." MT reads *lśwm lk šm*, "to make for yourself a (great and marvelous) name," but I follow LXX 17:21 *tou thesthai autō onoma* (= *lśwm lw šm*) and MT 2 Sam 7:23 *wlśwm lw šm*.

"a great and marvelous [name], driving out." MT 17:21 reads "[with] great and marvelous (deeds), driving out" *(gdlwt wnwrʾwt lgrš)*. MT 2 Sam 7:23 is corrupt: *wlʿśwt lkm hgdwlh wnwrʾwt lʾrṣk*. 4QSam$^{a}$ is fragmentary, [*wlʿ*]*śwt* g[*dlwh*] ("and to do the great thing"), but apparently briefer than MT 2 Sam 7:23 and close to LXX 2 Sam 7:23 (*tou poiēsai megalōsynēn*; Ulrich 1978: 67). The lemma of LXX 1 Chr 17:21 has some affinity to 4QSam$^{a}$ *mega kai epiphanes tou ekbalein* (= *gdwlh wnwrʾh lgrš*) and is adopted here. MT 1 Chr 17:21, and to a lesser extent 2 Sam 7:23, may assimilate toward an expression in Deut 10:21, "great and marvelous deeds" *(gdwlwt wnwrʾwt)*.

"nations" *(gwym)*. Tentatively reading with MT, LXX, and Josephus (*Ant.* 7.95) *(lectio brevior)*. MT 2 Sam 7:23 adds *wʾlhyw*, "and its gods," while LXX 2 Sam 7:23

*kai skēnōmata* and 4QSam[a] *w'hlym* have the nonsensical "and tents" (Ulrich 1978: 71, 161). It is possible, however, that LXX 2 Sam 7:23 and 4QSam[a] bear witness to an original lemma—either *gwym w'lhym,* "nations and gods" or *gwym w'lhyhm,* "nations and their gods"—that has been cut short due to haplography *(homoioteleuton).*

17:22. "you appointed" *(wttn).* Tg. follows MT 2 Sam 7:24 *wtkwnn lk,* "you established for yourself."

17:23. "O Yhwh." So MT and LXX. MT 2 Sam 7:25 "O Yhwh God."

"may it be confirmed" *(y'mn).* So MT and LXX. MT 2 Sam 7:25 "establish" *(hqym),* but LXX[L] 2 Sam 7:25 *pistōthēto* (= *y'mn*).

"do according to what you have promised" *(w'śh k'šr dbrt).* So MT and LXX[L] 17:23 and MT 2 Sam 17:25. This clause does not appear in LXX[AB] 17:23, but (corrupt) LXX 2 Sam 7:25 has *kai nyn kathōs elalēsas* (= *w'th k'šr dbrt*), "and now as you have spoken."

17:24. "may it be confirmed and may your name be magnified forever" *(wy'mn wygdl šmk 'd 'wlm).* Thus MT and and LXX[L]. Lacking in LXX[AB]. MT (and LXX) 2 Sam 7:26, "and may your name be magnified forever" *(wygdl šmk 'd 'wlm),* may reflect a haplography (*homoioarkton* from *wy'mn* to *wygdl*). LXX[AB] 1 Chr 17:23–24 have suffered a haplography from *'d 'wlm* in v. 23 (see previous TEXTUAL NOTE) to *'d 'wlm* in v. 24.

"Yhwh Sebaoth is God of Israel." I am partially following LXX, *Kyrie (Kyrie) pantokratōr theos (tou) Israēl.* The lemma of MT "Yhwh Sebaoth, God of Israel, God to Israel" *(yhwh ṣb'wt 'lhy yśr'l 'lhym lyśr'l)* conflates two variants, *'lhy yśr'l* and *'lhym (')lyśr'l,* found in the textual witnesses to Samuel: 4QSam[a] (and MT) 2 Sam 7:26 [*yhwh ṣb'*]*wt 'lhym 'l y*[*śr'l*], "Yhwh Sebaoth is God over Israel"; LXX[L] *pantokratōr ho theos epi ton Israēl* (LXX[B] omits due to haplography; McKenzie 1985: 78).

17:25. "indeed, you are Yhwh my God." So LXX[B] *hoti su Kyrie ho theos mou* (= *ky 'th yhwh 'lhy*). MT "indeed you are my God" *(ky 'th 'lhy)* has lost *yhwh* after *'th* due to haplography *(homoioteleuton).* The readings of MT 2 Sam 7:27 *(ky 'th yhwh ṣb'wt 'lhy yśr'l)* and 4QSam[a] ([*ky 'th yhwh*] *ṣb'wt 'lhy yś*[*r'l*]), "for you Yhwh Sebaoth are God of Israel," expand, probably under the influence of the divine epithets in the previous verse (McKenzie 1985: 52).

"you have disclosed to your servant." Literally, "you have uncovered the ear of your servant" *(glyt 't-'zn 'bdk).*

"your servant." So MT and LXX. MT and LXX 2 Sam 7:27 add the citation formula, "saying" *(l'mr).*

"to build for him a house" *(lbnwt lw byt).* So MT and LXX. MT 2 Sam 7:27 "a house I shall build for you" *(byt 'bnh-lk).*

"your servant has found courage" *(mṣ' 'bdk 't lbw).* Reading with MT, LXX, and 4QSam[a] 2 Sam 7:27. The phrase *'t lbw* was lost from MT and LXX 1 Chr 17:25 before *lhtpll.*

"to pray before you" *(lhtpll lpnyk).* So MT and LXX. MT 2 Sam 7:27 expands to "to pray to you this prayer" *(lhtpll 'lyk 't-htplh hz't).*

17:26. "Yhwh." So MT and LXX. MT 2 Sam 7:28 reads "Lord Yhwh" *('dny yhwh).*

"and your words will come true." Reading with MT, 4QSam[a] (*wdbryk* [*yhyw ʾmt*]), and LXX 2 Sam 7:28, which preface *wdbryk yhyw ʾmt* before *wtdbr ʿl-ʿbdk*, "and you have promised concerning your servant." 1 Chr 17:26 omits due to haplography (from *wdbryk* to *wtdbr*; McKenzie 1985: 52).

17:27. "you have been pleased to bless" *(hwʾlt lbrk)*. MT 2 Sam 7:29 *hwʾl wbrk* and 4QSam[a] *h*[*w*]*ʾl wbrk*, "be pleased and bless." LXX 1 Chr 17:27 *ērxai*, 2 Sam 7:29 *arxai*, and Syr. 2 Sam 7:29 *šrʾ* reflect *hḥl* "begin (to bless)."

"O Yhwh" *(yhwh)*. So MT, but missing from LXX due to haplography (*homoioteleuton* after *ʾth*, "you"). MT 2 Sam 7:29 (again) reads "Lord Yhwh" *(ʾdny yhwh)*.

"you have blessed and are blessed forever" *(brkt wmbrk lʿwlm)*. Thus MT. LXX 17:27 *eulogēsas kai eulogēson* [LXX[L] *kai eulogētai*] *eis ton aiōna*, "you have blessed and bless [it] [LXX[L] it has been blessed] forever." MT 2 Sam 7:29 *dbrt wmbrktk ybrk byt-ʿbdk lʿwlm*, "you have spoken, and may the house of your servant be blessed forever by your blessing"; 4QSam[a] [*dbrt wm*]*brktk* [*ybrk byt ʿbdk lʿwlm*], "you have spoken, and may the house of your servant be blessed forever by your blessing." It is possible that MT 1 Chr 17:27 has suffered haplography due to the similarity between *brk* (in *mbrktk*) and *bdk* (in *ʿbdk*; McKenzie 1985: 52–53), but the lemmata in Samuel and Chronicles are largely distinct.

## Notes

17:16a. "took his seat before Yhwh." The tent shrine of the Ark is probably in view (1 Chr 16:1, 37; 17:1). The king's response to Nathan's dynastic oracle (17:7–14) is one of prayer.

17:16b–19. David's prayer, like the dynastic oracle, contains a historical retrospect. The latter complements the former. The historical retrospect in the promises to David recounts Yhwh's past benevolence to David (vv. 7–8a), while the historical retrospect in David's prayer refers to Yhwh's benevolence in granting David a series of promises.

"who am I, O Yhwh God, and what is my house *(bêtî)* that you have brought me so far?" An allusion to the favors rehearsed in Nathan's third speech (vv. 7–14), pertaining to both David (vv. 7–10a) and his dynasty (*bayit*; vv. 10b–14). The expression is expanded to include Israel in David's later prayer (29:14). The king's query acknowledges a tremendous qualitative and quantitative gap between what David had proposed to do (build a temple) and what Yhwh has committed himself to do on behalf of David and his successor. For expressions of humility in other Chronistic speeches, see 1 Chr 24:14–16; 2 Chr 14:6; 20:6, 12 (Throntveit 1987: 95–96; De Vries 1989: 157).

17:18. "can David add to you for honor?" In expressing his gratitude to the God of Israel, David is faced with a conundrum—what he can give to God that God does not already have.

"as for you, you." In Nathan's dynastic oracle one finds a stress on the divine first person: "I, I took you from the pasture" (v. 7); "I have been with you wherever you went" (v. 8a); "I shall make a name for you like the name of the greatest in the land" (v. 8b); "I, I shall be a father to him" (v. 13a); "I shall not withdraw my loyalty from him as I withdrew it from your predecessor" (v. 13b); "I shall appoint him in my house and in my kingship forever" (v. 14). In David's response he echos a number of these promises in the second person, praising Yhwh's initiatives and requesting their fulfillment: "you, you have known your servant" (v. 18); "you have done this entire great deed" (v. 19); "you appointed your people Israel as your own people forever. And you, O Yhwh, you have become their God" (v. 22); "do according to what you have promised" (v. 23); "may the house of David your servant be established before you" (v. 24); "you will build for him a house" (v. 25).

"known your servant." At first glance, this declaration seems puzzling, if not superfluous. Has not God known David for some time? But the phrase probably has a more technical meaning, "to know" in the sense of "to recognize" (cf. Akk. *idû*, "to recognize" [politically]; Kalluveettil 1982: 84–85). In the ancient Near East, treaty relations often asked allies "to know" only their treaty partners and no others (Huffmon 1966). Such diplomatic usage illumines the reference here. David refers to the special recognition afforded him, "your servant," by Yhwh.

17:19. "according to your heart, you have done this entire great deed." Comparison with terminology appearing in ancient Near Eastern conveyances illumine this initially mystifying reference. The emphasis is on the freedom with which Yhwh has acted. Several documents in the fifth-century Aramaic papyri from Elephantine are helpful for comparative purposes because they stress the affection and thoughts of the donor to the donee (Muffs 1969: 36–50; 1992: 121–38; Porten and Greenfield 1984: 9–12; Szubin and Porten 1983: 38–41). A number of these texts such as settlement of a property claim, a testament, and a bestowal of dowry exhibit explicit and detailed unreserved language. The testamentary bequest (Szubin and Porten 1983: 35–46) dealing with the conveyance of a property from Maḥseiah to his daughter Mibṭaḥiah (AP 8) is relevant in this context. This document, which should be read in conjunction with three other documents relating to the same property (AP 5; 6; 9), reads in part:

> I give this house and land *(byt' znk 'rq)* to you during my life and at my death. You have right to it from this day and forever *('d 'lm)* and [so do] your sons after you. To whomever you wish, you may give it *(lmn zy rḥmty tntn)*. I do not have a son or daughter, brother or sister, woman or other man who has right to this land except you and your children forever. . . . Moreover, I, Maḥseiah, will not take [it] away tomorrow or any other day from your hand to give [it] to others. (AP 8.8–11, 18–19)

The precautions taken to ensure that only the daughter has rights over this property are extensive—indeed, too numerous to be listed here. The unconditional language is highly significant. Also relevant is the first-person declaration of the father. Muffs (1969: 133–35) argues that the donor in this and other related texts declares his total willingness to part with the property, thereby precluding the possibility of the donor's later invalidating his gift by declaring that he made it with reservations. Like the deity in the Davidic promises (1 Chr 17:13), the father explicitly renounces his claim to renege on his pledge. No coercion, mitigating circumstances, or rival claims have colored his decision. Maḥseiah abjures all previous deeds concerning the property and all future claims, including his own. Should he attempt such a claim, he will lose his case and have to pay a fine (AP 8.11–15; cf. *BP* 4; 6; 9; 10). The language of affection occurring in the Elephantine papyri illumines the reference to the deity's acting in accordance with his heart. Yhwh has acted freely. Hence, the king gives thanks to the deity for his tremendous generosity and devotion.

"to make known all the great deeds." The text plays on the relationship between the dynastic oracle taken as an individual act, "this entire great deed" *(kl-hgdwlh hzʾt)*, and Yhwh's other highly laudable actions, "all the great deeds" *(kl-hgdlwt)*. In 2 Sam 7:21 Yhwh does "this entire great deed to make known your servant" (see TEXTUAL NOTE). In other words, the dynastic oracle has the beneficial effect of publicizing a single individual—David. But the point is different in Chronicles. The great action Yhwh undertook on behalf of David—that is, his revelation through Nathan—will have the beneficial effect of publicizing all the rest of Yhwh's great actions undertaken on behalf of his people.

17:20–22. "O Yhwh." David's prayer is filled with exclamations, invocations, and ascriptions of praise. In these verses David's recounting of divine grace shifts from praising Yhwh for his revelation through Nathan (vv. 16b–19) to praising Yhwh for his marvelous actions on behalf of the people of Israel. The implication is that there is a continuity between God's dealings with the people and God's dealings with David.

17:20. "there is no one like you." The phraseology expressing Yhwh's incomparability *(yhwh ʾyn kmwk)* is nearly identical to Solomon's invocation at the temple dedication (1 Kgs 8:23//2 Chr 6:14), "Yhwh, God of Israel, there is no God like you" *(yhwh ʾlhy yśrʾl ʾyn kmwk ʾlhym)*. The phraseology also resonates with that found in a number of other contexts, for instance, MT Jer 10:6, "there is none like you, O Yhwh" *(mʾyn kmwk yhwh)*; Ps 86:8, "there is none like you among the gods, O Lord" *(ʾyn kmwk bʾlhym ʾdny)*; and Isa 45:5, "I am Yhwh, and there is no other" *(ʾny yhwh wʾyn ʿwd)*. See also Deut 32:39; Isa 45:6, 14, 18, 21, 22; 46:9; Joel 2:27; cf. Exod 15:11 (Weinfeld 1972a: 331 [#4 and #5]).

"and there is no God except for you" *(wʾyn ʾlhym zwltk)*. Again, there are similar statements to this monotheistic creed elsewhere in the HB, for instance in Isa 45:5, "I am Yhwh, and there is no other *(ʾny yhwh wʾyn ʿwd)*; except for me, there is no God *(zwlty ʾyn ʾlhym)*." What is unusual is the combination of the assertion, "O Yhwh, there is no one like you," with the claim that "there is no God except for you." The joining of the incomparability and monotheistic acclamations is striking, because the former presumes a divine council while the latter distances, if not negates, the other deities in the heavenly assembly (NOTES to 16:25–26).

"everything that we have heard with ears" (כל אשר-שמענו באזנינו). In Deuteronomistic contexts, this refers to the voice of God heard at Sinai (Deut 4:33; Weinfeld 1972a: 38, 207–8). These writers stress the people's own participation in and witness to major events initiated by God on their behalf (Deut 4:9; 7:19; 10:21; 11:7; 29:1–2; Josh 23:3; 24:7).

17:21. "who is like your people Israel (מי כעמך ישׂראל), a unique nation on the earth (גוי אחד בארץ)." Assertions of Yhwh's incomparability and unique status give way to assertions of Israel's unique status. The two sets of declarations are related. Unparalleled actions by Yhwh led to the formation of a distinct people. The phrase "your people Israel" has many parallels in Deuteronomy (4:20; 7:6; 14:2; 21:8; 26:15) and in Samuel-Kings (1 Sam 12:22; 1 Kgs 8:33, 34, 38, 43, 52).

"whom God went forth to redeem as a people for himself" (אשר הלך האלהים לפדות לו עם). The language is typical of Deuteronomy (7:8; 9:26; 13:6 [ET 13:5]; 15:15; 21:8; 24:18; S. Driver 1895: 101; Weinfeld 1972a: 326 [#1]). In this line of thought, Israel's distinctiveness lies in the unprecedented nature of its election. That Israel's rise to nationhood was unprecedented paradoxically magnifies its importance. On the reapplication of this important motif from the Tetrateuch and the Deuteronomistic History to Judah and the house of David, see Knoppers (2000a).

"to make for himself a great and marvelous name." The creation of a people from out of the midst of another nation functions as the means by which Yhwh gains an outstanding reputation. The Deuteronomic or Deuteronomistic name theology is a major subject in and of itself (Mettinger 1982).

"driving out nations from before your people, whom you redeemed from Egypt." The language and content is reminiscent of Deut 4:34–35, in which the Exodus is presented not only as involving a series of amazing events but also as demonstrating Yhwh's unique status (Weinfeld 1972a: 38–41; 1991: 212–30). The Exodus and Conquest are not prominent themes in the Chronicler's work; nevertheless, he makes selective reuse of them, especially when they occur in his sources (4th NOTE to 5:25).

17:22. "and you appointed your people Israel as your own people forever (ותתן את-עמך ישראל לך לעם עד-עולם). And you, O Yhwh, you have become their God (ואתה יהוה היית להם לאלהים)." On the former expression, compare Deut 4:20; 7:6; 14:2; 26:18–19; 28:9; 29:12; 1 Sam 12:22. On the latter, compare Deut 26:19; 29:12; Jer 7:23. The occurrence of the two expressions together echoes both the covenantal ratification in Deut 29:9–12 [ET 29:10–13] (Baltzer 1971: 102) and the Priestly formulation of the divine covenant with Israel (Exod 6:7; Lev 26:12). The application of such language to the relationship between God and Israel complements the application of sonship language to the relationship between God and David's successor in v. 13 (see NOTE).

17:23–24. These verses contain the only petitions found in David's prayer.

17:23. "as for the word that you have spoken about your servant and his house, may it be confirmed forever." In Nathan's oracle (vv. 7–14), there are a variety of promises, predicting David's greatness (v. 8b), Israel's peace and security (v. 9), the humbling of David's enemies (v. 10a), Yhwh's building of a dynasty for David (v. 10b), the future construction of a temple by David's offspring (v. 12), and the perdurable establishment of his throne (v. 14). But of all the assurances accorded to David in Nathan's oracle, David's requests focus on the promises directed toward his dynasty.

17:24. "may your name be magnified forever." Similar concerns for the greatness of Yhwh's reputation occur in the final speech of Samuel (1 Sam 12:22), the prayer of Solomon (1 Kgs 8:42//2 Chr 6:32), and select passages of Jeremiah (10:6; 44:26).

"Yhwh Sebaoth is God of Israel." Often translated, "Yhwh of hosts," *yhwh ṣĕbā'ôt* is an epithet associated with the personal divine name Yhwh. It is used with reference to the Ark in 1 Sam 4:4 and 2 Sam 6:2 and apart from the Ark in Pss 18:11 [ET 18:10] (//2 Sam 22:11), 80:2 [ET 80:1], and 99:1. As an epithet, Yhwh Sebaoth is an expansive statement of identity. Cross (1973: 68–71) hypothesizes that Yhwh was originally described as *ḏū yahwī ṣaba'ōt*, "he who creates the (heavenly) armies," a title of the divine warrior and creator (cf. Josh 5:14; 10:12; Judg 5:20; Hab 3:3–15; Isa 40:26). In this view, the epithet was an appropriate appellative for the deity who mustered the tribal militias and led Israel in its wars. In 1 Chr 17:24, however, this divine epithet is not used in the context of either a holy war or of a description of the Ark. David refers to a future event that may lead to further acclamation of Israel's deity. David's petition is that the divine confirmation of the promises made to him would lead to the recognition that "Yhwh Sebaoth is God of Israel."

"may the house of David your servant be established before you." Curtis and Madsen (1910: 230) speak of David's boldness in putting the rights of his house to rule alongside the right of Yhwh to be God of Israel. There is much validity to this claim, yet it does not go far enough. In David's prayer, there is an explicit juxtaposition of three figures—Yhwh, Israel, and David. God, people, and king are a unity. Davidic kingship, David hopes, will become a constitutive feature of Israelite identity.

"your servant has found courage to pray before you." David predicates his request for a divine confirmation of the dynastic promises on the fact of Yhwh's revelation itself: "you have disclosed to your servant that you will build for him a house."

17:26–27. "and now." Having rendered his petitions (vv. 23–24), David freely acknowledges his blessed position and (again) ascribes praise to Yhwh.

17:26. "O Yhwh, you are the God" *(yhwh 'th hw 'h'lhym)*. An asseveration of henotheism, if not monotheism. Williams (§88) argues for a slightly different translation of the article with *'lhym*, claiming that *h'lhym* has the force of "the true God." In this case, one would translate "O Yhwh, you are the true God." A similar expression, *yhwh hw' h'lhym*, appears in the mouths of important figures in the Deuteronomistic work: Moses (Deut 4:35, 39; 7:9), Raḥab (Josh 2:11), Solomon (1 Kgs 8:60), Elijah (1 Kgs 18:37), and Israel (1Kgs 18:39 [*bis*]; Weinfeld 1972a: 331 [#1]). In any case, the asseveration has a specific function in this context. Earlier, David addressed Yhwh, "you are my God" (אתה אלהי), in connection with the disclosure that Yhwh would build him a house (1 Chr 17:25). But in connection with the divine capacity to realize that promise, David addresses Yhwh differently, "you are the God" (אתה-הוא האלהים), thus underscoring Yhwh's power and sovereignty.

"and you have promised this good thing concerning your servant" *(wtbr 'l 'bdk hṭwbh hz't)*. References to "the good" or to "the good thing(s)" spoken by a superior to his servant, which occur in a number of contexts in the HB, clearly have benevolent overtones. Zenger (1968: 23–30), Fox (1973: 41–42), Malamat (1975), Kalluveettil (1982: 42–47), Levenson (1984a), and Weinfeld (1982: 27–53) contend that the phrases *dbr 'tw ṭbwt* (e.g., 2 Kgs 25:28), *dbr 't hṭwbh* (e.g., 2 Sam 7:28//1 Chr 17:26; 1 Sam 25:30), *hdbr hṭwbh* (e.g., Jer 33:14), and *dbrym ṭwbym* (e.g., 1 Kgs 12:7) have a more technical covenantal connotation. A treaty relationship involves the bestowal of favors on one party by another. On the basis of comparative evidence, there is some validity to this interpretation. In Akk. *ṭūbtu* or *ṭabūtū* ("friendship") can sometimes stand as a synecdoche for a treaty (Kalluveettil 1982: 43–44). Similarly, *ṭūbtu* (or Hitt. *atterūtu*) and *šalmu* ("peace"), when used with the verb *epēšu*, can mean "to enact a pact" (e.g., EA 136.8–32; KBo 1.10.57). Moran (1963: 173–76) translates *ṭbt'* in the Sefîre stelas as "'friendship, good relations,' with specific reference to the amity established by a treaty." Whether a formal covenant is in view in every instance in which the above expressions occur is, however, doubtful. Possible exceptions are Deut 23:7; 2 Sam 2:6; and even 2 Kgs 25:28 (Würthwein 1984: 481; Tadmor and Cogan 1988: 329; Becking 1990: 286–90). Nonetheless, the context in 1 Chr 17:26 (and 2 Sam 7:28) favors viewing the positive connotations of *hṭwbh hz't* as part of a structured covenantal relationship.

17:27. "you have been pleased to bless" *(hw'lt lbrk)*. As we have observed (see TEXTUAL NOTES), the structure and content of this verse differ from the parallel in 2 Samuel. There David thanks the deity and petitions him to consummate his pledge (2 Sam 7:25–29). David's last petition requests that Yhwh would bless (MT *hw'l wbrk*; 4QSam[a] *h[w]'l wbrk*) the house of his servant so that it might stand before Yhwh forever (2 Sam 7:29). But in Chronicles, David does not utter a prayer for a blessing. Once Yhwh blesses something, it is blessed forever. In Chronicles, the king lauds God for past action. Yhwh through his revelation to Nathan has already effected a blessing (1 Chr 17:19, 25–26). Hence, David thanks and praises the deity (Throntveit 1987: 56–58).

"indeed, you, O Yhwh, you have blessed and are blessed forever" (כי־אתה יהוה ברכת ומברך לעולם). The text of Samuel differs. In his concluding doxology in 2 Sam 7:29, David exclaims, "may the house of your servant be blessed by your blessing forever" (see TEXTUAL NOTES). Even though Chronicles refers to Yhwh's blessing, there is an additional blessing in the conclusion to David's prayer. Yhwh's blessing (upon David) is associated with the blessing of Yhwh. Upon blessing David's house, Yhwh is forever blessed.

## SOURCES AND COMPOSITION

Scholars generally agree that David's prayer in Samuel, like the Davidic promises, has been substantially overwritten and expanded by the Deuteronomist (Labuschagne 1960: 28–35; Weinfeld 1972a: 38–41; Cross 1973: 241–61; McCarter 1984: 239–41; Jones 1990: 70; Mayes 1983: 104; Mettinger 1976: 51; Van Seters 1983: 273; Veijola 1975: 74–80). As such, the prayer belongs to a series of

Deuteronomistic compositions that structure the history of Israel. To be sure, these scholars disagree whether this prayer was composed by the Deuteronomist or substantially edited by him. Whatever the precise compositional history of David's prayer in Samuel, our concern must be the organization and function of this prayer in Chronicles.

Indebted to the form, content, and structure of the Deuteronomistic History, the Chronicler employs a variety of speeches and prayers to unify his presentation of the monarchy. The Chronicler's writing, in fact, includes many more of these summarizing reflections, prayers, and speeches than the Deuteronomistic History does (Plöger 1957; Pratt 1987; Throntveit 1987). Recent studies of Chronicles agree in viewing David's prayer as one of these pivotal texts. Although he seems to have only lightly edited the text available to him, the Chronicler's own distinct perspective on David's prayer is clear both from close study of the prayer itself and by examination of its citation by later monarchs in the Chronicler's work.

## COMMENT

The appearance of David's prayer has struck some scholars as quite odd. Tsevat (1965) asks why David prays for something he has already received. De Vries (1989: 155) poses the issue more sharply. He speaks of "an aimless, anxiety-ridden prayer" that evinces a "theology of whining about for [sic] what God has already freely given." But David's prayer is neither superfluous nor pointless. It plays a strategic role in the Chronicler's larger presentation. There is both a synchronic and a diachronic significance to the placement of this piece. Synchronically, David's prayer praises God for his revelation through Nathan and implores Yhwh to actualize these dynastic promises. Most, but not all, of the assurances given to David pertain to the future. Nathan grants the king everything he wished for—and much, much more—but he delays the date for the implementation of most of these promises until the reign of David's heir. Given the postponement, a royal prayer is appropriate both as a forum for thanksgiving and as a petition for future fulfillment (v. 25). That David's specific requests focus exclusively on the dynastic promises (vv. 23–24) demonstrates how important these particular commitments were for the Chronicler, just as they were for the Deuteronomist before him. This does not mean that other divine commitments dealing with victory against David's enemies, peace for Israel, and the construction of a temple were unimportant. Rather, the Chronicler, like the Deuteronomist before him, viewed the dynastic promises as critical to the fulfillment of the others. If David's heir did not succeed him, most of the other divine assurances would become irrelevant. In the context of postmonarchic Judah, a time in which the splendor of the Davidic dynasty was a thing of the past, David's petitions may well have taken on additional significance, functioning as a prayer for a new realization of the divine promises (Williamson 1982b: 136).

Within the Chronicler's work, David's prayer also has a diachronic significance. It serves both as a bridge to Israel's communal past and as a bridge to its Jerusalem-centered future. As a bridge to Israel's past, it self-consciously integrates the Davidic promises into the larger history of God's dealings with Israel. The historical retrospect in David's prayer describes Nathan's revelation as "a great deed" (v. 19) and calls attention to the unique way in which Yhwh has dealt with his people (vv. 21–22). Yhwh's "great and marvelous deeds" on behalf of Israel, redeeming Israel from Egypt and driving out nations from before them, are essential to its distinctive heritage and identity. As Machinist (1991; 1994b) has observed, the Israelites, unlike the Egyptians and Mesopotamians, did not associate their history as coterminous with cosmogony. Instead, Israel's marginal status as newcomer was proclaimed as foundational to this people's special status. Throughout the centuries, Yhwh has been true to his people (v. 22). The Chronicler, like the Deuteronomist before him (2 Sam 7; 1 Kgs 8; Knoppers 1993c), pushes the trope a step further, hailing the newcomer status of David within Israelite history (vv. 16–18). Indeed, the very expressions the king uses in his prayer echo those used by other important figures in Israelite history (see NOTES). In David's prayer, the dynastic promises become an essential part of Israel's larger legacy. If the chosen heir succeeds and Yhwh fulfills the pledges made through Nathan, the promises to David will join the Exodus and Conquest as formative events in Israelite history (vv. 21–24). Indeed, the royal Davidic charter will call attention to Yhwh's other marvelous acts and contribute to Yhwh's reputation as an incomparable deity (vv. 19–20, 24).

As a bridge to the future, David's prayer anticipates the transition to his divinely chosen heir. David's prayer, in fact, draws further attention to the ties between Nathan's promises and David's seed. But the prayer also serves a broader purpose. David's very appreciative response to divine favor sets a standard for subsequent kings to emulate. Invocations, doxologies, and benedictions occupy a prominent place in this prayer. Later prayers (1 Chr 29:10–19; 2 Chr 1:8–10; 6:14–42; 20:6–12) echo these ascriptions of praise and thanksgiving. Like David's prayer, which occurs after the Ark of the Covenant has settled in Jerusalem, these royal prayers occur at critical points in the history of cult and kingdom. To be sure, later royal prayers each have their special concerns and contexts (Throntveit 1987: 51–88). Each responds to a distinctive situation. Yet by uttering public prayers in reaction to important moments in Israelite history, a number of David's successors continue the paradigm set by David. Like the Davidic promises, the Davidic prayer is formative.

# *XXII. "A Time for War": The Beginning of David's Foreign Campaigns (18:1–13)*

*Military Successes against the Philistines, Zobah, and Damascus*

1 Sometime after this, David defeated the Philistines, humbled them, and cap-

tured Gath and its dependencies from the control of the Philistines. [2]He also defeated the Moabites so that the Moabites became tribute-bearing vassals of David. [3]And David defeated Hadadezer, the king of Zobah toward Ḥamath, when he was on his way to set up his stela at the Euphrates River. [4]And David captured from him 1,000 chariots, 7,000 cavalry, and 20,000 foot soldiers. Then David hamstrung all of the chariot horses, except for 100 chariot horses, which he retained. [5]When the Aramaeans of Damascus came to support Hadadezer, the king of Zobah, David struck down 22,000 Aramaean men. [6]David stationed garrisons in Aram-damascus and the Aramaeans became David's tribute-bearing vassals. And Yhwh gave victory to David wherever he went.

*The Spoils of War and Tribute Brought to Jerusalem*

[7]Then David took the golden bow-and-arrow cases that belonged to the retainers of Hadadezer and brought them to Jerusalem. [8]And from Ṭibḥath and Kun, cities of Hadadezer, David captured a very large amount of bronze. With it Solomon made the bronze sea, the columns, and the bronze furnishings. [9]When Tou, the king of Ḥamath, heard that David had struck down all of the forces of Hadadezer, the king of Zobah, [10]he sent Hadoram his son to King David to sue for peace and to congratulate him for fighting against Hadadezer and defeating him, because Tou had often fought against Hadadezer. And (with Hadoram) were all kinds of gold, silver, and bronze objects. [11]King David also consecrated them to Yhwh, along with the silver and the gold that he exacted from all of the nations—from Edom, from Moab, from the Ammonites, from the Philistines, and from Amaleq.

*Abshai's Victory against the Edomites*

[12]Moreover, Abshai son of Zeruiah defeated the Edomites in the Valley of Salt—18,000. [13]He stationed garrisons in Edom and all of the Edomites became vassals of David. Yhwh gave victory to David wherever he went.

## TEXTUAL NOTES

18:1–13. This material is drawn from the author's version of 2 Sam 8:1–14. A portion of this material (2 Sam 8:2–8) is available in 4QSam$^{a}$.

18:1. "captured." So MT and LXX *(lectio brevior)*. A few Heb. MSS and Syr. follow MT 2 Sam 8:1 in adding "David."

"Gath and its dependencies" *(gt wbntyh)*. Reading with MT and LXX$^{L}$ *Geth kai tas thygateras autēs*. Cf. LXX$^{ABN}$ *Geth kai tas kōmas autēs*. MT and 4QSam$^{a}$ 2 Sam 8:1 have *mtg h'mh*, a puzzling expression that has been variously translated: "reins of the forearm" (Hertzberg 1964: 288), "the bridle of the mother (city)" (S. Driver 1912: 279), and "bridle of the water channel" (McCarter 1984: 243). Some (e.g., NRSV) simply transliterate "Metheg-ammah."

18:2. "the Moabites." 2 Sam 8:2 continues with a gruesome description of David's treatment of the captured Moabites: "and he measured them with a cord, causing them to lie down on the ground. He measured two lengths of cord for those who were to be put to death and one full length for those who were to be spared." Fragmentary 4QSam[a] also seems to presuppose this account. The Chronicler could have excluded this material from his own presentation as extraneous or unflattering to David. Alternatively, as Freedman (personal communication) points out, the material may have been absent from the Chronicler's *Vorlage* because of haplography (*homoioarkton* from "and he measured them" (וימדדם) in 2 Sam 8:2 to "and Moab became" (ותהי מואב) at the beginning of 2 Sam 8:3).

"and the Moabites became" (*wyhyw*). So MT and LXX[AB] 18:2 and perhaps 4QSam[a] *wyh*[*y*(*w*)]. MT 2 Sam 8:2 reads the expected *wthy*.

"tribute-bearing vassals of David." Literally, "servants to David, bearers of tribute" (עבדים לדויד נשׂאי מנחה). So 18:2 and 4QSam[a]. MT and Tg. 2 Sam 8:2 לדוד לעבדים נושׂאי מנחה, "to David as servants, bearers of tribute." See also the 3rd TEXTUAL NOTE to v. 6.

18:3. "Hadadezer" (*hddʿzr*). So MT 2 Sam 8:3 and MT 1 Chr 18:3. Many Heb. MSS and the versions read *hdrʿzr*. See also 2 Sam 8:5, 7, 8, 9, 10, 12; 10:16, 19; 1 Kgs 11:23; 1 Chr 18:5, 7, 8, 9, 10; 19:16, 19. Confusion between *dālet* and *rêš* is "a hardy perennial in Hebrew textual transmission" (Allen 1974b: 112). The patronym of 2 Sam 8:3 (MT, LXX, 4QSam[a]) "son of Reḥob" (בן רחב), which does not occur in Chronicles, may be an expansion based on 2 Sam 8:12 (McKenzie 1985: 53).

"Zobah toward Ḥamath" (*ṣwbh ḥmth*). So MT and LXX. The phrase "toward Ḥamath" (LXX[B] *Souba Hēmath*; LXX[L] *Souba en Haimath*) is absent from 2 Sam 8:3 and from Syr. and Vg. 1 Chr 18:3 because of haplography (*homoioteleuton*).

"Zobah" is usually spelled *ṣwbh* (2 Sam 8:3, 5[//1 Chr 18:3, 5], 12; 23:36; 1 Sam 14:47; 1 Kgs 11:23; 1 Chr 19:6; 2 Chr 8:3; Ps 60:[title]) but as *ṣwbʾ*, "Zoba," in 2 Sam 10:6, 8.

"when he was on his way" (בלכתו). The antecedent is unclear. It is possible to read the clause, as many do (e.g., Benzinger 1901: 58), with Hadadezer as the implied subject, "who was on his [i.e., Hadadezer's] way to set up his stela." But an equally likely antecedent would be the subject of the previous *wāw* consecutive clause, David (Curtis and Madsen 1910: 233; S. Driver 1892: 98–99). See further the NOTES to v. 3.

"to set up" (*lhṣyb*). So MT and perhaps LXX* 2 Sam 8:3 and LXX[AB] 1 Chr 18:3, which have the 1 aorist active inf. *epistēsai*, "to establish." MT 2 Sam 8:3 "to restore" (*lhšyb*).

"his stela" (*ydw*). On the use of *yd* to signify monument or stela, see 1 Sam 15:12 and 2 Sam 18:18 (S. Driver 1912: 125).

"at the Euphrates River" (*bnhr-prt*). So MT and LXX. MT 2 Sam 8:3, which lacks "Euphrates," is much more ambiguous (5th NOTE to v. 3). However, many Heb. MSS (and some of the versions) of 2 Sam 8:3 have *prt*.

18:4. "chariots" (*rkb*). So MT and LXX 1 Chr 18:4, as well as LXX, OL, and 4QSam[a] (*dr*[*kb wšbʿ*]) 2 Sam 8:4. The term "chariots" is lacking in MT 2 Sam 8:4.

"7,000." Reading with MT and LXX 1 Chr 18:4, as well as LXX and 4QSam[a] (*ʾlp*), instead of MT, 2 Sam 8:4 "1,700" (*ʾlp wšbʿ mʾwt*). See also 2 Sam 10:18, 1 Chr 19:18, and Josephus, *Ant.* 7.99.

18:5. "the Aramaeans of Damascus." Literally, "Aram-damascus." See also v. 6 and Ps 60:[title], "Aram-naharaim and Aram-zobah."

"Damascus." MT *drmšq*. For the sake of convenience, I am rendering *drmšq* according to the normal spelling of *dmšq*, "Damascus" (cf. LXX[ABL] *Damaskou;* LXX[S] *Damaskō*). A few Heb. MSS also have the more common *dmšq*, but MT Chronicles typically reads *drmšq* (1 Chr 18:5, 6; 2 Chr 16:2; 24:23; 28:5, 23).

"Hadadezer" *(hdd'zr)*. See the 1st TEXTUAL NOTE to v. 3.

18:6. "garrisons" *(nṣybym)*. So a few Heb. MSS, the versions, and 2 Sam 8:6. The term is missing from MT 1 Chr 18:6 because of haplography before "in Aram" *(bʾrm)*. Some prefer to translate *nṣybym* as "prefects" (so also in v. 13).

"Damascus" *(drmšq)*. Again, a few Heb. MSS have the more common *dmšq* (1st TEXTUAL NOTE to v. 5).

"David's tribute-bearing vassals" (לדויד עבדים נשׂאי מנחה). The wording of 2 Sam 8:6 is again slightly different, "to David as servants, bearers of tribute" (לדוד לעבדים נושׂאי מנחה; 3rd TEXTUAL NOTE to v. 2). Although the two Samuel readings (2 Sam 8:2, 6) are consistent, the variation in Chronicles creates a parallel chiasm between 18:2 and 18:6 (Kalimi 1995a: 221).

18:7. "golden bow-and-arrow cases" *(šilṭê hazzāhāb)*. Traditionally, "golden shields." The case for translating this expression as "golden bow cases" was made by Borger (1972). My adaptation follows the Akk. evidence compiled for *šalṭu*, "bow-and-arrow case" in *CAD š* (I) 271–72. The "bow-and-arrow case" *(šlṭ)* would be made of wood and, in this instance, plated with gold. The tomb of Aspathines, a dignitary of Darius I, depicts Aspathines carrying the bow case of Darius I. The accompanying inscription employs the Babylonian term *šalṭu*, "bow-and-arrow case," written with the logogram for wooden articles, to describe this object. Hence, *šeleṭ* is to be distinguished from *ʾašpâ*, "quiver."

"Hadadezer." See the 1st TEXTUAL NOTE to v. 3.

"to Jerusalem." So MT and LXX 1 Chr 18:7 and MT 2 Sam 8:7. 4QSam[a], LXX, and OL 2 Sam 8:7, as well as Josephus *(Ant* 7.104), add a reference to the invasion of Shishaq during the reign of Reḥoboam (which resulted in temple plunder). See 1 Kgs 14:25–26, 2 Chr 12:2–9, and the discussion of Ulrich (1978: 45–48).

18:8. "from Ṭibḥath" *(mṭbḥt)*. So MT. LXX[B] is similar, although it reflects a dittography of *mêm: ek tēs metabēchas* (= *mmṭbḥt*). MT 2 Sam 8:8 has *bṭḥ* through metathesis (cf. Syr. 2 Sam 8:8 *ṭbḥ;* LXX[L] [*Ma*]*tebak*). For the masc. form of Ṭibḥath, see Gen 22:24 "Ṭebaḥ."

"and from Kun" *(wmkwn)*. So MT. 4QSam[a] is fragmentary, "and from . . ." *(wm* . . . ). MT 2 Sam 8:8 *wmbrty*, "and from Berothai." LXX[B] 2 Sam 8:8 and LXX 1 Chr 18:8 are corrupt, *kai ek tōn eklektōn polemōn* (LXX[AN] and Arm. *poleōn*), reflecting either *wmbḥry*, "and from the (select) young men" or *mbrrwt*. If the underlying reading was *wmbḥry*, it would have to reflect both a *ḥêt/tāw* error and metathesis. See 2nd NOTE to v. 8 and 2nd TEXTUAL NOTE to 16:41.

"Hadadezer." See the 1st TEXTUAL NOTE to v. 3.

"David" (דויד). So MT and LXX. MT, LXX, and 4QSam[a] 2 Sam 8:8 "King David" (המלך דוד).

"a very large amount of bronze" (נחשת רבה). So MT. MT 2 Sam 8:8 נחשת הרבה.

"with it Solomon made the bronze sea, the columns, and the bronze furnishings." So MT and LXX. The statement is missing from MT 2 Sam 8:8, but 4QSam[a], LXX, OL 2 Sam 8:8 and Josephus (*Ant* 7.104–6) largely agree with the lemma of Chronicles. The textual evidence suggests that the Chronicler found this statement in his *Vorlage*.

"Solomon." Thus MT and LXX. The reading of Syr., "David," harmonizes to the context (vv. 1–8a).

"bronze sea" (*yām hannĕḥōšet*). Some prefer to translate less literally as "bronze tank."

"(and) the columns" (*wʾt hʿmwdym*). So MT and LXX (*lectio brevior*). Syr. adds *wtwrʾ dnhšʾ* (= *et boves aeneos*), "and bronze oxen," perhaps an assimilation toward 1 Kgs 7:44 and 2 Chr 4:15 (*wʾt-hbqr*).

18:9. "Tou" (*tʿw*). So MT. The lemma of LXX[BL] *Thōa* reflects metathesis (*twʿ*). LXX[AN] *Thoou*. LXX[BMN] (*Tho*[*u*]*ou*) and OL (*Thou*) 2 Sam 8:9 also reflect *tʿw*. MT 2 Sam 8:9 *tʿy*. A Hurrian or Luvian origin of the name has been suggested (Dion 1997: 76–77).

"Hadadezer." See the 1st TEXTUAL NOTE to v. 3.

"the king of Zobah." So MT and LXX 18:9, but wanting in MT 2 Sam 8:9.

18:10. "Hadoram" (*hdwrm*). Thus MT and LXX[L] (*Hadōram*). LXX[B] *Idouraam* (= *ydwrm*). The reading of Syr. *ywrm* "Joram" (**yāhū-rām*, "Yhwh is exalted") assimilates to MT 2 Sam 8:10 (*ywrm*). As to which lemma—*hdwrm* or *ywrm*—is earlier, the evidence points to *hdwrm*. To begin with, the reading of Josephus (*Ant.* 7.107), *Adōramos*, supports Chronicles. Second, the reading of *ywrm* may have resulted from a process of dissimilation, given the similarity in nomenclature between this prince and the chief of forced labor under David and Reḥoboam, "A/Hadoram" (*ʾ/hdwrm*; 2 Sam 20:24; 1 Kgs 12:18//2 Chr 10:18). Finally, the PN "Hadoram" (**haddu-rām*, "Haddu is exalted") makes the most sense from the standpoint of comparative Semitic (Dion 1997: 115–16).

"to sue for peace." Literally, "to ask him for peace." Kethib *lišʾôl-lô*; Qere and MT 2 Sam 8:10 *lišʾol-lô*. In both cases, LXX has *erōtēsai auton*, "to ask him."

"and to congratulate him." Literally, "and to bless him" (ולברכו).

"because Tou had often fought against Hadadezer." MT 1 Chr 18:10 and 2 Sam 8:10 literally read, "because the man of wars of Tou Hadadezer became" (*ky ʾyš mlḥmwt tʿw/y hyh hddʿzr*; 1st TEXTUAL NOTE to v. 3). The meaning seems somewhat clear, even if the syntax is not. The reading of LXX[B] *hoti anēr polemeos Thōa ēn tō Adraazar* may represent one attempt to render a difficult Heb. *Vorlage*. The alternate and shorter lemma of LXX 2 Sam 8:10 *hoti (anti)keimenos ēn tō Adraazar* (= *ky mtḥrh hyh bhddʿzr*) may be, however, closer to the original (McCarter 1984: 245).

"and (with Hadoram) were." MT (*wkl*) is elliptical. Syr. "by the hand of Joram" (= *byd ywrm*) is influenced by the verbiage of 2 Sam 8:10. Similarly, emending to *bkl* (*BHS*) or adding *bydw hyw* (*BHK*) after MT 2 Sam 8:10 is unnecessary. As Samuel Driver (1914: 537 [#27]) and Kropat (§24) point out, the Chronicler sometimes omits subjects or, less often, verbs from his sentences (e.g., 1 Chr 9:33; 15:13; 2 Chr 10:11, 14; 11:22; 15:3; 16:10, 12; 17:4; 18:3; 19:6; 21:15; 26:18; 28:21; 30:9, 17; 35:21). An alternative proposed by Roddy Braun (1986), and in more detail by Dirksen (1999), construes this clause with what follows at the beginning of v. 11: "as for all of the articles of gold, silver, and bronze, David dedicated them also." In this line of interpretation, the articles refer back to the spoil taken from Hadadezer and his retainers (vv. 3–8). While this reconstruction is possible, one wonders why the earlier text does not explicitly mention these gold and silver objects. Verse 7 only lists golden bow-and-arrow cases and v. 8 mentions a large amount of bronze, but there is no specific mention of silver articles. Moreover, there is an important contextual consideration that needs to be kept in mind. It would be odd for King Tou to sue for peace (vv. 9–10a) and not send along some sort of tribute to David.

"all kinds of gold, silver, and bronze objects" *(kl kly zhb wksp wnḥšt)*. So MT. The use of the *Nomen regens* in this clause is again typical of Chronistic style (Kropat, §19). MT 2 Sam 8:10 *kly-ksp wkly-zhb wkly-nḥšt*, "objects of silver and objects of gold and objects of bronze."

18:11. "he exacted" *(nś')*. So MT (maximum variation). LXX *elaben* (= *lqḥ*), "he took." As earlier in the verse, 2 Sam 8:11 *hqdyš*, "he consecrated."

"from all of the nations." So MT and LXX *(lectio brevior)*. 2 Sam 8:11 adds, *'šr kbš* "which he captured."

"from Edom." Reading with MT and LXX 1 Chr 18:11, as well as LXX 2 Sam 8:12. MT 2 Sam 8:12 reads "from Aram" (another *dālet/rêš* confusion; see 1st TEXTUAL NOTE to v. 3).

"from Amaleq." So MT and LXX. MT 2 Sam 8:12 adds "and from the plunder of Hadadezer, son of Reḥob, the king of Zobah."

18:12. "and Abshai son of Zeruiah" *(w'bšy bn-ṣrwyh)*. So MT and basically LXX *(kai Abessa huios Sarouias)*. On the PN "Abshai," see the 2nd TEXTUAL NOTE to 2:16. In 18:12, the witnesses to Chronicles differ from those to Samuel. MT 2 Sam 8:13 "and David made a name [i.e., built a memorial] upon his return [*wyʿś dwd šm bšbw*] from defeating Aram." LXX 2 Sam 8:13 *kai en tō anakamptein auton eptaxen ten Idoumaian* seems to reflect *wyšbw hkh 't 'dwm*, "and when he returned, he defeated Edom." This leads Benzinger (1901: 58–59), followed by Curtis and Madsen (1910: 235), to reconstruct *wbšwbw*, "and upon his return." But Benzinger's proposal leaves the name of the mother unexplained. On the basis of Ps 60:[title], which reads in part "when he [David] fought with Aram-naharaim and Aram-zobah, and Joab returned *(wyšb yw'b)* and defeated Edom *(wyk 't 'dwm)*," Rudolph (1955: 134) tries to remedy the deficiency in Benzinger's argument by reconstructing, "upon his return from Zobah" *(bšwbw mṣwbh)*. This latter proposal has some merit, but it neglects one of the most difficult, and likely original, features of the Chronicles (and Psalms) text: the attribution of a victory to someone other than David in a passage that otherwise highlights David's wartime victories (contra Kittel 1902: 76). In the course of transmission, the pressure would be to level the text by attributing all of the victories directly to David, especially in view of the summary statements in vv. 6 and 13.

"Edom." MT 2 Sam 8:13 "Aram" (another *dālet/rêš* confusion; see TEXTUAL NOTES to vv. 3, 11). LXX and Syr. 2 Sam 8:13 agree with Chronicles. Ps 60:[title] also has "Edom."

"18,000." So MT and LXX 1 Chr 18:12 and MT 2 Sam 8:13. Ps 60:[title] "12,000."

18:13. "he." Syr. and Arab. ("David") explicate.

"stationed garrisons (נציבים) in Edom." So MT *(lectio brevior)* and LXX[L] *(kai etheto en tē Idoumaia phrouran)*. The lemma of MT 2 Sam 8:14 evinces dittography: "he stationed in Edom garrisons, in all of Edom he stationed garrisons." The reading of LXX[B] 1 Chr 18:13 is confused, *kai etheto en tē koiladi phrouras*, "and he put garrisons in the valley."

# NOTES

18:1. "sometime after this" *(wyhy 'ḥry-kn)*. An inexact chronological notice of the kind regularly found in Chronicles (cf. *wyhy 'ḥrykn* in 2 Chr 20:1). The notice refers to the time of the dynastic oracle and prayer (1 Chr 17). The vague formulaic link with previous material, drawn from the author's *Vorlage* (2 Sam 8:1), introduces a new season in David's reign characterized by a series of foreign conflicts (18:1–20:8). In the Chronicler's highly complimentary and ordered presentation of David's career, this period—a "time for war" (Qoh 3:8)—is ordained by the deity (see COMMENT on 17:1–15). David's unmitigated success in battle realizes one of the promises made by the prophet Nathan in the dynastic oracle (17:10).

"defeated the Philistines." David engaged in battle against the Philistines earlier, successfully repelling two successive Philistine invasions (14:8–17). This new war against the Philistines is, however, different in that David is now on the offensive.

"humbled them" (ויכניעם). In the context of the Chronicler's work, this notice echoes and and begins to fulfill one of the promises Nathan made to David in the dynastic oracle, והכנעתי את-כל-אויביך, "I shall humble all your enemies" (17:10; 2nd NOTE). It is possible that Deut 9:3 stands behind the Chronicler's slight reformulation (17:10; cf. 2 Sam 7:11) of his source (Lorenzin 1996), but this is uncertain.

"captured Gath." In addition to subjugating his foe, David enlarges Israel's territory by seizing one of the main Philistine cities, Gath, along with its satellite villages. Gath has been traditionally associated with T. eṣ-Ṣafi, just south of Eqron (see 3rd NOTE to 8:13).

18:2. "Moabites." One of Israel's neighbors and occasional enemy to the southeast. Davidic friendship with Moabites is attested in 1 Sam 22:3–5, while a Moabite component in David's ancestry is attested in 1 Chr 2:5–15(//Ruth 4:13–22). The genealogy of Judah also mentions Judahite intermarriage with Moab (1 Chr 4:22). An earlier campaign against the Moabites is mentioned in 1 Sam 14:47, but not in Chronicles. In Chronicles, this is the first record of a war against Moab.

"tribute-bearing vassals" (לעבדים נשאי מנחה). The language reflects the world of international diplomacy (*ARAB* II, §§284, 510; J. Wilson 1969a: 235; Kalluveettil 1982: 66–69). In a relationship between two unequal powers, the weaker, subjugated state could become a client of the more powerful, conquering state (e.g., 2 Kgs 16:7; 17:3; 24:1; *KAI* 216.3). In such arrangements, attested widely in the ancient Near East (D. McCarthy 1981), minor parties usually retained a certain amount of autonomy over their internal affairs, but were obliged to manifest loyalty to their overlords by regularly dispatching tribute. Client obligations could also include the timely provision of military assistance, the renunciation of independent foreign diplomatic contacts, the extradition of refugees from the overlord's domain, and support for the succession of the overlord's designated heir.

18:3. "Hadadezer." More than one king with this name (= Hadad-ʿiḏr, "[the god] Hadad is [my] help") is attested in the history of Damascus (Pitard 1987: 99–100, 125–44).

"the king of Zobah." Much about Zobah's identity and location is uncertain (Dion 1997: 174–76). Most scholars would locate Zobah in the Biqâʿ Valley north of Damascus. Among the several small Aramaean states, Zobah appears as the most important rival of the fledgling Davidic monarchy (Pitard 1987: 90–94).

"toward Ḥamath." That is, in the direction of Ḥamath. The notice is important in light of the later mention that "Tou" was "the king of Ḥamath" (v. 9).

"when he was on his way." The subject is either Hadadezer (the nearest antecedent) or David (4th TEXTUAL NOTE to v. 3). In addition to the grammatical issue, there are geopolitical considerations that need to be weighed (McCarter 1984; Halpern 1996a; 2001). If Hadadezer was marching to the Euphrates, how would he encounter David? Israel was located to the southwest of Zobah, and the Euphrates was located to the northeast of Zobah. Conversely, if David is the antecedent, what is David doing marching all the way to the Euphrates? The answer may lie in the Chronicler's interpretation of his source (next NOTE).

"to set up his stela at the Euphrates River" (בלכתו להציב ידו בנהר-פרת). The change over against the more ambiguous Samuel, "when he was on his way to restore his monument at the river" (בלכתו להשיב ידו בנהר), the Chronicler's change reflects inner-biblical exegesis. In Samuel the monarch is journeying to restore (not establish) his monument at an unspecified river. Considering biblical and ancient Near Eastern usage of "the river" (הנהר; cf. Akk. *nāru*; *CAD* N [I] 373–74; Ephʿal and Naveh 1989: 195–96), the authors of Samuel may have had the Euphrates in view. Whatever the case, the Chronicler surmised as much from his source, because his text speaks explicitly of "the Euphrates River." In this respect, the interpretation of v. 3 belongs to the category of a literary clarification (cf. Kalimi 1995a). Nevertheless, given the geographical locations of Israel and Zobah, other suggestions have been proffered for the reference in Samuel, such as the Jordan (Halpern 1996a). Clearly, the contrast between crossing the Jordan River and crossing the Euphrates River has widely divergent implications for understanding the import of the text in question. The passage in Chronicles may have the Israelite monarch making a far-flung journey to the northeast and triumphing over his Aramaean opponent. It was customary for ancient Near Eastern kings to set up monuments commemorating their accomplishments and victories.

While some of these memorials, for instance, the Mesha stela (*KAI* 181; Smelik 1992), were erected in the conquering monarch's own territory, others, for instance, the Tel Dan stela (Biran and Naveh 1993; 1995), were erected in an area subjugated by the conquering monarch. Of special relevance to the reference in this verse is the aspiration of western kings to leave monuments at the Euphrates River, a traditional boundary. In this great ambition, some succeeded (e.g., Thutmosis I and Thutmosis III; J. Wilson 1969a: 239–40). If David is the subject of the disputed phrase (see TEXTUAL NOTE), the Chronicler places David in a select company of monarchs who traveled all the way to the eastern side of the Euphrates to set up their stelae. According to this line of interpretation, the king of Zobah would be engaged in a defensive maneuver, attempting to thwart a Davidic campaign that threatened the independence of Hadadezer's own state. If Hadadezer is the subject of the disputed phrase, David would be engaged in an aggressive maneuver against him. If this line of interpretation has merit, it seems unlikely that Hadadezer succeeded in setting up his own stela at the Euphrates.

18:4. "1,000 chariots, 7,000 cavalry, and 20,000 foot soldiers." The problem with large numbers in Chronicles has been discussed before (NOTE to 12:38). In this case, the problem is already apparent in the Chronicler's source (2 Sam 8:4).

"hamstrung all of the chariot horses." The reason is unclear. Was it because David's forces fought on foot (Pitard 1987: 90–94), or was it because David's forces already possessed a full complement of horses (Yadin 1963: 285)? McCarter (1984: 249) raises a third possibility, that of ritual punishment in the context of war (Josh 11:6–9). That David retains "100 horses" lends some credence to the second theory.

18:5. "Aramaeans of Damascus." The defeat of one state by an invading power may upset the balance of power in an entire region, especially affecting states neighboring the defeated kingdom. In later times, Damascus would become the capital of a unified, much larger Aramaean state (1 Kgs 11:23–25; Pitard 1987: 99–189; Dion 1997). But Damascus appears here as the capital of a local kingdom, one of a number of regional Aramaean states (cf. 2 Sam 10:1–19//1 Chr 19:1–19; Ps 60:[title]) of which Aram-zobah seems to be the most powerful.

"to support Hadadezer." That the army of Aram-damascus rallies to the cause of Hadadezer, the king of Zobah, suggests that the two were allies. In Akkadian and Hittite treaties, one state could be expected to provide military support if the territory of the other partner was invaded by a hostile power (Beckman, 2.§§29–35, 56–57; 4.§2; 5.§§3–4, 6; 6A.§8; 7.§§1–2, 4–6; etc.).

"22,000 Aramaean men." See the 1st NOTE to v. 4.

18:6. "stationed garrisons." David exercises control over his newly acquired vassal by stationing troops in the land. Such a formal presence by a major power in the territory of a client state was characteristic of many suzerain-vassal relationships (e.g., Beckman, 5.§7; 10.§§4, 12; 11.§19) and served two complementary purposes simultaneously: a security guarantee against hostile neighbors and a deterrent to seditious agitation within the client state.

"tribute-bearing vassals." Like the Moabites (NOTES to v. 2), these Aramaeans become Davidic clients.

"Yhwh gave victory to David." The position of this summary notice, repeated in

v. 13, is not premature (*pace* McCarter 1984: 249–50). The narrator is signaling the fulfillment of one of the divine promises made to the Israelite king, namely, that Yhwh would defeat David's enemies (17:8–10).

18:7. "golden bow-and-arrow cases." One of the major benefits of a successful military campaign was plunder. In this case, David retrieves precious articles for his newly established capital. As the narrator subsequently makes clear (v. 8), such spoil was not used simply for David's own enjoyment.

18:8. "Ṭibḥath." Mentioned already in the Amarna archives (*ṭu-bi-ḫi*; EA 179.15), in Thutmosis III's list of conquered Asian towns (*du-bi-ḫi*), and in the Papyrus Anastasi I letter (Albright 1934: 40; J. Wilson 1969b: 477), Ṭibḥath (masc. Ṭebaḥ) was a city in the Biqâʿ Valley. In Gen 22:24, Ṭebaḥ appears as a son of Abraham's brother Naḥor by a concubine. This makes him the eponymous ancestor of a collateral Aramaean tribe.

"Kun" (כון). Sometimes identified as Râs Baʿalbek in the Lebanon Valley. It appears as Ku-nú in Rameses III's list of conquered Asian towns (Albright 1934: 60). The domain controlled by Hadadezer was more than a single city-state. Ṭibḥath, Kun, and perhaps Berothai (2 Sam 8:8) are said to have belonged to his regime.

"the bronze sea, the columns, and the bronze furnishings." It was customary for pious kings in the ancient Near East to dedicate some of the spoil gained in war to the deities who granted them victory. Such public acts of piety were effected by donating plunder to appropriate sanctuaries in recognition of divine favor. A recently published north Syrian inscription on a trapezoid cast-bronze relief dating to the ninth century B.C.E., declares: "That which Hadad gave to our master Ḥazael from ʿUmqi in the year that our master crossed the river" (זי נתן הדד למראן חזאל מן עמק בשנת עדה מראן נהר; Eph'al and Naveh 1989). This Aramaic inscription is unusual, not so much in that the god Hadad is the subject, as in the fact that the inscription is inscribed on the booty itself. In the case of our text, the narrator makes a link between the dedication of David's spoil and its incorporation into the Temple subsequently built by his successor, Solomon (1 Kgs 7:13–47; 2 Chr 3:15–4:22; Josephus, *Ant* 7.106).

18:9. "Ḥamath" (modern Ḥamā) was situated on the middle Orontes significantly to the north of Zobah (cf. 2 Kgs 23:33; 25:21; Jer 39:5; 52:9, 27). Before coming under control of the Aramaeans, Ḥamath was a Neo-Hittite state (Pitard 1987: 87). See also the NOTE to 13:5.

"heard that David had struck down." As mentioned above (1st NOTE to v. 5), the invasion of one kingdom may have repercussions for neighboring states. Whether the conquest destabilizes or liberates neighboring kingdoms depends largely on particular historical circumstances and the nature of the relationships between the affected states. Whereas David's victory against Hadadezer led Aram-damascus (an ally of Aram-zobah) to challenge David (v. 5), the same victory brings a measure of relief to Tou, because Tou himself had suffered at the hands of Hadadezer (v. 10).

18:10. "Hadoram his son." That the king of Ḥamath dispatches his own son, rather than a ordinary messenger, underscores the gravity of his mission. Messengers could be ignored or be the subject of considerable abuse (Meier 1988).

"to sue for peace" (*lšʾl-lw lšlwm*). There is some merit to the traditional argument that Hadoram's objective was to establish or confirm a client-treaty relationship with David. Both the emissary (a prince) and the gifts he brings ("all kinds of gold, silver, and bronze objects") suggest that more than a courtesy visit is in view. Nevertheless, because neither Tou nor Hadoram is called a "servant" (*ʿbd*) of David, one should hesitate in defining this relationship as a vassal treaty. Based on ancient Near Eastern precedent, David's very reception of the gifts may engender a certain obligation on his part (Zaccagnini 1983: 206–7). To accept another ruler's gifts is essential to establishing or maintaining a partnership. Hence, it seems likely that the narrator considers the relationship to be founded on a mutual antipathy toward Hadadezer: "he who is an enemy to my enemies is a friend to me." Since Ḥamath was located to the north of both Damascus and Zobah, the establishment of an ongoing diplomatic relationship would be beneficial to both Tou and David.

18:11. "consecrated them to Yhwh." Ancient Near Eastern kings enjoyed sacral status, although exactly what this status amounted to differed in various political, social, and literary contexts. As mediators between the divine and human realms, kings represented their people to the gods through sacrifice, ritual, and prayer. Conversely, royalty represented the gods to the people by securing peace, prosperity, and justice on their behalf. In other words, the well-being of the monarchy was thought to be critical to the general well-being of society. In Chronicles David's hallowed character is illustrated by his sacrifices, his prayers, his care for the Ark, his appointment of and directions to the priests and Levites, and his piety in battle. David's critical status is also evident (in negative fashion) in the occurrence of a plague following his national census (21:1–22:1). Commensurate with his status as a pious king, David ritually dedicates the valuable articles he receives from Tou. In this manner, the author underlines the advantages that the Davidic monarchy brought to Yahwistic worship in Jerusalem.

"exacted from all of the nations." The narrator presents David's consecration as comprehensive. Everything that David receives from Edom, Moab, the Ammonites, the Philistines, and Amaleq, he dedicates to Yhwh.

"the Ammonites." Israel's neighbors to the east are not elsewhere mentioned in this chapter (cf. 2 Sam 11:1; 12:26–31). They occupy a prominent place in the later battle narratives of 1 Chr 19–20. The placement of this passage is an example of achronological historiography. This technique, sometimes called chronological displacement, involves deliberately narrating events out of strict chronological order to make a larger point (NOTE to 11:4–9). In the case of David's military campaigns, both Samuel and Chronicles foreground David's dedication of war booty gathered from all quarters to the deity responsible for his success.

"Amaleq." The Amaleqites are also not elsewhere mentioned in this record of David's campaigns. In fact, Chronicles, as opposed to Samuel (from which this reference is taken), does not record any Davidic campaign against or dealings with the Amaleqites (cf. 1 Sam 30:18; 2 Sam 1:1).

18:12. "Abshai" is one of a number of military heroes who help David secure victory against Israel's traditional foes (cf. 19:8–15; 20:1, 4–7). The authors of Samuel do not mention Abshai in this context (1st TEXTUAL NOTE to v. 12). According to MT 2 Sam 8:13, David constructed a memorial (literally, "made a name" [*wyʿś dwd šm*]) upon his return from defeating Edom (so LXX; MT "Aram") in the Valley of Salt.

"Zeruiah," the mother of Abshai, Joab, and Asahel, is mentioned often in Samuel and occasionally in Chronicles (1 Sam 26:6; 2 Sam 3:29; 16:9, 10; 18:2; 19:22; 21:17; 1 Chr 11:20; 19:11, 15). According to the Judahite genealogy (1 Chr 2:16; 2nd NOTE), Zeruiah was David's sister.

"Valley of Salt" (גיא המלח). The location is disputed. Some favor a location in traditional Edomite territory (2 Chr 25:11; 2 Kgs 14:7 [Kethib]), while others favor an identification with the Wâdī el-Milḥ, south of Beersheba. A third option involves identifying this valley with "the Valley of Craftsmen" (גיא חרשים) mentioned in 4:13–14 (Tadmor and Cogan 1988: 155).

18:13. "garrisons in Edom." See the 1st NOTE to v. 6.

"the Edomites became vassals of David." Like the Moabites (v. 2) and the Aramaeans (v. 6), the Edomites are consigned to a client relationship with David.

"Yhwh gave victory." Consistent with the ideology of sacral war, the narrator attributes ultimate responsibility for the conquests to Yhwh. The hand of God enables David to enjoy unmitigated military success "wherever he went."

## SOURCES AND COMPOSITION

First Chronicles 18:1–13 is paralleled by and taken from the Chronicler's *Vorlage* of 2 Sam 8:1–14. In a few instances, the Chronicler's narrative is briefer than that of Samuel (vv. 2, 11, 12). In a couple of instances, the Chronicler's narrative is more extensive (vv. 3, 8), but in the latter case the text-critical evidence from the versions and 4QSam[a] suggests that most of this material was already present in the Chronicler's *Vorlage*. It remains, therefore, to discuss those statements found in MT Samuel that are lacking in Chronicles. Two of these (vv. 11, 12) are fairly short and may perhaps best be explained on text-critical grounds—the Chronicler employed a version of Samuel that was similar, but not identical, to MT Samuel. In the third case (v. 3), the Chronicler may have omitted a patronymic (Kalimi 1994a: 81). The longer plus in 2 Sam 8:2, which is absent from Chronicles, may also be explained on textual grounds—haplography (1st TEXTUAL NOTE to v. 2). Alternatively, the author may have omitted this material about the treatment of Moabite captives as extraneous to his own narrative design. Certainly, the author displays a penchant elsewhere (already in 1 Chr 1) for omitting material that he considers to be irrelevant to his purposes. Whatever explanation one adopts for the Samuel material absent from 1 Chr 18:2, one is still left with a basic conclusion: The Chronicler seems to have made only slight changes from his *Vorlage*. In general, he has followed both the order and the content of 2 Sam 8 in writing his own work.

First Chronicles 18 introduces a new phase in David's reign, dominated by foreign military campaigns. Since the Chronicler devotes considerable coverage to this period (18:1–20:8), it will be useful to pay some attention to the literary devices by which he ties these disparate expeditions together. Drawing upon the Deuteronomistic History, the Chronicler organizes this period in David's reign into a string of pericopes of varied length with only brief connectives. At least some of the events alluded to in these chapters are presented out of chronological order (see 3rd NOTE to v. 11). In my judgment, the Chronicler's presentation is an excellent example of paratactic composition. Parataxis as a compositional technique is well attested in both ancient Greek historiography (Immerwahr 1966: 7–72; Lamberts 1970) and biblical historiography (Auerbach 1953; Van Seters 1983: 60–62). The primary principle of organization is neither strictly chronological nor dramatic (rising toward a climax). Although any given unit may be a unified composition, exhibiting its own coherence and set of internal correspondences, there may not be any explicit reference within the unit to the other units that together comprise this period in David's reign. Consistent with the conventions of parataxis, the brief transitions the Chronicler provides within or between these major units are, for the most part, only vaguely chronological.

18:1: "sometime after this" *(wyhy ʾḥry-kn)*.
19:1: "sometime after this" *(wyhy ʾḥry-kn)*.
20:1: "when it was the turn of the year" *(wyhy lʿt tšwbt hšnh)*.
20:4: "and sometime after this" *(wyhy ʾḥrykn)*.

In one case, the list of David's cabinet officers (18:14–17), there is no chronological marker. Recognition of the Chronicler's paratactic compositional technique elucidates the structure of David's reign. Since the author does not orchestrate intricate transitions between pericopes, he impels readers to draw analogies or contrasts between the events he depicts. The Chronicler aids this interpretive process through his employment of literary devices such as evaluative comments: "Yhwh gave victory to David wherever he went" (18:6, 13; cf. 18:14), speeches (19:12–13), dedication formulas (18:8, 11), and a prophecy/fulfillment schema (17:8–10; cf. 18:1–6; 19:17–18; 20:1–3, 8). These provide some thematic links between units. The Chronicler's ideology is also apparent in his recontextualization of the material he includes from his *Vorlage*. By connecting this phase of David's rule with the dynastic oracle and prayer that preceded it (1 Chr 17) and the Temple preparation and national political organization that follow it (1 Chr 22–29), the author conveys a larger sense of meaning and purpose to seemingly disparate episodes in David's public life.

## COMMENT

Discussing 2 Sam 8:2, Dennis McCarthy (1981: 287–88) remarks that this verse "sounds like a piece from Assyrian royal annals: punishment of the enemy, mercy for a remnant, and the imposition of tribute making them vassals." The observation holds true in a more general way of the entire passage under review; 1 Chr 18:1–13 consists of a series of battle and tribute reports. In this catalogue, the narrator describes neither the battles themselves nor military strategy in any detail. The numbers of royal troops are not given and only in three instances are the numbers of defeated troops provided (vv. 4, 5, 12). Summaries of Davidic successes are interrupted only by notices of war spoils, the dispatching of tribute, and royal dedications.

An overall consistency has been claimed for this impressive, highly stylized litany of victories. Whereas David's earlier triumphs were defensive in nature, David now takes the field in a series of offensives against a variety of foes. The king's success in war is evident in all directions: to the west against the Philistines, to the southeast against Edom, to the east against Moab, and to northeast against a number of discrete Aramaean states. The coffers of the state are enriched by the tribute flowing in from defeated nations. The upshot of these triumphs seems to be the establishment of a small empire situated between Egypt and Mesopotamia. To quote one commentator:

> David's kingdom was not only the first but also the greatest state to arise on the soil of Palestine. . . . Behind what is catalogued here in such a matter-of-fact way lies the supreme achievement of a man of whom it is twice intentionally said 'The Lord helped him'. Evidently his contemporaries and their successors regarded these deeds as a miracle. (Hertzberg 1964: 289)

But are such grandiose claims justified? There seems little doubt that the authors of these texts in Samuel and Chronicles glorify David. The Chronicler, in particular, idealizes David's reign. In the view of history advanced by the Deuteronomist and the Chronicler, warfare against Israel's neighbors was necessary to lay the foundations for the promised era of peace, which was to epitomize Solomon's reign (1 Kgs 5:17–19 [ET 5:3–4]; 1 Chr 22:8–9; Gabriel 1990). We will return to the importance and function of David's triumphs in the Chronicler's portrayal of the monarchy, but it will be useful first to examine the precise nature and ramifications of these victories.

If the Chronicler believed, or wanted readers to believe, that David succeeded in establishing a small empire, it is all the more important to study its conditions and nature. In this context, it is just as important to pay attention to what the text does not say as it is to pay attention to what it does say. Such considerations may help to elucidate not only the internal and external dynamics of the Chronicler's Davidic state but also its eventual decline. It may be appropriate to begin with the issue of territorial expansion. Only in one instance does a campaign lead to an actual increase in the size of the Davidic state—the acquisition of Gath from the Philistines (18:1). The other campaigns mentioned in 18:1–13 involve military triumph, tribute, vassalage or some combination of all three. In one instance, the campaign against Aram-zobah (vv. 3–4), a one-sided victory leads to great plunder (vv. 7–8), but not to the establishment of a client state. One hastens to add that victory and booty do not necessarily denote the establishment of a formal treaty relationship. A chieftain might vanquish the forces of another power and collect tribute, but not retain any form of dominion over the territory of the defeated party. Similarly, in the course of David's campaigns, Aram-zobah is humbled, but retains its independence.

A number of David's military victories do lead to client relationships: with the Moabites (v. 2), Aram-damascus (v. 6), and Edom (v. 13). In each of these three cases, the subjugated party is described as a "servant" (Heb. *ʿebed;* cf. Akk. *(w)ardu, (w)ardūtu*) of David (vv. 2, 6, 13). In two cases, the defeated parties, the Moabites and Aram-damascus, dispatch tribute *(minḥâ)* to David (vv. 2, 6). In the context of ancient Near Eastern diplomacy, the combination of becoming a servant and submitting tribute (Hitt. *argamannu;* Akk. *mandattu*) often signaled the inauguration of a vassal treaty (Kalluveettil 1982: 66–79). Regularly dispatching tribute was the characteristic way in which a client kept the oath and expressed his loyalty to his overlord. The discontinuation of tribute was tantamount to rebellion (e.g., 2 Kgs 17:4). Another feature of client relationships is evident in two cases. David stations garrisons in the lands of both Aram-damascus and Edom. The placement of troops in a client's territory, attested in a number of Hittite vassal treaties (Beckman, 5.§7; 10.§§4, 12; 11.§19), was designed to contribute to international stability and to discourage seditious agitation. It is quite possible that Tou the king of Ḥamath also established an ongoing relationship with David, but this is not entirely clear (2nd NOTE to v. 10).

In any event, the larger picture is clear. The peoples inhabiting regions neighboring Israel are not assimilated into a larger entity. The Philistines and residents of Aram-zobah remain independent in spite of military defeat. The states of Moab, Aram-damascus, and Edom become Davidic clients. The king of Ḥamath establishes some sort of relationship with David, but the territories and residents of Moab, Aram-damascus, Edom, and Ḥamath are not absorbed into Israel. Nor do they become Israelite provinces. It is the very nature of suzerainty treaties that client states retain significant autonomy. Even the Israel that David leads is, in the Chronicler's definition, a confederation of disparate tribes. These tribes may all be genealogically linked (1 Chr 2:1–8:40), but they never lose their tribal character. The rise of an Israelite state unifies these different sodalities, but it does not obliterate their individual traits. This means that the "kingdom" David put together was by its very nature tenuous. By successfully reducing the number of hostile states, David promotes domestic stability. By the same token, either the internal decline of the Israelite union or the renaissance of one or more of these neighboring states could easily lead to the dissolution of the geopolitical conditions Israel's leader created. Indeed, the Chronicler's account of subsequent diplomatic exchanges and battles during David's own reign (19:1, 6–8; 20:5–6) indicates the transitory nature of his military accomplishments.

Having explored some of the martial and diplomatic ramifications of David's victories, one should examine a related but more literary and theological issue: the place and function of David's triumphs in the larger presentation of the United Monarchy. A number of commentators have found the placement of this catalogue of Davidic victories in 2 Sam 8 and 1 Chr 18 to be odd. Some do not think that the sequence of the dynastic oracle and Davidic prayer (2 Sam 7) followed by wars (2 Sam 8) "sometime after this" (*wyhy ʾḥry-kn;* v. 1) is original. To this question another can be added. Why do the writers list David's dedications of war booty drawn from various defeated peoples (in 2 Sam 8 and

1 Chr 18) before David has actually defeated most of those peoples? Of the peoples mentioned or alluded to in v. 11 (Ḥamath, Edom, Moab, the Ammonites, the Philistines, and Amaleq), only Ḥamath, Moab, and the Philistines are subdued in the earlier narrative. What are the authors of Samuel and Chronicles up to?

Alt (1936) thought that the vague chronological notice in v. 1, "sometime after this," referred originally to the battle for Jerusalem narrated in 2 Sam 5 (and 1 Chr 11:4–9). In this reconstruction, the Deuteronomist, followed by the Chronicler, inserts the Davidic promises and prayer into a source comprising a series of battle narratives. Whatever the merits of this theory may be, the chronological link refers, in its present context, to the immediately preceding events—the dynastic oracle and Davidic prayer (1 Chr 17). Moreover, one can make the case that this present narrative arrangement makes eminent sense. As part of his dynastic oracle, Nathan assured David that Yhwh would be with David and would humble all of his enemies (17:10). The divine pledge is far-reaching. In the events narrated within 1 Chr 18 this pledge begins to find fulfillment. In rapid fashion, David subdues Israel's neighbors.

Other aspects of the narrative also resonate with Nathan's promises. Nathan pledged to David that David's own offspring would build the Temple that David himself was not allowed to build (17:12). There are hints in the narrative that the author already has this long-range prospect in view. Having taken the golden bow-and-arrow cases from Hadadezer's retainers, David brings them to Jerusalem (18:7). Having captured "a very large amount of bronze" from Ṭibḥath and Kun, David does (presumably) the same (v. 8). That a long-range objective is in view is confirmed by the narrator, who points out that Solomon used this bronze to make "the bronze sea, the columns, and the bronze furnishings" (v. 8). The dedication pattern is not limited, however, to the booty received from Hadadezer. The king takes the gold, silver, and bronze articles he receives from Tou the king of Ḥamath (v. 10), along with all of the silver and gold requisitioned from "all of the nations," and consecrates them to Yhwh (v. 11).

The use of achronology—David consecrates booty received from nations, such as the Ammonites, which he has not yet defeated—foregrounds the monarch's piety. In this respect, one can see David using the fulfillment of one of Nathan's promises (the subjugation of his enemies) to lay the foundations for the fulfillment of another (the construction of a centralized sanctuary by his son). The Chronicler's David is not a passive figure. He returns to Yhwh all that Yhwh has given him (29:14). His shedding "much blood" and fighting "great wars" (22:8) come to serve a higher purpose. When David subsequently prepares Solomon for his sundry duties, he can tell his divinely chosen successor of his preparations and endowment for temple construction: "In my humility *(bʿnyy)*, I have provided for the House of God—100,000 talents of gold and 1,000,000 talents of silver, as well as bronze and iron beyond weighing" (22:14). The setting aside of "gold, silver, bronze, and iron without number" (22:16) is but one means by which David contributes to the fulfillment of the dynastic oracle and enables his son to accomplish his divinely appointed role.

# XXIII. David's State Administration (18:14–17)

*The Just King and His Cabinet*

14 And David reigned over all Israel, exercising justice and equity for all of his people. 15 Joab son of Zeruiah was in charge of the army; Jehoshaphaṭ son of Aḥilud was registrar; 16 Zadoq son of Aḥiṭub and Aḥimelek son of Abiathar were priests; Shawsha was scribe; 17 Benaiah son of Jehoiada was in charge of the Cherethites and the Pelethites; and the first sons of David were at the king's side.

## Textual Notes

18:14–17. As the following TEXTUAL NOTES make clear, these verses are drawn from the author's *Vorlage* of 2 Sam 8:15–18. A different list of royal advisors and adjutants appears later (1 Chr 27:32–34). The relationship, if any, between the list in 27:32–34 and this list is discussed in SOURCES AND COMPOSITION to 27:25–34. There is also a second list of David's cabinet officers found in 2 Sam 20:23–26, paralleled in large part by 4QSam[a] (20:23–25), that closely resembles the list of 2 Sam 8:16–18. But the two Samuel accounts differ with respect to some details and the order in which the figures are arranged. Reference to some of the variations between the two Samuel inventories will be made in the TEXTUAL NOTES below.

18:15. "son of Zeruiah." So 18:15 and 2 Sam 8:16. Lacking in MT, LXX, and 4QSam[a] 2 Sam 20:23.

"in charge of" (*ʿl*). The use of the prep. *ʿl*, marking a burden or duty (Waltke and O'Connor, §11.2.13c), is amply attested epigraphically—in the Silwan Royal Steward inscription (Davies, §4.401.1) and in various Heb. seals and bullae (Davies, §§100.149.2; 501.2; 502.2; 503.2; 782.4; 860.2).

"the army" (הצבא). So MT and LXX 18:15, as well as MT and LXX 2 Sam 8:16. MT 2 Sam 20:23, "the entire army of Israel" (כל-הצבא ישראל).

"Aḥilud" (*ʾḥylwd*). So MT and LXX[L] 1 Chr 18:15, MT 2 Sam 8:16, as well as MT and 4QSam[a] 2 Sam 20:24. LXX[BS] 1 Chr 18:15 and 2 Sam 8:16 *Acheia* (= *ʾḥyh*, "Aḥijah"). LXX[B] 2 Sam 20:24 *Acheilouth*; Josephus, *Ant.* 7.110, 293 *Achilou*.

"registrar." The term *hypomnēmatographos*, which LXX[B] uses to render Heb. *mazkîr* (cf. 2 Chr 34:8; Isa 36:3, 22), is technical in nature. Cf. *epi (de) tōn hypomnēmatōn*, "in charge of the notes" (LXX 2 Sam 8:16; Josephus, *Ant.* 7.110); *anamimnēskōn*, "(the one) reminding" or "recording" (LXX 2 Sam 20:24). In the papyri from Ptolemaic Egypt *hypomnēmatographos* appears as a title of high rank, a writer of memoranda at the court of the Ptolemies (Gerleman 1946: 19, 44).

18:16. "Zadoq" *(ṣdwq)*. So MT and LXX^B. LXX^L *Saddouk* (= *Ṣadduq*).

"Aḥimelek" *(ʾḥymlk)*. I read with many Heb. MSS, LXX^BL *(Acheimelech)*, Vg., Syr., and MT 2 Sam 8:17. MT has "Abimelek" *(ʾbymlk)*. This is a case in which textual criticism and literary criticism intersect. The evidence provided by 1 Chr 18:16 and other contexts in Chronicles suggests that Abiathar was succeeded already in the time of David by his son Aḥimelek (or Abimelek, if one were to follow MT Chronicles). Admittedly, there are problems with this scenario. 2 Sam 20:25 lists David's priests as Abiathar and Zadoq. 1 Sam 22:20; 23:6; and 30:7 all indicate that Abiathar's father was Aḥimelek, while 1 Kgs 2:26 discloses that Abiathar served as a priest until David's death. One could argue for the MT Chronicles reading on the supposition that Abimelek was the son of Abiathar and the grandson of Aḥimelek. Yet Abimelek is never mentioned again in Chronicles. Other texts in 1 Chronicles do refer, however, to Aḥimelek (24:3, 6, 31). One of these texts refers explictly to this Aḥimelek as the son of Abiathar (24:6). For many scholars, this seemingly contradictory evidence demonstrates that both Samuel and Chronicles are corrupt. Wellhausen (1871), followed by Samuel Driver (1912), solves the problem by simply reversing the order, reading "Abiathar son of Aḥimelek," instead of "Aḥimelek son of Abiathar." This hypothesis is ingenious, but it suffers from two deficiencies. First, it does not explain precisely how the textual corruption occurred. Second, it basically ignores the evidence of Chronicles. Since the concern of this commentary is the original text of the Chronicler's work, the following comments focus on the issues raised by his text. In my judgment, it is possible to make progress in resolving the issue. In speaking of Aḥimelek as the son of Abiathar, the Chronicler may have thought in terms of papponymy, the practice of naming one's son after his grandfather (NOTE to 5:36). If 18:16 reflects papponymy, the two options—"Abiathar son of Aḥimelek" and "Aḥimelek son of Abiathar"—are not mutually exclusive. Aḥimelek would figure as the name of both the son and the father of Abiathar. Whatever the original reading in Samuel, the preponderance of textual evidence indicates that the Chronicler's *Vorlage* read Aḥimelek. See further the 2nd NOTE to v. 16.

"priests." So 18:16 and 2 Sam 8:17. The statement found in 2 Sam 20:26, "and Ira the Jairite was David's priest," is both lacking in the parallel accounts of 2 Sam 8:16–18 and 1 Chr 18:15–17 and in the two versions of David's cabinet found in Josephus (*Ant.* 7.110, 293).

"Shawsha" *(šwšʾ)*. So MT. LXX^B 18:16 and LXX^B $a_2$ 2 Sam 20:25 *Iēsous* (= *yšwʿ*). Tg. has *šyšʾ*, as in 1 Kgs 4:2 (cf. *Seisan*; Josephus, *Ant* 7.110). Syr. *sryʾ* follows MT 2 Sam 8:17 *śryh*, "Seraiah." The administrative list of MT 2 Sam 20:25 has *šyʾ* (Kethib) or *šwʾ* (Qere), while LXX^AN 2 Sam 20:25, LXX^ALN 1 Chr 18:16, and Josephus, *Ant.* 7.293 have *Sousa*.

18:17. "the Cherethites." Reading with MT 1 Chr 18:17, as well as 2 Sam 8:18, and 20:23. The erroneous lemma of LXX^B "the priests" *(tōn hiereōn)* may have been triggered by the proximity of *khnym* in v. 16.

"the Pelethites" *(hplty)*. So MT. A few Heb. MSS have *wʿl plty*, while a few others have the expected *wʿl-hplty*. Allen (1974b: 107) points out that LXX *phalteia* reflects metathesis (= *pltyh*). The plus of 2 Sam 20:24 (cf. Josephus, *Ant.* 7.293),

"Adoram was in charge of forced labor," is lacking in the catalogues of 18:15–18 and 2 Sam 8:16–18.

"the first sons of David." MT literally reads, "sons of David, the first" (בני־דויד הראשנים). The phrase has been interpreted in a number of ways (e.g., "David's sons were first ministers" [NJPS]). Since the masc. pl. הראשנים appears as an adj. in the attributive position after the masc. pl. construct chain "sons of David" (בני דויד), the natural meaning of the phrase would seem to be "the first(born) sons of David" or "the first (rank of) sons of David." On the text-critical variants, see next TEXTUAL NOTE.

"the first (sons of David) at the king's side" *(hr'šnym lyd hmlk)*. So MT and LXX[L] *(hoi prōtoi epi cheira tou basileōs)*. LXX[B] *hoi prōtoi diadochoi tou basileōs* could be translated as "the chief successors of the king" (note the use of *diadochos* in Acts 24:27). But according to Gerleman (1946: 17–18), the use of *diadochos* here (and in 2 Chr 16:11; 28:7) reflects the specific use of *diadochos* as a title of honor in civil and military organization under the Ptolemies. Given that this title falls into disuse at the end of the second century B.C.E., Gerleman uses this evidence as one means to date the Greek translation of Chronicles, *Paraleipomena* ("Introduction"). The reading of Josephus (*Ant* 7.110), "and the elder sons of David were next to him and guarded his person" *(hoi de presbyteroi paides autou peri to sōma kai tēn toutou phylakēn ēsan)*, may be derived from a text similar to 1 Chr 18:17. MT 2 Sam 8:18 reads *bny dwd khnym hyw*) "the sons of David were priests," while LXX 2 Sam 8:18 has *huioi Daueid aularchai ēsan*, "the sons of David were chiefs of the [royal] court." The evidence provided by the other versions to 2 Sam 8:18 is diverse (McCarter 1984: 254–55). The entire statement is wanting in the catalogue of 2 Sam 20:23–26. Gordon Wenham (1975) contends for an original *sknym*, "administrators." Many argue that the Chronicles reading results from a tendentious rewriting of Samuel, the MT Samuel 8:18 reading being original *(lectio difficilior)*. There is some merit to this argument, because references to administrative roles for members of the royal household are attested elsewhere in Chronicles (NOTE). Nevertheless, the text-critical evidence is complex. First, in the context of an administrative list, the verb *(hyw)* is unexpected. Second, the MT 2 Sam 8:18 lemma may have resulted from corruption (note the mention of priests in 2 Sam 8:17 [and 1 Chr 18:16]). A similar corruption has occurred in the textual transmission of 1 Chr 18:17 (see above). In short, the textual evidence suggests that *hr'šnym lyd hmlk* is the original Chronicles reading.

## NOTES

18:14–17. Readers will want to consult 2 Sam 8:15–18, from which these verses are largely taken.

18:14. "David reigned over all Israel." The narrative link with the preceding (David's military victories against foreign powers) presumes a connection between foreign affairs and domestic politics. The defeat of external enemies consolidates the king's position and leads the narrator to provide a description of the administrative personnel through which he rules his people.

"exercising justice and equity." In line with many ancient Near Eastern texts, the king is depicted as the supreme judge of his people (see COMMENT).

18:15. "Joab son of Zeruiah." Named immediately after David, Joab is consistently the second most powerful figure in the Davidic regime (1st NOTE to 11:6).

"in charge of the army." In Chronicles, Joab retains this important office throughout David's reign (1 Chr 27:34; cf. 2 Sam 17:25; 19:13).

"Jehoshaphaṭ son of Aḥilud." According to 1 Kgs 4:3, Jehoshaphaṭ son of Aḥilud also served as registrar during Solomon's reign.

"registrar" *(mazkîr)*. There has been a great deal of discussion as to what a *mazkîr* was and actually did. The traditional interpretation, reflected in my translation, is that of a royal secretary, whose duties included oversight of public records, hence "registrar" or "recorder." A different interpretation (e.g., Mettinger 1971: 52–62) sees the *mazkîr* as analogous to the Egyptian office of "speaker" *(whmw)*, whose responsibilities included reporting to the king and transmitting royal decrees. The second interpretation problematically assumes a substantial Egyptian influence in the organization of the Judahite royal court (Redford 1972). It should be added, however, that the two interpretations are not mutually exclusive. For comparisons between the *mazkîr* and the Greek *mnēmōn* (Dorian *mnamōn*), a magistrate who functioned as a kind of registrar handling titles and conveyances, see Avishur and Heltzer (2000: 42–46).

18:16. "Zadoq son of Aḥiṭub." On his Aaronide origins and status, see the 1st NOTE to 5:34 and the 1st NOTE to 12:29.

"Aḥimelek, son of Abiathar." The early history of the priesthood is one of the most intractable problems in the reconstruction of Israelite religion. In this respect, it may be helpful to keep the distinctive presentations of Samuel-Kings and Chronicles separate (2nd TEXTUAL NOTE to v. 16). In Samuel, Abiathar is a son of Aḥimelek and a descendant of Eli, the priest of Shiloh (1 Sam 1–4). After being the only survivor of Saul's massacre of the priests at Nob (1 Sam 22:6–23; Ps 52:2 [title]), Abiathar comes under David's protection and serves as one of David's priests until the time of David's death (1 Sam 23:6–13; 30:7–8; 1 Kgs 1:7, 19, 25, 42; 2:22, 26). The employment of one of these two priests is ended by Solomon, who deposes Abiathar for having leagued with Adonijah in his coup attempt (1 Kgs 1:7, 19, 25). For his part, Solomon bestows exclusive favor on Zadoq (1 Kgs 2:26–27, 35). The Chronicler's largely independent account of the priesthood differs from that of Samuel-Kings in a number of important respects. Like the Deuteronomist, the Chronicler posits both Zadoq and Abiathar as David's two priests (1 Chr 15:11). But at some undetermined time in David's reign, Abiathar's son Aḥimelek becomes one of David's priests, most probably as the replacement for his father (18:16). For his part, Abiathar does not appear again in Chronicles except as a patronymic for Aḥimelek (the Abiathar of 27:34 may be a different person). When David institutes the priestly divisions, the reference is to Zadoq of the sons of Eleazar and Aḥimelek of the sons of Ithamar (24:3). Sacerdotal registration occurs under the watch of, among others, Zadoq and Aḥimelek (24:6, 31). By the end of David's reign both Abiathar and Aḥimelek largely disappear, however, from the scene (1 Chr 27:17; cf. 27:34 [NOTE]). When all the important officers and members of the royal family endorse the accession of Solomon, Zadoq is the only priest present to do so (29:22). Neither Abiathar nor Aḥimelek appear during Solomon's reign. Neither, for that matter, does Zadoq! But the "house of Zadoq" is mentioned in the Judahite monarchy (2 Chr 31:10). In short, positing a succession of Abiathar by his son Aḥimelek best explains the evidence provided by Chronicles. One can argue, in fact, that it is impossible to make sense of both the Chronicler's references to Abiathar and Aḥimelek and the distribution of those references without assuming a priestly succession from Abiathar to Aḥimelek his son.

"priests." Both Zadoq and Aḥimelek are simply called "priests." The use of the technical terms "chief priest" or "high priest" is a later development, dating to the late monarchy or the Persian period. In Ugaritic texts, one occasionally comes across references to "the chief of the priests" (*rb khnm; KTU* 2.4.1–2; 6.6, 7, 8, 9, 10). The same title appears in Phoen. and Pun. sources (*rb khnm;* e.g., *KAI* 59; 81.8–9; 93.1–4; *CIS* 1 5950.1–4; 1 5955). There are some references to "the high priest" (*hkhn hgdwl;* 2 Kgs 12:11 [ET 12:10]; 22:4, 8; 23:4) and one reference to a "chief priest" (*khn hrʾš;* 2 Kgs 25:18) in the Deuteronomistic depiction of the late monarchy. But not all of these references are textually secure. In the presentation of Josiah's reign, for example, Ḥilqiah is called "the high priest" *(hkhn hgdwl)* in MT and LXX^B (2 Kgs 23:4), but the adjective "high" is *sub asteriscus* in the SyrH. Considering that the Chronicler lived during the late Achaemenid age, the time in which the high priesthood became firmly established in Jerusalem, it is not surprising that he occasionally applies the title "chief priest" to a few important figures in the United Monarchy (e.g., 1 Chr 27:5 [*hkhn rʾš*]) and the Judahite kingdom (2 Chr 19:11 [*khn hrʾš*]; 24:11 [*khn hrʾš*]; 26:20 [*khn hrʾš*]; 31:10 [*hkhn hrʾš*]). The authors of Chronicles also posit kinship organizations and hierarchies for priests within Levi similar to those posited for the other tribes. Hence, 1 Chr 24:31 can speak of the "heads of the ancestral houses of the priests and Levites" *(rʾšy hʾbwt lkhnym wllwym)*. The "leaders of the priests" (*śry hkhnym;* 2 Chr 36:14) share some of the blame for the Babylonian exile. The collocation "the high priest" *(hkhn hgdwl)* is, however, very rare in Chronicles (2 Chr 34:9).

"Shawsha was scribe." The name Shawsha is non-Semitic, possibly either Egyptian or Hurrian. In the ancient Near East, the presence of scribes was typical of both royal and Temple courts (1st NOTE to 2:55).

18:17. "Benaiah, son of Jehoiada." See the NOTES to 11:22 and 12:28.

"the Cherethites and the Pelethites." David's royal bodyguard (1st NOTE to 11:22).

"the first sons of David were at the king's side." Whatever the original reading in Samuel (see TEXTUAL NOTE), this reading makes good sense in the context of the Chronicler's presentation of royal polity. The author is envisioning a substantial royal court in which the king had many wives and offspring. The reference here is to David's leading sons, the firstborn or the first rank of male offspring, who would form a coterie around the reigning king. Such an arrangement would provide each wife with a representative near the throne as well as allow the king opportunities to pick out promising princes for advancement. Conversely, the reigning monarch could also keep an eye out for signs of restiveness and potential rebellion. In addition to David's employing his sons in his regime, two other kings make use of princes in governmental affairs. In the Chronicler's presentation of Reḥoboam's reign, Reḥoboam "appointed Abijah son of Maacah as head (ראש), as ruler (נגיד) among his brothers, because he intended to make him king" (2 Chr 11:22). Having publicly chosen a successor, Reḥoboam does not neglect his twenty-seven other sons. He distributed them "among all the lands of Judah and Benjamin and among all the fortified cities" (2 Chr 11:23). Reḥoboam provisioned "much food to the princes and sought (for them) a throng of wives" (2 Chr 11:23). The gainful employment of princes in royal administration is also attested in the depiction of Jehoram's accession. King Jehoshaphaṭ (Jehoram's father) gave his sons "many presents—silver, gold, and [other] precious gifts, in addition to fortified towns in Judah—but he gave the kingdom to Jehoram, because he was the firstborn" (2 Chr 21:3). Among other things, these texts suggest that monarchs could devolve limited political, administrative, or military responsibilities to their sons.

There is one other case in which a king employs a prince to create an efficient administration and effect a smooth transfer of power. David picks one of his sons (Solomon) to be his heir and grooms him for kingship by educating him in the art of governance, establishing an elaborate bureaucracy, making plans for the Temple, endowing the future temple, and cultivating widespread support both for Solomon and for the central sanctuary that Solomon is commissioned to build (1 Chr 22–29). The other princes, for their part, unanimously pledge their fidelity to Solomon (1 Chr 29:24). These maneuvers seem to serve at least three functions: consolidating a monarch's control over his realm, ensuring a smooth succession, and capitalizing on the availability of members of the royal household to oversee a realm.

The depiction of a princely role in state administration is unparalleled in Kings, but this does not mean the Chronicler's account lacks any connection whatsoever with historical reality. To begin with, the employment of male members of the extended royal family in administration is attested in other Near Eastern lands (Beckman 1995; Avishur and Heltzer 2000). Second, a significant number of ancient Hebrew seals and bullae have been found with the expression "son of the king" *(bn hmlk)*. There is also one "daughter of the king" *(bt hmlk)* seal dating to the seventh century (Davies, §100.781.2). All of these bullae (Davies, §§100.110.2; 100.506.2; 100.507.2; 100.508.2) and seals (Davies, §§100.072.2; 100.209.2; 100.252.2; 100.719.2; 100.760.3; 100.784.2) date to the late Judahite monarchy. Nevertheless, a caution must be introduced into this discussion. It is unclear how many of the officials bearing the title "son of the king" were actually descendants of the reigning monarch. Some may have been members of the extended royal family or descendants of earlier monarchs. Indeed, the locution "the first sons of David" implies a ranking among the king's progeny. The designation "son of the king" may have been used as a title for royal princes, male products of the royal harem, and high palace officials. See also the 6th NOTE to 27:32.

## SOURCES AND COMPOSITION

First Chronicles 18:14–17 is paralleled by and taken from the Chronicler's version of 2 Sam 8:15–18. The textual evidence suggests that the Chronicler generally followed his source closely, making only a few changes to his *Vorlage* (see TEXTUAL NOTES). Mention should be made of two other inventories of Davidic state officers. In 1 Chr 27:32–34 there is a list of Davidic officials that differs markedly from the present list, both in names and in titles. The only respect in which the two lists converge is in the listing of Joab as commander of the army. There is also, as we have seen (see TEXTUAL NOTES), a second list of David's cabinet in 2 Sam 20:23–26 (in addition to the list of 2 Sam 8:16–18). Second Samuel 8:16–18 and 20:23–26 are clearly parallel, differing only in certain details. Both texts enumerate the members of David's cabinet, but the arrangement of names and the number of offices in 2 Sam 20:23–26 diverge from those of 2 Sam 8:16–18. Unlike the list of 2 Sam 8:16–18, the list of 2 Sam 20:23–26 is not replicated in Chronicles.

## COMMENT

Since most ancient Mediterranean civilizations were monarchies, it is not surprising that scribes, especially those employed by the royal court, gave considerable thought to the nature and proper role of the monarchy. There were, of course, differences in royal ideology among various ancient Near Eastern states, but there were also some broad parallels. Kings were expected to be effective in administration, successful in war, supportive of the cult, and just in their dealings with their people (Oppenheim 1977: 102–4; Whitelam 1979: 17–38; Wyatt 1998). The king represented humanity to the deity and was critical to the prosperity of society. The king was supposed to be the guardian of the weak and vulnerable (Fensham 1962: 129–39; Weinfeld 1995: 45–56). But precisely because of the monarch's pivotal role in human affairs, a decline in the health of the state could reflect negatively on the king in office. Disarray in administration, economic disaster, repeated failure in war, neglect of temples, and the practice of injustice could prove to be highly problematic for royal reputations. In Samuel, David's failure to observe his kingly obligation of administering justice provides Absalom with an opportunity to ingratiate himself with the wider public and sow dissent against his father (2 Sam 15:2–6).

The account of Absalom's none-too-subtle criticism of his father's behavior draws attention to another feature of political life in the ancient Mediterranean world. Those propounding the virtues of royal rule were not the only ones to be heard on the issue. Dissenting voices could question royal corruption, the arrogation of power by a given king, or the abusive practices of lower-echelon figures within the government. The prophet Amos (6:1–8), for instance, derides the powerful of Samaria for enjoying a luxurious lifestyle while ignoring the ruin of Joseph (Wolff 1977: 291–316). In the book of Amos, the prophet censures the house of Jeroboam II and predicts the demise of Israel (Amos 5:2; 7:1–17; Andersen and Freedman 1989: 611–38; Paul 1991: 226–52). Micah (3:1–3, 9–11) castigates the heads of the house of Jacob and the rulers of the house of Israel for perverting justice and building Zion with blood. Employing the divine voice, Hosea (8:4) complains that "they have made kings, but not with my approval; they have made officers, but not with my knowledge." The officers of Judah (שׂרי יהודה) behave like those who shift field boundaries (Hos 5:10). Similarly, Isaiah (1:23) speaks of Jerusalem's officers (שׂריך) as rebels and companions of thieves. Indeed, in certain traditions injustice can warrant the removal of either human or divine leadership (1 Sam 8:3; Ps 82).

Disaffection with royal conduct is not unique to biblical texts. In the Ugaritic legend of Kirta (or Keret), King Kirta experiences a succession of problems that plague his kingdom (*CAT* 1.14–16). The king survives tremendous familial difficulties and international challenges, but not before one of his own sons beckons him to abdicate. How could a member of a royal household, the heir apparent, argue for his own father's resignation? Kirta's son Yaṣṣub strikes at the heart of royal ideology (Knoppers 1994a). According to Yaṣṣub, if a king fails to uphold justice, as determined by how he treats the most vulnerable members of society, he is not being kingly. For Yaṣṣub the institution of kingship must be honored, even if this means deposing the king presently in office—his father.

Listen, please, O Kirta, the Noble One.
Be alert and pay attention!
Like the most ruthless of raiders, you rule,
and [like] invaders you govern.
You have caused your hand to fall down in slackness;
you do not judge the cause of the widow,
nor try the case of the oppressed.
You do not banish those who plunder the poor,
you do not feed the orphan before you,
[nor] the widow behind your back.
Like a sister is a sickbed,
[like] a female companion is a bed of disease.
Descend from [the throne of your], kingdom that I may be king,
from [the seat of] your dominion that I myself may sit [on it].
(*CAT* 1.16.VI.41–54)

Yaṣṣub's subtle distinction between crown and king, not well received by his father (*CAT* 1.16.VI.54–58), provides him with sufficient cause to oust the monarch in office. Hence, Yaṣṣub's very rebellion against his father is conducted in the name of kingship.

Comparison with other ancient Near Eastern and biblical texts elucidates the

Chronicler's presentation of David's rule. Like other successful monarchs, David establishes and oversees a well-organized administration. The Chronicler's David is remarkably successful in his foreign campaigns and enjoys broad domestic support. Nevertheless, it requires courage for a leader to take the necessary risks to render justice, not just to some—the privileged and the powerful—but to all segments of society. This is precisely the claim made for David: he was "exercising justice *(mišpāṭ)* and equity *(ṣĕdāqâ)* for all of his people."

# *XXIV. Israelite Successes against the Ammonites and the Aramaeans (19:1–19)*

*Mission of Mercy or Reconnaissance Mission?*

1 Sometime after this, Naḥash the king of the Ammonites died, and his son
Ḥanun reigned in his stead. 2 And David thought, "I shall show loyalty to Ḥanun
the son of Naḥash, because his father showed loyalty to me." So David sent messengers with condolences to him concerning his father. When David's servants
went to the land of the Ammonites with his condolences to Ḥanun, 3 the Ammonite leaders said to Ḥanun, "Is David honoring your father in your sight because he
is sending you those offering condolences? Is not the purpose to explore the town,
to overthrow [it], and to search out the land that his servants have come to you?"
4 And Ḥanun took David's servants and shaved them, cutting their garments in
half up to the hip, and then he sent them away. 5 When they went and reported to
David concerning the men, he sent (others) to meet them, because the men were
greatly humiliated. And the king said, "Stay in Jericho until your beards grow back
and then return."

*The Ammonites Enlist the Aramaeans in Their Mobilization against David*

6 When the Ammonites saw that they had made themselves odious to David,
Ḥanun and the Ammonites sent 1,000 talents of silver to hire chariots and cavalry
for themselves from Aram-naharaim, Aram-maacah, and Zobah. 7 They hired for
themselves 32,000 chariots, as well as the king of Maacah and his army. And they
came and encamped before the waters of Rabbah. As for the Ammonites, they
were mobilized from their towns and arrived for battle.

*The Israelites Mobilize for War*

8 When David heard (of this), he dispatched Joab and the entire army of warriors. 9 And the Ammonites went forth and drew up for battle at the entrance of the
town, while the kings who had come were alone in the field. 10 When Joab saw
that the battle line was in front of him and in back of him, he made a selection of
all the elite troops in Israel and drew up to meet the Aramaeans. 11 As for the rest of
the army, he placed (it) under the command of Abshai his brother. When they
drew up to meet the Aramaeans, 12 he said, "If the Aramaeans prove too strong for
me, you will be my deliverance, and if the Ammonites prove stronger than you, I

shall deliver you. 13 Be strong and let us show ourselves strong for the sake of our people and for the sake of the towns of our God. And may Yhwh do what is right in his eyes."

14 When Joab and the army that was with him advanced before the Aramaeans for battle, they fled from before him. 15 When the Ammonites saw that the Aramaeans had fled, they also fled from before Abshai his brother and (re)entered the town. And Joab returned from (attacking) the Ammonites and came to Jerusalem.

*The Aramaeans Regroup with Reinforcements*

16 When the Aramaeans realized that they had been defeated by Israel, they sent messengers who brought out the Aramaeans living beyond the river. Shophach, the commander of Hadadezer's army, led them. 17 When this news was reported to David, he mobilized all Israel, crossed the Jordan, and came to Ḥelam. And David drew up (his forces) to meet the Aramaeans in battle.

*A Second Rout in Battle and the Collapse of the Ammonite-Aramaean Coalition*

Then they battled against him. 18 But the Aramaeans fled from before Israel and David killed 7,000 Aramaean charioteers as well as 40,000 foot soldiers. As for Shophach, the commander of the army, he put (him) to death. 19 When the clients of Hadadezer saw that they had been defeated by Israel, they made peace with David and served him. As for the Aramaeans, they were no longer willing to rescue the Ammonites.

## TEXTUAL NOTES

19:1–19. An earlier version of 2 Sam 10:1–19 is the source for this material (see SOURCES AND COMPOSITION). The text of 4QSam[a] is available for part of this passage: 2 Sam 10:4–7, 18–19.

19:1. "Naḥash the king of the Ammonites." So MT. LXX and 2 Sam 10:1 lack the PN.

"Ḥanun." So a few Heb. MSS. Syr., Tg., and MT 2 Sam 10:1. LXX[B] *Anan;* LXX[L] *Hannan.* Lacking in MT 1 Chr 19:1, perhaps because of haplography (*homoioteleuton* before *bnw*). Although confusion between *wāw* and *nûn* is not nearly as commmon as other consonantal confusions, it is attested—for example, in the textual transmission of Isaiah.

19:2. "because" *(ky).* So MT. LXX *(hōs),* Syr., and MT 2 Sam 10:2 *kʾšr.*

"messengers." So MT and LXX. MT 2 Sam 10:2 "by the hand of his servants."

"concerning *(ʿl)* his father." The variation with MT 2 Sam 10:2, "to *(ʾl)* his father," reflects a common confusion between the preps. *ʾl* and *ʿl* in Samuel-Kings and Chronicles (S. Driver 1912: 101).

"with his condolences to Ḥanun." Thus MT. The entire phrase is lacking in 2 Sam 10:2, while "to Ḥanun" is lacking in LXX[AB].

19:3. "Ḥanun." So MT and LXX 19:3. 2 Sam 10:3 adds "their lord."

"to explore *(lḥqr hʿyr)* the town." So LXX 19:3 and 2 Sam 10:3. MT 1 Chr 19:3 lacks "the town." The object was probably lost by haplography after *lḥqr (ho-*

*moioarkton)*. As MT 1 Chr 19:3 stands, the object of the (first) infs. is not "the town," as it is in Samuel, but "the land" (v. 3). It is possible that Chronicles speaks of the land, while Samuel speaks of the town, but later statements in Chronicles (vv. 7, 9, 15) make clear that a town is part of the larger narrative scene.

"to overthrow" *(lhpk)*. Reading with MT (maximum differentiation). LXX, largely followed by Syr., reads *kataskopēsai (tēn gēn)*, "to spy out the land." Some (e.g., Rudolph 1955: 136) read *wlḥpr*, "to spy," on the basis of LXX and Vg. *et investigent*, "and investigate." MT 2 Sam 10:3 places *lhpkh* ("to overthrow it," that is, the town) after *lrglh* ("to search it out"). Arnold Ehrlich (1914: 345–46) favors *hpk*, but argues for a translation "to examine" (cf. LXX) because *hpk* allegedly can mean "to overthrow" with Yhwh as subj. But this argument is specious. Although *hpk* can have a variety of nuances in BH ("to turn, change, overthrow, transform"), it never means "to examine, spy."

"the land." So MT 1 Chr 19:3. See the 2nd TEXTUAL NOTE v. 3.

"his servants have come." So MT and LXX. Syr. "he sent his servants" may have been influenced by MT 2 Sam 10:3, "David sent his servants."

"to you." Thus MT and LXX. Syr. "to us."

19:4. "and shaved them" *(wyglḥm)*. So MT and LXX. MT 2 Sam 10:4 provides more detail, *wyglḥ ʾt-ḥṣy zqnm*, "and he shaved half of their beards."

"the hip" *(hmpśʿh)*. So MT (maximum differentiation). LXX 19:4 *(tēs anabolēs)* resembles MT 2 Sam 10:4, which reads *štwtyhm*, "their buttocks."

19:5. "when they went." So MT and LXX. Lacking in Syr. and 2 Sam 10:5.

"and reported." So MT and LXX$^{L}$. LXX$^{AB}$ have the inf. "to report" *(apangeilai)*.

"concerning the men." So MT and LXX. The phrase is found neither in Syr. and Vg., nor in MT 2 Sam 10:5. That it is present in 4QSam$^{a}$, LXX, and OL 2 Sam 10:5 suggests that it was part of the Chronicler's *Vorlage*.

"stay in Jericho" *(šbw byrḥw)*. So MT and LXX 19:5 and MT 2 Sam 10:5. 4QSam$^{a}$ lacks the prep., *šbw yrḥw*. The evidence provided by LXX 2 Sam 10:5 is ambiguous.

19:6. "to David." So MT *(lectio brevior)*. LXX$^{BL}$ "the people of David."

"Ḥanun and the Ammonites sent." Thus MT and LXX 19:6, as well as perhaps fragmentary 4QSam$^{a}$. MT 2 Sam 10:6 reads simply, "and the Ammonites sent."

"1,000 talents of silver." So MT and LXX. Lacking in MT 2 Sam 10:6, but present in 4QSam$^{a}$.

"chariots and cavalry." So MT and LXX 19:6, as well as 4QSam$^{a}$. MT 2 Sam 10:6 "20,000 foot soldiers."

"for themselves" (להם). So MT and LXX. Lacking in MT 2 Sam 10:6 and 4QSam$^{a}$.

"Aram-naharaim." So MT and LXX, "Aram-mesopotamia" *(Syrias Mesopotamias)*. MT 2 Sam 10:6 "Beth-reḥob" *(byt rḥwb)*.

"Maacah." So MT and LXX. Lacking in MT 2 Sam 10:6, but present in 4QSam$^{a}$ *[m]ʾkh*.

"(and from) Zobah" *(wmṣwbh)*. So MT and LXX. This reading is evidently paralleled in 4QSam$^{a}$ 2 Sam 10:6 *[wmṣwb]h*. MT 2 Sam 10:6 "Zoba" *(ṣwbʾ)*.

19:7. "and they hired for themselves" (וישכרו להם). Tentatively following MT *(lectio brevior)*. But the plus of LXX[B] "chariots and cavalry" (*harmata kai hippeis* = *rkb wpršym*) could have been lost by haplography *(homoioteleuton)*. The entire clause is lacking in MT 2 Sam 10:7, but the spacing in 4QSam[a] suggests that the verb was part of this text.

"32,000 chariots." So MT and apparently 4QSam[a] [*šnym šlwšy*]*m ʾl̇p rkb*. LXX[B] has the same number, but again (see previous TEXTUAL NOTE) reads "chariots and cavalry" (= *rkb wpršym*). MT 2 Sam 10:6 reads, as we have seen, "20,000 foot soldiers."

"and his army" *(wʾt ʿmw)*. So MT and LXX. MT 2 Sam 10:6 "1,000 men." MT 2 Sam 10:6 continues with "and 12,000 men from the men of Ṭob," a phrase not found in Chronicles. A reference to [*wʾy*]*šṭwb* (cf. the PN found in LXX 2 Sam 10:6 *Eistōb* and Josephus *Istobos* [*Ant.* 7.121]) is found, however, in 4QSam[a].

"and they came and encamped before the waters of Rabbah. As for the Ammonites, they were mobilized from their towns and arrived for battle." Thus basically MT and LXX. These clauses are missing from MT 2 Sam 10:7. 4QSam[a] breaks off, but does include "as for the Ammonites, they were mobilized from their towns" ([*wbny*]*ʿmwṅ ṅʾspw mn h*[*ʿry*]*ṁ*).

"(the) waters of Rabbah" *(my rbh)*. Following the textual reconstruction of Rothstein and Hänel (1927: 351), Noordtzij (1937: 163), Rudolph (1955: 137), et al. MT *(mydbʾ)* "Medeba"; LXX[B] *Maidaba*; $e_2$ *Mēdaba*; *bb*′ *Mēnadaba*. The Moabite town of Medeba (Moabite *mhdbʾ*), being significantly to the south (about 9.5 km south of Ḥeshbon), seems out of place here (Num 21:30; Josh 13:9, 16; Isa 15:2; *KAI* 181:8, 30), unless Joab and his forces crossed the Jordan at the northern end of the Dead Sea and approached Rabbath-ammon from the south (Yadin 1963: 272–74). Reading with MT, Aharoni (1979: 296, 319) concedes that the battle of Medeba involves the Aramaeans coming to the defense of the Moabites, not the Ammonites. In defense of their proposal for reading *my rbh*, Rothstein and Hänel cite 2 Sam 12:27, which mentions "the town of waters" *(ʿyr hmym)* in the context of Rabbah's capture (2 Sam 12:27–29). One might add that the letters *dālet* and *rêš* are easily confused in the scripts of most periods.

"for battle." Rudolph (1955: 137) adds *ʾyš ʾyš* on the basis of 2 Sam 10:6 (*homoioteleuton* from v. 6), but MT 2 Sam 10:6 *(ʾlp ʾyš wʾyš ṭwb)* is itself corrupt (Ulrich 1978: 155).

19:8. "he dispatched Joab." On this 1 Chr 19:8, 2 Sam 10:7, and 4QSam[a] agree. But later in this verse, the textual witnesses to Samuel and Chronicles again diverge.

"the entire army of warriors." MT has "every army, the warriors" *(kol-ṣābāʾ haggibbôrîm)*. I am repointing MT along the lines of MT 2 Sam 10:7, "all of the army—the warriors" *(kol-haṣṣābāʾ haggibbôrîm)*, *haggibbôrîm* being in apposition to *kol-haṣṣābāʾ*. In sortal apposition a broad class is followed by a narrower term of the same type (Waltke and O'Connor, §12.3b). The reading of LXX interprets the Heb. along the same lines, "all the army of warriors" (*pasan tēn strateian tōn dynatōn* = *kol-ṣĕbāʾ haggibbôrîm*). Syr. and Vg. are similar. A second possibility (e.g., S. Driver 1912: 288; Budde 1902: 248) is to emend to "all of the army and the warriors" *(kol-haṣṣābāʾ wĕhaggibbôrîm)*. A third possibility is to strike either *haggibbôrîm* (and read simply *kol-haṣṣābāʾ*, "the whole army"; A. Ehrlich 1914: 346) or *kol-haṣṣābāʾ* (and read simply *haggibbôrîm*, "the warriors"; McCarter 1984: 268).

19:9. "entrance of the town" *(ptḥ hʿyr)*. So MT. Syr. follows MT 2 Sam 10:8, "entrance to the gate" *(ptḥ hšʿr)*. LXX 1 Chr 19:9 *pylōna tēs poleōs*, "gate of the town" *(šʿr hʿyr)*.

"while the kings who had come were alone in the field." MT 2 Sam 10:8 reads differently, "while Aram-zoba, Reḥob, the men of Ṭob, and Maacah were alone in the field." Some (e.g., Budde 1902: 249) think that the Chronicles reading is earlier, the Samuel text being a later elaboration. But, if so, it is odd that Chronicles would mention only kings and make no mention of the armies themselves.

19:10. "the battle line." Literally, "the face of battle" (פני-מלחמה). If the subj. were the masc. pl. construct, one could say that the collective is being used with a sg. verb (GKC § 145k; 1 Sam 4:15; Job 16:16). But the subj. may be the f. sg. noun מלחמה, so the use of the f. sg. verb היתה is to be expected.

19:11. "Abshai." So MT. LXX *(Abessa)*, Syr., and Vg., as well as MT 2 Sam 10:10, *ʾbyšy*. See the 2nd TEXTUAL NOTE to 2:16.

"they drew up" (ויערכו). So MT, LXX[B], and $e_2$. LXX[AN] *b*b'y and MT 2 Sam 10:10, "he drew up."

19:12. "I shall deliver you" *(whwšʿtyk)*. So MT and LXX. MT 2 Sam 10:12 *hlkty lhwšyʿ lk*, "I shall go to deliver you."

19:13. "be strong and let us show ourselves strong for the sake of our people and for the sake of the towns of our God." So MT and LXX[ALN] 19:13, as well as MT and LXX 2 Sam 10:12. Lacking in LXX[B].

19:14. "advanced" *(wygš)*. So MT 19:14 and 2 Sam 10:13 (maximum differentiation). LXX 1 Chr 19:14 *kai paretaxato*, "and drew up" (= *wyʿrk*).

"before the Aramaeans for battle" *(lpny ʾrm lmlḥmh)*. Syr. 19:14 is similar to MT 2 Sam 10:13, which reads "for battle with the Aramaeans" *(lmlḥmh bʾrm)*.

19:15. "they also fled" *(wynwsw gm hm)*. So MT. MT 2 Sam 10:14 is shorter, "and they fled" *(wynwsw)*, but see LXX 2 Sam 10:14.

"from before Abshai his brother" *(mpny ʾbšy ʾḥyw)*. So MT and Tg. Some (e.g., Kittel 1902: 78) would preface "from before Joab" on the basis of LXX[B], "from before Joab and from before his brother" (= *mpny ywʾb wmpny ʾḥyw*). LXX[AN] are more expansive, identifying the brother as "Ab(i)shai" (= *mpny ywʾb wmpny ʾbyšy ʾḥyw*). LXX[L] "from before Ab[i]shai brother of Joab" (= *mpny ʾbyšy ʾḥy ywʾb*). Some delete "his brother" *(ʾḥyw)* on the basis of MT 2 Sam 10:14, "from before Abshai" *(mpny ʾbšy)*. Rudolph (1955: 138) would read *ʾḥy ywʾb*, "the brother of Joab" (the PN presumably corrupted into *wybʾw*). But Chronicles is consistent in its usage; note the appearance of "Abshai his brother" *(ʾbšy ʾḥyw)* in v. 11.

"and Joab returned *(wyšb ywʾb)* from [attacking] the Ammonites and came *(wybʾ)* to Jerusalem." A reconstruction based on Vg. and Syr. 19:15 and MT 2 Sam 10:14 *(wyšb ywʾb mʿl bny ʿmwn wybʾ yrwšlm)*. MT (and LXX[B]) 19:15 simply reads "and Joab came to Jerusalem" *(wybʾ ywʾb yrwšlm)*. In defense of MT, one could say that the lemmata of 1 Chr 19:15, "and they entered the town *(wybʾw hʿyrh)* and Joab came to Jerusalem" *(wybʾ ywʾb yrwšlm)*," reflect the occasional use of the verb *bw'* in the *qal* with the meaning "to return" (1 Kgs 22:27; Isa 23:1; Prov 7:20; *HALOT* 112–13). But the evidence for a haplography seems strong, especially if the Chronicler's *Vorlage* read *wyšb yw'b m'l bny 'mwn wyb' yw'b yrwšlm* (*homoioarkton* from *wyšb yw'b* to *wyb' yw'b*).

19:16. "they sent messengers who brought out" *(wyšlḥw ml'kym wywṣy'w)*. So MT. LXX has the sg., "he sent messengers and brought out." MT 2 Sam 10:16, "Hadadezer sent and brought out" *(wyšlḥw hdd'zr wyṣ')*.

"beyond the river." So MT and LXX. MT 2 Sam 10:16 adds *wyb'w ḥylm*, which has been variously interpreted as "and their army came" or "and they came to Ḥelam" (Wellhausen 1871: 180; Kittel 1902: 78). Syr. and Tg. 1 Chr 19:16 follow MT 2 Sam 10:16, at least in part. See further the 2nd TEXTUAL NOTE to v. 17.

"Shophach" *(šwpk)*. Thus MT and LXX[L]. LXX[BN] "Shophar" *(Sōphar)*; LXX[A] *Sōbach*. MT 2 Sam 10:16 "Shobach" *(šwbk)*; LXX[B] *Sōbach*. Josephus (*Ant.* 7.127) reads *Sebekos* and adds that this commander brought 80,000 foot soldiers and 10,000 cavalry.

"Hadadezer." On the spelling, see the 1st TEXTUAL NOTE to 18:3.

19:17. "the Jordan." So MT and LXX. Lacking in Syr.

"and came to Ḥelam" *(wyb' ḥl'mh)*. Reading with MT and LXX *(paregenonto eis Ailam)* 2 Sam 10:17. See also "Ḥelam" *(ḥylm)* in 2 Sam 10:16 (2nd TEXTUAL NOTE to v. 16). As Benzinger (1901: 60), Rothstein and Hänel (1927: 354), and Goettsberger (1939: 147) point out, MT 1 Chr 19:17 "and came to them" *(wyb' 'lhm)* is corrupt. The entire expression is lacking in Syr. LXX[B] reads "and came upon them" (*ep' autous* = *'lyhm*).

"and David." Reading with a few Heb. MSS, Syr., Vg. 19:17, and MT 2 Sam 10:17. MT 1 Chr 19:17 prefaces "and he drew up for them" *(wy'rk 'lhm)*. Rudolph (1955: 138) follows MT 1 Chr 19:17, supposing that a haplography occurred in the text of Samuel *(homoioarkton)*, but a dittography is more likely after *wyb' ḥl'mh* (or *wyb' 'lhm*, if one follows MT) and before *wy'rk dwyd*.

"David drew up (his forces) to meet the Aramaeans." So MT (and Tg.) 19:17 *(wy'rk dwyd lqr't 'rm)*. LXX[BS] read differently, "the Aramaeans deployed opposite David" *(kai paratassetai Syros ex enantias Daueid)*. Similarly, MT 2 Sam 10:17, "and the Aramaeans drew up (their forces) to meet David" *(wy'rkw 'rm lqr't dwd)*.

19:18. "7,000." So MT, LXX, and Tg. MT 2 Sam 10:18 "700." Unfortunately, 4QSam[a] is fragmentary, having only *šb*[ʿ] extant.

"charioteers." Literally, "chariots" *(rkb)*.

"foot soldiers" *('yš rgly)*. So MT and LXX. Josephus (*Ant.* 7.128) agrees with Chronicles, as do LXX[L] and OL 2 Sam 10:18. MT and LXX[B] 2 Sam 10:18 have "cavalry" *(pršym)*.

"Shophach." 2 Sam 10:18 "Shobach" (3rd TEXTUAL NOTE to v. 16).

"he put (him) to death" (המית). So MT, LXX, and Tg. Syr. "he put (him) to death there [= *šm*]" assimilates toward the more expansive lemma of MT 2 Sam 10:18 and 4QSam[a], "he struck [Shobach] so that he died there" (הכה וימת שם).

19:19. "when the clients of Hadadezer saw" (ויראו עבדי הדדעזר). Thus MT, LXX, and Tg. MT 2 Sam 10:19 reads more expansively, "when all of the kings, (the) clients of Hadadezer saw" (ויראו כל-המלכים עבדי הדדעזר).

"they made peace with David and served him." So MT, LXX, and Tg. MT 2 Sam 10:19, "they made peace with Israel and served them."

"as for the Aramaeans, they were no longer willing to rescue the Ammonites" *(wlʾ ʾbh ʾrm lhwšyʿ ʾt bny ʿmwn ʿwd)*. Reading with MT and LXX. MT 2 Sam 10:19, "and the Aramaeans were afraid to rescue the Ammonites again" *(wyrʾw ʾrm lhwšyʿ ʿwd ʾt-bny ʿmwn)*.

# Notes

19:1. "sometime after this" *(wyhy ʾḥry-kn)*. The same vague chronological notice appears at the beginning of the battle campaigns narrated in 1 Chr 18. The formulaic link with previous material is drawn from the Chronicler's *Vorlage* (2 Sam 10:1). See further SOURCES AND COMPOSITION for 18:1–13.

"king of the Ammonites." Samuel and Chronicles depict a series of clashes between the kings of Israel and Ammon. Other texts presuppose better relations between the two peoples and their leaders (2 Sam 23:37; 2 Sam 10:1–2//1 Chr 19:1–2; 1 Kgs 11:1, 7; 14:21, 31; 1 Chr 11:39; 2 Chr 24:26). In the Deuteronomistic History, the Ammonites exhibit a royal polity before the Israelites do, in the time of the chieftains (Judg 11:12–13). There is, however, much uncertainty as to the age during which the Ammonites actually developed a regional polity (Kletter 1991; Hübner 1992; Younker 1999). From the vantage points of epigraphy (Aufrecht 1999a) and archaeology (B. MacDonald 1999), the Ammonites are best attested in the Iron II period. An Ammonite regional culture persists through the sixth century and into the Persian period. Based on recent epigraphic studies, there has been some discussion that Ammon, like Yehud, was a regional province during the Persian era (Herr 1999).

"reigned in his stead." The death of a king could usher in a period of instability and uncertainty. Even if an heir had been appointed before the king's death, the transition to the reign of that heir could be a time of vulnerability. Moreover, given that international pacts were made between the leaders of nations, and not between the nations themselves, a ruler's death could effectively undo diplomatic agreements. For this reason, monarchical succession is a common issue in international treaties. Stipulations calling on the client to support the designated heir of his overlord are a regular feature of suzerainty treaties. The arrangements made by the great Assyrian king Esarhaddon to ensure that his clients recognized his appointed heir are elaborate (VTE §10). But commitments from a suzerain to a client can also be found. In his treaty with Kupanta-Inara of Mirā-Kuwaliya, Muršili II reinforces the right of Kupanta-Inara to his father's house and land despite his father's transgressions (Friedrich 3.7.12–22; 24.8–21). Similarly, Muwatalli guarantees Alakšandu that his heir will occupy his throne even though his subjects may not want him (Friedrich 5.1.A.71–81; B.7–10; cf. 5.4.37–46). The absolute promise of succession within a particular dynasty is a striking feature of the treaty of Tudḫaliya IV with Ulmi-Tešup (KBo 4.10: obv. 9–13). Indeed, the guarantee of succession to the throne for a client's issue is common in Hittite treaties (Friedrich 1.8.23–28; 6.5.31–40; Weidner 6: rev. 13–16; 7.I.49–54). The stability afforded by dynastic succession within the house of a loyal subject was advantageous to the Hittite crown. The death of a monarch would necessitate the dispatching of messengers to the court of the treaty partner to ensure that the treaty would remain in force without any interruption (Moran 1963: 80). Apparently no such provisions were in force in the diplomatic ties between David and Naḥash. Naḥash's death led to a mutual reexamination of Israelite-Ammonite relations.

19:2. "I shall show loyalty *(ʾeʿĕśeh-ḥesed)* to Ḥanun." The use of the noun *ḥesed* can indicate covenantal relations. Nevertheless, even if a formal covenant existed between the two states, it is possible that such a covenant did not include provisions dealing with succession (see 3rd NOTE to v. 2).

"the son of Naḥash." According to 1 Sam 11:1–13, Naḥash was an enemy of Saul. This foe of Saul was also apparently a friend of David. According to MT 2 Sam 17:27, Abigail the daughter of Naḥash (and wife of David) was the sister of Joab's mother Zeruiah (cf. LXX 2 Sam 17:27; 1 Chr 2:12–17). Relations between the Davidic dynasty and the Ammonite elite continued in later generations. Reḥoboam's mother was Ammonite (2 Chr 12:13).

"sent messengers with condolences." The loyalty of Naḥash to David leads David to send an overture to Naḥash's successor. In the same way, Ḥiram (Ḥuram in Chronicles) of Tyre, who enjoyed good relations with David, sent his servants to Solomon following David's death (1 Kgs 5:15 [ET 5:1]).

19:3. "Ammonite leaders" (שׂרי בני-עמון). Budde (1902: 247) calls attention to the role played by advisors in influencing another young king—Reḥoboam at the Council of Shechem (1 Kgs 12:6–14//2 Chr 10:6–14). In each case, the new monarch miscalculates.

"to explore the town." The comments by Ḥanun's advisors may seem paranoid, but they should be interpreted in the context of the Chronicler's larger presentation of David's military successes. From the perspective of the omniscient narrator, David's messengers were sent with the best of intentions. But to Ḥanun's counselors, David's string of victories against the Philistines (14:8–17; 18:1), the Moabites (18:2), the Edomites (18:12–13), and certain Aramaean states (18:3–11) established a imperialistic pattern that they could ignore only at their peril.

19:4. "cutting their garments in half." That is, half in breadth, not half in length (S. Driver 1912: 287). David's aides have one entire side of their garments cut off up to the hip, an obvious humiliation. Relevant to this indignity is the mention of an Ammonite oppression against Reuben and Gad in the version of 1 Sam 11 preserved by 4QSam[a]. The beginning of 1 Sam 11 in 4QSam[a] states that the Ammonites gouged out the right eyes of Reubenites and Gadites and otherwise struck terror and dread in Israel. According 4QSam[a], Naḥash continued to terrorize Jabesh-gilead until the residents of this town concluded a pact with him.

"sent them away." Ḥanun's act is designed to humiliate, but this provocation sets in motion a series of incidents, the ramifications of which extend far beyond Israelite-Ammonite relations.

19:5. "Stay in Jericho." The quarantine furnishes David's aides with the requisite time to recover and regain their dignity. Jericho also functions as an intermediary station in Aḥaz's reign. There, Jericho serves as a way station for the return of Judahite prisoners of war following Judah's devastating loss to Israel (2 Chr 28:5–15).

19:6. "odious to David." Having discovered that they incurred David's wrath, the Ammonites are faced with a strategic decision: to make amends with the offended party or continue the state of hostility? Considering that the royal advisors had advocated the provocation against David's messengers in the first place, it comes as no surprise that the Ammonites mobilize their forces and draw on the forces of their allies to fight against Israel. The Ammonite leaders undoubtedly believed that they could effectively counter any military threat that David might pose to them. Otherwise, they would have never counseled their impressionable king to insult David in the first place.

"1,000 talents of silver." The Ammonite leadership attempts to renew or initiate an alliance with another set of Israel's enemies to counter the menace posed to them by an offended David. Two later Judahite monarchs—Asa (1 Kgs 15:16–21\\2 Chr 16:1–5) and Aḥaz (2 Kgs 16:5–9; 2 Chr 28:16–21)—also employ a diplomatic strategy of appealing to a third party to counter (northern) Israelite threats to their realms (Parker 1997: 76–104). Kilamuwa of Sam'al (*KAI* 24.7–8) and Panamuwa II of Sam'al (according to his son Bir-Rākib; *KAI* 215.6–8), who lived about a century later, used a similar strategy in appealing to the Assyrian crown to ward off threats to their own regimes. Note the explicit description of Aḥaz's offer of silver and gold to the Assyrian king as a "gift" or "bribe" (*šōḥad;* 2 Kgs 16:8). For an example of the same diplomatic device used much earlier to fend off an invasion of Ugarit, see RS 17.340.

"Aram-naharaim." Literally, "Aram of the two rivers," the two rivers being the Euphrates and the Tigris. Aram is listed as one of Shem's descendants in the universal genealogy of 1:17. Aram-naharaim is mentioned in the heading of Ps 60, which seems to deal with the exploits of David and Joab as narrated in both 2 Sam 8(//1 Chr 18) and 2 Sam 10(//1 Chr 19).

"Aram-maacah." A small Aramaean state, Maacah was located in the Golan, southwest of Damascus and northeast of the Sea of Kinneret (or Galilee). See Deut 3:14; Josh 12:5; 13:11; and the 3rd NOTE to 4:19.

"Zobah." Located in the Biqâʿ Valley north of Damascus (2nd NOTE to 18:3).

19:7. "32,000 chariots" *(rkb)*. The text is elliptical. The Ammonites hired presumably more than just chariots. The number is unbelievably high, but the text-critical evidence indicates that this fantastic figure was part of the author's *Vorlage* (2nd TEXTUAL NOTE to v. 7).

"and his army." Literally, "(and) his people" *(ʾammô)*. In war narratives the term *ʿam* can refer to military troops, the people under arms (e.g., Num 20:20; 31:32; Josh 8:1, 3, 11; 10:7; 11:7; Judg 5:11, 13; 20:2, 10; 1 Sam 11:11; 14:17; 2 Sam 1:12; 2:26; 12:28, 29; 1 Kgs 20:15; 2 Kgs 13:7; 18:26; 1 Chr 19:7; 20:3; 21:5).

"waters of Rabbah." Rabbah, or Rabbath-ammon (modern Amman), was the royal city of Ammon (Deut 3:11; Josh 13:25; 2 Sam 17:27; Jer 49:2, 3; Ezek 21:25

[ET 21:20]; 25:5; Amos 1:14). Second Samuel 12:27 mentions "the town of waters" *(ʿyr hmym)* in the context of Rabbah's capture (2 Sam 12:27–29). The Rabbah that appears in the district of Judah (Josh 15:60) refers to a different site (Aharoni 1979: 174, 326).

19:9. "entrance of the town." That is, the entrance to the town of Rabbah. The Ammonites deliberately prepare for battle at a different location from that of their Aramaean allies so that their coalition can challenge David on two fronts.

"the kings who had come were alone in the field." The text is again elliptical. Only the king of Maacah is explicitly mentioned earlier (v. 7). The text alludes to the kings of Aram-Naharaim, Aram-maacah, and Zobah, and by implication to their forces as well (vv. 6–7). Note the parallel in MT 2 Sam 10:8, "while Aram-Zoba, Reḥob, the men of Ṭob, and Maacah were alone in the field."

19:10. "in front of him and in back of him." The Israelites are presented with the unenviable task of fighting two separate battles simultaneously. This raises the issue of how Joab will allocate Israel's military assets to deal with the unusual challenge.

"a selection of all the elite troops." Literally, "the picked men," deemed to be "the flower of the army" (Curtis and Madsen 1910: 239), are designated to fight against the Aramaeans. Even though the Aramaean forces were comprised of mercenaries, they were a more formidable opponent than the Ammonites.

19:12. "he said." Joab is second in importance only to David in the Chronicler's construction of David's reign (3rd NOTE to 20:1). His brief speech bears some resemblance to the features displayed by other military orations in the HB (Weinfeld 1972a: 45–51). It begins with an imperative for courage in the face of an impending threat, appeals to the patriotism of the combatants, and concludes with a prayer, "And may Yhwh do what is right in his eyes" (v. 13).

19:13. "for the sake of our people" *(ʿammēnû)*. I am translating *ʿam* in its normal sense as "people." It is possible to construe the term more narrowly as "army," as in v. 7 (2nd NOTE), but Joab's speech seems to have the broader populace in view.

"the towns of our God" *(ʿārê ʾĕlōhênû)*. Some scholars have found this to be an odd expression, but it comports with sacral-war ideology, which construes conflicts between rival states as ultimately conflicts between their gods. What the narrator's use of this expression assumes is that at least part of the territory being fought over is claimed by the Israelites. Given the territorial perquisites ascribed to the tribes of Manasseh (Josh 13:29–33; 1 Chr 5:23–26; Ezek 48:4–5) and of Reuben and Gad (Josh 13:15–28; 1 Chr 5:1–22; Ezek 48:6–7), as well as the assertions of King Mesha of Moab about how he reversed Israelite hegemony in various parts of his land (*KAI* 181:5–26), this seems a plausible assumption to make.

19:15. "also fled." Assyrian monarchs, in their royal inscriptions, vaunt their military prowess by describing the panic of enemy troops upon their encounter with the might of the Assyrian army (M. Weippert 1972: 478–80). Such a state of chaos leads to significant losses for the army abandoning the battle. In this particular case, the very genius of the coalition's strategy—the two-pronged attack—contributes to its undoing. Having witnessed the Aramaean mercenaries taking flight, the Ammonites also take flight. The two-pronged attack becomes a two-stage panic.

"(re)entered the town" (ויבאו העירה). On the use of the verb *bw'* in the *qal* with locative *hê*, see also Gen 12:11; 41:57; Num 14:24; Judg 11:16; 2 Kgs 6:4. The Ammonite retreat into the town from which many of them originally deployed—Rabbath-ammon—leads to a cessation of hostilities. Joab elects to return home rather than continue the campaign by launching a siege on the city. The following year Joab will return with the elite of his army to ravage the land of Ammon and begin a siege (20:1).

19:16. "messengers." In a new phase of hostilities, the scope of the war widens further. The Aramaeans successfully appeal for help from their kinsmen.

19:"the river." In the HB, "the river" (הנהר) usually designates the Euphrates (e.g., Gen 2:14; 15:18; Deut 1:7; 2 Kgs 23:29 [//2 Chr 35:20]; 24:7; 1 Chr 5:9), but the Jordan and the Yarmuk have also been mentioned as possibilities (e.g., Stoebe 1994; Halpern 1996a). See further, the 3rd NOTE to 18:3.

"the commander of Hadadezer's army." Given Zobah's earlier defeat at the hands of David (18:3–4), the leaders of this state had ample incentive to resist Israel's military ascendancy.

19:17. "Ḥelam." In 2 Sam 10, Ḥelam is spelled in two slightly different ways: *ḥylm* (v. 16) and *ḥl'm* (v. 17). The second spelling conforms to Egyptian *(ḥl'm)* evidence. There are some indications (Goldstein 1976: 301; McCarter 1984: 273) that Ḥelam was a region, not a town, in the northern Transjordan (LXX Ezek 47:16 *Ēliam*; 1 Macc 5:26: *Alelama*). A region would be consistent with the following battle description, which depicts a clash in the open country, rather than a siege of a town.

"drew up (his forces)." Unlike the previous campaign led by Joab, David takes charge of this campaign himself.

19:19. "the clients of Hadadezer *(ʿbdy hddʿzr)* saw." On the use of Heb. *ʿebed*, "servant" to indicate client or vassal status, see the NOTES to 18:2. The defeat of the Aramaeans under Shopach of Zobah has larger geopolitical implications. Given the weakened state of their patron, Hadadezer, his former political servants are free to seek out new diplomatic alignments.

"made peace with David and served him" *(wyšlymw ʿm-dwyd wyʿbdhw)*. The use of the *hipʿil* of the verb *šlm* ("to make peace") reflects the ratification of an alliance (cf. Deut 20:12; Josh 10:1, 4; 11:19; 1 Kgs 22:45 [ET 22:44]; Job 5:23; 22:21). The use of this verb (or its cognates) to depict the conclusion of a treaty is also attested in Mari Akk. (*salāmum;* Knoppers 1993b: 84–85). That the verb *šlm* occurs together with an expression of service *(ʾbd)* indicates that Hadadezer's clients conclude vassal treaties with David (Gabriel 1990: 45–48). David's victories (cf. 1 Chr 18:5) give rise, therefore, to a new balance of power in the region. A prominent Aramaean state loses its clients to a new competitor in Syria-Palestine.

"no longer willing to rescue." The new balance of power in the region, tilted in Israel's favor, leaves the Ammonites isolated from their former allies. The victories of Joab and David succeed in disrupting the traditional military ties between the Ammonites and the Aramaeans, because the Aramaean states can no longer afford to risk military assets to maintain such ties.

## Sources and Composition

The material in 1 Chr 19:1–19 is paralleled by 2 Sam 10:1–19, but there are, as we have seen, a large number of variants among the textual witnesses to these texts. How does one account for so many differences between the two passages? There are three main explanations. Some believe that the Chronicler freely rewrites his *Vorlage* resulting in a substantially different, albeit occasionally confused, account from that found in 2 Sam 10 (Curtis and Madsen 1910; Willi 1972; Williamson 1982b: 140–41). In the view of Curtis and Madsen, for example, the Chronicler paraphrases, rewrites, interprets, omits, simplifies, magnifies, confuses, expands, substitutes, and abridges the text of Samuel. Within this scholarly tradition, there is a subset of commentators who think that they can identify the source of the distinctive elements within the Chronicler's text. These scholars (e.g., Curtis and Madsen 1910: 238–41; McCarter 1984: 267–68) believe that the text of 1 Chr 19 (and so also Josephus) has been elaborated with intrusive materials from 2 Sam 8.

Scholars of a second group acknowledge reinterpretation and adaptation in Chronicles, but maintain that MT and LXX Samuel are also developed texts. They call attention to the variants among MT, LXX, and OL Samuel and point to parallels between 2 Sam 8 and 2 Sam 10 as evidence that the text of Samuel has been reworked and glossed. In line with the view that Samuel went through a number of stages of development, these scholars (e.g., Keil 1873: 227–33; Rothstein and Hänel 1927: 359–60) believe that the Chronicler's *Vorlage* may have differed somewhat from MT Samuel. Again, there is a subset of scholars within this tradition (Noth 1960: 194–96; Hertzberg 1964: 305; Eissfeldt 1965: 276) who contend that the battle of Ḥelam (2 Sam 10:15–19//1 Chr 19:16–19) is but a rewritten version of the battle against Hadadezer (2 Sam 8:3–8//1 Chr 18:3–8). Second Samuel 8:4 (and 1 Chr 18:4), for example, mentions 20,000 foot soldiers captured by David, while 2 Sam 10:6 (but not 1 Chr 19:7) also mentions 20,000 foot soldiers. They suggest that the descriptions of the Ammonite-Aramaean wars in 2 Sam 10 may have been influenced by the descriptions of the Aramaean wars in 2 Sam 8. The problem, then, for these scholars is not so much 1 Chr 19 as it is 2 Sam 10, which they see as a reworking of 2 Sam 8.

A third group (Auld 1994: 34–36, 49–50; 1999; Ho 1995) takes a radically different approach to the relationship between Samuel and Chronicles, contending that both Samuel and Chronicles represent alternate or competing appropriations of an earlier story of Judah's kings. The various textual witnesses to Samuel and Chronicles (MT, $LXX^{B}$, $LXX^{L}$, etc.) are employed to reconstruct a shorter shared text for the authors of Samuel and Chronicles. In some respects, this position returns the discussion to a time before the work of de Wette (1806–07), who influentially argued that Chronicles is dependent upon Samuel-Kings (see "Introduction"). The editors of Samuel and Chronicles are each said to have developed a common, albeit relatively short, source.

How does one decide among these three very different explanations of the relationship between the text of Chronicles and Samuel? It is appropriate to make some observations. The subsidiary stance within the second position, in my judgment, understates the dissimilarities between the narratives in 2 Sam 8 and 10. Nevertheless, both the second position (the larger scholarly tradition of which this perspective is but one part) and the third position (a shared common source) display some commendable features (Knoppers 1995d). These positions recognize that the development of the text of Samuel is a complex and significant issue. Most scholars within the second and third traditions argue that because of development in the Samuel text, Chronicles may be used as a major witness to reconstruct the text of Samuel. In some instances Chronicles may even furnish a more primitive reading than Samuel. But what of the larger claims made by scholars holding to these positions? Fortunately, the Dead Sea Scrolls shed some welcome light on longstanding problems. The availability of 4QSam$^{a}$ affords some control in assessing the relative merits of the three theories (Ulrich 1978: 152–56). It will be helpful to take a close look at some of the differences between 2 Sam 10 and 1 Chr 19 in which 4QSam$^{a}$ is also extant. Our first case study will be the variations in the textual witnesses to the Ammonite appeal to the Aramaeans (2 Sam 10:6; 1 Chr 19:6–7).

| | |
|---|---|
| *Samuel* | |
| MT | – – –[no price given]<br>Aram-bet-reḥob and Aram-zobah |
| LXX$^{B}$ | – – –[no price given]<br>Aram-bet-reḥob |
| LXX$^{L}$ | – – –[no price given]<br>Bet-reḥob and Aram-zobah |
| 4QSam$^{a}$ | 1,000 talents of silver<br>[Aram-naharaim, Aram-ma]ʿakah, [and Zob]ah |
| *Chronicles* | |
| MT | 1,000 talents of silver<br>Aram-naharaim, Aram-maacah, and Zobah |
| LXX | 1,000 talents of silver<br>Aram-naharaim, Aram-maacah, and Zobah |
| *Josephus* | |
| *Ant.* 7.121 | 1,000 talents<br>Souros, the king of the Mesopotamians |

As this comparison makes clear, Chronicles is more like one of the Samuel witnesses (4QSam$^{a}$) than the others (MT Samuel and LXX Samuel). The parallels are, in fact, remarkable. Chronicles and 4QSam$^{a}$ are in substantial agreement over against MT and LXX Samuel. To a large extent, Josephus also follows the witness of 4QSam$^{a}$ and Chronicles. This evidence suggests that the Chronicler's *Vorlage* for these verses resembled 4QSam$^{a}$.

To determine whether the affinity between the readings of 4QSam$^{a}$ and Chronicles is coincidental or something more substantial, it will be useful to compare the texts of Samuel and Chronicles elsewhere in this chapter. The following chart provides the major parallels and variations in the textual witnesses as to what the Ammonites hire (2 Sam 10:6b; 1 Chr 19:7).

| | |
|---|---|
| *Samuel* | |
| MT | 20,000 foot soldiers |
| | the king of Maacah |
| | 1,000 men |
| | 12,000 men of Ṭob |
| LXX[B] | 20,000 foot soldiers |
| | the king of Maacah |
| | the king of Amalēm |
| | 1,000 men |
| | Eistōb, 12,000 men |
| LXX[L] | 20,000 foot soldiers |
| | the king of Maacah |
| | 1,000 men |
| | Eistōb, 12,000 men |
| 4QSam[a] | [32,0]00 chariots |
| | the king of Maacah |
| | Ishṭob |
| *Chronicles* | |
| MT | 32,000 chariots |
| | the king of Maacah and his army |
| LXX | 32,000 chariots and cavalry |
| | the king of Maacah and his army |
| *Josephus* | |
| *Ant.* 7.121 | 20,000 foot soldiers |
| | the king of Micha |
| | ———[no mention of 1,000 men] |
| | Istobos, 12,000 hoplites |

The preceding comparison demonstrates that there are significant variants not only between Samuel and Chronicles, but also between the witnesses to Samuel. In this case, 4QSam[a] shares some readings with both Samuel ("the king of Maacah" as opposed to "the king of Maacah and his army") and Chronicles ("32,000 chariots"). In one instance, it shares an error (*ʾyš ṭwb* as a PN: Ishṭob) with LXX Samuel *(Eistōb)* and Josephus *(Istobos)*. Chronicles lacks any equivalent to either. In this sample, the text of Josephus resembles the witnesses to Samuel to a much greater extent than his text resembles Chronicles.

One final case study is appropriate: the losses inflicted by David on the Aramaeans (2 Sam 10:18; 1 Chr 19:18). Unfortunately, the evidence provided by 4QSam[a] is too fragmentary to be of much help. Nevertheless, the evidence provided by the witnesses to Samuel and Chronicles is diverse enough to warrant close scrutiny.

| | |
|---|---|
| *Samuel* | |
| MT, LXX[B] | 700 chariots and 40,000 cavalry |
| Syr. | 1,700 chariots, 4,000 cavalry, |
| | and a great army |
| LXX[L], OL | 700 cavalry and 40,000 foot soldiers |

*Chronicles*

MT, LXX 7,000 cavalry and 40,000 foot soldiers

*Josephus*

*Ant.* 7.128 7,000 cavalry and 40,000 foot soldiers

Our final sample shows that striking differences can exist among the textual witnesses to Samuel. In this instance, Chronicles shares one important reading ("40,000 foot soldiers") with LXX$^{L}$ Samuel, OL Samuel, and Josephus over against MT and LXX$^{B}$ Samuel. In another instance ("700 cavalry"), LXX$^{L}$ Samuel and OL Samuel share features with both MT Samuel ("*700* chariots") and Chronicles ("7,000 *cavalry*"). In this latest case, Josephus ("7,000 cavalry") follows Chronicles. This comparison bears on the issue of the *Vorlage* used by the author of Chronicles. The evidence provided by Syr., LXX$^{L}$, OL 2 Sam 10:18 and Josephus suggests that the Chronicler may have simply reproduced the figures that were present in his source.

Based on these preceding comparisons, it will be useful to draw some broader conclusions. The various figures attested in Josephus, Chronicles, and the witnesses to Samuel demonstrate that the critical issue is not simply the testimony of Samuel as compared to Chronicles. There are divergent witnesses to the text of Samuel itself. One of these witnesses, 4QSam$^{a}$, bears a number of important parallels to MT and LXX Chronicles. This important evidence lessens the likelihood that both the authors of Chronicles and the authors of Samuel drew from a common source. Two related conclusions seem much more probable, namely, (1) that the Chronicler drew upon a divergent text of Samuel with affinities to 4QSam$^{a}$ and (2) that multiple textual witnesses existed for these books, especially for Samuel. MT, LXX, and 4QSam$^{a}$ indicate that in the last centuries B.C.E., texts of Samuel were extant that were at points much closer to MT and LXX Chronicles than to MT Samuel. The same comparisons also shed some light on the work of Josephus. As Ulrich (1978: 233–56) points out, the Samuel text used by Josephus was intimately affiliated with the 4QSam$^{a}$ tradition and was closer to the Old Greek tradition (and Chronicles) than it was to MT.

Given that some of the witnesses to Samuel resemble Chronicles, at least in part, one should refrain from assuming that the Chronicler has deliberately and thoroughly altered his *Vorlage*. One can and should argue the opposite position. Many of the textual variants in Chronicles did not result from the Chronicler's own hand. The textual evidence suggests that most were already present in the Chronicler's source. This is not to claim that Chronicles, or 4QSam$^{a}$ for that matter, preserves a pristine version of the text. The differences between the witnesses to Samuel indicate that MT Samuel and 4QSam$^{a}$ are each developed texts. Each represents a textual tradition that has undergone change and development over time. Hence, if the text of David's war against the Aramaean coalition is a "glossators' carnival" (Ulrich 1978: 153), this carnival has to include Samuel itself.

The point about textual traditions among the witnesses to Samuel brings us back to Chronicles. The Chronicler's narration of David's wars not only warrants study in its own right but also reflects one of the major witnesses to the text of Samuel. The author may have made some additions and adjustments to his *Vorlage*, but the evidence indicates that in many cases he simply reproduced the text before him.

## Comment

The record of David's wars against the Ammonites and Aramaeans illustrates how an isolated incident can escalate into a international crisis. The text begins with a review of the formerly positive diplomatic relations between the leaders of two neighboring nations. When these relations break down because of an Ammonite provocation, war breaks out. But this diplomatic fracas between two states quickly develops into a much wider war. In dealing with the Ammonites, Israel is not dealing with an isolated people, but with a nation that has ties to a number of other regional powers. By acquiring mercenaries from Aram-naharaim, Aram-maacah, and Zobah, the Ammonite king succeeds in involving Aramaean states in his campaign against Israel. This multinational strategy is, however, unsuccessful. Both the Aramaean mercenaries and the Ammonites flee before Joab and Abshai. To be sure, the Israelite victory is limited. When the Aramaeans take flight and the Ammonites retreat to their town, Joab chooses not to continue the campaign. It is one thing to fight a pitched, open-field battle, but quite another to lay siege to a town (Eph'al 1983: 91–94). Joab and his army elect to return to Jerusalem.

Nevertheless, Joab's journey home to his capital does not signal the end of hostilities. The events set in motion by the Ammonite-Aramaean coalition acquire a momentum of their own. Having been overcome by Israel's army, the Aramaean partners appeal for help from their Aramaean allies "beyond the river." The dimensions of the war widen further. What began as a humiliation of David's messengers becomes a series of international conflicts involving many states. Broadening the war does not achieve the desired result. The coalition under the leadership of Shopach of Zobah is trounced by David.

The net result of these conflicts is a political realignment in ancient Palestine. In this respect, Ḥanun could not have anticipated the far-ranging results of his mistreatment of David's aides. He suffers defeat in battle at the hands of the power he insulted and ends up losing perhaps his most important set of allies, the Aramaeans. The Ammonites will later experience a devastating invasion (20:1–3). The state most responsible for inaugurating the series of international conflicts is not alone in suffering considerable losses. The association of Aramaean states, in particular Zobah, experiences not only defeat, but also a major shift in its international standing. Aram-zobah takes command of the Aramaean coalition only to lose another war to David. More important, Zobah's satellites switch their allegiance from Zobah to Israel. Whereas Zobah previously commanded a prominent position as the most powerful of a number of regional Aramaean states, Israel's victories erode Zobah's prominence. Zobah is confronted with a new political order in which its former clients serve the very foe that defeated it. The great beneficiary of all of this is, of course, Israel. In the Chronicler's presentation,

Israel's king does not seek out war, but he certainly benefits from it. David succeeds not only in overcoming a number of Israel's enemies and severing some of the ties that formerly bound these enemies together, but also in establishing his own influence and network of alliances in the region.

# *XXV. The Completion of the Foreign Military Campaigns (20:1–8)*

*The Sack of Rabbah and the Destruction of Other Ammonite Towns*
1 When it was the turn of the year, the time when kings go forth (into battle),
Joab led out the elite of the army and razed the land of the Ammonites. He also
came and besieged Rabbah, while David was staying in Jerusalem. When Joab attacked Rabbah, Joab sent messengers to David saying, "You go capture Rabbah,
lest I capture it and my name be invoked there." Then David mobilized the army,
went to Rabbah, captured it, and tore it down. 2 And David seized Milkom's crown
from his head and found the weight to be a talent of gold. On it was a precious
stone, and it was set on David's head. And the booty that he brought out of the
town was very great. 3 After he brought out the people who were in it, he tore (it)
asunder with a saw, iron picks, and axes. Thus David did to all the towns of the
Ammonites. Then David and the whole army returned to Jerusalem.
*More Conflicts with the Philistines*
4 And sometime after this, war broke out with the Philistines in Gezer. Then
Sibbekai the Ḥushathite struck down Sippai, one of the descendants of the Rephaim, and they were humbled. 5 And there was war again with the Philistines. And
Elḥanan the son of Jair struck down Laḥmi the brother of Goliath the Gittite. The
shaft of his spear was like a weavers' beam. 6 And there was war once again in Gath.
There was a man of (great) stature. His digits were twenty-four—six (on each
hand) and six (on each foot). He too was descended from Rapha. 7 Although he
harrassed Israel, Jonathan the son of David's brother Shimea struck him down.
8 These were descended from Rapha in Gath and they fell at the hand of David
and at the hand of his aides.

## TEXTUAL NOTES

20:1–8. The material in this chapter is drawn from a variety of different sections of 2 Samuel. Verse 1 is taken from 2 Sam 11:1; 12:26a, 27–29, while vv. 2–3 are taken from 2 Sam 12:30–31 and vv. 4–8 are taken from 2 Sam 21:18–22.

20:1. "when it was the turn of the year" *(wyhy lʿt tšwbt hšnh)*. Literally, "when it was the time of the turn of the year." MT 2 Sam 11:1 lacks *ʿt (wyhy ltšwbt hšnh)*.

"(the) kings" *(hmlkym)*. Reading with MT and LXX 20:1, as well as LXX, OL, Tg., and Vg. 2 Sam 11:1. MT 2 Sam 11:1 "the messengers" *(hmlʾkym)*.

"Joab led out" *(wynhg ywʾb)*. So MT and LXX *(ēgagen)*. MT 2 Sam 11:1 reads differently, "and David sent Joab" *(wyšlḥ dwd ʾt-ywʾb)*. The Chronicler's text reflects the use of *nhg* in LBH to signify "to direct" or "to lead out" (e.g., Isa 11:6; 60:11; Song 8:2; 2 Chr 25:11).

"the elite of the army" *(ḥyl hṣbʾ)*. So MT. This lemma is better explained as reflecting a different *Vorlage* from MT 2 Sam 11:1 ("and his servants with him and all Israel") than as being a paraphrase of MT 2 Sam 11:1 (contra Curtis and Madsen 1910: 241). LXX 20:1 *pasan tēn dynamin tēs stratīas* is expansionary.

"the land of the Ammonites." So MT and LXX. MT 2 Sam 11:1 reads simply "the Ammonites" (**בני עמון**).

"he also came" *(wybʾ)*. So MT, LXX$^{BL}$ *(ēlthen)*, and LXX$^{AN}$ *(ēlthan)*. MT 2 Sam 11:1 is lacking due to haplography (**wybʾw* before *wyṣrw*).

"and besieged" *(wyṣr)*. Following MT. MT 2 Sam 11:1 "and they besieged" *(wyṣrw)*.

"when Joab attacked" *(wyʿk ywʾb)*. So MT and LXX$^{AN}$. LXX$^{B}$ and $c_2$ *kai epataxen*, "and he attacked." The lemma of Syr., "and captured" (= *wylkd*), may have been influenced by the longer lemma of 2 Sam 12:26, "and Joab fought against Rabbah of the Ammonities and captured the royal city" *(wylḥm ywʾb brbt bny ʿmwn wylkd ʾt-ʿyr hmlwkh)*.

"Rabbah." Reading with MT and LXX *(lectio brevior)*. Syr. explicates by adding "their town" (= *ʿyrm*).

"and Joab sent messengers to David saying, 'You go capture Rabbah, lest I capture it and my name he invoked there.' Then David mobilized the army, went to Rabbah, captured it" (**וישלח יואב מלאכים אל-דויד לאמר לך לכד אתה את-רבה פן-אלכדה אני ונקרא שמי עליה ויאסף דויד את-העם וילך רבתה וילכדה**). A restoration based on LXX cursives ij (*kai apesteilen Iōab angelous pros Daueid legōn elthōn prokatalabou tēn Rhabba su hopōs mē prokatalobōmai autēn egō kai klēthē to onoma mou ep autēn kai synēgage Daueid ton laon kai eporeuthē eis Rhabba kai prokatelabeto autēn*; Brooke, McLean, and Thackeray 1932: 450 mistakenly attribute the plus to cursives iy) and the substantially longer lemma of MT 2 Sam 12:27–29 (**וישלח יואב מלאכים אל-דוד ויאמר נלחמתי ברבה גם לכדתי את-עיר המים ועתה אסף את-יתר העם וחנה על-העיר ולכדה פן-אלכד אני את-העיר ונקרא שמי עליה ויאסף דוד את-כל-העם וילך רבתה וילחם בה וילכדה**). See also Josephus (*Ant.* 7.160). Cursive g of 1 Chr 20:1 adds a similar plus (to that of cursives ij) after *kai kateskapsen autēn* (= **ויהרסה**). The material present in cursives ij, but lacking in MT and LXX$^{ABL}$ 1 Chr 20:1, was lost because of haplography *(homoioteleuton)* from "Rabbah" (**רבה**) to "and he captured it" (**וילכדה**). Alternatively, one could posit a slightly shorter loss of the following: "and Joab sent messengers to David saying, 'You go capture Rabbah, lest I capture it and my name be invoked there.' Then David mobilized the army and went to Rabbah" (**וישלח יואב מלאכים אל-דויד לאמר לך לכד אתה את-רבה פן-אלכדה אני ונקרא שמי עליה ויאסף דויד את-העם וילך רבתה**; cf. *BHS*). In this case, the haplography *(homoioteleuton)* would be from "Rabbah" to "Rabbah." A haplography seems all the more likely, because there is a disjunction between v. 1, which describes exclusive action by Joab, and vv. 2–3, in which David suddenly appears on the scene. Given the differences between the lemma of cursives ij and 2 Sam 12:27–29, the argument that the plus in LXX Chronicles results from parallel assimilation toward MT and LXX Samuel (Allen 1974a: 87) is not compelling.

"and tore it down" *(wyhrsh)*. So MT and LXX^B. Both MT 2 Sam 12:26, "and he [Joab] captured the royal city" *(wylkd ʾt-ʿyr hmlwkh)*, and MT 2 Sam 12:29, "and he [David] fought against it and captured it" *(wylḥm bh wylkdh)*, read differently.

20:2. "Milkom" *(milkōm)*. A reconstruction based on the evidence provided by different witnesses. The divine name *milkōm* is reflected in Vg. *(Melchom)* and Arab. A double reading is evident in LXX^ABN 20:2 (and LXX 2 Sam 12:30) *Molchol* (LXX^B; LXX^AN* *Molchom*; $c_2$ *Molmoch* [reflecting metathesis]) *basileōs autōn*, "Molchol their king." Cursives $be_2$ lack the name, while cursive $c_2$ lacks "their king." MT 20:2 and MT 2 Sam 12:30, as well as Josephus (*Ant.* 7.161) read simply "their king" *(malkām)*. As Wellhausen (1871: 186) observes, the pronominal suf. in MT's "their king" *(malkām)* lacks an antecedent. For a similar set of text-critical variants (*milkōm*, *malkām*, etc.), see the witnesses to 1 Kgs 11:5, 7, 33 (Knoppers 1993c: 141–43, 186–88).

"and found the weight to be *(wymṣʾ hmšql)* a talent of gold." MT *wymṣʾh mšql*, "and he found it, a weight." I am following the suggestion of Benzinger (1901: 60–61) to read the *hê* as the article on the following noun *mšql*, hence, "he found the weight" (= *wymṣʾ hmšql*). This may explain the lemma of LXX, "the weight of it was found (to be)" (*kai heurethē ho stathmos autou*; Rehm 1937: 21). Syr. is similar. An alternative would be to read "he found its weight (to be)" *(wymṣʾ mšqlh)*. MT 2 Sam 12:30 "and its weight (was)" *(wmšqlh)*.

"on it" *(bh)*. So MT and LXX. Lacking in MT 2 Sam 12:30, perhaps due to haplography (McCarter 1984: 311).

"and it was *(wthy)* set on David's head." Literally, "and it was on David's head." The antecedent is not clear: is it the crown or the stone? Both "stone" *(ʾbn)* and "crown" *(ʿṭrh)* are f. sg. nouns, hence the f. sg. of the verb *(wthy)* agrees with either noun. McCarter (1984: 311) objects to the crown as the antecedent because of the weight involved (one talent of gold), but what would it mean to place a stone on David's head?

20:3. "tore (it) asunder" *(wyśr)*. Reading the relatively rare verb *śwr* with MT *(lectio difficilior)*. Cf. *maśśôr*, "saw" in Isa 10:15. The lemmata of LXX^L 2 Sam 12:31 and LXX^AB 1 Chr 20:3 *kai dieprisen* ("and he sawed") and 1 Chr 20:3 cursives *bb′ eprisen*, "he sawed," support MT. Cf. $e_2$ *eneprēsen*, "he set on fire." Kittel (1902: 79), Arnold Ehrlich (1914: 347), *BHS*, NAB, et al. follow MT 2 Sam 12:31 in reading "and he set" *(wyśm)*. But *wyśr* is more likely to be the earlier reading *(lectio difficilior)*. A related and highly important question is the nature of the implied object ("it"). Is David hacking apart (or "setting," if one follows MT 2 Sam 12:31) the resident Ammonites (so most commentators) or the town (note the earlier reference, "who were in *it*")? The town is more likely to be the intended antecedent. First, David is said to have brought the people out of the town. If the writer wished to claim that David killed the people, this could have easily been done within the city itself. Second, the tools David uses are suited to working with physical objects in construction or, as the case may be, destruction. Third, the following summary, "thus David did to all the towns of the Ammonites," points to the town of Rabbah as the object.

"with a saw" *(bmgrh)*. So MT and LXX *(en priosin)*. In 1 Kgs 7:9, a "saw" *(mgrh)* is used to cut stone for the temple.

"with iron picks" *(bḥryṣy hbrzl)*. The translation is provisional. The text refers to sharp iron instruments of some sort. Similarly, LXX "with iron (carpenter) axes" *(en skeparnois sidērois)*. Aside from the appearance of *ḥryṣ* in 2 Sam 12:31, the noun is only found elsewhere in 1 Sam 17:18. The expression *ḥrwṣy hbrzl* appears, however, in Amos 1:3. NJPS translates both expressions as "(with) iron threshing boards," but *ḥryṣ*, defined as "iron pick," should be distinguished from *ḥrwṣ*, defined as "threshing sled" (Anderson and Freedman 1989: 237–39).

"and with axes." Reading *wbmgzrwt* with one Heb. MS 20:3 and MT 2 Sam 12:31. MT 1 Chr 20:3 has "and with saws" *wbmgrwt*, perhaps an assimilation toward *bmgrh* earlier in the verse. The phrase is lacking in LXX[AB] 20:3, perhaps because of haplography (Allen 1974a: 114). LXX[L] "and with threshing machines" *(kai en tois tribolois)*. MT 2 Sam 12:31 continues with an enigmatic statement, "(axes) of iron, and he caused them to pass with the brick kiln *(mlbn)*" (Qere).

"all the towns of the Ammonites" (כל ערי בני-עמון). So MT, LXX[AN], and Josephus (*Ant.* 7.161). LXX[BL] "all of the Ammonites" (= כל בני-עמון).

"then David and the whole army returned *(wyšb)* to Jerusalem." So MT (and LXX). See also the last TEXTUAL NOTE to 19:15.

20:4. "broke out" *(wtʿmd)*. The appearance of the verb *ʿmd* does not signify textual corruption (Curtis and Madsen 1910: 244), but reflects the usage of *ʿmd* in LBH with the meaning "to arise" or "to happen" (Dan 8:22–23; 11:2–4; 12:12; Esth 4:14; Qoh 4:15; Sir 47:1, 12). See also LXX *(kai egeneto)* and Syr. The addition of MT 2 Sam 21:18 "again" *(ʿwd)* is unnecessary in Chronicles, given the lack of any earlier reference to the Philistines.

"in Gezer" *(bgzr)*. So MT and LXX *(en Gazer)*. MT 2 Sam 21:18 "in Gob" *(bgwb)*; LXX[B] 2 Sam 21:18 "in Gath" *(bgt)*. 1QSam "of mighty men."

"Sibbekai" *(sbky)*. So MT 20:4, MT 2 Sam 21:18, and 1QSam. LXX[B] 1 Chr 20:4 *Sobachai*; LXX[AN] *Sobbochai*; LXX[L] *Sobakch(e)i*.

"the Ḥushathite" *(haḥûšātî)*. So MT 20:4 and MT 2 Sam 21:18. LXX[B] *Thōsathei* likely reflects an inner-Greek error (Allen 1974b: 19). LXX[L] *ho Essath(e)i* (= *haḥiššātî*); LXX[AN] *ho Ousathi*. LXX[L] 2 Sam 21:18 and Josephus (*Ant.* 7.301) "the Hittite."

"Sippai" *(spy)*. Reading with MT and LXX[L] *Sapph(e)i*. Cf. LXX[B] *Saphout* (= **spw;* Allen 1974b: 118). Arm. *Sapʿii;* MT 2 Sam 21:18 "Saph" *(sp)*. Cf. LXX[LMN] 2 Sam 21:18 (McCarter 1984: 449). The two spellings, *sp* and *spy*, reflect two different versions of the same name.

"one of the descendants" *(mylydy)*. So MT and perhaps LXX *(apo tōn huiōn)*. MT 2 Sam 21:18 *ʾšr bylydy*, "who was among the descendants."

"of the Rephaim" *(hrpʾym)*. So MT. LXX "of the giants" *(tōn gigantōn)*. Some Heb. MSS have *hrpʾ*, perhaps in anticipation of *hrpʾ* in vv. 6 and 8. MT 2 Sam 21:18 *hrph*, "Raphah." See the 5th NOTE to v. 4.

"and they were humbled" *(wyknʿw)*. Thus MT. LXX[ABL] *(kai etapeinōsen auton)* "and he humbled him" (= *wyknyʿw*). Proposals to emend to *wyknyʿw*, "they humbled" (Rehm 1937: 58) or to "from Canaan" (*mn-knʿn;* Rudolph 1955) are difficult to sustain. The phrase, lacking in 2 Sam 21:18, is likely the Chronicler's own addition (see NOTE).

20:5. "war." So MT and LXX. MT 2 Sam 21:19 adds, "in Gob" *(bgwb)*. Cf. MT 2 Sam 21:16, 18.

"Jair" *(yʿyr)*. Thus Qere and LXX$^{BL}$ *(Iaeir)*. Kethib "Jaur" *(yʿwr)*. MT 2 Sam 21:19, "son of Jarre-oregim" *(bn yʿry ʾrgym)* is corrupt (S. Driver 1912: 354).

"Laḥmi." So MT. LXX$^{B}$ $c_2$ *Elemee* likely reflects an inner-Greek corruption (Allen 1974b: 35). MT 2 Sam 21:19 "a Bethleḥemite" *(byt hlḥmy)*.

"brother of Goliath" *(ʾḥy glyt)*. Reading with MT and LXX. MT 2 Sam 21:19 "Goliath" *(ʾt glyt)*. On the force of the Chronicler's assertion, see the NOTES to v. 5.

20:6. "a man of (great) stature" *(ʾyš mdh)*. So MT and LXX, "an enormous man" *(anēr hypermegethēs)*. Cf. 1 Chr 11:23 *(ʾyš mdh);* Isa 45:14 *(ʾnšy mdh);* Num 13:32 *(ʾnšy mdwt)*. Qere 2 Sam 21:18 "a man of Midian" *(ʾyš mdyn);* Kethib, "a man of Madon" or "a man of strife" (*ʾyš mdwn;* cf. Jer 15:10; Prov 22:10; 25:24; 26:21).

"his digits." So MT and LXX. MT 2 Sam 21:20 is more expansive, "and the digits of his hands and the digits of his feet."

"twenty-four." So MT and LXX. MT 2 Sam 21:20 adds "(in) number."

"six (on each hand) and six (on each foot)." The number is repeated to convey a distributive sense (GKC §134q; Waltke and O'Connor, §7.2.3c).

"was descended from Rapha" *(nwld lhrpʾ)*. Thus MT. LXX *houtos ēn apogonos gigantōn*, "he was a descendant of the giants." Cf. LXX$^{ABN}$ 20:8 *houtos egeneto Rhapha* and 2 Sam 21:20, 22 *autos etechthē ho (tō) Rhapha*. LXX$^{L}$ 2 Sam 21:20 *apogonos Titanos* (b -*nōn*), "descendant (of the) Titan(s)." Josephus (*Ant.* 7.301) *progonous tous Gigantas*, "giants for ancestors." I am construing הרפא as a proper name, "Rapha" (cf. 1 Chr 8:2 *rpʾ*; BDB 952; Avigad and Sass 1997), but others see a designation of "the giants" (NRSV), another designation of "the Rephaim" (NAB), or "the Rapha" (NJPS). See also the 2nd NOTE to v. 6.

20:7. "Jonathan." Reading with MT, LXX, and Josephus (*Ant.* 7.304). Arab. 20:7 and some LXX cursives of 2 Sam 21:21 have "Jonadab," as in 2 Sam 13:3.

"Shimea" *(šimʿāʾ)*. Reading with MT 20:7, Qere 2 Sam 21:21 *šimʿāʾ*, and some witnesses to LXX 2 Sam 21:21. LXX$^{B}$ 1 Chr 20:7 and Josephus (*Ant.* 7.304) have *Sama(a)*, but this is precisely the same lemma that LXX$^{AB}$ *(Samaa)* have for MT's "Shimea" in 1 Chr 2:13. LXX$^{AN}$ 1 Chr 20:7 *Samaas*. MT 1 Sam 16:9 and Syr. 1 Chr 20:7 "Shammah" *(šmh)*. Kethib 2 Sam 21:21 *šimʿî* "Shimei."

20:8. "these" *(ʾēl)*. I read with MT *(lectio difficilior)*. On the form, compare Pun. *ʾlʾ* and *ily*, Aram. *ʾl*, and Eth. *ʾella*. This form of the pl. demonstrative pron. is found elsewhere only in the Pentateuch, but always as *hāʾēl* (Gen 19:8, 25; 26:3, 4; Lev 18:27; Deut 4:42; 7:22; 19:11). The *Sebir* follows MT 2 Sam 21:22 in reading the expected *(ʾēlleh)*. LXX 1 Chr 20:8, which reads *houtos*, continues with, "all of these four were giants" *(pantes ēsan tessares gigantes)*. Given the lemmata of LXX 1 Chr 20:8 and MT 2 Sam 21:22, "these four" *(ʾet-ʾarbaʿat ʾēlleh)*, some add *ʾarbāʿâ toʾēl* (or *ʾēlleh*), thus reading "these four." But Chronicles only mentions three, unlike Samuel, which mentions a fourth figure (2 Sam 21:15–21).

Moreover, LXX might be explained as reflecting an early Heb. gloss, *klm ʾrbʿt rpʾym* (Allen 1974a: 197). In any case, there is no compelling reason to adopt the reading of LXX, because this reading seems to assimilate toward Samuel.

"were descended." The vocalization of MT (*nûllĕdû*) is irregular. Many repoint the Heb. as *nôlĕdû* (GKC §69t; Curtis and Madsen 1910: 244). Cf. the 3 pl. 1st aorist pass. indic. of *gennaō* in bye$_2$ (*egennēthēsan*). See also the 1st TEXTUAL NOTE to 3:5.

"Rapha." So MT and LXX$^B$ (maximum differentiation). LXX$^L$ has the more common "the Rephaim," *tō Rhapha(e)in*. See also the 5th TEXTUAL NOTE to v. 6.

"at the hand of David and at the hand" (*byd-dwyd wbyd*). So MT 20:8 and MT 2 Sam 21:22. It is possible to posit metathesis and read *bdy dwyd wbyd*, "at the hands of David and at the hand" (Rudolph 1955: 14), but then one would expect to find *bydy dwyd wbyd*.

## NOTES

20:1. "when it was the turn of the year" (*wyhy lʿt tšwbt hšnh*). The beginning of v. 1 is drawn from the Chronicler's *Vorlage* of 2 Sam 11:1. What the text leaves ambiguous, later interpreters seek to clarify. Targum 1 Chr 20:1 specifies that this action took place at the end of the year, during the spring month of Nisan (rather than at the other turn of the year, autumn). Josephus (*Ant.* 7.129) makes a similar distinction, differentiating between David's campaign against the Aramaeans (1 Chr 19:17–19), which ended in the winter, and Joab's campaign, which began in the following spring.

"the elite of the army" (*ḥyl ḥṣbʾ*). The expression recurs in 2 Chr 26:13. The phrase has different connotations from the expression that occurs earlier in 1 Chr 19:8 (and 2 Sam 10:7), "the entire army of warriors" (*kol-haṣṣābāʾ haggibbôrîm*; 2nd TEXTUAL NOTE to 19:8). It is important to observe that the context is different in Samuel. There David directs Joab, "his servants with him, and all Israel" (וישלח דוד את־יואב ואת־עבדיו עמו ואת־כל־ישׂראל) into Ammon (2 Sam 11:1). In Chronicles Joab, without direct orders from David, leads an elite unit of warriors on a campaign into Ammon.

"and razed the land of the Ammonites." The assertion is to be understood against the backdrop of the Ammonite-Israelite clashes described earlier (1 Chr 19). There Joab played a major role in securing victories against both the Ammonites and the Aramaeans (19:8–15). Although it is sometimes maintained that the Chronicler manifests an exclusive interest in glorifying David, he has no difficulty with a military foray led by Joab. The author freely recognizes achievements by David's armed forces and generals. It is no criticism of a commander in chief that he attracts outstanding soldiers and officers (11:11–47; 12:1–39; 13:1; 18:15). It is no defect of David that his generals experience success on the battlefield (18:12; 19:8–15; 20:1), nor is it a mark against David that some of his troops emerge victorious from single combat against formidable foes (20:4–7). On the contrary, inasmuch as these triumphs occur while David serves as Israel's king, they redound to the good reputation of both David and Israel.

"while David was staying in Jerusalem." The connotations of this notice differ markedly from those in the Chronicler's source. In Samuel the notice provides the troubling setting for the story of David's affair with Bathsheba—this is a king who is deliberately staying home from waging battle. But in Chronicles, the same notice is incidental, providing the reader an explanation as to David's whereabouts when Joab, on his own initiative, leads an elite unit into Ammonite territory. Hence, not only does Chronicles completely omit the story of David's liaison with Bathsheba (2 Sam 11:2–12:25), but it also changes the circumstances of Joab's military venture into Ammon.

"attacked Rabbah." Having omitted the entire story of David and Bathsheba, the Chronicler rejoins his source (2 Sam 12:26a, 27–29) in narrating the continuation of the siege of Rabbah. On the variations from Samuel, see the TEXTUAL NOTES.

"lest I capture it." In Chronicles a strategic foray led by Joab and "the elite of the army" is so successful that the Ammonite defenses are near a state of complete collapse, hence the commander tactfully requests that his king come and complete the conquest. David complies by mobilizing "the army," arriving on scene, finishing the siege, and capturing Rabbah.

20:2–3. This material is drawn from the author's *Vorlage* of 2 Sam 12:30–31.

20:2. "Milkom." The national deity of the Ammonites. Previously only attested in biblical literature (1 Kgs 11:5, 7, 33; 2 Kgs 23:13; LXX Amos 1:15; Jer 49[= LXX 30]: 1, 3; Zeph 1:5), Milkom is now also attested epigraphically, appearing on a variety of Ammonite seals in PNs and in formulaic phrases (Aufrecht 1989; Hübner 1992). The name may also appear in the first line of the ninth-century Amman Citadel inscription ([*m*]*lkm;* Jackson 1983: 10–13).

"Milkom's crown." The context suggests that the crown belonged to a statue representing Milkom. Such divine images were to be found in the inner sanctuaries of temples dedicated to those deities.

"from his head." That is, from the head of (the statue of) Milkom. There is not a little satire in the narrator's remark. While the Ammonites undoubtedly distinguished between the deity and the image representing that deity, the Israelite writer, a devotee of aniconic worship, collapses the distance between the divine and the divine image. Compare the satire directed against the Philistine deity Dagon and his statue in 1 Sam 5:1–5. The parodies directed at the images of other gods in Isa 44:9–20 and 45:14–25 are more comprehensive (Dick 1999: 20–45).

"booty . . . was very great." In the Chronicler's theology, tribute or booty from the nations is one mark of divine blessing (Wellhausen 1885: 203–10; Dillard 1984b: 164–72).

20:3. "who were in it" (*'šr bh*). That is, in Rabbah.

"thus David did to all the towns of the Ammonites." A similar summary follows Josiah's cultic reform campaign in Samarian territory, "and he [Josiah] did to them according to all that he had done to Bethel" (2 Kgs 23:19; cf. 1 Kgs 13:2, 32). With this brief statement, the Deuteronomist makes a large claim, namely, that

Josiah defiled these northern shrines in the same way that he conducted his cultic reform in Bethel (2 Kgs 23:15–18; Knoppers 1994e: 209–12). In 1 Chr 20:3, the narrator claims that David ravaged the other Ammonite towns in the same way he ravaged Rabbah. Such a major campaign would damage the economic infrastructure of Ammon. By the same token, it is important to recognize what the author does not claim. He does not assert that David made the Ammonites his political servants or that he exacted regular tribute from them.

"the whole army." Literally, "all of the people" (2nd NOTE to 19:7).

20:4–8. These verses, drawn from the author's *Vorlage* of 2 Sam 21:18–22, portray conflicts with the Philistines in personal terms. The clash that breaks out in Gezer, for example, is settled by Sibbekai's striking down Sippai. The result is a humiliation for the Philistines (v. 4). In this respect, the battle depicted in v. 4 (and elsewhere in vv. 5–8) is a combat of champions, a type of warfare attested in Mesopotamia, Egypt, and Greece (Yadin 1963.2: 266–67; Sasson 1974). Rather than being simply settlements of personal rivalries (duels), these contests have larger repercussions for the armed forces from which the heroes are drawn.

20:4. "And sometime after this" *(wyhy ʾḥrykn)*. Identically vague connecting clauses appear at the beginning of chs. 18 and 19 (*wyhy ʾḥry-kn;* SOURCES AND COMPOSITION to 18:1–13).

"Gezer." Located some 24 km southeast of Gibeon, Gezer may have served as a border between Philistine and Israelite territory (Halpern 1996a). In 14:16, David and his troops are said to have defeated the Philistine army "from Gibeon to Gezer."

"Sibbekai the Ḥushathite." Mentioned earlier (11:29) as one of David's valiant warriors, he reappears later as the one in charge of David's military division during the eighth month (27:11). On the Judahite town of Ḥushah, see the 3rd NOTE to 4:4.

"one of the descendants." Instead of the standard translation of *ylyd* as "born," "son," or "descendant," some scholars (McCarter [1984: 449–50] provides a summary) favor translating *ylyd* as "votary" or "a member of a military group." This is possible, but the traditional interpretation has much to commend it. The context in Chronicles is concerned with the unusual, if not formidable, features of Israel's Philistine opponents, such as great stature, six-fingered hands, and six-toed feet. Hence, the connection with the "Rephaim" makes sense. Note also the expression *ylydy hʿnq*, "the descendants of Anaq" (Num 13:22, 28; Josh 15:14). Like the Rephaim, "the descendants of Anaq" *(bny hʿnq)* appear as giants. According to Deut 9:2, they are "a people great and tall" (and are understood as such in LXX). The Anaqim are associated geographically with both Ḥebron and Philistia (Num 13:22, 33; Josh 15:14; Judg 1:20).

"Rephaim." The term "Rephaim" has multiple meanings. In some contexts, it refers to the shades, dead humans who reside in the underworld (Isa 26:14, 19; Ps 88:11 [ET 88:10]; Job 26:5; Prov 2:18; 9:18; cf. *KAI* 13.7–8; 14.8; 177.1). But in other contexts, including this one, the term refers to an ancient race of giants or warriors (cf. Gen 14:5; 15:20; Deut 2:11, 20; 3:11, 13; Josh 12:4; 13:12).

"and they were humbled." That is, the Philistines. This phrase, not found in

Samuel, is one of the Chronicler's additions to his *Vorlage* (see TEXTUAL NOTE). The use of the verb "to humble" *(knʿ)* is typical of Chronistic style (e.g., 1 Chr 17:10; 18:1; 2 Chr 7:14; 12:6, 12; 13:18; 28:19; 30:11; 32:26; 33:12, 19, 23; 34:27). The verb is used here as a generalizing summary, following the description of the contest between Sibbekai and Sippai, to comment on the fate of the Philistines (introduced at the start of v. 4). In this manner, the Chronicler reinforces the point made in 18:1, narrating another conflict against the Philistines: David "humbled them" (*knʿ* in the *hipʿil*). Both notices point to the fulfillment of one of Nathan's promises, namely, that Yhwh would humble *(knʿ)* all of David's enemies (17:10).

20:5. "Elḥanan the son of Jair." Elḥanan appears as one of David's valiant warriors in 11:26. Indeed, the heroic exploits of 20:4–8 recall the lists of warriors and chieftains who rally to David over the course of his early career (11:11–47; 12:1–39). These soldiers play an instrumental role in Israel's battles against its enemies.

"Laḥmi the brother of Goliath." The text harmonizes two different claims found in Samuel. According to 1 Sam 17:50, David killed the Philistine giant, identified as Goliath of Gath (1 Sam 17:4). But, according to 2 Sam 21:19, Elḥanan killed Goliath the Gittite. By having Elḥanan kill the brother of Goliath the Gittite, and not Goliath himself, the Chronicler accommodates both claims. Bertheau (1873: 190) and Willi (1972: 138–39) recognize the textual innovation, but point to corruption in the Chronicler's *Vorlage* as a trigger motivating the unusual assertion. But there is no clear evidence to suggest that the *Vorlage* was as corrupt as MT 2 Sam 21:19 is. The Chronicler's comment is best explained in exegetical terms rather than in text-critical terms. He attempts to reconcile two different claims found in Samuel (*pace* Auld 1996). Another such textual blend is evident in the presentation of Josiah's Passover (2 Chr 35:13). There the Chronicler asserts that the Passover lamb was boiled *(bšl)* in fire *(ʾš)*, according to the custom *(kmšpṭ)*. As Fishbane (1985: 135–36) points out, the author harmonizes two different pieces of Pentateuchal legislation regulating the preparation of the paschal offering: roasting (Exod 12:9) or boiling (Deut 16:7). That the Chronicler is fully aware of both pieces of legislation is apparent in his use of vocabulary: fire *(ʾš)* in accordance with Exod 12:9 and boiling *(bšl)* in accordance with Deut 16:7. In this manner, the writer accommodates two distinct legal traditions. But such harmonizations, however much they reconcile different claims, create their own hermeneutical challenges. This is apparent in the Targum's treatment of our passage. The authors of the Targum were undoubtedly aware that in spite of the summary in v. 8 "they fell at the hand of David," none are explicitly said to have done so. Lest the Chronicler's harmonization of 1 Sam 17:50 and 2 Sam 21:19 detract from David's glory, Tg. 1 Chr 20:5 corrects it by asserting that David (and not Elḥanan) killed Laḥmi, Goliath's brother on the day that David killed Goliath himself. Hence, the *traditio* of Tg. 1 Chr 20:5 creates a new *traditum* distinct from the claims found in both Samuel and Chronicles, presenting David as the slayer of both Laḥmi and Goliath. In so doing, it brings the text of Chronicles into conformity with the summary in v. 8.

"Goliath the Gittite." See 1 Sam 17:4, 23; 21:10; 22:10; 2 Sam 21:19.

"weavers' beam." Also the weapon of choice of Benaiah's foe in 11:23 (cf. 1 Sam 17:7).

20:6. "Gath." One of the principal Philistine cities. Some commentators wish to emend the text to "Gob" or "Gezer" (see TEXTUAL NOTES), but the notice makes sense in the context of the Chronicler's work. According to 18:1, David "captured Gath and its dependencies from the control of the Philistines." Hence, the presumption of Israelite access to traditionally Philistine-dominated territory is justified. What the text indicates, however, is that territorial hegemony over other peoples was tenuous.

"descended from Rapha" (הרפא). Rapha (see also v. 8) appears as the eponymous ancestor of the three Philistine warriors mentioned in vv. 4–7. The spelling in Chronicles (רפא) over against Samuel (רפה; 2 Sam 21:16, 18, 20, 22) is insignificant. In PNs, a final *ʾālep* is often interchangeable with a final *hê* (Fowler 1988: 165–66). One of the Ugaritic texts, RS 24.252 (= *KTU* 1.108) mentions a figure *rpʾu*, who seems to be associated with the same locales, *ʿṯtrt* and *hdrʿy* (= Ashtaroth [עשתרות] and Edrei [אדרעי]), as those of Og of Bashan, whom the Deuteronomistic History presents as the last of the remaining Rephaim (Deut 3:11, 13; Josh 12:4–5; 13:12). In this line of interpretation, the Rephaim (רפאים), mentioned in 1 Chr 20:4, are descendants of Rapha. The same legendary figure may be referred to in Stephen's polemical speech against the Jewish authorities in which he cites a version of LXX Amos 5:26, "And you took up the tent of Moloch, and the star of the deity Raiphan" (Acts 7:43; Pope 1977a: 177). But the Heb. "Kiyyun" of Amos 5:26 points toward Akk. *kayamānu*, "steady one," an appellation of the god (and planet) Saturn (Paul 1991: 196).

20:7. "Jonathan." To be distinguished from the Jonathan (Joḥanan) related to Saul (12:5) and from the Jonathan (Joḥanan) of the tribe of Gad (12:13).

"David's brother Shimea." For the genealogy, see 2:13–16.

20:8. "fell at the hand of David." The general summary derives from 2 Samuel. The text does not explicitly list any of these unusual foes as being directly victimized by David himself.

## SOURCES, COMPOSITION, AND STRUCTURE

For the material in this chapter, the Chronicler has carefully culled his source (Samuel) and excised coverage of David's personal and family struggles, as well as coverage of Israel's internal political affairs. The writer has thereby excluded an enormous amount of material found in 2 Samuel relating to David's reign. Given the omission of so much narrative, it is important to examine what the author retains. Synoptic study of Samuel and Chronicles reveals that the Chronicler keeps almost all of the information pertaining to Israel's foreign wars. The parallels and omissions may be outlined as follows:

| *Event* | *2 Samuel* | *1 Chronicles 20* |
|---|---|---|
| Joab and the Ammonites | 11:1 | 1a |
| David and Bathsheba | 11:2–12:25 | — |
| Joab at Rabbah | 12:26a, 27–29 | 1b |
| Joab and David | 12:27–29 | — |
| Booty and Destruction | 12:30–31 | 2–3 |
| Amnon's Rape of Tamar | 13:1–22 | — |
| Absalom's Murder of Amnon | 13:23–39 | — |
| Absalom's Rehabilitation | 14:1–33 | — |
| Absalom's Revolt | 15:1–12 | — |
| David's Flight | 15:13–16:14 | — |
| Advice to Absalom | 16:15–17:20 | — |
| David vs. Absalom | 17:21–18:8 | — |
| Death of Absalom | 18:9–19:1 | — |
| David's Consolidation | 19:2–44 | — |
| Sheba's Revolt | 20:1–26 | — |
| Execution of Saulides | 21:1–14 | — |
| David and the Philistines | 21:15–17 | — |
| Contests with the Philistines | 21:18–22 | 4–8 |

The author's selection from and recontextualization of his sources has led him to edit the material he retains from his *Vorlage*. This is especially evident with respect to Joab's foray into Ammon and the circumstances relating to David's remaining in Jerusalem (NOTES to v. 1), but it is also evident with respect to the clashes with the Philistines (NOTES to vv. 4–8).

The carefully organized chapter naturally falls into two separate sections: the Israelite invasion of Ammon (vv. 1–3) and the assorted Israelite battles against the Philistines (vv. 4–8). The transition to the invasion of Ammon in v. 1, "When it was the turn of the year, the time when kings go forth [into battle]," calls attention to this unit's links with the Israelite-Ammonite conflicts reported in 1 Chr 19. The invasion itself is subdivided into reports of different stages in the Israelite campaign led by Joab and David. Like the first section, the second section is introduced by a temporal transition, "And sometime after this" (v. 4). Again, like the first section, the narrative dealing with wars against the Philistines is subdivided into reports of individual battles. Each of these subsections is introduced by similar introductions:

v. 4 "And sometime after this, war broke out with the Philistines in Gezer" (ויהי אחריכן ותעמד מלחמה בגזר)

v. 5 "And there was war again with the Philistines" (ותהי-עוד מלחמה את-פלשתים)

v. 6 "And there was war once again in Gath" (ותהי-עוד מלחמה בגת)

Each of these notices introduces reports of duels between individual Israelite warriors and their Philistine adversaries. A summary (v. 8) concludes the last of the three subsections.

# COMMENT

As the preceding discussion demonstrates, the Chronicler is both dependent upon his version of Samuel and extremely selective in what he retains from his source. Consistent with his presentation in previous chapters (18:1–19:19), the author maintains his focus on David's military campaigns. To put this remarkable presentation in perspective, it is necessary to compare it with Samuel. As interpreted by the prophet Nathan in his parable and judgment oracle against David (2 Sam 12:1–12), the affair with Bathsheba is a major turning point in David's reign. The consequences of David's conspiracy against Bathsheba's husband, Uriah, transform David's tenure from one of international and domestic success to one of great internal upheaval. As Nathan pointedly informs David following David's murder of Uriah, "The sword will not depart from your house forever" (2 Sam 12:10). In this regard, Nathan's judgment oracle qualifies his earlier dynastic oracle (2 Sam 7:5–16) and prepares both David (and readers) for trouble. Episodes of tremendous familial strife and political upheaval ensue, during which the king is continually confronted with enemies from within his state, military, and family. Israel itself is internally divided. At stake for David is not only his grip on his realm, but also his life. To be sure, the monarch is eventually able to return to Jerusalem and regain some measure of control over the various factions that deserted him. He and his troops even experience some success against foreign adversaries (2 Sam 21:15–22). Nevertheless, he never regains complete control over his family. Nor does David, judging from the series of uprisings of Sheba (2 Sam 20) and Adonijah (1 Kings 1) against him, ever regain the domestic support he enjoyed previously.

The Chronicler is heavily dependent upon Samuel for his account of David's reign. He adds relatively little to the material he draws from Samuel. Nor does he, in this case, rearrange the contents of the material that he retains. It is, therefore, all the more amazing how much his presentation differs from that of his *Vorlage*. He exhibits an adroitness in selecting only those scenes that are necessary to his own narrative design. The author's work does not minimize David's private, familial, and state struggles; it gives no attention to them whatsoever. Following his portrayal of Nathan's dynastic oracle and David's prayer (1 Chr 17), the author presents a series of foreign campaigns (1 Chr 18–20). As the table in SOURCES, COMPOSITION, AND STRUCTURE illustrates, the narratives drawn from 2 Samuel are presented sequentially, resulting in a remarkably unified presentation. This means that David never faces a domestic challenge to his authority. Nor does the body politic ever divide into factions. Once acclaimed by all Israel at the inception of his rule (11:1–3), David never loses his people's undivided support.

Why the Chronicler presents such a different picture of David is a question that has been asked since antiquity. Given the vast amount of coverage devoted to David's career, this is also an issue that affects how one understands the purpose of Chronicles itself. Almost all scholars speak of an idealization of David in Chronicles. This standard view has considerable merit, but it overlooks the degree to which the depiction of David in Samuel is also a historiographical construct that involves stylization. In any case, one should push further and inquire as to why the Chronicler presents such a highly polished and distinctive presentation of David. To their credit, Japhet (1993a) and Steussy (1999) pursue this matter. They point to the Chronicler's reluctance to relate the private affairs of the public figures within his history. While this historiographical tendency is certainly apparent in Chronicles, the situation in Samuel is not so simple. There David's personal, familial, and domestic political troubles are all intimately related. Indeed, the close ties between David's personal politics and state politics drive the plot. The very fact that David is driven into exile while Absalom and "the Israelites" take control in Jerusalem indicates that more than the monarch's personal life is in view.

Complicating matters further is the Chronicler's highly complimentary picture of Israel. If David is idealized in Chronicles, so are the people he leads. Surprisingly, the portrayal of a valiant, highly effective, and unified Israel has received little or no attention from scholars. In the presentation of Samuel, which is more nuanced than some recognize, Israel is factionalized, even riven. David's problem is not simply divisions within his own family, but also deep divisions within the nation he leads. Some of the factions are tribal, but others seem to be intratribal. Even during David's return to Jerusalem, he faces opposition. One could make the case that some of these disputes result from David's own mismanagement, but in any case, they complicate Israel's national life.

The issues of David's reputation and Israel's reputation are very much related and provide some insight into the Chronicler's distinctive presentation. To appreciate the force of David's campaigns (1 Chr 18–20), it is helpful to situate these wars in the context of the Chronicler's larger presentation. In my judgment, the Chronicler uses Nathan's dynastic oracle (17:1–15) as a charter by which he organizes the remainder of David's reign (1 Chr 18–29; Knoppers forthcoming [e]). Nathan's promises have both dynastic and national implications, forbidding David from building the Temple, but also providing David with a series of divine commitments. One important pledge is victory over all of David's enemies (17:8, 10). David's initial string of successes against the Aramaeans, Moabites, Edomites, and Philistines (1 Chr 18) signals that Yhwh is keeping his pledge. The victory motif continues as David, Joab, and the Israelite army enjoy a series of triumphs over the Ammonites and a group of Aramaean states. These victories earn David a formidable reputation among his contemporaries (17:9; 18:9–11, 14; 19:19; 20:8).

Having picked a theme for this phase of David's reign, the author sticks with it. He only includes material from his *Vorlage* that fits the topic of foreign conflict. The effect of the selection and recontextualization is dramatic. The battles of 1 Chr 20 are not appendices to long and lively narratives about the king's domestic troubles, as they are in Samuel, but a continuation of the major subject matter introduced in 1 Chr 18. God's promise to humble *(knʿ)* David's enemies (17:10) is echoed in the notices that the Philistines were humbled (*knʿ*; 18:1; 20:4). Unlike *Florilegium* (4Q174 1:1–10; Brooke 1985), which in its interpretation of the dynastic oracle places the vanquishing of enemies in the future, Chronicles situates these conquests within David's reign.

But Nathan's promise that Yhwh would humble all of David's enemies is closely related to other promises. The triumphs of David, Joab, Abshai, and the rest of Israel's warriors end the unruly state of affairs that the Israelites experienced in previous centuries. In Nathan's dynastic oracle, Yhwh assures David that "evildoers will no longer wear them down as in the past, ever since the days I commanded chieftains over my people Israel" (17:9–10). In the Chronicler's construction of history, David's success and Israel's success are intimately related. His many and, in the case of the Philistines, repeated victories secure Israel's position. To quote Nathan again: "I shall make a place for my people Israel and I shall plant them so that they will reside in it and be disturbed no longer" (17:9).

The achievement of Israelite security through military conquest lays, in turn, the groundwork for the fulfillment of other promises: the establishment of the scion's kingdom and the construction of the Temple. In Chronicles much of the remainder of David's reign, in which the story of the census (1 Chr 21) serves as a transition, is devoted to preparing for the completion of these goals. This involves readying the designated heir for his tasks (22:7–16; 28:9–10, 20–21), organizing a national administration (23:2–27:34), drawing up plans for the Temple (22:2–5; 28:11–19), securing the enthusiastic endorsement of all Israelites (22:17–19; 28:1–8; 29:1–9, 20–25), and praying for their success (29:10–19). The postdynastic charter phases of David's reign follow the order of the charter itself.

By arranging his presentation in such a careful and highly stylized manner, the Chronicler creates an image of David's reign (and Solomon's following it) as Israel's normative age. Chronicles acknowledges the authority of the law of Moses (Shaver 1989; Dörrfuß 1994; Spawn 2002), but neither the Exodus nor the wilderness wanderings appear as ideal ages. Mosaic law, not Israelite polity in the time of Moses, is incumbent upon Israel. For the Chronicler, the time of the Judges is a period of considerable upheaval (1 Chr 17:9–10; cf. 2 Chr 15:3–6). The record of the Judahite monarchy is mixed, a time of both accomplishments and disasters. The epoch of David and Solomon is, however, a classical age. During this era Israel experiences unprecedented prosperity, success, and unity. Israel's foundational institutions—the Davidic monarchy, the city of Jerusalem, the Temple—take definitive shape in this period. For the Chronicler, not only these institutions themselves but also their configuration in the United Monarchy represent a normative legacy for Israelites. Later monarchs are evaluated according to the standard David and Solomon establish.

Given his concern to present the Israel of David (and Solomon) as normative, the Chronicler omits material found in Samuel and Kings that might compromise the paradigm he wishes to promote. To function as a model, history must display some consistency. Achieving such uniformity means that material in Samuel depicting fractious disputes will not be recounted. Such material would tarnish the high standard the Chronicler wishes to create. Recognition of the author's larger literary design elucidates a minor feature in the presentation of David's foreign wars. If the Chronicler consistently includes all of the material that is found in Samuel pertaining to David's foreign wars, why does he exclude 2 Sam 21:15–17 (paralleled in 1QSam), dealing with David's encounter with the Philistines? It may have been omitted, as Botterweck (1956: 427) argues, because of the danger posed to the perpetuity of the Davidic promises implied by the reference to extinguishing the lamp *(nēr)* of Israel (2 Sam 21:17). But these verses could also have been left out because of their depiction of David as a weary and defenseless warrior. As with the material relating to internal political strife, the inclusion of this incident would unnecessarily complicate the depiction of the United Monarchy. In Chronicles David knows only success in battle.

# *XXVI. The Census and Plague: David as Repentant Sinner (21:1–22:1)*

*David's Census*

1 An adversary took his stand against Israel and incited David to take a census of
Israel. 2 Then David said to Joab and the officers of the army, "Go number Israel
from Beer-sheba to Dan and then bring back (the outcome) to me so that I may
know their number." 3 But Joab responded, "May Yhwh add to his people one
hundred times! Is not my lord the king? All of them are servants of my lord. Why
does my lord seek this? Why should there be guilt upon Israel?" 4 But the command of the king prevailed upon Joab. So Joab set forth and traveled through all
Israel and came (back) to Jerusalem. 5 Then Joab provided the tally, the muster of
the people, to David. All Israel had 1,100,000 men who drew the sword, while
Judah had 470,000 men who drew the sword. 6 But Levi and Benjamin he did not
count among them, because the command of the king was abhorrent to Joab.
7 This thing was evil in the sight of God and so he struck Israel.

*David's Confession and Choice of Punishment*

8 Then David said to God, "I have sinned greatly in doing this thing. Forgive the
transgression of your servant, because I have acted very foolishly." 9 And Yhwh
spoke to Gad (the) seer, 10 "Go and speak to David saying, 'Thus said Yhwh: I am
extending three (choices) to you. Choose one of them for yourself and I shall do it
to you.' " 11 When Gad came to David, he said to him, "Thus said Yhwh, 'Choose
one of the following for yourself: 12 a three-year famine, three months of your succumbing to your foes, with the sword of your enemy overtaking (you), or three
days of the sword of Yhwh accompanied by a plague in the land and a messenger
of Yhwh wreaking destruction in every territory of Israel.' Now decide with what
word I shall return to my sender." 13 And David replied to Gad, "I am in great distress. Let me fall into the hand of Yhwh, because his compassion is exceedingly
great. But into the hand of man let me not fall."

*The Plague and David's Intercession*

14 Then Yhwh set a plague in Israel and there fell from among the Israelites
70,000 people. 15 And God sent a messenger to Jerusalem to destroy it; but, as he
was about to destroy (it), Yhwh saw and repented of the evil. Then he said to the
destroying messenger, "Enough! Now stay your hand!" And the messenger of
Yhwh was standing by the threshing floor of Ornan the Jebusite. 16 And David

lifted his eyes and saw the messenger of Yhwh standing between the earth and the heavens with his sword drawn in his hand, outstretched against Jerusalem. Then David and the elders, dressed in sackcloth, fell on their faces. 17 And David said to God, "Was it not I, I who said to number the people? I was the one who sinned and did great evil. But as for these sheep, what have they done? O Yhwh my God, may your hand be upon me and upon the house of my father. But as for your people, let (them) not be subject to a plague."

*The Site Purchased from Ornan*

18 Then the messenger of Yhwh said to Gad to say to David that David should go up to establish an altar to Yhwh on the threshing floor of Ornan the Jebusite. 19 So David went up in accordance with the command of Gad, who spoke in the name of Yhwh. 20 When Ornan turned and saw the king, his four sons with him hid themselves, covering themselves with sackcloth. Meanwwhile, Ornan continued threshing out the wheat. 21 Then David came to Ornan. When Ornan looked and saw David, he went forth from the threshing floor and bowed before David, nose to the ground. 22 And David said to Ornan, "Give me the place of the threshing floor that I may build upon it an altar to Yhwh. At the full price give it to me so that the plague upon the people will end." 23 Ornan replied to David, "Take (it) for yourself and may my lord the king do what is good in his own eyes. See I give the oxen for the burnt offerings, the threshing sledges for wood, and the wheat for the cereal offering—all of these I give." 24 But King David said to Ornan, "No, I shall indeed buy them at full price, for I shall not lift up to Yhwh what is yours nor offer the burnt offerings for nothing." 25 Then David gave 600 shekels of gold to Ornan for the place.

*David's Offerings and Yhwh's Answer*

26 David built there an altar to Yhwh and lifted up burnt offerings and offerings of well-being. He called upon Yhwh and he answered him with fire from the heavens upon the altar of burnt offering and (it) consumed the burnt offering. 27 Then Yhwh spoke to the messenger and he returned his sword to its sheath. 28 At that time, when David saw that Yhwh answered him at the threshing floor of Ornan the Jebusite and he sacrificed there, 29 the Tabernacle of Yhwh that Moses had made in the wilderness, and the altar of the burnt offering were at that time at the high place in Gibeon. 30 But David was not able to go before it to seek God, because he was terrified on account of the sword of the messenger of Yhwh.

*The Site of the Future Temple*

22:1 And David said, "This will be the House of Yhwh God and this will be the altar of the burnt offering for Israel."

## Textual Notes

First Chronicles 21:1–27 is largely taken from the Chronicler's *Vorlage* of 2 Sam 24:1–25, while 1 Chr 21:28–22:1 is unique to Chronicles. 4QSam$^{a}$ is available for 2 Sam 24:16–20.

21:1. "an adversary" (*śāṭān*). So MT and LXX$^{ABN}$ (*diabolos*). LXX$^{L}$ *Satan*. MT

2 Sam 24:1 reads, "and Yhwh was angry again against Israel and incited David." Tg. conflates the reading of 2 Sam 24:1 with that of 1 Chr 21:1, "and Yhwh raised up Satan." This is the only mention of *śāṭān* in Chronicles and it requires some discussion. Most translations render *śāṭān* as a proper name, "Satan." This is possible (e.g., LXX^L), but *śāṭān* is normally an indefinite noun (Num 22:22, 32; 1 Sam 29:4; 2 Sam 19:23 [ET 19:22]; 1 Kgs 5:18 [ET 5:4]; 11:14, 23, 25; Ps 109:6). As Japhet (1989: 145–49) and Day (1988: 127–45) have argued, the most plausible meaning for the noun *śāṭān* is "an (anonymous) adversary." The celestial adversary of Yhwh in Job 1–2, a kind of prosecuting attorney in the divine council, is rendered with the definite article *haśśāṭān*. See also the use of *haśśāṭān* in Zech 3:1, 2, rendered with the article in LXX (*ho diabolos*). To put the case somewhat differently, if *śāṭān* is being used as a proper name in 21:1, whether of a certain (otherwise unknown) human person named Satan or of a divine intermediary ("Satan"), this is the only instance in the entire HB in which the term has such a denotation. It thus seems preferable to interpret *śāṭān* according to its normal usage as an indefinite noun.

"to take a census." Literally, "to number" (*limnôt*). Indirect discourse is found in both MT and LXX 21:1, whereas 2 Sam 24:1 has direct discourse, "(incited David) against them saying, 'Go and take a count.' "

"Israel." So MT and LXX. In anticipation of 2 Sam 24:9, 2 Sam 24:1 adds "and Judah."

21:2. "the officers of the army" (*śry hḥyl*). So LXX 21:2. Cf. MT 2 Sam 24:2 *śr hḥyl*. MT 1 Chr 21:2 "the officers of the military force" (literally, "the people," *hā'ām*).

"go number Israel." So MT and LXX. MT 2 Sam 24:2 "traverse (*šwṭ*) through all the tribes of Israel." The use of the verb "to number" (ספר) in this context is virtually synonymous with the verb "to muster" (פקד) used in other sources (Weiss 1968: 127–29).

"from Beer-sheba to Dan." So MT and LXX^AB. A Chronistic locution (1st NOTE to v. 2). LXX^L follows MT 2 Sam 24:2 in reading the more typical "from Dan to Beer-sheba."

"bring back" (*hābîʾû*). The verb is in the *hipʿil*, so the common translation "come back" is inadequate.

21:3. "is not my lord the king?" (*hlʾ ʾdny hmlk*). Following MT (maximum variation). LXX 21:3 and 2 Sam 24:3 read, "and the eyes of my lord the king see" (= *wʿyny ʾdny hmlk rʾwt*).

"all of them are servants of my lord." So MT and LXX. Lacking in MT 2 Sam 24:3.

"why should there be guilt upon Israel?" Reading with both MT and LXX (see NOTE). Lacking in Samuel.

21:4. "but the command of the king prevailed upon Joab" (*wdbr-hmlk ḥzq ʿl-ywʾb*). So MT and LXX^AN. Cursive $c_2$ *kai epischysen ho logos tou basileōs kai egeneto kai ēlthen Iōab*. LXX^B lacks the entire expression. MT 2 Sam 24:4, which is similar to MT 1 Chr 21:4 (*wyḥzq dbr-hmlk ʾl-ywʾb*), is followed in part by LXX^L *kai ischyse to hrēma tou basileōs*.

"Joab." MT 2 Sam 24:4 adds "and the officers of the army."

"so Joab set forth." So MT and LXX^L^. MT 2 Sam 24:4 again adds "and the officers of the army" (שׂרי החיל). The expression is lacking in LXX^B^.

"and traveled through all Israel and came (back) to Jerusalem." Thus MT and $LXX^{ALN}$. The words, "and traveled through all Israel" do not appear in $LXX^{B}$. MT 2 Sam 24:4–8 present a much longer text than either MT or LXX Chronicles, including a detailed description of Joab's journey through various territories.

21:5. "1,100,000 men who drew the sword." So MT and LXX. MT 2 Sam 24:9 "800,000 warriors who drew the sword." $LXX^{L}$ 2 Sam 24:9 "900,000" (cf. Josephus, *Ant.* 7.320).

"while Judah had 470,000 men who drew the sword." So MT and (basically) $LXX^{AL}$. The collocation is missing from $LXX^{BN}$ and $c_2$ due to haplography by *homoioteleuton* (from "men who drew the sword" to "men who drew the sword").

"470,000 men." So MT. $LXX^{AL}$ "480,000 men." MT 2 Sam 24:9 "500,000 men." $LXX^{L}$ 2 Sam 24:9 "400,000 warriors" (cf. Josephus, *Ant.* 7.320).

21:6. "but Levi and Benjamin he did not count among them because the command of the king was abhorrent to Joab." So MT. The entire verse is not found in Samuel.

"was abhorrent." Reading *ntʿb* with the MT (maximum variation). $LXX^{B}$ $hc_2$ *kateischysen*, "was anticipated"; $LXX^{AN}$ *prosōchthisen* ("angered, offended"); $LXX^{L}$ *katetachynen*. $LXX^{B}$ $hc_2$ may reflect *nbʿt* due to metathesis (Allen 1974b: 11). Another possibility is that $LXX^{B}$ assimilates toward the phraseology of 21:4, "but the command of the king prevailed upon Joab" *(wdbr-hmlk ḥzq ʿl-ywʾb)*. See also Spottorno (2001: 78).

"to Joab" *(ʾt-ywʾb)*. So MT and $LXX^{B}$. A few LXX witnesses reflect the expected prep. *ʾl*. Rudolph (1955: 142) reads MT *ʾt* as signifying a prep. ("bei") with the *nipʿal* of *tʿb*.

21:7. "this . . . and so he struck" *(hzh wyk)*. Thus MT and LXX (maximum variation). Syr. *ʿl dmnʾ dwyd* (= *ʿl ʾšr spr dwyd*). Chronicles and Samuel differ here. MT 2 Sam 24:10 lacks "this thing was evil in the sight of God." Moreover, in Chronicles, it is Yhwh who regards the census as iniquitous and strikes Israel *(wyk ʾt-yśrʾl)*. MT 2 Sam 24:10 "and the heart of David struck him *(wyk lb dwd ʾtw)* sometime after he had numbered the people."

21:8. "this thing." So MT and LXX. Lacking in MT Sam 24:10.

"forgive." The Heb. is a *hipʿil* impv., literally, "pass over" *(hʿbr-nʾ)*. Similarly, LXX *periele dē*.

"foolishly." MT Sam 24:11 adds "and David arose in the morning."

21:9. "seer" *(ḥzh)*. So $LXX^{B}$ *(horōnta)*. MT Sam 24:11 "the prophet, the seer [of David]" *(hnbyʾ ḥzh)*. MT and $LXX^{L}$ 1 Chr 21:9 (as well as MT 2 Sam 24:11) continue with an expansion of specification: "of/to David saying" (cf. $LXX^{AN}$). Some LXX cursives "saying."

21:10. "extending" *(nōṭeh)*. So MT. MT Sam 24:12 "lifting (over)" *(nōṭel)*. Similarly, LXX 1 Chr 21:10 *airō*, "I raise, lift."

21:11. "he said to him." So MT and LXX 21:11, but the prefatory plus of MT 2 Sam 24:13, "and he reported to him," may have been lost by haplography (*homoioarkton* from *wygd* to *wyʾmr*).

" 'thus said Yhwh, "Choose (one of the following) for yourself" ' " *(qbl-lk)*. So MT and LXX. MT Sam 24:13 lacks "thus said Yhwh" and reads *htbw' lk*, "will come to you" instead of *qbl-lk*. But LXX^BLM 2 Sam 24:13 read *eklexai seautō*, "choose for yourself."

21:12. "three years." So MT and LXX 21:12 as well as LXX 2 Sam 24:13. MT Sam 24:13 "seven years."

"famine." So MT and LXX. MT Sam 24:13 adds "in your land," probably in anticipation of "in your land" *(b'rṣk)* later in the verse.

"succumbing *(nsph)* to your foes." So MT (maximum variation). Kittel (1902: 82) would read *nskh* in line with LXX *(pheugein)* and Vg. *(fugere)*. MT Sam 24:13 is similar, "take flight *(nsk)* before your foes."

"with the sword of your enemy overtaking (you)" *(wḥrb 'wybyk lmśgt)*. So MT. For "overtaking" *(lmśgt)*, LXX^B has *tou exolethreusai*, "destroying utterly," while LXX^L has *tou katadiōkein se* (= *lk mśgt*). MT Sam 24:13 reads differently, *whw' rdpk*, "while he pursues you."

"the sword of Yhwh accompanied by a plague in the land and a messenger of Yhwh wreaking destruction in every territory of Israel." MT (and LXX) thus anticipate the sequence of events depicted in vv. 14–15. The shorter and more imprecise version of MT 2 Sam 24:13, "and a plague in your land," is probably the more original reading.

"now decide with what word I shall return to my sender." So MT and LXX^B. MT 2 Sam 24:13 "now know and decide with what word I shall return to my sender."

21:13. "I am in great distress." Thus MT 21:13 and MT 2 Sam 24:14 *(lectio brevior)*. LXX 21:13 adds "and (all) the three," *(Stena moi) kai ta tria* (LXX^AN adds *tauta*) *sphodra*. Similarly, LXX^MN 2 Sam 24:14 adds *kai ta tria*.

"let me fall." So MT and LXX 21:13, as well as LXX 2 Sam 24:14. MT 2 Sam 24:14 "let us fall."

"because his compassion is exceedingly great" *(ky-rbym rḥmyw m'd)*. So MT (and LXX^B *hoti polloi hoi oikteirmoi autou sphodra*, "because his many mercies are great"). MT 2 Sam 24:14 "his compassion is great" *(ky-rbym rḥmyw)*.

21:14. "a plague in Israel." So MT and LXX. MT 2 Sam 24:15 adds puzzling *mhbqr wʿd-ʿt mwʿd*, usually rendered as "from morning until (the) appointed time" (but see McCarter 1984: 506). LXX 2 Sam 24:15 *hōras aristou* (= *ʿt sʿd*[?], "dinnertime").

"and there fell from among the Israelites 70,000 people." So MT and LXX. MT 2 Sam 24:15 "and there died among the people from Dan to Beersheba 70,000." The appearance of the phrase "from Dan to Beersheba" not only agrees with regular usage in Samuel-Kings (3rd TEXTUAL NOTE to v. 2), but it also brings the implementation of the plague into conformity with David's mandate for the scope of the census (2 Sam 24:2).

21:15. "and God sent a messenger" *(wyšlḥ h'lhym ml'k)*. So MT and LXX (maximum differentiation). Benzinger (1901: 63) emends to *wyšlḥ ml'k h'lhym lydw* ("and the messenger of God set his hand"), thereby bringing the text of Chronicles more into line with that of MT 2 Sam 24:16, *wyšlḥ ydw hml'k* ("and the messenger set his hand"). Eupolemus expands by naming the angel, *Dianathan* (Eusebius, *Praep. ev.* 9.30.6), although this PN may be a corruption of *dia Nathan*, "through Nathan" (Wacholder 1974: 142).

"as he was about to destroy" *(khšḥyt)*. So MT and LXX *(hōs exolothreuen)*. Instead of *k-* many Heb. MSS and Tg. preface the prep. *b-* *(bhšḥyt)*. Rudolph (1955: 142) emends by adding the suf., *khšḥytw.* The phrase is lacking in MT 2 Sam 24:16.

"the destroying messenger" (למלאך המשחית). Thus MT and LXX. 2 Sam 24:16 "the messenger destroying the people" (למלאך המשחית העם).

"enough! Now" *(rb ʿth)*. So MT Chronicles and Samuel. LXX has the 3rd-per. sg. pres. impv. "let it suffice you" *(hikanousthō soi)*.

"and the messenger of Yhwh was standing by the threshing floor of Ornan the Jebusite" *(wmlʾk yhwh ʿwmd ʿm grn ʾrnn hybwsy)*. Paralleled in 4QSam[a] [*wmlʾk y*]*ḣwh ʿwmd* ʿ[*m grn* ʾ]*rnʾ h*[*yb*]*ẇśy*. MT 2 Sam 24:16 is slightly different, "and the messenger of Yhwh was by the threshing floor of Araunah the Jebusite" *(wmlʾk yhwh hyh ʿm grn hʾwrnh hybwsy)*.

"Ornan" *(ʾrnn)*. LXX *Orna*; Tg. *ʾrwn* ("Arwan"). MT 2 Sam 24:16 is corrupt; Kethib *hʾwrnh* (Qere *ʾrwnh*); cf. *ʾrnyh* in 2 Sam 24:18 and *ʾrwnh* in 2 Sam 24:20. 4QSam[a] *ʾrnʾ*.

21:16. "and David lifted his eyes and saw the messenger of Yhwh standing between the earth and the heavens with his sword drawn in his hand, outstretched against Jerusalem. Then David and the elders, dressed in sackcloth *(mksym)*, fell on their faces." So Chronicles and Josephus (*Ant.* 7.327). 4QSam[a] is quite close to Chronicles, "and David lifted his eyes and saw the messenger of Yhwh standing between the earth and the heavens with his sword drawn in his hand, outstretched against Jerusalem. Then David and the elders fell on their faces ([*wypl dwyd whzqnym ʿl pn*]*yhm*), covering themselves *(mt*[*ksym*]*)* in sackcloth." MT 2 Sam 24:17 "and David said to Yhwh, when he saw the messenger striking the people." The statements were lost to MT 2 Sam 24:16 by haplography (*homoioarkton* from *wyśʾ* to *wyʾmr dwd* at the beginning of 2 Sam 24:17 and 1 Chr 21:17; Cross 1961: 141).

"between the earth and the heavens." So MT and LXX. A few Heb. MSS, Syr., and Arab. have the inverse, "between the heavens and the earth." The reference in Eupolemus also speaks of the angel as above *(epanō)* the place (Eusebius, *Praep. ev.* 9.30.5).

21:17. "David said to God, 'Was it not I, I who said to number the people?' " So MT and LXX. MT 2 Sam 24:17 reads simply, "and he [David] said, 'Behold.' " See the following TEXTUAL NOTE.

"I was the one who sinned and did great evil" *(ʾny hwʾ ʾšr-ḥṭʾty whrʿ hrʿwty)*. I read with MT. LXX[B] *kai egō eimi ho hamartōn* (LXX[L] adds *kai*) *kakopoiōn ekakopoiēsa*, "I am the sinner; I committed iniquity." It is unclear whether, as Allen (1974a: 50) argues, the translator is using the ptc. to paraphrase his Heb. *Vorlage*. MT 2 Sam 24:17, "I have sinned and I have acted wickedly" *(hnh ʾnky ḥṭʾty wʾnky hʿwyty)*. 4QSam[a] bears some similarities to LXX 21:17, [ʾ]*nky hrʿh hrʿty*, "I the shepherd did evil" (cf. LXX[L] and OL Samuel, as well as Josephus, *Ant.*

7.328). McCarter (1984: 507) thinks that *hrʿh* was lost to MT Samuel and that an original *hrʿty* became *hʿwty* through confusion between *wāw* and *rêš* and the occurrence of metathesis. But Rofé (1990: 118) argues that MT 2 Sam 24:17 assimilates toward the formula found in 1 Kgs 8:47, "we have sinned and committed iniquity" *(ḥṭʾnw whʿwynw)*. Cf. Ps 106:6; Job 33:27; Dan 9:5.

"these sheep." Literally, "these of the flock."

"O Yhwh my God, may your hand be upon me and upon the house of my father. But as for your people, let [them] not be subject to a plague" *(yhwh ʾlhy thy nʾ ydk by wbbyt ʾby wbʿmk lʾ lmgph)*. So MT and LXX*. MT 2 Sam 24:17, "may your hand be upon me and upon the house of my father" *(thy nʾ ydk by wbbyt ʾby)*, lacks the final clauses of 1 Chr 21:17 (see NOTE).

"to a plague" *(lmgph)*. So MT. LXX *eis apōleian*, "for destruction." Since this is the only case in which LXX renders *apōleia* for the noun *mgph* (Hatch and Redpath 1897: 151c–152a), it raises the possibility of a different *Vorlage*. In v. 22, LXX has *plēgē* for MT's *mgph*.

21:18. "then the messenger of Yhwh said to Gad to say to David that David should go up to establish an altar to Yhwh on the threshing floor of Ornan the Jebusite." Chronicles displays a more elaborate relay of instructions (involving the divine messenger) than that depicted in Samuel. 2 Sam 24:18 simply reports, "and Gad came to David on that day and said to him, 'Go up, establish an altar to Yhwh on the threshing floor of Araunah the Jebusite.' "

21:19. "in accordance with the command" *(bdbr)*. The versions and 2 Sam 24:19 read the expected *kdbr* (cf. *bdbr* in Num 31:16 [P]; 1 Kgs 13:5, 9, 32).

"who spoke in the name of Yhwh" *(ʾšr dbr bšm yhwh)*. So MT and LXX. MT 2 Sam 24:19 "which Yhwh commanded" *(kʾšr ṣwh yhwh)*.

21:20. "when Ornan turned" *(wyšb)*. So MT and LXX. Vg. *(porro Ornan cum suspexisset)* follows MT 2 Sam 24:20 (and 4QSam[a]) in reading *wyšqp*.

"the king" *(hmlk)*. Reading with one Heb. MS and LXX 21:20. So also MT 2 Sam 24:20, and Josephus (*Ant.* 7.13). MT 1 Chr 21:20 "the messenger" *(hmlʾk)*.

"and four *(wbʾrbʿt)* of his sons with him." Reading with MT and LXX. Some (e.g., Rudolph 1955: 148) favor emending to "and when (his sons) saw (him)," *wbrʾtw (ʾtw)*. MT 2 Sam 24:20 reads differently, "and his servants coming over to him" *(wʾt-ʿbdyw ʿbrym ʿlyw)*.

"hid themselves, covering themselves with sackcloth" *(mtḥbʾym mtksym bśqym)*. A reconstruction. MT simply reads "hid themselves," while LXX[B] $c_2$ transliterate the Heb. *methachab(e)in*. LXX[AN] *krybomenoi;* e *kryptomenoi;* $ye_2$ (and Arm.) *kryboumenous; bb′ poreumenous.* Supposing a haplography *(homoioteleuton)*, Rudolph (1955: 148) adds "from underneath the sheaves," *mittaḥat hāʾălummîm*. The phrase is lacking in MT 2 Sam 24:20, but as reconstructed by McCarter (1984: 507), it forms part of a longer lemma in 4QSam[a] *[mtḥbʾym mtksym] bśqym*.

"meanwhile Ornan continued threshing out the wheat" *(wʾrnn dš ḥṭym)*. So MT and LXX 21:20 and 4QSam[a] *(wʾrnʾ dš ḥṭym)*. Lacking in MT 2 Sam 24:20.

21:21. "then David came to Ornan *(ʿd-ʾrnn)*." So MT and LXX. Some emend to "came to the threshing floor *(ʿd-hgrn)*." The entire clause is wanting in MT 2 Sam

24:20. 4QSam[a] is fragmentary, but space considerations would seem to require some such statement.

"when Ornan looked and saw David" *(wybṭ ʾrnn wyrʾ ʾt-dwyd)*. So MT and LXX[L]. These words do not appear in LXX[AB] *kai Orna exēlthen ek tēs halō*, "and Ornan went forth from the threshing floor." But it is possible that the words found in MT and LXX[L] were lost to LXX[AB] by haplography. Indeed, given a possible reconstruction of 4QSam[a] ([*wybṭ ʾrnʾ wyrʾ ʾt-dwd*]), a haplography seems likely.

"he went forth from the threshing floor." Reading with MT and LXX. Lacking in Syr. MT 2 Sam 24:20 "and Araunah went forth."

"and bowed before David, nose to the ground." So MT and LXX. MT 2 Sam 24:20 "and bowed before the king, his nose to the ground."

21:22. "and David said to Ornan." MT 2 Sam 24:21 prefaces a query, "and Araunah said, 'why has my lord the king come to his servant?' "

"give me the place of the threshing floor that I may build upon it an altar to Yhwh" *(tnh-ly mqwm hgrn wʾbnh-bw mzbḥ lyhwh)*. So MT and LXX. 2 Sam 24:21 "to purchase from you the threshing floor to build an altar to Yhwh" *(lqnwt mʿmk ʾt-hgrn lbnwt mzbḥ lyhwh)*.

"at the full price *(ksp mlʾ)* give it to me." Reading with MT and LXX. Lacking in Samuel. The terminology in Chronicles reflects the influence of Gen 23:8–20, Abraham's purchase of the cave of Machpelah (Bertheau 1873; Williamson 1982b; Zakovitch 1985). The phrase *ksp mlʾ* is found only in 1 Chr 21:22, 24 and Gen 23:9.

21:23. "take (it) for yourself *(qḥ-lk)*, and may my lord the king do *(wyʿś)*." Thus MT and LXX 21:23, as well as many witnesses to LXX 2 Sam 24:22. MT 2 Sam 24:22 "may my lord the king take and go up" *(wyqḥ wyʿl)*.

"see I give the oxen" *(rʾh ntty hbqr)*. Thus MT and LXX. MT 2 Sam 24:22 lacks "I give." Cf. Gen 23:11, *hśdh ntty lk whmʿrh ʾšr-bw lk ntty lʿyny bny-ʿmy nttyh lk*, "the field I give to you and the cave which is within it I give to you in the sight of my people."

"for the burnt offerings." Reading with MT. LXX follows MT 2 Sam 24:22 in reading the sg. "for the burnt offering."

"the threshing sledges" *(whmwrgym)*. LXX[B] has the sg. *kai to arotron*.

"for wood" *(lʿṣym)*. MT 2 Sam 24:22 reads more expansively *wkly hbqr lʿṣym*, "and the gear of the oxen for wood" (NJPS).

"the wheat for the cereal offering." Lacking in MT 2 Sam 24:22.

"all of these I give" *(hkl ntty)*. MT 2 Sam 24:23, "all of these (things) Araunah gives, O king, for the king" *(hkl ntn ʾrwnh hmlk lmlk)*. MT 2 Sam 24:23 continues with, "and Araunah said to the king, 'may Yhwh your God favor you.' " This statement is not found in Chronicles. Chronicles does not distinguish between the god of Ornan and the god of David. Both the reference by Ornan to "Yhwh your God" (2 Sam 24:23) and the reference by David to "Yhwh my God" (2 Sam 24:23) do not appear in Chronicles.

21:24. "at full price" *(bksp mlʾ)*. MT 2 Sam 24:24 *mʾwtk bmḥyr*, "from you at a price." The difference in terminology, *ksp mlʾ* vs. *mḥyr*, is deliberate (3rd TEXTUAL NOTE to v. 22).

"for I shall not lift up to Yhwh what is yours" *(ky lʾ ʾśʾ ʾšr-lk lyhwh)*. So MT and LXX. MT 2 Sam 24:24 "I shall not lift up to Yhwh my God" *(lʾ ʾʿlh lyhwh ʾlhy)*.

"nor offer the burnt offerings" *(wĕhaʿălôt ʿôlâ)*. So MT 21:24 and 2 Sam 24:24 *(ʿōlôt)*. One Heb. MS 21:24 reads *wĕhaʿălitî*, while LXX has the inf. *tou anenegkai* with *holokautōsin*. Tg. 21:24 is similar.

"for nothing" *(hinnām)*. So MT 21:24 and MT 2 Sam 24:24. LXX 1 Chr 21:24 "as a gift" *(dōrean)*.

21:25. "and David gave to Ornan." MT 2 Sam 24:24 "and David purchased."

"600 shekels of gold." Thus MT and LXX. The reading of Syr., "50 shekels of gold," assimilates toward the number of 2 Sam 24:24, "50 shekels of silver."

"to Ornan for the place" *(lʾrnn bmqwm)*. So MT and LXX$^{AN}$ *(peri tou topou)*. LXX$^{B}$ (and $mc_2$) *en tō topō*. Instead of referring to a site, 2 Sam 24:24 refers to "the threshing floor and the oxen" (2nd TEXTUAL NOTE to v. 22).

21:26. "he called upon Yhwh." So MT and LXX. Tg. "he prayed before Yhwh." The statement is lacking in 2 Sam 24:25, perhaps due to haplography (*homoioarkton* from *wyqrʾ* to *wyʿtr*).

"and he answered him with fire from the heavens upon the altar of burnt offering." The divine response differs in Samuel (NOTE). After depicting David's sacrifice of burnt offerings and offerings of well-being, Samuel states that Yhwh accepted David's "supplication for the land" (2 Sam 24:25).

"the altar of burnt offering *(mzbḥ hʿlh)* and (it) consumed the burnt offering *(wtʾkl ʾt-hʿlh)*." Following LXX (cf. Syr. and Arab.) *kai katanalōsen tēn holokautōsin*, "and consumed the burnt offering." The clause *wtʾkl ʾt-hʿlh* has been lost from MT by haplography *(homoioteleuton)*. In this instance literary considerations shed light on this text (see NOTE). It is likely that the author is imitating the verbiage of older passages: "and fire went forth from before Yhwh upon the altar and consumed the burnt offering *(wtʾkl ʿl-hmzbḥh ʾt-hʿlh)* and the fatty portions upon the altar" (Lev 9:24); "and the fire of Yhwh fell and consumed the burnt offering *(wtʾkl ʾt-hʿlh)*" (1 Kgs 18:38); "the fire from heaven consumed the burnt offering *(wtʾkl ʾt-hʿlh)* as well as the sacrifices, and the glory *(kābôd)* of Yhwh filled the house" (2 Chr 7:1).

21:27. "then Yhwh spoke to the messenger and he returned his sword to its sheath." Again, the version of Samuel is different, stating simply that "the plague was averted from Israel" (2 Sam 24:25).

21:29. "the high place." So MT and LXX, which transliterates *bamōth* (LXX$^{B}$) or *bama* (LXX$^{A}$). A few Heb. MSS and LXX$^{Aal}$ add explicating, "which" (= *ʾšr*).

22:1. "this will be the House of Yhwh God" (זה הוא בית יהוה האלהים). The Heb. could be more literally translated, "this is it, the house of Yhwh the God."

"the altar." Reading המזבח. MT מזבח has lost the initial *hê* after זה. Cf. LXX *to thysiastērion*. The whole clause could be more literally translated, "this is the altar of the burnt offering for Israel."

# NOTES

21:1. "an adversary" *(śāṭān)*. This is the first and most famous difference between the texts of 2 Sam 24 and 1 Chr 21. Why does the Chronicler attribute the idea for the census to an enemy *(śāṭān)* and not to Yhwh (2 Sam 24:1)? The use of *śāṭān* instead of Yhwh cannot be convincingly attributed to a shift in metaphysics from the preexilic to the postexilic age, because Chronicles nowhere else evinces an inherently dualistic view of reality. The Chronicler is as much of a monist as the Deuteronomists are (Knoppers 1994e: 229–54). A more convincing explanation for the switch in subjects emerges after one considers the challenge that the Samuel narrative posed for the Chronicler's ideology (Knoppers 1995b). For the Chronicler, musters are an appropriate feature of national administration (1 Chr 9:1; 11:11; 12:24; 23:3; 27:1–34; 2 Chr 2:1 [ET 2:2]; 17:13–19; 25:5; 26:11–13; 31:12–19; Wright 1993: 90–92). Moreover, the Chronicler was a firm believer in the principle of proportionality in divine-human relations (Ben Zvi 1993). Given these facts, the author risked presenting his audience with an untenable scenario. If he did not alter his *Vorlage*, Yhwh would be prompting David to do something good and then punishing him for doing it.

"took his stand" (ויעמד). The context of this narrative differs markedly from the context in Samuel. There the census and plague narrative is introduced by the words, "and Yhwh again became angry with Israel and incited David to number Israel." The author of 2 Sam 24 is alluding to an earlier instance of divine wrath against the people: the story of the famine in 2 Sam 21 (Caquot and de Robert 1994: 575–89, 627–43). The situation varies greatly in Chronicles. Whereas in Samuel Yhwh induces David to number Israel to implement Yhwh's anger against the people, in Chronicles there is no sign of divine displeasure until Joab implements David's command to undertake a census (21:7). Nor is there any earlier famine or national catastrophe in David's reign. The idea for the census stems from one of David's unnamed adversaries, who "took his stand against Israel" (ויעמד על-ישׂראל; cf. Judg 6:31; Ezra 10:15). Having just experienced a string of impressive military victories against the Ammonites, Edomites, Arameans, Moabites, and the Philistines (1 Chr 18–20), David uncritically falls prey to the designs of one of his opponents. This difference from Samuel accomplishes, therefore, two things. By attributing the census to the instigation of an anonymous adversary, the Chronicler simultaneously excuses Yhwh from any responsibility for the census and casts a pall over David's entire plan (contra Curtis and Madsen 1910: 246). In the context of the larger narrative, the issue becomes not so much the census as that one of David's enemies has successfully induced him to order such a maneuver. The Chronicler's narrative underscores David's accountability.

"and incited" *(wyst)*. The use of the verb *syt* (always in the *hipʿil*) usually carries negative connotations in Chronicles (2 Chr 18:2; 32:11, 15; Ackroyd 1973a: 144). Even if one were to allow a more neutral translation of *syt*, "to persuade" (2 Chr 18:31; Wright 1993: 93), the use of the verb with this particular subject *(śāṭān)* suggests that the circumstances surrounding this particular census are highly suspicious. David's census is not a valiant response to the (military) threat posed by a foe, but the product of that anonymous enemy's activity.

"David." Gunn and Fewell (1993: 125–28) think that, because of the corporate emphasis in the introduction and conclusion to the census narrative (2 Sam 24:1, 25), the author of 2 Sam 24 displays a primary interest in Israel. If so, this only amplifies the contrast with 1 Chr 21:1–22:1. In both the introduction and conclusion, the figure of David is prominent (21:1; 22:1).

"a census of Israel." Scholars disagree about why a census should incur divine wrath (Exod 30:11–16; Num 1:2–54; 26:2–65). McCarter (1984: 512–14) provides a helpful survey of opinion on the interpretation of the story in Samuel. Vis-à-vis the story in Chronicles, the question has been raised whether there is a problem with the census at all. Large numbers of people and troops are usually an indication of divine blessing in Chronicles (Wright 1993: 89–92). In the view of Wright (1993), Joab, not David, is to blame for Israel's crisis. By failing to complete the census (21:6), Joab jeopardizes the fate of his nation (cf. 27:23–24). Innocent David vicariously accepts divine punishment to save his kingdom. Nevertheless, there is no clear indication that the Chronicler blames Joab for the disaster that befalls Israel (Bailey 1994: 87–90). Moreover, the Chronicler, as we have seen, actually accentuates David's stigma more than the narrator of 2 Sam 24 does. Even more so in Chronicles than in Samuel, David is guilty. Johnstone (1998: 128–40) contends for a strong link to Exod 30, arguing that David failed to give proper consideration to the Tabernacle and the Levites. In this line of interpretation, the problem was (again) not the census itself, but the fact that David failed to require, as Exod 30:12 stipulates, that Israelites submit a ransom (כפר), while they are being mustered. Two questions immediately arise, however. First, Chronicles mentions other musters (1st NOTE to v. 1)—why do none of these fail for want of a levy or expiation payment? Second, why are Benjamin and Levi not spared since they did not participate in the census at all? In brief, Wright and Johnstone insightfully draw attention to the positive functions of musters in Chronicles, but one has also to recognize that the Samuel story may have carried a certain force, in spite of the changes the Chronicler made to it. In his rewriting, the Chronicler shifts attention from the census itself to the circumstances surrounding the census. In Chronicles the context of the pan-Israel muster becomes highly problematic for King David (see previous NOTES).

21:2. "from Beer-sheba to Dan." The southern and northern limits of the Israelite kingdom. On the Chronicler's south to north orientation, see also 1 Chr 13:5; 2 Chr 19:4; 30:5 (cf. Neh 11:30).

21:3. "is not my lord the king?" Joab's objections are more pointed in Chronicles than the diplomatically worded objections are in Samuel (TEXTUAL NOTES to v. 3). In Chronicles, Joab's role as second in command (1st NOTE to 11:6) is clear. He warns his superior that the proposed census will have negative ramifications for Israel. In this manner, the Chronicler lays the burden of responsibility for the census squarely on David's shoulders.

"guilt upon Israel?" Only in Chronicles does Joab explicitly describe David's plan as bringing "guilt (*ʾāšmâ*) upon Israel." The terminology used in Chronicles is significant. Joüon 1938: 454–59) and Milgrom (1976: 3–12) observe that the term *ʾāšām* can connote both the wrong and the retribution. In other words, David's wrongdoing will inevitably lead to punishment. See also the more general comments of Johnstone (1986: 119–26; 1998: 127–131).

21:5. "the people" *(hāʿām)*. In the sense of the people under arms, the army (2nd NOTE to 19:7). See further the 3rd NOTE to v. 5.

"1,100,000 men . . . while Judah had 470,000 men." In the former instance, the number totals more than the "800,000 warriors" (and the "500,000 men") mentioned in MT 2 Sam 24:9. The Chronicler may have drawn a number of inferences from his source. If he thought that the "800,000" and the "500,000" represented a total of 100,000 for each tribe (twelve tribes, plus the tribe of Levi), he may have concluded that the deletion of Levi and Benjamin should reduce the census total by 200,000 warriors (Curtis and Madsen 1910: 248; R. Klein 1997: 275). This calculation is based on the assumption that the figure for Israel in Samuel ("800,000") reflects only the population of the northern tribes, while that of Chronicles ("1,100,000") reflects Israel and Judah together. Yet Chronicles also mentions "470,000" men for Judah. Some (e.g., R. Klein 1997: 275) think this latter notation represents a later addition to the text, but it might also be the case that the figures in the Chronicler's *Vorlage* were not the same as those that appear in MT 2 Sam 24:9 (TEXTUAL NOTES to v. 5).

"who drew the sword." The text makes clear that the particular kind of census on which Joab embarks is martial in nature. David wishes to determine troop strength in his kingdom. The assemblage of warriors to David's cause (11:11–12:39) is a prominent theme in the Chronicler's presentation of David's early career.

21:6. "But Levi and Benjamin he did not count among them." Only in Chronicles does Joab refuse to complete the muster. Whereas Samuel provides a detailed presentation of Joab punctilously implementing the muster throughout the entire land (2 Sam 24:4–8), the shorter version of the muster in Chronicles presents Joab as deliberately excluding Benjamin and Levi because "the command of the king was abhorrent to Joab" (21:6). It is unclear why Joab excludes these two particular tribes. It may be that Joab excludes Levi because this tribe was excepted from being numbered among the Israelites for military service (Num 1:49; cf. 2:33; Benzinger 1901: 62–63). Benjamin may have been omitted because the holy site of Jerusalem was considered to lie within its borders. But with respect to Levi, this tribe is counted among those who supply warriors to support David (1 Chr 12:27–29). Whatever the reasons for the omissions, the point is that Joab refused to provide David with full compliance because he bristled at the order itself. In this manner, Joab sought to undermine David's command.

21:7. "this thing was evil in the sight of God and so he struck Israel *(wyk ʾt-yśrʾl)*." The circumstances by which David realizes his guilt differ from those in Samuel. The evaluative comment that "this thing was evil in the sight of God" is lacking in 2 Sam 24:10. Moreover, 2 Sam 24:10 has David repent, "and the heart of David struck him" *(wyk lb dwd ʾtw)*, sometime after he had numbered the people. In Chronicles, it is Yhwh who deems the census to be evil and strikes Israel.

Warned by Joab that his census would bring guilt upon Israel, David requires an overt, albeit unspecified, display of divine displeasure against Israel to realize his error. Only then does David confess any wrongdoing.

21:8. "I have sinned greatly in doing this thing." The reference to "this thing" *(haddābār hazzeh)* alludes to the offense mentioned in the previous verse: "this thing" (*haddābār hazzeh*; v. 7), suggesting that this particular census is improper (Bailey 1994: 88–89). In v. 17, the same point recurs: David unambiguously reaffirms that he alone is to blame for the calamity that has befallen his people and threatens to overwhelm Jerusalem.

"forgive the transgression of your servant." The Chronicler, like the author of Samuel, has David openly confess his guilt and request that Yhwh remit his misdeed (2 Sam 24:10). David is not passive. Unlike Saul, who dies in his rebellion (1 Chr 10:13–14), and Aḥaz, who stubbornly compounds his guilt (2 Chr 28), David is immediately repentant. He does not attempt to shift the blame to others. In accordance with the psalmist's admonition not to ignore one's transgression (Ps 32:3–5), the king confronts the consequences of his actions. Note how pointed his admissions of wrongdoing are: "I have sinned greatly *(ḥāṭāʾtî mĕʾōd)*. . . . I have acted very foolishly *(niskaltî mĕʾōd)*."

"I have acted very foolishly." This is not the first time that David has erred (in Chronicles). At the beginning of David's reign, he dared his warriors to fetch him a drink of water from the cistern in his hometown of Bethleḥem (11:17). When the deed was accomplished, David realized his folly, refused to drink it, and offered the water as a libation to Yhwh (11:18). In both cases, David responds appropriately to (potential) disasters of his own making.

21:9. "Yhwh spoke to Gad [the] seer *(ḥōzeh)*." The terminology is significant. In Chronicles many, but not all, kings have a prophet *(nābîʾ)* or a prophetess *(nĕbîʾâ)*:

| | |
|---|---|
| David | (1 Chr 16:22; 17:1; 29:29) |
| Solomon | (2 Chr 9:29) |
| Reḥoboam | (2 Chr 12:5, 15) |
| Abijah | (2 Chr 13:22) |
| Asa | (2 Chr 15:8) |
| Jehoshaphaṭ | (2 Chr 18:5, 6, 9, 11, 12, 21, 22; 20:20) |
| Jehoram | (2 Chr 21:12) |
| Joash | (2 Chr 24:19) |
| Amaziah | (2 Chr 25:15, 16) |
| Uzziah | (2 Chr 26:22) |
| Ḥezeqiah | (2 Chr 28:9; 29:25; 32:20, 32) |
| Josiah | (2 Chr 34:22; 35:18) |
| Zedeqiah | (2 Chr 36:12) |
| General | (2 Chr 36:16) |

If a second prophetic figure is mentioned, that figure will usually be called a seer (1 Chr 21:9; 25:5; 29:29; 2 Chr 9:29; 12:15; 19:2; 29:25, 30; 33:18, 19; 35:15) or a visionary (*rōʾeh*; 1 Chr 9:22; 26:28; 29:29; 2 Chr 16:7, 10; Micheel 1983). The typology is fairly consistent. Conversely, it is abnormal for a king to have a seer or a visionary, but not a prophet. Nathan is David's prophet, while Gad is usually mentioned as his seer. The different terminology need not denote a hierarchy and in no way diminishes Gad's status. According to the Chronicler, Gad "spoke in the name of Yhwh" (v. 19).

21:10. "three (choices)." A contrast has been drawn between the much-belated repentance of Saul in Samuel and David's immediate acknowledgment of his guilt (2 Sam 12:13; 1 Chr 21:8; Sternberg 1987: 512–14). But there is also a contrast between the treatment of David following his sin with Bathsheba and the treatment of David following his implementation of the census. In both 2 Sam 12:13 and 2 Sam 24:10, David requests that his sins be remitted. Nathan accedes to this request (2 Sam 12:13) even as he pronounces that the child will die (2 Sam 12:14). But Gad never directly responds to David's plea for forgiveness in either Samuel or Chronicles. Instead, he offers David a choice of three punishments.

"choose one of them for yourself." The divine command to Gad is elliptical. The punishments are not fully described until Gad communicates with David (Sternberg 1987: 384).

21:12. "a three-year famine." The punishments described by Gad—three years of famine, three months of subjugation by enemies, three days of pestilence—underscore David's national importance. Indeed, the collective nature of these penalties reflects a cardinal tenet of ancient Near Eastern royal ideology, that a people may experience weal or woe contingent upon the standing of its king with the divine realm (Knoppers 1994a). If Israel earlier benefited from its election of David to be its king, Israel now suffers for his error.

"three days of the sword of Yhwh accompanied by a plague in the land and a messenger of Yhwh wreaking destruction in every territory of Israel." The Chronicler's version of the three options stresses the choice between human punishment and divine punishment (Micheel 1983: 22–23). By contrast, Samuel's third option is simply couched as "a plague in your land" (2 Sam 24:13). In Chronicles, as opposed to Samuel, there is also a close correlation between what Gad predicts (in this choice) and what actually happens.

21:13. "David replied to Gad, 'I am in great distress.' " Both Samuel and Chronicles present David as being in a state of considerable apprehension (2 Sam 24:14). But both texts also present David as an astute participant in the negotiations that determine his fate.

"let me fall into the hand of Yhwh." The third option (see 2nd NOTE to v. 12) is rather severe but David picks it anyway because he would rather fall under the discipline of Yhwh than under the discipline of his human enemies. In this respect, David has learned his lesson. Rather than fall prey again to the designs of one of his opponents (21:1), the king places his nation's fate in the hands of it's God.

"his compassion is exceedingly great." David's reasoning for choosing a divinely administered penalty—divine mercy—is well-founded, given the character of Yhwh as "a God compassionate and gracious, slow to anger, and abounding in loyalty and truth" (Exod 34:6; NOTES to v. 15).

"let me not fall." The Chronicler arranges David's response chiastically, thus calling attention to the quality of divine compassion as the determining factor in his choice.

a let me fall
 b into the hand of Yhwh,
  c because his compassion is exceedingly great.
 b′ but into the hand of man
a′ let me not fall.

21:14. "there fell from among the Israelites 70,000 people." That Israel, and not David himself, directly suffers for David's crime is a matter of debate among the early interpreters (e.g., Tg. 1 Chr 21:13; *b. Yoma* 22b).

21:15. "Yhwh saw and repented of the evil." Earlier David repented after Yhwh struck Israel. Now Yhwh, upon seeing the destruction caused by his messenger, repents (*nḥm*) as well. Given the earlier divine decree to punish David, the question naturally arises as to what Yhwh saw that changed his mind. The Targum offers two answers: the ashes from the binding of Isaac (and therefore the covenant with Abraham) and the heavenly sanctuary (Le Déaut and Robert 1971b: 60; McIvor 1994: 116; cf. Tg. 2 Chr 6:2).

"Enough! Now stay your hand!" Unbeknownst to David, Yhwh halts his messenger's killing spree before that messenger destroys Jerusalem.

21:16. "his sword drawn." Given his location, "standing between the earth and the heavens," the messenger of Yhwh (*mal'ak yhwh*) is very much a threat to David and Jerusalem. See also Num 22:22–35; Josh 5:13–15; 2 Chr 32:21 (Mosis 1973: 115–16; Sugimoto 1990: 63–65).

"outstretched against Jerusalem." Even with the repentance of Yhwh, it is not entirely clear, as some have supposed, that the threat to Jerusalem has completely passed. David is unaware of Yhwh's repentance. Hence, he proceeds under the assumption that Jerusalem is the next target of the divine agent's wrath. Those commentators who would either excise 21:16ff. as a later gloss or view the information provided in these verses as incidental to the progress of the story underestimate the importance of the different roles played by the characters in this narrative (*pace* von Rad 1930: 101; Willi 1972: 174). The reader is informed that Yhwh constrained the activities of his messenger (21:18), but there is no indication that David knows anything about this development. From David's perspective, the threat remains until Yhwh tells his messenger to sheath his sword (21:27). In Chronicles there are two stages in the cessation of the pestilence (Rofé 1990: 114–15).

"David and the elders, dressed in sackcloth." Given that David witnesses Yhwh's envoy with an unsheathed sword, perched between heaven and earth, in a menacing pose against Jerusalem, it is no wonder that David and the elders fall on their faces. In the context of this apparent threat to the population of Jerusalem, one finds David again interceding with God, pleading with him to reconsider his plan of destruction.

21:17. "I was the one who sinned and did great evil" (*'ny hw' 'šr-ḥṭ'ty whr' hr'wty*). The contrite David of Chronicles is even more explicit about his responsibility than the David of Samuel. In MT Samuel David confesses, "I have sinned and I have acted wickedly" (*hnh 'nky ḥṭ'ty w'nky h'wyty*). But in Chronicles David's plea to Yhwh on behalf of his people is more pointed. David reminds God that it was he (David) who issued the command to number Israel and that it was he (David) who "sinned and did great evil."

"these sheep, what have they done?" Like the plaintiff of Ps 51:5 [ET 51:3], who confesses, "I know of my rebellions, my sin is continually before me," David reaffirms that he committed the crime. But he also questions the punishment. David proposes to attenuate the negative effects that the king can have on the fate of his people as a nexus between the heavenly and earthly realms. In both Samuel and Chronicles, David implores Yhwh to vent his wrath against the perpetrator (David) and not against the innocent populace of Jerusalem. In this regard, the grounds for David's appeal resonate with the Chronicler's standard of justice (B. Kelly 1996), which some have simplistically referred to as a "theology of immediate retribution."

"may your hand be upon me and upon the house of my father" *(thy nʾ ydk by wbbyt ʾby)*. Along with the authors of Deuteronomy (7:9–10; 24:16), Jeremiah (31:28–30), and Ezekiel (18; 33:12–20), David makes a case for limiting the scope of divinely administered punishment of humans to the guilty parties themselves. Or if vicarious punishment (Exod 20:4–6; cf. 34:6–7) is to characterize divine-human relations, suffering for the sins of others should be limited to the members of one's family (Levinson 1992: 46–61). Hence, in this case, the king ingeniously requests that he not be considered above the law, but in accordance with it (cf. Deut 17:14–20; 1 Sam 12:14–25).

"let [them] not be subject to a plague." David's plea manifests a chiastic design:

a  but as for these sheep, what have they done?
  b  O Yhwh my God, may your hand be upon me
  bʹ  and upon the house of my father.
aʹ  but as for your people, let (them) not be subject to a plague.

This feature of David's legacy, his ability as an intercessor, was credited to him by various early interpreters: Sir 47:11; *Miqṣat Maʿaśê ha-Torah* (4Q398 14–17 ii 25–26); *Pss. Sol.* 17:21; *Apoc. Sedr.* 14:4; *Midr. Ps.* 3:4; 6:9; 26:2; 51:3; 100:2; 116:8; *b. ʿAbod. Zar.* 4b/5a; *b. Ḥul.* 89a; *b. Yoma* 22b; *Pirqe R. El.* 17; 43. In the Qurʾān, David appears as an exemplary penitent (s. 38:10–27) and as representative of Judaism, alongside Jesus as representative of Christianity (s. 5:78).

21:18. "said to Gad to say to David that David should go up to establish an altar to Yhwh." The divine authorization for the altar is more explicit here than in 2 Sam 24:18. In Samuel Gad simply tells David to establish an altar for Yhwh at the threshing floor, but in 1 Chr 21:18 the messenger of Yhwh tells Gad to inform David that David should construct an altar.

21:19. "in accordance with the command of Gad." If the Chronicler accentuates David's responsibility for the census and his intercession on behalf of his people, he also accentuates David's diligence in following the directions of the divine messenger.

21:22. "give me the place *(māqôm)* of the threshing floor." In the Chronicler's version of the negotiations between David and Ornan, David repeatedly refers to the threshing floor as a *māqôm* (vv. 22, 25), a term that in certain contexts can designate a sacred precinct or sanctuary, not only in Heb. (e.g., Deut 12:5, 11, 14, 18, 21, 26; 14:23, 24, 25; 15:20; Josh 9:27) but also in Phoen. and perhaps in Pun. (Tomback 1978: 195–96; Krahmalkov 2000: 308). The choice of terminology does not seem to be accidental. In the introduction to his description of Solomon's construction of the Temple, the Chronicler avers that Solomon built this edifice on Mount Moriah, the place *(māqôm)* where Yhwh appeared to David at the threshing floor of Ornan the Jebusite (2 Chr 3:1). Hence, the Chronicler draws a connection between the choice of this site and the Aqedah (Gen 22; Kalimi 1990b: 345–62). Josephus (*Ant.* 7.333–34) and the Targum make the connection with Genesis 22 explicit.

21:23. "all of these I give" *(hakkōl nātattî)*. The narrative plays on the different nuances of the verb *ntn* (NOTE to v. 22; NOTE to v. 25). David wants Ornan to give (i.e., sell) him the threshing floor (twice in v. 22), but Ornan raises the stakes in the transaction by repeatedly volunteering to give (i.e., donate) not only the threshing floor but also the wood and oxen for the sacrifices (v. 23). Eventually, David gives (i.e., pays) Ornan 600 shekels of gold for the entire package (v. 25). A similar play on *ntn* is found in the story of Abraham's negotiations (Gen 23:8–20).

21:24. "no, I shall indeed buy them" *(lō' kî-qānōh 'eqneh)*. The king has to make his intentions clear (see previous NOTE). Both 21:22–24 and 2 Sam 24:21–24 depict David demanding repeatedly to pay for the threshing floor, the ox, and the wood so that he might avert the outbreak of a plague among the people of Jerusalem. As Williamson (1982b: 149–50) and Zakovitch (1985: 181) have shown, the terminology used to describe David's land purchase (1 Chr 21:22–25), even more so than that used in Samuel (2 Sam 24:22–24), replicates the terminology used to describe Abraham's purchase of the cave of Machpelah (Gen 23:8–20). I use the term *replicate,* rather than *assimilate,* because the similarities between 21:22–25 and Gen 23:8–20 seem to result from deliberate authorial (and not scribal) activity. There are also some parallels between David's encounter with Ornan and the meeting between the divine messenger and Gideon at Ophrah (Judg 6:11–24; Willi 1972: 157).

"at full price" *(bksp ml')*. Like Abraham negotiating with the Hittite Ephron for the cave of Machpelah, the Chronicler's David repeatedly insists that he pay full price for the threshing floor of Ornan the Jebusite. In purchasing the threshing floor of Ornan the Jebusite, David, no less than Abraham before him, must own the property (and hence secure the legal right to the land) before he can carry out his obligation.

21:25. "David gave *(ntn)* 600 shekels of gold to Ornan." Fifty shekels of gold for each of the twelve tribes of Israel (Rashi). The "full price" David disburses to build an altar and offer burnt offerings at this site—600 shekels of gold—dwarfs the price paid by either the David of Samuel (50 shekels of silver) or the Abraham of Genesis (400 shekels of silver; Gen 23:15–16). The exorbitant payment for the threshing floor highlights the significance a conscientious David ascribes to securing this site.

21:26. "built there an altar to Yhwh and lifted up burnt offerings and offerings of well-being." Consistent with royal ideology, David acts as the representative of his people to the divine realm. As we have seen, the authors of both Samuel and Chronicles portray disaster upon the body politic as the consequence of David's sin. The Chronicler, however, seizes upon the national implications of David's misdeed to demonstrate the national implications of David's intercession and obedience.

"he called upon Yhwh" *(wyqrʾ ʾl-yhwh)*. This assertion is not found in Samuel. One is tempted to say that the Chronicler's David observes the Deuteronomistic mandate to invoke Yhwh at his chosen place. In Deuteronomistic terms, the central sanctuary bears Yhwh's name and one is to call upon him there (1 Kgs 8:43 [//2 Chr 6:33], 52; 2 Kgs 20:11; Jer 7:10–11, 14, 30; 32:34; 34:15 [all Jer C]; Weinfeld 1972a: 325). But the expression *qrʾ ʾl-yhwh,* is ubiquitous in the HB as an act of piety (e.g., Judg 16:28; 1 Kgs 17:20; Isa 55:6; 58:9; Joel 1:14; Pss 4:1, 3; 18:4, 7 [ET 18:3, 6]; 86:3, 5, 7; 2 Chr 14:10 [ET 14:11]; cf. Isa 64:7; Pss 14:4; 79:6).

"and he answered him." The version of the divine acceptance of David's offerings contrasts with the account in Samuel. After depicting David's sacrifice of burnt offerings and offerings of well-being, Samuel states that Yhwh accepted David's "supplication for the land" (2 Sam 24:25). This notice ends the narrative, because the altar has served its purpose; "the plague was averted from Israel" (2 Sam 24:25). To be sure, the offerings on the altar also end the threat of divine wrath in Chronicles. Yhwh tells his messenger to sheath his sword (21:27); the peril to Jerusalem has passed. But the additional material in Chronicles, specifically the divine confirmation of David's sacrifices, establishes David's altar as an enduring fixture in Israelite worship.

"fire from the heavens." Only in Chronicles does Yhwh answer David's burnt offerings, offerings of well-being, and invocation by sending down heavenly fire. The imagery is highly significant. In portraying this miraculous divine affirmation of David's altar, the Chronicler draws upon the divine response to the institution of the Tabernacle altar in the Priestly Code. When Aaron and his sons use the Tabernacle altar for the first time, "fire came forth from before Yhwh and consumed the burnt offering and the fatty portions upon the altar" (Lev 9:24). A similar divine response attends Elijah's sacrifice at Mount Carmel (1 Kgs 18:37–38). By sanctioning the altar built at the threshing floor of Ornan in a similar way to his sanctioning of the Tabernacle altar, Yhwh publicly designates this place *(māqôm)* as a new sacred precinct.

21:27. "returned his sword to its sheath." Thus decisively ending the threat to Jerusalem, temporarily suspended in vv. 15–16.

21:28–30. "at that time, when David saw." These verses should probably be regarded as a later addition. The technique used to interpolate the additional material in vv. 28–30 is inverted quotation (Beentjes 1982) or Seidel's Law (Seidel 1955–56). The writer reuses phraseology from vv. 26–27 to frame his own addition. Verse 28 refers to v. 26, but reformulates its terms in basically reverse order.

| | |
|---|---|
| 26a. *wybn šm dwyd mzbḥ lyhwh* | 28b. *wyzbḥ šm* |
| 26b. *wyqrʾ ʾl-yhwh wyʿnhw* | 28a. *ky-ʿnhw yhwh* |

Having modeled his explanation on the description of Solomon's journey to Gibeon (2 Chr 1:3–6), he returns his readers to the original narrative at the end of v. 30 by referring to the events of v. 27 (again) in basically reverse order.

| | |
|---|---|
| 27a. *wy'mr yhwh* | 30c. *yhwh* |
| 27b. *lml'k* | 30b. *ml'k* |
| 27c. *wyšb ḥrbw 'l-ndnh* | 30a. *ky nbʿt mpny ḥrb* |

Many scholars have acknowledged that this material is parenthetical within this chapter (Curtis and Madsen 1910: 254; Rudolph 1955: 148; Dion 1985: 114–117; Japhet 1989: 141–42; Williamson 1982b: 150–51). But the material is more than parenthetical; its content conflicts with the force of earlier verses (Kittel 1902: 79–81). The author of vv. 28–30 draws on material in vv. 26–27 and 2 Chr 1:3–6 to excuse David's offering sacrifice away from the Tabernacle altar. But David is explicitly commanded to do so (1 Chr 21:18). Not the Chronicler, but a later scribe is bothered by the story's evidence for divinely approved worship away from the Gibeon altar.

22:1. "the House of Yhwh God." David seizes upon the divine action and declares the site to be the home of the future Temple (cf. 2 Chr 2:2–4 [ET 2:3–6]; 3:1–2). Hence, the Chronicler construes the mandate to construct an altar at this particular location, not as an ad hominem emergency maneuver to avert divine wrath, but as a decisive turning point in the history of Israelite religion. How much the story in Samuel functions as a justification for the site of the Temple is debated. Hertzberg (1964: 410–11), for example, describes the Samuel story as the *Hieros Logos* of the Jerusalem Temple cult. But the connections between the threshing floor and the future site of the Temple are not made explicit in the Samuel text itself (Wellhausen 1885: 178–80). In any case, the situation is clear in Chronicles. David immediately begins to gather workers and materials for the construction of the Temple (22:2–4). He also begins to prepare his son for the construction of the central sanctuary, describing its purpose in glowing terms (22:5–16). The rest of David's reign consists of preparing for the construction of the Temple and establishing an elaborate national administration to assist his chosen successor, Solomon (1 Chr 22–29). In this respect, the Chronicler's story of the census functions as a bridge between two highly important periods in David's career: the campaigns against Israel's neighbors (18:1–20:8) and the preparations for the transition to the reign of his successor and the construction of a temple (22:1–29:30). Just as Yhwh provided Moses with a plan *(tabnît)* for the Tabernacle, David provides Solomon with a plan *(tabnît)* for the central sanctuary (28:11, 18, 19; cf. Exod 25:9, 40). It will only be a matter of time before the Tabernacle will be brought to Jerusalem from Gibeon to find its place in the Temple. That the central sanctuary simultaneously incorporates and succeeds previous cultic arrangements is emphasized in the depiction of Solomon's temple dedication. After the Ark of the Covenant and the Tent of Meeting are brought into the Temple and Solomon utters his dedicatory prayers, divine intervention occurs again: "the fire from heaven consumed the burnt offering as well as the sacrifices, and the glory *(kābôd)* of Yhwh filled the house" (2 Chr 7:1).

"this will be (*zh hw'*) . . . and this will be (*wzh*)." In consistently employing the singular, David implies that the Jerusalem altar and sanctuary will supersede all previous altars and sanctuaries. Given the larger context, David's words take on the force of a prophecy (Abadie 1997: 83). Indeed, in later Jewish and Christian tradition David would come to be viewed as a prophet himself (11QPs[a] 27:11; Acts 2:30; Josephus, *Ag. Ap.* 1.177–79; *Ant.* 7.337; *Barn.* 12:10; Jerome, *Comm. Gal.* 3.5; *y. Soṭah* 9:12; *b. Soṭah* 48b; cf. Heb 11:32; Fitzmyer 1972). The divine response to David's sacrifice also serves an important long-range objective in divine-human relations. The impressive divine reaction to David's offerings, as interpreted by David, resolves a dualism in the national cultus that had existed since the Ark was brought into Zion. The much celebrated arrival of the Ark in the City of David establishes Zion as a national shrine (16:1), but it also left Israel with two major official sanctuaries: Jerusalem and Gibeon (see the NOTES to 16:37–42). Even though the Ark was stationed in David's tent, the Tabernacle *(mškn)* of Yhwh remained in Gibeon, attended by Zadoq and his kin (16:39; cf. 2 Chr 1:3–6; 1 Kgs 3:4). Each of these cult centers is associated with its own complement of ritual trappings. The Chronicler sanctions the Gibeon shrine, commenting that the sacrifices performed there accorded with "all that was written in the Torah of Yhwh" (16:40). But in the Chronicler's ideology of a unified national cult, which draws upon both Deuteronomic and Priestly traditions, the Ark and the Tabernacle belong together. Given the Deuteronomic mandate for one central sanctuary, the existence of two national shrines can only be temporary. It is this situation that David's obedience and Yhwh's dramatic intervention resolve.

"the altar of the burnt offering for Israel." The Chronicler, more so than the Deuteronomist, maintains a consistent interest in the fate of the Jerusalem altar (2 Chr 4:1, 19; 5:12; 6:12, 22; 7:7, 9; 8:12; 15:8; 23:10; 29:18–21; 32:12; 35:16). The connections between David's successful campaigns, the construction of David's altar, and the Temple also appear in a fragmentary text (4Q522) from Qumran that mentions the name of Joshua (Puech 1992; 1998). The text predicts David's taking of "the rock of Zion" and the construction of the Temple. The summary of David's reign by Eupolemus also underscores the connection between this altar and the Temple. Eupolemus writes that David wanted to build a temple for God and asked him to reveal the site. An angel obliged (Eusebius, *Praep. ev.* 9.30.5). In this manner, Eupolemus manages to avoid dealing with the census altogether.

## SOURCES AND COMPOSITION

The principal source for the census and plague story is not in dispute. For 1 Chr 21:1–26, the Chronicler relied heavily upon his *Vorlage* of 2 Sam 24:1–25. The more pertinent question is: How much did the Chronicler change his source? Differences among the textual witnesses to Samuel (e.g., MT, LXX, 4QSam[a], Josephus) and Chronicles suggest a complex picture of textual development. One should not presume that whenever MT Chronicles differs from MT Samuel, this discrepancy results from the Chronicler deliberately altering his source. On the contrary, the parallels between 4QSam[a] and Chronicles indicate that the Chronicler was remarkably conservative in quoting his *Vorlage* (Lemke 1965; Ulrich 1978: 1–37). The common traits shared by 4QSam[a] and MT (and LXX) Chronicles that are not shared by MT Samuel point to some distance between the texts of MT Samuel and Chronicles (see TEXTUAL NOTES).

The Chronicler's conservatism in quoting his source does not tell the whole story, however, about his compositional technique. He both selected from (e.g., 1 Chr 21:4; cf. 2 Sam 24:4–8) and supplemented his *Vorlage* (1 Chr 21:27–22:1). Through recontextualization and smaller additions (e.g., 21:6–7a) the Chronicler innovates (Dion 1985: 114–17; Wright 1993: 87–89). Hence, whatever the causes for the discrepancies among the various textual traditions, one must ultimately deal with the text of Chronicles as best one can reconstruct it.

## COMMENT

The story of David's census and plague is a *crux interpretum* in the Chronicler's depiction of an illustrious reign. Following the failure and death of Saul (10:1–14), David initiates a most auspicious era in Israelite history. Unanimously acclaimed by all Israelites, David is victorious in war, successful in cult, adept in politics, and diligent in administration. Given this highly stylized and flattering portrait of David, scholars are puzzled by the incorporation of the census and plague account from 2 Sam 24. David's census is a major blemish in an otherwise glorious career. How does one explain this apparent anomaly? It will be useful to survey contemporary criticism as a prelude to the approach taken here. (For a longer discussion, see Knoppers 1995b.)

Some ascribe the appearance of the story in Chronicles, at least in part, to an interest in exegesis (W. E. Barnes 1896: 427; Willi 1972: 170–71). This interpretive strategy calls attention to how the Chronicler reinterprets and reapplies his *Vorlage*, but functions only as a penultimate explanation of the text. The question remains why the Chronicler retains and reworks this particular incident. Japhet (1993a: 370–90) offers a different explanation, viewing the inclusion and shaping of this story as proof of the Chronicler's abilities as an honest broker of history. As with his depiction of other monarchs, the Chronicler balances the positive and negative aspects of David's career. Nevertheless, one wonders why the author's quest for balance does not lead him to include more negative material about David (contrast 2 Samuel and 1 Kgs 1–2) and include corresponding negative material for Solomon, the other king in the United Monarchy whom the Chronicler idealizes. The Chronicler omits, in fact, all of the explicitly critical material about Solomon in Kings from his work (Knoppers 1990: 423–29). The comparison with the sanitized Solomon of 2 Chr 1–9 makes the errant David of 1 Chr 21 all the more striking.

Perhaps the majority of commentators attribute the inclusion of this story to an authorial concern to validate Ornan's threshing floor as the future site of the Temple (Noth 1987: 34, 55–56; Galling 1954: 59–62; Rudolph 1955: 141–49; Ackroyd 1973a: 73–77; Mosis 1973: 104–24; Williamson 1982b: 142–51; Im 1985: 145–53; R. Braun 1986: 212–18; De Vries 1989: 177–80). The Chronicler tolerates some unsavory details about David because the story of the census "culminates in the providential choice of a site for the Temple" (W. E. Barnes 1909: 52). This influential theory highlights the important links that the Chronicler posits between this incident and the construction of the Temple, but fails to explain major characteristics of the census and plague story. To begin with, David is the main character throughout the story. He is mentioned twenty-four times in 21:1–22:1 (Wright 1993: 98–104). In contrast, the Temple is explicitly mentioned only at the story's very end. If the Chronicler wished to validate the Temple, it is unclear why he consistently keys on the figure of David. Similarly, why does he include, indeed supplement, earlier parts of the narrative that underscore David's folly? Why does he not temper or even omit portions of his *Vorlage* that reflect negatively on David's conduct?

In my judgment, the issue of David's unblemished character has been misconstrued (Knoppers 1995b). The aforementioned explanations assume that the criticism of David in the narrative is a problem. The inclusion of the census story is thought to undercut David's role as an exemplary king. It is precisely this assumption that needs to be reexamined. David's acknowledged culpability does not disqualify him from serving as a paradigmatic figure to the Chronicler's audience. The portrayal of David is more complex. The stress on royal responsibility may be understood in the context of a larger movement characterized by wrongdoing, confession, intercession, renewed obedience, and divine blessing. The story of the census, plague, and establishment of a permanent altar underscores the highly positive consequences of David's ability to confront and manage his own failure. David's unequivocal admission of guilt, his mediation on behalf of Israel, his diligent observance of divine instructions, and his securing a site for the future Temple contribute positively to his legacy.

Approaching David as the model of a repentant sinner elucidates prominent features of the story. Because the writer portrays David's transgression as part of a broader process beginning with repentance and ending with divine blessing, he has no interest in denying royal culpability. On the contrary, the first part of the census narrative clarifies and accentuates the king's responsibility for the plague, while the latter part of the narrative accentuates the positive outcome of his intercession and obedience. The stylized movement that the author creates from Davidic transgression to a miraculous divine affirmation of his sacrifices serves two purposes. First, it enables the writer to present the establishment of David's altar as a permanent fixture in the history Israel's cult. The Chronicler draws upon Deuteronomic and Priestly theologies to present David's altar as the focal point around which the venerable but separate institutions of the Ark and the Tabernacle can find a common home. Second, the extraordinary contrast between the initial punishment of royal infraction and the divine forgiveness amplifies the significance of David's intercession with Yhwh. The common hope expressed in

Psalms for Yhwh to have compassion on and reverse the plight of the supplicant (Westermann 1981: 64–71, 181–213; W. Holladay 1993: 49–52; P. Miller 1994: 55–134) is realized in the Chronicler's version of the census and plague.

The portrait of the king as an intercessor raises the larger issue of the author's understanding of David's significance. There are, as many have stressed, multiple images of David within the HB: shepherd, warrior, musician, administrator, lyricist, politician, singer, sinner, king, husband, paramour, and father. Given this diversity, it is only to be expected that later interpreters concentrated upon certain aspects of David's reputation and neglected others. Writing toward the end of the biblical period, the Chronicler was himself an early interpreter who was likely familiar with many, if not all, of these representations of David. Considering the multiple images of David available to the Chronicler, it would be startling to see him fixate upon one. Yet this is what many have claimed. Of the many disparate portraits of David, the Chronicler's presentation has often been associated, not always approvingly, with that of David as cult founder. Wellhausen (1885: 182), for instance, claims:

> See what Chronicles has made of David! The founder of the kingdom has become the founder of the temple and the public worship, the king and hero at the head of his companions has become the singer and master of ceremonies at the head of a swarm of priests and Levites; his clearly cut figure has become a feeble holy picture, seen through a cloud of incense.

Such a one-sided presentation of David's significance can be easily qualified by recognizing the martial, dynastic, administrative, and political aspects of David's leadership in 1 Chr 11–29. David is a cult founder in Chronicles (Welch 1939: 55–96; Mosis 1973: 101–55; De Vries 1988; Riley 1993; Dyck 1998). But David's establishment and structuring of worship in Jerusalem is only one aspect of his reputation, albeit a very important one.

Close scrutiny of this chapter reveals that there are compelling reasons to recognize an additional dimension of the Davidic legacy in Chronicles. The image of David as the model of a repentant sinner is a constituent element in the depiction of this king. The David of the census story is a person of confession and supplication par excellence, a human sinner who repents, seeks forgiveness, intercedes on behalf of his people, and ultimately secures the site of the future Temple. Precisely because David is a pivotal figure, David's repentance and intercession are paradigmatic. The Chronicler's conviction that errant Israelites have both the opportunity to reform and the potential to make new contributions to their nation is evident in the reigns of Reḥoboam (2 Chr 12:5–12), Jehoshaphaṭ (2 Chr 19:1–11), Amaziah (2 Chr 25:5–13), and even Manasseh (2 Chr 33:10–17; B. Kelly 1996). But this principle is formatively and preeminently at work in David's career. In the context of a national disaster of his own making, David is able to turn a catastrophe into the occasion for a permanent divine blessing upon Israel. First Chronicles 21 is an example of, rather than the exception to, the Chronicler's idealization of David. The Chronicler's David is a multidimensional figure whose exemplary significance is not limited to a single facet of his public career.

# *XXVII. Materials, Artisans, and a New King for the Temple (22:2–19)*

*David's Initial Preparations for the Temple*

2 David gave orders to gather the resident aliens who were in the land of Israel
and appointed masons for cutting hewn stones to build the House of God. 3 Iron
in abundance for nails for the doors of the gates and for the clasps David provided,
as well as bronze in abundance beyond weighing 4 and innumerable cedar logs,
because the Sidonians and the Tyrians brought cedar logs in abundance to David.
5 And David thought, "My son is an inexperienced youth, and the House that is to
be built for Yhwh must be exceedingly great to win fame and glory throughout all
lands. Let me provide, therefore, for it." So David provided (materials) in abundance before his death.

*Instructions to Solomon*

6 Then David called for his son Solomon and commanded him to build a house
for Yhwh, the God of Israel. 7 And David said to Solomon, "My son, I myself had it
in mind to build a house for the name of Yhwh my God, 8 but the word of Yhwh
came to me saying, 'Much blood you have shed and great wars you have waged.
You will not build a house for my name, because you have shed much blood to the
earth before me. 9 A son has been born to you; he, he will be a man of rest. I shall
give him rest from all of his surrounding enemies; indeed, Solomon will be his
name and peace and quiet I shall give to Israel in his days. 10 As for him, he will
build a house for my name. He, he will become my son and I shall become his father. And I shall establish the throne of his dominion over Israel forever.'

11 "Now, my son, may Yhwh be with you so that you will become very prosperous and build the House of Yhwh your God as he promised concerning you.
12 Only may Yhwh give you insight and understanding so that when he puts you in
command over Israel you may observe the Torah of Yhwh your God. 13 Then you
will become very prosperous, if you are careful to carry out the statutes and the
judgments that Yhwh commanded Moses concerning Israel. Be strong and resolute; neither fear nor be dismayed. 14 In my humility, I have provided for the
House of God: 100,000 talents of gold and 1,000,000 talents of silver, as well as
bronze and iron beyond weighing, because there was so much of it. I have also
provided wood and stones and you will add to them. 15 And with you in abundance are artisans—masons, stonecutters, and carpenters—with every kind of skill
in every kind of work 16 pertaining to gold, silver, bronze, and iron without number. Arise and act and may Yhwh be with you."

*Instructions to Israel's Leaders*

17 Then David commanded all the officers of Israel to help Solomon his son.
18 "Is not Yhwh your God with you? He has given you rest on every side. Indeed,
he has given all the inhabitants of the land into my hand. The land is subdued before Yhwh and before his people. 19 Now dedicate your hearts and your lives to
seeking Yhwh your God. Arise and build the sanctuary of Yhwh God to bring the

Ark of the Covenant of Yhwh and the holy furnishings of God into the House that is to be built for the name of Yhwh."

## TEXTUAL NOTES

22:2–19. This material is unique to Chronicles. The writer draws from or alludes to a number of earlier texts, but there is no direct parallel in Samuel-Kings to this narrative and private speech.

22:2. "gave orders." Literally, "and said" *(wy'mr)*. The use of *'mr* to signify "command" is common in LBH (BDB 56).

"to gather" *(lknws)*. In the *qal* and the *piʿel*, the verb *kns* reflects late usage (Esth 4:16; Qoh 2:8, 26; 3:5; Neh 12:44; Rooker 1990: 156–57).

"the resident aliens" *(hgrym)*. So MT *(lectio brevior)*. LXX *(pantas tous prosēlytous)*, Syr., and Vg. add "all" (= *kl*), perhaps in anticipation of 2 Chr 2:16 [ET 2:17], *kl h'nšym hgrym*. Influenced by his versions of 1 Kgs 5:29–30 (ET 5:15–16) and 2 Chr 2:16–17 [ET 2:17–18], Josephus (*Ant.* 7.335) adds that David ordered a census of aliens (180,000) and assigned them specific tasks.

"and appointed" *(wyʿmd)*. Reading with MT *(lectio brevior)*. Syr., Vg., and Arab. add *mnhwn* (= *mhm*), while LXX$^L$ adds *autous*. These lemmata may have been influenced by the verbiage of 2 Chr 2:17 [ET 2:18] *(wyʿś mhm)*.

22:3. "for the clasps." Given the meaning of the verbal root *ḥbr* as "to unite" or "to bind," most scholars have construed the relatively rare pl. fem. ptc. *mĕḥabbĕrôt* as "things to connect," that is, "(iron) clamps" (e.g., Keil 1873: 243). LXX has *kai tous stropheis*, "and the sockets" (in which the pivots of doors would move). Elsewhere the *mĕḥabbĕrôt* appear only in 2 Chr 34:11, but there the *mĕḥabbĕrôt* are explicitly associated with wood. Based on the assumption that *ʿēṣîm lammĕḥabbĕrôt* in 2 Chr 34:11 refer to "wooden beams," Dirksen (1995b: 23–24) contends for a similar meaning here. But *ʿēṣîm lammĕḥabbĕrôt* in 2 Chr 34:11 can just as well be rendered "wood for the couplings" (NJPS). Priestly usage in reference to the Tabernacle may be useful for comparative purposes: *ḥōbĕret*, "thing joined" or "seam" (Exod 26:4, 10; 36:17); *maḥberet*, "joint" or "set" (Exod 26:4; 28:27; 36:11, 17; 39:20; Cazelles 1980: 195–96).

22:5. "and David thought." Literally, "and David said (to himself)." Cf. Gen 20:11; 26:28; 1 Sam 20:26; 2 Sam 5:6; 12:22; Isa 49:4; Mal 1:7; Ruth 4:4.

"my son." So MT *(lectio brevior)*. LXX adds explicating "Solomon."

"an inexperienced youth" *(naʿar wārāk)*. Although the term *naʿar* can occasionally designate a certain type of public servant, military official, or member of a professional guild in Heb., Ammonite, and Phoen. (J. MacDonald 1976; *DNWSI* 739–40), age and experience seem to be the issues here. In this respect, LXX *paidarion hapalon*, "a tender youth," captures the nuance of the Heb.

"must be exceedingly great" *(lĕhagdîl lĕmaʿlâ)*. An example of the internal (i.e., inwardly transitive) *hipʿil* (Waltke and O'Connor, §27.2g). Both the expression and the placement of the inf. are typical of Chronistic style in which *lĕmaʿlâ* is often employed as an intensive, "exceedingly" (S. Driver 1895b), rather than to signify "upwards," as in earlier Heb. Similarly, the Chronicler sometimes uses the prep. *l-* with the inf. at the end of sentences (S. Driver 1914: 537 [#32]).

"let me provide" *(ʾkynh)*. Emending the text by prefacing "I" *(ʾny)* is unnecessary (contra Rudolph 1955: 150). On the use of the cohortative to express self-encouragement, see GKC §108b.

"for it" *(lw)*. It is also possible to translate *lw* as "for him," that is, for Solomon.

22:7. "my son" *(bny)*. Reading with Qere, many Heb. MSS, Tg., and Vg. *(fili mi)*. Kethib *bnw*, hence, "(David said to Solomon) his son." LXX *Teknon*, "son." Given the orthographic similarity between *wāw* and *yôd* in ancient scripts dating from different periods, it is extremely difficult to determine which reading is earlier. See also v. 11, "now, my son," and v. 6, "his son" (*bnw*; cf. 23:1).

"I myself had it in mind" *(ʾny hyh ʿm-lbby)*. The cliché *hyh ʿm-lbb* occurs often in Chronicles: 1 Chr 28:2; 2 Chr 1:11; 6:7–8(//1 Kgs 8:17–18); 9:1(//1 Kgs 10:2); 24:4; 29:10. Cf. Josh 14:7 *(kʾšr ʿm-lbby)*.

22:8. "the word." Tg. explicates, "the word of prophecy from before."

22:9. "I shall give" *(ʾtn)*. So MT (maximum variation). A few Heb. MSS and Syr. have "there will be" *(yhyh)*, as earlier in the verse.

22:10. "and I shall become his father" *(wʾny-lw lʾb)*. So MT *(lectio brevior)*. The Heb. is elliptical. A few MSS, LXX$^{Aal}$, Syr., Vg., and Arab. add the expected verb *ʾhyh*.

"the throne." Thus MT. Many Heb. MSS preface *ʾt*.

"his dominion" *(malkûtô)*. LXX *basileias autou*, "his kingdom." Given that *malkût* normally designates "royalty" or "kingship," one might be tempted to posit a different *Vorlage* (i.e., *mamlākâ*). But one cannot make such a fixed and fast distinction between *mamlākâ* and *malkût* in Chronicles (*pace* De Vries 1987), because *malkût* can mean "kingdom," especially in LBH (BDB 575; S. Driver 1914: 536 [#9]).

"over Israel" *(ʿl yśrʾl)*. So MT. LXX *en Israēl*, "in Israel." The expression *ʿl yśrʾl* does not appear in either 2 Sam 7:13 or its parallel 1 Chr 17:12.

22:11. "so that you will become very prosperous" *(wĕhiṣlaḥtā)*. Another example of the internal *hipʿil* (Waltke and O'Connor, §27.2g). Normally the *hipʿil* would take an object.

"as he promised concerning you" *(kʾšr dbr ʿlyk)*. The rendering of the Heb. by LXX picks up the nuance of the verb *dbr* with the prep. *ʿl* (BDB 180), *hōs elalēsen peri sou*, "as he spoke concerning you."

22:12. "when he puts you in command over Israel." The syntax of MT is difficult. MT literally reads, "and he commands you *(wyṣwk)* over Israel." NRSV provides one interpretation, "when he gives you charge over Israel," while NJPS offers another, "and put you in charge of Israel." LXX seems to reflect a different *Vorlage*, *kai katischysai se epi Israēl*, "and to strengthen (= *ḥzq*) you over Israel." Cf. Vg. *ut regere possis Israhel*. If one were inclined to emend the text, the proposal of Arnold Ehrlich (1914: 348–49) to read *wlṣwt ʾt*, "to command," is more likely than either of Rudolph's two proposals (1955: 150): *wĕyēṣer rak* or *wĕyēṣer yaṣṣîb*. On the verb, see also Deut 31:14, 23; Josh 1:9.

"you may observe the Torah of Yhwh your God." Again, the syntax is difficult.

MT literally reads, "and to observe *(wlšmwr)* the Torah of Yhwh your God." The precise relationship of this clause to the two previous clauses ("only may Yhwh give you insight and understanding and/when he puts you in command over Israel") is disputed. Compare the translation of NRSV, "when he gives you charge over Israel you may keep the law of the LORD your God" (cf. Kittel 1902: 84) with that of NJPS, "and put you in charge of Israel and the observance (of the teaching of the LORD)." Kropat (§7.2) argues that when an inf. (with *l-*) follows a finite verb, the inf. may be translated with a personal subject. The more expansive version of LXX *kai tou phylassesthai kai tou poiein (= wlšmwr wlʿśwt)*, "and to keep and to carry out (the law)," may have been influenced by the verbiage of v. 13, *ʾm-tšmwr lʿśwt*, "if you are careful to carry out (the statutes)."

22:13. "you will become very prosperous" *(taṣlîaḥ)*. See the 1st TEXTUAL NOTE to v. 11.

22:14. "in my humility" *(bĕʿonyî)*. So MT. The translation of BDB (777), "in spite of my frustration," is ad hoc. In this context, the noun seems to signify a self-imposed restraint. This certainly is the way the versions have construed *bĕʿonyî*: Tg. *bsgwpy wbṣwmy*, "in my affliction and in my fasting"; LXX *kata tēn ptōcheian mou*, "according to my beggary"; Vg. *in paupertatula mea*, "in my poverty." Note the assertion in David's later speech, *kĕkol-kōḥî*, "commensurate with all of my ability, [I have set aside for the House of my God]" (1 Chr 29:2; GKC §119o). Also relevant is the use of the verb *ʿnh*, "to be afflicted, humbled." Ps 132:1, for example, reads, "Remember, O Yhwh, with respect to David all of his self-denial" (*ʿunnôtô*; Knoppers 1998). There is no other instance of a *puʿal* inf. construct of *ʿnh* (Waltke and O'Connor, §25.1b). Nevertheless, there are no compelling reasons to doubt the integrity of the reading (Briggs and Briggs 1907: 469; Kraus 1993: 472). LXX Ps 132:1 *tēs prautētos autou* may represent *ʿonwātô* ("his humility"). Both the content and the context suggest that *ʿnh* refers to humility or self-denial (Perles 1895: 65; Halpern 1981a: 17; Seow 1989: 151). Similarly, Oesterly (1959: 531) draws attention to the use of *ʿnh (puʿal)* in Lev 23:29 to designate self-denial through abstinence from work on the Day of Atonement (cf. Lev 23:28, 30–32).

"100,000 talents of gold." So MT *(lectio difficilior)*. Josephus (*Ant.* 7.340) presents a smaller number, "10,000 talents of gold." On the Chronicler's use of fantastic numbers, see the NOTE to 12:38.

"1,000,000 talents of silver." Again, Josephus (*Ant.* 7.340) presents a smaller number, "100,000 talents of silver."

"because there was so much of it" *(ky lrb hyh)*. Translating according to sense. Similarly, LXX *hoti eis plēthos estin*.

22:15. "and with you." Many witnesses to LXX add the impv. *prosthes*, "you must add."

22:16. "pertaining to gold, silver, bronze, and iron without number." Does the phrase "without number" *(ʾyn mspr)* refer to the gold, silver, bronze, and iron ("in quantities without limit"; NJPS) or to the artisans (v. 15)? If the clause referred to materials, one would expect the phrase "beyond weighing" (*ʾyn mšql*; cf. v. 14). The confusion results from the author's architectonic arrangement of vv. 14–16:

"beyond weighing (אין משקל) . . . so much of it (לרב)" (v. 14) "in abundance (לרב) . . . without number (אין מספר; vv. 15–16)

The phrase "without number" refers to the innumerable workers David provided on Solomon's behalf. So also (apparently) LXX *ouk estin arithmos* and Syr., which repeats "workers" before each metal and concludes by stating "they [masc. pl.] could not be numbered."

22:17. "his son." Reading with MT *(lectio brevior)*. Some LXX cursives add *legōn*, "saying" (= *l'mr*), while LXX$^{L}$ adds *kai eipen*, "and he said" (= *wy'mr*).

22:18. "into my hand" *(bydy)*. So MT and LXX$^{L}$. LXX$^{B}$ *en chersin*, "in (the) hands." LXX$^{AN}$, Syr., Vg. have the 2nd-per. pl. suf., *en cheiri humōn* (= *bydkm*, "into your hand").

"and before his people" *(ʿmw)*. Given the context, one could also translate "and before his army" (2nd NOTE to 1 Chr 19:7).

22:19. "dedicate your hearts." Literally, "give *(tnw)* your hearts." The verb *ntn* can mean "dedicate" or "present" both in Heb. (BDB 679) and in Phoen. (*ytn*; Speiser 1963; Knoppers 1992a: 106–8; Krahmalkov 2000: 219).

"to seeking" *(ldrwš)*. So MT. Syr. reads "pray."

# NOTES

22:2. "gave orders." Having received a dramatic and unambiguous divine confirmation that Ornan's threshing floor would be the future site of the altar and temple (COMMENT on 21:1–22:1), David hastens to prepare for their construction (22:2–5). The immediate and considered attention David gives to this major project is but one aspect of his highly positive legacy in Chronicles.

"to gather" *(lknws)*. The verb is used in a variety of administrative, political, and agricultural contexts in late texts (Qoh 2:8; 3:5; Ezek 22:21; 39:28; Esth 4:16; 1 Chr 22:2). Conscription was a normal way for ancient Near Eastern kings to implement public works. Within Kings there is a debate about how Solomon procured labor for building the Temple. According to 1 Kgs 5:27–32 [ET 5:13–17] (cf. 11:28; 12:4), Solomon conscripted labor from Israel, but according to 1 Kgs 9:20–22 (cf. 3 Kgdms 10:23–25) Solomon did not impose conscription upon any Israelites. From a Deuteronomic (Deut 17:14–17) point of view, Solomon's imposition of a corvée upon Israel could be viewed as a blight upon his reign. The Chronicler resolves this issue by omitting the controversial part of 1 Kgs 5:27–32 [ET 5:13–17] and including 1 Kgs 9:20–22 within his own composition (2 Chr 8:7–9). One could argue that the Chronicler extends the indenture of resident aliens by having not only Solomon but also David implement their conscription (1 Chr 22:2; 2 Chr 2:16–17 [ET 2:17–18]). But 2 Sam 20:24 suggests that David also introduced some sort of forced labor.

"the resident aliens" *(haggērîm)*. Biblical authors accord different kinds of status to resident aliens (Japhet 1989: 334–51; van Houten 1991; Bultmann 1992). Although in some texts the *gērîm* appear as foreigners, perhaps remnants of the Canaanite population, in Chronicles the "aliens" have more of a mediate status.

Although not enjoying the status of full Israelites, they are entitled to participate in some public activities (1 Chr 22:2; 2 Chr 2:16–17 [ET 2:17–18]; 30:25; cf. 1 Chr 16:19). On the application of the term to Israelites, see the NOTE to 29:15.

"the land of Israel" (ארץ ישׂראל). The expression is relatively rare in the HB (1 Sam 13:19; 2 Kgs 5:2, 4; 6:23; Ezek 27:17; 40:2; 47:18). Proportionately, the expression occurs more commonly in Chronicles (1 Chr 22:2; 2 Chr 2:16 [ET 2:17]; 30:25; 34:17; cf. 1 Chr 13:2 ארצי ישׂראל), but its use is undefined. It seems to refer to the geographical habitat—whether real or ideal—of the Israelite people (cf. 22:5; Willi 1994a). Hence, in individual cases such a habitat may overlap with the habitats of other peoples.

"masons" (*ḥōṣĕbîm*). Solomon will employ some 80,000 of these to work on the Temple (2 Chr 2:17 [ET 2:18]).

"hewn stones" (*ʾabnê gāzît*). According to Exod 20:25, stone altars were not to be built with hewn stones. Deuteronomy 27:5–6 is even more explicit, stipulating that an altar must be made of unhewn stones upon which no iron has been wielded (Fishbane 1985: 159–61; Olyan 1996b). But the reference in v. 2 is to the Temple building and not to its altar.

22:3. "in abundance" (*lrb*). This expression is characteristic of the Chronicler's writing, occurring some thirty-five times in Chronicles (S. Driver 1895b: 248–49; Curtis and Madsen 1910: 33 [#105]). It serves as a *leitmotiv* in this chapter. David provides abundantly to ensure the success of his son (22:3, 4, 5, 8, 14, 15; cf. 29:2, 21; Josephus, *Ant.* 7.336).

"David provided (*hēkîn*)." The use of the verbal root *kwn* in the sense of "to set up" or "to prepare" is characteristic of Chronistic style (Curtis and Madsen 1910: 30 [#54]).

"bronze in abundance beyond weighing." To be used for the columns (2 Chr 3:15–17), the altar (2 Chr 4:1), the molten sea (2 Chr 4:2–5), and other objects (e.g., 2 Chr 4:6).

22:4. "the Sidonians and the Tyrians." The authors of Samuel, Kings, Chronicles, and Ezra posit a history of commercial relations between the Phoenicians and the Israelites. Ḥuram of Tyre sent David cedar, stonemasons, and carpenters to build David a palace (1 Chr 14:1; 2 Chr 2:3; cf. 2 Sam 5:11). Here, David sets aside "innumerable cedar logs" for the Temple project. Similarly, Solomon obtains Lebanon cedar, cypress, and algum wood from Ḥuram of Tyre for the Temple (2 Chr 2:7–8, 10–15 [ET 2:8–9, 11–16]; cf. 1 Kgs 5:15–32 [ET 5:1–18]). In Ezra, the returned exiles pay food, drink, and oil to the Tyrians and the Sidonians to bring them cedar from Lebanon for the rebuilding of the Temple (Ezra 3:7). In this manner, the editors of Ezra establish links between the First and Second Temples ("Introduction").

22:5. "David thought." In the later interpretation of Eupolemus, the prophet Nathan commanded David to provide Solomon with all the necessary building materials to construct the temple (Eusebius, *Praep. ev.* 9.30.7–8).

"an inexperienced youth" (*naʿar wārāk*). The phrase recurs in 29:1, also in reference to Solomon. The term *naʿar* can connote immaturity (e.g., 2 Sam 18:5; Jer 1:6; 1 Kgs 3:7; 1 Chr 22:5; 2 Chr 13:7). Of David's many sons, Solomon was one of the youngest (2 Sam 13:21b [LXX, 4QSam[a]]; 1 Kgs 1:12, 17; 2:22). Indeed, in the later interpretation of Eupolemus, Solomon was only twelve years old when he took office (Eusebius, *Praep. ev.* 9.30.8). But 2 Sam 12:24 only states that Solomon was born after the Syro-Ammonite war. The Chronicler uses a similar phrase to *naʿar wārāk* in reference to Reḥoboam *(naʿar wĕrak-lēbāb)* to explain how Jeroboam was able to wrest the northern kingdom away from Solomon's ill-prepared son (2 Chr 13:7). In his incubation at Gibeon (as depicted in 1 Kgs 3:7, but not in the parallel 2 Chr 1:9–10), Solomon refers to himself as a "young boy" *(naʿar qāṭōn)*. On the expression *naʿar qāṭōn*, see also 1 Kgs 11:17; 2 Kgs 2:23; 5:14. Solomon's challenge, as depicted in his dream at Gibeon, is to rule "a great people too numerous to be numbered" (1 Kgs 3:8; cf. 2 Chr 1:9–10). Although Solomon's youthful inexperience is also at issue here, building the central sanctuary is presented as his major challenge.

"exceedingly great." In Chronicles Israel's God is more than a national deity. Yhwh reigns in heaven and rules over all the kingdoms of the earth (2 Chr 20:6; 32:19; cf. 2 Kgs 19:15–16). For the Chronicler, there is only one supreme deity—"Yhwh is the God" (*yhwh hûʾ hāʾĕlōhîm;* 2 Chr 33:13; cf. 1 Chr 16:24–26; 17:20). Because Israel worships an incomparable God (1 Chr 29:10–12; 2 Chr 32:19), the House built in his name must reflect his incomparability (2 Chr 2:4–5 [ET 2:5–6]). Hence, David sets about planning a magnificent structure.

"to win fame and glory throughout all lands." In the ancient Near East, palace-temple complexes communicated the power of a king (and his gods) to his people, to his clients, and to foreign emissaries. Since the Temple testifies to Yhwh's reputation, the international function of the Jerusalem sanctuary is a concern of both David and Solomon. At the Temple's dedication, Solomon intercedes for those foreigners who, having heard of "your [Yhwh's] great name and your mighty hand and your outstretched arm," journey to Jerusalem to pray at the Temple (2 Chr 6:32–33//1 Kgs 8:41–43). By the same token, the converse is true. If Israel proves unfaithful and Yhwh banishes the people from the land, the demolished shrine will become "a byword among all peoples" (2 Chr 7:20).

22:6. "called for his son Solomon." It is clear from the context that David has already picked Solomon to be his successor. Nevertheless, there is no indication that this decision has been proclaimed publicly either to the officers of his regime or to the elite in Jerusalem. In this respect, one should distinguish a series of steps in the process through which a succession may occur: the royal decision to designate an heir, the public pronouncement(s) to this effect, and the actual public installation (and anointing) of the king designate. Similarly, in the "apology" of Esarhaddon, one may observe a series of steps in the succession of Ashurbanipal, such as Esarhaddon's decision to choose Ashurbanipal, the education of the crown prince, and the public installation (H. Tadmor 1983). When the actual installation took place, the royal family, the court, and the state officials all swore an oath of allegiance. Similarly, the other royal princes, state officials, military officers all throw their support to Solomon at the time of his accession (29:23–24).

22:7–16. "said to Solomon." The first of many speeches David delivers to a variety of audiences, orchestrating a smooth transition to his son's rule. This particular speech has the character of a private communication from father to son (vv. 6, 7, 11). The text presents a Solomonic succession, even though there has not yet been a public announcement to this effect. Initially, David's efforts focus on gathering materials for the Temple (vv. 2–5), but since he recognizes that he will not, and cannot, be around to see the structure actually built, he alerts Solomon both to the succession and to his task in constructing the Temple.

22:7. "I myself had it in mind to build a house for the name of Yhwh my God" (אני היה עם-לבבי לבנות בית לשם יהיה אלהי). An echo of 1 Kgs 8:17–18. There Solomon quotes Yhwh as saying that David "did well" (הטיבת) by intending to build a house for the name of Yhwh (יען אשר היה עם-לבבך לבנות בית לשמי; 1 Kgs 8:18; cf. 2 Sam 7:1–2; 1 Chr 17:1). What David rightly intended to do, but was proscribed from doing, his son was divinely called to do. What Solomon attributes to David in Kings, David attributes to himself in Chronicles.

22:8. "but the word of Yhwh came to me, saying." The citation that follows (vv. 8–10) is largely drawn from Nathan's dynastic oracle (17:7–14). But this by no means exhausts the content of this oration. Included are allusions to other texts as well as the Chronicler's own contributions.

"much blood you have shed." The text three times asserts that David cannot build the Temple because of his spilling of blood (22:8[bis]; 28:3). The writer underscores his point by means of a chiastic arrangement.

a Much blood you have shed and great wars you have waged (דם לרב שׁפכת ומלחמות גדלות עשׂית).
  b You will not build a house for my name (לא-תבנה בית לשמי),
a′ because you have shed much blood to the earth before me (כי דמים רבים שׁפכת ארצה לפני).

The precise force of this important assertion is not clear and requires some discussion. The repeated references to David's spilling of blood have elicited basically three explanations.

One line of interpretation is to see David's shortcoming as cultic in nature: a "holy work needs clean hands" (Rudolph 1955: 151; cf. Williamson 1982b: 154). Ritual uncleanness bars David from temple building. This view calls attention to the fact that David is forbidden to participate in a central activity relating to the cult. Yet there are shortcomings to this interpretation. To begin with, David is not barred from other sorts of cultic activities. Moreover, the cleanliness stipulations do not present war conduct as ipso facto rendering a person unclean (e.g., Lev 15:2–33; 17:10–16; 18:3–30; 20:9–16; 21:1–23; Deut 20:1–20), although contact with a corpse does (Num 5:2–4; 6:6). Why, then, would the Chronicler disqualify David on this count?

A second line of interpretation finds fault with David on ethical grounds. Citing depictions of shedding blood (*šāpak dām*) as a guilty act, including murder (e.g., Gen 9:6; 37:22; Deut 19:10; Ezek 22:4, 9, 12; Lam 4:13), some scholars contend that David's shedding blood constitutes an ethical lapse. "David has done wrong and is guilty before God" (Dirksen 1996c: 53; cf. Fishbane 1985: 424–26). In one version of this interpretation, the backsliding is associated with the census, which resulted in much loss of life (B. Kelly 1998). This line of interpretation commendably draws attention to the distinction between the warrior David and the peaceful Solomon in the typology of the United Monarchy. The question of who would (or did) build the long-awaited central sanctuary could not be attributed solely to historical exigency. Temple building was of high, one might say of highest, importance. The matter of who could build the promised shrine had to be a matter of a deliberate divine decree (R. Braun 1986: 224; Dirksen 1996c: 53–55). One may add that, at least in one instance in Samuel, David is directly accused of being a "man of blood" (איש דמים; 2 Sam 16:8). The accusation carries criminal overtones. There are obstacles, however, to sustaining this line of interpretation. The Chronicler never accuses David of incurring bloodguilt (Num 35:33–34) or of committing accidental or intentional homicide (Deut 19:10–13; 21:8–9; 2 Kgs 24:4; Jer 7:6). One must be careful to distinguish between the Chronicler's views and those of other biblical authors, even if he is indebted to older works. Moreover, if one were to assume that the author drew upon older passages to level such an accusation against David, one might expect him to do the same with other figures such as Moses and Solomon (2 Chr 8:3), who—although responsible for shedding blood—also had much to do with sanctuary construction. Finally, if David was guilty of an identifiable sin, such as the shedding of (innocent) blood, one might expect to see national consequences because such an action could, for example, pollute and contaminate the land (Lev 35:33–34; cf. 2 Chr 36:12–21). The corporate consequences of David's census are, as we have seen, a case in point (1 Chr 21:1–13). But there are no national implications pointed to here; the injunction against David's building the Temple is personal in nature.

A third approach, attested already in antiquity (e.g., Josephus, *Ant.* 7.337), is to identify David's waging of wars with bloodshed. David's "paradoxical and tragic flaw" is his shedding of blood in battle (Japhet 1993a: 397–98; cf. Goettsberger 1939: 163; McKenzie 1999b; Muray 2001: 457–60). This line of interpretation presumes that the Chronicler is interpreting and rewriting the text of Kings. There, David's preoccupation with waging war leaves him unable to go about constructing a temple. In explaining to Ḥiram of Tyre how he came to build the Temple, Solomon contrasts the wars that beset David with "the rest Yhwh my God has given me roundabout; there is neither adversary nor trouble" (1 Kgs 5:18 [ET 5:4]). Because Yhwh was placing David's enemies "under the soles of his feet" (1 Kgs 5:17 [ET 5:3]), David was not able to build the central sanctuary. In Chronicles, David also wages "great wars" (1 Chr 11:4–9; 14:8–17; 18:1–20:8; 22:8). David is even deemed by Yhwh to be a "man of wars" (איש מלחמות; 28:3). These many battles do not simply preoccupy David; they also render him unfit to construct the Temple (28:3; cf. 1 Kgs 2:31; Ps 79:3; GKC §124n). In this respect, the Chronicler's evaluation has more gravity than that offered by the Deuteronomist (Dirksen 1996c; B. Kelly 1998; McKenzie 1999b). According to Murray (2001), the Chronicler's negative judgment draws upon not only Kings, but also the purification legislation of Num 31:19–24 (relating to warriors and captives). The writer links this material to the references to manslaughter in Num 35:30 and the pollution of the land through shedding blood in Num 35:33–34.

I am attracted to a modified version of the third view, but would readily admit that it is not perfect. With a few possible exceptions (e.g, 1 Sam 25:31), most OT authors do not associate "shedding blood" with conduct in war. Cases of self-defense, judicial execution, and war are, in fact, usually considered to be exceptions to the rule that killing defiles (Gen 4:8–12; 9:6; Exod 22:1 [ET 22:2]; Num 35:33; 2 Sam 21:1; 1 Kgs 2:5–6; Ezek 36:17–18). Yet, in each case in which David's shedding of blood is mentioned in the Chronicles, that action is associated with his waging of war (1 Chr 22:8 [*bis*]; 28:3; cf. Eupolemus, "he was defiled because of human blood and because of many years of warfare" [Eusebius, *Praep. ev.* 9.30.6]). It seems counterproductive to decouple the two. In this context, a further question should be raised: why would the shedding of blood in war render David unworthy to build the Temple? Addressing this question involves relating a number of features of older biblical presentations to each other. To begin with, as Murray (2001) observes, the corpse contamination legislation of Num 31:19–24 (cf. Num 19:16) requires Israelite warriors who had killed the enemy to remain outside the Israelite camp for seven days and to undergo a two-stage purification ritual. In this respect, one can affirm some basic tenets of the third view, while allowing a ritual aspect (view 1) to the overall explanation. Moreover, the references to David's shedding blood are important in light of other earlier biblical texts. It seems unlikely that the Chronicler held to a firm and absolute distinction between the act of pouring out blood in sacrifice and the act of pouring out blood in homicide. A number of earlier writers believed that blood embodied life (e.g., Gen 6:9; Deut 12:23; Lev 17:11) and, as such, was allotted to God (Sperling 1992: 761). Concomitantly, blood is forbidden to Israelites in biblical legislation (Lev 3:17; 7:22–26; Deut 12:23–25). Because blood belonged to God, those who spilled blood through acts of violence might attempt to conceal the blood of their victim from God's sight (Gen 37:26; 1 Sam 26:20; Ezek 24:7–8). In David's case, however, there was no hiding the fact. Yhwh specifically speaks of David's shedding blood "to the earth before me." Moreover, David had not simply spilled blood, he had, as the text repeatedly tells us, spilled "much blood."

One can recognize that the issue of why Israel's reverend king was barred from building the Temple proved to be a historical, hermeneutical, and theological challenge for the writer. It was customary in ancient Near Eastern societies for successful monarchs to give thanks to the deities who supported them by building temples in their honor. In the Chronicler's construction of the past, David was not an average king. He managed to achieve one military and political success after another. How could this figure, the Chronicler's favorite monarch, not build a scared shrine to the God of Israel who had so resolutely supported him? The author could not deny some of the basic facts provided in his source, although he could modify and elaborate upon the reasons provided by that source to account for such a momentous divine decision.

The author was faced with another difficulty. If the Chronicler had simply taken over the defense provided by the Deuteronomist, the Chronicler would undermine distinctive dimensions of his own presentation of David's career. The David of Samuel-Kings was beset by wars, because he had to wage not only a series of campaigns against Israel's foreign foes but also against rebellions within his own house. Much of the so-called "Succession Narrative" or "Court History of David" (2 Sam 9–20*; 1 Kgs 1–2*) is concerned with the struggle among David's sons as to who might succeed him. The Chronicler does not recount, however, such a struggle for the succession to the Davidic throne. The royal succession is an entirely smooth one and all of David's other sons endorse chosen Solomon (29:23–24). The Chronicler has David, in fact, spend the last part of his life in peace, grooming his son for the succession, assembling a national administration, and preparing for the construction of the promised central sanctuary (1 Chr 22–29). The explanation of David being distracted by war would not suffice in the context of the Chronicler's own portrayal of the Davidic monarchy.

The Chronicler chose not to abandon the explanation provided in Kings, but to reinterpret and modify it by recourse to other texts, applying the notion of "shedding blood" (*šāpak dām*) to David's conduct in war. The issue was neither a matter of time management nor a moral lapse on David's part. David's many military campaigns, fought in the name of Yhwh, had left him ritually unfit to build the Temple of Yhwh, the "Holy House" (בית הקדש; 1 Chr 29:3). Because David's wars had rendered him ineligible to build the central sanctuary, there was no question of his doing so even after "the land was subdued before Yhwh and before his people" (נכבשה הארץ לפני יהוה ולפני עמו; 22:18). In this way, the Chronicler sought to provide a more substantive and contextually appropriate explanation than the preoccupation-with-war explanation found in his source. The Chronicler's selective interpretation, extension, and application of older texts are, however, ad hoc. The legislation of Num 31:19–34 allows warriors to purify themselves and re-enter the camp after seven days. No such ritual is offered to David. The author does not specifically cite any legislation to justify his evaluation. Nor does he level this type of charge against other kings. It is true that the ideal kingdom is one that is at peace (Mosis 1973: 94–100, 151; Fishbane 1985: 397; Gabriel 1990: 65–72). Nevertheless, given the ad hoc nature of the argument, it is misleading to generalize a Chronistic theology of pacifism from the judgment rendered against David.

22:9. "a man of rest" (*'îš mĕnûḥâ*). Solomon is "not a man who procures peace but one who enjoys peace" (Keil 1873: 245). In Kings Solomon does both. He procures peace by pacifying internal opposition to his rule (1 Kgs 2), and he enjoys peace because he does not have to confront external threats (or any further internal threats) until relatively late in his reign (1 Kgs 11:14–43; but see 11:21–22, 25; Knoppers 1993c: 160–64).

"his name." The Chronicler, followed by Josephus (*Ant.* 7.337–38), puns on the name "Solomon" (*šĕlōmōh*) and the word for "peace" (*šālōm*). Cf. Eupolemus (Eusebius, *Praep. ev.* 9.34.20). Aside from the fact that David has defeated Israel's enemies, such repose is assured because "peace (*šālōm*) and quiet (*šeqeṭ*) I [Yhwh] shall give to Israel in his days." On the reuse of Samuel-Kings, see further Kalimi (1995b: 37).

22:10. "as for him, he will build a house for my name" (הוא יבנה בית לשמי). Possibly a direct allusion to 17:12, "as for him, he will build a house for me" (הוא יבנה-לי בית), although it is more probable that the author had 1 Kgs 5:19 [ET 5:5] in view, "your son . . . he, he will build the House for my name" (בנך . . . הוא-יבנה הבית לשמי). Whatever the case, the rest of 1 Chr 22:10 is largely an inverted quotation of 17:12–13. By reversing the sequence of the three clauses in 17:12–13, the author calls attention to the fact that he is quoting this source.

| *1 Chronicles 17:12–13* | *1 Chronicles 22:10* |
|---|---|
| a. I shall establish his throne forever | c. He, he will become my son |
| b. I, I shall be a father to him, | b. and I shall become his father. |
| c. and he will be a son to me | a. And I shall establish the throne of his dominion over Israel forever. |

"he will become my son and I shall become his father." On the force of this technical language, see the 1st NOTE to 17:13.

"and I shall establish the throne of his dominion over Israel forever." The expansion over against 17:12, "and I shall establish his throne forever," does not seem to be accidental. That the Davidic throne carries authority "over Israel" *(ʿl yśrʾl)* coheres with the Chronicler's repeated contention that the Davidic promises pertain to all members of all of the Israelite tribes, whether southern or northern (2 Chr 13:5; Knoppers 1990; 1993a).

22:11. "may Yhwh be with you." The text plays on the theme of presence—whether divine or material, present or future. The wish for divine presence is repeated by David at the conclusion of his oration (v. 16). In between these two requests for divine presence, David expounds on what he has provided for Solomon, "and with you in abundance *(wʿmk lrb)* are artisans . . ." (v. 15).

"so that you will become very prosperous *(wĕhiṣlaḥtā)*." The terminology recalls the speech of Yhwh to Joshua at the inception of Joshua's tenure as Israel's leader (Josh 1:2–9; Porter 1970; Williamson 1976; R. Braun 1986). As with David and Solomon, such speeches mark the transition between two eras. In the aftermath of Moses' death, Yhwh instructs Joshua on the terms of his mission, predicating the overall success of Israel's conquest upon vigilant observance of "this scroll of the Torah"—"only then will you prosper *(taṣlîaḥ)* your way, and only then will you be very successful" (Josh 1:8).

"as he promised concerning you" *(kʾšr dbr ʿlyk)*. Another allusion to Nathan's dynastic oracle (17:7–14). Consistent with the Chronicler's concentration upon the singular, "I shall appoint him in my house and in my kingship forever" (1 Chr 17:14; cf. 2 Sam 7:16), he speaks of the singular (Solomon) here.

22:12. "insight and understanding" *(śēkel ûbînâ)*. At Gibeon Solomon requests "wisdom and knowledge" (*ḥokmâ ûmaddāʿ*; 2 Chr 1:10; cf. 1 Kgs 3:9). In Chronicles David anticipates Solomon's request. This is one means by which the Chronicler ties the reign of Solomon to that of David. David knows, so to speak, what Solomon will need before Solomon thinks of it himself. The connection between wisdom and the observance of divine statutes is also characteristic of Deuteronomistic thought (Weinfeld 1972a).

"observe the Torah of Yhwh your God" (לשמור את-תורת יהוה אלהיך). If the relationship between these clauses and the previous clause is properly construed (see TEXTUAL NOTE), David is expressing a concept of divine-human relations similar to that expressed in 29:12–14. Israelites have a sacred obligation to obey their

God. But divine gifts, in turn, help Israelites honor their commitments to the deity. In formulating such a theology, the Chronicler was probably influenced by Jeremiah (31:31–34) and Ezekiel (36:22–29; 37:14; 39:28–29).

22:13. "you will become very prosperous, if . . ." Summonses to obey Yhwh's statutes and judgments are ubiquitous in Deuteronomy (e.g., 7:11; 11:32) and the Deuteronomistic History (Weinfeld 1972a: 332–39), but the linkage between obedience and prosperity finds its closest parallel in the Deuteronomistically worded speech of Yhwh to Joshua (1:2–9; 2nd NOTE to v. 11). In both cases, the focus is upon an individual leader, even though this leader is part of a larger corporate entity (Josh 1:2–3, 10–15; 1 Chr 22:17–19). The behavior of these authorities will be instrumental in determining Israel's future course. In the case of Joshua, the success of the Conquest is at stake, while in the case of Solomon, temple construction is at stake.

"be strong and resolute" (*ḥăzaq weʾĕmāṣ*). This formula of encouragement is familiar from Deuteronomistic contexts (e.g., Deut 31:6, 7; Josh 1:18; 10:25; Weinfeld 1972a: 343 [#11]). Although the collocation appears in Moses' speech to Joshua (Deut 31:23), it is especially prominent in Yhwh's speech to Joshua, appearing three times (Josh 1:6, 7, 9). The expression is adopted by the Chronicler, who uses it in both martial and nonmartial contexts (1 Chr 22:13; 28:20; 2 Chr 32:7).

"neither fear nor be dismayed" (*ʾal-tîrāʾ wĕʾal-tēḥat*). Another expression often found in Deuteronomic, Deuteronomistic, and other contexts (Weinfeld 1972a: 344 [#12]) that is adopted by the Chronicler (1 Chr 28:20; 2 Chr 20:15, 17; 32:7). In some contexts, the expression relates to readying troops before battle (e.g., Deut 31:7–8; Josh 10:25; 2 Chr 20:15–16; 32:7; Conrad 1985: 6–78). But both the Deuteronomist, in his presentation of Yhwh's speech to Joshua (1:7–8), and the Chronicler expand its coverage to include observing divine statutes (Weinfeld 1972a: 5, 11; Fishbane 1985: 384). Not so much physical strength, but spiritual fortitude is necessary for the success of Joshua and Solomon.

22:14. "in my humility" (*bĕʿonyî*). Internal reallocation of state resources is critical to the king's capacity to provide for his son. Through self-denial, David is able to set aside enormous quantities of materials to build the sanctuary. A similar instance of self-restraint, perhaps the source for our text, is attributed to David in Ps 132 (see TEXTUAL NOTE). The psalmist's summons to Yhwh to remember David (Ps 132:1) is associated with David's oath to Yhwh that he will find Yhwh an appropriate sanctuary (Ps 132:2–5). David avoids his house and abstains from sleep until he finds a domicile for "the Mighty One of Jacob" (Ps 132:3–5).

"100,000 talents of gold and 1,000,000 talents of silver." The incredible figures easily dwarf those mentioned in Kings to describe Solomon's riches. There Ḥiram dispatches 120 talents of gold to Solomon as his annual tribute (1 Kgs 9:14). The queen of Sheba also brings 120 talents of gold to Solomon, along with an incomparable quantity of spices and precious stones (1 Kgs 10:2, 10). The joint expedition of Ḥiram and Solomon nets Solomon the enormous sum of 420 talents ($LXX^B$ = 120; 2 Chr 8:18 = 450) from Ophir (1 Kgs 9:28). An even larger figure is used to describe the wealth Solomon garners through tribute: 666 talents of gold annually (1 Kgs 10:14). Nevertheless, all of these numbers pale in comparison with the "100,000 talents of gold and 1,000,000 talents of silver" that David sets aside from state coffers for Solomon's use. The point is not realism, but extravagance. The gifts are deliberately excessive. Successful ancient Near Eastern kings were supposed to endow the construction and refurbishment of shrines. Temple complexes (and palaces) could only succeed with great attention being paid to logistics, planning, and the requisition of extensive sums of labor and materials. To take one example, the great Assyrian king Esarhaddon, who reigned in the early seventh century B.C.E., boasts in his royal inscriptions of all the effort he expended rebuilding Esagil, the great Babylonian temple complex destroyed by Esarhaddon's own father Sennacherib. Letters from priests to Esarhaddon confirm the tremendous scope of this work, mentioning the construction of courtyards, shrines, and battlements (Cole and Machinist, §161), the deposit of precious stones (Cole and Machinist, §161), the use of cedar for the main gate and to roof the shrines (Cole and Machinist, §§162–64), the employment of precious metals and gems (Cole and Machinist, §§166, 174), and the use of much gold for a variety of decorative purposes (Cole and Machinist, §§174, 179). In the case of Chronicles, the author portrays David as a great king whose endowments are designed to ensure that Solomon succeeds in his task. Indeed, the size of the endowments are so outrageously high that Solomon need not even worry about embarking on one of the normal means of gaining wealth—raids and campaigns against one's neighbors. David enables Solomon to rule effectively without recourse to war. The use of such fantastic numbers (NOTE to 12:38) may have led Eupolemus to speculate how David was able to procure such large amounts of gold bullion (Eusebius, *Praep. ev.* 9.30.8).

"and you will add to them." Solomon cannot be passive—the mere recipient of his father's largesse—he has his own work to do (2 Chr 2:1–9 [ET 2:2–10]).

22:15. "artisans." The Chronicler carefully lays the groundwork for his presentation of Solomon's reign to complement that of David. When Solomon later tells Ḥuram of Tyre of his temple-construction plans, he need only ask for one specialist. Aside from this technical help, Solomon can draw upon the coterie of craftsmen "whom David my father provided me" (2 Chr 2:6 [ET 2:7]).

"with every kind of skill (*ḥākām*)." The term *ḥākām* is used to describe both the artisans of the Tabernacle (Exod 28:3; 31:6; 35:10; 36:1, 2, 4, 8) and the artisans of the Temple (2 Chr 2:6, 12, 13 [ET 2:7, 13, 14]). This is but one way in which the Chronicler ties the two sacred institutions together.

22:16. "arise and act and may Yhwh be with you." At first glance, the composition of vv. 13–16 seems cumbersome. Some commentators are, in fact, inclined to excise vv. 14–16 as a later addition (e.g., Rudolph 1955: 151; R. Braun 1986: 226; Throntveit 1987: 43). But the puzzling configuration of these verses results partially, at least, from the overall design that the Chronicler imposes on his material. He frames David's provisions with moral exhortations to Solomon (vv. 13, 16).

*Exhortation*
[13]Be strong and resolute; neither fear nor be dismayed.
*Materials*
[14]In my humility, I have provided for the House of God: 100,000 talents of gold and 1,000,000 talents of silver, as well as bronze and iron beyond weighing, because there was so much of it. I have also provided wood and stones and you will add to them.
*Artisans*
[15]And with you in abundance are artisans—masons, stonecutters, and carpenters—with every kind of skill in every kind of work
*Materials*
[16]pertaining to gold, silver, bronze, and iron without number.
*Exhortation*
Arise and act and may Yhwh be with you.

The chiastic arrangement underscores the fact that the reigning monarch has given his son and chosen successor more than moral support. It is one thing to designate an offspring for succession; it is quite another thing for that offspring to succeed. Even in instances in which a reigning monarch arranged for a succession or a coregency, other claimants to the throne could oppose the succession after the reigning monarch died. Esarhaddon's contested accession is a case in point. That Sennacherib took all kinds of precautions to ensure that Assyrian clients did not contest Esarhaddon's accession did not prevent Esarhaddon's princely rivals from doing so. The Chronicler's David does his best to thwart such a possible outcome. Not only has David set aside abundant and varied materials for the sanctuary project (vv. 14–16a), thereby alluding to his earlier actions (vv. 2–5), but he also furnishes Solomon with artisans to work with these materials to ensure that the project becomes a reality (v. 15). In this way, the temple project will not become an undue burden on the shoulders of David's successor.

22:17–19. Some scholars view this address, spoken to Israel's leaders, as anticipating the public addresses of 28:2–10, 20–21 and therefore deem it to be secondary (Rudolph 1955: 151–52; Noth 1987: 112; R. Braun 1986: 226–27). Throntveit (1987: 44) argues that its insertion was occasioned by the great insertion of 1 Chr 23–27, which separated David's (presumably) private (22:7–16) and public addresses (28:2–29:19). This is quite possible, but the grounds by which all of 1 Chr 23–27 have been excised from the Chronicler's work have been vigorously challenged by some recent scholars (see "Excursus: The Composition of 1 Chronicles 23–27"). With respect to the present context, more attention needs to be given to the manner in which unevenness in the text has resulted both from the citation of older biblical passages and from the modeling of this composition upon earlier patterns, especially those texts depicting the Moses-Joshua transition (see SOURCES AND COMPOSITION). Deuteronomy 31 and Josh 1, from which the author drew various formulas, contain a variety of speeches delivered to various audiences at various times. Deuteronomy 31 contains, in fact, no fewer than seven distinct speeches (vv. 1–6, 7–8, 10–13, 14, 16–21, 23, 25–29). The insertion of the long poem in Deut 32 (introduced in Deut 31:30) adds yet a further complication in the progress of the narration. There is undeniably some repetition among the orations in these chapters and among their recipients, but this repetition may have little bothered the writer, who employed this variegated material in plotting his own composition. In other words, the elaborate sequence of speeches marking the transition from Moses to Joshua may well have influenced how the Chronicler depicted David's final years and Solomon's rise to power.

22:17. "then David commanded" (**ויצו דויד**). During the final period of David's reign, he makes a series of public addresses in which he instructs Solomon (22:7–16; 28:9–10, 20–21), the officers in his kingdom (22:17–19; 29:1–5, 20), and the masses as a whole (28:2–8). In this particular case, he urges the assembled officials to support his designated heir, follow divine statutes, and build the Temple. The mention of a series of instructions by the head of state requires some discussion. In ancient Mediterranean kingdoms, state functionaries have their roles defined by and take their directions from temple or royal overseers (Weinfeld 1976: 379–414). The so-called "instructions" from the "Great King" of Ḫatti to his lords, princes, and bodyguards reveal something of what sovereigns demanded of their dependents (von Schuler 1957: 1–52; Goetze 1960: 69–73; Güterbock and van den Hout 1991: 3–41). In these texts, high officials are admonished to fulfill their duties and warned not to enter into treasonable acts against the king or his dynasty. Instruction texts typically begin with a preamble, the name and title of the king who is giving the instructions, and the instructions, each followed by a corresponding loyalty oath (von Schuler 1957: 2–7; cf. Weinfeld 1976: 392–402). The instructions conclude with a summary prohibition of oath breaking and a special prohibition of breach or nonobservance of any provision (von Schuler 1957: 2; Korošec 1931: 18–57, 89–107). In one such instruction to princes, lords, and high officials, twenty-one sections are devoted to instances in which princes and lords must prove their loyalty (von Schuler 1957: 23–29). These include prohibitions against libel (§18), against conspiracy with fugitives (§11), against acknowledging rival claims to the throne by the king's relatives (§3), the obligation to report a conspiracy (§5), and to render timely assistance (§2). The instructions to high officials include the obligation to maintain silence with regard to confidential communications (§24), to report the disappearance of the king's relatives (§25), and to report any evil threatening the king (§28; Goetze 1957: 95–105; von Schuler 1957: 2–4; Beckman 1992: 45–49). It seems likely that these functionaries had to swear an oath of loyalty, placing themselves, if the oath were broken, under the vengeance of the gods invoked (Goetze 1964: 32).

Comparison with Hittite instruction texts reveals both similarities and differences with the instructions given in Chronicles. Both the instruction texts and Chronicles document an array of royally appointed officials supported by the crown. Both point toward a strong central authority to whom these officials are obligated. In neither case are the relationships between various types of officials systematically developed. But there are also differences between the two. The speeches in Chronicles orient themselves to a few specific issues: support of the heir apparent, compliance with divine ordinances, and construction of the Temple. The accompanying texts in 1 Chr 23–27 are long in enumerations of titles, names, and patronymics and short in explications of responsibilities. The converse is true of the Hittite instructions. Hence, one can posit only an indirect relationship, at most, between the elaborate instruction texts found in the ancient Near East and the shorter kinds of instructions found in Chronicles.

"all the officers of Israel *(kl-śry yśr'l)*." The text does not specify who these leaders were, but the larger point seems clear. In Kings, Solomon succeeds his father (1 Kgs 1) and consolidates his kingdom by pacifying, eliminating, and exiling his domestic foes (1 Kgs 2). Solomon's actions appear drastic, although he acts at his aged father's bidding (1 Kgs 2:1–9; Knoppers 1993c: 57–77). In Chronicles such a dramatic effort is totally unnecessary because David has mobilized elite backing for Solomon. One means by which David galvanizes support for Solomon is to allude subtly to the mandate imposed by Deuteronomic law to build the central sanctuary (see below; cf. 29:5–9, 23–24). Indeed, the establishment of rest and security for Israel is in and of itself an imperative for building the Temple. According to Deuteronomic law, once Israel becomes safely established in its land, Israelites are to bring their designated offerings to "the site where Yhwh your God will choose to set his name" (Deut 12:10–11). Given this timetable, Israel's leadership has no choice but to act. This is no time for dissension, much less a struggle of rival claims to the succession. The Temple must be built.

22:18. "is not Yhwh your God with you?" The peace resulting from the conquest of Israel's enemies indicates that Yhwh is present with Israel (v. 18; cf. 28:20). Whereas the presence of God with Solomon is a future wish (vv. 11, 16), the presence of God with Israel forms the grounds for David's exhortation.

"given you rest on every side" (והניח לכם מסביב). Drawing upon certain features of the Deuteronomistic History (e.g., 1 Kgs 5:4–5, 17–19 [ET 4:24–25, 5:3–5]), the Chronicler portrays Solomon's tenure as an unprecedented time of rest and peace (1 Chr 22:9; 2 Chr 6:4–5, 40–41). To be sure, the rest given by Yhwh in Chronicles is not simply a onetime affair (Deut 12:10–12; 25:19), but a present possibility for later generations (von Rad 1966b: 94–98). That this would be so is not an indication of how far the theological concept of rest has degenerated by the time of the Chronicler's writing (contra von Rad), but of how the Chronicler understands the workings of divine justice. To begin with, the Deuteronomistic History does not speak with one voice on the issue of when the promised rest is achieved (Josh 1:13, 15; 21:41–43; 22:4; 23:1; 2 Sam 7:1, 11; 1 Kgs 5:4–5, 17–18 [ET 4:24–25, 5:3–5]; 8:56), a point von Rad concedes. Second, from the Chronicler's vantage point, it would be unfair to associate peace exclusively with any one king or with any one particular period. That the time of sanctuary construction should follow the establishment of national security does not preclude Israel's enjoyment of subsequent times of peace. If rest from one's enemies is linked in some fashion to the broader issues of loyalty and obedience, then such rest should be available to Israel in a variety of periods (2 Chr 13:23 [ET 14:1]; 14:4–5 [ET 14:5–6]; 15:15; 20:30; 32:22 [LXX]).

"given all the inhabitants of the land into my hand." Not the Israelites, but the Canaanites are in view (Num 32:22, 29; Josh 2:24; 18:1; 23:3–5, 9–13; 24:11, 18). David has consolidated Israel's geopolitical status and secured its international borders (1 Chr 11:4–9; 14:8–17; 18:1–20:8). The author's assertion that David's conquest of his enemies marks a major moment in David's career finds an interesting parallel of sorts in one of the superscriptions to the Greek Psalms (Psalm 96). The superscription, *Tō Dauid hote hē gē autou kathistatai* ("Relating to David, when his land was set in order"), is not found in MT and most likely belongs to early Jewish (Greek) exegetical tradition (Pietersma 2001). The additions of such psalm titles, or the addition of further details in already existing titles, is a fascinating aspect of the history of early biblical interpretation. Many such psalm superscriptions are evidently based on the content of the individual psalms themselves (Childs 1971). In LXX Psalm 96, David's gaining complete control over the land becomes the occasion for singing a new song to Yhwh (v. 1) and for celebrating Yhwh's dominion over the nations (vv. 7–10). In Chronicles, David's gaining complete control over his enemies becomes the occasion for a new round of major royal initiatives that are focused on preparing for Solomon's reign and the construction of the long-awaited central shrine.

"the land is subdued before Yhwh" *(wnkbšw h'rṣ lpny yhwh)*. An expression drawn from the Priestly writers to describe the result of conquest (Num 32:22, 29; Josh 18:1). Here, the divine warrior has effected his victories not through Moses and Joshua, but through David. In this respect, the peace and tranquility that characterize Solomon's reign already punctuate the final portion of David's reign.

22:19. "seeking *(drš)* Yhwh your God." The verb *drš* has cultic overtones in certain biblical contexts, such as Chronicles (S. Driver 1895b: 304–5), and at Qumran (Wagner 1978: 298–304). Here "seeking God" is connected with the construction of "the sanctuary of Yhwh God." See also the last NOTE to 10:13.

"arise and build the sanctuary of Yhwh God" (מקדש יהוה האלהים). Baltzer (1971: 77–88) points out that investiture ceremonies of Hittite clients included two acts: the vassal's oath to the Hittite overlord and the oath of the vassal's people to their king. There are some differences between such ceremonies and the situation depicted here, but there are also some parallels. David instructs his successor and defines the terms of his success. Having urged on his son, David addresses the officers, commanding their assistance for his son and their support for the projected Temple.

"the Ark of the Covenant of Yhwh." David prepares for what he hopes is the final movement of Israel's ancient palladium (2 Chr 5:2), presently situated in the tent that he established for it (15:1, 25–16:6; 17:1).

"the holy furnishings of God" *(kělê qōdeš hā'ělōhîm)*. The authors of Chronicles and Ezra take a consistent interest in sacred artifacts, especially those associated with the Temple. The temple vessels have been called, in fact, "a continuity theme" in Chronicles, Ezra, and Nehemiah (Ackroyd 1987: 56–59). This theme begins, as we have seen, with David's ritual dedication of his spoils (18:7–8, 10–11). It is present in the depiction of Solomon (2 Chr 5:1, 5) and continues during the Judahite monarchy (2 Chr 13:11; 15:18; 24:14; 25:24; 28:24; 29:26). The theme is advanced despite the exile (2 Chr 36:7, 10, 18), finding a resumption in the early postexilic community (Ezra 1:7–11). It continues during the time of Ezra (7:19–20; 8:26–28, 33–34) and Nehemiah (10:39; 13:5–9). In pursuing this "holy vessels" theme, the writers of Ezra and Nehemiah establish clear links between their contemporary situation and that of the monarchy. But this important theme of continuity and return is anticipated within Chronicles itself (Knoppers 1999e). Following the genealogical introduction to the people of Israel (1 Chr 2:3–9:1a) and the brief notice of Judah's exile (9:1b), the account of their return places much emphasis on the fact that the Persian period community perpetuates both monarchic and Sinaitic forms of Israel's worship (COMMENT to 9:2–34). In this context, the author observes that "all the holy furnishings" (*kol-kĕlê haqqōdeš;* 9:29) are (again) part of the Levitical responsibilities in the Jerusalem cult.

## SOURCES AND COMPOSITION

First Chronicles 22 is unique. Because there is no direct parallel in Samuel-Kings to David's preparations and speeches in 1 Chr 22, many scholars have surmised that the Chronicler must have had access to extra-biblical sources in composing this material. Such an assumption is likely to be mistaken. It is clear that the author drew heavily upon a variety of older biblical passages to write most of this material (see NOTES). Most prominent among these are Joshua's installation speech (Josh 1:2–9) and Nathan's dynastic oracle (1 Chr 17:12–13)—explicitly cited in David's oration (1 Chr 22:7–16), Solomon's letter to Ḥiram (1 Kgs 5:17–18 [ET 5:3–4]), and Solomon's first dedicatory blessing (1 Kgs 8:17–19). Less visible in the style and language of 1 Chr 22, but still informing its presentation, is the demand for and the timing given to the establishment of a central sanctuary in Deut 12. Given the allusions to or citations of prestigious texts, the clear signs of the Chronicler's own style (S. Driver 1895b; Curtis and Madsen 1910: 256–60), and the late linguistic usage evident throughout the chapter (Margain 1974; TEXTUAL NOTES), one can say that this chapter represents a Chronistic composition. The author has employed different biblical materials, rearranged them according to his own purposes, and added his own contributions. The result is a work that clearly reflects the author's own priorities and themes.

The astute reuse of older biblical texts deserves closer study. In his speech to Solomon, David explicitly cites ("the word of Yhwh came to me, saying"; v. 8) another speech, a divine communication, that forms the basis (vv. 8–10) of his exhortations to Solomon (vv. 11–16). The appeal to an authoritative divine utterance is explicit, effected through an inverted quotation of Nathan's dynastic oracle (1st NOTE to v. 10). When David begins his instructions to Solomon, he appeals again to this *traditum* ("as he promised concerning you"; v. 11). Yet the Chronicler's citation goes well beyond its source. In his historical retrospect (vv. 8–10) David also alludes to the aggadic transformations of Nathan's dynastic oracle in 1 Kgs 5:17–18 [ET 5:3–4] and 8:17–19. To these citations and allusions the Chronicler adds his own material, most notably the explanation of why David was not allowed to build the Temple.

If the reworking of the dynastic oracle of 2 Sam 7 in 1 Kgs 5 and 8 represents a double literary shift (Fishbane 1985: 415), the reuse of this material in Chronicles represents a triple literary shift. The citation of certain Davidic promises, presented in reverse sequence, is decontextualized from its original setting. Combining part of Nathan's speech with revisions of that speech found in other literary contexts creates a new literary entity. The Chronicler's *traditio* ingeniously arranges Solomon's transformations of the dynastic promises in a new setting so that David recounts them himself. Moreover, the Chronicler's additions to these sources are not incidental to the larger presentation, but are pivotal to an understanding of the roles of David and Solomon in the United Monarchy. David's quotation of a divine communication turns out to be much more than that.

The resourceful rewriting of the relationship between the Davidic dynasty and temple construction is ingeniously augmented by the reuse of speeches orchestrating the transition from Moses to Joshua (Deut 31:7–8, 23; Josh 1:2–9). To these speeches should be added two other major addresses: the commission of Joshua in Num 27:15–23 (usually attributed to Priestly tradition) and the oration of Moses that opens the book of Deuteronomy (1:6–3:29). In the former piece, Yhwh instructs Moses to lay his hand upon Joshua and invest him with some of Moses' authority so that the "entire Israelite community might heed [him]" (למען ישמעו כל-עדת בני-ישׂראל; Num 27:18–20). Although the latter Deuteronomistic speech prefaces a great variety of statutes, laws, historical summaries, and other speeches, it also has the Moses-Joshua succession in view. In one context, Moses proclaims that of all the Israelites, only Caleb and Joshua will enter the promised land. These were the two individuals who had remained loyal to Yhwh (Deut 1:34–36, 38–40). Moses, along with the Israelites, would be denied the privilege, because they had incensed the deity (Deut 1:35, 37). Moses is to imbue Joshua with strength (אתו חזק; NJPS), because it will be Joshua who will allot the land to Israel (Deut 1:38). In a later context, Moses revisits the Joshua succession and recounts his pleading with Yhwh to let him cross over the Jordan (Deut 3:23–25). But Moses' appeal is to no avail. Although he is allowed to view the land from the summit of Pisgah, Moses is commanded to "strengthen and fortify" (חזקהו ואמצהו) Joshua because Joshua will be the one to cross over before the people and allot the land to them (Deut 3:28).

Following the rehearsal of a long series of statutes, commandments, and ordinances, delivered in a sequence of addresses, Moses returns to the issue of succession. Having summoned Joshua, Moses urges Joshua, in the presence of "all Israel," to be "strong and resolute" (חזק ואמץ) because Joshua will be entering the land with this people and apportioning it to them (Deut 31:7). Employing formulas of encouragement known from other Deuteronomistic contexts, Moses provides his successor with a series of assurances. "As for Yhwh, he will go before you, he will be with you, he will not fail you or abandon you. Neither fear nor be dismayed!" (לא תירא ולא תחת; Deut 31:8). Joshua is later summoned to witness a theophany and another speech, in this case from Yhwh to Moses (Deut 31:14–21). At the conclusion of this episode, Moses again charges Joshua and provides similar words of encouragement (Deut 31:23; cf. 32:44). The final speech to Joshua, narrating the transition in leadership, occurs following the death of Moses and is cast as a direct speech from Yhwh to Joshua (Josh 1:1–9).

The repeated appearance of the succession motif both prior to and subsequent to the proclamation of Deuteronomic law (however one defines its extent) is highly important in considering how the Solomonic succession provides the backdrop for the administrative reorganization of the kingdom (1 Chr 23–27). When the Chronicler wrote his work, the model he imitated was itself repetitive and highly elaborate. Given the nature of the model from which he worked, it is no accident that the Chronicler framed both the old Deuteronomic law code and the decrees governing the Levites, priests, and other officials with speeches that narrate, among other things, the theme of a major leadership transition.

Within 1 Chr 22, the influence of the installation speech of Josh 1:2–9 is, as we have seen (see NOTES), especially prominent in David's instructions to Solomon (1 Chr 22:11–16), sharing with Josh 1:2–9 a formula of encouragement ("be strong and resolute; neither fear nor be dismayed"; v. 13), a description of the task (vv. 11–13), and an assurance of divine aid ("arise and act, and may Yhwh be with you"; v. 16; Lohfink 1962; Baltzer 1971; D. McCarthy 1971; Romerowski 1986). In each case, the task addresses the unfulfilled legacy of the outgoing leader. That task is, moreover, explicitly associated with and predicated upon obedience to the Torah. Hence, the Chronicler incorporates Solomon's commission within a larger literary context that is modeled upon an earlier, highly auspicious transition in Israelite leadership. One function of this typology is to present David as a new kind of Moses who acknowledges his unfulfilled dream, but commendably prepares a successor to carry on. Another is to recast the transition from David to Solomon as a smooth and orderly process, supervised and blessed by God. A third is to draw two pivotal moments—Sinai and Zion—together.

## COMMENT

In modeling the David-Solomon succession after the Moses-Joshua succession, the Chronicler has consciously avoided modeling this transition after the David-Solomon succession in Samuel-Kings. From the Chronicler's references and allusions (e.g., 1 Chr 22:7–19), one can be sure that he knew at least some of his (biblical) source material well. The author's restraint is all the more remarkable when one recognizes that the Deuteronomistic History contains a number of speeches (e.g., 2 Sam 12:7–12; 1 Kgs 2:1–9; 3:4–15) that punctuate David's latter reign and Solomon's succession. One of these orations, David's last words to Solomon (1 Kgs 2:1–9), contains exhortations to obey Yhwh's laws, statutes, and commandments and reformulates the dynastic promises (1 Kgs 2:2–4). But of these three speeches, the Chronicler directly employs only the Gibeon dream account (in revised form) within his own history (2 Chr 1:7–12).

To this it could be objected that the Chronicler, given his concern with the Temple and the promises to David, had to turn elsewhere to find an alternative to the helter-skelter picture of David's final days in Samuel-Kings. There is certainly some truth to this observation (see below), but the editing of Samuel-Kings does evince a clear concern with the fulfilment of the dynastic promises (Knoppers

1993c: 57–77). In Samuel-Kings the realization of the divine promises to David has everything to do with the rise and reign of Solomon. In Deuteronomistic perspective, David is the royal exemplar who wages war, follows divine statutes, and receives divine promises. But David is thwarted in some of his chief ambitions, battling his own demons as well as foreign and familial foes (2 Sam 12–20). The latter part of his reign is dominated by palace intrigues and civil war. As a result of some machinations, an unlikely candidate, one of David's youngest sons, succeeds his father (1 Kgs 1). At David's bidding (1 Kgs 2:1–9), Solomon systematically—one could say ruthlessly—ends the internal strife besetting the kingdom (1 Kgs 2:13–46). Having consolidated the realm, Solomon receives divine promises (1 Kgs 3:4–15). The divine revelation at Gibeon individuates Solomon's reign, equipping him for the tasks that lie ahead (Knoppers 1993c: 77–82). The peace and security Israel enjoys during the time of Solomon fulfill one of the divine promises made to David in Nathan's oracle, namely, that Israel would "live in security and be disturbed no longer" (2 Sam 7:10). In Samuel-Kings the reigns of David and Solomon therefore complement and validate each other (Knoppers 1993c: 83–122). Not only is Solomon the promised "seed" prophesied by Nathan (2 Sam 7:12) who establishes David's kingdom, but Solomon also ushers in Israel's promised peace (2 Sam 7:10–11). The attainment of peace, prosperity, and rest in the time of Solomon serves to vindicate David's conquests and wars. The dynastic oracle and Davidic prayer, in turn, anticipate and validate the reign of Solomon. The Chronicler's elaborate pairing of David and Solomon as an ideal team who together bring all traditional Israelite aspirations and institutions to their culmination (R. Braun 1973; 1986: xxxii–xxxv; Williamson 1976; Dillard 1987: 1–7) is already latent within the Deuteronomistic work.

The question that must be addressed is not whether David and Solomon complement one another in Samuel-Kings, but how. In the Deuteronomistic work David has his role to play, but it is Solomon who ultimately salvages many of Nathan's promises. Succession, consolidation, peace, prosperity, and temple construction are all associated with his reign. This leads to a conclusion about the Chronicler's purposes that differs from that traditionally offered (e.g., Curtis and Madsen 1910: 259). The Chronicler rewrites the transition from David to Solomon according to the Moses-Joshua model, not to diminish Solomon's reputation, but to redeem the reputations of David and Israel. The new version of the David-Solomon relationship has to do with temple building, but goes beyond it. There are larger exegetical, political, and social issues at stake. The formulations of Samuel-Kings undoubtedly presented a number of problems for the author. If the establishment of a dynasty was itself contingent upon the reign of one of David's "seed" (2 Sam 7:12), would it not make sense for David to do everything in his power to lay the groundwork for the transition in power? In Samuel, David sires a variety of sons through a variety of marriages. Given the import of Nathan's provisions concerning succession, how could David not prepare for the accession and reign of one of these offspring? If so much was at stake, why was so little done? How could the king allow his family situation to deteriorate so badly in his final years that it threatened the future of his state (2 Sam 12–20; 1 Kgs 1)? There are also the related issues of national identity and national solidarity. Given that Nathan's promises contained provisions for an unprecedented era of peace for Israel, how could Israelites act in such a counterproductive, if not self-destructive, manner during the latter part of David's tenure? Finally, there is the Temple that David was barred from building. Given the magnitude of Nathan's promises (2 Sam 7:5–16), why did David not at least make some preliminary preparations so that this project could succeed, as pledged (2 Sam 7:13), in the next generation?

By modeling the David-Solomon succession after the drawn-out and deliberative Moses-Joshua succession, the Chronicler redresses these deficiencies in the presentation of Samuel-Kings. David realizes that his own legacy is at stake and moves decisively to appoint a successor and to facilitate his task (Wright 1991). He meticulously lays the groundwork for the accession and reign of his son by explaining first to him and then to Israel's elite his plans for the future. David anticipates various kinds of needs—material, political, and spiritual—that Solomon might have in order for him to complete his divinely appointed role. At considerable cost (22:14), David supplies these needs "in abundance" (*lrb;* 22:3, 4, 5, 14, 15). In Chronicles, as in Kings, Solomon ascends to power while David is still on the throne, but in Chronicles David unifies the kingdom before Solomon takes his seat. The transition is effected through a variety of means: the reigning king's personal preparation of his heir (22:7–16), his provision of materials for the construction of the Temple (22:1–5), and his organization of elite support for the scion (22:17–19).

David's reconfigured reign anticipates signature features of Solomon's reign. In Kings, Solomon's wealth is a divine bequest granted in response to Solomon's request for wisdom (1 Kgs 3:4–14). In Chronicles Solomon requests wisdom (2 Chr 1:8–10), but David has already anticipated Solomon's needs. Solomon's wealth becomes in part a Davidic bequest. David's self-denial results in the setting aside of enormous quantities of gold, silver, and bronze for his son's use (22:2–4, 14). The generosity of the people and officers (*śrym;* 29:6–9) also contributes to Solomon's affluence. In Kings God provides Solomon with wisdom as a gift to fulfill his specific request (1 Kgs 3:12). But in Chronicles Solomon's wisdom first appears in conjunction with a Davidic request. David petitions Yhwh to accord to Solomon "insight and understanding" (22:12). Finally, in Kings the inception of the promised era of rest begins with the consolidation of Solomon's reign (1 Kgs 2:12, 46). In Chronicles Solomon's reign is also depicted as the long-awaited era of peace (22:9). Indeed, Solomon is "a man of rest" (22:9). But the time of national peace begins already in the latter part of David's reign (22:18; 23:25). Israel's reverend king announces that "the land is subdued before Yhwh and before his people" (22:18). In conformity with the dictates of Deuteronomic law (Deut 12:8–11), this security compels David to begin making plans for constructing the central sanctuary.

By anticipating certain features of Solomon's reign in his depiction of David's reign, the Chronicler melds the two together. David's establishment of security and peace is foundational to the success of Solomon's major initiatives. The narrator later boasts of the benefits Israel experiences during Solomon's tenure

(2 Chr 8:17–9:28). In this respect, 1 Chr 22–29 are as much as a prelude to Solomon's reign as the denouement to David's. Victories against Israel's neighbors (1 Chr 18–20) realize one of the Davidic promises, while David's provisions for Solomon's accession to power lay the foundation for the attainment of others. The beneficiary of his father's preparations, Solomon is but "an inexperienced youth," and the challenges ahead are formidable. Yet the forward-looking policies of an aging David (22:5) establish the contours of his son's reign and ensure its success.

## EXCURSUS: THE COMPOSITION OF 1 CHRONICLES 23–27

A recently published Neo-Babylonian economic text dating to the first year of the reign of Nabonidus presents a fascinating glimpse into the intricate relationship between temple and state, between temple officials and royal personnel. In response to a request from Šum-ukîn son of Bêl-zêri (a royal official) and Kalbaia son of Iqišaia, the king grants to these individuals 6,000 *kur* of arable land, 400 oxen, and 100 cows to replace the loss of 400 cattle (Joannès 1982: 136–41). During the first year of the arrangement, the Eanna Temple is to consign to Šum-ukîn and Kalbaia 3,000 *kur* of barley for seed as well as 10 talents of iron. They, in turn, will be responsible for delivering annually 25,000 *kur* of barley and dates to the banks of the canals to the Lady of Uruk. Moreover, the offspring born to the cows are to be presented to the messenger of the king, who will mark them with the brand of the Lady of Uruk. The wealth of Šum-ukîn and Kalbaia will thus be tied to the temple. Befitting its importance, the charter is executed in the presence of a variety of officials including the governor of the land, the chief of the sacrificers, the governor of the *Bît Ada*, the chancellor *(rab unqâtu)*, the chief of the army *(rab kiṣir)*, the chief of the troops *(rab ṣabbu)*, the governor of Uruk *(šākin ṭēmi uruk)*, and Nabu-šar-uṣur the *rêš šarri*. The document witnesses to the close relations that could exist among temple, civic, military, and royal officials. Temple administrators served ultimately at the behest of the king. Indeed, given the close links between temple and state governance, a change within the political administration in the capitals of the Neo-Babylonian and Persian realms could result in the turnover of top temple officials (Wright 1989).

One also reads about ties among the governance of the state, the governance of the military, and the governance of the cult within 1 Chr 23–27. Priests, Levites, judges, gatekeepers, military leaders, and tribal officers all make appearances as an inveterate David makes a series of appointments in anticipation of his successor's reign. When seen against the backdrop of the close ties that could exist between temple and state officials in the Neo-Babylonian and Achaemenid eras, the close ties posited between David and the assorted officials in his kingdom become all the more intriguing. Most of the scholarship on these difficult chapters has not been focused, however, on these larger social, political, and religious issues. Rather, commentators have wrestled with the fundamental question of authorship. Do these chapters—largely comprising lists of Levites, priests, officials, and gatekeepers—stem from sources in the Chronicler's employ, from the Chronicler himself, from later editors, or from anonymous glossators? Useful overviews of the larger discussion may be found in Graham (1990), Wright (1989; 1992), and Peltonen (1996). Is it possible that all of these points of view are valid in the sense that these chapters resulted from a variety of hands?

One unfortunate consequence of this preoccupation with sources and redactions over the course of the past two centuries is that the larger picture becomes lost as scholars focus on the origins and date of individual textual fragments. I wish to return to the social, political, and religious concerns raised by these chapters, specifically, how the materials relating to administrative appointments made at the close of David's reign contribute to the larger picture of his legacy. Nevertheless, it is necessary to begin with the issue of literary (dis)unity. The complexity of the questions force us to deal with arcane source-critical and redaction-critical issues at some length.

The issue of composition for this material is very much related to the composition of the speeches in 1 Chr 22 and 28–29. Many commentators who have viewed the materials in 1 Chr 23–27 (or 1 Chr 23–26; Welch 1939: 81–96) as at least partially secondary have also viewed parts of 1 Chr 22 and 28–29 as secondary. The implications of whatever stance one takes on compositional issues are profound, considering the length of the material in question: 1 Chr 23–27 (160 verses) and 1 Chr 22; 28–29 (70 verses). The diverse topics covered by these chapters may be summarized as follows:

Elite Summit (23:1–2)
Levitical Census (23:3–5)
The Three Levitical Divisions (23:6–23)
David's Revision of the Levitical Legal Age (23:24–27)
The Assignment of Levitical Duties (23:28–32)
The Twenty-four Priestly Courses (24:1–19)
The Remaining Levites (24:20–31)
The Selection of Singers (25:1–5)
The Establishment of Twenty-four Courses (25:6–31)
The Divisions of Gatekeepers (26:1–12)
The Casting of Lots for Guard Duty (26:13–19)
Supervision of the Treasuries (26:20–28)
Supervision over Regional Affairs (26:29–32)
Introduction to the Census of David's Military Leaders (27:1)
Twelve Divisions; Twelve Officers (27:2–15)
Thirteen Tribal Officers (27:16–24)
Royal Supervisors (27:25–31)
Royal Advisors and Adjutants (27:32–34)

Taken together, this material is more extensive than some biblical books are. Whatever position one takes on the issue of sources and redaction also affects how one views the nature and purpose of the larger work itself. At stake are the Chronicler's positions on royalty, priests, Levites, singers, gatekeepers, sacrifice, and temple polity.

The case for attributing virtually all of the material in these chapters to later hands is based on the following five considerations (e.g., Noth 1957: 112–15; Rudolph 1955: 152–85; Michaeli 1967: 118–38; Willi 1972: 194–204; Mosis 1973: 44; Im 1985: 153; R. Braun 1986: 228–64; Throntveit 1987: 6–7; Welten 1991; Dörrfuß 1994: 158–71; Steins 1995: 283–335). First, 1 Chr 23 begins with David's appointment of "his son Solomon to reign over Israel" (23:1), but Solomon's accession is not addressed until 28:5–21. Second, the language used in 28:1, describing David's great assembly in Jerusalem purportedly repeats the language of 23:2, in which David gathers together "all of the officers of Israel along with the priests and the Levites." According to one version of this interpretation, all of the material in 23:2–27:34 has been inserted through the technique of *Wiederaufnahme* (repetitive resumption). The author(s) of the interpolation created an editorial seam by narrating another convocation (28:1) corresponding to the earlier gathering (23:2). According to another version of this line of interpretation, only the material in 23:2–26:32 (or 23:1–26:32) is an insertion. The author of the new material at the beginning of 1 Chr 27 switches subjects from sacred matters to secular matters. Whether this author was the Chronicler himself or some later editor is disputed.

Third, there is a significant amount of repetition among the speeches that surround the material in 1 Chr 23–27 (from 1 Chr 22 to 1 Chr 28–29). That this repetition occurs is seen as proof that the same editors who inserted material in 1 Chr 23–27 supplemented earlier versions of the speeches in 1 Chr 22 and 28–29. Fourth, the lists within 1 Chr 23–27 are deemed to be confused and incoherent. If this material, which is thought to have stemmed from a variety of later hands, is removed from the primary edition of the Chronicler's history, the work is said to be more internally consistent and straightforward. Finally, the content of these chapters is considered by some to be inconsistent with the character of the author's work as a whole. The passages in question concern the Levites, priests, choristers, gatekeepers, Levitical supervisors, military officers, and royal advisors, but both the preceding speeches (in 1 Chr 22) and the succeeding speeches (in 1 Chr 28–29) fail to mention such officials (Noth 1957: 112–13). If one subtracts the reference to "the priests and Levites" in 23:2 (so Noth), there are no remaining references to the priests and Levites in 1 Chr 22–29.

In excising chapters 23–27 (or chapters 23–26) from the Chronicler's work, these commentators do not suppose that this material is a unity. Quite the contrary, they see different layers of composition within the lists. For example, Steins (1995), who has authored the most extensive treatment of these chapters, distinguishes between two distinct levels within the insertion of 23:2–26:32: a musician/gatekeeper redaction (23:2f., 6–24a, 25f., 28–32; 24:1–19; 26:1–12a*, 13*, 14–16a, 19, 20, 21*, 22, 24–28) and a communal layer (23:3f., 24b, 27; 24:20–31; 25:1–31; 26:12, 13, 16b–18, 21, 29–32). As for 27:1–34, Steins sees this material as belonging to the final redaction of the book.

If some scholars have excised 1 Chr 23–27 from the Chronicler's work completely, others have taken more nuanced positions, differentiating between disparate levels and types of composition within these chapters. Some have contended that the Chronicler inserted the various lists himself, even though he did not himself author them (Benzinger 1901: 68–81; Goettsberger 1939: 165, 191; Kleinig 1993: 55). This raises larger questions as to the function of source criticism in assessing the nature of the Chronicler's work (Peltonen 1999). Others argue for a series of editions and additions to a basic text authored by the Chronicler (Kittel 1902: 85–102; Ackroyd 1973a: 81–82; Williamson 1979a; 1982b: 157–78; De Vries 1988; 1989: 186–215; Riley 1993: 86–87). The nature and extent of these editions and additions differ, however, according to how scholars conceive of them. Some (e.g., Williamson) envision an original, pro-Levitical work authored by the Chronicler (23:6b–13a, 15–24; 25:1–6; 26:1–3, 9–11, 19; 26:20–32) that was substantially supplemented by a later pro-Priestly editor (23:3–6a, 13b–14, 25–32; 24:1–19, 20–31; 25:7–31; 26:4–8, 12–18; 27:1–34). Others (e.g., Galling 1954: 63–78) contend for a succession of Chroniclers, the second of whom was more Levitically oriented than the first. Yet others envision a more complicated, multistage development (e.g., Rothstein and Hänel 1927: lxiv–lxvi).

In recent years, a third point of view has gained some momentum. According to these scholars (e.g., Japhet 1989; 1993a: 406–11; Wright 1989; 1991; 1992; Selman 1994a: 218–48; Schniedewind 1995), most, if not all, of the material in 1 Chr 23–27 was set there by the Chronicler himself. These scholars have raised a number of objections to the thesis that the material in chapters 23–27 is secondary. I would acknowledge (along with those holding the second point of view) that there are a number of additions present in 1 Chr 23–27. Nevertheless, I would agree with the proponents of both the second and the third views that at least a basic core of the material in 1 Chr 23–27 is original to the Chronicler's work. Indeed, to their arguments others may be added. First, there is no real sense in which either 1 Chr 28 or 1 Chr 29, for that matter, repeat or pick up on the assertion of 23:1, that David "appointed his son Solomon to reign over Israel" *(wymlk ʾt-šlmh bnw ʿl-yśrʾl)*. Solomon does not begin to reign until David leaves office and dies (29:25–30). Chapters 28 and 29 consist largely of speeches by David instructing Solomon and exhorting the assembled authorities. In spite of the talk by some modern scholars of a coregency between David and Solomon, Solomon is publicly anointed toward the very end of David's reign (29:22). There is no indication in the final period of David's reign—as portrayed in either 1 Chr 23–27 or in 1 Chr 28–29—that Solomon exercises any form of power while David is still in office. Solomon is an entirely passive figure; he does not act.

Only in presenting the death notice for David does one read that "Solomon his son reigned in his stead" *(wymlk šlmh bnw tḥtyw)* (29:28). Indeed, Solomon's reign is introduced with the observation that "Solomon, the son of David, strengthened himself *(wayyitḥazzēq)* over his kingdom and Yhwh his God was with him and exalted him exceedingly" (*waygaddĕlēhû lĕmāzʿĕlâ*; 2 Chr 1:1). The notice resonates with an earlier comment about the royal transition, "And Yhwh made Solomon exceedingly great *(waygaddēl yhwh ʾet-šĕlōmōh lĕmaʿlâ)* in the sight of all Israel" (1 Chr 29:25). The Chronicler often uses the verb *ḥzq* (normally in the *hitpaʿel*) to characterize a king's consolidation of his rule either at the beginning of his reign or at the start of a commendable new period in his reign (Knoppers 1990). To be sure, these observations do not prove unity of authorship.

On the contrary, they could be used to claim that much (or all) of chapters 28–29 is part of a larger addition, or set of additions, to the text. But, in any case, they indicate that 23:1 does not constitute indubitable evidence to sever 23:2–27:34 from 28:1–29:30.

Second, assuming, for the sake of argument, that 28:1 signals a repetitive resumption of 23:2 (but see below), this would not in and of itself entail an interpolation. The use of *Wiederaufnahme* can be authorial as well as editorial (B. Long 1987). In this context, one is reminded of the positions of Bertheau (1873: 190–213), Benzinger (1901: 68–80), Welch (1939: 81–96), and Goettsberger (1939: 165–66). These scholars point to a change in subject matter: overseers and military officials (27:1–34) as opposed to Levites, priests, and doorkeepers (23:1 or 23:2–26:32). One could also point to a possible seam within the material separating David's Levitical appointments (23:2–26:32) from his other appointments (27:1–34). Both sections begin with a census. In the case of 23:3–5, "the Levites were numbered from the age of thirty years and up." This first census counts temple overseers, officials, judges, gatekeepers, and choristers, while the second census (27:1) counts ancestral heads, leaders of thousands and of hundreds, and officials. Indeed, the techniques of ring composition and repetitive resumption are in ample evidence elsewhere within Chronicles (Kalimi 1995a). If each instance of *Wiederaufnahme* signaled a secondary insertion, one would be left with a significantly truncated work (Japhet 1993a: 408; cf. Steins 1995: 283–88).

Third, the repetition between the beginnings of chapter 23 and chapter 28 is a very important consideration. Yet, one wonders whether the repetition between the two assemblies is more apparent than real (Williamson 1979a; 1982b; De Vries 1989; Wright 1989; 1991; Japhet 1993a). The first text (23:2) speaks of a gathering *(ʾsp)* of officers, priests, and Levites *(kl-śry yśrʾl whkhnym whlwym)*, while the second (28:1) speaks of David's assembling *(qhl)* a much broader national convocation in Jerusalem, consisting of "all Israel's officers—the tribal officers, the officers of the divisions, those serving the king, the officers of the thousands, the officers of the hundreds, and the officers in charge of all the property and livestock for the king and for his sons, along with the eunuchs, warriors, and every valiant warrior" *(kl-śry yśrʾl* śry *hšbṭym wśry hmḥlqwt hmšrtym ʾt-hmlk wśry hʾlpym wśry hmʾwt wśry kl-rkwš-wmqnh lmlk wlbnyw ʿm-hsrysym whgbwrym wlkl-gbwr ḥyl)*. While it is true that the technique of *Wiederaufnahme* does not require word-for-word repetition, there is not as much overlap between the two as some have assumed. The amount of material thereby interpolated (five chapters) would be unusual but not impossible (e.g., Josh 13:1–23:2; for a different view, see Japhet 1993a: 407–8).

More to the point, at least some of the leaders depicted in the second assembly were not yet appointed at the time of David's earlier speeches to Solomon (22:6–16) and to the Israelite officers (22:17–19). The references seem to be part of a larger pattern. The mention of "the officers of the tribes" *(śārê haššĕbāṭîm)* alludes to the earlier appointment of such officials (27:16–22). Prior to the discussion of David's latter reign, these officials never appear. The reference to "the officers of the divisions *(hammaḥlĕqôt)*, those serving the king" (28:1) is also interesting because it alludes to David's establishment of divisions among the Levites (23:6), priests (24:1), gatekeepers (26:1, 12, 19), and officers (27:1, 2–5–15). Prior to David's establishment of divisions (23:6), the term *maḥălōqet* (**maḥlĕqâ*) is never used in Chronicles. Similarly, the reference to "the officers in charge of all the property and livestock of the king" *(śry kl-hrkwš-wmqnh lmlk)* points to the list of such officials in 27:25–31. Note that the summary statement—"all of these were officers of King David's property" *(kl-ʾlh śry hrkwš ʾšr lmlk dwyd)*—in 27:31 anticipates the language used in 28:1. Prior to the mention of the officers who were in charge of the royal estates (27:31), the term *rĕkûš* is never used in Chronicles. A similar situation holds for the mention of officers overseeing the royal holdings of livestock (*miqneh*; 28:1; cf. 27:29–31). The term *miqneh* appears a few times in the genealogies in reference to the possessions of individual tribes (5:9, 21; 7:21). Elsewhere, it only occurs with reference to the possessions of Judahite monarchs (see below). Finally, the mention of "the officers of the thousands, the officers of the hundreds" *(śry hʾlpym wśry hmʾwt)* in 28:1 resonates with the introductory notice of 27:1—"the officers of thousands and of hundreds, and the officials—those serving the king" (*śry hʾlpym whmʾwt wšṭryhm hmšrtym ʾt-hmlk*; Wright 1991). In this case, however, David is not creating a new institution, but employing an old one. There are earlier references in the discussion of David's reign to these officers (4th NOTE to 26:26).

To this it could be objected that part of 28:1 is redactional, the result of an editor's conforming an earlier version of this verse to the material added later in 1 Chr 23–27 (e.g., Rudolph 1955: 185). Alternatively, one could argue that 23:1 is original and that 23:2–28:1 are secondary. But one is still left with later references and allusions to the arrangements associated with David's latter years. These include the divisions of officials (e.g., 28:13, 21), the treasuries of the house of God and the treasuries of the dedicated gifts (28:12; cf. 26:20, 22 [see NOTES]), and the mention of "Jeḥiel the Gershonite," head of the descendants of Laadan (29:8; cf. 26:21 [3rd NOTE]). There are also some references to the priests and Levites (28:13, 21; cf. 29:22). Nor do these references all stem from material that Noth (1957: 112–13) deems to be later additions (28:18b–19, 21a; 29:6). If these citations presuppose some or all of the material in 1 Chr 23–27, do they prove that the Davidic arrangements are original to the Chronicler's work or that the subsequent references are themselves the work of later editors? In any case, the subtraction of the verbiage in 28:1 that parallels the verbiage in 1 Chr 23–27 does not leave a statement that neatly parallels 23:2.

The observation of Noth about the distinctive character of 1 Chr 23–27 is complex because it strikes at the heart of how one goes about ascertaining the central features of the Chronicler's work. The issues are both historiographical and form critical. The excision of 1 Chr 23–27 and various other genealogies and lists succeeds in conforming the Chronicler's work to the literary character of the Deuteronomistic History. But is the Chronicler's writing like the Deuteronomistic History, a composition in which genealogies and lists are uncommon (von Rad, Noth, Rudolph), or is the Chronicler's writing like the Priestly work and Ezra-Nehemiah, in which lists and genealogies are common (Curtis and Madsen,

Rothstein and Hänel, Japhet)? In my judgment, the Chronicler's work is like the Priestly work and Ezra-Nehemiah in certain respects and like the Deuteronomistic History in other respects (Knoppers 1999a). The Chronicler's writing is like both and neither. The Chronicler draws on earlier works, but his writing evinces his own distinctive style and character ("Introduction"). In any case, one's determination about the form of the Chronicler's work should be derived from the work itself. If one excises most of the lists and genealogies from the Chronicler's work on the basis of an a priori determination about its form, one may be left with not only a truncated work but also a version that distorts the original's character.

One way of getting at the issue of the distinctive nature of the Chronicler's work is to investigate whether the institutions that appear in 23:2–27:34 are unique to this section of Chronicles. Are the references to the various officials mentioned in David's latter reign peculiar, or do they reappear in other sections of the work? If the references and arrangements are unique, this would increase the likelihood that all of this material (23:2–37:34) was added by later editors. If not, this would increase the likelihood that at least some of the material was integral to the Chronicler's original work. In one case, the reference is practically unique. That the tribal officers are only referred to in 27:16–22, 28:1; and 29:6 suggests that the list of 27:16–22 is secondary. But references to other officials mentioned in 28:1 are attested in later parts of the work. To be sure, some of the references are so general—the "warriors and every valiant warrior" *(hgbwrym wlkl-gbwr ḥyl)*—that this is not surprising. But other references are more specific. Mention is made of "the divisions" *(hammaḥlĕqôt)* of Levitical and priestly officials with reference to the reign of Solomon (2 Chr 5:11; 8:14) and the reforms of Jehoiada (2 Chr 23:8), Ḥezeqiah (2 Chr 31:2, 15, 17), and Josiah (2 Chr 35:4, 10).

The narration of the monarchy also contains a series of references to the property *(rĕkûš)* of Judahite kings (cf. 1 Chr 27:31; 28:1). The term *rĕkûš* appears only in nonsynoptic portions of the Chronicler's version of Judahite history. In one instance the reference is to holdings taken away from an aberrant king, Jehoram (2 Chr 21:14, 17), while in other instances the reference is to holdings accumulated under some of Judah's most successful kings, Jehoshaphaṭ, Ḥezeqiah, and Josiah (2 Chr 20:25; 31:3; 32:29; 35:7). Aside from the mention of the officers overseeing David's livestock (*miqneh*; 28:1; cf. 27:29–31), this term appears in two different contexts: (1) a few times in the genealogies with reference to the possessions of individual tribes (1 Chr 5:9, 21; 7:21) and (2) a few times in the monarchy with reference to the acquisitions or possessions of some of Judah's better kings, Asa, Uzziah, and Ḥezeqiah (2 Chr 14:14; 26:10; 32:29).

One could contend that the overlap in terminology is coincidental or that the references in David's reign were added by an editor to set the stage for the later references in the Judahite monarchy. Alternatively, one could contend that both the references in David's reign and the references in the Judahite monarchy are part of a single layer in the work. Nevertheless, three points need to be kept in view. First, the references all appear in nonsynoptic passages; these are not citations that were mindlessly borrowed from Samuel-Kings. Second, the distribution of the references in the Judahite monarchy is not random. There is a correlation between

Judah's better monarchs and the sort of activities and holdings outlined above. Much as David is presented as an exemplary king who reorganized the Levites and priests, instituted the divisions, and acquired many possessions, so some of Judah's better kings observe (or reinstitute) the Levitical and priestly divisions and possess much land and livestock. Conversely, Chronicles does not attribute the successful acquisition or possession of royal estates and livestock to any of Judah's derelict monarchs. Nor do Judah's negatively evaluated kings observe the priestly and Levitical divisions introduced by David. The third point is related to the second. In the context of the Chronicler's work, which evinces many highly typological features, it would be unusual for the Chronicler not to anticipate major positive features of Judahite reigns with standard features of the United Monarchy. Some of Judah's better leaders (Asa, Jehoshaphaṭ, Jehoiada, Uzziah, Ḥezeqiah, and Josiah) renovate, but David and Solomon set the benchmark against which later monarchs are evaluated. This indicates that if much of the material in 23:2–27:34 has been added by later editors, these editors have carefully integrated their own work into earlier stages of the composition. Their additions conform to the larger pattern established by the Chronicler himself.

We have been evaluating critically the various criteria by which some scholars have deemed all of 1 Chr 23:2–27:34 and some of 1 Chr 22 and 28–29 to be secondary. We have seen that some of these criteria are problematic. More difficult to assess are the arguments that the repetition in the speeches and the character of certain lists indicate that some of these materials are later additions. It seems likely that some of the lists are secondary, but the issue pertaining to the speeches is especially difficult because, as we have seen (see SOURCES AND COMPOSITION to 22:2–19), the transfer of leadership from David to Solomon has been modeled after the elaborate and drawn-out transfer of leadership from Moses to Joshua. Since the Moses-Joshua transition is depicted in (the present text of) Numbers, Deuteronomy, and Joshua as punctuated by all sorts of speeches and long narrative interruptions, it is unclear how much of the repetition in Chronicles may stem from the conscious application of the literary technique of *imitatio* and how much it may stem from additions to an older, significantly shorter, and internally consistent *Grundschrift*. Such considerations leave open the question of which individual passages within 1 Chr 23–27 have resulted from the work of later editors and scribes. These issues may be best addressed by means of an examination of each individual unit within 1 Chr 23–27.

Returning to the issues raised at the beginning of this excursus, it may prove useful to reflect on the function of the arrangements elaborated in 1 Chr 23–27 in the context of the larger work. In what follows, my focus will be on the present text of Chronicles. The author of 1 Chr 23:1 introduces David's appointment of Solomon as his successor against the background of David's becoming "old and advanced in years" *(zqn wšbʿ ymym)*. To put his house in order and prepare for the reign of his son, the elderly king sets in motion a series of administrative arrangements that will serve his son and kingdom for generations to come. Many of these appointments specifically involve the tribe of Levi (23:3–26:32) and concern the staffing arrangements associated with the Temple. Other appointments involve non-Levitical civil servants and officials (27:1–34). A census is mentioned to demarcate both sets of groups (23:3–5; 27:1). In the narration of David's career, all of these activities and appointments occur at the end of his reign. "Among the last commands of David," the Levites were subjected to a census (23:27). In referring to the Levitical supervisors over regional affairs (26:29–32), the writer comments that these appointments occurred during the "fortieth year of the reign of David" (26:31), that is, during the final year of his reign (29:27). David dies "at a ripe old age, full of days, riches, and honor" (*bśybh ṭwbh śbʿ ymym ʿšr wkbwd*; 29:28). The references to David's dotage in 1 Chr 23–29 mean that a great portion of the literary coverage devoted to his career is focused on the last year(s) of a very long life.

The flurry of activity occurring at the end of David's life recalls the flurry of activities characterizing the end of Joshua's life. Following the many narratives dealing with Israel's entry into and conquest of the land (Josh 1–12), we read that "Joshua was old (and) advanced in years" (*wyhwšʿ zqn bʾ bymym*; 13:1). The notice about Joshua's old age becomes the occasion for a divine pronouncement about the unfinished work to which Joshua has yet to attend, "And Yhwh said to him, 'As for you, you are old (and) advanced in years *(ʾth zqnt bʾt bymym)* and very much land remains to be possessed' " (13:1). In the case of Joshua, the issue is not an impending transition to a young and inexperienced leader as it is with David (1 Chr 22:5; 29:1). Rather, much work remains to be done before Joshua's tasks are completed. These are territories yet to be conquered (13:2–7) and tribal allotments to be apportioned among Israel's many sodalities (13:8–19:48). Land is yet to be distributed to Caleb (15:13–19) and to Joshua himself (19:49–51). Other tasks involve designating towns of refuge (20:1–9), allocating towns for the Levites (21:1–42), and dismissing the Transjordanian tribes to their territories (22:1–10). Finally, Joshua has to settle (along with Phineḥas) a dispute over the erection of an altar by the Transjordanian tribes (22:11–34). All of the initiatives relating to the casting of lots, the division of land among Israel's tribes, and matters pertaining to the Transjordanian tribes occur during the final period of Joshua's life. That this is so can be seen by the introduction to Joshua's final address, which calls attention to his dotage, "Long after Yhwh had given rest to Israel from all of their surrounding enemies and Joshua was old (and) well advanced in years *(wyhwšʿ zqn bʾ bymym)*, Joshua summoned all Israel—its elders, heads, judges, and officials—and said to them, 'As for me, I am old (and) advanced in years' " (*ʾny zqnty bʾty bymym*; 23:1–2).

Given the repetitive resumption between Josh 13:1 and 23:1–2, it is readily understandable that scholars have debated whether some or perhaps all of the material between the notices of Joshua's old age (13:1; 23:1–2) was interpolated by later writers. Most modern scholars do not believe that all of the sections within 13:1–23:2 belong to the original composition of the book. Many see the work of more than one editor within these chapters. In this respect, the composition of Joshua raises similar issues to those raised about the composition of 1 Chr 23–27. The question arises, however, about what the accumulation of all these materials comes to. What is their function within the larger narration of the book? In the case of Joshua, one finds a very active and productive leader during the final years of his public career. The more material added to this section of the book, the more the land takes on added significance and Joshua's legacy grows. The extended literary coverage devoted to the tribal allotments, the towns of refuge, the Levitical towns, and the fortunes of the eastern tribes lends gravity to this period in Joshua's life. When Moses' successor dies at an extremely old age—110 (Josh 24:29), he bequeaths his own considerable patrimony to his people. Not only the taking of territory, but also its organization, supervision, and distribution are of serious consequence for Israel's life in the land.

In 1 Chr 23–27 the appointment of various leaders and the assignment of courses to such officials contribute to the larger picture of David's reign as a time of significant change for Israel. This is an important consideration no matter what position one takes on the composition of the material in question. The administrative arrangements portrayed in 1 Chr 23–27 order the Jerusalem bureaucracy for generations to follow. The temple personnel, civic officials, and military officers all receive their appointments in turn. The latter reign of David witnesses the creation and consolidation of an array of state positions and service arrangements centered in the city of Jerusalem. To be sure, some of the personnel, such as the priests and Levites, predate the monarchy. But they achieve their definitive form vis-à-vis the Temple in the age of David. Inasmuch as many of Judah's better kings, such as Asa, Jehoshaphaṭ, Uzziah, Ḥezeqiah, and Josiah, institute arrangements recalling the formative reign of David, they appear as reformers and not as innovators. They return Jerusalem and the kingdom of Judah back to the standards established centuries earlier by the founding father of their dynasty.

Considering that some of the arrangements depicted in 1 Chr 23–27 involved temple and civic officials who were active in the author's own time, the author's depiction of their assignments many centuries earlier sanctions their assignments in the present. In this context, it must be remembered that the Second Temple was authorized and largely funded by an external authority (the Persian crown). As such, the Second Temple built under Zerubbabel and Jeshua was not only a new institution, but also one in which foreign benefactors had played a major role (Ezra 1:1–4, 7–11; 4:3; 6:1–22). The focus of the authors of Chronicles is on the First Temple and not the Second. Nevertheless, these writers validate contemporary sacerdotal arrangements and aspirations by recourse to native precedents in Israel's past. Institutions of the Second Temple period are authorized by their creation during the planning of the First Temple. In this manner, Second Temple officials could claim a commission for their duties and rota that stretched back to the very beginning of the First Temple. Major families living in postexilic Jerusalem could argue that their positions were established by no less an authority than David himself. The implicit parallels between the First and Second Temples were also important for those residents of Yehud who wished to cultivate patronage of their shrine. The Second Temple gains prestige through association with the First. In supporting the Jerusalem sanctuary of their own day, the residents of Yehud were honoring and preserving one of their national institutions.

As additions were made by later writers to 1 Chr 23–27, this new material reinforced the importance of the actions undertaken by Israel's reverend king during his seniority. More and more assignments made during the Persian and Hellenistic periods came to be associated with the monarch who first prepared for the establishment of the centralized House of God. If the Ancestral era marks Israel's birth as a people, the Sinaitic era marks the time in which Israel receives its national code of conduct, and the life of Joshua marks the time in which Israel receives and divides its land, the Davidic era marks the time in which the institutions associated with the Jerusalem Temple achieve standard definition. The Levites, priests, gatekeepers, musicians, treasurers, overseers, and supervisors all receive authorization in their centralized work assignments. The more material added to this section of the book, the more Jerusalem's importance grows and David's legacy is enhanced. In this respect, 1 Chr 23–27, no less than other materials in Chronicles depicting the careers of David and Solomon, contribute to a larger picture of the United Monarchy as a golden age for the people of Israel.

# *XXVIII. David's Levitical Appointments (23:1–32)*

*Elite Summit*

1 When David was old and replete with days, he appointed his son Solomon to
reign over Israel. 2 And he gathered together all of the officers of Israel along with
the priests and the Levites.

*Levitical Census*

3 And the Levites were numbered from the age of thirty years and up. Their
head count was 38,000 men. 4 Out of these, 24,000 were overseeing the work of
the Temple of Yhwh, 6,000 were officials and judges, 5 4,000 were gatekeepers,
and 4,000 were praising Yhwh with instruments he made for offering praise.

*The Three Levitical Divisions*

6 Then David partitioned them into divisions corresponding to the sons of Levi:
Gershon, Qohath, and Merari.

*The Gershonites*

7 Belonging to the Gershonites: Laadan and Shimei. 8 The sons of Laadan: the
head was Jeḥiel, and Zetham and Joel—three. 9 The sons of Jeḥiel: Shelomoth,
Ḥaziel, and Haran—three. These were the ancestral heads of Laadan. 10 The sons
of Shimei: Jaḥath, Ziza, Jeush, and Beriah. These were the sons of Shimei—four.
11 Jaḥath was the head and Ziza was the second, but Jeush and Beriah did not produce many sons and so they became one ancestral house, according to one enrollment.

*The Qohathites*

12 The sons of Qohath: Amram, Izhar, Ḥebron, and Uzziel—four. 13 The sons
of Amram: Aaron and Moses. And Aaron was set apart so that he could consecrate
the most sacred objects, he and his sons forever, to make offerings before Yhwh, to

serve him, and to pronounce blessings in his name forever. [14]As for Moses, the man of God, his sons were reckoned among the tribe of Levi. [15]The sons of Moses: Gershom and Eliezer. [16]The sons of Gershom: Shubael the head. [17]The sons of Eliezer: Reḥabiah the head. Eliezer had no other sons, but the sons of Reḥabiah increased abundantly. [18]The sons of Izhar: Shelomoth the head. [19]The sons of Ḥebron: Jeriah the head, Amariah the second, Jeḥaziel the third, and Jeqameam the fourth. [20]The sons of Uzziel: Micah the head and Isshiah the second.

*The Merarites*

[21]The sons of Merari: Maḥli and Mushi. The sons of Maḥli: Eleazar and Qish. [22]But Eleazar died without having any sons, only daughters, so the sons of Qish, their kinsmen, married them. [23]The sons of Mushi: Maḥli, Eder, and Jeremoth—three.

*David's Revision of the Levitical Legal Age*

[24]These were the sons of Levi by their ancestral houses, the ancestral heads according to their enrollments by their head count of names, the ones doing the work for the service of the Temple of Yhwh from the age of twenty and up. [25]For David said, "Yhwh the God of Israel has given rest to his people and has taken up residence in Jerusalem forever [26]and so the Levites no longer need to carry the Tabernacle along with all of its furnishings for its service." [27]For among the last commands of David, this was the census of the sons of Levi from the age of twenty years and up.

*The Assignment of Levitical Duties*

[28]Indeed, their appointment was to be at the side of the sons of Aaron for the service of the Temple of Yhwh, (to be responsible) for the outer courts, the chambers, the purity of all sacred objects, and the work for the service of the Temple of God; [29]and for the rows of bread, the choice flour for the cereal offering, the unleavened wafers, the griddle, the well-mixed (cakes), and all measures of capacity and length; [30]also to stand every morning to give thanks and to praise Yhwh, and likewise in the evening, [31]and whenever burnt offerings are offered to Yhwh for the sabbaths, new moons, and festivals, with the number (being set) according to the prescription concerning them, perpetually before Yhwh. [32]They were also to keep the watch of the Tent of Meeting, the watch of the sacred objects, and the watch of the sons of Aaron, their kinsmen, for the service of the Temple of Yhwh.

# TEXTUAL NOTES

23:1. "his son." So MT *(lectio brevior)*. LXX$^{B}$ adds "in his stead" *(tḥtyw)*, a phrase that appears in a similar context in 29:28 (Allen 1974b: 102). Alternatively, *tḥtyw* may have been lost by haplography after *bnw (homoioteleuton)*.

23:3. "and . . . were numbered." Thus MT *(nipʿal)* and LXX$^{L}$ anz. LXX$^{AB}$ and Tg. "and they numbered."

23:4. "overseeing." The use of *nṣḥ* to denote supervision is characteristic of Chronicles (1 Chr 15:21; 2 Chr 2:1 [ET 2:2]; 34:12–13), of Ezra (3:8–9), and of fifty-five psalm headings (Curtis and Madsen 1910: 32 [#74]).

"officials" (*šōṭĕrîm*). So MT. The lemma of LXX, grammateis, "clerk," may have influenced Syr., "scribes" (so also Syr. 2 Chr 19:11 "scribes" for MT *šōṭĕrîm* and LXX *grammateis*). But Weitzman (1999: 189) observes that Syr.'s rendering of "scribe" for Heb. *šōṭĕr* is common in the Peshiṭta of Exodus, Deuteronomy, and Joshua.

"the work of the Temple." Thus MT. LXX "the works of the Temple."

23:5. "4,000 were gatekeepers." So MT. That this phrase does not appear in LXX$^{B}$ probably results from a haplography (by *homoioarkton* from "4,000" to "4,000"). The summary of Josephus (*Ant.* 7.363) confirms the presence of 4,000 gatekeepers.

he made." So LXX$^{B}$ (*epoiēsen*), Josephus *Dauidēs kateskeuase* (*Ant.* 7.364), and Vg. (*fecerat*). MT's "I made to praise" (*ʿśyty*) may have arisen to differentiate the subject of the verb from the nearest antecedent (Yhwh). The proposal (Begrich in *BHK*) to add *bkly šyr mšmʿym* assimilates the phraseology toward that used in other contexts (e.g., 15:16; 16:42).

"for offering praise." So MT and LXX*. Literally, "he made (*ʿśh*) to praise." Following the suggestion of Rothstein and Hänel (1927), Begrich (*BHK*) proposes to insert "to Yhwh" (*lyhwh*) with many Heb. MSS and some witnesses to LXX at the end of the verse (after "praising"). But MT seems to be more original (Rudolph 1955: 154). Syr. adds a reference to David's acts of charity.

23:6. "partitioned them." MT has the *nipʿal* of *ḥlq*. On the basis of some Heb. MSS, LXX, Vg., and Tg., I read the *piʿel*. Reading the *hipʿil* is also possible (e.g., A. Ehrlich 1914: 349), but the *hipʿil* is much more rare. Compare the use of this verb in MT 1 Chr 24:3 (*nipʿal*) and 24:4 (*hipʿil*).

"Gershon." So MT and LXX$^{AN}$. The reading of LXX$^{BL}$ *Gedsōn* reflects a *dālet*/*rêš* confusion (TEXTUAL NOTE to 6:1). Syr. lacks the prep. *l-* found in MT.

23:7. "the Gershonites." So MT. LXX and Syr. have PNs. LXX$^{B}$ *Parosōm* and $c_2$ *Parosom* may reflect two inner-Greek confusions (*p*/*gi* and *ni*/*m*; Allen 1974b: 6, 19). LXX$^{L}$ *Gedsōn*.

23:8. "Laadan: the head was Jeḥiel." So MT and LXX. Tg. construes "head" with what precedes rather than with what follows (Jeḥiel), thereby promoting Laadan.

"Zetham" (*ztm*). Thus MT and Tg. LXX$^{B}$ *Zethom*; LXX$^{L}$ *Zēthan*. Syr. *ywtm*. The PN, meaning "olive (tree)," belongs to the category of plant names. See Noth (1928: 230).

23:9. "the sons of Jeḥiel." I adopt the emendation proposed by Kittel (1902: 86), followed by Galling (1954: 64), Myers (1965a: 158), and Hognesius (1987), to read Jeḥiel (see v. 8). MT v. 9 reads, "the sons of Shimei: Shelomoth, Ḥaziel, and Haran—three. These were the ancestral heads of Laadan." Since the previous clause deals with the descendants of Shimei, the appearance of the summary "these were the ancestral heads of Laadan" is surprising. Both the appearance of "these were the ancestral heads of Laadan" at the end of v. 9 (cf. vv. 7–8) and the recurrence of "the sons of Shimei" in v. 10, suggest that v. 9 or v. 10 is corrupt. The phrase "the sons of Shimei" is considered to be a gloss by some (e.g., Benzinger 1901: 69). Williamson (1982b: 161) thinks that this Shimei is a different Shimei from the Shimei appearing in vv. 7 and 10, but if this were so, the segmentation of the genealogy would break down. Goettsberger (1939: 167) takes a different approach, construing "Shelomith, Ḥaziel, and Haran—three. These were the ancestral heads of Laadan" to be an addition, misplaced from another context. But with slight emendation (reading "Jeḥiel" instead of "Shimei"), the text makes sense. A scribe's eye may simply have inadvertently slipped from *bny yḥy'l* to the following two occurrences of *bny šmʿy* in v. 10. A slightly divergent sequence appears, however, in 1 Chr 26. There Laadan represents a Gershonite ancestral house and Jeḥiel (or the Jeḥielites) appears as an offspring of Laadan (1 Chr 26:21; TEXTUAL NOTE). But Zetham and Joel descend from Jeḥiel (26:22).

"Shelomoth." Reading *šlmwt* with Kethib, Syr., and Arab. Qere, LXX^A^, Vg., Tg., and Arm. "Shelomith" *(šlmyt)*—a *wāw/yôd* confusion. LXX^B^ (and $c_2$) *Alōtheim* is corrupt. On the name *(šlmy/wt)*, see also the witnesses to 1 Chr 23:18; 24:22; 26:25, 28; 2 Chr 11:20; Ezra 8:10. Noth's inference (1928: 165) that "Shelomith" is normally a f. name (see Lev 24:11; 1 Chr 3:19) seems to be confirmed by the discovery of a Persian period seal with the words "belonging to Shelomith, maidservant of Elnatan the governor" (*lšlmyt 'mt 'lntn pḥ*[*w'*]). See further Avigad (1976: 11–13 [# 14]) and Davies (§106.018.1). The affix *-ôt* in "Shelomoth" is hypocoristic (cf. Jeremoth; v. 23).

"Ḥaziel." Thus MT, Tg., and perhaps LXX^ALN^ *Aziēl*. The lemmata of LXX^B^ *Eieiēl* and $c_2$ *Iēeil* may be influenced by *yḥy'l* in v. 8.

"Haran." So MT and LXX^A^. LXX^B^ *Haidan* and $c_2$ *Edan* reflect a *dālet/rêš* confusion.

23:10. "Jaḥath." So MT. LXX^B^ *Ieth*.

"Ziza" *(zyz')*. Reading with one Heb. MS, LXX^BL^, and Vg. *(Ziza)*. MT and Tg. "Zina," reflect a *zayin/nûn* confusion. Syr^A^ has *zbydh*, while other witnesses to Syr. may reflect "Zabdi" *(zbdy)*. See also 4:37 *(zyz')* and 23:11 (below).

"Jeush" *(yʿwš)*. So MT and Tg. The reading of LXX^B^ *Yōas* (also in v. 11) reflects metathesis.

23:11. "Ziza." So LXX^BL^. MT "Zizah" *(zyzh)*. See also the 2nd TEXTUAL NOTE to v. 10.

"one ancestral house." Inserting *'ḥd*, "one," as proposed by Rothstein and Hänel, and followed by *BHK* and *BHS*, thus "they became one ancestral house, according to one enrollment."

23:13. "so that he could consecrate (the) most sacred objects" *(lĕhaqdîšô qōdeš qŏdāšîm)*. MT literally reads "to consecrate himself [or it]" *(lhqdyšw)*, most sacred objects." One Heb. MS has "to draw near" *(lhqryb)*, while another Heb. MS lacks the 3rd-per. masc. sg. suf. *(-ô)*. Translations of the Heb. vary. One possibility is that *qŏdeš qŏdāšîm* refers to Aaron himself, hence "to sanctify himself a most holy one" (e.g., Bertheau 1873; Curtis and Madsen 1910). But the expression *qōdeš qŏdāšîm* is not used elsewhere to refer to Aaron (as "a most holy one"). Some (e.g., KBL 1078) see a solution in following Vg. (and Syr.) *ut ministraret in sancto sanctorum.*

But there are two problems with this. First, a reference to "the Holy of Holies" would be couched as *qōdeš ha-qŏdāšîm* (e.g., 1 Chr 6:34; 2 Chr 3:8, 10). Second, the appearance of *ministraret* may represent an assimilation to *lšrtw* later in the verse. The text is probably referring to the *sancta*, the "most sacred objects" *(qōdeš qŏdāšîm)*, often mentioned by the Priestly source (5th NOTE to v. 13). The 3rd-per masc. sg. suf. *(-ô)* most likely refers not to Aaron as an object, but to Aaron as a subject, hence "for his consecrating" or, less literally, "so that he could consecrate."

"to make offerings" *(lĕhaqṭîr)*. So NRSV, a better translation than "to burn incense."

23:14. "his sons." So MT and LXX$^{AB}$. Some witnesses (e.g., LXX$^{L}$ and Tg.) preface the copula.

"were reckoned among" *(yqr'w 'l)*. A similar expression (in the *nipʿal*) occurs in Gen 48:6 and Ezra 2:61 (= Neh 7:63).

23:16. "the sons of Gershom." The language is formulaic as only one son is mentioned (TEXTUAL NOTE to 2:8). LXX* *huioi Gērsam* (cf. 15:7; 26:24).

"Shubael" *(šwb'l)*. Following LXX$^{AB}$ *Soubaēl* (cf. *bb'* *Soubiēl;* $e_2$ *Sōbiēl*) and 24:20; 25:20 (cf. 25:4; Noth 1928: 32,199). The lemma of MT, "Shebuel" *(šbw'l)*, has suffered metathesis. Alternatively, the MT spelling could reflect paradigm pressure from the PNs of the *lĕmû'ēl, pĕnû'ēl, yĕmû'ēl, qĕmû'ēl* type (Layton 1990b: 50–51). In this context, it is relevant to observe that Syr. has the more common "Samuel" *(šĕmû'ēl)*.

23:17. "Reḥabiah" *(rḥbyh)*. So MT. LXX$^{AN}$ (and Arm.) *Raabia*. Syr.$^{A}$ reflects *rḥmyh*.

23:18. "Shelomoth." So LXX$^{AB}$ *Salōmōth* (see also LXX 24:20; 25:4, 20). MT and $e_2$ "Shelomith" (שלמית; 2nd TEXTUAL NOTE to v. 9).

23:19. "Jeriah" *(yryhw)*. Thus MT. Some of the following variants reflect a *dālet/rêš* confusion: LXX$^{B}$ *Idoud;* LXX$^{AN}$ *Ieria;* *bb'* *Ieddi;* $e_2$ *Ieddidia;* Tg. *yryh;* Syr. *ywr'*. Cf. MT *yryh* in 26:31 (LXX$^{B}$ *Toudeias* < *Ioudeias* = *ydyh*).

"Jeḥaziel" *(yḥzy'l)*. So MT and Tg. LXX$^{B}$ *Oziēl* may reflect "Uzziel" (see v. 20) or perhaps Ḥaziel. LXX$^{A}$ *Iaziēl;* Vg. *Iazihel*. See also the variants to 1 Chr 16:6 and 2 Chr 20:14.

23:22. "their kinsmen" *('ḥyhm)*. So MT and LXX. Taking Qish as the subject, Tg. expands to "the brother of their father" (*'ḥy 'byhn;* McIvor 1994: 122).

23:23. Maḥli." Thus MT. LXX$^{B}$ *Moolei*.

"Eder." So MT. LXX$^{B}$ (and $c_2$) *Aidath*.

"Jeremoth" *(yĕrēmôt)*. So MT and Tg. The PN *yĕrēmôt* also appears in MT 7:8; 8:14; 25:22; Ezra 10:26, 27, but the form *yĕrîmôt* appears in MT 1 Chr 7:7; 12:6; 24:30; 25:4; 27:19; 2 Chr 11:18; 31:13 (Noth 1928: 39, 226). In both 1 Chr 23:23 and 24:30, LXX$^{B}$ and $c_2$ read *Areimōth*. The form *yĕrîmôt* seems to be reflected in this v. (cf. 8:14; 12:6) and in 24:30 by LXX$^{AN}$ *Iarimōth* (in 24:30 *Ierimōth*), LXX$^{L}$ *Ierimōth*, and Vg. *Ierimoth*. In 1 Chr 7:7, 8; 25:4; 27:19; 2 Chr 31:13, LXX offers *Ierimōth*, while in 2 Chr 11:18 it reads *Ierimouth*. The name *yrymwt* is attested on a seventh-century Heb. seal (Davies, §100.361.1).

23:24. "according to their enrollments" *(lipqûdêhem)*. The significance of *pqwd* is disputed (*HALOT* 956–57). The most likely meaning in this context is that of an enrollment in a census (e.g., Exod 30:14; 38:21, 25; Num 1:44, 46; 2:4; 4:42; 26:22, 25, 27, 37, 43, 47, 57, 63; 31:14, 48; cf. Exod 38:25).

"the ones doing the work" *(ʿśy hmlʾkh)*. So many Heb. MSS and some of the versions, which read the pl. (e.g., LXX^BL *poiountes*). MT *ʿśh hmlʾkh*, "the one doing the work" *(ʿśh hmlʾkh)*. LXX^BL also read a pl. object *(ta erga)*. There is a similar discrepancy between MT and the versions in 2 Chr 24:12; 34:10, 13, reflecting a *hê/yôd* confusion.

23:25. "has taken up residence." Literally, "tented" *(škn)*. See 17:9 and the NOTE to v. 25.

23:27. "among the last commands of David" *(bdbry dwyd hʾḥrnym)*. LXX is similar, *entois logois Daueid tois eschatois*. It is possible to render MT as "according to [or 'among'] the last deeds of David" (so NJPS following Qimḥi). Vg. *Iuxta praecepta quoque David novissima*. Tg. is expansionary, "by the words which he prophesied and spoke at the end."

"this was the census of the sons of Levi" *(hmh mspr bny-lwy)*. The use of the pl. pron. *hmh* most likely refers to the Levites *(bny-lwy)*. Perhaps *mspr bny-lwy* should be understood as a compound subject (GKC § 146).

23:28. "indeed, their appointment" *(ky mʿmdm)*. So MT. LXX^BL "for he stationed them," *hoti estēsen autous* (= *ky ʿmdm*?).

"to be at the side of (ליד) the sons of Aaron." The translation of NRSV, "to assist the sons of Aaron," leads the reader. The prep. phrase ליד consistently denotes proximity (1 Sam 19:3; Ps 140:5; Prov 8:3; Neh 11:24; 1 Chr 18:17; Knoppers 1999a).

"and (the) work" *(wmʿśh)*. So MT. LXX *kai epi ta erga*, "and for the works" (= *wlmʿśy* or *wʿl hmʿśy*). Similarly, Vg. *et in universis* (= *wʿl kl*). Note the related constructions earlier in v. 28 and later in v. 29.

23:29. "and for the rows of bread." So MT and LXX^L. LXX^B lacks the connective. Hence, LXX^B connects with v. 28b "and over the works of the service of the Temple of God for the rows of bread" (followed by Curtis and Madsen, 1910; Rothstein and Hänel, 1927; Rudolph, 1955).

"the well-mixed (cakes)." The meaning of the rare term *murbeket* is disputed: REB "pastry"; NAB "mixing"; NJPS "well soaked" (defended by Milgrom 1991: 399–400). The root of this *hopʿal* fem. ptc., *rbk*, may be compared to Akk. *rabāku*, "to make a concoction," and to Akk. *rabaka* "(dough) to mix" (AHw 933b). The other two relevant biblical texts are Lev 6:14 [ET 6:21], "It will be made on a griddle *murbeket* with oil, you will bring it," and Lev 7:12, "choice flour *murbeket*, cakes mixed in oil." In Talmudic Heb., *rbykh* refers to "pulp of flour mixed with hot water and oil" (Jastrow 1442).

"and all measures of capacity and length" *(wlkl-mśwrh wmdh)*. LXX^AB read *kai eis pan metron*, "and for every measure," due to haplography of *wmdh (homoioteleuton)* after *mśwrh*.

23:30. "and likewise in the evening" *(wkn lʿrb)*. Thus MT and LXX *(lectio brevior)*. Syr. adds *lʿrb*, thus creating a parallel with *bbqr bbqr* earlier in the verse. Alternatively, as Freedman (personal communication) points out, *lʿrb* may have been lost by haplography after *lʿrb* (parablepsis).

23:32. "(and) the watch of the sacred objects." So MT and LXX^L. The phrase can also be translated as "(and) the watch of the holy place" *(w't-mšmrt hqdš)*. Lacking in LXX[AB] due to haplography (*homoioarkton* after *'t-mšmrt 'hl-mw'd*). *BHS* misrepresents the case when it posits LXX's minus as *hqdš wmšmrt*.

"and the watch of the sons of Aaron" *(wmšmrt bny 'hrn)*. Thus MT and LXX. Rudolph (1955: 158) deletes the connective on the basis of Num 8:26.

## Notes

23:1. "replete with days" *(śāba' yāmîm)*. The expression is analogous to Akk. *balāṭa šebû*, "full of life" or "satisfied with life" (*AHw* 1207; *CAD* Š/2 253). The attainment of this stage in life is presented as an honor (so also 29:28). Similar expressions are used to describe the venerable status of Abraham (Gen 25:8), Isaac (Gen 35:29), and Job (42:17).

"he appointed his son Solomon to reign over Israel." Chapter 23 begins with an intriguing development: an elderly David designates his chosen heir to rule over the people. The transition from David to Solomon involves a combination of private and public events. Earlier, David had privately spoken to Solomon about the planned succession (22:7–16) and charged "all the officers of Israel" to help Solomon (22:17). Here, David appoints Solomon before he gathers together the priests, Levites, and the same group of officials—"all of the officers of Israel" (23:2). Appreciating the force of the transition involves, therefore, making distinctions between what the author tells his readers, what David tells Solomon in private, what David tells Solomon in public, what David tells some officials, and what David tells all of Israel's leadership. In this case, the author employs a notice about David's designation of Solomon to remind his readers about the coming transition in kingship. In Samuel-Kings the end of David's rule is marked by rebellion and near chaos, but in Chronicles David himself takes command of his declining years by preparing the nation for a shift in power. To this end he convenes select leaders, "all of the officers the priests and the Levites." The mention of leadership—Solomon, the officers, the priests, and the Levites—bears a broadly inverse relationship to the order in which these are discussed in the text: Levites (23:3–32), priests (24:1–19), Levitical choristers and gatekeepers (25:1–26:19), officers and various officials (26:20–27:34), and Solomon (28:9–10, 20–21). The transition from the tenure of the founding father to that of his son calls for the organization of a national administration. Solomon, in turn, may gainfully employ these sundry officials to implement the goals that Yhwh and David have established for him (17:11–14; 22:7–16). The reign of Solomon will realize the movement from a cultus centered around ark and tent to one that is centered around a stationary temple, hence many of David's instructions deal with the extensive preparations that are necessary to complete this project successfully. Particular needs are staffing, schedules, and role (re)definition.

23:2. "he gathered together" *('sp)*. This summit of select officials in the state bureaucracy forms the background to David's other major administrative initiatives outlined in the narratives and lists of 23:3–27:34. As with many other assemblies portrayed in Near Eastern texts, for example, the Hittite assembly (Beckman 1982), David's summit involves officials who have a stake in the central bureaucracy. The civil officials ("the priests and the Levites") and leaders ("all of the officers of Israel") are summoned by the king and are subject to him. Subsequent to this elite summit, David will reorganize the ranks of these functionaries. At the conclusion of this administrative (re)organization, David assembles *(qhl)* a much larger national convocation to prepare the way for Solomon's rule (28:1–29:25).

23:3. "the Levites were numbered." The writer does not say who conducted the census. Given the use of the *nipʿal,* one could translate reflexively, "the Levites numbered themselves." In any case, the procedure redounds to the good reputation of David and the other Israelite authorities, because this enumeration, unlike the pan-Israel census of 1 Chr 21, proceeds according to the dictates of Num 1:47–49 and 2:33. According to these texts, the Levites were not to be numbered with the other tribes, but were to be subject to their own census (Num 3–4). In the earlier census, David's instructions were subverted by Joab, who did not number the tribes of Levi and Benjamin (1 Chr 21:6) because he found David's order to be repugnant. This separate census honors Levi's special status.

"thirty years and up." This was the earlier custom according to one source (Num 4:3, 23, 30, 35, 39, 43). A divergent tradition lists the minimum legal age as twenty-five (Num 8:23–26). Unlike the Priestly writers, who posit a retirement age of fifty for certain kinds of Levitical work, this text does not mention any maximum age. See also the 2nd NOTE to v. 24.

"their head count" *(msprm lglgltm)*. In referring to a census, this terminology is reminiscent of that used in the Priestly writings (Exod 16:16; 38:26; Num 1:2, 18, 20, 22; 3:47).

"38,000 men." A more impressive total than the Levitical census numbering 8,580 in the time of Moses (Num 4:36–48). As in the Priestly censuses (Num 1–4; 26), only males are counted. On the Chronicler's use of incredibly high numbers, see the NOTE to 12:38. Inflated numbers are, of course, also characteristic of the Priestly source (Milgrom 1990: 336–39).

23:4. "out of these." In this particular census, attention is paid not only to numbers but also to professional specialization: overseers, officials, judges, gatekeepers, and musicians (vv. 4–5).

"24,000." The large number of overseers, approximately 63 percent of the total, reflects the high priority given to temple building.

"overseeing the work of the Temple of Yhwh" *(lnṣḥ ʿl-mlʾkt byt-yhwh)*. In Chronicles the construction of the Temple occurs under the supervision of the Levites. When the Temple is repaired in the reign of Josiah (2 Chr 34:8–13), the Levites have a supervisory role, and gatekeepers, musicians, scribes, and officials are present once again. Similarly, in the time of the restoration, Levites have a prominent role in temple construction. Zerubbabel, Jeshua, and the rest of their kin, the priests and the Levites, begin rebuilding the Temple (Ezra 3:8–9). As in the time of David, the Levites are appointed "to oversee the work of the Temple of Yhwh" (*lnṣḥ ʿl-mlʾkt byt-yhwh;* Ezra 3:8). These and other parallels (see the following NOTES) suggest that the author (or editor) of the opening chapters of Ezra shared some affinities in perspective with the author of this material in Chronicles. In the present form of Chronicles and Ezra, the building of the Second Temple is modeled after the building of the First Temple (as depicted in Chronicles). See the introduction for discussion on the relationship between Chronicles and Ezra-Nehemiah.

"6,000 were officials *(šōṭĕrîm)* and judges *(šōpĕṭîm)*." It is not necessary to understand all these judges and officials as having some supervisory role in temple construction itself (*pace* Curtis and Madsen 1910: 262). Of the total 38,000, only one group, albeit a sizable majority of 24,000, are explicitly said to be construction supervisors. In Chronicles, the Levites serve in a variety of capacities (COMMENT on 26:1–19). For instance, in the reign of Jehoshaphaṭ, he sends his own officers *(śryw)*, as well as certain Levites and priests, throughout Judah's towns on teaching missions (2 Chr 17:7–9). Later in his reign, the king institutes further reforms. Having earlier assigned troops and prefects to all the fortified towns (2 Chr 17:2), Jehoshaphaṭ stations judges *(šōpĕṭîm)* within each of these sites (2 Chr 19:5) and appoints a court in Jerusalem, staffed by Levites, priests, and ancestral heads (2 Chr 19:8; cf. 1 Chr 23:6–23 below).

23:5. "4,000 were gatekeepers." Their divisions and responsibilities are outlined in 26:1–19.

"4,000 were praising Yhwh." One of the main Levitical duties established earlier in David's reign (15:16–21; 16:4–38) and reaffirmed at the conclusion of the partition into divisions (23:30–31). The appointments and divisions of choristers appear in 1 Chr 25. The Levitical responsibility to praise Yhwh is a consistent feature of the Chronicler's depiction of monarchical history (Kleinig 1993). It continues in the restoration, when the foundation of the Second Temple is established. During this time, Levites, in particular the sons of Asaph, are stationed "to give praise to Yhwh" (Ezra 3:10–11). The parallel between the procedures observed at the First and Second Temples seems deliberate, because the writer notes that this was done "as King David of Israel had ordained" (Ezra 3:10).

"instruments he made for offering praise." The antecedent is not altogether clear. Is it Yhwh or is it David? The former is a possibility as some ancient cultures attributed the invention of musical instruments to gods or demigods. But within Hebrew tradition, such invention could be attributed to humans. For instance, the author of Gen 4:21 depicts the antedeluvian figure Jubal as the ancestor of "all who play the lyre and the pipe." Given David's longstanding association with song and music, it is not surprising that some biblical authors, especially late authors, credit him with the invention or craftsmanship of musical instruments in Israel (Amos 6:5; Neh 12:36; 2 Chr 7:6; 29:26; LXX Ps 151:2). For a different view of Amos 6:5, arguing that this text refers to David's improvisational skills on musical instruments, see Andersen and Freedman (1989: 563–64).

23:6. "divisions" *(maḥlĕqôt)*. The prospect of Solomon's rule, the construction of the Temple, and the advent of centralized worship at one national sanctuary lead to the establishment of a system of divisions and courses among the Levites, priests, singers, gatekeepers, and military officials. Some earlier Priestly writers envisioned Israelite tribes as being made up of tribal divisions (Josh 11:23; 12:7; 18:10), but this highly stylized and elaborate system represents an important new development (COMMENT on 1 Chr 24:1–31). The system of divisions allows for continuous service in Jerusalem by a variety of groups.

"corresponding to the sons of Levi: Gershon, Qohath, and Merari." The tripartite segmentation of the Levites in vv. 6–23 recalls that of earlier sources (Exod 6:16–19; Num 3:17–39; 1 Chr 6:1–33). David's system of divisions follows, therefore, the traditional segmentation of Levi's lineage.

23:7. "Gershonites." The list in vv. 7–23 features collateral segmentation; the largest genealogical depth is four generations.

"Laadan and Shimei." Laadan reappears in 26:21, but elsewhere Shimei is consistently paired with Libni (Exod 6:17; Num 3:18; 1 Chr 6:2, 5, 14). The reason for the discrepancy is unclear. Zöckler (1877: 143) opines that Laadan was a descendant of Libni, but this may simply harmonize two variant traditions.

23:9. "The ancestral heads," or clan chiefs *(rāʾšê hāʾābôt)*, were in charge of their ancestral houses, a prominent form of social organization in the Achaemenid period (1st NOTE to 15:12).

23:10. "The sons of Shimei." Having outlined Laadan's descendants, the author returns to the other Gershonite: Shimei (v. 7).

"Jaḥath." As opposed to the sequence depicted here, Shimei appears as the son of Jaḥath in 6:27–28.

"Jeush" *(yʿwš)*. The PN ("may he come to help") appears in the Edomite genealogies (Gen 36:5, 14, 18; 1 Chr 1:35), elsewhere in Chronicles (1 Chr 7:10; 8:39; 2 Chr 11:19), and on an eighth-century Samaria ostracon (Davies, §3.048.3). But Jeush, along with Ziza and Beriah, are not elsewhere attested as sons (or descendants) of Shimei.

23:11. "one ancestral house." Cf. 24:3, 19.

23:12. "The sons of Qohath." On Qohath and the Qohathites, see Gen 46:11; Exod 6:16–18; Num 3:17–30; 4:2–15; 10:21; 26:57–58; Josh 21:4, 5, 10, 20, 26. Within Chronicles the Qohathites are prominent in the genealogies (1 Chr 5:27–41; 6:1–7, 18, 23, 39, 46, 51, 55; 9:32). But Qohathites also make appearances in the monarchy (1 Chr 15:5; 2 Chr 20:19; 29:12; 34:12). See further the 1st NOTE to 15:5.

"Amram, Izhar, Ḥebron, and Uzziel." These four are also listed as sons of Qohath in Exod 6:18; Num 3:19, 27; 1 Chr 6:3 [see NOTES]. Cf. 1 Chr 6:7.

23:13. "The sons of Amram." In presenting Aaron and Moses *(ʾahărōn ûmōšeh)* as brothers and sons of Amram, this statement comports with earlier genealogies (e.g., Exod 6:18–20; 1 Chr 5:29). The text does not develop Aaron's lineage in this context (cf. Num 3:1–4; 1 Chr 5:27–29). The writer's primary concern is the organization, age, and duties of the Levites.

"Aaron." That the writer contextualizes Aaron within the larger Levitical lineage is highly significant, because in Chronicles Aaronides are, broadly speaking, Levites (2nd NOTE to 5:29).

"set apart" *(wayyibbādēl)*. The author launches into a digression on the sacerdotal responsibilities of Aaron and his sons. Digressions and anecdotes are a common feature of genealogies in the Near Eastern and classical worlds, but this one requires some explanation because Aaron's own lineage is not presented in this chapter. The digression recalls a pattern found in the Priestly writing. There one of the summaries of Levitical duties (Num 1:50–53) occurs in the context of an Israelite census that excludes the tribe of Levi itself (Num 1:1–54). An explanation for the noninclusion of the Levites becomes the occasion for a summation of their special duties. Similarly, in this context, the noninclusion of the Aaronides in the Levitical divisions becomes the occasion for an explanation—"Aaron's being set apart"—and a synopsis of Aaron's priestly responsibilities. The description of priestly duties here is more extensive than that given for the priests serving at Gibeon (16:39–40). The synopsis shows some indebtedness to the Priestly writers and, to a lesser extent, to Ezekiel (see COMMENT).

"consecrate" *(haqdîš)*. In biblical literature one finds both laypeople and their leaders consecrating items for sacral use (Exod 28:38; Lev 27:14–22). In both Kings (e.g., 2 Kgs 12:19) and Chronicles (e.g., 1 Chr 26:26–28), one also finds monarchs, as patrons of the cult, consecrating booty to the Temple. Indeed, one reason that Solomon builds the Temple, according to the Chronicler, is "to consecrate it" *(lĕhaqdîš lô)* to Yhwh (2 Chr 2:3 [ET 2:4]). Of the various sacerdotal duties, one was to handle and, if need be, purify items that Israelites consecrated to Yhwh (Exod 28:38; Lev 22:2–16; 27:26). This priestly responsibility also seems to be evident in the eighth-century Ivory Pomegranate inscription, *lby*[*t yhw*]*h qdš khnm* (Davies, §99.001).

"the most sacred objects" *(qōdeš qŏdāšîm)*. The phrase *qōdeš qŏdāšîm* can represent a number of things: the holy food associated with the cult of the Tabernacle (Lev 2:3) and the Temple (Ezra 2:63//Neh 7:65), the most holy offerings or donations (Lev 21:22; Num 18:10; Ezek 42:13; 44:13), or the most holy *sancta*, that is, the most holy furnishings associated with the Yahwistic cult (Exod 28:1–30:10; 40:10; Num 4:4–15, 19; 2 Chr 31:14). In some cases, the entire Tabernacle complex may be in view (e.g., Exod 30:29; Milgrom 1976: 35–37). Of the various possibilities, the reference here is probably to the most holy *sancta*. In line with the position of the Priestly writers (e.g., Num 4:4–20), reaffirmed by the authors of Ezekiel (e.g., 44:15–16), the Chronicler maintains that only the priests, defined here as the sons of Aaron, are qualified to have direct contact with the most sacred objects, which were ipso facto potentially lethal (Haran 1978: 187–88; Milgrom 1990: 343–44). Hence, after Aḥaz desecrates the sacred vessels situated in the Jerusalem Temple, it is up to the priests to reconsecrate them during Ḥezeqiah's reforms (2 Chr 29:16–19).

"he and his sons forever" *(hû'-ûbānāyw ʿad-ʿôlām)*. The author is careful to state that the Aaronic prerogative applies not only to him but also to his descendants. In this way, the writer links the perquisites of a central figure of the Ancestral era to those of the Aaronide priests of his own time.

"to make offerings before Yhwh." This mandate to the Aaronides is detailed in a number of contexts (e.g., Exod 29:38–42; 30:1–10; Lev 8:1–9:24; 16:1–28; 1st NOTE to 6:34). But not all biblical writers speak with one voice on this issue. The story of the revolt headed by Qoraḥ, Dathan, Abiram, and On against Moses and

Aaron centers on the question of who may become a priest (Num 16). Many scholars believe that this episode and others like it reflect struggles between different priestly houses in ancient Israel over the right to offer sacrifices at major shrines, including the Jerusalem Temple (Cross 1973: 198–206). To take another example, Ezekiel's confirmation of the exclusive rights of the priests to sacrifice is coupled with a demotion of the Levites. Because the Levites led the "house of Israel" astray, they may no longer offer sacrifices before Yhwh (Ezek 44:12–13). The very fact that this demotion occurred indicates that some Levites offered sacrifices in former times (Haran 1978: 58–83).

"to serve him" *(lšrtw)*. The priests serve Yhwh by, among other things, serving at the altar, performing rites, and ministering in the sanctuary (Num 3:6; 4:12; Ezek 44:15–27).

"to pronounce blessings." See Lev 9:22–23; Deut 10:8; 21:5; Num 6:23–27; Ps 129:8; 1QS 1.18, 21; 2.1, 11; 5.5; 1Q28a 2.19 (cf. 2 Sam 6:18; 1 Chr 16:2). One such benediction, a version of the Priestly blessing (Num 6:23–26), dating to the sixth century BCE, appears on an amulet found in Ketef Hinnom just outside old Jerusalem (Barkay 1986; 1992b).

"in his name." There is a link between priestly blessings made in Yhwh's name and the well-being of Israel. In Num 6:27, Yhwh affirms that the priests "will place my name upon the people of Israel and I shall bless them."

23:14. "Moses." In Leviticus and Numbers, Moses plays an essential role in anointing and consecrating the *sancta* (the Tabernacle and its furnishings), the priestly personnel (Aaron and Aaron's sons), and their vestments. However indispensable Moses' role is to these foundational events in the history of the Israelite cult in general and to the establishment of the priesthood in particular, this indispensable role does not translate into the achievement of priestly status, at least as far as Moses' descendants are concerned. In Priestly theology, the descendants of Moses are treated as Levites genealogically (Num 26:59). For this reason, the census of Num 3 mentions the lineage of Aaron and Moses, but lists only the descendants of Aaron. In stating that the descendants of Moses "were reckoned among the tribe of Levi," the author agrees with Priestly dogma. Milgrom (1990: 15) points out that in the Pentateuch whenever Moses and Aaron are mentioned together, Moses' name always precedes Aaron's. The only exception occurs in the genealogies, which mention Aaron first (the older brother) and Moses second (Exod 6:20; Num 3:1; 26:59) because they are concerned with priestly pedigree. The same holds true for Chronicles. In the genealogies and lists, Aaron precedes Moses (1 Chr 5:29; 23:13).

"the man of God." Some scholars (e.g., Willi 1972: 228) believe that the title presents Moses as a prophet, while Schniedewind (1995: 50–54) contends that the title refers to Moses as a legislator par excellence. The two interpretations are not mutually exclusive (Deut 18:15–19; 34:11–12). If the early interpreters are any indication of the text's original significance, some element of prophecy is in view. Instead of calling Moses "the man of God," Tg. speaks of him as "the prophet of Yhwh." See also *Jub.* 1; 1Q22 1.7–11; 4Q365 23.4; 4Q377 2.2; 4Q378 3.26; 4Q393.3.

23:15. "Gershom." This son of Moses (Exod 2:22; 1 Chr 26:24; cf. Judg 18:30) is to be distinguished from Gershom the son of Levi (1 Chr 5:27; 6:1, 5, 47, 56; 15:7).

23:16. "Shubael." Although he appears elsewhere in Chronicles (1 Chr 24:20; 25:20; 26:24), this son of Gershom is otherwise unattested in the HB. The Targum associates this son of Gershom with the son of Gershom named Jonathan, who is mentioned in Judg 18:30. The PN *šbʾl* is found on a sixth-century(?) jar handle from Gibeon (Davies, §22.021.1).

23:17. "Eliezer." The son of Moses by this name (Exod 18:4; 1 Chr 26:25) is to be distinguished from other individuals with the same name (1 Chr 7:8; 15:24; 27:16; 2 Chr 20:37; Ezra 8:16; 10:18, 23, 31).

"Reḥabiah." Like "Shubael," this name reappears in 1 Chr 24:21 (cf. 26:25).

23:18. "Izhar" was one of the sons of Qohath (Exod 6:18–21; Num 3:19; 16:1; 1 Chr 5:28; 6:3, 23; 23:12). The sons of Izhar are listed in earlier sources as Qoraḥ, Nepheg, and Zichri (Exod 6:21; cf. Num 16:1; 1 Chr 6:22–23). The gentilic of "Izhar" occurs in Num 3:27; 1 Chr 24:22; 26:23, 29.

"Shelomoth the head." In the Qohathite genealogies (e.g., Exod 6:21; Num 3:19; 16:1; 1 Chr 5:27–28; 6:3, 7–13, 18–23) Shelomoth does not appear. See further 1 Chr 24:22.

23:19. "sons of Ḥebron." The Levite Ḥebron appears in a number of earlier contexts (Exod 6:18; Num 3:19; 1 Chr 5:28; 6:3). The gentilic occurs in Num 3:27; 26:58; 1 Chr 26:23, 30–31. There are, however, different accounts of Ḥebron's offspring within Chronicles. In 15:9 Ḥebron's son (or descendant) is listed as Eliel. Two Ḥebronites are listed by name in 26:30–31, "Ḥashabiah" and "Jeriah the head" (cf. "Jeriah the head" here). To complicate matters further, "Jeriah, Amariah the second, Jeḥaziel the third, and Jeqameam *(yĕqamʿām)* the fourth" are mentioned as among the descendants of the Hebronite named Shelomoth in 24:22–23.

"Amariah *(ʾămaryāh)* the second." The name *ʾmryhw*, "Yhwh has said," and its shortened form *ʾmryh* occur relatively infrequently in the Bible, apart from the late literature *(ʾmryh* 1 Chr 5:33, 37; Ezra 7:3; 10:42; Neh 10:4 [ET 10:3]; 12:2, 13; *ʾmryhw* 1 Chr 24:23; 2 Chr 19:11; 31:15). The name is common in priestly contexts (e.g., 1 Chr 5:33, 37; 2 Chr 19:11; Ezra 7:3). But *ʾmryhw* is also attested on two eighth-century graffiti from Beersheba, six seventh—to sixth-century jar handles from Gibeon, a seventh—to sixth-century seal from Qiriath-jearim, and a seventh—to sixth-century seal from the vicinity of T. Beit Mirṣim. The PN *ʾmryw* is attested at Kuntillet ʿAjrûd.

"Jeḥaziel the third." The name occurs only in Chronicles (1 Chr 12:5; 16:6; 24:23; 2 Chr 20:14) and Ezra (8:5).

23:20. "The sons of Uzziel: Micah the head and Isshiah the second." In earlier tradition, Uzziel appears as one of four sons of Qohath (Exod 6:18; Num 3:19, 27; 1 Chr 6:3). According to Exod 6:22, the sons of Uzziel were Mishael, Elzaphan, and Sithri. Leviticus 10:4 mentions Mishael and Elzaphan. It is unclear why the genealogy in Chronicles differs from that found in Exodus and Leviticus. In ancient societies genealogical details were not always fixed, but were subject to change according to the social needs of particular generations (R. Wilson 1977). In any case, the version found here is not accidental; it reappears in slightly different form in 1 Chr 24.

"Micah *(mykh)* the head." Also listed as a son of Uzziel in 24:24–25. Cf. 5:5; 8:34–35; 9:40–41.

"Isshiah *(yiššîyyāh)* the second." Another name, "Yhwh exists" or "Yhwh is (there) for me," that occurs only in Chronicles (1 Chr 7:3; 24:21, 25) and Ezra (10:31). Isshiah appears as the brother of Micah in 1 Chr 24:25. De Vries (1989: 194–95) speculates that the final names in each of the ancestral houses mentioned in the table (e.g., Isshiah) happened to be Levitical contemporaries of the Chronicler. Note, however, that some of the new names extend to more than one generation.

23:21. "The sons of Merari." Maḥli and Mushi are also presented as sons of Merari in Exod 6:19, 1 Chr 6:4, and 1 Chr 24:26. Numbers 26:57 lists as Levitical families the Gershonites, the Qohathites, and the Merarites, while the following verse mentions the Libnites, the Ḥebronites, the Maḥlites, the Mushites, and the Qoraḥites. On Merari, see further the 3rd NOTE to 6:1.

"Maḥli." See also 1 Chr 24:28 and Ezra 8:18–19 (in which Ḥashabiah and Jeshaiah of Merari are also mentioned). As a gentilic, see Num 3:20, 33 in which Maḥli and Mushi are listed as clans of Merari.

"Mushi." See Exod 6:19; Num 3:20; 1 Chr 6:4, 32; 23:23; 24:26, 30.

"Qish." The information concerning Maḥli's offspring is unique to Chronicles. On the name *qyš*, see 1 Chr 24:29 (as the son of Maḥli), 2 Chr 29:12 (as a descendant of Merari), the hypocoristicon "Qishi" in 1 Chr 6:29, and what is likely to be the full name "Qishaiah" (LXX *Keisaiou*) in 1 Chr 15:17 (see TEXTUAL NOTE).

23:22. "without having any sons, only daughters." This is a case that bears only some similarities to the case of the daughters of Zelopheḥad (contra Curtis and Madsen 1910), who petition Moses, Eleazar, and the chieftains of Israel concerning the inheritance of their father (Num 27:1–5; cf. 36:1–12; 1 Chr 7:15). The future of this inheritance was threatened because Zelopheḥad had no sons. Recognizing the just cause of Zelopheḥad's daughters, Moses rules that in such cases the property may be transferred to a daughter (Num 27:6–11). Here, however, there is no transfer of property to the daughters of Eleazar. Instead, a type of levirate marriage seems to be operative (Gen 38; Deut 25:5–10; Ruth 4). In levirate law, a widow who had no sons would be taken as a wife by her husband's brother. By performing this duty, the levir would be preserving his deceased brother's inheritance. But the parallel with levirate law is also imperfect, because in 1 Chr 23:22 it is the daughters who marry, not their mother. In this respect, the case depicted in Num 36:1–12 is relevant. Moses responds to the petition brought by one of the Josephite clans by decreeing that daughters among the Israelite tribes who lay claim to their father's patrimonial estate because they have no surviving male siblings must marry within their tribe. Thus shares within one tribe cannot be transferred to another tribe. In accordance with this ruling, Zelopheḥad's daughters all marry sons of their uncles (Num 36:11). Hence, in neither the case of the daughters of Zelopheḥad nor in the case of levirate law do women actually inherit property. Rather, the daughters bridge a gap between male generations by preserving a patrilineal estate (Bird 1992: 953). This differs from the situation in first millennium Babylon (van der Toorn 1996b) and from the situation of the Jews in Elephantine, where women could own property (*TAD* B2.5; B2.6; B2.8; Porten 1968) and inherit property (*TAD* B2.1:4–6; B2.3; Szubin and Porten 1982; 1983). In the case of the situation depicted by the authors of Numbers, the transfer of property of the daughters of Zelopheḥad allows his inheritance to survive. Similarly, by marrying their kinsmen—the sons of Qish—the daughters of Eleazar ensure that Eleazar's inheritance will continue.

23:23. "Maḥli, Eder, and Jeremoth" (see TEXTUAL NOTE) also appear as sons of Mushi in 24:30.

23:24. "by their ancestral houses *(lbyt 'btyhm)*, the ancestral heads *(r'šy h'bwt)* according to their enrollments *(lpqwdyhm)* by their head count of names *(bmspr šmwt lglgltm)*." The technical language has been often misunderstood by scholars. The vocabulary recalls that used in the censuses of Exod 30:11–16; Num 1; 3–4; 26 (Scolnic 1995: 39–40). The pan-Israel census of Num 1, in particular, is important for understanding the verbiage used in this verse. The census of Num 1 proceeds by ancestral houses *(lbyt 'bwtm)*, with all males *(kl-zkr)* registered in a tally of names *(bmspr šmwt)* by their heads (*lglgltm*; v. 2). In other words, the census comprises more than just a general head count. Each individual's name is registered. Focusing on the internal structure of each tribe, the census of Num 1 takes the ancestral house as its basic social unit. Within each ancestral house, numbering is the responsibility of the ancestral head (Num 1:5–15). Each ancestral head or clan chief makes a head count, according to name, of the males in his household. After the head counts procured by the clan chiefs are added together for each tribe, the result is presented to Moses and Aaron (Num 1:19–43). The sum total for all the tribes is then tabulated (Num 1:45–46). The clan-based organization of the pan-Israel census in the wilderness is, therefore, quite different from the centralized method employed by David and Joab in their pan-Israel census (2 Sam 24; 1 Chr 21).

If David's organization of the Levites recalls the pattern of the pan-Israel census of Num 1, it does so only in part. Whereas 1 Chr 23:3–5 refer to a census, 23:7–23 comprise a genealogically based list of Levitical divisions (re)established by David. The tripartite division honors the genealogical segmentation of the Levites dating to the wilderness period (Num 3–4), which follows the descendants of Levi's three sons: Gershon, Qohath, and Merari. The list subsequently follows the subdivision of the Gershonites, Qohathites, and Merarites into ancestral houses. As with the muster of Num 1, the register in 1 Chr 23 lists a variety of ancestral heads. The text explicitly mentions ancestral houses (vv. 9, 11) and ancestral heads (vv. 8, 11, 16, 17, 18, 19, 20) in two of the divisions appointed by David. By virtue of the summary in v. 24, the existence of clan chiefs among the Merarites (vv. 21–23) is implied as well. In this respect, the questions posed by some scholars (e.g., De Vries 1989: 194) about whether vv. 7–23 are truly a genealogy are on the mark. If vv. 7–23 were simply a genealogy, one might expect it to be much more thorough. Similarly, if vv. 7–23 were simply a list of individual appointees, it would be most odd for King David (unless he were a hopelessly corrupt ruler) to be appointing dead people and their deceased descendants. As the text stands, no section of the Levitical list appears to extend anywhere near the time of David. In short, these verses comprise neither a genealogy nor a list of appointees, but a table of organization that follows a broad genealogical outline. David's partitioning of the Levites honors their genealogical segmentation, even though he will revise both their minimum age (vv. 25–27) and their job description (vv. 28–32).

The mention of clan chiefs and ancestral houses recalls certain features of the organization of the Israelites in the wilderness period (Num 1). The list of subdivisions within each of the three major divisions (1 Chr 23:7–11, 12–20, 21–23) revises and extends the genealogical outline of the Levites found in Num 3–4. If the purpose of the pan-Israel muster of Num 1 is to determine how many males of military age Moses and Aaron have at their disposal, the Levitical census of 1 Chr 23:3–5 determines how many Levites are available to David and what their professional specializations are. The ensuing Davidic organization of the Levites into divisions and ancestral houses (vv. 6–23) selectively reuses and extends the Levitical genealogies of Num 3–4 to address another more specific issue: "the work for the service of the Temple of Yhwh" (v. 24). Hence, it should come as no great surprise that the table of organization (vv. 7–23) is soon followed by a summary of Levitical duties at the projected Temple (vv. 28–32).

"from the age of twenty and up" *(mbn ʿśrym šnh wmʿlh)*. As long recognized by commentators, there is a tension between the age given in v. 3 (thirty) and the age given here and in v. 27 (twenty). See further SOURCES AND COMPOSITION.

23:25. "has taken up residence." Literally, "tented" *(škn)*. The text plays on the meaning of an important Priestly concept. In Priestly theology, Yhwh is a transcendent deity whose sanctuary is portable. As Israel moves from place to place, the sanctuary has to be dismantled and later reassembled. The deity's relationship to the sanctuary comports with its movable nature: Yhwh tabernacles with his people at his portable sanctuary. Like the Priestly writers, the Chronicler uses the verb *škn*, but he infuses it with new meaning. The United Monarchy witnesses the construction of a permanent sanctuary in Jerusalem. As in the Priestly writing, Yhwh is transcendent. But Yhwh now tents "in Jerusalem forever" *(ʿd-lʿwlm)*. The Temple is depicted as a constituent institution of Israel's collective life. This means that the reorganization and expansion of Israel's civil service has authority not just for Solomon but also for subsequent generations. When some of Judah's reforming kings, such as Joash under the guidance of Jehoiada (2 Chr 24:4–15), Ḥezeqiah (2 Chr 29–31), and Josiah (2 Chr 34:8–13; 35:3–19), refurbish the Temple and reorganize its civil service, they do so along the lines that David first established. Indeed, "the writing of David and the document of Solomon his son" are invoked to commend and inform Josiah's reforms (2 Chr 35:4).

23:26. "its service" *(ʿăbōdātô)*. In the Priestly source, the standard meaning of the term *ʿăbōdâ* (occurring some seventy times) is physical labor or work (Milgrom 1970: 60–83; 1991: 7–8). But in Chronicles and other late biblical books *ʿăbōdâ* can have a broader meaning, denoting cultic service (3rd NOTE to 6:33).

23:27. "among the last commands of David." NRSV sets all of vv. 27–32 apart as the words of David, a continuation of the speech began in vv. 25–26. The issue is that v. 27 speaks of David's orders in the third person. NAB addresses this problem by repositioning v. 27 directly after v. 24. NAB is then able to present vv. 25–26, 28–32 as direct speech. This is possible, but it does not seem necessary to rearrange the text to make sense of it. It is more likely that in vv. 27–32 the author is paraphrasing the words of David. After quoting David's revision of the minimum Levitic age of service (vv. 25–26), the author describes the Levitical duties (vv. 28–32).

23:28. "their appointment." The depiction of Levitical duties in vv. 28–32 engages a number of earlier biblical texts, both legal (the Priestly source) and prophetic (Ezekiel) in nature. Japhet (1989: 92) contends that the language of "appointment" *(mʿmd)* recalls Deut 10:8, in which Yhwh "set the tribe of Levi apart to bear the Ark of the Covenant of Yhwh to stand *(lʿmd)* before Yhwh to serve him *(lšrtw)*." The language used is important. The term *mʿmd* to denote "appointment," "position," or "office" recurs elsewhere in Chronicles (2 Chr 35:15), in Sir 33:12, and in the writings found at Qumran (e.g., 1QIsa 22:19). But in 1 Chr 23, as in P, it is the priests who serve *(lšrtw*; v. 13) Yhwh. Of the various writings that make up the Pentateuch, the Chronicler's description of Levitical duties is most indebted to Priestly lore. The Chronicler's description of Levitical responsibilities is, however, not simply traditional. Like David's revision of the minimum Levitical age, the description goes beyond earlier precedent (see the following NOTES).

"for the service of the Temple of Yhwh." In other words, the summary is not meant to be an exhaustive tabulation of all Levitical duties (*pace* R. Braun 1986: 230–34). Rather, vv. 28–32 address what the Levite responsibilities are to be vis-à-vis the Temple.

"the chambers" *(hallĕšākôt)*. The term *liškâ* can refer generally to a cella, or chamber, of the Temple (2 Kgs 23:11; Ezek 42:13; 44:19; Ezra 10:6; 1 Chr 9:26, 33; 28:12) or more particularly to a storeroom within the Temple (Ezra 8:29; Neh 10:38–40 [ET 10:37–39]; 13:5–8; 2 Chr 31:11). It is difficult to reconstruct the precise nature, purpose, and size of all the rooms found at the sides, and perhaps rear, of the Temple (C. Meyers 1992: 358). Nehemiah 10:39 [ET 10:38] mentions "the storerooms of the treasury" *(hallĕšākôt lĕbêt hāʾôṣār)*. In the elaborate temple complex envisioned by the authors of Ezekiel (42:13–14; 44:19), at least some of the rooms—"the holy chambers" *(liškôt haqqōdeš)*—were reserved exclusively for the priests. In Chronicles it is unclear whether a more general or a more particular meaning is intended. In any case, the differentiation called for by Ezekiel seems to be unrealized in Chronicles, Ezra, and Nehemiah. The Levites who serve alongside the priests (v. 28) have responsibility for the chambers. The text of 1 Chr 9:26 refers to gatekeepers (Levites) who were in charge of the chambers and treasuries of the Temple, while 9:33 mentions singers and Levitical ancestral heads who were in the chambers. During the reforms of Ḥezeqiah, Levites were in charge of preparing the temple chambers for Israel's gifts (2 Chr 31:11–12). But the texts in Ezra and Nehemiah do not describe the chambers that served as storeooms as the specific domain of the Levites. In fact, Neh 13:4 mentions that a priest (Eliashib) was in charge of the temple chambers. The precise status of this Eliashib is disputed (Williamson 1985: 386).

"the purity of all sacred objects" *(ṭohŏrat lĕkol-qōdeš).* Two other translations are possible: "the purity of everything holy" or "the purity of all sacred donations." On the latter meaning of *qōdeš*, see Lev 22:10, 14. The text refers to cleansing or the establishment of ceremonial cleanliness (Lev 13:7, 35: 14:2, 23, 32; 15:13; Num 6:9; Ezek 44:26; 2 Chr 29:15; 30:19; Ringgren 1986: 293). In Chronicles, the purity of the *sancta* is a special responsibility of the Levites, even though they serve in this capacity alongside the priests (v. 28). Similarly, in Neh 12:45, the guarding of purity *(mišmeret haṭṭohŏrâ)* is ascribed to the priests and Levites "in accord with the command *(miṣwat)* of David and of Solomon his son."

23:29. "the rows of bread" *(leḥem hammaʿăreket).* In P (Exod 25:30; 35:13; 39:36; Lev 24:5–9) the relevant expression is "the bread of the presence" *(leḥem happānîm)*, a phrase that also appears in 1 Sam 21:7 and 1 Kgs 7:48(//2 Chr 4:19). The "rows of bread" or "bread of the presence" are characteristic of both tabernacle and temple worship (Exod 25:30; 35:13; 39:36; Lev 24:5–9; Neh 10:33; 1 Chr 9:32 [see NOTE]; 2 Chr 13:11). In Leviticus the bread of the presence could only be eaten by Aaron and his sons and had to be changed every sabbath (24:8–9). The instruction to (re)place the showbread is, according to Lev 24:8, "an everlasting covenant" *(bryt ʿwlm).*

"the choice flour" *(sōlet).* In Akk., *siltu* can refer to "shavings" (cf. *salātu*, "to split into many parts") or to a certain food used as an offering (*CAD* S 267). Arab. *sult* can designate a roasted grain. In Heb. *sōlet* designates a fine flour or semolina that was likely made from wheat (Exod 29:2; Lev 2:1, 4, 5; 2 Kgs 7:16; Milgrom 1991: 179). This semolina *(sōlet)* is to be distinguished from ordinary flour *(qemaḥ).* See also the 2nd NOTE to 9:29.

"the unleavened wafers" *(rĕqîqê hammaṣṣôt).* Compare Akk. *raqāqu*, "to be thin, small;" *raqqaqu*, "very thin" (*AHw* 957); Arab. *ruqāq*, "flat loaf of bread;" *raqqa*, "to be(come) thin, delicate, fine;" and see Exod 29:2; Lev 2:4; 7:12; Num 6:15.

"the griddle." The meaning of the term *maḥăbat* has been the subject of some discussion. The term refers to a metal plate, tray, or "griddle" (NJPS) that would be used for baking or roasting. The authors of Leviticus mention a "cereal offering on a *maḥăbat*" (Lev 2:5) and an offering "prepared with oil on a *maḥăbat*" (Lev 6:14 [ET 6:21]; 7:9). The book of Ezekiel speaks of the prophet placing his face against an iron *maḥăbat*, thereby creating a kind of iron wall between him and the city of Jerusalem (Ezek 4:3). If *maḥăbat* designates a pan or griddle, there is no firm evidence that *maḥăbat* also denotes a cake for an offering (contra REB; *HALOT* 288). Rudolph (1955: 158) reads this term *(maḥăbat)* with the following *(murbāket)* as designating a flat, round cake. Similarly, NJPS: "the cakes made on the griddle and soaked" (NJPS). But the syntax *(wĕlammaḥăbat wĕlammurbāket)* suggests that these are two different terms. Moreover, *ḥbytym* may designate what may be made on a *maḥăbat.* MT 1 Chronicles 9:31 speaks of the Levite Mattithiah being "responsible for making the flat cakes" *(ʿl mʿśh hḥbtym).*

"measures of capacity and length." The *mśwrh* is a measure of volume (Lev 19:35; Ezek 4:11, 16), while the better-attested *mdh* is a measure of length (Exod 26:2, 8; 36:9, 15; Josh 3:4; Ezek 48:30, 33; 2 Chr 3:3). That the Chronicler presents the Levites as the keepers of standard measures is important because his stance on this issue differs from that of a variety of earlier authors (contra Zöckler 1877: 144). In Lev 19:35–36, the responsibility for maintaining standard measures lies with the entire community, the *ʿdt bny yśrʾl* mentioned in Lev 19:2 (Gerstenberger 1996: 280–81). Similarly, fair standards and weights are the responsibility of the Israelites in Deut 25:13–16. Finally, in Ezekiel, responsibility for a system of standard measures lies with the political authorities. The author of Ezek 45:9–12 implores the "princes" *(nśyʾy)* of Israel to maintain balanced weights and standards with respect to ephahs, baths, homers, and shekels.

23:30. "to give thanks and to praise Yhwh." On this standard Levitical duty in Chronicles, see the NOTES to 16:4, 7–38 and 23:5.

23:31. "and whenever burnt offerings are offered" *(wlkl hʿlwt ʿlwt)*. The Levites are to be present during the lifting up of burnt offerings, but they do not offer sacrifices themselves (contra Büchler 1899: 131). The duties of the Levites and Aaronides are complementary, but largely distinct. The role of the Levites is to serve alongside the Aaronides (v. 28). This means that they are "to give thanks and to praise" (v. 30) whenever the Aaronides present burnt offerings.

"burnt offerings." As the context (v. 30) implies, these were to be offered both morning and evening. In ancient Mesopotamia also, it was standard practice to feed the gods twice daily (Frankfort 1948). The priests at the Tent of Meeting (Num 18:3–4) and at the Temple were supposed to present burnt offerings morning and evening (Exod 29:38–42; Num 28:3–8; 2 Chr 13:11). Such worship is, in the words of Solomon (2 Chr 2:4), "Israel's everlasting obligation" *(lĕʿôlām zōʾt ʿal-yiśrāʾēl)*.

"sabbaths, new moons." See, for instance, Lev 23:3 and Num 28:9–15. Solomon builds the Temple to "offer sacrifice before him [Yhwh] aromatic incense, and for the regular arrangement [of showbread], and for burnt offerings morning and evening, for the sabbaths and for the new moons, and for the festivals of Yhwh our God" (2 Chr 2:3 [ET 2:4]).

"festivals." According to biblical law, ancient Israel observed three major annual feasts: Passover and Maṣṣot (Num 28:16–25), Pentecost (Num 28:26–31), and Tabernacles (Num 29:12–38). The number three is explicitly mentioned in the summary of festivals provided by Solomon (2 Chr 8:13; cf. 31:3). For other versions of these festivals, see Exod 23:14–17; Lev 23:4–44; Deut 16:1–17 (Haran 1978: 290–300).

"with the number (being set) according to the prescription *(kĕmišpāṭ)* concerning them." The number of burnt offerings would vary according to the occasion. By using the citation formula *kĕmišpāṭ* (also popular in Qumran halakic texts; 11QT 15.3; 18.5; 22.10; 28.5, 8; 50.7, 17), the Chronicler presents David as a conserver of authoritative tradition.

"perpetually *(tāmîd)* before Yhwh." The adverb *tāmîd* carries the sense of continuity and regularity. A number of cultic activities were to be performed in perpetuity (Exod 25:30; 29:38; Lev 6:13; 24:3; Deut 11:12; 1 Kgs 10:8). According to the divine decree given through Moses, "regular burnt offerings" should characterize Israel's cult "throughout your generations" (Exod 29:42). Cessation of such offerings could be viewed as catastrophic for Israel (2 Chr 29:7–16; Dan 8:11–13; 11:31; 12:11).

23:32. "the watch *(mišmeret)* of the Tent of Meeting." In speaking of a "watch" *(mišmeret)*, the author is referring to guard duty (2nd NOTE to 25:8). The term also has this meaning in P, where it occurs some forty-three times (Milgrom 1976: 8–16; 1991: 7), and elsewhere in Chronicles. On the military dimensions of Levitical responsibilities, see the NOTE to 12:27.

"the watch of the sacred objects" *(mišmeret haqqōdeš)*. Two translations of this expression are possible: "the watch of the sacred objects" and "the watch of the sanctuary." In the first instance, *haqqōdeš* designates the *sancta*, the sacred objects associated with, and sometimes including, the sanctuary (Num 3:31; 4:15; 7:9; 31:6; 1 Chr 9:29). In the second instance, the term refers to either the sanctuary itself (Exod 28:29, 35; 36:1–6; Lev 4:6; 10:4, 18; 1 Chr 29:3) or to one particular area within this sanctuary—the holy place as opposed to the most holy place (Exod 26:33–34; 2 Chr 5:11; 29:7; cf. 2 Chr 35:3). The combination of terms *(mišmeret haqqōdeš)* points toward the translation "watch of the sanctuary." The usage in 1 Chr 23:32 contrasts, therefore, with the teachings of the Priestly writers. According to Num 18:5, the priests, that is, Aaron and his sons, are to have responsibility for *mišmeret haqqōdeš*, "the guard duty of the sanctuary" (i.e., the holy place). Hence, there is good reason to believe that the author of 1 Chr 23 is contesting or modifying Priestly law by depicting the Levites as guards of the sanctuary (Milgrom 1976: 82–83; Hanson 1979). See further the COMMENT.

"the watch of the sons of Aaron, their kinsmen." In Priestly lore, one of the Levitical duties was to guard the priests (Num 3:7; 18:2–3).

"for the service of the temple of Yhwh" *(laʿăbōdat bêt yhwh)*. The Priestly writers often speak of the Levitical responsibility for the work *(ʿăbōdâ)* of the Tent of Meeting. Chronicles affirms this historic service (vv. 25–26), but transfers its relevance to the Temple. Within the last two pericopes of chapter 23, the author mentions the Levitical service of the House of God five times (vv. 24, 26, 28[bis], 32). By employing similar terminology to that used by the Priestly writers, the author stresses a fundamental continuity in Levitical responsibilities from their work at the Tabernacle to their work at the Temple. But in Chronicles this older Priestly terminology is infused with new meaning (3rd NOTE to 6:33).

## SOURCES AND COMPOSITION

The compositional history of 1 Chr 23 is fiercely debated. Some scholars contend for a series of additions and editions to a basic text that can be as narrowly defined as vv. 1–6a (Welch 1939: 84–85) or as broadly as vv. 6b–13a, 15–24 (Williamson 1979a; 1982b). Others (e.g., Japhet 1993a: 406–21; Wright 1991; 1992; Selman 1994a: 218–28; Schniedewind 1995) attribute the entire chapter to the Chronicler. The sharp disagreement extends even to those scholars who date all of the chapter to a time after the Chronicler. Noth (1957: 114–15), for example, contends for three stages of composition (vv. 3–5, 6b, 7–24aα; vv. 6a, 24aβ, 25–26, 28–32; vv. 24b, 27), each of which postdates the Chronicler. Dörrfuß (1994:

159–66) provides a convenient history of scholarship. The chapter falls into five major parts.

| | | |
|---|---|---|
| I. | Summit | vv. 1–2 |
| II. | Levitical Census | vv. 3–5 |
| III. | Levitical Divisions | vv. 6–23 |
| IV. | New Age for Legal Service | vv. 24–27 |
| V. | Levitical Duties | vv. 28–32 |

Aside from the relationship of the opening verses to the opening verses of 1 Chr 28 ("Excursus: The Composition of 1 Chronicles 23–27"), there are three major compositional issues:

1. the relation of the list of divisions that David establishes (vv. 7–23) to the Levitical census (vv. 3–5) and to the notices that precede (v. 6) and follow it (v. 24)
2. the discrepancy in the legal minimum age of the Levites between v. 3 (age 30) and vv. 24, 27 (age 20)
3. whether either or both of the duty lists, pertaining to the priests (vv. 13–14) and the Levites (vv. 28–32), are later additions to the text

The NOTES to vv. 6 and 24 address the first issue by pointing out that scholars have been led astray by two unwarranted assumptions about the makeup of 1 Chr 23: first, that the census (vv. 3–5) must be a key to the organization of all that follows, and second, that the list of vv. 7–23 is a misplaced or confused genealogy. Because the census (vv. 3–5) pertains to the Levitical population and professional specialization, it is relevant for the material dealing with specialists (officials, judges, gatekeepers, etc.) in 1 Chr 24–27. By the same token, the census is only partially relevant for the description of Levitical duties (vv. 28–32) because this description only affects those Levites who are associated with the sanctuary and its service (as repeatedly stated in vv. 24, 26, 28, 32). It is, therefore, inappropriate to expect a one-for-one correspondence between the groups mentioned in vv. 3–5 and those mentioned in vv. 28–32. Similarly, it is illusory to expect a correspondence between the administrative list of vv. 7–23, introduced in v. 6 and summarized in v. 24, and the census of vv. 3–5. The outline of vv. 7–23 comprises not a genealogy, as many have supposed, but a table of organization that follows a broad genealogical outline. This administrative arrangement bears some resemblance to the organization of the Israelite tribes, especially that of Levi in the Priestly source, but is implemented with a view toward temple service (1st NOTE to v. 24). David's partitioning of the Levites into divisions honors and slightly redraws their genealogical segmentation into a variety of ancestral houses. Yet the partitioning is not simply an act of conservation, as it is associated with a revision of the Levitical minimum age (vv. 25–27) and a restructuring of the Levitical work profile (vv. 28–32).

The third issue, the nature of the duty lists of the Levites and priests, deals primarily with content, but it also involves the issue of form. Form-critical reasons have occasionally been given for deleting the duties of the priests (vv. 13–14) and the Levites (vv. 28–32) from the primary composition of 1 Chr 23, but as we have seen (3rd NOTE to v. 13), these reasons are not strong. They fail to consider the extent to which genealogies in ancient Israel, Mesopotamia, and Greece incorporate comments, anecdotes, and other digressions. Issues of content will be dealt with in the COMMENT below.

It remains, then, to address the second issue, the legal minimum age. No fewer than five different solutions have been proposed to explain the discrepancy:

1. David initially numbered the Levites from thirty years old to comply with custom (Num 4:3) and subsequently numbered the Levites from twenty years old because there was no longer a need to transport the Tabernacle (e.g., Qimḥi; Koester).
2. The author draws upon two variant traditions, both of which he incorporates into his own account (e.g., Bertheau; Schniedewind).
3. One of the two readings is a mistake (e.g., Keil).
4. One (or both) of the readings is a later addition to the text (e.g., Kittel; Rudolph; R. Braun) or is part of a pro-Priestly redaction of Chronicles (e.g., Welch; Williamson; De Vries).
5. The writer has David introduce a (postexilic) innovation, distinguishing between the age of those who could be involved in the construction of the Temple (v. 3) and those who could serve (v. 24) in such a sanctuary (e.g., Curtis and Madsen).

My own view is a combination of views 1 and 5. To be sure, one cannot rule out views 2, 3, and 4 completely. The Chronicler may have drawn upon extra-biblical sources for the composition of this chapter. Such a theory could help to explain both some unique features of the list, such as its mention of certain ancestral heads who are unattested elsewhere in biblical literature, and some minor inconsistencies, such as the differences between certain names in the list of David's Levitical divisions and names that appear in the Levitical genealogies elsewhere. Granting the possibility of sources, one should press the question further. Assuming, for the sake of argument, that the author had access to extra-biblical sources, why did he not reconcile them on the issue of age? Unlike the issue of certain names, the issue of the minimum Levitical age is not incidental to the composition of 1 Chr 23. It forms an essential element in two sections of the text (vv. 3–5 and 24–27). In other words, even if one appeals to a theory of extra-biblical sources, the discrepancy remains to be explained.

Similar considerations hold true for views 3 and 4. It is possible that all or part of vv. 24–27 are a later interpolation. But if vv. 24–27 are a later gloss, how does one explain other texts in Chronicles and Ezra (see below) that also feature the age of twenty as the legal age for Levites? Moreover, assuming, for the sake of argument, that vv. 24–27 are a later addition or part of a secondary or tertiary redaction, why would a later redactor introduce a contradiction into the text? Why would later writers and editors multiply tensions and not seek to alleviate them? Examples from Qumran of glosses inserted into biblical texts point in the opposite direction (Tov 1994). Such interpolations are usually of an explanatory or explicative nature. In any event, appealing to putative additions or redactions simply postpones explanation and does not, in itself, constitute a fully adequate accounting of the difficulties inherent within the text.

In my judgment, the author has David innovate and thereby ratify a postexilic practice. The writer harkens back to a change made in the time of a legendary figure, Israel's founding father of Jerusalem, to authorize a much later invention. In this context, the appeal to the traditional segmentation of Levi maintained by David (vv. 6–23) is also critical. Even as David innovates beyond earlier practice, he honors the force of traditional Levitical genealogy. "Consecration by time" could be at least as powerful an ideology in the ancient world as "consecration by God" in the face of competing claims and threats (Finley 1982: 18). The distinction made in 1 Chr 23 on the issue of age does not involve, however, temple construction as opposed to temple service (contra Curtis and Madsen 1910). The minimum age seems to be pertinent to both situations. The minimum age of twenty for Levitical service appears in the reforms of Ḥezeqiah (2 Chr 31:17). Similarly, in the restoration, Levites are appointed "from the age of twenty and up" *(mbn ʿśrym šnh wmʿlh)* to supervise the building of the Second Temple (Ezra 3:8). Rather than being tied to a distinction between temple construction and temple service, the innovation is tied to the change from a portable sanctuary to a permanent one. The introduction of a new minimum age "from the age of twenty and up" (v. 24) is linked to a royal decree: "for *(ky)* David said, 'Yhwh the God of Israel has given rest to his people and has taken up residence in Jerusalem forever, and so the Levites no longer need to carry the Tabernacle along with all of its furnishings for its service' " (vv. 25–26). In speaking of the porterage of the Tabernacle, the Chronicler is alluding to the situation described by the Priestly writing. In Num 3–4, the Levitical duties include dismantling, transporting, and reassembling the Tabernacle. This hard labor is linked to the minimum and maximum ages of service (twenty-five or thirty to fifty Num 4:2–3, 21–23, 29–30, 34–35, 38–39, 42–43, 46–47; 8:23–26). Given Yhwh's decision to reside in Jerusalem permanently, the earlier decree is now obsolete.

By explicitly linking the change in minimum age to the transition from a portable sanctuary to a stationary sanctuary, the author accomplishes two things. First, he has Israel comply, initially at least, with legal precedent (v. 3). In this manner, the Chronicler acknowledges and confronts the weight of antecedent tradition. Second, the writer defends a postexilic innovation by relativizing the very law David and Israel initially follow to the pre-Davidic stage of Israelite history. With the advent of the permanent divine residence in Jerusalem, a change of the minimum age is justified. Hence, one "of the last commands of David" revises the earlier standard. What begins as an authoritative *traditum* becomes a temporary precedent, honored but consigned to the pre-temple phase of Israel's existence.

## COMMENT

Formidable objections have been raised about the originality of the duty rosters of the priests and Levites. Some argue that the content of vv. 13–14 and 28–32 is fundamentally inconsistent with what they deem to be the Chronicler's staunchly pro-Levitical views. Indeed, certain scholars (e.g., von Rad 1930: 80–118; De Vries 1988) think that a major reason, if not the major reason, for the Chronicler's writing a national history is to advance the cause of the Levites. Whereas the duty lists of 1 Chr 23 distinguish between the responsibilities of the Levites and the priests, even subordinating the former to the latter, the Chronicler himself holds that the Levites can participate in the temple cult (Williamson 1979a; 1982b). Welch (1935: 172–84, 217–44; 1939: 77) even claims that the Chronicler holds to an absolute equality between the Levites and priests. These scholars see the Chronicler taking one side in a long dispute within ancient Israel concerning issues of cult and priesthood. The Chronicler purportedly stands with Deuteronomy, which speaks of "Levitical priests" and holds that any Levite, in principle, can become a priest (Haran 1978: 61–63), and not with the Priestly work and Ezekiel, which draw clear distinctions between the status and functions of priests and Levites.

Given their understanding of the Chronicler's attitude toward cultic affairs as decidedly pro-Levitical, how do these scholars approach the distinct sections on the priests and the Levites in 1 Chr 23? Welch (1935: 172–84, 217–44; 1939: 55–96), Williamson (1979a; 1982b), Roddy Braun (1986: 235–36), De Vries (1989: 191–96), and others contend that while the original Chronicler was pro-Levitical, a later pro-Priestly editor brought the Chronicler's work into conformity with Priestly theology. In this line of interpretation, vv. 13–14 and 28–32 stem from a pro-Priestly reviser who couches the duties of the Levites as subservient to and distinct from those of the Aaronides (vv. 13–14).

However little disagreement exists that the lists of duties in vv. 13–14 and 28–32 are indebted to Priestly lore, there is substantial disagreement about what this indebtedness comes to. The Priestly presentation of Levitical and Aaronide duties in Numbers has itself been subject to a variety of interpretations. Büchler (1899) and Curtis and Madsen (1910) acknowledge the indebtedness of the Levitical responsibilities (within vv. 28–32) to certain texts in the Priestly writing, but disagree what the specific sources are. These scholars point to tensions between the duty roster of the Levites in Chronicles and some of the duty rosters of Numbers. The writer of Num 3:28, for example, speaks of the Levites as "those keeping watch over the sanctuary" (*šōmrê mišmeret haqqōdeš*). In Num 3:31 the Levites, specifically the Qohathites, have responsibility for guarding the *sancta* (the ark, the table, the lampstand, the altars, the sacred vessels, and the screen). This evidence would seem to comport with the use of the expression *mišmeret haqqōdeš* in 1 Chr 23:32 to describe one of the Levitical responsibilities. So far so good. But does the Levitical *mišmeret haqqōdeš* conflict with other Priestly dogma? According to Num 18:5, the priests (Aaron and his sons) have responsibility for *mišmeret haqqōdeš*, "the guard duty of the sanctuary" (or "holy place"). Given the testimony of Num 18, Curtis and Madsen maintain that the Chronicler consulted only Num 3, and not Num 18, in composing 1 Chr 23. Büchler thinks that the Chronicler had access to a Priestly source, but confused it.

There are, then, two related issues. The first is whether the Levitical duty roster in 1 Chr 23:28–32 is pro-Priestly, and hence to be considered as a later addition.

The second is ascertaining whether the Priestly writing itself speaks with more than one voice on the specific responsibilities of the Levites and priests. Because of the disagreement and confusion about the Priestly sources for the discourse on Levitical responsibilities in 1 Chr 23:28–32, it is necessary to give some sustained attention to the Priestly presentation of Levitical duties. Is there some fundamental contradiction between the lists of duties in Num 3–4 and 18 that the author of 1 Chr 23:28–32 exploits to his own advantage? Are the Levites in Chronicles merely "janitors" in charge of the physical equipment of the sanctuary, as Myers (1965a: 161) claims? To anticipate my conclusions, there is no compelling reason to think either that the writer of 1 Chr 23:28–32 used only Num 3 or that the position evinced in Num 3 is fundamentally different from that of Num 18. There are three basic problems with the way the issue is usually approached. One is the way in which the pertinent section of 1 Chr 23 (vv. 28–32) is interpreted, a second is the way in which scholars have understood the Priestly writing, and a third is a failure to recognize the degree to which the Chronicler is more than an exegete of the Priestly materials. Of a certainty, the Chronicler draws upon his Priestly *Vorlage*, but he does so to pursue his own agenda. As will become clear in the following discussion, the writer formulates his own distinctive position, even as he draws upon older sources.

To begin with the first point, the Chronicler's account of Levitical responsibilities takes the form of a summary that does not spell out all that the duties require. It is clear that the author generally portrays Levitical and Aaronide responsibilities as complementary: "their appointment was to be at the side of the sons of Aaron for the service of the Temple of Yhwh" (v. 28). The stress on complementarity is highly important because the author does not always clearly distinguish where Levitical duties end and Priestly duties begin. The writer does not specify how the Levites, serving alongside the Aaronides, were to be responsible "for the outer courts, the chambers," and so forth. That they bear some responsibility for these tasks is itself significant. The author employs terminology that is familiar from the Priestly source and Ezekiel, but he uses it in a different way. Both the Priestly writing and Ezekiel are fairly clear on the separate and distinct tasks of Levites and priests (see below), but in Chronicles what does it mean that the Levites serve alongside the Aaronides for "the purity of all sacred objects?" Does this mean that the Levites were to be on the watch against contamination of these vessels by lay encroachment? Does it suggest that the Levites, along with the priests, were to purify *(ṭhr)* the sacred objects? Or does it indicate that the Levites were to replace the priests in purifying the sacred utensils? The text does not say. In any case, the use of Priestly language in a new and different context should caution against reading too much Priestly theology into the text. That the use of Priestly language signifies a pro-Priestly position has to be proved, not assumed.

If the Priestly language in 1 Chr 23:28–32 has been overinterpreted as a reflex of Priestly theology, the Priestly writing has been underinterpreted. By this I mean that the duties of the Levites in the Priestly writings are more involved and nuanced than many commentators on Chronicles have recognized. I speak of positions because commentators dispute whether certain texts in Numbers stem from the Holiness (H) or Priestly (P) writers (Milgrom 1991: 13–42; Levine 1993: 48–73; Knohl 1995: 1–45). Since both H and P belong within the larger Priestly tradition, the issue of sources within the Priestly tradition need not detain us. Within the narrative flow of Numbers, chapter 18 does represent a development beyond the material in chapters 3–4, but one can make the case for a fundamental continuity between these chapters. To put it somewhat differently, there are some changes in the responsibilities of the priests in the wake of the rebellion by Qoraḥ the Levite, Dathan, Abiram, On, and the 250 chieftains of Israel against Moses and Aaron (Num 16), but these changes do not materially affect the presentation of Levitical duties in either the Priestly source or in Chronicles. In Num 3:7–8 the Levites are instructed to do the work of the Tabernacle and to guard all of the furnishings of the Tent of Meeting (cf. Num 1:53; Milgrom 1990: 20–21). While the Gershonites (Num 3:25–26) and Merarites (Num 3:36–37) are given some general moving tasks (dismantling, unloading, loading, and reassembling), the Qohathites are given the special responsibility of transporting and guarding the most sacred objects (Num 3:31). What the Priestly writers mean by this becomes clear in their subsequent discussions of Qohathite duties. Only when Aaron and his sons finish covering the sacred objects and their furnishings (Num 4:5–14) are the Qohathites permitted to come and lift them (Num 4:15). The Qohathites are entitled neither to come into direct contact with the *sancta* (Num 4:15) nor to view them (Num 4:20). The result of such encroachment would be death (Num 4:15, 19). Hence, the Priestly writers assert that the Levites (i.e., the Qohathites) have responsibility for the most sacred objects in transit (Num 4:4), but they define carefully what this responsibility does and does not entail. The Priestly writers also assert that the Levites, like the Aaronides (Num 8:26), have a responsibility for the Tent of Meeting (Num 4:18–19). The Levites are to do the work of the Tent of Meeting (Num 8:15; 16:9). One of the additional Levitical tasks is to guard the sanctuary (or the *sancta*) against encroachment by ordinary Israelites (Num 8:18–19; Milgrom 1970: 16–59). Another is to assist the Aaronides in their tasks (Num 3:6; 8:13, 19). Nevertheless, these Levitical responsibilities involve neither officiating within the Tent of Meeting nor having direct contact with the most sacred objects (Milgrom 1990: 148–49). In Priestly theology the Aaronides and the Levites share custody of the Tabernacle, but each of these groups is assigned a distinct set of responsibilities.

After narrating the story of the disastrous results of Qoraḥ's rebellion (Num 16:1–35) and the ensuing plague upon the people (Num 17:1–26 [ET 16:36–17:13]), the Priestly writers address the issue of Levitical and Priestly responsibilities again (Num 18). The revisitation of duties and relationships is necessary not simply because of Qoraḥ's thwarted aspirations for priesthood (Num 16:3, 10–11) but also because the Israelites are no longer inclined to resort to Yhwh at the Tabernacle, lest they perish (Num 17:27–28 [ET 17:12–13]). The earth's swallowing Qoraḥ and his 250 followers coupled with the plague's causing 14,700 deaths have worked too well. A way must be found to convince Israelites to worship again at the Tabernacle. The solution, presented to Aaron (in Num 18), lies basically with the priests and not with the people themselves (Milgrom 1990). It does not directly address the force of Qoraḥ's earlier protests, but it does address the relations between Levites and priests. The Levites are to assist the Aaronides (Num 18:2) and to guard them (Num 18:3). The Levites are also to police the Tent of Meeting against lay encroachment (Num 18:3, 22–23). But the Levites are not to encroach upon the holy furnishings and the altar, lest both they and the Aaronides die (Num 18:3). As in Num 3–4, the Levites continue to have responsibility for the work of the Tent of Meeting (Num 18:4, 6, 21). Given their labors, the Levites are entitled to the tithe (Num 18:23–24). The priests, for their part, are to perform their duties at the altar and behind the curtain (Num 18:7). The priests are responsible for offering sacrifices and for the sacred donations made by Israelites to Yhwh (Num 18:7–10). The priests are entitled to certain perquisites from these sacred gifts (Num 18:11–19).

Like the Levites, the priests have to police the Tent of Meeting. If the Levites guard the Tent against lay encroachment (Num 18:2–3, 22–23), the priests are to guard the Tent and the courtyard altar against (Levitical) encroachment (Num 18:4–5). The priests have responsibility for "the watch over the holy place" *(mišmeret haqqōdeš)*. In short, the Levites and priests share custody of the Tent of Meeting, but within this shared custody there is a hierarchy of status and responsibilities (Milgrom 1990: 423–24). By enforcing the system of protective Levitical and priestly cordons around the Tabernacle, the priests may avoid incurring guilt in their administration of the Tabernacle, its associated rites, and its furnishings. In the aftermath of the revolt and plague, it becomes clear that the priests themselves will bear the consequences if any unqualified (or disqualified) personnel successfully encroach upon the altar or shrine (Num 18:1, 7; cf. 3:10). The basic difference between the duties meted out before and after Qoraḥ's insurrection involves, therefore, not so much the rules themselves as the penalties for breaking those rules. Qoraḥ, his followers, and the people suffered the consequences for his encroachment. But henceforth the priests are told that they will bear both "the guilt of the sanctuary" and the "guilt of your priesthood" (Num 18:1). In other words, because the priests oversee the sanctuary, they bear primary responsibility for any intrusion (Num 18:1).

This brief discussion of Levitical and priestly duties at the Tent of Meeting elucidates the Chronicler's presentation of Levitical duties. The Levites are responsible for the *sancta* at least in two respects. The Qohathite branch of the Levites is responsible for the *sancta* when the *sancta* are in transit. The Levites (all three branches) are responsible for guarding the Tent of Meeting. With the advent of a permanent sanctuary (1 Chr 23:28–32), only the latter responsibility is paramount (contra von Rad 1930: 107–9). Hence, the Chronicler speaks of (only) the Levitical "watch of the sacred objects." In this respect, scholars have been right in what they asserted, but wrong in what they assumed. The Chronicler affirms that the Levites have duties with respect to the sanctuary and the *sancta*. This is an important indication of their status (see further below). But there is no compelling evidence to suggest that such duties entail sacrificing or directly handling the most sacred *sancta*.

We have seen that the Levitical duty roster of 23:28–32 engages and draws upon relevant Priestly formulations in Numbers. But is the summary of Levitical assignments (vv. 28–32) basically a restatement of Priestly doctrine? At least one scholar of the Priestly writing thinks not, noting discordance between the demands of P and the discourse of David (Milgrom 1976: 13–15, 82–83). His impressions can be reinforced and extended. A related issue is the comparison between priests and Levites: Does the synopsis of vv. 28–32 underscore the Levites' subordination to the priests? In my judgment, there is substantial evidence to suggest that the roster represents a new extension beyond the Priestly writings and Ezekiel. Rather than constituting evidence for a pro-Priestly redactor of Chronicles, the summary of Levitical duties is evidence for the Chronicler's own distinctive position, a *via media* among the positions of Deuteronomy, Ezekiel, and the Priestly source (Knoppers 1999a).

To be sure, some of the duties that the Chronicler assigns to the Levites seem to be traditional: for example, to guard the priests and the Tent of Meeting against lay encroachment (v. 32). Other duties represent, however, a new development. The Levites have primary responsibility for ritual cleanliness, "the purity of all sacred objects" (v. 28), and for maintaining a system of balanced measures (v. 29). As opposed to the testimony of the Priestly source and Ezekiel, the Levites are in charge of the "watch of the sacred objects" (v. 32). This represents a double shift. In Numbers the Qohathite Levites are responsible for the *sancta* while they were in transit. In general, the priests have primary responsibility for the "watch of the holy place" (*mišmeret haqqōdeš*; Num 18:5). This exclusive Priestly prerogative of the priests is staunchly defended by Ezekiel, who proclaims that the consecrated areas of his projected temple are to be attended only by priests (40:45–46; 43:18–27; 44:8, 15–16; 46:20; 48:11). By contrast, the Levites are servitors, appointed over the temple gates, guards who perform various temple chores (Ezek 44:11–14). But in Chronicles all Levites—Qohathites, Merarites, and Gershonites alike—have primary responsibility for the "watch of the sacred objects." By quoting one phrase from the Priestly writings *(mišmeret haqqōdeš)* in a new context, the author radically alters its import.

In addition to their obligations in guarding the holy place, the Levites are responsible for the musical liturgy: "to give thanks and to praise Yhwh" every morning and evening and during the festivals (vv. 30–31). Such a mandate for the Levites was previously established by David vis-à-vis the Ark (16:1–38). The verbal and musical dimensions of ancient Near Eastern worship should not be dismissed as inconsequential or as unrelated to the practice of sacrifice (G. Anderson 1991b; Knoppers 1995b). Such public actions were a meaningful component of corporate worship. Having responsibility for musical liturgy in itself means that the Levites participate in the cultus of the Temple. Whenever holocausts are offered by the priests, music is offered by the Levites (v. 31).

In this manner, the writer advances an understanding of the relationship between the Levites and Aaronides different from that of the Priestly writings and Ezekiel. Whereas the Priestly writers consistently stress that the Levites are to serve *(šrt)* the Aaronides (Num 3:6; 8:26; 18:2), the Chronicler states that the appointment of the Levites is to be "at the side of the sons of Aaron" (v. 28). The

Chronicler stresses cooperation and complementarity, not competition and hierarchy. The emphasis on the coordinate responsibilities of Levites and priests is not unique to this text (1 Chr 9:10–34; 28:12–13; 2 Chr 5:2–14; 7:1–10; 13:9–12; 23:1–11; 29:3–36; 31:2–21; 34:8–13; 35:1–19). A basic kinship between the Levites and the Aaronides is maintained (v. 32). The sons of Aaron (v. 13) are ultimately Levites (v. 6). They share a common genealogy.

But the author does not jettison all distinctions between the two. The Aaronides have a distinct status within the tribe of Levi (secured by birth) and a different function—to consecrate the most sacred *sancta*, to make offerings, and to pronounce blessings in Yhwh's name (v. 13). The sons of Aaron are "officers of the sanctuary and officers of God" (24:5). In this regard, the stance of Chronicles bears more affinities to the stance of the Priestly writing than it does to the stance of Deuteronomy. Nevertheless, the Chronicler offers a new collateral understanding of the relationship between priests and Levites. Similar verbiage has misled scholars into thinking that there is more contiunuity between P and Chronicles than is warranted by the evidence. The writer draws on Priestly terminology, but he does so to expand Levitical responsibilities and to blur some of the clear distinctions advanced by the Priestly writers and defended by Ezekiel. In Chronicles, as opposed to P, both the Levites and the priests are "holy" (*qdš*; 2 Chr 23:6). The Levites are referred to as "those holy to Yhwh" (2 Chr 35:3). If Ezekiel demotes the Levites, Chronicles gives them a new promotion.

Last but not least, the Levitical work profile, "for the service of the Temple of Yhwh" *(laʿăbōdat bêt yhwh)*, represents a development over against the Priestly source and Ezekiel. In this case, Chronicles uses almost the same language as P, "the work *(ʿăbōdâ)* of the Tent of Meeting," but gives it a much broader meaning and application. For P, *ʿăbōdâ* is normally "work," the labor associated with assembling, maintaining, guarding, dismantling, and moving the Tent of Meeting. But in Chronicles *ʿăbōdâ* stands more broadly for "(cultic) service." That the Chronicler quotes the Priestly source to authorize his own position has a double benefit, underscoring continuity in orthopraxis from the time of Moses to the time of David and authorizing an innovation. The Chronicler's *traditio* of a Priestly *traditum* becomes itself a new *traditum*, normative for kings, priests, and Levites in the Temple period(s) of Israel's national life.

# *XXIX. Priestly and Levitical Courses (24:1–31)*

*The Twenty-four Priestly Courses*

1 And as for the descendants of Aaron: their divisions. The sons of Aaron: Nadab
and Abihu, Eleazar and Ithamar. 2 Nadab and Abihu died before their father without having any sons, so Eleazar and Ithamar served as priests. 3 And David parti-

tioned them, along with Zadoq from the sons of Eleazar and Aḥimelek from the
sons of Ithamar, by their duty in their service according to their ancestral houses.
[4]When the sons of Eleazar were found to be more numerous as head warriors
than the sons of Ithamar, they partitioned them: of the sons of Eleazar sixteen
heads of ancestral houses and of the sons of Ithamar eight ancestral houses. [5]They
partitioned them by lots, one like the other, because they were officers of the sanctuary and officers of God—from the sons of Eleazar and from the sons of Ithamar.
[6]And Shemaiah son of Nethanael, the scribe from the Levites, registered them in
the presence of the king, the officers, Zadoq the priest, Aḥimelek son of Abiathar,
and the heads of the ancestral houses of the priests and the Levites. One ancestral
house was picked out for Eleazar and one (ancestral house) was picked out for
Ithamar.

[7]The first lot fell to Jehoiarib,
the second to Jedaiah,
[8]the third to Ḥarim,
the fourth to Seorim,
[9]the fifth to Malchijah,
the sixth to Mijamin,
[10]the seventh to Haqqoz,
the eighth to Abijah,
[11]the ninth to Jeshua,
the tenth to Shecaniah,
[12]the eleventh to Eliashib,
the twelfth to Jaqim,
[13]the thirteenth to Ḥuppah,
the fourteenth to Ishbaal,
[14]the fifteenth to Bilgah,
the sixteenth to Immer,
[15]the seventeenth to Ḥezir,
the eighteenth to Happizzez,
[16]the nineteenth to Pethaḥiah,
the twentieth to Jeḥezqel,
[17]the twenty-first to Jachin,
the twenty-second to Gamul,
[18]the twenty-third to Delaiah,
the twenty-fourth to Maaziah.

[19]These were their duties corresponding to their service: to enter the House of
Yhwh according to their custom at the directive of Aaron their ancestor as Yhwh
the God of Israel had commanded him.

*The Remaining Levites*

[20]As for the rest of the descendants of Levi:
belonging to the sons of Amram: Shubael;
belonging to the sons of Shubael: Jeḥdeiah;
[21]belonging to Reḥabiah: belonging to the sons of Reḥabiah, Isshiah was the head;

22 belonging to the Izharites: Shelomoth;
belonging to the sons of Shelomoth, Jaḥath;
23 the sons of Ḥebron: Jeriah the head, Amariah the second, Jeḥaziel the third, and Jeqameam the fourth;
24 the sons of Uzziel: Micah;
belonging to the sons of Micah: Shamir;
25 the brother of Micah: Isshiah;
belonging to the sons of Isshiah: Zechariah;
26 the sons of Merari: Maḥli and Mushi;
the sons of Jaaziah: Bani;
27 the sons of Merari—belonging to Jaaziah: Bani, Shoham, Zakkur, and Ibri;
28 belonging to Maḥli: Eleazar and Ithamar, but Eleazar died and did not have any sons;
29 belonging to Qish: the sons of Qish, Jeraḥmeel;
30 the sons of Mushi: Maḥli, Eder, and Jerimoth.
These were the descendants of the Levites by their ancestral houses.
31 They also cast lots exactly as their kin the sons of Aaron (did) in the presence of King David, Zadoq, Aḥimelek, and the heads of the ancestral houses of the priests and Levites, the ancestral head exactly as his youngest kinsman.

## TEXTUAL NOTES

24:1. "the descendants of Aaron." Reading with MT, which, along with LXX$^{AL}$, records two instances of the phrase בני אהרן in v. 1 (the second before "Nadab and Abihu"). LXX$^{B}$ is the *lectio brevior* because it lacks the second occurrence. Nevertheless, LXX$^{B}$ may reflect haplography.

"their divisions." So MT. LXX$^{BL}$ lack "their."

"and Abihu" (ואביהו). Reading with MT (so also in v. 2). LXX has *kai Abioud* as in 5:29 (2nd TEXTUAL NOTE). See also the witnesses to Exod 6:23; Lev 10:1; Num 3:4.

24:3. "David partitioned them." On the basis of the versions, I read the *piʿel*. MT has the *nipʿal* of *ḥlq* (1st TEXTUAL NOTE to 23:6).

"by their duty." Reading the sg. with MT *lipquddātām* (cf. 1st TEXTUAL NOTE to v. 19). The term may carry connotations of a duty group both here and in v. 19 (*HALOT* 958).

"according to their ancestral houses" (לבית אבותם). Reading with LXX *kat' oikous patriōn autōn*. Lacking in MT due to haplography (*homoioteleuton* from בעבדתם to לבית אבותם). See also vv. 4, 6, 30, 31.

24:4. "head warriors" *(rāʾšê haggibbôrîm)*. So a few Heb. MSS, LXX*, and Vg. MT "male heads" *(rāʾšê haggĕbārîm)*. In fourth-century B.C.E. orthography, both words (*hgbrym* and *hgbwrym*) could have been written the same way, without the medial *wāw*. Compare 7:11; 9:26; 11:10; 23:3; 26:12 (see TEXTUAL NOTE).

"ancestral houses." So MT and LXX. The lemma of a few Heb. MSS, Syr., and

Tg., "their ancestral houses," assimilates toward the expression at the close of the verse.

24:5. "one like the other." Literally, "these with these" (אלה עם-אלה). NJPS renders, "both on an equal footing."

"officers *(śry)* of (the) sanctuary" *(qōdeš)*. LXX "officers of the holy things" (= *qŏdāšîm*).

"officers of God." So MT. LXX "officers of Yhwh." Either reading is preferable *(lectio difficilior)* to Syr.[A] "officers of the priests."

"and from the sons (ומבני) of Ithamar." So many Heb. MSS, Syr., Vg., and Tg. MT "and among the sons (ובבני) of Ithamar" (a *bêt/mêm* confusion). LXX has *en*, "among," in both cases (Eleazar and Ithamar).

24:6. "registered them." Literally, "wrote them" (ויכתבם).

"one *('ḥd)* ancestral house was picked out *('ḥz)* for Eleazar." So MT. LXX, Syr., and Vg. read "one" *('ḥd)* in both instances, but this leaves the final instance of *'ḥz* in the verse unexplained (see next TEXTUAL NOTE).

"and one *('ḥd)* (ancestral house) was picked out *('ḥz)* for Ithamar." Reading with a few Heb. MSS, LXX, Syr., and Vg. MT's "and picked out, picked out *(w'ḥz 'ḥz)* for Ithamar" has suffered corruption. Dequeker (1986: 100) emends MT to בית-אב אחד אחז לאלעזר ואחד ואחז אחד לאיתמר, hence "one ancestral house was picked out for Eleazar and one more, and one was picked out for Ithamar." The proposal is ingenious but it presupposes both corruption and an important haplography, which disturbs the symmetry of the Heb.

24:9. "Mijamin." So MT and LXX[AL] *Miamin (lectio difficilior)*. LXX[B] "Benjamin" suggests the possibility of a *bêt/mêm* confusion, but the PN "Mijamin" is attested elsewhere in the Persian period, and in most instances, the references are to priestly names (Neh 10:8 [ET 10:7]; 12:5; 1 Chr 24:9; cf. Ezra 10:25).

24:11. "Jeshua." Reading with MT and LXX. Syr. "Elisha."

24:12. "Jaqim." Reading with MT and LXX[BL]. LXX[A] "Eliakim."

24:13. "Ishbaal" *(yšb'l)*. Reading the *lectio difficilior* with LXX[A] *Isbaal*, abb' *Iesbaal*, $e_2$ *Iesbal*, Vg. *Isbaal*. MT "Jeshebeab" *(yšb'b)*.

24:15. "Ḥezir." So MT, LXX[L] *Chēz(e)ir*, and Vg. *Ezir*. LXX[B] *Chēzein;* LXX[A] *Iēzeir;* Syr. *'ḥzy'* (= *Aḥaziah?).

24:19. "their duties." Reading the pl. *pĕquddōtām* (cf. Syr. and Vg.). Note the pl. antecedent *'lh* (Kittel 1895: 70; Rudolph 1955: 160–62). MT and LXX have the sg. *pĕquddātām*.

24:20. "Shubael" *(šwb'l)*. So MT and LXX[AN] *(Soubaēl)*. LXX[B] and $c_2$ *Iōbaēl;* bb' *Soubiēl;* $e_2$ *Sōbiēl*. See also 25:20; 26:24 (cf. 25:4; Noth 1928: 32, 199); and the 2nd TEXTUAL NOTE to 23:16.

"belonging to the sons of Shubael" (לבני שובאל). So MT, LXX[AN], and many cursives: "Shubael of [LXX[L]: and Abijah to] the sons of Shubael." Lacking in LXX[B] due to haplography.

"Jeḥdeiah" (יחדיהו). LXX[B] *Iadeia;* LXX[L] *Iadaia;* LXX[AN] *Iadeia Aradeia.*

24:21. "belonging to the sons of Reḥabiah" *(lbny rḥbyhw)*. So MT. LXX[L] *tois huiois Abia* (bb' *Sabia*) *Iōsias*. Lacking in LXX[AB] perhaps due to haplography *(homoioteleuton)*. Compare the pattern in vv. 20 and 22.

"Isshiah" (ישיה). Thus MT, LXX$^{AN}$ *(Iesias)*, and Arm. LXX$^{L}$ *Yōsias*. Lacking in LXX$^{B}$.

24:23. "and (the) sons of Ḥebron" *(wbny ḥbrwn)*. Reading in part with LXX$^{L}$ (cf. Arm.) *tois huois Chebrōn Ieddi(a) ho archōn* "(to) the sons of Ḥebron, (PN) the head." Some suggest reconstructing "for the Ḥebronites" or "Ḥebron the head." This reconstruction may be compared with 23:19, "the sons of Ḥebron." The reading of MT "and Benay" *(wbny)* is incomplete. Two Heb. MSS (in the margins) have "and the sons of Ḥebron." LXX$^{AB}$ have a similar *Vorlage* to MT, but interpret the consonants differently: LXX$^{B}$ "sons"; LXX$^{A}$ "and sons."

"Jeriah." Reading with MT. LXX$^{B}$ *Iēdeimou;* LXX$^{AN}$ *Iediou;* LXX$^{L}$ *Ieddi(a)*.

"the head." A restoration based on the parallel in 23:19. Many commentators, believing that a haplography *(homoioteleuton)* has occurred, restore *lbny yryhw*, "belonging to the sons of Jeriah," on the basis of the pattern found in vv. 20, 21, 22, 24, and 25. But Amariah is the brother (and not the son) of Jeriah (23:19).

24:24. "Shamir." So Qere, many Heb. MSS, and the versions (Tg. *šmyr;* LXX *Samēr;* Vg. *Samir*). Kethib "Shamur."

24:26. "the sons of Jaaziah" *(bny yʿzyhw)*. There is significant textual confusion in vv. 26–27. The relationship between "the sons of Jaaziah" (similarly, LXX$^{B}$ $c_2$ *huioi Ozeia*) and what precedes is unclear. Benzinger (1901: 71) and Curtis and Madsen (1910: 274) preface the connective *wāw*, while Kittel (1902: 90) rewrites as *wgm bny*. The confusion continues in the remainder of vv. 26–27. For the PN, cursives $be_2$ and Arm. seem to have a conflation of readings: *Ozia (b Iozias) huios autou Bonneia* (*b Bonnia;* Arm. *Bunia*) *huios autou*. Cursive b′ *Iozias ho huios autou*. Rudolph (1955: 164) proposes "among his sons, his son Jaaziah" *(bbnyw yʿzyhw bnw)*. But the text may be intentionally ambiguous (see NOTE).

"Jaaziah" *(yʿzyhw)*. Thus MT *(lectio difficilior)*. On the basis of LXX$^{B}$ $c_2$ *Ozeia*, *BDB* and *BHK* read the more common "Uzziah" *(ʿzyhw)*, but this is unnecessary (Noth 1928: 28, 203).

"Bani" *(bny)*. Reading in part with LXX$^{AN}$ *huioi Bonni*. MT, which reads *bnw*, "Benno" (so Vg. *Benno*) or "his son," has experienced a *wāw/yôd* confusion. The lemma is lacking in LXX$^{B}$, but it is possible either that LXX$^{B}$ has suffered an inner-Greek haplography (Allen 1974b: 52) or that the LXX *Vorlage* was defective due to haplography from **bny yʿzyhw bny* (v. 27) *bny mrry* to *bny yʿzyhw* (v. 27) *bny mrry*. The PN "Bani," a hypocoristicon of "Banaiah" (בניהו; Noth 1928: 38, 172), is common in late texts (1 Chr 6:31; 9:4 [TEXTUAL NOTE]; Ezra 10:29; Neh 3:17; 8:7; 9:4; 10:14 [ET 10:13]; 11:22; cf. 2 Sam 23:36).

24:27–30a. These verses are lacking in Syr.

24:27. "the sons of Merari." This phrase is attested by all witnesses, but it is unclear why it is repeated from v. 26. A dittography may have occurred in the text or the text may reflect a double reading (see the preceding and following TEXTUAL NOTES).

"belonging to Jaaziah: Bani." MT "belonging to Jaaziah: Benno." For the latter, LXX$^{AB}$ have "his sons." See the last TEXTUAL NOTE to v. 26. Kittel (1902: 90), followed by NJPS, reads with MT and translates "by his son [Jaaziah]."

"(and) Shoham" *(wšhm)*. Thus MT. *BHK* and *BHS* delete the *wāw* on the basis of LXX, but the LXX readings reflect *yšhm* (LXX$^{B}$ $c_2$ *Isoam;* LXX$^{AN}$ *Issoam;* LXX$^{L}$

*Iessam*), which may be a corrupt form of *wšhm* (Allen 1974b: 119). On the PN, see Noth (1928: 223).

24:28. "(Eleazar) and Ithamar, but Eleazar died." So LXX (*kai Ithamar kai apethanen Eleazar* = ואיתמר וימת אלעזר). MT simply reads "Eleazar." The material was probably lost by haplography (*homoioteleuton* from "Eleazar" to "Eleazar").

"and (he) did not have any sons" (*wl'-hyh lw bnym*). So MT. Many Heb. MSS have the pl. verb, *wl'-hyw lw bnym*, but the meaning is not affected "and sons were not to him."

24:29. "Qish" (*lqyš*). So MT and LXX. Some emend to "and Qish" (*wqyš*).

"sons of Qish." Reading with MT. A few Heb. MSS and Vg. have the sg.

24:30. "Jerimoth" (ירימות). See the 3rd TEXTUAL NOTE to 23:23.

24:31. "the ancestral head." The Heb. is unusual, literally "the ancestral heads" (אבות הראש).

"exactly as (*lĕʿummat*) his youngest kinsman." The same idiom (*lĕʿummat*) occurs earlier in the verse.

# NOTES

24:1–19. "and as for the descendants of Aaron: their divisions" (ולבני אהרן מחלקותם). The phrase functions as a rubric for all of vv. 1–19. A similar phrase introduces the next section (v. 20): "and as for the rest of the descendants of Levi" (ולבני לוי הנותרים). The earlier depiction of a Levitical census (23:3–5) forms the backdrop for much of the material that one finds in chapters 23–27. Within these chapters, the subject sometimes switches back and forth from the Levites to the priests. The register of Levitical appointments (23:6–23) includes a brief description of priestly duties (23:13). This material is later followed by a description of Levitical duties and their relationship to priestly duties (23:28–32) and a register of priestly courses (24:1–19). The priests are organized into twenty-four divisions, which cast lots for places (see COMMENT). The very format of the presentation underscores the fact that the priests and Levites are related to one another. The order of the presentation followed in these chapters—Levites followed by priests—may be surprising to those familiar with the Priestly work. In the Priestly sections of the Pentateuch, one hardly reads about the Levites and their duties until one reaches the book of Numbers (chapters 3–4). Considerable attention is devoted in Exodus to the outfitting, consecration, and ordination of Aaron and his sons (Exod 28–29). Much of Leviticus is concerned with the various types of offerings and the priests responsible for them. The presentation in Chronicles reflects a contention that the priests are a subdivision of the tribe of Levi and that the priestly and Levitical functions are to be coordinated in the operation of the cult (Knoppers 1999a). The addition of another section dealing with Levites (1 Chr 24:20–31; see SOURCES AND COMPOSITION) following the priestly courses (narrated in vv. 1–19) only underscores the links between the priests and Levites.

24:1. "descendants of Aaron." The nomenclature is highly significant. In

Chronicles, the priests are most often referred to and defined as the sons of Aaron (2nd NOTE to 5:29).

"their divisions." Earlier David partitioned the descendants of Levi into "divisions" (*maḥlĕqôt;* 1st NOTE to 23:6). The text now introduces the "divisions" (*maḥlĕqôt*) among the priests. The rubric identifies the author's interest. He is concerned not simply with the genealogy of the descendants of Aaron but rather with the internal classification of these priests and their rotation of service at the Temple.

"Nadab and Abihu, Eleazar and Ithamar." This roster of Aaron's sons replicates the rosters found in Exod 6:23 and 1 Chr 5:29.

24:2. "died before their father." That is, they perished during the lifetime of their father. The author is alluding to the untimely demise of Nadab and Abihu, but he does not explain it. For evidence of a similar compositional technique at work in the genealogies, see the NOTES to 2:3. According to Num 3:4, Nadab and Abihu offered strange fire before Yhwh and were subsequently consumed by fire themselves (see also Lev 10:1–7). Their deaths left Eleazar as the older of Aaron's two remaining sons.

24:3. "Zadoq . . . Aḥimelek." Chronicles posits a close relationship between David and the officers of the two major Aaronide families (1 Chr 15:11; 18:16–17; 25:1; cf. 2 Sam 8:18; 15:35; 17:15; 1 Kgs 1:7, 39). On Aḥimelek's ancestry and status during David's regime, see the 2nd NOTE to 18:16.

"Eleazar . . . Ithamar." See the 1st NOTE to 5:29.

"by their duty" (*lipquddātām*). The text employs the same terminology in referring to the establishment of administrative (1 Chr 26:30) and martial positions (2 Chr 26:11; Welten 1973: 82–83). Cf. Num 3:36; 4:16; Ps 109:8; 1 Chr 23:11. The priests, as civil servants, were counted as part of David's earlier assembly (23:2).

"in their service" (בעבדתם). Whereas the Priestly writers speak of service (by which they largely mean labor) with exclusive reference to the Levites, the Chronicler speaks of service with a broader sense (cultic service) and employs the term with reference to both the Levites and the priests. This disparity in meaning and usage is an important distinction between the views of the Priestly writers and those of the Chronicler (3rd NOTE to 6:33).

24:4. "more numerous." In the system of priestly divisions depicted here, the descendants of Eleazar dominate. Whatever the precise situation in earlier times, this statement comports with postexilic reality in which the Zadoqites (from the sons of Eleazar) dominated the priesthood. Descendants of Ithamar were, however, not entirely unattested (Ezra 8:2).

"they partitioned." That is, David, Zadoq, and Aḥimelek (v. 3). The division into sacerdotal courses represents a joint effort on behalf of the king and his two (chief) priests. Such a division into courses honors the traditional principle of genealogy and social organization—the "ancestral house" (בית אבות)—found within the Levite tribe (vv. 3, 4, 6). The system envisioned by the author is hierarchical, traditional, and patriarchal in nature.

24:5. "one like the other." In spite of the numerical superiority of Eleazar's descendants, Eleazar's descendants were not accorded any special prerogatives in the casting of lots.

"officers of the sanctuary and officers of God." One reason for the relatively equal treatment accorded the two families is that both contained leadership figures of an excellent pedigree. Commensurate with the priests' responsibilities over the sanctuary, there is a close association between the priests and altar worship (NOTES to 6:34). The titles "officers of the sanctuary" and "officers of God" reflect the privileged position the sons of Aaron enjoy in the Chronicler's work. Precisely because of their important standing, the priests share responsibility, together with monarchs and the people themselves, for the fate of the nation. Consistent with this notion, "the officers of the priests" *(śārê hakkōhănîm)* bore some of the blame for the Babylonian exile (2 Chr 36:14).

24:6. "Shemaiah son of Nethanael, the scribe from the Levites." The Chronistic interest in scribes and record keeping is again evident (1st NOTE to 2:55). This particular Shemaiah is not otherwise attested.

"one ancestral house." The writer stresses that the principle of an alternating order of lots was maintained (at least, at the beginning). In this system, no family within the Eleazarite and Ithamaride branches could go out of order and directly follow another family from within its own branch. The ancestral houses are a fundamental component in the organization of the Levites (e.g., 23:11; 24:4, 6, 30–31) as they are in the organization of other tribes (1st NOTE to 15:12).

24:7. "Jehoiarib." Given that "the first lot fell" to him, "Jehoiarib" (יהויריב) has a privileged place in the system of twenty-four courses. By contrast, "Joiarib" (יויריב) appears near the end of the list in Neh 12:12–21 (12:19). The author of 1 Macc 2:1 connects the origins of the Hasmoneans with the class of Jehoiarib (see COMMENT).

24:7b–18. "Jedaiah." The list of Ezra 2:36(//Neh 7:39) makes a connection between the "house of Jeshua" and the "sons of Jedaiah," but it is unclear to which Jeshua the text is referring (Ezra 3:2; Hag 1:1; cf. 1 Chr 24:11) and whether this connection is original to the list (Williamson 1985: 35). Along with "Jehoiarib," the PNs "Jedaiah" (v. 7), "Ḥarim" (v. 8), "Malchijah" (v. 9), "Mijamin" (v. 9), "Abijah" (v. 10), "Shecaniah" (v. 11), "Bilgah" (v. 14), and "Maaziah" (v. 18) appear in one or both of the lists in Neh 10:3–14 and 12:1–25 (allowing for some textual variation). Conversely, many of the following names appear infrequently and are not otherwise attested as PNs in sacerdotal contexts: "Seorim" (v. 8), "Jaqim" (v. 12), "Ḥuppah" (v. 13), "Ishbaal" (or "Jeshebeab" in MT; v. 13), "Ḥezir" (v. 15), "Happizzez" (v. 15), and "Gamul" (v. 17; Noth 1928: 182).

24:10. "Haqqoz" *(haqqôṣ)*. According to Ezra 2:61–63(//Neh 7:63–65), his descendants were barred from the priesthood after the return because they could not authenticate their pedigree by finding their record in the genealogies. But in Chronicles, the pedigree and status of "Haqqoz" are not in doubt.

"Abijah" *(ʾăbîyāh)*. In addition to the citation in this passage (vv. 7b–18), note the mention of a Qohathite Levite in 6:13 (cf. Neh 10:8; 12:4, 17).

24:11. "Jeshua" *(yēšûaʿ)*. Some equate this Jeshua with the head of "the house of Jeshua" mentioned in Ezra 2:36(//Neh 7:39), but the Ezra 2 roster contextualizes Jeshua's house by mentioning "the sons of Jedaiah" (cf. 1 Chr 24:7).

24:12. "Eliashib" *(ʾelyāšîb)*. A well-known priestly name in late texts (Ezra 10:6; Neh 3:1, 20; 12:10, 22; 13:4, 7, 28).

24:14. "Immer." Along with the descendants of Jedaiah (v. 7) and Ḥarim (v. 8), the descendants of Immer returned from exile with Zerubbabel (Ezra 2:36–39// Neh 7:39–42). The priestly name "Pashḥur," mentioned in Ezra 2:38; 10:22; Neh 7:41; 10:4, is, however, not mentioned here.

24:15. "Ḥezir." A very rare PN in the HB (Neh 10:20). Cf. *Ḫiziru* (EA 336.3; 337.4).

24:16. "Pethaḥiah." Among its few attestations, "Pethaḥiah" appears as a Levitical PN (Ezra 10:23; Neh 9:5).

"Jeḥezqel." Apart from being the name of the famous priest and prophet (Ezek 1:3; 24:24; Sir 49:8), the PN "Jeḥezqel" occurs only here.

24:17. "Jachin." Along with a Jehoiarib and a Jedaiah, a Jachin appears in the roster of returning priests in 9:10(//Neh 11:10).

"Gamul." In the calendrical documents found at Qumran, Gamul heads the lists. Gamul is, in fact, said to be in service already at the time of creation (4Q319 IV 10–11, 4Q320 1 i 3–5; 3 i 10–12; 4 ii 10–14).

24:18. "Delaiah" *(dlyhw)*. The PN does not appear elsewhere in this form (except Jer 36:12), but a "Delaiah" *(dlyh)* appears in the priestly register of Ezra 2:60(//Neh 7:62). The PN *(dlyh)* appears elsewhere in the HB (Neh 6:10; 1 Chr 3:24) and at Elephantine (*TAD* A4.7:29; 4.8:28; 4.9:1).

24:19. "their duties *(pĕquddōtām)* corresponding to their service." A summary statement closing the list of vv. 7–19, detailing the system of courses established by David and the (chief) priests.

"as Yhwh the God of Israel had commanded him." The use of the citation formula, referring to an Aaronic directive, pertains to the way that the priests are supposed to enter the Temple. In other words, David's division of the priests into twenty-four courses affects their schedule of service, but not their ritual preparation. The recourse to an otherwise unattested divine command to Aaron is unusual. Inasmuch as they refer to any human figure, Chronistic citations of earlier law usually mention Moses (Dörrfu*ß* 1994).

24:20–31. "the rest of the descendants of Levi." At first glance, this introductory rubric seems puzzling. Why does the author speak of "the rest of" the Levites, if the singers, gatekeepers, and officers mentioned in 1 Chr 25–27 are also Levites? The most likely reference for this allusion is the genealogically based list in 23:7–23. This second list purports to supplement the earlier one (see also the NOTE to 24:1–19). Yet as many have have noticed, this second list of Levites (24:20–31) shares many names with the earlier catalogue in 23:7–23. In some cases, the second roster goes a second generation beyond the first. The new account also differs from the earlier account in the order it presents and in the surprising relationships it posits among certain names. The new roster only mentions Qohathites and Merarites. As opposed to the earlier catalogue (23:7–11), no Gershonites are included. This is unexpected, given that Gershon was Levi's firstborn

(2nd NOTE to 6:1). Hence, the relationship between this register and the previous register is not a simple one (see SOURCES AND COMPOSITION).

24:20–25. "sons of Amram." This section of the list is devoted to one Levitical branch: the Amramites. Amram was a son of Qohath (6:3). As in the earlier Levitical genealogies (5:27–41), the Qohathites appear first. The coverage can be compared with 23:12–20 (see following NOTES).

24:20. "Shubael" is listed as a son of Gershom in 23:16 (cf. 25:20; 26:24), but this "Shubael" is more broadly linked to Amram, the father of both Aaron and Moses.

"Jeḥdeiah" ("may Yhwh give joy") was not mentioned in the earlier lineage (23:12–20). The PN (יחדיהו) occurs elsewhere only as one of David's civil servants in charge of she-asses (27:30).

24:21. "Isshiah was the head." Ostensibly, Isshiah would be the head of Reḥabiah's ancestral house. This would comport with the pattern found in 23:17. Nevertheless, many details of this brief lineage remain obscure. There Reḥabiah is listed as a son of Eliezer, the son of Moses. Here Reḥabiah has no stated parentage. The present roster extends Reḥabiah's genealogy a generation beyond the earlier account by mentioning Isshiah. In 23:20 Isshiah is listed as the second son of Uzziel.

24:22. "Izharites." Like Amram, Izhar was a son of Qohath (1st NOTE to 23:18).

"Shelomoth." That this Izharite has a son named "Jaḥath" extends the lineage of 23:18 one generation.

24:23. "Ḥebron." Like Amram, Ḥebron was a son of Qohath (2nd NOTE to 6:3). His descendants are listed as Jeriah, Amariah, Jeḥaziel, and Jeqameam *(yĕqamʿām)*, which comports with 23:19. On the context of the earlier register, see the 1st NOTE to 23:19.

"Amariah *(ʾămaryāhû)* the second." On the PN *ʾmryh(w)*, "Yhwh has said," see the 2nd NOTE to 23:19.

"Jeḥaziel." The name occusrs only in Chronicles (1 Chr 12:5; 16:6 [2nd NOTE]; 24:23; 2 Chr 20:14) and Ezra (8:5). Given the context, one might have expected "Uzziel".

24:24. "Uzziel: Micah." Micah is listed as the head of the "sons of Uzziel" in 23:20. The other son listed there is "Isshiah" (see NOTE to 24:21 and following NOTES).

"sons of Micah: Shamir." Again, this list goes a generation further than the earlier list (23:20) in mentioning "Shamir." Elsewhere in the HB, "Shamir" appears only as a place-name (Josh 15:48; Judg 10:1).

24:25. "brother of Micah: Isshiah." As one expects, given the testimony of 23:20.

"the sons of Isshiah: Zechariah." Another detail not found in the earlier roster (23:20).

24:26–30. "sons of Merari." This section of the larger list (vv. 20–31) is devoted to one lineage branch: the Merarites. The coverage is more substantial than in 23:21–23. On the Merarites, see 3rd NOTE to 6:1.

24:26. "Jaaziah." The writer of vv. 26–27 links this figure with the Merarites, but the association is somewhat loose. The claim that Jaaziah was a son of Merari would be unique in the HB (see TEXTUAL NOTE). Merari's sons are usually listed as simply Maḥli and Mushi (Exod 6:19; Num 3:20; 1 Chr 6:4, 32; 23:21). Rather than blatantly contradict this tradition, the writer may have chosen to leave the precise relationship somewhat ambiguous. If this were not the case, he could have simply listed Merari's sons as Maḥli, Mushi, and Jaaziah (in 24:26).

24:27. "Bani, Shoham, Zakkur, and Ibri." This material is not found in the earlier account (23:21–23).

"Shoham" appears only here as a PN (see TEXTUAL NOTE).

"Zakkur" (זַכּוּר). This PN occurs mainly in late texts (Num 13:4; Ezra 8:14 [Qere]; Neh 3:2; 10:13 [ET 10:12]; 12:35; 13:13; 1 Chr 4:26; 24:27; 25:2, 10), but see also the Aram. *zkr* inscription (A.1.4; Gibson 1975: 12–14).

"Ibri." Elsewhere "Ibri" appears only as the gentilic "Hebrew" (*ʿibrî;* Gen 14:13; 40:15; Exod 3:18; 5:3; 7:16; 9:1, 13; Jonah 1:9).

24:28. "Maḥli." Along with Mushi, one of the two sons of Merari (1st NOTE to 6:4). See also the NOTES to 23:21.

"Eleazar" is also mentioned as a son of Maḥli in 23:21.

"Ithamar." Not mentioned in the roster of 23:21–23. There Qish appears as Maḥli's other progeny. The PN "Ithamar" usually signifies the fourth son of Aaron (1st NOTE to 5:29), as it does in 24:1–6.

"did not have any sons." For a fuller explanation, see the NOTE to 23:22.

24:29. "Qish" *(qyš)*. In 23:21, "Qish" explicitly appears as a son of Maḥli. Here, his parentage is unstated. On the name, see the 3rd NOTE to 6:29.

"Jeraḥmeel." The relevant register in 23:22 mentions the fact that Qish had offspring, but does not name any of them.

24:30. "Maḥli, Eder, and Jerimoth" also appear as sons of Mushi in 23:23.

"these were the descendants of the Levites by their ancestral houses" (אלה בני הלוים לבית אבתיהם). This summary is very close to and may be a partial quotation of 23:24, "These were the sons of Levi by their ancestral houses" (אלה בני-לוי לבית אבתיהם).

24:31. "cast lots exactly as their kin the sons of Aaron." The implication seems to be that the Levites cast lots and then rotated by courses just as the priests did (cf. vv. 3–6). The mention of David, Zadoq, Aḥimelek, and the ancestral heads legitimates the whole operation. The text also alludes to the alternating system of singling out ancestral houses within the major Levitical branches (cf. v. 6). Nevertheless, there seem to be some contrasts between the two operations. For instance, the earlier text mentions that "they (i.e., David, Zadoq, and Aḥimelek) partitioned them by lots" (ויחלקום בגורלות; v. 5).

"the ancestral head exactly as his youngest kinsman" (אבות הראש לעמת אחיו הקטן). Again, the casting of lots occurs without granting special privileges to any one party. The earlier text uses a similar expression, "one like the other" (אלה עם-אלה; v. 5).

# Sources and Composition

There is little disagreement that vv. 1–19 are a unity. Many have contended that this material represents a secondary insertion within 23:2–27:34 (e.g., Albright 1926: 99; Williamson 1979a: 258; R. Braun 1986: 238–39; Dequeker 1986: 96; De Vries 1989: 200), while others (e.g., Wright 1989: 105–13; Japhet 1993a: 423–32) argue that this material belongs to the primary level of composition within this chapter. Many of the issues relate to larger questions dealing with the purpose of the Chronicler's original work: Was it pro-Priestly or pro-Levitical? If one adopts, for instance, the former position, vv. 1–19 may not belong to the Chronicler's original composition. I have argued elsewhere (Knoppers 1999a) that this oft-stated dichotomy between the rights of Levites and priests is reductive and does not do justice to the complexity and subtlety of the Chronicler's work. Similarly, the author's stance toward the priests cannot be said to be unabashedly pro-Zadoqite. As we have seen, Chronicles privileges not only Zadoq but also Aaron and Levi. In this respect, the Chronicler's position may not be neatly aligned with that of any previous biblical writer (e.g., Deuteronomy, the Priestly work, Ezekiel). The Chronicler is an independent author who is perfectly capable of formulating his own distinctive position even as he draws upon older works.

The literary issues presented by vv. 1–19 are dealt with effectively in Wright's dissertation (1989) and need not be repeated here. He points to a number of signs that vv. 1–19 belongs to its larger literary context. One issue not addressed by Wright requires some discussion. The text of v. 7 mentions that "the first lot fell to Jehoiarib." Since Mattathias the Maccabee traced his ancestry to the family of Jehoiarib (1 Macc 2:1), 1 Chr 24:1–19 is thought by some to date to Maccabean times. In this line of thinking, vv. 1–19 (or vv. 7–19) were written sometime in the second century B.C.E. to justify the Maccabees' claim to the priesthood and to privilege their position. That Jehoiarib's lot wins him the first course purportedly vouchsafes Mattathias's station. The argument assumes what it needs to prove, namely either that the Maccabees had some connection to the Qohathite house of Jehoiarib or that both such a priestly figure and a corresponding system of courses needed to be created. Given the way that genealogies worked in antiquity, neither of these two scenarios seems convincing. It is more likely that the opposite is true. The privileged position of Jehoiarib's family at the Jerusalem Temple, established in the text of Chronicles, was probably known to the Maccabees and their apologists. What the author of 1 Maccabees attempted to do, genealogically speaking, was to link the ascendancy of a relatively new figure (Mattathias) to a venerable pedigree. To concoct such a respected figure out of whole cloth would make little sense because it would gain the Maccabees little with their subjects. To postulate, however, a tie with a priestly figure already established in the past would legitimate a claim to respectability in the present. One should press the matter further. The recourse to Jehoiarib and his primary position in the system of priestly courses at the Jerusalem Temple provides some insight into the history of Chronicles. It suggests that the text of 1 Chr 24:1–19 was, in all likelihood, both known and established by the time the authors of 1 Maccabees wrote their work.

If there is much debate about the place of the priestly courses (vv. 1–19) in the composition of Chronicles, the same cannot be said for the roster of Levites (vv. 20–31). Most view this material as secondary, and with good reason. There are both parallels and important differences between this list and the Levitical list that occurs earlier in chapter 23. The second list deals only with the Qohathites (cf. 23:12–20) and Merarites (cf. 23:21–23). No Gershonites are mentioned in 24:20–31 (cf. 23:7–11). The parallels and differences may be sketched in the diagram on p. 839.

The important differences between the two accounts are, for the most part, not so problematic (for further details, see the NOTES). These could be explained simply by the theory that someone wanted to provide an alternative account of the roster in 23:12–23. It is the parallels between the two tallies that are more difficult to explain. These suggest some sort of relationship between the two texts. This possibility becomes more likely when one considers that the second register extends some of the lineages of the first an additional generation, indicating that the second is at least partially derivative (Benzinger 1901: 70–71; Kittel 1902; Curtis and Madsen 1910: 272–74; Williamson 1982b: 165; R. Braun 1986: 238–39). Another interesting feature of the second list—its omission of any mention of the sons of Gershon—also comports with this theory. In preparing the second list the writers updated and corrected those features of the first list in which they took an avid interest. The fact that the earlier material dealing with the Gershonites (23:7–11) was not recapitulated may be due to a lack of interest in or a disagreement with this roster. Wright (1989: 113–16) notes, in this context, that the Gershonite section (23:7–11) contains information about internal leadership functions (23:7–8, 11), whereas the other two sections dealing with the Qohathites (23:12–20) and Merarites (23:21–23) do not. One purpose of the new list dealing exclusively with the Qohathites (24:20–25) and Merarites (24:26–30) may have been to correct this deficiency (24:21, 23, 30). Nevertheless, it should be pointed out that the new material dealing with the Merarites also lacks any clear references to ancestral heads.

Given the references and allusions in vv. 20–31 to the account of vv. 1–19, it seems likely that when vv. 20–31 was written, the author(s) had access to the earlier material in vv. 1–19. The parallel that the writers draw between the (re)organization of the priests and that of the Levites (v. 31) shows an awareness of the earlier material dealing with the priestly courses (vv. 7–19). The authors of vv. 20–31 do not precisely explain, however, whether the Levites mentioned (vv. 20–30) were or could have been (re)organized in courses. In brief, vv. 20–31 belong to a later stage of development in the text. The authors of this material had access both to the material in 23:6–23 and to the priestly material in 24:1–19.

In adding this new register, the authors of vv. 20–31 strategically positioned their material to frame the earlier material dealing with the priestly courses (vv. 1–19).

a The Descendants of Levi (23:6–23)
  b Priestly Courses (24:1–19)
a′ The Remaining Descendants of Levi (24:20–31)

A. QOHATHITES

1. 23:12–20

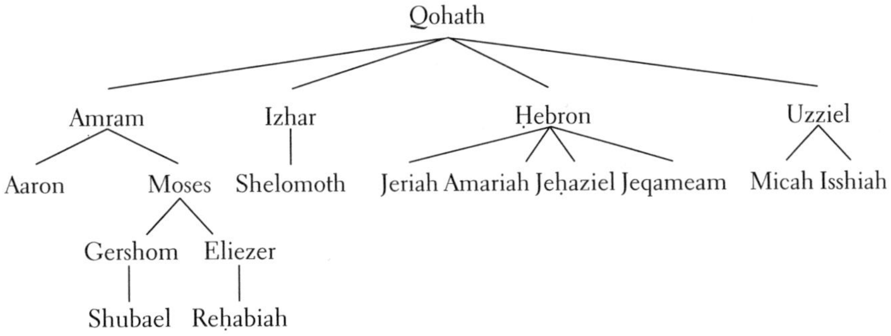


2. 24:20–25

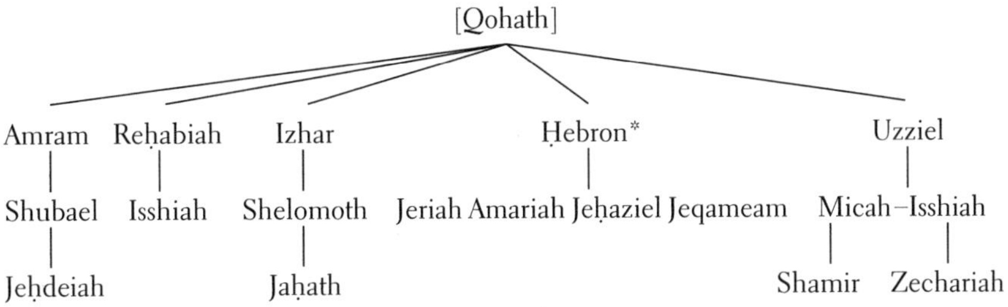


*Reconstructed (1st TEXTUAL NOTE to v. 23).

B. MERARITES

1. 23:21–23

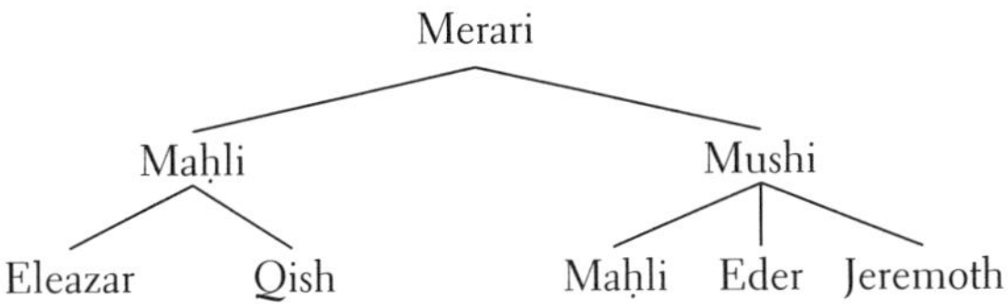


2. 24:26–30

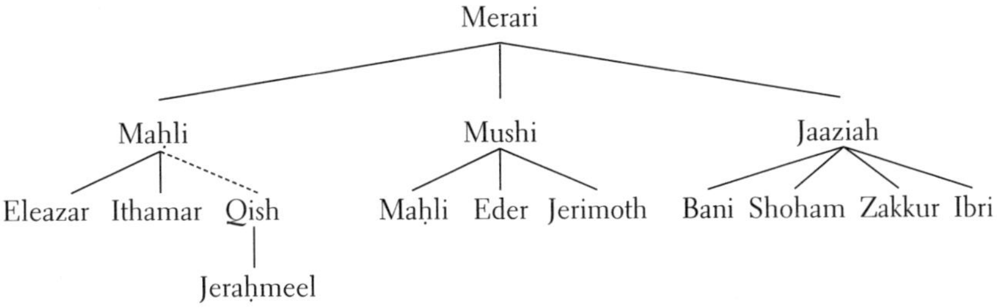

The literary technique of chiastic composition is well-attested elsewhere in Chronicles (Kalimi 1995a). In the genealogical introduction to the people of Israel, priestly lineages (5:27–41; 6:35–38) envelop Levitical genealogies (6:1–34). Similarly, related genealogies of Judahites (2:3–55; 4:1–23) frame the genealogy of David in 1 Chr 3. In each case cited, the editors have employed genealogies or catalogues to impose a larger literary unity upon diverse materials. This attention to sequence and position indicates that the editors performed their work in accordance with a larger literary design and purpose.

## COMMENT

Within the unique view of history promulgated in Chronicles, the reign of David functions paradoxically as the normative age for temple administration. It is during David's tenure that the major arrangements and appointments are established for Israel's national sanctuary. That this central shrine does not yet exist is no obstacle to embarking on extensive and detailed preparations to ensure its proper operation. If Solomon's reign marks the time in which the long-awaited Temple is finally built, David's reign marks the time in which the Temple is formally requested, planned, designed, endowed, equipped, organized, scheduled, and staffed. David does everything but actually build the shrine. Solomon receives not only a peaceful and secure kingdom but also an elaborate administrative apparatus to run it. Earlier preparations included securing a divinely sanctioned site for the Temple (21:18–22:1), assembling workers and materials (22:2–5), privately instructing the designated heir (22:6–16), charging Israel's officers (22:17–19), conducting a Levitical census (23:3–5), partitioning the Levites into divisions (23:6–23), adjusting the Levitical minimum age (23:24–27), and (re)defining the Levitical work profile (23:24–32). Israel's reverend king then turns his attention to another important component of the Levite tribe: the "divisions" of the priests (24:1).

In consultation with his two major priests, Zadoq from the sons of Eleazar and Aḥimelek from the sons of Ithamar, David partitions the priests into courses. Establishing a rotation of courses for the priests is an important contribution to the orderly process of creating and staffing a temple. The (re)organization of the sacerdocy to perform this highly critical role calls attention to one of the principal functions of the priests, to be "personal attendants" to Yhwh in his house (Leithart 1999). Inasmuch as ancient Near Eastern temples served multiple functions and were dedicated to serving specific deities, it was the responsibility of priests to perform a variety of duties, including ministering to these deities and safeguarding the sanctity of such dwellings against encroachment and desecration. Because sacred precincts normally did not shut down for extended periods of the year, some sort of system had to be devised to assure ongoing service of the divine.

It is relevant to note in this context that neither David nor his two major priests give any attention to instructing the sacerdocy who were to serve at the Temple. A brief description of priestly duties was furnished earlier in 23:13 (see NOTES). Presupposing a priestly work profile or at least some sort or sacerdotal "prescription" *(mišpāṭ)* governing how priests were to enter the sanctuary, a prescription commanded by Yhwh and established by Aaron (v. 19), the text concerns itself with documenting a clear rotation of priestly attendants at the Temple. The establishment of such a rota is designed to be a permanent institution. Since the directions pertain to ancestral houses, and not simply to individual priests within these houses at a particular time, the succession can theoretically last as long as the Temple lasts and as long as the ancestral houses in the phratries of Eleazar and Ithamar last.

In the scenario depicted in 24:1–19, each division was to work its appointed turn in rotation until a round was completed and a new round began (1 Chr 24:1; 26:1, 12, 19; 27:1–15; 28:1, 13, 21; 2 Chr 5:11; 8:14; 23:8; 31:2, 15, 17; 35:4, 10). In this respect, the rota established for the priests is but the first of a series of administrative innovations to ensure that the projected sanctuary has a full complement of personnel at any time during the year. The divisions in Chronicles consistently number twenty-four, suggesting that each course was responsible for approximately two weeks of temple service per (lunar) year. Some commentators have also tried to reconstruct twenty-four divisions in the genealogically based list of 1 Chr 23, but the text resists such attempts (see the TEXTUAL NOTES to 23:6–23).

Although attributed to David's initiative, the development of a rota of twenty-four divisions is first attested in the Chronicler's work. Chronicles ratifies a late Persian or Hellenistic institution by recourse to a policy implemented during Israel's classical age. To be sure, scholars have argued that the lists of priests mentioned in Nehemiah (10:2–9 [ET 10:1–8]; 12:1–7, 12–21) also bear witness to a system of courses, perhaps twenty-two in number (Benzinger 1901: 48, 72–73; Williamson 1979a; 1985: 341–64). Indeed, the very sequence of names in these Nehemiah lists seems to be significant. Like the system outlined in 24:1–19, one of the registers in Nehemiah (12:12–21) mentions the ancestral houses of the priests it lists. But the priestly names occurring in these rosters are not explicitly numbered, as they are in Chronicles. Nor do the Nehemiah texts contain any explicit references to a system of courses. To complicate matters further, the names shared by the two major sets of Nehemiah lists (10:2–9 [ET 10:1–8] and 12:1–7, 12–21) admit to some variation in content and order. LXX Neh 12 (vv. 1–3, 7, 12–14) presents a substantially shorter text than MT Neh 12 (vv. 1–7, 12–21). Hence, textual variants make it impossible to be sure about the exact number in each list. Interestingly enough, only some of the ancestral names mentioned in the lists of Neh 10:2–9 [ET 10:1–8] and 12:12–21 overlap with those of Chronicles. Most of the ancestral priestly names differ, in fact, from those that appear here (see NOTES). The registers in Nehemiah may be regarded as steps toward the system appearing in Chronicles (Williamson 1979a; 1985), but the path is not a straight one.

Of the priestly rosters mentioned in Nehemiah and Chronicles, it was the system described in 24:1–19 that proved to be the most influential. Understanding the system of rotating watches in Chronicles is critical to understanding the calendar steadfastly maintained by the Qumran covenanters (4Q317; 4Q319; 4Q320; 4Q321; 4Q322; 4Q323; 4Q324a; 4Q324b; 4Q324c; 4Q325; 4Q326; 4Q327; 4Q328; 4Q329a; 4Q330; 4Q334; 4Q337; 4Q394; 6Q17; 11Q19; 11Q20; Talmon 1989: 147–85; VanderKam 1998: 71–90; Ben-Dov 2001; Glessmer 2001). In the elaborate and sophisticated calendrical documents found at Qumran, festivals and sabbaths are all aligned with a detailed enumeration of successive priestly divisions. The number, names, and sequence of priestly courses in these documents match those of 1 Chr 24. Because the twenty-four priestly courses served in a regular succession as defined by the model presented in Chronicles, weeks and days could be designated by following these courses. Another indication of the influence of the priestly watches found in Chronicles is that Jehoiarib begins the lists of courses found in the Palestinian *Piyyutim* and in a number of ancient inscriptions, in which the courses are consecutively numbered (Talmon and Knohl 1995: 295). In this context, some of the Qumran scrolls differ. The calendrical scroll 4Q321, for instance, begins its cycle on the fourth day of service in the week of Gamul (course twenty-two in Chronicles). This choice of a beginning point may reflect the covenanters' opposition to the Hasmoneans, who claimed descent from Jehoiarib (see SOURCES AND COMPOSITION).

It is sometimes claimed that the system attested in the Dead Sea Scrolls involves a change from twenty-four to twenty-six courses, reflecting a solar calendar of fifty-two weeks. While the covenanters did use a solar calendar (cf. *1 En.* 72–82; *Jub.* 6; VanderKam 1998), this claim misrepresents the nature of the innovative adjustments made by the Qumran covenanters. Rather than add new priestly families into the mix and thus add new courses, the covenanters employed existing ancestral houses and staggered their service over a six-year cycle (Talmon and Knohl 1995: 296; Talmon 2001). This meant that in a given year twenty courses would serve two terms of one week, while four courses would serve three terms of one week.

The diverse types and numbers of calendrical documents in early Jewish sources testify, among other things, to the influence of the system of priestly courses found in Chronicles. Of course, the calendrical disputes within early Judaism, which are enormously important and complicated developments, go far beyond the world of the Chronicler's work. On these matters, see the recent treatments of Talmon and Knohl (1995), Beckwith (1996), VanderKam (1998), and Talmon (2001). For our purposes, it is sufficient to say that the text of Chronicles played a foundational role in a variety of later calculations. The rotation of priestly courses is attested in the works of Josephus (*Ant.* 7.366; *Life* 2; *Ag. Ap.* 2.8), in early Christian sources (Luke 1:5), and in rabbinic sources (*b. Ber.* 12a; *b. Ket.* 27a; *b. Menaḥ.* 107b; *b. Sukkah* 55b–56b; *b. Taʿan* 27b; *b. Yoma* 26a; *m. Sukkah* 5:8; *m. Tamid* 5:1; *t. Taʿan.* 2.1ff.; *y. Yoma* 2:39d). It remained in play until the destruction of the Second Temple in 70 C.E.

# *XXX. Twenty-four Courses of Choristers (25:1–31)*

*The Selection of Singers*

1 And David and the army officers set apart the sons of Asaph, Heman, and Jeduthun for service, those prophesying to the accompaniment of lyres, harps, and cymbals. Their census by their headcount of working men, according to their service, was:

2 belonging to the sons of Asaph: Zakkur, Joseph, Nethaniah, and Asarelah—the sons of Asaph under the command of Asaph, who prophesied under the command of the king;

3 belonging to Jeduthun: the sons of Jeduthun—Gedaliah, Izri, Jeshaiah, Shimei, Ḥashabiah, Mattithiah—six, under the command of their father Jeduthun, who, to the accompaniment of the lyre, prophesied in thanksgiving and praise to Yhwh;

4 belonging to Heman: the sons of Heman—Buqqiah, Mattaniah, Uzziel,
Shubael, Jerimoth, Ḥananiah, Ḥanani, Eliathah, Giddalti, Romamti-
ezer, Joshbeqashah, Mallothi, Hothir, Maḥazioth—5 all of these
were sons of Heman, the seer of the king, in divine matters to exalt his
cause. So he gave to Heman fourteen sons and three daughters. 6 All
of these were under the command of their father for the singing in the
House of Yhwh, to the accompaniment of cymbals, harps, and lyres
for the service of the House of God, under the command of the king.

*The Establishment of Twenty-four Courses*

Asaph, Jeduthun, and Heman: 7 their census with their kin—trained in singing
to Yhwh, all (of whom were) skillful—was 288. 8 And the lots fell duty corresponding to duty, the small the same as the great, the skillful along with the apprentice.

9 The first lot fell for Asaph—to Joseph: he and his brothers and his sons—12;
the second (to) Gedaliah: he and his brothers and his sons—12;

10 the third, Zakkur: his sons and his brothers—12;

11 the fourth, Izri: his sons and his brothers—12;

12 the fifth, Nethaniah: his sons and his brothers—12;

13 the sixth, Buqqiah: his sons and his brothers—12;

14 the seventh, Jesarelah: his sons and his brothers—12;

15 the eighth, Jeshaiah: his sons and his brothers—12;

16 the ninth, Mattaniah: his sons and his brothers—12;

17 the tenth, Shimei: his sons and his brothers—12;

18 the eleventh, Uzziel: his sons and his brothers—12;

19 the twelfth, Ḥashabiah: his sons and his brothers—12;

20 the thirteenth, Shubael: his sons and his brothers—12;

21 the fourteenth, Mattithiah: his sons and his brothers—12;

22 the fifteenth, Jerimoth: his sons and his brothers—12;

23 the sixteenth, Ḥananiah: his sons and his brothers—12;

[24]the seventeenth, Joshbeqashah: his sons and his brothers—12;
[25]the eighteenth, Ḥanani: his sons and his brothers—12;
[26]the nineteenth, Mallothi: his sons and his brothers—12;
[27]the twentieth, Eliathah: his sons and his brothers—12;
[28]the twenty-first, Hothir: his sons and his brothers—12;
[29]the twenty-second, Giddalti: his sons and his brothers—12;
[30]the twenty-third, Maḥazioth: his sons and his brothers—12;
[31]the twenty-fourth, Romamti-ezer: his sons and his brothers—12.

## Textual Notes

25:1. "the army officers" *(śry hṣbʾ)*. So MT and LXX *(hoi archontes tēs dynameōs)*. The proposal of Curtis and Madsen (1910: 279), followed by Rudolph (1955: 164) and Roddy Braun (1986: 240) to read the following *lʿbdh* as a gen. modifying *hṣbʾ*, "chiefs for the serving host," is unwieldy.

"set apart" *(wayyabdēl)*. Reading with MT. LXX$^{BL}$ have *kai estēse(n)*, "he placed," where one would expect *kai diestēse(n)*, "and he set apart."

"Jeduthun" *(ydwtwn)*. So MT. The lemma of LXX$^{B}$ *Ideithōn* (cf. Vg. *Idithun*) replicates that of 16:42 (LXX$^{B}$ *Ideithōn*). LXX$^{L}$ *Idithoum*.

"those prophesying" *(hannābîʾîm)*. Reading with the Qere, many Heb. MSS, LXX$^{AB}$ *bb′* (*apophthengomenous*, "chanting"), Vg., and Tg. (GKC §93oo). Note also the pres. act. ptc. in ye$_2$, *prophēteuontas*. Kethib "the prophets" *(hannĕbîʾîm)*. Arm. *Qui praedixerunt*.

"their census by their head(count)" *(msprm lglgltm)*. So LXX$^{B}$, "their census by their head(count)" *(kata kephalēn autōn)*. LXX$^{L}$ *kata kephalēn andrōn*. MT "their census" has the *lectio brevior*, but *lglgltm* was probably lost by haplography *(homoioteleuton)* after *msprm*. Cf. 1 Chr 23:3, 24.

25:2. "and Asarelah" *(ʾśrʾlh)*. Reading the *lectio difficilior* with MT and LXX$^{L}$ *Aseirēla*. LXX$^{B}$ and c$_2$ *Eraēl* (< *ʾśrʾl?). A few Heb. MSS and some witnesses to Tg. "and Asharelah." Goettsberger (1939: 176) believes that a haplography occurred and reconstructs *wʾśrʾl ʾlh*, "and Asarel—these are." Rudolph (1955: 164) goes a step further and reconstructs *wʾśrʾl ʾrbʿh ʾlh*, "and Asarel—these four." This latter proposal ingeniously effects a symmetry between Asaph and Heman (v. 5) and Jeduthun (v. 3), but the parallel in v. 14 (MT) reads "Jesarelah" *(yśrʾlh)*.

"who prophesied" *(hnbʾ)*. So MT. A few Heb. MSS and LXX *(tou prophētou)* read "the prophet" (= *hnbyʾ*).

25:3. "Izri" *(yṣry)*. Reading with MT v. 11. MT *ṣry* has lost initial *yôd*, while LXX *Sourei* (= *ṣwry*) may reflect metathesis.

"(and) Shimei" *(wšmʿy)*. Reading with a few Heb. MSS and LXX$^{B}$ *(Semeei)*. MT omits due to haplography (*homoioarkton* after "[and] Jeshaiah" [*wyšʿyhw*]). That MT has suffered corruption is confirmed both by the total of "six" later in the verse and the appearance of Shimei in v. 17.

"to the accompaniment of the lyre, prophesied" *(bakkinnôr hannibbāʾ)*. So MT and LXX *(lectio difficilior)*. LXX$^B$ *en kinyra anakrouomenos*; cf. Vg. *qui in cithara prophetabat*, "who prophesied with the lyre."

"in thanksgiving" *(ʿal-hōdôt)*. The translation "in charge of giving thanks" (Kleinig 1993: 152) is also possible.

25:4. "Uzziel" *(ʿzyʾl)*. Reading with MT and LXX$^{AN}$. LXX$^B$ and $c_2$ have *Azaraēl*, "Azarel," as does MT in v. 18 *(ʿzrʾl)*. There LXX$^B$ and $c_2$ have *Azaria*, but LXX$^L$ has *Oziēl* (= *ʿzyʾl*) in both cases. The same reading appears in Syr., *ʿzyʾl*. See also the 3rd TEXTUAL NOTE to 16:5 (cf. 23:20; 24:24).

"Shubael" *(šûbāʾēl)*. Reading with LXX. MT has "Shebuel" *(šĕbûʾēl)*, but MT and LXX v. 20 have "Shubael." See also the 2nd TEXTUAL NOTE to 23:16.

"Jerimoth" *(yrymwt)*. Reading with MT. LXX$^B$ has *Ieremōth*, "Jeremoth," as does MT in v. 22 *(yrmwt)* and 7:8. LXX$^L$ *Iereimōth*. LXX$^B$ v. 22 *Ereimōth*; LXX$^L$ *Iereimouth*. MT 24:30 *yrymwt*. See further the 3rd TEXTUAL NOTE to 23:23.

"Ḥanani." Reading with MT and LXX. Syr. breaks off after "Ḥanani" and resumes at the end of v. 6 ("and Heman").

"Eliathah" *(ʾlyʾth)*. LXX$^B$ $c_2$ *Ēliathath*; LXX$^L$ *Ēliatha*. MT v. 27 "Elithah" *(ʾlyth)* has elided the *ʾālep*. Syr. *ʾlyb*.

25:5. "in divine matters" *(bĕdibrê hāʾĕlōhîm)*. For the locution, see also 2 Chr 29:15, "according to the command of the king *(kĕmiṣwat hammelek)* in matters of Yhwh" *(bĕdibrê yhwh* (cf. 1 Chr 26:32; 2 Chr 19:11; Rothstein and Hänel 1927: 450). The phrase could also be rendered "by the commands of God." The translation of NJPS, "[who uttered] prophecies of God," is quite free.

"to exalt his cause." Reading *lĕhārîm qarnô*. The lemma of MT *lĕhārîm qeren*, "to exalt a horn" (i.e., power), is problematic. Does this phrase refer to Yhwh as its object or to Heman? Many (Keil, Benzinger, Kittel, Zöckler, Curtis and Madsen, A. Ehrlich) would connect this phrase with what follows in v. 6. The divine gift of many children to Heman heightened his prestige. The suf. *wāw* was dropped before the connective *wāw* in *wayyittēn* (haplography). To these considerations, another may be added. Those texts which speak of exalting someone's horn (*qeren* with the *hipʿil* of *rwm*) have God as subject and (a) human(s) as object (1 Sam 2:1, 10; Pss 75:11 [ET 75:10]; 89:18 [ET 89:17]; 92:11 [ET 92:10]; 112:9; 148:14; Lam 2:17). A different solution would be to reinterpret the MT as signifying "to blow the horn loudly." This is unlikely because this use of *qrn* with the verb *rwm* is unattested.

25:6. "lyres for the service of the House of God." Reading with MT. Although LXX's "lyres" is the *lectio brevior*, the phrase "for the service of the House of God" was likely lost by haplography.

"Asaph, Jeduthun, and Heman." So MT. LXX and Tg. preface the connective *wāw*. Rudolph (1955: 166) thinks that the phrase is a gloss to "all of these."

25:8. "and the lots fell." So MT. LXX "and these lots fell."

"lots" *(gôrālôt)*. Some advocate punctuating as a construct *(gôrĕlôt)*.

"duty corresponding to duty" *(mišmeret lĕʿummat mišmeret)*. So a few Heb. MSS and Tg. MT, which simply reads *(mišmeret lĕʿummat)*, has suffered haplography. On the expression, compare משמר לעמת משמר, "watch corresponding to watch" (1 Chr 26:16; MT Neh 12:24).

"the small the same as the great" *(kaqqāṭōn kaggādôl)*. The prep. *k-* is repeated to convey a comparative sense (Williams, §256).

25:9. "for Asaph." Thus MT and LXX. This may be an addition caused by dittography as Benzinger (1901: 75) and Arnold Ehrlich (1914: 350) maintain (לאסף ליוסף). Kittel (1902: 95) and Roddy Braun (1986: 243) regard it as a gloss.

"to Joseph: he and his brothers and his sons—12." A restoration based, in part, on LXX *huiōn autou kai adelphōn autou* ($ic_2$ *autōn*), which appears before *tō Asaph* (but after *tō Asaph* in $LXX^{L}$). Note also the general claims of Josephus (*Ant.* 7.367; cf. *Life* 1) that the Levites, like the priests, were divided into twenty-four courses (each serving one week in rotation). MT lacks the phrase, but such a reconstruction is demanded by the numerical total of 288 (= 24 x 12) in v. 7.

"the second." Thus MT and $LXX^{L}$. $LXX^{ABN}$ add *Hēni(a)* due perhaps to dittography (*Hēneia* < *Sēne* = *šny*; Rudolph 1955: 168).

25:14. "Jesarelah" *(yśrʾlh)*. So MT, followed by $LXX^{A}$ *Isreēla* (*pace* Allen 1974b); $LXX^{B}$ *Iseriēl;* $LXX^{L}$ ($ye_2$) *Iezrei.* MT v. 2 "Aśarelah" *(ʾśrʾlh)*. Goettsberger (1939: 179) emends to "Asarel" *(ʾśrʾl)*.

25:17. "Shimei." So MT. Two Heb. MSS and Vg. *(Semeiae)* have the theophoric, "Shemaiah."

25:18. "Uzziel." See the 1st TEXTUAL NOTE to v. 4.

25:22. "Jerimoth." See the 3rd TEXTUAL NOTE to v. 4.

25:24. "Joshbeqashah." Thus MT (so also v. 4). $LXX^{B}$ and $c_2$ *Bakata;* $LXX^{L}$ *Iesbok;* Syr. "Eliashib" *(ʾlyšb)*.

25:27. "Eliathah." So MT v. 4 (see last TEXTUAL NOTE), $LXX^{L}$ *Ēliatha,* and some Tg. MSS. MT *ʾĕliyyātâ* has lost the internal *ʾālep* in *ʾĕlîʾātâ* ("my God has come").

25:28. "Hothir" *(hôtîr)*. Thus MT and $LXX^{L}$ *Hōtheir.* $LXX^{B}$ *Hēthei;* $e_2$ *Hōsthēr;* $c_2$ *Eiskēthēr;* Syr. *ytr.*

25:29. "Giddalti" *(gdlty)*. Reading with MT. $LXX^{B}$ *Godomathei;* $c_2$ *Godolomathi;* $LXX^{L}$ *Godollath.* Syr. *(y)rby.*

25:30. "Maḥazioth." So MT. $LXX^{B}$ $c_2$ *Meazōth;* $LXX^{L}$ *Maaziōth.* Tg.* "Maḥaziah."

25:31. "Romamti." So MT. LXX* *Rōṃ huioi* may reflect **rwmbty* > *rwm bty* > *rwm bny* (Allen 1974b: 110).

## NOTES

25:1. "the army officers" *(śry hṣbʾ)*. For those who accept this reading of MT (see TEXTUAL NOTE), two explanations predominate. One construes "the army officers" as military commanders, while the other sees an allusion to Israel's leaders in their role as Yhwh's host (cf. Exod 12:17, 41). The two options are not mutually exclusive (1 Chr 26:26; 2 Chr 33:11). Many commentators have expressed astonishment that army commanders should have a say in the establishment of courses for the singers. But both the army commanders and the Levitical choristers are state employees. The projected sanctuary is to be paid for and endowed by the head of state with unbelievable amounts of wealth. The Chronicler's temple, when built, will be the most valuable edifice in the land. Who gets to serve in that institution is, therefore, not simply a sacerdotal or aesthetic issue but also a security issue. In this context, it is worth noting that some of the traditional Levitical duties, such as guard duty (23:32), are military in nature. Indeed, the book devotes significant attention to the gatekeepers, whom David appoints as the Temple's police force (26:1–19). In the ancient Near East and Egypt, sacral and martial affairs cannot be entirely disentangled. For example, in New Kingdom Egypt, it was easy for officials to move from military or civil service into priestly service, or vice versa (te Velde 1995: 1734). In commenting on the structure of the military in ancient Greece, Finley (1982: 18) observes that, "in principle, there was no separation between the civil and military 'departments' of government." Within the Chronicler's work, the martial dimension of Levitical service is apparent at the beginning of the Chronicler's depiction of David's reign, when the Levites send 4,600 warriors to join David "at Ḥebron to turn the kingdom of Saul over to him" (12:24; 1st NOTE to 12:27). Military roles and titles are not reserved exclusively for the Levites (narrowly defined). Also involved in the early pan-Israel muster is "Zadoq, a valiant young warrior, along with his ancestral house" (1st NOTE to 12:29). In later times, the Maccabean revolution was led by a militant family of priests.

"set apart" *(wayyabdēl)*. The verb denotes separation, whether of the priests from the Levites for their duties (23:13), of the priests (or the priests and/or the Levites) from the people at large (Num 8:14; 16:9, 21; Deut 10:8), or of Jewish husbands from their foreign wives (Ezra 10:8, 16). Using the verb in this particular context establishes a parallelism between David's choice and investiture of the singers, of the Levites, and of the priests (Myers 1965a: 171). Japhet (1993a: 444) goes farther in claiming that the Chronicler ascribes to David a system of singers "parallel in every detail to that of the priests and the Levites."

"the sons of Asaph, Heman, and Jeduthun." These represent three distinct families or guilds of singers. Based on 15:17 (see NOTE), one might expect the third eponym to be Ethan, not Jeduthun. The text of Chronicles does not speak with one voice on this issue. The triumvirate of Asaph, Heman, and Ethan appears in the genealogy of 6:16–32. But most texts depicting the age of the monarchy refer to Jeduthun. First Chronicles 16:5, 7, 37 speak of Asaph, whom David appoints to serves at the Ark of the Covenant in Jerusalem, while 16:41–42 speak of Heman and Jeduthun, whom David appoints to serve at the Tabernacle in Gibeon (cf. 9:16). As in 25:1, Heman and Jeduthun are accompanied by musical instruments (16:42). See further SOURCES AND COMPOSITION to 16:4–43.

"Asaph." From the Levitical phratry of Gershon (6:24–27; NOTE). On his appointment under David, see the 1st NOTE to 16:5.

"Heman." From the Qohathite phratry of Levi (6:18–23). See further the 2nd NOTE to 6:18.

"Jeduthun." On his identity and status, see the 2nd NOTE to 16:38.

"their census by their headcount." Who conducted the census is unclear. One possibility is "the sons of Asaph, Heman, and Jeduthun." During the preparations for the second attempt to bring the ark up to Zion, David tells "the Levitical officers to appoint their kinsmen as singers" (15:16). The Levites then appoint various kinsmen to fulfill this duty (15:17–24). Musters are a regular feature of the administrative reorganization associated with David's reign (23:3–5; 27:1–15; 1st NOTE to 21:1).

"working men" *(ʾanšê mĕlāʾkâ)*. One might initially be surprised that singers are referred to in this way, but the Levites are civil servants employed by the king. Cf. 1 Chr 26:29; Neh 11:16.

"for service" *(laʿăbōdâ)*. That is, cultic service (Knoppers 1999a: 64; COMMENT on 1 Chr 23). The singers have their own distinctive role to play among the sanctuary staff. If the Levites prepare sacrifices (23:28–29) and the priests offer sacrifices (23:13, 31), the singers praise Yhwh while such sacrifices are being offered (23:30–31). See also the 1st NOTE to v. 6.

"those prophesying *(hnbyʾym)* to the accompaniment of lyres, harps, and cymbals." The allusion to prophecy is both striking and recurrent. The author of v. 2 speaks of the descendants of Asaph as prophesying "under the command of the king," while v. 3 speaks of the descendants of Jeduthun as prophesying "to the accompaniment of the lyre *(bakkinnôr)*." The concept of prophecy in Chronicles is broader than some have imagined. At least one priest, Zechariah, prophesies (2 Chr 24:19–22). Yhwh communicates his will through the prophets both in ad hoc matters and in law, "for the commandment *(hmṣwh)* is by the hand of Yhwh through his prophets" (2 Chr 29:25; Japhet 1993a: 440). Seers and prophets also compose royal chronicles (1 Chr 29:29; 2 Chr 9:29; 12:15; 13:22; 33:19; Orlinsky 1974: 43). In rabbinic (Grözinger 1982: 99–107) and early Christian sources (Luke 1:67–79; 2:27–35; 10:21–22; Eph 5:15–20; cf. Matt 13:35; Mark 12:36; Acts 1:20; 4:25–26) the link between prophecy and song is well-established. The Targum to Chronicles repeatedly associates the singers' words with prophecy (vv. 2, 3, 5).

25:2. "Zakkur, Joseph, Nethaniah, and Asarelah." Of the four, only Zakkur is elsewhere attested as a descendant of Asaph (Neh 12:35).

"the sons of Asaph." The material in this chapter presupposes that cultic appointments could be transmitted within families for several generations. Such a depiction comports with evidence from various ancient Mediterranean lands of hereditary offices in cultic affairs. Priestly offices were handed down through many generations, for example, in Egypt (te Velde 1995: 1733–35).

"who prophesied *(hnbʾ)* under the command of the king." That seers might be commissioned to prophesy under the jurisdiction of the king should not be surprising. Zakkur, king of Ḥamath and Luʿash in central Syria during the early eighth century B.C.E., declares that in the midst of an enemy siege, "I lifted my hands to Baʿl Sha[may]n and Baʿl Shamay[n] answered me [and spoke] to me through seers *(ḥzyn)* and through intermediaries *(ʿddn)*" (*KAI* 202.11–12). At least some of those male and female figures with the prophetic title *āpilu/āpiltu* ("answerer") at Mari were occasionally supported by distributions from the royal stores (Huffmon 1976: 698). But how closely these figures were tied to the cult is debated. Certainly, the *muḫḫûs* ("ecstatics") at Mari played regular cultic roles and sometimes delivered cultic messages (Dalley 1984: 127–33; R. Wilson 1980: 103–4). But there are cases in which an *āpilu* could be assertive in communicating his advice to the king (Huffmon 1997: 11–12). In the Neo-Assyrian period *maḫḫûs* seem to have been a regular fixture of the royal court. Also of relevance to the prophetic designation of singers in 1 Chr 25 is the prophetic title *assinnu* found at Mari and elsewhere (*CAD* 1/2 341–42). The *assinnu* refers to a member of the cultic staff of the goddess Ishtar (*Annunītum* at Mari) associated with singing and special dress (Huffmon 1976: 698). In New Kingdom Egypt, higher priests could be called prophets (te Velde 1995: 1734). As noted below (2nd NOTE to v. 3), the existence of prophetic singers at the Temple is not attested in the Deuteronomistic History. There is, however, evidence within the Deuteronomistic History for the existence of court prophecy. Nathan, for example, seems to have been quite comfortable in the Jerusalem royal court (2 Sam 7//1 Chr 17). His support for Solomon's accession was one important factor in the latter's success (1 Kgs 1:11–27). That such figures should be subject to the king is not surprising since he appointed and sustained them (e.g., 1 Kgs 22:1–23//2 Chr 18:1–22). Our passage points to arrangements that extend, however, beyond the life of a single monarch. Chapters 23–27 narrate the establishment of institutions and arrangements that will serve not only Solomon but also subsequent kings. David's charge *(mišmeret)* to the singers is their *raison d'être* in an age dominated by the Temple. That the text repeatedly speaks of the activities of both the three—Asaph, Jeduthun, and Heman—and their sons (vv. 1–5) underscores the foundational nature of David's arrangements.

25:3. "Gedaliah, Izri, Jeshaiah, Shimei, Ḥashabiah, Mattithiah." This information is found only here. Of these six "sons of Jeduthun," Mattithiah (1 Chr 15:18, 21; 16:5), Jeshaiah (1 Chr 26:25; Ezra 8:19), Shimei, and Ḥashabiah (1 Chr 6:30; 9:14; 25:19; 26:30; Ezra 8:19; Neh 3:17; 10:11; 11:15) are elsewhere attested as Levitical names.

"in thanksgiving and praise to Yhwh." It is sometimes intimated that singers are a postexilic interest, if not a postexilic phenomenon. But there is extra-biblical evidence for the existence of court singers already in the monarchic period. According to Assyrian sources, both male and female singers were sent by Ḥezeqiah to Sennacherib as part of his tribute payment to Sennacherib (Oppenheim 1969: 288). That such singers are not mentioned in the Deuteronomistic History may be explained by the peculiar interests of its writers. Although the Deuteronomists are highly concerned with the centralization of the Yahwistic cult in Jerusalem and the elimination of all other cults, Yahwistic or otherwise, they ironically take little sustained interest in the inner workings of the temple cult they do so much to promote (Noth 1957: 100–110; Knoppers 1994d).

25:4. "the sons of Heman." Of the names listed, the following are attested elsewhere as Levitical names: Mattaniah (2 Chr 29:13), Uzziel (1 Chr 15:10; 23:12, 20; 24:24; 2 Chr 29:14; Neh 3:8), Shubael (1 Chr 24:20; 26:24), and Jerimoth (1 Chr 23:23; 24:30).

"Eliathah, Giddalti, Romamti-ezer. . ." The names in the latter part of v. 4 are onomastically unparalleled. Since at least the nineteenth century (Ewald 1870:

680), it has been generally acknowledged that the names beginning with Ḥananiah *(ḥnnyh)* originally comprised some kind of poetic verse. Whether this poetry was part of a source or part of a later addition is debated (see SOURCES AND COMPOSITION).

25:5. "the seer" *(ḥōzeh)*. The term appears in a variety of literary contexts. The recently published materials from Deir ʿAllā refer to Balaam as "a seer of the gods" *(ḥzh ʾlhn)* who saw a vision *(mḥzh)* as a result of the gods coming to him (I.1; Hackett 1984: 27). The use of *ḥōzeh* here is not unique in Chronicles. It may be compared with Gad, the "seer" of David (21:9; cf. 29:29), Asaph "the seer" (2 Chr 29:30), and "Asaph, Heman, and Jeduthun—seers [*ḥôzê;* see LXX *hoi prophētai,* the other versions, and 1 Esd 1:15, *hoi para;* cf. MT *ḥōzēh*]) of the king" (2 Chr 35:15). Other seers mentioned in Chronicles include "Jedo" (MT *yeʿdô*) during the reign of Jeroboam (2 Chr 9:29), "Iddo" *(ʿiddô)* during the reign of Reḥoboam (2 Chr 12:15), and "Jehu" (*yēhûʾ*; 2 Chr 19:2) during the reign of Jehoshaphaṭ (Micheel 1983: 71–80). More general references to seers occur at the close of Manasseh's reign (2 Chr 33:18–19). Many of the allusions and references are to written works (1 Chr 29:29; 2 Chr 9:29; 12:15; 33:19). There does not seem to be any hierarchy between those called "prophets" and those called "seers." Iddo, for instance, is also called a "prophet" (*nābîʾ*; 2 Chr 13:22). In this case, Heman the seer, like Gad before him (21:9), seems to have held a position in the royal court.

"in divine matters." The author is referring to the cultic context in which the Hemanites exercise their responsibilities. The authors of Chronicles make some distinctions between cultic affairs and royal affairs, even though they recognize some connections between them (Knoppers 2001a). For this reason, King Uzziah finds himself in trouble after he displays great arrogance by entering the Temple and making offerings upon the incense altar (2 Chr 26:16–17). Confronted and admonished by the priests, Uzziah becomes angry only to be struck by leprosy. He spends the rest of his days as a leper cut off from the Temple (2 Chr 26:18–21). The distinction between divine and royal matters maintained in Chronicles (e.g., 1 Chr 26:31–32) may be compared with distinctions observed by other late writers, for example, the differentiation between the office of governor and the office of high priest in the dyarchic leadership of Zerubbabel the governor of Judah (פחת יהודה) and Jeshua the high priest (הכהן הגדול; Hag 1:1, 12, 14; 2:2, 4, 21–23; Zech 4:6; 6:11; Ezra 2:2; 3:8–13 [cf. 1 Esd 5:56–65]; 5:1–2; Neh 7:7). Attention may also be drawn to the careful distinction made in the program of Ezekiel between the office of "prince" (נשׂיא) and the positions held by the priests (37:24–28; 44:1–3; 45:1–25; 46:1–10, 12, 16–18; 48:21–22).

"fourteen sons and three daughters." Large families consistently appear as a sign of blessing in Chronicles (1 Chr 14:3 [see NOTE]; 26:4–5; 2 Chr 11:18–22; 13:21; 21:1–3; Dillard 1984b: 167). Each of the fourteen sons is mentioned, but the three daughters go unnamed. Nevertheless, both sons and daughters sing at the Temple (v. 6).

25:6. "to the accompaniment of cymbals, harps, and lyres." The instruments appear in the opposite order of their appearance in v. 1. The inversion is no accident; it is part of a larger literary artifice by which the basic order of clauses in v. 1 is reversed in v. 6.

a David and the army officers set apart the sons of Asaph, Heman, and Jeduthun
  b for service
    c prophesying to the accompaniment of lyres, harps, and cymbals
    c′ singing . . . to the accompaniment of cymbals, harps, and lyres
  b′ for the service of the House of God
a′ under the command of the king. Asaph, Jeduthun, and Heman

The sophisticated use of Zeidel's Law (inverted quotation) effectively envelops the material dealing with the appointment of twenty-four singers stemming from the descendants of Asaph, Jeduthun, and Heman. The literary arrangement creates a parallel between prophesying and singing. At the same time, the concluding frame forms a bridge to the introduction of the twenty-four courses of twelve singers.

"under the command of the king." The descendants of Asaph, Heman, and Jeduthun have their respective roles to play "singing in the House of Yhwh," but the monarch is ultimately the one in charge of all the proceedings. Commissioned by David and the army officers (v. 1), the singers are accountable to royal authority. A similar situation is depicted earlier. The "sons of Asaph: Zakkur, Joseph, Nethaniah, and Asarelah" serve "under the command of Asaph, who prophesied under the command of the king" (v. 2). See also 6:16–17.

"Asaph, Jeduthun, and Heman." The three patronyms serve as organizing principles for the singers. Some commentators wish to distance Asaph, Jeduthun, and Heman from their descendants as prophets. In other words, it is conceded that the original three—Asaph, Heman, and Jeduthun—are regarded as prophets (in some sense), but not their sons. The difficulties with this view are twofold. First, the sons are also said to prophesy (v. 1). Second, even if the descendants were not included, the picture of the original three would still be significant because of the connection between eponymous ancestors and their descendants. The authors of Chronicles, writing during the Persian period, many centuries after David's reign, were interested in justifying institutions of their own time by recourse to what they regarded as Israel's classical past. The traditions begun by Asaph, Heman, and Jeduthun are carried on by their descendants. Given this vital linkage—very much the point of the chapter—the two cannot be dissociated.

25:7. "trained in singing to Yhwh." The Levites belong to a select group. The choice of 288 skilled singers may be compared with the general total of 4,000 for all of the Levitical singers gathered by David (23:5). The number of singers in the list of returnees is 128 (Ezra 2:41) or 148 (Neh 7:44).

"288." The calculation reflects twelve singers for each of the twenty-four courses. The summary number anticipates the detailed list that follows (vv. 9–31), but it ironically does not include the three eponymous ancestors themselves, Asaph, Heman, and Jeduthun.

25:8. "the lots fell." As with the priests (24:5) and the remaining Levites (24:31) a lottery is held to determine the twenty-four courses for the singers. The same principle is operative here as that governing the earlier lotteries: "the small exactly as the great, the skillful along with the apprentice" (cf. 24:5, 31). Most think that the lottery refers to the establishment of rotating divisions (compare the *maḥlĕqôt* in 23:6; 24:1), but Japhet (1993a: 446) defends the minority view that it refers to the division of duties within the groups of singers.

"duty *(mišmeret)* corresponding to duty." The writer, like other biblical authors sometimes uses the term *mišmeret* to refer to guard duty (NOTE to 9:27). In some instances (Josh 22:3; Ezek 40:46; 44:8; Neh 12:45; 2 Chr 13:11), *mišmeret* can refer more broadly to an obligation, charge, or duty.

"the skillful along with the apprentice." Because the summary of v. 7b speaks of all the singers as skillful, some (e.g., Rudolph 1955: 166) excise this phrase as a later addition.

25:9. "Asaph." That the first lot falls for him indicates an "advantage" (Curtis and Madsen 1910: 276) for his descendants. Nevertheless, the Asaphites occupy the smallest portion (four) of the twenty-four courses assigned to the singers. Of the sons of Asaph, Heman, and Jeduthun, the sons of Heman receive the lion's share of the courses (fourteen).

"Joseph." See the 1st NOTE to v. 2.

"he and his brothers and his sons." Some speak of the artificiality of an arrangement in which the figure twelve appears for each of the twenty-four singers in the lottery. But the lots fall to Joseph and the other twenty-three, and not specifically to their kin. It is unclear whether the author is envisioning Joseph selecting twelve of his brothers and sons to accompany him in his responsibilities or whether some other system is in play to arrive at the figure of a dozen.

"Gedaliah." See the 1st NOTE to v. 3.

25:10. "Zakkur." See the 1st NOTE to v. 2.

25:11. "Izri." A relatively rare name (the gentilic of *yēṣer*), only attested here and in v. 3 as a Levitical name.

25:12. "Nethaniah." Referring to Nethaniah of v. 2 (see 1st NOTE). The PN *ntnyhw*, "Yhwh has given," also appears on Heb. bullae, seals, and ostraca (Davies, §§2.023.8; 2.056.1; 25.001.2; 25.002.1; 100.031.1; 100.032.1; 100.870.2).

25:13. "Buqqiah." Only attested here and in v. 4. The hypocoristicon בקי appears in some late texts (Num 34:22; Ezra 7:4; 1 Chr 5:31; 6:36) and on a recently published seventh-century seal (Lemaire 1999: 111). The name בקיהו appears on the eighth-century "Ophel" ostracon (Davies, §4.101.1).

25:14. "Jesarelah." Undoubtedly, the same figure as "Asarelah" (v. 2; see the TEXTUAL NOTES). "Jesarelah" is the last Asaphite to be chosen. The remaining figures to be chosen by lot are all descendants of Heman and Jeduthun.

25:15. "Jeshaiah." See the 1st NOTE to v. 3.

25:16. "Mattaniah." See the 1st NOTE to v. 4.

25:17. "Shimei." See the 2nd TEXTUAL NOTE to v. 3.

25:18. "Uzziel." See the 1st NOTE to v. 4.

25:19. "Ḥashabiah" *(ḥšbyh)*. Mentioned earlier in v. 3 *(ḥšbyhw)*.

25:20. "Shubael." See the 1st NOTE to v. 4.

25:21. "Mattithiah" is the last descendant of Jeduthun to be chosen (on the name, see the 1st NOTE to v. 3). The remaining ten figures to be chosen by lot are all descendants of Heman. Despite the numerical superiority of the Hemanites in this context, Heman's descendants do not appear in either Ezra or Nehemiah.

The sons of Asaph appear in Ezra (2:41; 3:10), and the sons of both Asaph and Jeduthun appear in Nehemiah (11:17).

25:22. "Jerimoth." See the 1st NOTE to v. 4.

25:23. "Ḥananiah." Only attested here and in v. 4 as a Levitical name.

25:24. "Joshbeqashah." Only attested here and in v. 4.

25:25. "Ḥanani." The name of Nehemiah's kin (1:2; 7:2), but only attested here and in v. 4 as a Levitical name.

25:26. "Mallothi." Only attested here and in v. 4.

25:27. "Eliathah." Apart from its appearance in v. 4 (TEXTUAL NOTE), the name is otherwise unattested in the HB.

25:28. "Hothir." Only attested here and in v. 4.

25:29. "Giddalti." Only attested here and in v. 4.

25:30. "Maḥazioth" *(maḥăzîʾôt)*. The PN Maḥazioth is attested only here and in v. 4.

25:31. "Romamti-ezer." See the 2nd NOTE to v. 4.

## SOURCES AND COMPOSITION

As with every chapter in Chronicles, there is no scholarly consensus about the compositional history of 1 Chr 25. Steins (1995: 320–27) thinks that the entire chapter was one part of a larger expansion of an older version of 1 Chr 23–26. But many view vv. 1–6 (or vv. 2–6) as the original core of this chapter, later subject to a long expansion in vv. 7–31. Williamson (1979a) provides an overview and defense of this latter position. Discrepancies between some of the names in vv. 1–6 and those that follow in vv. 9–31 have been overstated, however. At least some of these differences can be explained text critically (see TEXTUAL NOTES). Similarly, what some view as repetition between the two sections, for instance, "their census" in vv. 1 and 7, could just as easily be viewed as a sign of literary unity. That the rota is determined by the casting of lots (v. 8) rather than by Davidic choice (v. 1) is not a clear sign of secondary composition. David does not usually micromanage every aspect of cultic affairs (e.g., 15:16–24), and based on the precedent of the earlier gathering (23:3) and lotteries (24:5, 31), one expects the priests and Levites to have some involvement in the process.

Some commentators also see the order of names in vv. 9–31 as a sign of a later hand. The beginning of the list (vv. 9–21) alternates the names found in vv. 2–4a, and then the remainder of the list (vv. 22–31) retains not only the names but also the order of the names found in v. 4b. That there is an imbalance in the selection of personnel can be shown by the chart on p. 854, which categorizes the order of lots cast according to the three ancestors of the Levitical singers.

The outline shows the paucity of Hemanites selected in the initial rounds and the absolute dominance of Hemanites in the latter rounds. But is this phenomenon proof of composite authorship? The same evidence has been explained as reflecting an essentially binary system of casting lots (Japhet 1993a: 447–48).

| | *Asaph* | *Jeduthun* | *Heman* |
|---|---|---|---|
| 1. (v. 2) | Joseph (v. 9a) | | |
| 2. (v. 3) | | Gedaliah (v. 9b) | |
| 3. (v. 2) | Zakkur (v. 10) | | |
| 4. (v. 3) | | Izri (v. 11) | |
| 5. (v. 2) | Nethaniah (v. 12) | | |
| 6. (v. 3) | | Buqqiah (v. 13) | |
| 7. (v. 2) | Jesarelah (v. 14) | | |
| 8. (v. 3) | | Jeshaiah (v. 15) | |
| 9. (v. 4a) | | | Mattaniah (v. 16) |
| 10. (v. 3) | | Shimei (v. 17) | |
| 11. (v. 4a) | | | Uzziel (v. 18) |
| 12. (v. 3) | | Ḥashabiah (v. 19) | |
| 13. (v. 4a) | | | Shubael (v. 20) |
| 14. (v. 3) | | Mattithiah (v. 21) | |
| 15. (v. 4b) | | | Jerimoth (v. 22) |
| 16. (v. 4b) | | | Ḥananiah (v. 23) |
| 17. (v. 4b) | | | Joshbeqashah (v. 24) |
| 18. (v. 4b) | | | Ḥanani (v. 25) |
| 19. (v. 4b) | | | Mallothi (v. 26) |
| 20. (v. 4b) | | | Eliathah (v. 27) |
| 21. (v. 4b) | | | Hothir (v. 28) |
| 22. (v. 4b) | | | Giddalti (v. 29) |
| 23. (v. 4b) | | | Maḥazioth (v. 30) |
| 24. (v. 4b) | | | Romamti-ezer (v. 31) |

Moreover, to make the case that vv. 7–31 are secondary, scholars have to acknowledge that some of the parallel material in the earlier verses is either part of the same addition or the result of a tertiary redaction (e.g., Petersen 1977; R. Braun 1986).

To put matters somewhat differently, one can concede that the second portion of the chapter (vv. 7–31) may be the result of a second hand who has organized the choristers into twenty-four courses. But the second writer has skillfully inserted this new material to correspond to the details provided in the earlier account (vv. 1–6). Both major sections have suffered some corruption in transmission (see TEXTUAL NOTES), but the chapter still shows clear signs of unity and stylization. The descendants of Asaph, Heman, and Jeduthun listed in vv. 2–4 all reappear in the rota mentioned in vv. 9–31. The summary total of 288 (v. 7) matches the total of descendants listed in vv. 9–31. The first section opens with the appointment of the sons of Asaph, Heman, and Jeduthun (v. 1a). The "census" *(mspr)* of their working men features an enumeration of twenty-four individuals, based upon the tripartite organization of Asaphites, Hemanites, and Jeduthunites (vv. 1b–6).

The second reference to "their census" *(msprm)* mentions the triumvirate again (vv. 6b–7), along with a summary total (288), to prepare readers for what is to follow—a lottery for twenty-four rounds of twelve singers involving the descendants of Asaph, Heman, and Jeduthun (v. 8). The rest of this section consists of a formulaic account of the results of this lottery (vv. 9–31). The organization of the whole chapter betrays a certain logic. The former section provides names, family information, lines of authority, and tasks, while the latter provides names, information about the rota, and numerical allotments. As one might expect, the names mentioned in vv. 2–4 are all repeated in a new order in vv. 9–31. The second section is thus consequent upon the first. If the tally of singers in vv. 2–4 is based upon the triumvirate listed in vv. 1 and 6b, the rota in vv. 9–31 are based upon the enumeration of the descendants of this triumvirate in vv. 2–4.

The reworked song in v. 4b is a subsidiary compositional issue. If one were to take the list of choristers' names in vv. 23–31 as the primary source (Torczyner 1949), the reconstructed verse(s) would look quite different. But most commentators have sought to reconstruct this song, or this series of incipits, from the list in v. 4b.

| | |
|---|---|
| *ḥānēnî yāh* | Be compassionate to me, O Yhwh, |
| *ḥānēnî* | Be compassionate to me. |
| *ʾēlîʾ ʾāttâ* | You are my God; |
| *giddaltî wĕrōmamtî ʿôzrî* | I have magnified and I will exalt my helper; |
| *yôšēb qāšâ mallôtî* | Living in adversity, I have spoken; |
| *hôtîr maḥăzîʾôt* | Be generous with revelations. |

If this reconstruction, however speculative, has merit, the reworking of an older verse need not be seen as the result of a later addition. Other explanations are possible. The reworking could have involved a source in the author's employ, or it could have been done by the author himself. The former is more likely to be true, however because the text presents the terms as names (*pace* Goettsberger 1939: 177). That this is the case is confirmed by the general correspondence between the names in the list of vv. 2–4 and the same names in a new order in the list of vv. 9–31.

One question remains to be addressed. What is the relevance of reworking but not effacing the "incipits of hymns sung by the Levitical singers" (Myers 1965a: 173)? Why did the author not completely rewrite the irregular terms? Or, to put it differently, what are the consequences of incorporating such odd proper names? One effect is that the list exhibits artificiality (Japhet 1993a: 438). A second follows from the fact that the lineaments of the older poetic verse are still visible in the litany of names. Even in their present context, the names collectively comprise a greater whole. In this respect, the meaning of the names is significant. The act of naming was an important exercise in the ancient Semitic world (e.g., Gen 2:19–20). The name of a person could be construed as an indication of that person's character (e.g., Gen 2:23; 17:5, 15; 32:23–32). Similarly, when the authors of the Babylonian creation story *Enūma eliš* (Dalley 1989: 233) begin to depict the watery masses with which creation begins, they write:

When the heavens above were yet unnamed
nor the earth below pronounced by name . . . (I.1)

If the beginning of this work posits primordial matter, it ends with accomplishment, order, and peace. The Babylonian creation story concludes with lengthy accolades as the gods and goddesses bestow fifty names on Marduk, the new king of the gods (VI-VII). Such names are regarded not simply as labels attributed to a god or a person but also as a conveyance of power in themselves. When seen against the importance attached to naming in the ancient Semitic world, the singers' names in v. 4b are significant. Their sequence embodies verses of praise to Yhwh. In this respect, there is a larger symmetry between the office of chorister and the names of David's Levitical singers.

## Comment

The Hebrew Scriptures present David's legacy as multifaceted. One recurring image of David in Samuel is that of a musician. Through his playing, David dispels evil spirits (1 Sam 16:14–18, 23; 18:10; 19:9; cf. 2 Sam 6:5, 14). Another recurring image of David in Samuel is that of a singer (e.g., 2 Sam 1:17–27). The incipit of 2 Sam 22:1 reads, "and David spoke (דבר) the words of this song to Yhwh on the day that Yhwh saved him from the hand of all his enemies and from the hand of Saul." The introduction (2 Sam 23:1) to the last words of David describes him as "the anointed of the God of Jacob and the favorite of the songs of Israel" (נעים זמרות ישׂראל; NJPS). In this fascinating but textually difficult piece, David declares that "the spirit of Yhwh has spoken through me" (2 Sam 23:2). These images are, of course, by no means unique to Samuel. David's role as a musician appears in other contexts (e.g., Amos 6:5; Neh 12:36). Many of the psalm superscriptions associate these poetic pieces with David (Cooper 1983; Auwers 1999). In later tradition David becomes the psalmist par excellence, the "the sweet singer of Israel." The statement about "David's Compositions" (at Qumran) claims that David wrote 3,600 psalms (11Q5 37.4–10). The halakic document MMT$^{d}$ from Qumran speaks of the Hebrew Scriptures as "the book of Moses and the books of the prophets and David" (4Q397 14–21; C.9–10). This intriguing description seems to align the figure of David (and his psalter) with an emerging third division of the Scriptures (Flint 2000: 180).

The images of David as a singer and a musician are also found in Chronicles, but they are not highlighted. When referring to the dedication of the House of Yhwh, Chronicles speaks of the Levites as those "with instruments of song that King David made to praise Yhwh" (2 Chr 7:6). As one of his reforms, Ḥezeqiah orders the Levitical singers "to praise Yhwh with the words of David and Asaph the seer" (2 Chr 29:30). Although certainly important, such references are relatively uncommon. The Chronicler seems to assume the portrayals of David as a singer, composer, and musician, but he does not make them his first priority. One of the most prominent images of David in Chronicles is that of the person who is most responsible for the arrangement of Israel's sacred music. King David ensures that singing and music become a constituent component of his people's corporate worship (1 Chr 15:16; 16:4, 7, 37–38; 2 Chr 29:25). The Chronicler's David is not so much a bard as he is the founder, organizer, and patron of Israel's national orchestra and choir. He sees to it that singers are an essential component of the temple staff and that priestly sacrifices are accompanied by Levitical hymns. Just as the priests, the sons of Aaron, are organized into a system of twenty-four courses to serve the Temple's needs on an annual basis, so the Levitical singers, the sons of Asaph, Heman, and Jeduthun, are organized into a system of twenty-four courses (25:1–31). In Chronicles, both the priestly courses and the Levitical courses are constituent features of David's legacy to ancient Israel.

The picture of the sons of Asaph, Heman, and Jeduthun "prophesying" is especially striking. What role does this prophesying play in the portrayal of the Levitical singers David commissions and reorganizes? Many commentators have been taken aback by this unique feature of the presentation and attribute it to a lost source. Even if one were to explain the terminology by recourse to a putative source, one would hardly think that the author would give it such a prominent place in his presentation if he did not agree with it. We are dealing, after all, with more than one incidental reference. The chapter begins with David and the army commanders setting "the sons of Asaph, Heman, and Jeduthun for service, those prophesying to the accompaniment of lyres, harps, and cymbals." Subsequent verses continue the theme. The descendants of Asaph are to prophesy "under the command of the king" (v. 2), and the descendants of Jeduthun are to prophesy "to the accompaniment of the lyre" (*bakkinnôr;* v. 3).

But what do these references to Asaph, Heman, and Jeduthun as prophesying mean? As Japhet (1993a: 441) observes, the "exact manner in which the performing of sacral music is regarded as prophecy is not made clear by the references in Chronicles." Nevertheless, some explanations are better than others. The theory that the prophecy depicted is extemporaneous or improvisational in character (e.g., A. Ehrlich 1914: 350) fails to convince because the context clearly shows that David is establishing an institution that is to serve the central sanctuary in perpetuity. David commissions the sons of Asaph, Jeduthun, and Heman to perform a regular duty (*mišmeret;* v. 8). In this regard, David's appointment of the singers is similar to his appointment of the priests (24:1–19) and the Levitical gatekeepers (26:1–19). Each of these groups is singled out to perform a customary service in the Jerusalem cultus. Just as the appointments of the priests and gatekeepers are regarded as permanent, so the appointment of the singers should be thought of in the same way.

Another less-than-fully-satisfying interpretation is the claim that the singers prophesied in the sense of singing inspirational songs (e.g., Köberle 1899: 4). That the singing had an effect on the participants in worship services is undoubtedly true. Nevertheless, this understanding dilutes the import of the verb *nb'*. If the author wished to speak simply of inspired songs, he could have used the verbs *šîr* or *zimmēr* (Kleinig 1993: 154). Moreover, the three singers are all called seers. Heman is referred to as a "seer" (*ḥōzeh*) in v. 5, and Asaph is called "the seer" in 2 Chr 29:30. As we have seen (1st NOTE to v. 5), Asaph, Heman, and Jeduthun are called "seers (*ḥôzê*) of the king" (2 Chr 35:15). Similarly, the argument that the singers only acted as prophets (Schniedewind 1995: 186–88) fails to consider the context (see above) and import of *nb'* in Chronicles (1 Chr 25:1, 2, 3; 2 Chr 18:6, 7, 9, 11, 17; 20:37). Chronicles never uses this verb, whether in the *nipʿal* (as here) or in the *hitpaʿel* in nonsynoptic passages, to depict temporary or false prophecy. In other words, if the singers only acted as prophets, they did so on a regular basis.

Finally, the action by David and the army leaders pertains to the three families of singers, not simply to the singers themselves (see NOTES). Hence, the argument that the author wished to limit prophecy solely to Asaph, Heman, and Jeduthun is not compelling. One can argue about the syntax of vv. 2–3, but v. 1 clearly establishes David's initiative as affecting "the sons" of Asaph, Heman, and Jeduthun. Demonstration that David's actions affect the descendants and not exclusively the singers themselves is found in a later context. In 2 Chr 20:14 the Levite Jaḥaziel *(yaḥăzî'ēl)*, a descendant of Asaph, delivers a prophetic speech to King Jehoshaphaṭ and the assembly *(qhl)* as they face a horde of invading foes (2 Chr 20:15–17). To be sure, he does not use the divine citation formula ("thus said Yhwh"), but "the spirit of Yhwh" does envelop him. In any case, his words are more than a selective reuse of older scriptures. He provides the king and the gathered people with specific instructions on their conduct and fate. In short, Jaḥaziel plays a prophetic role in the setting of a grave national crisis.

Whether Asaph, Heman, and Jeduthun and their descendants should be called cultic prophets is fiercely debated. Some contend for a continuation of cultic prophecy from the preexilic period to the postexilic period (Mowinckel 1962: 53–73; von Rad 1930: 113–15; Gese 1974; A. Johnson 1979: 130; Myers 1965a: 171–73; Williamson 1982b: 166), while others (Petersen 1977: 62–68, 85–87; De Vries 1989: 207) speak of a transformation of preexilic prophecy to postexilic (cultic) prophecy. To complicate matters, the new social and political conditions obtaining in Yehud (as opposed to preexilic Judah) inevitably affected the institution of prophecy (Petersen 1991a; Albertz 1994: 443–522). Some connection to the cult is, in my judgment, undeniable. To begin with, prophecy is responsible both for the promise of the Temple (17:12; Kleinig 1993: 149) and the location of its site (21:18–22:1; Knoppers 1995b). The chapter opens with David and the army leaders setting apart the sons of Asaph, Heman, and Jeduthun "for (cultic) service" (25:1). The singers are to sing whenever the priests offer sacrifices (23:30–31). Given the very nature of their office, the Asaphites, Hemanites, and Jeduthunites have an indelible connection to the nation's central shrine.

Second, a connection between prophecy, music, and song is not new, but depicted in a variety of older sources. Young Saul is told that he will meet a band of prophets coming down from the high place with various musical instruments "prophesying" (1 Sam 10:5; cf. 1 Sam 19:19–24). After reluctantly agreeing to deliver a prophecy to Kings Jehoram and Jehoshaphaṭ, Elisha responds, "Get me a musician" (קחו-לי מנגן; 2 Kgs 3:15). It is after the music begins that the spirit of Yhwh descends upon Elisha and he begins to prophesy (2 Kgs 3:15–20). Ezekiel, a prophet with a priestly pedigree, is described as "a singer of bawdy songs," someone who has "a sweet voice and plays skillfully" (Ezek 33:30–33; NJPS). It has become customary for some to draw a clear distinction—if not an opposition—

between prophets and priests, and between prophecy and song; nevertheless, it seems implausible to deny a connection between them, at least in some cases (1 Sam 1:9–3:21; Jer 23:11; 29:26; 35:4; Zech 7:3; Lam 2:20; Neh 6:10–14; Lindblom 1962: 78–80, 207–10).

The more important and relevant question is not whether there was such a thing as cultic prophecy envisioned by the writer, but in what sense did he understand the Levitical singers' cultic activities as prophetic? In posing the question in this way, I do not mean that such Levitical singing was the definition, much less the quintessence, of prophecy for the authors of Chronicles. Prophecy in Yehud was a complex and variegated phenomenon (Petersen 1991b; Berquist 1995; S. Cook 1995). One cannot and should not reduce it to a single feature. The Chronicler is no exception to this complexity; he recognizes a variety of prophets, seers, and prophetic interpreters (Micheel 1983; Schniedewind 1995; 1997). One of the problems underlying some traditional explanations of the singers' charge as prophesying is the unspoken assumption that singing is simply a matter of praising a particular deity. In Chronicles this is certainly part of the story, but not all of it. When David wishes to bring the Ark to its designated place in Zion, he tells the Levitical officers "to appoint their kinsmen as singers—with musical instruments: harps, lyres, and cymbals—making themselves heard by raising a joyful sound" (15:16). After the Ark has made its successful pilgrimage, singing becomes part of the ongoing Levitical responsibilities: "He stationed some of the Levites as ministers before the Ark of Yhwh to commemorate, to give thanks, and to give praise to Yhwh, the God of Israel" (16:4). The model established by David is honored by some of Judah's better kings. One of Ḥezeqiah's reforms decrees that Yhwh should be praised with the words of David and Asaph the seer (2 Chr 29:30).

But if the Levitical singers praise God, they also minister to the people on behalf of Yhwh. Asaphite Jaḥaziel may serve as an example (2 Chr 20:14–17). He delivers a message that expresses Yhwh's will for king and people. In this sense, the Levitical singers, like the prophets, have an intermediary role between Yhwh and the larger populace (R. Braun 1986: 245; Kleinig 1993: 188–89). But there may be another sense in which the Levitical singers may be said to prophesy. In the Chronicler's time, temple psalmody itself may have been regarded as the result of divine inspiration (Liver 1987: 87). Certainly, when "David first put Asaph and his kinsmen in charge of giving thanks to Yhwh" (16:7), the hymn sung by the sons is but a medley of selections from the psalms (16:8–36). Indeed, one of the reasons why Asaph, Heman, and Jeduthun might be called seers is that they are deemed to be composers and performers of psalms sung at the Temple. They are to prophesy to the accompaniment of musical instruments. The precise composition of the psalter in the time of the Chronicler is not altogether clear, but it seems pertinent to observe that of the various psalm superscriptions, two mention Jeduthun (39; 62), twelve mention Asaph (50; 73–83), and one mentions Heman (88). Asaph, Heman, and Jeduthun are also accorded some authority in Chronicles. The text of 2 Chr 35:15 assumes that the arrangements made by not only David but also by Asaph, Heman, and Jeduthun are authoritative for later generations: "The singers, the sons of Asaph, were by their station according to the commandment of

David, and Asaph, Heman, and Jeduthun—seers (*ḥôzê;* 1st NOTE to v. 5) of the king" (2 Chr 35:15).

In classical and medieval Judaism a complex debate surrounded the nature of the biblical psalms: Were these compositions songs of praise to God, Israel's response to Yhwh, or were these compositions God's designated hymns for Israel, part of Yhwh's revelation to his people? Strong arguments were offered for each of these positions in the context of a larger debate (Kugel 1988: 134–36; Simon 1991). If the reconstruction above has merit, this medieval debate was anticipated, at least in some respects, in the late Persian and early Hellenistic era. Part of the job description for the Asaphites, Hemanites, and Jeduthunites was to offer songs of praise to Yhwh at the Temple. This they did on various occasions. But if the hymns they sang to musical accompaniment were themselves regarded as resulting from divine inspiration, the Levitical singers could also be said to prophesy to the people on behalf of God.

# *XXXI. The Gatekeepers (26:1–19)*

*The Divisions of Gatekeepers*

[1]As for the divisions of the gatekeepers: belonging to the Qoraḥites: Meshelemiah son of Qore, of the sons of Abiasaph. [2]Meshelemiah's sons were Zechariah the firstborn, Jediael the second, Zebadiah the third, Jathniel the fourth, [3]Elam the fifth, Jehoḥanan the sixth, Elioenai the seventh; [4]belonging to the sons of Obed-edom: Shemaiah the firstborn, Jehozabad, Joaḥ, Sakar, Nethanael, [5]Ammiel, Issachar, Peullethai—for God blessed him. [6]To his son Shemaiah were born sons who ruled their ancestral house because they were valiant warriors. [7]The sons of Shemaiah: Othni, Rephael, Obed, Elzabad; and his kinsmen, warriors, Elihu and Semachiah. [8]All of these were among the descendants of Obed-edom; they, their sons, and their kinsmen were warriorlike in strength for the service—62 belonging to Obed-edom. [9]Meshelemiah had sons and brothers, warriors—18. [10]Ḥosah of the sons of Merari had sons: Shimri was the head (even though he was not the firstborn, his father appointed him as head), [11]Ḥilqiah the second, Ṭebaliah the third, Zechariah the fourth. All the sons and brothers of Ḥosah—13. [12]These were the divisions of the gatekeepers by head warriors (with) duties corresponding to those of their kinsmen to serve at the House of Yhwh.

*The Casting of Lots for Guard Duty*

[13]And they cast lots by ancestral houses, small and great alike, gate by gate. [14]The lot for the east (gate) fell for Shelemiah. Now Zechariah his son was an insightful counselor. When they cast lots for him, his lot came out to be the north (gate). [15]For Obed-edom, the south (gate), and for his sons, the storehouses; [16]and for Ḥosah, the west (gate), the chamber gate by the ascending road, watch corresponding to watch. [17]At the east there were six daily; at the north, four daily; at the

south, four daily; and at the storehouses, two; [18] at the west, four; at the road, two; at the colonnade, two. [19] These were the divisions of the gatekeepers pertaining to the sons of the Qoraḥites and the sons of the Merarites.

# TEXTUAL NOTES

26:1–19. There are a number of important text-critical variants between MT and LXX in this section, not all of which can be attributed to corruption in LXX. There are also a number of difficulties with MT.

26:1. "the gatekeepers." Reading *laššōʿārîm.* MT *lĕšōʿārîm.* LXX$^{B}$ *tōn phylōn;* LXX$^{AN}$ *tōn pylōn;* LXX$^{L}$ *pylōn* (cf. 1 Chr 27:16: LXX$^{B}$ *tōn phylōn;* LXX$^{L}$ *tōn pylōn*).

"belonging to the Qoraḥites" (לקרחים). So MT. LXX$^{ABN}$ *huioi Koreeim* (LXX$^{AN}$ *Kore*); LXX$^{L}$ *tois Korēnois* (cf. *huioi* in 25:9–31). The LXX readings may go back to **huiois ho Kore* (Allen 1974a: 150). Syr. *dʾḳym dwyd mlkʾ nṭwrʾ*, "which David, king of the guard, appointed." The Arab. is similar.

"Meshelemiah" (משלמיהו). LXX$^{B}$ *Mosolaēl;* LXX$^{AN}$ *Mosollam.* The reading of LXX$^{L}$ *Selemia(s)* here, in v. 2 (MT *mšlmyhw;* LXX$^{B}$ *Mosolēa;* LXX$^{AN}$ *Masellamia;* $c_2$ *Mosalēl*), and in v. 9 (MT *mšlmyhw;* LXX$^{B}$ *Mosomameid;* LXX$^{AN}$ *Mes(s)ollemia*) congrues with v. 14 MT *šlmyhw* (LXX$^{Bh}$ and $c_2$ *Salameia*). In v. 14, LXX$^{L}$ again has *Selemia.* On the PN משלמיהו ("Yhwh compensates" or "Yhwh provides a replacement"), see Stamm (1965: 420).

"Abiasaph" *(ʾăbîʾāsāp).* A reconstruction, "my (divine) father has gathered (in the harvest)," that partially follows LXX$^{B}$ and $c_2$ *Abia Saphar.* The related PN "Ebiasaph" *(ʾebyāsāp)* in MT 6:8, 22; 9:19 evinces a corruption of the initial vowel (dissimilation) and a contraction of the second *ʾālep.* Note that some Heb. MSS for 6:8, 22 render the older form *ʾăbîʾāsāp* (see TEXTUAL NOTES). Cf. the textual witnesses to Exod 6:24 (MT *ʾăbîʾāsāp;* SP *ʾbysp;* LXX *Abiasaph*). The lemma of MT 1 Chr 26:1 (and LXX$^{L}$ *Asaph*), "Asaph" *(ʾāsāp)*, recalls the common PN, the Gershonite Asaph (6:24–28), but *ʾāsāp* is in all likelihood a shortened form of a longer PN, such as *ʾāsap-ʾēl* or *ʾăbîʾāsāp.*

26:2. "Jediael" *(ydyʿʾl).* So MT and LXX$^{L}$ *(Iadiēl).* LXX$^{B}$ *Iderēl;* $c_2$ *Idreēl;* $e_2$ *Iaēl;* cf. 7:6 *Iadiēl;* 11:45 *Iediēl* (for MT *ydyʿʾl*).

"the second." Thus MT. LXX* lacks ordinals for Jediael, Zebadiah, and Jathniel in v. 2 and for Elam, and Jehoḥanan in v. 3. This, along with other textual evidence, raises the question of whether MT represents the original text (TEXTUAL NOTE to vv. 4–5).

"Zebadiah" *(zbdyhw).* So MT (maximum variation). A few Heb. MSS, LXX$^{B}$ *(Zacharias)*, and Syr. read the more common "Zechariah" *(zkryhw)*, which assimilates to "Zechariah" earlier in the verse.

"Jathniel" *(ytnyʾl).* So MT. Aside from the missing *tāw*, LXX$^{B}$ and $c_2$ *Ienouēl* reflect a common *wāw/yôd* confusion. Rudolph (1955: 170) prefers to follow LXX$^{L}$ *Nathanaēl (ho tetartos)*, "Nathanael (the fourth);" Syr. (and Arab.) *ntnʾyl*, but MT has the *lectio difficilior.* On the issue of ordinals in MT and LXX, see TEXTUAL NOTE to vv. 4–5.

26:3. "Elam" (*ʿylm*). LXX$^{B}$ $c_2$ *Iōlam* (*ʿwlm*) reflects a *wāw/yôd* confusion.

"Jehoḥanan" (*yhwḥnn*). So MT. The lemma of LXX$^{B}$ and $c_2$ *Iōnas* assimilates toward a nearby name. LXX$^{L}$ *Iōnathan.*

"Elioenai." Following the reading of LXX$^{B}$ *Eliōēnai* and $c_2$ *Eliōnais* (cf. LXX$^{L}$ *Eliōnai*). Note LXX 4:36 *Eliōnai* for MT *ʾlywʿyny.* MT's "Eliehoenai" (*ʾlyhwʿyny*) is suspicious, while Syr. has simply *ydʿy.* On the form proposed here, see also *ʾlywʿyny* in MT 1 Chr 3:24, 7:8; Neh 12:41; and the TEXTUAL NOTE to 8:20.

"the seventh." That the ordinal (*ho hebdomos*) appears in witnesses to LXX contrasts with the lack of ordinals for the previous five names (TEXTUAL NOTES to vv. 2 and 4–5).

26:4–5. "Jehozabad, Joaḥ, Sakar, Nethanael, Ammiel, Issachar, Peullethai." Beginning with Jehozabad and ending with Peullethai, MT provides ordinals, hence" Jehozabad the second, Joaḥ the third, Sakar the fourth, Nethanael the fifth, Ammiel the sixth, Issachar the seventh, Peullethai the eighth." I am reading with LXX* which lacks all of these ordinals for the descendants of Obed-edom (*lectio brevior*). The tradition represented by MT has assimilated toward the use of ordinals elsewhere in this section (TEXTUAL NOTES to vv. 2–3).

26:4. "Shemaiah the firstborn." Thus both MT and LXX.

"Joaḥ." So MT. LXX$^{B}$ and $c_2$ *Iōath*; cf. LXX 2 Chr 29:12 *Iōach.*

"Nethanael." Thus MT and LXX$^{L}$. LXX$^{B}$ and $c_2$ read two names, *Naas* and *Ieiēl.*

26:5. "Issachar." See the 2nd TEXTUAL NOTE to 2:1.

"Peullethai" (*pʿlty*). LXX$^{B}$ and $c_2$ *Iaphthoslaathi*; LXX$^{L}$ *Phellathi.* On this unique PN, see Noth (1928: 189). Cursive $c_2$ continues with a concluding rubric, "these were the sons of Obed-edom."

26:6. "to his son." Thus MT (*lectio brevior*). LXX adds "of (his) firstborn Rhosai" *tou prōtotokou Rhōsai*; (LXX$^{AN}$ *tou prōtotokō Rhōsai*). In this context, LXX follows the pattern exhibited in vv. 2–4, which lists the firstborn of both Meshelemiah and Obed-edom. The lemma *Rhōsai* may be a corruption of *rʾš* (Spottorno 2001: 73).

"who ruled" (*hmmšlym*). LXX has a PN (*tou prōtotokou*) *Rhōsai.* Arnold Ehrlich (1914: 350) proposes *hēm mōšĕlîm,* "they were ruling," but the ptc. with the article can have a relative function (Waltke and O'Connor, §37.1c; 37.5b).

"their ancestral (*ʾbyhm*) house." So MT. LXX$^{B}$ is similar *ton oikon ton patrikon autou.* A few Heb. MSS, LXX$^{L}$, and Tg. have the expected *ʾb(w)tm.*

"valiant warriors" (*gibbôrê ḥayil*). Cf. 5:24; 7:5. LXX has *dynatoi* as in 26:9.

26:7. "Shemaiah" (*šmʿyh*). Thus MT and LXX$^{L}$. LXX$^{B}$ and $c_2$ *Samai* (= *šmʿy*).

"Elzabad" (*ʾlzbd*). So MT. A few Heb. MSS and LXX* preface the connective. LXX$^{B}$ *Elēzabath* may reflect **ʾlyzbd,* but see 12:13.

"and his kinsmen." So a few Heb. MSS and LXX$^{L}$. MT *ʾeḥāyw,* "his kinsmen." On the basis of LXX$^{BNh}$ and $c_2$ *kai Achioud,* LXX$^{A}$ *kai Achiou,* Allen (1974b: 68) revocalizes *'ăḥiyyô*. Arm. has a double reading, *Achiu et fratres eius*. The name אחיו is attested elsewhere in 1 Chronicles (8:31; 9:37) and at Elephantine (*TAD* A4.4:7; B2.1:15; 2.2:18; 2.6:38; 2.10:19; B3.1:22; 2.2:12; 3.6:17; 3.11:18). But the context favors reading "and his kinsmen."

"warriors" *(bĕnê ḥayil)*. So MT and LXX* *(huioi dynatoi)*. It is not necessary to view this phrase, along with the earlier expression in v. 6, "(and) his kinsmen, warriors," as a gloss (so some), patterned after "they were valiant warriors" *(gibbôrê ḥayil)* in v. 6. Note the appearance of the later summary המה ובניהם ואחיהם, "they, their sons, and their kinsmen" (v. 8).

"Elihu." So MT, LXX[AN], and Arm. A few Heb. MSS preface the connective. LXX[B] and $c_2$ *Ennou*.

"Semachiah" *(sĕmakyāhû)*. So MT and LXX[L] *(Samachia)*. LXX[B] *Sabcheia*; $c_2$ *Sabakcheia*. At the end of v. 7, some witnesses to LXX add *kai Isbakōm*, perhaps reflecting a doublet in the Greek (Rothstein and Hänel 1927: 464).

26:8. "all of these" *(kl-'lh)*. Thus MT. LXX "all" *(kl)*.

"their sons, and their kinsmen." The sequence is transposed in LXX[ABN], "their kinsmen, and their sons."

"warriorlike in strength" *('îš-ḥayil bakkōaḥ)*. So MT and LXX[L]. LXX[B] *poiountes dynatōs* may not represent MT (*pace* Allen 1974b: 112).

"for the service" *(lʿbdh)*. Thus MT. LXX is similar, *en tē ergasia*.

"62." Thus MT and LXX. Cf. 16:38 "68."

26:9. "Meshelemiah." So MT. LXX[B] *Mosomameid*; LXX[AN] *Mes(s)ollemia*; LXX[L] and Arm. *Selemia*.

"warriors" *(bĕnê ḥayil)*. LXX has *dynatoi* as in v. 6.

"18." LXX adds "warriors."

26:10. "Shimri was the head." Thus MT. The LXX translators interpreted the consonantal text of their *Vorlage* differently, *phylassontes tēn archēn*, "who were observing the headship."

"the firstborn." Reading *hbkwr*. MT has lost the article due to haplography after *hyh*.

"as head." So MT *(lectio brevior)*. LXX[B] "as head of the second division" *(tēs diaireseōs tēs deuteras)*. One hesitates to call LXX expansionistic because of the minus in LXX at the beginning of MT v. 11 (see next TEXTUAL NOTE).

26:11. "Ḥilqiah" *(ḥlqyhw)*. So MT. The reading of LXX[B] in v. 10, *tēs diaireseōs*, may reflect *ḥăluqqâ* (cf. 2 Chr 35:5; Allen 1974b: 156).

"Ṭebaliah" *(ṭblyhw)*. So MT. LXX[ALN] preface *Chelk(e)ias ho deuteros* ("Chelkias the second"). LXX[B] *Tablai* reflects a different *Vorlage* (the hypocoristicon of *ṭblyhw*). Cursives bb' *Tabeēl*; $ye_2$ *Tabaiēl*. Rudolph (1955: 170) cites Köhler in reading *ṭoblĕyāhû*.

26:12. "by head warriors." Following LXX[ABLN] *tois archousi tōn dynatōn* (= *lĕrā'šê haggibbôrîm*. MT "by head males" or "by male leaders" *(lĕrā'šê haggĕbārîm)*. In fourth-century B.C.E. orthography, the terms *hgbrym* and *hgbwrym* could have been written the same way, without the medial *wāw*. See 24:4 (TEXTUAL NOTE).

26:13–27:34. This section of the text is lacking in many of the witnesses to the

Peshiṭta Weitzman (1999: 309–13) provides a hopeful discussion of the Syriac evidence.

26:13. "gate by gate" (לשער ושער). The sg. noun is repeated syndetically, as it often is in late texts, to indicate diversity (Waltke and O'Connor, §7.2.3c).

26:14. "Shelemiah" (שלמיהו). One initially expects משלמיהו, "Meshelemiah," given the testimony of vv. 1, 2, 9. But the PNs שלמיהו and משלמיהו (3rd TEXTUAL NOTE to v. 1) probably refer to the same person. Cf. יהויכין, "Jehoiachin" (2 Kgs 24:6, 8, 12, 15; 25:27; Jer 52:31; 2 Chr 36:8), יכניהו, "Jeconiah" (Jer 27:20; 28:4), and כניהו, "Coniah" (Jer 22:24, 28: 37:1; Davies, §§1.003.15; 2.049.1). The PN שלמיהו appears in a variety of ancient Heb. inscriptions (Davies, §§1.009.7; 13.001.4; 100.144.2; 100.230.3; 100.333.1; 100.879.1).

"now Zechariah" *(wzkryhw)*. So MT and LXX. On the basis of Vg. *(porro Zachariae)*, some (e.g., Kittel 1902: 97; A. Ehrlich 1914: 351) read *wlzkryhw.*

"his son" *(bnw)*. LXX "sons of" *(bny)*, hence "for Shelemiah and Zechariah sons of."

"an insightful counselor" *(yôʿēṣ bĕsekel)*. LXX is again different: *Sōaz* (LXX^A *Iōias;* LXX^N *Iōas*) *tō Melcheia*, hence "(sons of) Soaz/Joaṣ. For Melchia (they cast lots)."

26:15. "and for his sons" *(wlbnyw)*. So MT. On the basis of LXX *katenanti,* many commentators read *lpny*, "before."

"the storehouses" *(bêt hāʾăsuppîm)*. So MT. The cognate Akk. *asuppu* means "outbuilding" and refers to a method of construction, while the later Heb. refers to use and function (*CAD* 1/2 349). Cf. Syr. *ʾswpʾ*. V. 17 *ʾăsuppîm*, "storehouses"; cf. Neh 12:25 *ʿăsuppê haššĕʿārîm*. In this verse LXX^B *(esephein)* and $c_2$ *(esephē)* transliterate, while LXX^L *Asaph* and Arm. *Asapʿay* assimilate to the common PN. Syr.^A *spʾ* perhaps reflects **hassippîm*.

26:16. "for Ḥosah." MT prefaces "for Shuppim" *(lšpym)*. LXX^BL preface *eis deuteron*, which reflects a different *Vorlage* from that of MT (= *lšnym*). It seems best to strike *lšpym* as a dittography of *hāʾăsuppîm*. LXX^L continues with *tois prothyrois* (= *lassippîm*), an addition triggered by a dittography of the similar phrase in v. 15b.

"the chamber gate." Reading with LXX, *tēn pylēn pastophoriou* (= *lišket*), hence "the chamber gate." So also Curtis and Madsen (1910: 286), who point to the use of *pastophorios* for *lišket* or *liškâ* in 1 Chr 9:26; 23:28; 28:12; 2 Chr 31:11; Jer 35:4; Ezek 40:17, 44. MT "Shallecheth gate" *(šaʿar šalleket)*; Vg. *quae ducit* (= *š* + *leket*). Rudolph (1955: 172) is dubious about the LXX lemma, but there is no need to force the case for MT. Its puzzling form can be explained by methathesis. One should add, however, that the entire phrase, "the chamber gate by the ascending road," may be an early gloss on "the west (gate)," which precedes it.

"by the ascending road" *(bmslh hʿwlh)*. A longstanding crux in 1 Chr 26:16, 18 and 2 Chr 9:11. The relatively rare term *mĕsillâ* is not rendered in LXX, but "ascending" *(hʿwlh)* is translated (contra Torrey 1910: 104) by *tēs anabeseōs* (cf. LXX 2 Chr 20:16; 32:33, in each case for *mʿlh*). On the basis of contextual considerations, *mĕsillâ* is usually translated "highway" in Isa 11:16 and Judg 21:19, that is, a road or path through open country (cf. *HALOT* 606). The expression is often rendered "on the ascending highway" here. The problem is that *měsillâ* seems to denote part of some larger architectural complex in each of its appearances in Chronicles. One hastens to add that the location of this *měsillâ* is in Jerusalem (cf. *měsillâ* in 2 Kgs 18:17; Isa 7:3; 36:2) and does not designate a road connecting separate towns. Whether such graded and surfaced roads even existed in pre-Roman periods is a matter of debate (Tidwell 1995). Dorsey (1985: 385–91) helpfully calls attention to the use of Akk. *mušlālu*, "gatehouse, gate," a term that occurs in a number of royal Assyrian inscriptions. A *mušlālu*, which had some sort of a superstructure, could serve as a city gate, a palace gate, or a gatehouse. Whether *mušlālu* should be distinguished from a regular gateway in containing an outer stairway (*AHw* 684; cf. *mslh hʿwlh* here) is disputed (Van Driel 1969: 30). Old Babylonian, Old Assyrian, and Neo-Assyrian texts refer to *mušlālus* as places in which justice is dispensed, for example, the gateway of a palace (*CAD* 10 277). Both the archaeological evidence from several sites and the Akk. testimony are of some help in making sense of *měsillâ* in Chronicles. A *měsillâ* seems to have been an approach road, leveled, graded, and surfaced, from the base of a tell to the main city gate (Tidwell 1995). Such a path could continue into the city itself and serve, on certain occasions, as a *via sacra* to the gate of a palace or temple.

"watch corresponding to watch" *(mšmr lʿmt mšmr)*. Keil (1873: 277), Rothstein and Hanel (1927: 468), and Rudolph (1955: 172) connect this phrase with v. 17.

26:17. "at the east there were six daily." This reconstruction is based on LXX* *pros anatolas hex tēn hēmeran* (= *lmzrḥh lywm ššh*). MT reads "at the east *(lmzrḥ)* there were six Levites *(hlwym ššh)*." In MT *lywm* has become corrupted to *hlwym*.

"at the storehouses." See the 2nd TEXTUAL NOTE to v. 15.

"two" *(šnym)*. Reading with LXX* *(lectio brevior)*. The reading of MT, $LXX^{ALN}$, and Arm., "two (by) two" *(šnym šnym)*, may be explained either as a simple dittography or as a displacement of *šnym* from the end of v. 18, where MT is lacking. The second *šnym* is also lacking in a few Heb. MSS.

26:18. "at the west." MT prefaces *lapparbār*, an addition from v. 18b. $LXX^{B}$ is even more expansionary, *eis diadechomenous kai tō Hiossa*, "for the relief gatekeepers and to Ḥosah." The LXX in this verse is much longer and more troubled than MT. Some of the LXX readings can be explained either as internal developments within the Greek text or as expansions based on vv. 15–16 (Allen 1974b: 100). But a few of LXX's readings may provide clues about the origin of problems in MT (see below).

"four." So MT. LXX *meta tēn pylēn tou pastophoriou treis*, "with the chamber gate—three."

"at the road, two" (למסלה שנים). Thus MT. The major plus contained in LXX partly results from a dittography of the material in earlier verses: ($LXX^{B}$) *phylakē katenanti phylakēs tēs anabeseōs pros anatolas tēs hēmeras hex kai tō* ($c_2$ *tōn*) *borra tessares kai tō notō tessares kai esepheim duo*, "watch opposite watch, of the ascent toward the east, six daily; and at the north, four; and at the south, four; and (at the) storehouses, two."

"at the colonnade" *(lapparbār)*. So MT. The origins of the rare term *parbār* have been long debated (Grelot 1961; 1964; Runnalls 1991). The translation of

LXX[B] "for relief (gatekeepers)" *(eis diadechomenous)* is a conjecture based on a title used in the Alexandrian court (Thackeray 1907). The proposed translations of *parbār* include "forecourt" based on *parvār*, "forecourt, vestibule" (*HALOT* 962); "temple precinct," based on Vg. *in cellulis* and the context of 2 Kgs 23:11 *parwārîm* (Kittel 1902: 97; Montgomery 1951: 539–40; Tadmor and Cogan 1988: 288–89); "open space" (Rothstein and Hänel 1927: 469); and "congregating area" (Rudolph 1955: 172). My translation is based on the recurrence of *prwr* in the *Temple Scroll* (11QT, esp. §§35.9–15; 37.6; 42.1–11; Yadin 1983: 1.235–39; 1983: 2.150–51, 156–60, 178–79), where it designates a stoa or colonnaded porch, located to the west of the היכל ("hall" [of the Temple]). The *parwār* in the *Temple Scroll* may designate a stoa that served as a "place of ritual separation," as Runnalls argues, but no such specification occurs in this context. Mention should also be made of "Parvaim" (פרוים), which occurs in the context of the description of Solomon's Temple construction (2 Chr 3:6). But "Parvaim" should be connected with the "land of Parvaim" (מת לפרוין), a far-off mountain or land that occurs in the *Genesis Apocryphon* (1QapGen 2:23) from Qumran (Cave 1) and is described as the home of Enoch (Grelot 1961: 34). Some associate this latter "Parvaim" (or "Parvain") with the garden of the righteous ones mentioned in *1 En.* 60:23 (Grelot 1964).

"two." This reconstruction is informed by the double occurrence of *šnym* at the end of MT v. 17 (see the TEXTUAL NOTE) and by the conclusion to LXX v. 18, *kai pros dysmais tessares kai eis ton tribon duo diadechomenous*, "and at the west, four; and for the path, two relief (gatekeepers)."

26:19. "pertaining to the sons of the Qoraḥites" *(lbny hqrḥy)*. LXX[Bh] and $c_2$ *tois huiois Kaath* (= Qohath); LXX[AN], Syr., Vg. *(filiorum Core)* read *tois huiois (tou) Kore* (= *qrḥ*). Similarly, Tg. "for the sons of Qoraḥ."

# NOTES

26:1–19. "the divisions *(maḥlĕqôt)* of the gatekeepers." This material is unique to Chronicles. Part of David's major administrative reorganization involves integrating and assigning the gatekeepers. The text counts the gatekeepers as Levites (cf. Ezra 2:42, 70; Neh 11:19) and provides them with Levitical pedigrees (1 Chr 26:1–12). The casting of lots for these sanctuary guards provides the Levitical families they represent with permanent assignments at the temple complex in Jerusalem (vv. 13–19). On the system of *maḥlĕqôt* for priests and Levites, see the 1st NOTE to 23:6. Gatekeepers were active in David's earlier reign when he brought the Ark to Jerusalem (15:18, 23, 24). Once the palladium was at rest in Zion, sanctuary guards were stationed by it (16:38). The Tabernacle at Gibeon was similarly protected (16:42). Of the various officials David gathered to prepare for the transition to Solomon's reign, 4,000 were gatekeepers (23:5). The gatekeepers are, however, a class of Levites whose responsibilities may encompass more than guard duty (see COMMENT). See also the last NOTE to 15:18.

26.1. "the Qoraḥites." Qoraḥ was a descendant of Levi through his second son, Qohath (6:7–8, 22–23). The 1st NOTE to 9:19 discusses the pedigree and place of the "Qoraḥites." Chapter 26 presents gatekeepers from the Qohathite line of Qoraḥ (vv. 1–9) and from the Merarite line (vv. 10–11). No gatekeepers stemming from Levi's other son, the firstborn Gershon (6:1), appear.

"Qore." Similarly, 9:19 presents Qore as a descendant of Qoraḥ through Abiasaph.

"Abiasaph" *(ʾbyʾsp)*. A descendant of Qohath through Qoraḥ (Exod 6:16–21; 1 Chr 6:7–8, 22; 9:17–19).

26:2. "Zechariah." In the list of returnees from exile, Zechariah the descendant of Meshelemiah (so MT) is mentioned as a gatekeeper at the entrance of the Tent of Meeting (9:21).

26:4–8. "the sons of Obed-edom." This information is unique. The eight sons of Obed-edom are not attested elsewhere.

26:4. "Obed-edom." In Chronicles Obed-edom consistently appears as a Levite, one of whose functions is to serve as a gatekeeper (15:18, 24; 2nd NOTE to 13:13). No statement of ancestry appears for him here (see SOURCE AND COMPOSITION). To complicate matters further, the authors of Chronicles may have held to the existence of two individuals by the name of Obed-edom. A musician by this appellative appears in 15:21 and 16:5. The text of 16:38 distinguishes between an Obed-edom with 68 kinsmen and Obed-edom son of Jeduthun (so Qere; Kethib *ydytwn*, "Jedithun"), who serves together with Ḥosah (cf. "Ḥosah" in 26:10) as a gatekeeper. The present context suggests, but does not directly claim, a connection between Obed-edom and Qoraḥ of the Qohathite phratry (cf. Exod 6:21, 24; 1 Chr 6:7–9; 9:19). In this list of gatekeepers, the Merarites do not appear until v. 10.

26:5. "for God blessed him." Large families are a indelible sign of blessing in the Chronicler's theology (3rd NOTE to 25:5). In the case of Obed-edom, his house "and all that he had" experienced a godsend when the Ark of the Covenant resided with him for three months (13:13–14).

26:6. "valiant warriors" *(gibbôrê ḥayil)*. The use of such terminology belies the view that the author viewed the gatekeepers as minor clerical functionaries (see COMMENT).

26:7. "The sons of Shemaiah: Othni." Unlike the situation with Meshelemiah (vv. 2–3), no ordinals are given for Shemaiah's sons.

"Semachiah" *(sĕmakyāhû)*. The PN appears on two recently published seals (Avigad and Sass 1997: §282; Deutsch and Heltzer 1999: 50). The hypocoristicon *smk* appears many times more on seals and seal impressions (Avigad and Sass 1997: §§59; 101; 119; 214; 281; 283; 347; 366; 389; 689; 694; 861).

26:8. "for the service" *(laʿăbōdâ)*. The gatekeepers' work is seen as making its own contribution to the life of Israel's national cult. The NOTE to 9:13 discusses *ʿăbōdâ* as cultic service.

26:10. "Ḥosah." A Merarite gatekeeper who is assigned to Jerusalem earlier in David's reign (4th NOTE to 16:38).

"the sons of Merari." One of the three major Levitical phratries (1 Chr 6:1, 14,

32, 48, 62; 9:14; 15:6, 17; 23:6, 21; 24:26, 27; 2 Chr 29:12; 34:12; Ezra 8:19). See the 3rd NOTE to 6:1.

"even though he was not the firstborn." The Chronicler's work recognizes the force of primogeniture. Nevertheless, there are exceptions to the pattern. Fathers could ignore primogeniture and appoint another son as head or crown prince (1 Chr 5:1–2; 2 Chr 11:22; De Vries 1987: 65–66; Knoppers 2000b). The translators of the Peshiṭta noticed the unusual presentation in Chronicles and sought to explain it by maintaining that the firstborn son had died.

26:12. "the gatekeepers by head warriors" (השערים לראשי הגבורים). A concluding rubric to the list of gatekeepers in vv. 1–11. Because the author's concern is with the number of authority figures within the gatekeepers' ranks, it seems risky to compare the select numbers given here (a total of 93) with the comprehensive numbers in other lists (e.g., 212 in 1 Chr 9:22; 139 in Ezra 2:42; 138 in Neh 7:45; and 172 in Neh 11:19) with a view to drawing larger historical or redaction-critical conclusions. (For a different view, see Roddy Braun 1986: 251.)

"duties" *(mišmārôt).* On this meaning of *mišmeret,* see the 2nd NOTE to 25:8.

"corresponding to those of their kinsmen." That is, corresponding to the priests and singers, who also appear as part of the larger Levitical civil service (24:5, 19, 31; 25:8).

26:13. "small and great alike." Because the lottery was held to determine which family was to serve at which gate, the number of members within a particular family did not determine or affect the process of selection.

"gate by gate." The text is programmatic. What David establishes, Solomon implements. He installs the gatekeepers in their duties, in conformity with the command of David, "gate by gate" (2 Chr 8:14–15). Similarly, during Josiah's Passover, the author observes that the Levites were at their post and the "gatekeepers were at every gate" (2 Chr 35:15).

26:14. "Shelemiah." The pattern found earlier with the twenty-four priestly courses (1 Chr 24) and the twenty-four courses of singers (1 Chr 25:7–31) is replicated here. After the officials have been selected and numbered, lots are cast to determine their order or place of service.

"an insightful counselor." This is the only clue as to why Zechariah was chosen for his own lot. Since there were only two major Levitical families included (1st NOTE to v. 1), one of the families was split to accommodate the gatekeeping needs of the temple complex and its immediate environs. In the case of Qoraḥite Zechariah (v. 2), "his lot came out to be the north (gate)."

26:15. "the south (gate)." The reference here would seem to indicate that the southern gate and the storehouses were in close proximity (cf. 2 Chr 25:24; Neh 12:25). In any event, Obed-edom and his sons had responsibility for both.

26:16. "Ḥosah." See v. 10 (4th NOTE to 16:38).

"the chamber gate." The term *liškâ* can refer generally to a cella, or chamber, of the Temple or more particularly to a storeroom within the Temple (3rd NOTE to 23:28). The chambers *(hallĕšākôt)* of the Temple were the responsibility of the Levites.

26:18. "at the west." Neither MT nor LXX specifies precisely who served here.

"at the colonnade, two." If this reconstruction is correct (see TEXTUAL NOTES), there were a total of twenty-four gatekeepers on duty at any one time: six at the east, four at the north, four at the south, two at the storehouse, four at the west, two at the road, and two at the colonnade.

26:19. "the sons of the Qoraḥites and the sons of the Merarites." No Gershonites are mentioned in this summary (cf. 23:6; 1st NOTE to v. 1). Instead, the Gershonites play a prominent role in the administration of the treasuries (26:21–22).

## SOURCES AND COMPOSITION

Many commentators think that at least part of 1 Chr 26 is original to this section of the work (23:2–27:34). The view that vv. 1–19 do not stem from the Chronicler's hand (e.g., Rudolph 1955: 173) is tied to the assumption that the Chronicler was responsible for authoring not only Chronicles but also Ezra-Nehemiah. Hence, one reason for viewing vv. 1–19 as a later addition is because the categorization of the gatekeepers in this chapter varies from those found in Ezra and Nehemiah. But if these books stem from different hands, some discrepancies between them are not a problem. For those scholars who deem only part of the chapter to be original, the most common tendency is to view vv. 4–8 (von Rad 1930: 116–18) or vv. 4–8 and 12–18 (Rothstein and Hänel 1927: 469–73; Williamson 1982b: 169–71; R. Braun 1986: 250–51) as secondary. In fact, some (Myers 1965a: 177; R. Braun 1986: 251) think that the present version of 1 Chr 26 is one of the latest parts of the Chronistic work, transforming and updating the material in 1 Chr 9:17–44 and 16:37–43. In contrast, Welch (1939: 91–93) opines that vv. 4–8 and 14–18 were added to the text from an older source, perhaps by the Chronicler himself. Steins (1995: 327–31) takes a different approach, contending that vv. 12–13 and 16b–18 are part of a later "musician-gatekeeper" expansion of an older text: vv. 1–12a*, 13*, 14–16a, 19. The older material, an integral part of the original text of 23:2–26:32, gave primary emphasis to the appointment of priests, Levites, gatekeepers, and supervisors of the temple treasuries.

In defending the possibility of later additions, more attention has been paid to vv. 4–8 than to vv. 12–18 (or to vv. 14–18). The discussion of Obed-edom's descendants (vv. 4–8) is understandably deemed to be intrusive, because it interrupts the discussion of Meshelemiah's descendants (vv. 1–3, 9). Moreover, Obed-edom is given no genealogical pedigree. As for vv. 12–18, the appearance of "Shelemiah" (v. 14), instead of the expected "Meshelemiah" (vv. 1, 2, 9), is said to confirm that vv. 12–18 stem from a later hand than the hand who authored vv. 1–3.

It is certainly quite possible that vv. 4–8 are intrusive, because v. 9, mentioning the sons and brothers of Meshelemiah, continues the discussion of vv. 2–3, dealing with "Meshelemiah's sons." To the reasons given above, another can be added. Within the list of Obed-edom's descendants there is an *inclusio*. The pericope begins with "belonging to the sons of Obed-edom" (*wlʿbd ʾdm bnym*; v. 4) and ends with "belonging to Obed-edom" (*lʿbd ʾdm*; v. 8).

But the question should be pressed further. Granting the addition of vv. 4–8, why did an editor add this material? It seems plausible that the editor introduced the list of Obed-edom's descendants to provide Obed-edom with a Levitical pedigree. In so doing, he may have shaped the list of Obed-edom's descendants to conform to the style of the surrounding material. Certainly, in their present form, the list of Obed-edom's descendants (vv. 4–8) shares a considerable number of literary features with the rest of the gatekeepers' list (vv. 1–3, 9–12). These include the concern with the firstborn (v. 4; cf. vv. 2, 10; also LXX v. 6), the use of ordinals in MT (vv. 4–5; cf. vv. 2–3, 11; but see the TEXTUAL NOTES), the repeated mention of sons and kinsmen (v. 8; cf. vv. 9, 11), the motif of divine retribution, a well-recognized characteristic of the Chronicler's theology (v. 5), and the recurrence of martial terminology, such as "warriors," and "valiant warriors," and "warriorlike in strength" (vv. 6, 7, 8; cf. vv. 9, 30, 31, 32). One should add that the association of Obed-edom (whatever his original pedigree [13:13]) with the Levites is a distinctive aspect of the Chronicler's work (1 Chr 15:18, 21–24; 16:38; 2 Chr 25:24). This increases the likelihood that his appearance here is no accident.

As for the composition of the rest of the work (specifically, vv. 12–19), the arguments for multiple editions are not compelling. To be sure, MT exhibits a number of difficulties, but at least some of these are best explained at the level of text-criticism (see TEXTUAL NOTES) rather than at the level of redaction-criticism. The rubrics in vv. 1–19 exhibit a unified design. The first section opens with an introduction to the gatekeepers' divisions (v. 1) and ends with summary of these divisions (v. 12). The introduction to the following section mentions the casting of lots according to ancestral houses (v. 13). The final rubric again refers to the gatekeepers' divisions (v. 19). That the concluding summary mentions only the Qoraḥites and the Merarites is no argument against this overall unity, because no new figures (non-Qoraḥites and non-Merarites) are introduced in the intervening list of duties and stations (vv. 12–18).

On a positive level, there are signs of unity. First, there is a correspondence between the personnel selected (vv. 1–12) and the personnel involved in the lotteries (vv. 13–19). Second, this correspondence extends to Obed-edom. Like the other figures in vv. 1–12, Obed-edom and his sons (vv. 4–8) are included in the lottery (v. 15). Furthermore, the reference in 2 Chr 25:24 to Obed-edom (in the context of King Joash's plundering the Temple) presupposes that Obed-edom and his descendants had some official role at the House of God. It is true that among all of the figures listed in 1 Chr 26:1–19, there is one apparent exception to the pattern of congruence. The name "Shelemiah" (v. 14) appears instead of the expected "Meshelemiah" (vv. 1, 2, 9). But while the discrepancy holds true for MT, it does not hold for all textual witnesses (e.g., $LXX^{L}$). Moreover, the discrepancy can be explained by recognizing that we are dealing, in all likelihood, with two variants of the same name (see TEXTUAL NOTES). In any case, it seems ill-advised to predicate one's redactional reconstruction on a reading that is textually disputed.

Finally, there are a number of correspondences between the selection of and lottery for the gatekeepers and the selection of and lottery for the priests, singers, and Levites. The rubric of v. 12 alludes to a correlation between the gatekeepers' duties and those of the other Levites, stating that all are to serve at "the House of Yhwh" (23:24, 28, 32; 24:19; 25:6). The next section, dealing with the casting of lots according to ancestral houses (26:13), echoes the pattern of casting lots found in earlier sections. The establishment of courses by lot for the priests (24:7–18) and the singers (25:9–31) also follows the selection of these personnel (24:1–6; 25:1–8). There are additional parallels listed in the NOTES. To be sure, one could argue that these various correspondences are the result of an editor or scribe who patterned them after the material in earlier sections, but if so, the distinction between an author and an editor is not of great consequence.

# COMMENT

In discussing the gatekeepers, who dominate 1 Chr 26, scholars have paid much more attention to questions of composition than to questions of vocation. Because of this lack of interest in definition of task, it seems appropriate to pay some attention to it. What did gatekeepers actually do in the ancient world, and how did the Chronicler, in particular, construe their task? Some have viewed the gatekeepers in Chronicles as minor clerical functionaries. Such a determination might seem surprising in light of the positive, even martial, descriptions of the gatekeepers in this chapter. Nevertheless, the "minor clerics" view has been influential both because the gatekeepers belong to a priestly order and because of the supposition that by the time of the Chronicler the descriptions of the gatekeepers as "valiant warriors" and "warriors" had become merely "honorific" (R. Braun 1986: 249). In recent years, another view has come to the fore, presenting the gatekeepers as an important "paramilitary inner-city security force" (Wright 1990: 69). The latter view is, in my judgment, closer to the mark because it has evidentiary support elsewhere in Chronicles and parallels in ancient Near Eastern lore. As we shall see, gatekeepers perform multiple functions, but the martial aspect is prominent.

First, the fact that Levites are mentioned as gatekeepers should not mislead readers into thinking that the role of gatekeepers was only formal in nature. Priests performed guard duty, for instance, in Mari (ARM 10.50.16–17). Certain police functions for temple staff are also attested in early Mesopotamia (Postgate 1994a) and in Ḫatti, as evident in the "Instructions for Temple Officials" (*KUB* 13; Milgrom 1990: 341–42). One of the mid-fifth-century temple-tariff inscriptions from Kition mentions "men who were at the door of the shrine" (לאדמם אש על דל קצר) who received payment for their work in the month of Etanim (*KAI* 37.A.5). (On the textual reconstruction, see Masson and Sznycer 1972: 21–68.) Xenophon's *Cyropaedia* (8.1–9), which attributes the establishment of "the gate of the king" (cf. Dan 2:49) to Cyrus, implies that this institution had some military associations (Wright 1990: 75). In the *Temple Scroll* from Qumran (11QT), one sees a similar emphasis placed on military capability and high character (Weinfeld

1980). The 12,000 men whose assignment is to guard the king need to be "warriors" (איש מלחמה), "men of truth" (אנשי אמת), and "God fearers" (יראי אלוהים; 11Q19 57.6–8). It is also pertinent to observe that in the account of Diodorous Siculus dealing with the kings of ancient Egypt, the royal security detail consisted of men who not only were at least twenty years old and of impeccable character but also were "sons of the most distinguished priests" (*Bibl.* 1.70.2).

In the Priestly source, guards for the Tabernacle are of Levitical pedigree (Num 3:5–43; Milgrom 1990: 341–42). Similarly, David's provisions for the Ark and the Tabernacle include Levitical gatekeepers for both institutions (1 Chr 15:18, 23; 16:38, 42). The Hittite "Instructions for the Royal Bodyguard" (*IBoT* I 36) does not address the pedigree of gatekeepers, but it does mention some of their duties (Güterbock and van den Hout 1991). These include staying at one's post, preventing illicit passage, and asking permission for and getting a substitute should it be necessary to relieve oneself (§§6–10). Finally, mention should be made of an undated ancient Hebrew bulla that also attests to the martial aspect of gatekeeping responsibilities: *lʿzryhw šʿr hmsgr,* "belonging to Azaryahu, gatekeeper of the prison" (Davies, §100.858).

Second, the use of military imagery to describe the gatekeepers belies the view that "gatekeeper" is only an honorific title. The men chosen to be gatekeepers are "warriorlike in strength" (*ʾîš-ḥayil bakkōaḥ;* v. 8), "valiant warriors" (*gibbôrê ḥayil;* v. 6), "warriors" (*bĕnê ḥayil;* vv. 7, 9), and "head warriors" (*rāʾšê haggibbôrîm;* v. 12). The Chronicler commonly uses the term *ḥayil* in military contexts (Wright 1990: 71–73). This should not be surprising. To be an effective police force, proper temperament, character, and training would be necessary. Since one of their chief obligations is to guard the gates of the sanctuary precincts, the quality of the gatekeepers had to be up to a certain standard. In Chronicles the central sanctuary is a magnificent edifice, endowed with countless amounts of precious gold, silver, and material objects. The security force assigned to such a structure would have a major responsibility to fulfill. Far from having the impression that the gatekeepers were minor clerical functionaries, one is left with the impression that the Levites chosen were some of the finest personnel available. The list of assignments (vv. 13–19) is inherently martial in nature.

Third, security work is one of the roles the gatekeepers play elsewhere in the monarchy. In the Chronicler's version of Jehoiada's *coup,* the gatekeepers are prominent (2 Chr 23:1–15), a fact that is all the more striking because the gatekeepers are not mentioned in the parallel of 2 Kgs 11:4–16. When the gatekeepers' task in overthrowing Athaliah is complete and young Joash is safely in power, they resume their role as a police cordon around the Temple. In so doing, the gatekeepers protect the shrine's sanctity (2 Chr 23:18–21).

In addition to policing the temple gates, the gatekeepers perform other functions. One of these functions is stewardship, a role that is evident in the reign of Ḥezeqiah. Qore, who was a gatekeeper of the eastern gate, was in charge of the voluntary offerings, the giving of a contribution (*tĕrûmâ;* Milgrom 1990: 426–27) to Yhwh, and the dedicated gifts (*qōdeš haqqŏdāšîm;* 2 Chr 31:14). To assist him in his work, Qore had a staff of six, whose responsibilities included the distribution of offerings in priestly towns and the registry of priests, Levites, and their dependents (2 Chr 31:14–19). The work of stewardship is also apparent in the Chronicler's treatment of Josiah's reforms. In Josiah's Temple-repair project, some of the Levites employed were scribes, officials, and gatekeepers (2 Chr 34:13). The scribes, officials, and gatekeepers do not appear in the parallel (2 Kgs 22:3–7), which speaks instead of carpenters, laborers, and masons.

The relevance of sanctuary management and upkeep becomes clearer when one considers that the gatekeepers performed their duties not only for the Temple proper but also for its storehouses. Since temples in the ancient Near East functioned as major depositories, Levitical supervision over the Temple treasuries would involve some oversight of Temple revenue. To put it somewhat differently, if temples were banks, the Temple storehouses could be viewed as bank vaults (Wright 1990: 76). Hence, when King Joash of Israel chooses to plunder Judah's wealth, he seizes, among other things, "all the gold and the silver, as well as the furnishings that were found in the House of God with Obed-edom" (2 Chr 25:24). The most likely source for the allusion to Obed-edom, which is not found in the parallel of 2 Kgs 14:14, is this chapter's detailing the prominence of Obed-edom and his sixty-two relatives as guards for the Temple (vv. 4–8, 15, 17).

The link with the temple treasuries is apparent in Josiah's reign. There the gatekeepers collect, not disburse, sanctuary revenue (2 Chr 34:14–16). To help pay for the restoration of the shrine, the guardians of the threshold serve as tax collectors, gathering silver for the temple renovations. Such revenue was collected from Manasseh, Ephraim, all of the remnant of Israel, Judah, and Benjamin (2 Chr 34:9). Given the opportunity or threat of embezzlement, the need to perform such duties truthfully was critical to the venture's success (2 Chr 34:12; cf. 1 Chr 9:22). According to 1 Chr 9:17–27, the gatekeepers resumed their duties in the Persian period. In this context, appeal is made to the precedent established by David and Samuel(!) the seer (9:22). The gatekeepers were (re)appointed to serve as guards on all four sides of the sanctuary: east, west, south, and north (9:23–24). Their kinsmen in the villages were also required to lend assistance every seven days on a regular schedule (9:25). Four chief gatekeepers *(gibbôrê haššōʿărîm)* were in charge of the temple chambers and treasuries (9:26).

None of this information about the gatekeepers is available in Samuel-Kings. All of it stems from Chronicles. The multiple roles these figures play are more than honorific and formal. To be sure, the gatekeepers are not of primary interest to the author. They hardly dominate the pages of his work. Nevertheless, the gatekeepers are an integral component of the larger Levitical sodality. By contrast, the status of the gatekeepers in Ezra-Nehemiah and their relationship to the Levites is much disputed (see NOTES). In Chronicles this security force fulfills a variety of administrative functions—guard duty, revenue collection, temple repair, and revenue disbursement. As such, the gatekeepers are critical to temple stewardship and are portrayed positively.

# *XXXII. The Levitical Supervisors (26:20–32)*

*Supervision of the Treasuries*

20 And the Levites, their kinsmen, were in charge of the treasuries of the House of God and the treasuries of the dedicated gifts. 21 The sons of Laadan the Gershonite. Belonging to Laadan the Gershonite: Jeḥiel. 22 The sons of Jeḥiel, Zetham and Joel, were in charge of the treasuries of the House of Yhwh. 23 Belonging to the Amramites, the Izharites, the Ḥebronites, the Uzzielites: 24 Shubael, a descendant of Gershom the son of Moses, was commander over the treasuries. 25 And his kinsmen, belonging to Eliezer: his son Reḥabiah, his son Jeshaiah, his son Joram, his son Zichri, and his son Shelomoth. 26 This Shelomoth and his brothers were in charge of the treasuries of all the dedicated gifts that King David, the clan chiefs, the officers of the thousands and of the hundreds, and the officers of the army dedicated. 27 That which they took from the war spoils they dedicated to strengthen the House of Yhwh. 28 All that Samuel the seer dedicated, as well as Saul son of Qish, and Abner son of Ner, and Joab son of Zeruiah—everything that someone dedicated was under the charge of Shelomoth and his brothers.

*Supervision over Regional Affairs*

29 Belonging to the Izharites: Chenaniah and his sons were responsible for the outlying work with respect to Israel as officials and judges. 30 Belonging to the Ḥebronites: Ḥashabiah and his kinsmen, warriors, 1,700 in charge of the supervision of Israel beyond the Jordan westward for all matters of Yhwh and for the service of the king. 31 Of the Ḥebronites, Jeriah was the head of the Ḥebronites. The genealogical lines of his ancestors were sought out in the fortieth year of the reign of David and among them were found valiant warriors in Jaazer of Gilead. 32 As for his kinsmen, warriors, 2,700 ancestral heads, King David appointed them to be in charge of the Reubenites, the Gadites, and the half-tribe of Manassites, for every matter of God and for (every) matter of the king.

## TEXTUAL NOTES

26:20. "their kinsmen" (*'ḥyhm*). Following LXX, *(hoi) adelphoi autōn* (cf. Arm. *una cum fratribus*). MT "Aḥijah" (*'ḥyh*), hence "and the Levites: Aḥijah." See further de Lagarde (1883: 4).

26:21. "(the) sons of Laadan." So MT and LXX$^{L}$. LXX "these are the sons of Chadan" (LXX$^{A}$ *Ledan;* $e_2$ *Daadan;* LXX$^{N}$ *De(a)dan*). There is considerable confusion in both MT and LXX v. 21, but reconstructing "from the sons of Laadan" (Rudolph 1955: 172) is unnecessary, given the pattern at the beginning of v. 22, "the sons of Jeḥiel(i)."

"the Gershonite" (הגרשני). I read the gentilic *(lectio brevior)*. Cf. LXX$^{Bh}$ and $c_2$ *Gērsōnei*. MT expands to "(the) sons of the Gershonites" *(bny hgršny)*. LXX$^{AN}$ "(belonging) to the Gershonites."

"belonging to Laadan" *(llʿdn)*. So MT and LXX$^{L}$. LXX$^{B}$ exhibits some confusion, reading *tō La(a)dan kai Iaieēl* ($c_2$ *Iaiaipa*) *tou (iou) huioi* ($c_2$ *huiou*) *Ieiēl.* Allen (1974b: 135) posits an inner-Greek haplography, but I am more inclined to think of an expansion of specification after the second *llʿdn*. MT (and LXX) add "the ancestral heads of Laadan" *(rʾšy ʾbwt llʿdn)*.

"Jeḥiel." Reading with LXX, which consistently has *I(a)eiēl* (= Jeḥiel) here and in v. 22. MT "Jeḥieli" (*yḥyly*; vv. 21–22) assimilates to the gentilics in vv. 21 and 23.

26:22. "the sons of Jeḥiel." Again, some (e.g., Curtis and Madsen 1910: 286) excise as a gloss.

"Joel" *(yôʾēl)*. So MT and LXX$^{ABN}$; cf. cursives ce "Uzziel" *(Oziēl)*. MT continues with "his brother"; cf. LXX* "the brothers"; Vg. "his brothers." Rothstein and Hänel (1927) follow Vg., but Rudolph (1955: 174) is probably right in regarding the lemma as a gloss on *bny* at the beginning of the verse. The persons mentioned are listed as brothers in 23:8.

26:23. "the Amramites, the Izharites, the Ḥebronites, the Uzzielites." Thus MT. LXX *(Ambram, Issaar, Chebrōn, Ozeiēl)* does not read gentilics in this verse.

26:24. "Shubael." So LXX$^{AN}$ *Soubaēl* and Vg. *Subahel.* LXX$^{L}$ *Sōbiēl.* LXX$^{B}$ and $c_2$ "Joel" *(Iōēl)*. MT "Shebuel." See further the 2nd TEXTUAL NOTE to 23:16.

"a descendant of Gershom." Thus MT. LXX "the one of Gershom," *ho tou Gērsam.*

"the son of Moses." Thus MT. LXX$^{B}$ *tou Mōsē.*

"commander *(nāgîd)* over the treasuries." So MT and LXX$^{AN}$. LXX$^{B}$ and $c_2$ *epi tōn thēsaurōn*, "over the treasuries," have lost *nāgîd (epistatēs)* by an inner-Greek haplography *(homoioarkton)*.

26:25. "and his kinsmen" *(wʾḥyw)*. So MT. Benzinger (1901: 78) follows LXX *(kai tō adelphō)* by reading "and to his brother" (= *wlʾḥyw*).

"to Eliezer: his son *(bnw)* Reḥabiah." Thus MT and LXX$^{AN}$. LXX$^{B}$ "to Eliezer: Reḥabiah *(Rhabias)* the son *(huios = bn)*." It may be that LXX originally read "the son *(bn)* of Reḥabiah."

"his son Jeshaiah." Thus MT. Because LXX$^{B}$ consistently lacks the expression "his son" in this verse in conjunction with Jeshaiah, Joram, Zichri, and Shelomoth, all these figures are presented as progeny of Eliezer.

"Shelomoth." Reading with Kethib and LXX$^{ABal}$. Qere, LXX$^{L}$, Syr., Tg., and Vg. "Shelomith." See "Shelomoth" at the beginning of v. 26 and the TEXTUAL NOTES to 23:9, 18.

26:26. "Shelomoth." So MT and LXX *(Salōmōth)*. Many Heb. MSS and LXX$^{L}$ "Shelomith."

"the officers" *(lśry)*. Many (e.g., Keil 1873: 279) read the expected *w(l)śry*, citing Tg. and 29:6. One might add $c_2$, which prefaces *kai* to *ch(e)iliarchoi* (LXX$^{ABN}$).

26:27. "that which they took" *(ʾšr nśʾ)*. Partially following LXX, *ha elaben ek* (LXX$^{AN}$ add *tōn*) *poleōn* (LXX$^{A*}$ and Theodoret *polemōn*) *kai ek tōn laphurōn*

(= *ʾšr nśʾ*[*w*] *mn-hʿrym wmn-hšll*, "that which [t]he[y] took from [the] cities [or: wars] and from the plunder"). The minus with respect to MT, "that which they took," may be attributed to haplography (*homoioteleuton* from *ṣbʾ* to *nśʾ*).

"from the war spoils." Reading MT, "from the wars and from the plunder," as a hendiadys.

"they dedicated" *(hiqdîšû)*. So MT *(lectio brevior)*. LXX *kai hēgiasen apʾ (tōn) autōn*, "and dedicated some of them."

"to strengthen *(lḥzq)* the House of Yhwh." Thus MT. LXX is again expansionary, *tou mē kathysterēsai tēn oikodomēn tou oikou tou theou*, "that the building of the house of God would not be delayed."

26:28. "and all *(wkl)* that Samuel the seer dedicated" *(hăhiqdîš)*. LXX* reads somewhat differently, "and over all the holy things of God *(kai epi* [= *wʿl-kl*] *pantōn tōn hagiōn tou theou)* Samuel the prophet *(Samouel tou prophētou)*."

"Abner." So MT *(ʾabnēr)* 26:28; 27:21; as well as MT 1 Sam 14:50, 51; 17:55; 1 Kgs 2:5, 32. The readings of LXX$^{B}$ *Abennēr;* LXX$^{L}$ *Abenēr* reflect *ʾăbînēr*, the spelling sometimes found in MT Samuel (1 Sam 14:50; 2 Sam 2:17). The LXX translators seem to have worked from a *Vorlage* that was orthographically more developed than MT Chronicles is (2nd TEXTUAL NOTE to 2:16). On the PN *ʾăbînēr*, "my (divine) father is a lamp," or *ʾabnēr*, "the (divine) father is a lamp," see Noth (1928: 167) and more comprehensively Layton (1990b: 145–50).

"everything that someone dedicated" *(kol hammaqdîš)*. Thus MT. On the use of the article *h-* for the relative pron. *ʾšr*, see Kropat (§29). Since LXX reads *pan ho hēgiasen* ("all that someone dedicated"), it is unnecessary to reconstruct *hammiqdāš* or *hamĕquddāš* (contra Benzinger 1901: 78; Rudolph 1955: 176). LXX$^{L}$ and Theodoret *kai pas ho hagiazōn*.

"was under the charge of" *(ʿal yad)*. So MT. LXX *dia cheiros*, "by the hand of."

"Shelomoth." Reading with LXX*; MT "Shelomith" (last TEXTUAL NOTE to v. 25).

26:29. "for the outlying work" *(lammĕlāʾkâ haḥîṣônâ)*. That is, the work outside Jerusalem in more remote regions. The translation of REB, "secular affairs," misapprehends the Heb.

"officials and judges" *(lšṭrym wlšpṭym)*. Thus MT. LXX *tou grammateuein kai diakr(e)inein* (= *lswprym wlšpṭym*). It is difficult to tell which of these two readings is the more primitive; they may simply be ancient variants (cf. 2 Chr 34:13).

26:30. "in charge of the supervision of Israel" *(ʿal pĕquddat yiśrāʾēl)*. The term *pĕquddâ* can carry the general sense of an appointment or duty (Num 3:36; 4:16; Ps 109:8), but the term can refer more specifically to an administrative obligation (1 Chr 23:11; 24:3, 19; cf. Akk. *piqittu; AHw* 865) or even to a duty group (2 Chr 26:11; 2nd TEXTUAL NOTE to 24:3).

26:31. "of the Ḥebronites." So MT and LXX$^{B}$ *(tōn Chebrōnei)*. Cursives ag *tōn Chebrōn*.

"Jeriah" *(yryh)*. A few Heb. MSS have *ydyh*. LXX$^{B}$ $c_2$ *Toudeias*, a mistake for *Ioudeias* = *ydyh*), itself reflecting a *dālet/rêš* confusion. The same *dālet/rêš* confusion characterizes the variants for "Jeriah" *(yryhw)* in 23:19 (see TEXTUAL NOTE).

"the genealogical lines of his ancestors" *(ltldwtyw lʾbwt)*. So MT. LXX *kata geneseis autōn kata patrias*.

"the reign of David." Thus MT. LXX *tes basileias autou*, "of his reign."

"valiant warriors" *(gibbôrê ḥayil)*. LXX *anēr dynatos*, "a strong man" (= *ʾyš ḥyl*; cf. 26:6, 9).

"Jaazer of Gilead" *(yʿzyr glʿd)*. This seems to be how LXX translators understood their *Vorlage*; $LXX^{B}$ $c_2$ *Rhiazēr tēs Galaadeitidos*; $LXX^{L}$ *Iazēr tēo Galaaditidos*.

26:32. "warriors" *(bĕnê ḥayil)*. $LXX^{ABN}$ have *huioi hoi dynatoi*, although *huioi dynatoi* may have been the original LXX reading (Allen 1974a: 160). See also the TEXTUAL NOTES to 26:6, 9, 31.

"2,700" *(ʾlpym wšbʿ mʾwt)*. So MT and $LXX^{B}$ *disch(e)ilioi heptakosioi (lectio difficilior)*. $LXX^{A}$ *chilioi heptakosioi*, "1,700"; $LXX^{N}$ and Arm. *chilioi pentakosioi*, "1,500." The number given by $LXX^{A}$ assimilates to "1,700" in v. 30.

"ancestral heads." Some scholars view this as a gloss, based on v. 31a.

"for every matter *(dābār)* of God and for (every) matter *(dābār)* of the king." So MT. LXX* "for every command *(prostagma)* of Yhwh and for (every) matter *(logon = dābār)* of the king." LXX may (*prostagma = ḥq* in 1 Chr 16:17; 22:13; 29:19; 2 Chr 33:8; 34:31; = *mṣwh* in 2 Chr 29:15, 25; 30:6, 12; 31:21) or may not (*prostagma = dbr*; 2 Chr 19:10) reflect a different *Vorlage* from that of MT.

## NOTES

26:20–28. This section of chapter 26 falls naturally into two related parts. The first section (vv. 20–28) deals with those Levites who were appointed to oversee "the treasuries of the House of God/Yhwh" (vv. 20, 22) and the "treasuries of the dedicated gifts" (vv. 20, 26). Two Levitical groups administer the treasuries: the Gershonites (vv. 21–22) and the Amramites (vv. 23–26). The second section (vv. 29–32) deals with Levitical supervision of the regions to the west and east of the Jordan River (NOTE to vv. 29–32).

26:20. "their kinsmen." That is, the kinsmen of the gatekeepers (vv. 1–19). Both the gatekeepers and the supervisors were drawn from the ranks of the Levites.

"treasuries *(ʾôṣĕrôt)* of the House of God." Both the temple treasuries and the palace treasuries are mentioned often in Samuel, Kings, and Chronicles (see COMMENT), but the provenance of the treasuries of the dedicated gifts (see also v. 26) is more difficult to pinpoint. Were these treasuries separate from the shrine and palace treasuries or, as is more likely to be the case, did they form part of the temple treasuries?

"the dedicated gifts" *(haqqŏdāšîm)*. The precise meaning of the term *haqqŏdāšîm*, "the holy things," can be interpreted in different ways, depending on context. Here and in v. 26 it seems to designate the holy offerings or donations (Lev 21:22; Num 18:10; 1 Kgs 7:51; 15:15; 2 Kgs 12:5, 19; Ezek 42:13; 44:13; 2 Chr 29:33; 31:12). In the present setting, such donations are the responsibility of the Qohathites (vv. 23–28).

26:21. "Laadan" is traced to the Gershonite phratry (2nd NOTE to 23:7) in a telescopic lineage. The writer begins with Laadan and proceeds to provide a one-generation lineage from Laadan's son Jeḥiel to his sons Zetham and Joel (v. 22). In such highly compacted Chronistic genealogies, the stress is on tying someone (or a group) in the classical past, that is the United Monarchy, to their forebears in the Ancestral age.

"the Gershonite." Gershon was the firstborn of Levi (2nd NOTE to 6:1). In the previous discussion of gatekeepers, no Gershonites appeared. There the Qohathites (vv. 1–9) and the Merarites (vv. 10–12) dominated.

"Jeḥiel." See the 1st TEXTUAL NOTE to 23:9. In 23:8, Jeḥiel appears, along with Zetham and Joel, as sons of Laadan. But in 26:22, Zetham and Joel appear as sons of Jeḥiel. In 23:9 the sons of Jeḥiel are Shelomoth, Ḥaziel, and Haran. In spite of these disagreements, the sources agree that Jeḥiel was a Gershonite. This is also true of 29:8: "the treasury of the House of Yhwh under the care of Jeḥiel the Gershonite."

"the treasuries of the House of Yhwh." Whereas the treasuries for the dedicated gifts are the responsibility of the Qohathites, the temple treasuries are the responsibility of the Gershonites. The text dealing with the staffing of the treasuries in the time of the return only mentions "the treasuries of the House of God" (9:26).

26:23. "the Amramites, the Izharites, the Ḥebronites, the Uzzielites." These four families all descend from Qohath (Exod 6:18; Num 3:19, 27; 1 Chr 6:3; 23:12; cf. 1 Chr 6:7), who represents a highly important Levitical phratry (1st NOTE to 5:28). In the litany that follows, the "Amramites" (26:24–25), the "Izharites" (v. 29), and the "Ḥebronites" (vv. 30–32) all appear. No specific "Uzzielites" are listed, however.

"Amramites." Amram, the firstborn son of Qohath (1st NOTE to 6:3), was the father of both Aaron and Moses.

"Izharites." Izhar was the second son of Qohath (1st NOTE to 23:18).

"Ḥebronites." Ḥebron was the third son of Qohath (2nd NOTE to 6:3).

"Uzzielites." Uzziel was the fourth son of Qohath (3rd NOTE to 6:3).

26:24. "Shubael." This descendant of Gershom (23:15–16; 24:20) should not be confused with the Hemanite (25:4, 20) of the same name. The author provides a highly condensed genealogy, beginning with Shubael, skipping intermediate stages, and proceeding to Gershom the son of Moses. It is often supposed, understandably so, that the text exhibits some irregularity in referring to Shubael's function as "commander over the treasuries," when the earlier rubric referred specifically to "the treasuries of the House of God and the treasuries of the dedicated gifts" (v. 20). The "treasuries of the House of Yhwh" are assigned to Jeḥiel's sons, Zetham and Joel (v. 22), while "the treasuries of the dedicated gifts" are assigned to Shelomoth and his kin (v. 26). What, then, of Shubael? One possibility may be the use of a source that the author did not completely overwrite (see SOURCES AND COMPOSITION). Another possibility is that the author is referring to a traditional claim of the Amramites to oversee the treasuries, as evidenced by Shubael's serving in this capacity. Shubael's precedent may thus explain why one of the descendants of his kinsmen (through Eliezer) is given the charge over "the treasuries of the dedicated gifts" (v. 26).

"Gershom." On this son of Moses, see Exod 2:22 and 1 Chr 23:15.

"commander" *(nāgîd)*. The title *nāgîd*—"commander," "king-designate," or "leader"—is used for a variety of different positions (7th NOTE to 11:2).

"over the treasuries." The temple complex was the home of some of the nation's cherished valuables. In this respect, ancient Near Eastern shrines were important both as places of worship and as depositories.

26:25. "his kinsmen." Literally, "his brothers." The reference is to a collateral line, that of Shubael's kinsmen who belonged to Eliezer, the brother of Gershom. The expression is used because all of the descendants listed in vv. 24–25 stem from two brothers, Gershom and Eliezer, who were both sons of Moses (10th NOTE to 23:14). As happens quite often in the genealogies, the writer links a person in (what he considers to be) his nation's classical age to a forefather in the Ancestral age. A five-generation descending lineage begins with Eliezer, the brother of Gershom, and ends with a contemporary of David, Shelomoth.

"Reḥabiah." According to 23:17, Reḥabiah had many progeny, but these descendants are not individually named.

"his son Jeshaiah" *(yšʿyhw)*. In 24:21, the name of Reḥabiah's son is spelled *yšyh*.

"his son Joram." The linear genealogical pattern "$PN_1$, his son $PN_2$, his son $PN_3$" is relatively rare in Chronicles, but is found in the Davidic genealogy (3:10–14, 16, 21).

26:26. "Shelomoth." This descendant of Reḥabiah is to be distinguished from the Izharite Shelomoth (23:18; 24:22) and from the Gershonite Shelemoth (23:9).

"dedicated gifts" *(haqqŏdāšîm)*. See the 3rd NOTE to v. 20.

"dedicated" *(hiqdîš)*. There are other cases in which a king (18:7–11), people (Exod 28:38), or layperson (Lev 27:14–22) dedicates an item for sacral use. Indeed, Solomon builds the Temple "to dedicate it" *(lĕhaqdîšô)* to Yhwh (2 Chr 2:4). But in this case, one finds a cross section of Israel's civil and military leadership represented, "King David, the clan chiefs, the officers of the thousands and of the hundreds, and the officers of the army." In this idealized presentation, everyone who had a major hand in winning any battle dedicated at least some of the spoils to the Temple.

"the officers of the thousands and of the hundreds." The language is traditional. The same sort of military terminology, referring to units of thousands, hundreds, or tens, is attested elsewhere in the Bible (Exod 18:21, 25; Deut 1:15; 1 Sam 8:12). Similar terminology is evident in Assyrian sources (Ahlström 1995: 600) and in the Hittite "Instructions for the Royal Bodyguard" (e.g., §11.63; Güterbock and van den Hout 1991: 10). In Chronicles "the officers of the thousands" *(śry hʾlpym)* were instrumental in bringing the Ark to Jerusalem (15:25). The reference here also recalls the rally of tribal clans to David in 12:21, 24–39. In David's reorganization of Israel's national administration "the officers of the hundreds" *(śry hmʾwt)* and "the officers of the thousands" *(śry hʾlpym)* consistently play a supporting role (26:26; 27:1; 28:1). The use of "a thousand" to signify a military brigade continues to be attested in later times (e.g., 1 Macc 5:13; Goldstein 1976: 299).

26:27. "to strengthen the House of Yhwh." As Curtis and Madsen (1910: 288) observe, Chronicles normally employs the verb *ḥzq* (*piʿel* or *hipʿil*) in building contexts to denote repair (2 Chr 11:11, 12; 24:5, 12; 26:9; 29:3; 32:5; 34:8, 10). The verb *ḥzq* is used thirty-one times with this sense in Nehemiah (e.g., 3:4, 19). In the view of the LXX translators *(tou mē kathysterēsai tēn oikodomēn tou oikou tou theou)*, this was done so "that the building of the House of God would not be delayed." But the very act of strengthening something presumes that it already exists. Hence, the author either anachronistically assumes the existence of a standing temple or depicts military, prophetic, and political leaders as endowing the future shrine's upkeep. The repair of shrines was viewed as a pious act in antiquity (Ahlström 1982; 1995). If the latter interpretation holds, Israel's military and civil leadership is credited with having the foresight to plan not only for the building of the House of God but also for refurbishing it in later generations.

26:29–32. The second part of this section of chapter 26 (NOTE to vv. 20–28) deals with Levitical overseers in the king's employ who have judicial, administrative, and cultic responsibilities in outlying regions within Israel. These officials are drawn from the ranks of the "Izharites" (v. 29) and "Ḥebronites" (vv. 30–32) mentioned in the earlier introduction (v. 23). In the Chronicler's work, the best Judahite kings exercise proper rule in Jerusalem and project their power into the countryside. In this respect, David is a model for others to follow.

26:29. "Izharites." In earlier sources, the "sons of Izhar" are listed as Qoraḥ, Nepheg, and Zichri (Exod 6:21; cf. Num 16:1; 1 Chr 6:22–23). In 1 Chr 23:18, "Shelomoth the head" is mentioned as a son (or descendant) of Izhar.

"Chenaniah" *(knnyhw)*. A Levitical officer by the same name is said to have wielded authority in the porterage of the Ark because of his expertise (15:22).

"the outlying work with respect to Israel" *(lmlʾkh hḥyṣwnh ʿl-yśrʾl)*. In Nehemiah certain Levites are assigned "the outside work for the House of God" (Neh 11:16). In Chronicles, one finds a distribution of assignments for the Levites, apportioned according to their ancestral affiliations. The Amramites (v. 24) are given authority over the treasuries, while the Izharites serve in an administrative capacity over regional affairs in the Cisjordan and the Transjordan.

"officials and judges" *(šṭrym wlšpṭym)*. In the Levitical census of 23:3–5, "6,000 were officials *(šōṭĕrîm)* and judges *(šōpĕṭîm)*." The use of these civil servants in judicial and administrative capacities is not unique. In Deuteronomy the people are to appoint "judges and officials" *(šōpĕṭîm wĕšōṭĕrîm)* in all of their towns (16:18–20). Deuteronomic legislation also calls for employing sacerdotal officials as judges *(šōpĕṭîm)* at the central shrine (Deut 17:8–13; 19:17; 21:5). In Deuteronomic legislation, the king does not enjoy a primary, much less a formative, role in the organization and administration of justice (Deut 17:14–20; Knoppers 1996b; 2001d). "The judge" *(hšpṭ)* in residence or "Levitical priests" *(hkhnym hlwym)* officiate as magistrates at Israel's central sanctuary (Deut 17:8–13). But in Chronicles the king plays a much more formative role in the organization and distribution of justice (Knoppers 1994b). One of Jehoshaphaṭ's initial reforms is to assign troops and prefects to all of his fortified towns (2 Chr 17:2). In the second round of his reforms, he stations judges *(šōpĕṭîm)* within each of these towns (2 Chr 19:5). The extent to which the author envisions the officials as collecting taxes (the earlier context in 1 Chr 26:20–28 deals with the administration of the treasuries) is not known. Governmental intervention in the countryside was not unknown in later times (1 Macc 2:17–38).

26:30. "Ḥebronites." As the context makes clear (vv. 30–32), these Qohathite Levites bear some major administrative responsibilities on behalf of the crown (1st NOTE to v. 23).

"Ḥashabiah" (חשביהו). The late PN (1 Chr 25:3; 2 Chr 35:9) and its variant חשביה are quite common in sacerdotal circles (Ezra 8:19, 24; Neh 10:11; 11:15, 22; 12:21, 24; 1 Chr 6:30; 9:14; 25:19; 27:17), but it is not unique to those contexts (Neh 3:17).

"beyond the Jordan westward" (מעבר לירדן מערבה). The expression is quite unusual (literally, "from beyond the Jordan to the west"). Cf. מ/בעבר לירדן ימה, "(from) beyond the Jordan to the sea" (Josh 5:1; 22:7).

26:31. "Jeriah" *(yryh)*. Jeriah *(yryhw)* is also mentioned as "head" of Ḥebron's sons in 23:19. There his male siblings are also listed.

"the fortieth year of the reign of David." In the Chronicler's reckoning, David ruled for forty years (29:27). The authors of the material relating to David's administrative arrangements consistently situate these initiatives in the final stage of David's reign (23:1). Note also the claim that "among the last commands of David," the Levites were subject to a census (23:27).

"Jaazer of Gilead" *(yʿzyr glʿd)* is said to belong to the Amorites (Num 21:24 [LXX], 32; 32:1–3, 35). Although Jaazer is mentioned in other texts (Josh 13:25; 21:39; 2 Sam 24:5; 1 Macc 5:8; 2 Macc 10:24–38 [*gzr*]; Goldstein 1976: 297–98; 1983: 391–99), its precise location is disputed (B. MacDonald 2000: 106–8). Most would place it south of the Jabbok and west of the Jordan River. Specific suggestions include Khirbet Jazzir, at the head of the Wâdī Šuʿayb, and Khirbet eṣ-Ṣâr, about 11 km west of Rabbath-ammon. Particularly interesting in the present context is the appearance of Jaazer in the lists of Levitical towns (Josh 21:39; MT 1 Chr 6:66 [cf. LXX *Gazēr*]). In this instance, the Transjordan—the home of Reuben, Gad, and Half-Manasseh—receives special mention as an area administered directly by David's civil servants. The text presumes a long reach for Jerusalem's central authorities. Noticing the occurrence of Jaazer in the Levitical town lists, some scholars (e.g., Aharoni 1979: 302) take the analysis a step further. The sites in these lists were purportedly administered by Levites because they were part of the government's land holdings. The theory has an advantage over less plausible theories (e.g., Curtis and Madsen 1910), but the Levitical-town hypothesis also has its problems. It is unclear, for instance, why supervisors are not listed for the other towns as well. Moreover, if our passage is to be cited as evidence for a central administrative strategy, that strategy may not be keyed to the Levitical towns at all. The references in vv. 30 ("Israel beyond the Jordan") and 32 ("the Reubenites, the Gadites, and the half-tribe of Manassites") are geographical and tribal in nature. Historically speaking, one cannot discount another factor: the author's interest in this area is related to the circumstances of his own time. The land of Gilead in the Transjordan was the home of not a small number of Jews during the Maccabean era (1 Macc 5:17–54; cf. Josephus, *Ant.* 12.329–330; Goldstein 1976). The beginnings of this population growth may have taken place in the age of the Chronicler.

26:32. "kinsmen." Along with the tasks meted out to the other Ḥebronites, Ḥashabiah and his kinsmen (v. 30) have, therefore, a major responsibility (vv. 30–32).

"the Reubenites, the Gadites, and the half-tribe of Manassites." The author(s) of Chronicles takes a special interest in the Transjordan (COMMENT on 5:1–26).

"for every matter *(dābār)* of God and for (every) matter *(dābār)* of the king." The expression, *dbr-yhwh* (or *h'lhym*)/*dbr-hmlk*, "matter(s) of Yhwh (or God)/matter(s) of the king," is only found in Chronicles (1 Chr 26:30, 32; 2 Chr 19:11). The differentiation made in Ezra 7:26 *(dtʾ dy-ʾlhk wdtʾ dy mlkʾ)* between "the law of your God and the law of the king" is similar. On this critical Persian period distinction, see further the 2nd NOTE to 25:5.

## SOURCES AND COMPOSITION

The larger issues in reconstructing the composition of 1 Chr 26 have been dealt with in our earlier discussion of the material pertaining to the gatekeepers (26:1–19). It remains to discuss the material directly outlining the purview of the Levitical supervisors. As with vv. 1–19 there are some significant text-critical issues with vv. 20–32 that inevitably affect any source-critical or redaction-critical reconstruction. In this context, lower criticism is very much tied to higher criticism *(Introduction)*.

In its present form vv. 23–32 are a single unit. The rubric mentioning "the Amramites, the Izharites, the Ḥebronites, the Uzzielites" (v. 23) is followed by subsections pertaining to the first three of these families: the Amramites (vv. 23–28), the Izharites (v. 29), and the Ḥebronites (vv. 30–32). Against the background of these three specific Qohathite clans, the material relating to Gershonite Laadan (vv. 21–22) stands out. But even here one can discern that an effort has been made to integrate this notice into a larger context. The introduction of v. 20 mentions that both "the treasuries of the House of God and the treasuries of the dedicated gifts" are the charge of the Levites. The former treasuries of the House of Yhwh are administered by Laadan's descendants (v. 22), while the treasuries of the dedicated gifts are administered by (Amramite) Shelomoth and his kinsmen (v. 26).

In spite of these signs of unity, there are also some significant signs of disunity. The text speaks of "the Amramites, the Izharites, the Ḥebronites, (and) the Uzzielites" (v. 23), yet no Uzzielites appear in the list that follows (vv. 24–32). This may suggest the partial citation of a source (Williamson 1982b: 171–72) or the use of a truncated source. The introduction speaks of the treasuries both of the House of God and of the dedicated gifts (v. 20), yet the text enigmatically speaks of

Shubael as "commander over the treasuries" (v. 24; NOTE). Some names in the passage overlap with names in earlier lists (especially 23:7–20), yet the configuration of relationships among the names sometimes varies between the two texts (NOTES). All of this evidence suggests that an editor has employed and only partially revised or supplemented a source (e.g., Williamson 1982b; R. Braun 1986; Steins 1995; Dirksen 1998a). Unfortunately, the precise contours of such a putative source are not easily recovered. Steins (1995: 327–31) thinks that a primary layer of vv. 20, 21*, 22, 24–28* has been supplemented by vv. 21, 29–32 as part of a larger "musician-gatekeeper" expansion. By contrast, Dirksen (1998a: 145–49) reconstructs a source in vv. 21b, 22–24, 29, 30 that has been supplemented in vv. 20, 21a, 25–28, 31, 32 by the author of 1 Chr 23–27.

## COMMENT

Having outlined the assignments of priests, Levites, and gatekeepers at the projected Jerusalem Temple, the authors turn to the deployment of Levites in other positions within the royal administration. The depiction of Levitical supervision over the treasuries and outlying regions in David's domain presupposes a centralized state with a significant degree of influence in peripheral areas. These remote areas are portrayed as integral components of a larger domain rather than as semi-independent or marginal territories. Some Levitical functionaries are employed as overseers over the treasuries, while others are employed to supervise political and judicial affairs on the west and east banks of the Jordan River. The Davidic regime thus has a long reach, but such a system of governance does not do away with the older tribal system altogether. The civil servants are all drawn from one tribe (Levi) and serve members of all the other tribes (e.g., v. 32). The central government coexists with traditional sodalities.

This picture is broadly congruent with Chronistic theology. In the highly stylized portrayal of the Judahite monarchy, strong kings (or formerly weak monarchs who have mended their ways) build public structures, support the Jerusalem shrine, accumulate large armies, maintain contacts with tribal leaders, reclaim lost people and territories, gainfully employ the priests and Levites, receive tribute, implement new initiatives, and institute nationwide reforms. Weak kings (or formerly strong monarchs who have lost their way) yield territory, lose wars, send tribute to other powers, forfeit recognition, neglect the Jerusalem Temple and its attendant cultus, support other sanctuaries, and often suffer harm. In this respect, the reign of David and that of his successor, Solomon, create a positive paradigm to which later kings may aspire.

In what follows, I will focus on the changing fortunes of the treasuries as a foray into the world of the Chronistic theology (see further Knoppers 1999e). The national treasuries (*ʾôṣĕrôt*), whether of shrine or palace (vv. 22, 24, 26), are a consistent interest of both the Deuteronomist (1 Kgs 7:51; 14:26; 15:18; 2 Kgs 12:18; 14:14; 16:8; 18:15; 20:13–15; 24:13) and the Chronicler (1 Chr 9:26; 26:20–26;

27:25–28; 28:12; 29:8; 2 Chr 5:1; 8:15; 11:11; 12:9; 16:2; 25:24; 32:27–29; 36:18). That this is so should not be surprising. In the ancient Near East, palace and temple complexes—as places of worship and as fortified depositories—were home to many of the nation's valuables. Both the Samuel-Kings and Chronicles chart the history of the treasuries during the heyday of the United Kingdom, the repeated despoliations in the era of the dual monarchies, and the disaster of the Babylonian exile. What is particularly revealing in comparing these two major works is the extent to which Chronicles presents this record more positively than Samuel-Kings does. In Chronicles one also finds a systematic attempt to relate the fortunes of the national treasuries to larger themes in Israelite life.

In the Deuteronomistic History, the reign of Solomon marks a period of unprecedented prosperity and peace. The Temple and palace are built (1 Kgs 6–7), the Temple is dedicated (1 Kgs 8), and tribute flows into Jerusalem from the nations (1 Kgs 10). But this time of opulence and glory comes to an abrupt end with Solomon's sins and the advent of the divided monarchy (1 Kgs 11:1–12:20). In later times the temple treasuries do not fare very well. In narrating the history of Judah, the Deuteronomists mention a series of temple and palace plunderings by a variety of monarchs (Meier 1984; Mullen 1992; Na'aman 1995a). If, economically speaking, Solomon marks a time of unparalleled wealth and grandeur, the divided monarchy marks a time of repeated assaults of the temple and palace treasuries. Raids are carried out by both foreign and domestic kings. The first foreign monarch to do so is Shishaq, who fleeces the palace and temple treasuries during the reign of Reḥoboam (1 Kgs 14:26). More than three centuries later, Nebuchadnezzar empties the same during Jehoiachin's brief and ill-fated reign (2 Kgs 24:13). During the reign of Zedeqiah, Nebuzaradan, the chief guard of Nebuchadnezzar, burns and destroys the House of God itself (2 Kgs 25:9, 13–17). In addition to raids by these foreign monarchs, there is one incident of an Israelite king, Jehoash, who plunders the Jerusalem treasuries during the reign of Amaziah (2 Kgs 14:14).

Kings also describes how some Judahite kings plunder their own treasuries to achieve a variety of foreign-policy goals. Asa takes "all the silver and the gold remaining in the treasuries of the House of Yhwh and the treasuries of the royal palace" and dispatches them to Ben-hadad of Damascus to induce the Syrian king to ward off an attack against Judah by Baasha of Israel (1 Kgs 15:18). Joash takes a more direct approach. He seizes all the dedicated gifts of his predecessors—Jehoshaphaṭ, Jehoram, and Aḥaziah—along with the gold found in the palace and temple treasuries and sends them all to Ḥazael of Aram to convince him to desist from launching a campaign against Jerusalem (2 Kgs 12:18). Aḥaz employs a similar strategy to the one successfully implemented by Asa. He sends the silver and gold from the palace and temple treasuries to Tiglath-pileser III of Assyria as a bribe *(šōḥad)* to ward off a joint attack by Rezin of Syria and Peqaḥ of Israel (2 Kgs 16:8). King Ḥezeqiah, who delivers all of the silver found in the Temple and in the palace treasuries to Sennacherib (2 Kgs 18:15), also dispatches bullion gained by stripping the gold from the temple doors and posts, which Ḥezeqiah himself had plated (2 Kgs 18:16). In Kings there is one other incident that involves the national coffers. Ḥezeqiah is faulted for showing off his treasuries to the Babylonian embassies of Merodoch-baladan (2 Kgs 20:13–15), an event that carries the stigma of being linked to a future Babylonian deportation (2 Kgs 20:14–18).

Of all the kings of Judah mentioned, only one, Asa, actually makes a donation of dedicated gifts (those of his fathers) to the House of God, presumably to the temple treasuries (1 Kgs 15:15). But this same king soon takes "all the silver and gold remaining in the treasuries of the house of Yhwh and the treasuries of the royal palace" and dispatches them to Ben-hadad as a treaty inducement (1 Kgs 15:18). The long history of despoliations ends with the looting of the Temple during the reign of Jehoiachin (2 Kgs 24:13) and the destruction of the Temple (2 Kgs 25:9, 13–17) during the reign of Zedeqiah. These last two incidents are associated with a series of exiles (2 Kgs 24:10–12, 14–17; 25:1–7, 11–12, 18–26) that result in an empty and devastated land.

The testimony of Chronicles is both more complex and more hopeful. The picture differs from Kings in four important respects. First, the writer dwells on the establishment and endowment of the treasuries in the United Monarchy. His presentation of the treasuries includes significant involvement by both David and Solomon. In contrast, the Deuteronomist first raises the issue of the temple treasuries in his presentation of Solomon's reign (1 Kgs 7:51). To be sure, Solomon's endowment of the central sanctuary is made possible by David's beneficence (2 Sam 8:9–12), but the Deuteronomistic treatment of David does not contain any explicit reference to endowments for the national treasury. In Samuel-Kings, the reign of Solomon, and not that of David, features incomparable prosperity (1 Kgs 3:4–14; 10:23–25; Knoppers 1992b: 411–17).

The Chronicler's treatment of David contains a series of extended references to the treasuries in particular and to Israel's wealth in general. In his treatment of David's military triumphs, the Chronicler, unlike the Deuteronomist, overtly connects David's war dedications (1 Chr 18:7–8a, 9–11//2 Sam 8:7–11) with Solomon's Temple. The bronze David captures from Hadadezer is employed by Solomon to construct "the bronze sea, the columns, and the bronze furnishings" (1 Chr 18:8b). The emphasis on the complementarity of David and Solomon's reigns is a hallmark of the Chronicler's presentation of the United Monarchy (R. Braun 1973; 1976; Williamson 1976). To prepare for the transition to his son's reign, an elder but still lucid monarch establishes a national administration to serve Solomon (23:1–27:34). Part of this planning involves the appointment of Levitical supervisors for the treasuries of the Temple and the treasuries of the dedicated gifts (26:20–26). The Gershonites are put in charge of the former, while the Qohathites are put in charge of the latter. In addition to the appointments made for these treasuries, appointments are made both for the royal treasuries and for the treasuries in the country, towns, and citadels (27:25).

David not only anticipates the construction of the House of God along with its associated treasuries, but he also—through the aegis of God's spirit—designs these structures. In his second speech to Solomon, David delivers the model *(tabnît)* for the entire temple complex, including the temple courts, chambers, furniture, and utensils (28:11–19). Much like inspired Moses before him, who produces a plan *(tabnît)* for the Tabernacle and its furnishings (Exod 25:9, 40), David bequeaths a plan for the Temple, along with its appurtenances, to his heir. The grand architectural design includes blueprints for "the treasuries of the House of God and the treasuries of the dedicated gifts" (1 Chr 28:12). A related part of this strategic planning involves endowments. According to 26:26, the treasury of the dedicated gifts housed donations made by David, the ancestral heads, and the commanders of thousands and hundreds. War spoils were used to strengthen the House of Yhwh (26:27). Major benefactors, whose dedications make their way to the treasury, include Samuel the seer, Saul son of Qish, Abner son of Ner, and Joab son of Zeruiah (26:28). It seems that in Chronicles any Israelite contemporary of David who was of any consequence and who ever waged war makes a dedicatory gift. In his speech to the entire assembly (29:1–5), David makes a concerted pitch to enlarge this elite circle of benefactors. He speaks of his generosity toward the House of God, including the setting aside of a considerable supply of gold and silver, but he also beckons those gathered to make their own freewill offerings. The assembly *(qāhāl)* does not disappoint. The military, clan, and tribal leaders all make incredibly generous donations to the work of the Temple, involving thousands of talents of gold, darics, silver, bronze, and iron (29:6–7). The plentiful gifts for the Temple provided by these leaders include (precious) stones to the temple treasury (29:8).

The endowments created in the time of David are put to good use by Solomon. He brings David's dedicatory gifts, the silver, the gold, and all of the furnishings into the treasuries of the Temple (2 Chr 5:1). David's provisions for the Levitical supervisors are also implemented. In Solomon's reign there was no departure from "the command of the king concerning the priests and the Levites in any matter, including the treasuries" (2 Chr 8:15). As in Kings, Solomon's reign is a time of heightened prosperity (2 Chr 1:5–17; 9:22). Tribute flows in from the nations (2 Chr 8:17–9:28). Together with the material on David's reign, the references to Solomon's accomplishments create an enduring and highly positive image of the United Monarchy's legacy for subsequent generations. The self-denial practiced by David and Israel's leaders is rewarded by Solomon's achievements. In Chronicles, the Temple is not simply a royal chapel planned by one Davidic king and built by another but also the patrimony of all the people. Similarly, the very success of the national treasuries results from both royal and popular largess. David and Solomon establish a consistent pattern of support for and enhancement of national institutions.

David's planning and endowments are properly exploited by Solomon, but the era of the dual monarchies is not such a success. In his narration of Judahite history, the Chronicler follows Samuel-Kings in recording a series of Jerusalem temple despoliations by domestic and foreign foes (2 Chr 12:9; 16:2; 25:24). But the important deviations between the two works are of both a historical and a theological nature. To begin with, Chronicles does not mention all of the despoliations recorded in Kings (1 Kgs 14:26; 15:18; 2 Kgs 12:18; 14:14; 16:8; 18:15; 20:13–15). In agreement with his source, the author mentions raids on the shrine or palace treasuries during the reigns of Reḥoboam (1 Kgs 14:26//2 Chr 12:9), Asa (1 Kgs

15:18//2 Chr 16:2), Amaziah (2 Kgs 14:14//2 Chr 25:24), and Aḥaz (2 Kgs 16:8//2 Chr 28:21), although his version of these despoliations sometimes varies markedly from that of Kings (Knoppers 1999e).

But there are also two omissions that directly affect the larger history of Judah. The treatment of King Joash (2 Chr 24:1–27) makes no mention of his pillaging the temple and palace treasuries to prevent a potential attack on Jerusalem by King Ḥazael of Syria (2 Kgs 12:17–18). The writer also makes a number of important changes to the Deuteronomistic account of Ḥezeqiah's reign, including his relationship to the temple and palace treasuries. The Chronicler does not include any account of Ḥezeqiah's looting of "all the silver found in the House of Yhwh and in the treasuries of the royal palace" as a tribute payment to King Sennacherib of Assyria (2 Kgs 18:15). Nor is there any mention of Ḥezeqiah's stripping of the temple doors and posts to augment his tribute payment to the Assyrian king (2 Kgs 18:16). In short, the entire tribute episode in Kings (2 Kgs 18:13–16) is missing from Chronicles. Finally, the Chronicler only briefly and obliquely alludes to Ḥezeqiah's reception of the Babylonian envoys of Merodoch-baladan, in which he showed them his entire storehouse, the silver, gold, spices, and fine oil—"all that was found in his treasuries" (2 Kgs 20:12–13). The whole matter of the Babylonian envoys is summarily mentioned as a divinely administered test of Ḥezeqiah's character (2 Chr 32:31). The implication may be that he failed this test, but the whole matter is shrouded in ambiguity (Ackroyd 1987). In any event, the Chronicler makes no connection between this particular incident and a future Babylonian exile. The effect of these omissions is to reduce the number and pattern of treasury raids found in Kings.

Second, the presentation also differs from that of Kings in that the Chronicler overtly posits times of economic renewal for Jerusalem and Judah. Some recoveries are marked by the construction of new treasuries or storehouses *('ôṣĕrôt)* or new contributions to them, but others are not. In any event, the larger picture is clear. Despoliations are balanced by periods of recovery and the amassing of wealth by some of Judah's kings. The first such reformer is, in fact, the first king of the independent state of Judah, Reḥoboam. Following the disaster of Israel's secession, he recovers and oversees a number of reforms (2 Chr 11:5–23). These include strengthening the fortified towns and locating storehouses *('ôṣĕrôt)* of food, wine, and oil within these towns (2 Chr 11:11–12).

King Asa also institutes a series of positive reforms. But as in the Deuteronomistic History, Asa's legacy vis-à-vis the treasuries is mixed. Asa both makes a number of dedications to the Temple (2 Chr 15:18) and empties the shrine and royal treasuries to induce Ben-hadad to attack an invading Baasha of Israel (2 Chr 16:2). But the Chronicler distances the two incidents from one another by placing them within two distinct phases of Asa's reign, one long and progressive (2 Chr 14:1–15:19) and the other short and regressive (2 Chr 16:1–10). This brings us to an important theological difference between the two works. In the Deuteronomistic History, royal raids on national treasuries are not an integral element in the evaluation of a king's reign. Four out of six kings associated with treasury raids are rated positively: Asa (1 Kgs 15:11–14), Joash (2 Kgs 12:3–4 [ET 12:2–3]),

Amaziah (2 Kgs 14:3–4), and Ḥezeqiah (2 Kgs 18:3–6). Moreover, the one king who is associated with two negative treasury incidents, Ḥezeqiah, happens to be one of the most highly esteemed kings in the entire work (2 Kgs 18:3–6). The Deuteronomistic judgments of northern and southern kings center on whether a king supports the centralization of the Yahwistic cultus in Jerusalem *(Kultusreinheit)* and whether he eliminates other cults *(Kultuseinheit)*. One could argue that the larger pattern of treasury onslaughts contributes toward a larger sense of doom, but whether a given monarch raided the treasuries is not a productive theological concern in evaluating the record of that monarch.

The situation is different in Chronicles. The author integrates royal actions toward the treasuries into his larger presentation and evaluation of a monarch's reign. He does this in a variety of ways. In the case of Asa, whom he evaluates positively (2 Chr 14:1–3), he situates his contributions to the treasury in the productive stage of Asa's tenure, while he consigns the raid on the treasuries to the regressive part of his tenure. In the case of Reḥoboam, whom the Chronicler evaluates negatively (2 Chr 12:14), he consigns the raid on the treasuries to one of the regressive periods of his reign (2 Chr 12:1–9), while he contextualizes Reḥoboam's construction of treasuries to one of the reform periods of his reign (2 Chr 11:1–23). In the case of Ḥezeqiah, whom the author evaluates most highly (2 Chr 29:2), he does not mention a treasury raid at all. Quite the contrary, Ḥezeqiah builds treasuries and endows them. By employing these disparate textual strategies, the Chronicler does more than offer a variant picture from that of Kings. He creates a larger sense of balance and coherence within his narration.

The period of renewal in Asa's reign is matched by one in his successor Jehoshaphaṭ's reign. In the first part of his tenure, unparalleled in Kings, Jehoshaphaṭ implements reforms, deploys troops, and fortifies cities (2 Chr 17:1–2). In so doing, he grows stronger and more widely respected. Yhwh's establishment of Jehoshaphaṭ's realm is echoed in the acclamation of his people. All of Judah brings tribute to the new king, who, like Solomon, experiences "riches and honor in abundance." In fact, some of Judah's neighbors send great tribute *(minḥâ)* and silver to Jehoshaphaṭ (2 Chr 17:11). Jehoshaphaṭ, in turn, builds fortresses and storage towns *(ʿārê miskĕnôt)* in Judah (2 Chr 17:12–13a).

The positive contributions made by one reformer, Jehoshaphaṭ, are renewed by another, Ḥezeqiah (2 Chr 32:27–30). Ḥezeqiah builds himself treasuries *(ʾôṣĕrôt)* to house silver, gold, precious stones, shields, and a variety of expensive utensils (2 Chr 32:27). This is but one indication of the great prosperity that attends his latter reign (2 Chr 32:28–30). That King Ḥezeqiah builds and endows the national treasuries marks a complete reversal of the picture in Kings. There, as we have seen, Ḥezeqiah despoils the temple treasuries to ward off an invading Sennacherib (2 Kgs 18:13–16). In Kings the end of Ḥezeqiah's reign is marred by the specter of a future Babylonian exile, but in Chronicles the end of Ḥezeqiah's reign is largely a story of economic success. In constructing and supporting the national treasuries, Ḥezeqiah's reign recalls some of the glories of the United Monarchy.

The point in discussing the accomplishments and wealth of Judah's kings is not that the Chronicler portrays the history of the divided monarchy as a glorious age.

He clearly does not. The time of David and Solomon is the highpoint of Israelite history. But the Chronicler does present Judah's economic fortunes as mixed—a record of both substantial declines and substantial recoveries. More important than the question of whether the Judahite monarchy was good or bad is the pattern established during this age. Virtually every regression is followed by a recovery. Each monarch has the wherewithal to reverse the course set by his ancestors and, indeed, to reverse his own course (von Rad 1962b; B. Kelly 1996). In this, the Chronicler's writing departs markedly from the pattern evident in the final edition of the Deuteronomistic History, a work that has been described by one scholar as a history of destruction (Japhet 1989). For the Chronicler, the looting of the palace or temple treasuries by some kings is offset by the prosperity and dedications of others.

The third way in which the Chronicler revises the Deuteronomistic presentation of the national treasuries is in his version of Judah's final years of independence. The Chronicler's depiction of the events leading up to the Babylonian exile is less severe and more temperate than that of the Deuteronomistic work. Whereas the final chapters of Kings depict a series of devastating exiles and temple lootings, Chronicles briefly depicts two plunders, one during the reign of Jehoiachin, which sends the sanctuary furnishings to Babylon (2 Chr 36:7, 10), and another during the reign of King Zedeqiah, which dispatches all of the sanctuary furnishings along with the temple treasures to Babylon (2 Chr 36:18). The final destruction of the Temple and plundering of its contents is described in only two verses (2 Chr 36:18–19; cf. 2 Kgs 25:9, 13–17). The Chronicler's version of the temple plunder and destruction has two complementary effects. It plays down the devastation wrought by the Babylonian invasions (Japhet 1989), and it creates a continuity theme vis-à-vis the temple vessels (Ackroyd 1987). Whereas Kings presents two temple lootings, the first of which results in the deportation of the temple and palace treasures (2 Kgs 24:13) and the second of which results in the destruction of the Temple and all its contents (2 Kgs 25:9, 13–17), Chronicles consistently portrays a Babylonian destination for both the temple furnishings (2 Chr 36:7, 10) and the temple and palace treasures (2 Chr 36:18). Given the emphasis in Ezra-Nehemiah (e.g., Ezra 1:7–11; 2:68–69; 5:14–15; 6:5) on the return and reuse of the temple furnishings, one can say that in Chronicles, Ezra, and Nehemiah there is a clear continuity between the pre- and postexilic ages.

But a positive fate for the sanctuary furnishings is adumbrated in Chronicles itself. This brings us to the fourth way in which the handling of the national treasuries differs from that of Samuel-Kings. The genealogical introduction contains an account of the (re)establishment of services for the Second Temple (1 Chr 9:23–33). This passage mentions that four chief gatekeepers *(gibbôrê haššōʿărîm)* are placed in charge of the temple chambers and treasuries (9:26). The pattern of disruption and recovery that characterizes the history of the Judahite monarchy is also present here. Although the story of Israel's development in the land is ended by the Babylonian deportations (2:3–9:1), it is resumed in the Persian period (9:2–34). The exile becomes only an interruption in the ongoing story of Israel and its national institutions.

The theme of continuity in spite of upheaval is also present at the end of the monarchy. Although Chronicles retells the disaster of the Babylonian exile, along with the destruction of the Temple, the book ends with the summons of King Cyrus of Persia to rebuild the Jerusalem Temple (2 Chr 36:22–23). In this respect, the treatment of the sanctuary's fate is a good example of the generally optimistic view of history found within this book. By mentioning the decree of Cyrus authorizing the rebuilding of the Temple, the work ends by pointing back, however tentatively, toward the foundations first laid by David centuries earlier.

# *XXXIII. Military and Tribal Officers (27:1–24)*

*Introduction to the Census of David's Non-Levitical Leaders*

1 The sons of Israel by their census: the ancestral heads, the officers of thousands and of the hundreds, and the officials—those serving the king for every matter of the rotating divisions, month by month throughout all of the months of the year. Each division had 24,000.

*Twelve Divisions; Twelve Officers*

2 In charge of the first division for the first month: Jashobeam son of Zabdiel
3 from the sons of Perez and the head of all of the army officers for the first month. [2 His division had 24,000.]

4 In charge of the division of the second month: Dodai the Aḥoḥite. His division had 24,000.

5 The third army officer for the third month: Benaiah son of the chief priest Jehoiada. His division had 24,000.
6 That one, Benaiah, was a warrior of the Thirty and in command of the Thirty. His son Ammizabad was in command of his division.

7 The fourth for the fourth month: Asah-el brother of Joab, and after him Zebadiah his son. His division had 24,000.

8 The fifth for the fifth month: the officer Shammoth the Zeraḥite. His division had 24,000.

9 The sixth for the sixth month: Ira son of Iqqesh the Teqoaite. His division had 24,000.

10 The seventh for the seventh month: Ḥelez the Pelonite, of the sons of Ephraim. His division had 24,000.

11 The eighth for the eighth month: Sibbekai the Ḥushathite, of the Zeraḥites. His division had 24,000.

12 The ninth for the ninth month: Abiezer the Anathothite, of the Benjaminites. His division had 24,000.

13 The tenth for the tenth month: Mahrai the Neṭophathite, of the Zeraḥites. His division had 24,000.

14 The eleventh for the eleventh month: Benaiah the Pirathonite, from the sons of Ephraim. His division had 24,000.

15 The twelfth for the twelfth month: Ḥeldai the Neṭophathite, of Othniel. His division had 24,000.

*Thirteen Tribal Officers*

16 In charge of the tribes of Israel:
for the Reubenites: the commander was Eliezer son of Zichri;
for the Simeonites: Shephaṭiah son of Maacah;
17 for the Levites: Ḥashabiah son of Qemuel;
for Aaron: Zadoq;
18 for Judah: Eliab, of the brothers of David;
for Issachar: Omri son of Michael;
19 for Zebulun: Ishmaiah son of Obadiah;
for Naphtali: Jerimoth son of Azriel;
20 for the sons of Ephraim: Hoshea son of Azaziah;
for the half-tribe of Manasseh: Joel son of Pedaiah;
21 for the half-tribe of Manasseh in Gilead: Iddo son of Zechariah;
for Benjamin: Jaasiel son of Abner;
22 for Dan: Azarel son of Jeroḥam.

These were the officers of the tribes of Israel.
23 But David did not take a census of those less than twenty years of age because God had promised to make Israel as numerous as the stars of the heavens.
24 Joab son of Zeruiah began to number (them), but he did not finish. Wrath came upon Israel on account of this and the census was not entered into the book of the chronicles of King David.

# Textual Notes

27:1. "(and) the sons of Israel by their census" *(wbny yśrʾl lmsprm)*. For the terminology, see also vv. 23–24.

"the officers of thousands and of the hundreds." The construct chain with a single construct and two absolutes is unusual (1st TEXTUAL NOTE to 28:13).

"the officials" *(šṭrym)*. A restoration. MT "their officials" *(šṭryhm)*; LXX "scribes" (*grammateis* = *swprym*).

"the king." Reading with MT *(lectio brevior)*. LXX prefaces *tō laō kai*, "to the people and." Allen (1974a: 145–46) thinks that the formulation of LXX 27:1 has been influenced by a marginal comment on 26:32, but it is also possible that this phrase was lost by haplography *(homoioarkton;* את-העם ו before את-המלך "the king").

"for every matter of the (rotating) divisions" (לכל דבר המחלקות). LXX presents a slightly different text and sequence, *eis pan logon tou baslieōs kata diaireseis* (= לכל דבר המלך למחלקות), "for every matter of the king according to divisions."

"rotating." Literally, "the one coming in and the one going out" *(hbʾh whyṣʾt)*. Again, LXX reads somewhat differently, "every matter of coming in and going out" (*pan* [LXX$^{LN}$ *panta*] *logon tou eisporeuomenou kai ek* [LXX$^{L}$ *eis*] *poreuomenou*). The expression "coming in and going out" often refers to military or administrative experience (Num 27:17; Deut 28:6; 31:2; Josh 14:11; 1 Sam 18:13; 2 Sam 5:2;

Isa 37:28; van der Lingen 1992: 59–66). Hence, at Gibeon Solomon speaks of himself as "a small youth," an inexperienced leader who "does not know how to go out or to come in" (1 Kgs 3:7; Knoppers 1993c: 81–82). In this context, the locution has a literal meaning, referring to rotating shifts.

"each." Literally, "the one" *(hʾḥt)*. On the use of *ʾḥt* (and *ʾḥd*) to mark an indefinite noun, see Waltke and O'Connor (§13.8a).

27:2. "Jashobeam" *(yšbʿm)*. So MT. LXX$^{B}$ *Sobal;* LXX$^{A}$ *Isboam;* $c_2$ *Sobaa;* LXX$^{L}$ *Iesboam;* Arm. *Iezbaal.* On the basis of Arm. and certain witnesses to 2 Sam 23:8 (MT *yšb bšbt;* LXX$^{B}$ *Iebosthe;* LXX$^{L}$ *Iesbaal*); 1 Chr 11:11 (MT *yšbʿm;* LXX$^{B}$ *Iesebada;* bb′ *Iessebaal*); and 12:7 (MT *yšbʿm;* LXX$^{B}$ *Sobokam;* LXX$^{ALN}$ *Iesbaam;* Arm. *Iezbaam*), some reconstruct an original "Ishbaal" *(ʾyšbʿl)*. "Ishbaal" may well be the original Samuel reading as Wellhausen (1871: 212), Budde (1902: 319), and McCarter (1984: 82, 489) all suggest, but Chronicles presents, in this instance, a different or later stage of textual development.

"son of Zabdiel." So MT and LXX (maximum differentiation). The textual witnesses to Chronicles and Samuel differ about Jashobeam's patronymic (3rd TEXTUAL NOTE to 11:11).

27:3. "Perez" *(prṣ)*. So MT. LXX *Phares.*

"the head of all of the army officers" *(hrʾš lkl-śry hṣbʾwt)*. LXX* *archōn pantōn tōn archontōn* lacks the article.

"his division had 24,000." A restoration. In MT (and LXX), this clause appears as the final clause of v. 2 *(wʿl mḥlqtw ʿśrym wʾrbʿh ʾlp)*. Hence, the transition from v. 2 to v. 3 reads "son of Zabdiel. His division had 24,000." Transposing this clause to the end of v. 3 has the double merit of clearing up the awkward sequence of v. 2 and of conforming vv. 2–3 to the pattern regularly followed in vv. 4–15.

27:4. "Dodai" *(dwdy)*. So MT and LXX$^{L}$ (b′ *Dodai;* bye$_2$ *Dōdai*). Arm. *Dudayi.* Cf. LXX$^{B*}$ *Dōdeia* (= *dwdyh*); $c_2$ *Dōleia;* LXX$^{A}$ *Dōeia.* The text of 11:12 prefaces אלעזר בן-, "Eleazar son of" (cf. Kethib 2 Sam 23:9 *ʾlʿzr bn-ddy*). Cf. 1 Chr 11:26 "Elḥanan son of Dodoi from Bethleḥem" (TEXTUAL NOTE). In 11:12 we read "Dodai" *(dwdy)* with LXX$^{BL}$ *Dōdai.* The reading of MT 11:12 and of Qere 2 Sam 23:9, "Dodo" *(dwdw)*, reflects a *wāw/yôd* confusion. Note also Kethib 2 Sam 23:9 *ddy.* Some (e.g., Zöckler 1877: 151; Kittel 1902: 99; Curtis and Madsen 1910: 290) restore the full reading of 11:12, but it is difficult to determine what precisely would have triggered such a haplography.

"the Aḥoḥite." So LXX *(lectio brevior)*. MT adds "and his division and Miqloth the commander." The whole phrase is lacking in LXX* and may have arisen as an insertion through repetitive resumption (from *wmḥlqtw* to *wʿl wmḥlqtw*). Note the suspicious "Miqloth" *(mqlwt)* after *wmḥlqtw.*

27:5. "the chief priest." Reading *hkhn hrʾš* with LXX *ho hiereus ho archōn.* Cf. 2 Chr 31:10; Ezra 7:5. MT *hkhn rʾš.*

27:6. "a warrior of the Thirty" *(gbwr hšlšym)*. Thus MT and LXX. Many Heb. MSS and Tg. read "a warrior among the Thirty" *(gbwr bšlšym)*, thus assimilating toward the formulation of (MT) 2 Sam 23:24.

"and in command of the Thirty" *(wʿl-hšlšym)*. So MT and LXX*. Believing that a haplography has occurred, Rudolph (1955: 178) omits the initial *wāw* (cf. cursives hze$_2$) and prefaces "and was placed" *(wyśm)* to "in command of the Thirty" *(ʿl hšlšym)*.

"his son Ammizabad was in command of his division" *(wʿl mḥlqtw ʿmyzbd bnw)*. So LXX and Vg. MT lacks "in command of" (= *ʿal*).

27:7. "after him" *(ʾḥryw)*. Thus MT. LXX$^{B}$ "and the brothers" (= *whʾḥym; pace* Allen 1974b: 127). LXX$^{L}$ and Arm. conflate the two readings.

27:8. "Shammoth" *(šmwt)*. Reading with MT 11:27 *(šmwt)* and LXX$^{B}$ 11:27 *Sammaōth* (= *šmwt*). MT 27:7 "Shamhuth" (*šmhwt;* cf. LXX$^{L}$ *Samaōth*) reflects the combination of two readings: MT 1 Chr 11:27 *šmwt* and MT 2 Sam 23:25 *šmh*.

"the Zeraḥite" *(hzrḥy)*. The lemma of MT, "the Izraḥite" *(hyzrḥ)*, found only here, reflects metathesis of the gentilic (*yôd*). Cf. LXX$^{B}$ *ho Esrae;* LXX$^{A}$ *ho Iezrael;* LXX$^{L}$ *ho Iezra*. MT 11:27 "the Harorite" (*hhrwry;* cf. 11:34, 35); LXX$^{B}$ 11:27 *ho hadi*. MT 2 Sam 23:25 "the Ḥarodite" *(hḥrdy)*. See further the TEXTUAL NOTES to 11:27.

27:10. "the Pelonite" *(hplwny)*. So MT. LXX$^{B}$ *ho ek phallous*. MT 2 Sam 23:26 has "the Palṭite" *(hplṭy)*, but LXX$^{ALMN}$ 2 Sam 23:26 reflect *hplwny*.

27:11. "Sibbekai" *(sbky)*. See also 1 Chr 11:29 and 2 Sam 23:27.

27:12. "of the Benjaminites." So Kethib *(labbenyĕmînî)*. Qere *labbēn yĕmînî* (GKC §127d). LXX$^{B}$ *ek gēs Beniamein*.

27:15. "Ḥeldai." So MT (cf. LXX$^{A}$ *ho Choldai*). LXX$^{B}$ *Choldeia;* ye$_2$ *Holdia;* bb′ *Hoddia*. MT 11:30 "Ḥeled" (LXX$^{B}$ *Chthaod;* LXX$^{A}$ *Helad;* c$_2$ *Choaod*). MT 2 Sam 23:29 reads erroneously *ḥēleb* (McCarter 1984: 492).

27:18. "Eliab." So LXX* *(Eliab)* and MT 2:13 *(ʾlyʾb)*. Rudolph's notion that MT 27:18 "Elihu" *(ʾlyhw)* represents David's eighth, elsewhere unnamed, son seems far-fetched.

"Issachar." See the TEXTUAL NOTE to 2:1.

27:19. "Ishmaiah" *(yšmʿyhw)*. LXX *Samaias* and Syr. reflect "Shemaiah" (= *šmʿyhw*).

"Azriel" *(ʿzryʾl)*. So MT here and in MT 1 Chr 5:24; Jer 36:26. LXX$^{B}$ *Esreiēl* (= *ʿēzrîʾēl*) is adopted by Kittel (1895: 71). LXX$^{ALN}$ *Oziēl* (= *ʿzyʾl*).

27:20. "Azaziah" *(ʿzzyhw)*. A few Heb. MSS "Uzziah" *(ʿzyhw)*. LXX *ho tou Ozeiou* (e$_2$ *Aziou;* djmpqtz *Ozaziou*).

27:21. "the half-tribe of Manasseh" *(ḥăṣî šēbeṭ hammĕnaššeh)*. So a few Heb. MSS, LXX$^{AB}$, and Vg., which have the standard expression in Chronicles, *ḥṣy šbṭ (h)mnšh* (1 Chr 5:18, 23, 26; 12:38; 26:32; 27:21; cf. Num 32:33; Deut 29:7; Josh 4:12; 13:7; 18:7; 22:9, 10, 11, 13, 15, 21). The other pertinent expression is *mṭh ḥṣy mnšh*, "half-tribe of Manasseh" (Num 34:14; Josh 12:6; 13:29; 21:27; 22:1; 1 Chr 6:46, 56). MT and LXX$^{L}$ *ḥăṣî hammĕnaššeh*, "Half-Manasseh."

"Iddo" *(yiddô)*. Thus MT. LXX$^{BL}$ *Iaddai* (= *ydy*) reflect a common *wāw/yôd*-confusion.

"Zechariah" *(ṣĕkaryāhû)*. So MT, LXX$^{L}$, and Tg. LXX$^{B}$ *Zabdeiou* (= *ṣbdyhw*) reflects a *dālet/rêš* confusion.

"Jaasiel" *(yaʿăśîʾēl)*. LXX$^{AN}$ *Asiēl* (= *ʿśyʾl*); LXX$^{B}$ *Aseiēr*.

"Abner." Thus MT and cursives djpqtz *(ʾabnēr)*. LXX$^{ABLN}$ *Abennēr* and cursives eh *Abenēr* reflect *ʾăbînēr* (2nd TEXTUAL NOTE to 26:28).

27:22. "Jeroḥam" *(yrḥm)*. Thus MT. LXX[AB] *Iōram* (= *ywrm*); LXX[L] *Ieroam*; $e_2$ *Ieroboam*.

27:24. "the census *(hmspr)* . . . in the book" *(bspr)*. So LXX (maximum differentiation). MT *hmspr* . . . *bmspr* is corrupt, the second *mspr* arising due to influence of the first.

## NOTES

27:1. "by their census" *(mspr)*. The noun *mispār*, "number," both here and in vv. 23–24 denotes a census (1st NOTE to 23:3).

"the officers of thousands and of the hundreds." These military commanders are one of the traditional leadership groups who support David's major initiatives (4th NOTE to 26:26).

"serving the king for every matter of the rotating divisions" (המחלקות). A standard administrative procedure in David's latter reign (1 Chr 23–27) is to implement rotating shifts of personnel to ensure that the major Jerusalem institutions enjoy continuous service (e.g., 23:6 [see NOTE]; 24:1–31; 25:8–31; 26:1–12). The system established here—twelve monthly relays of 24,000 soldiers, each headed by a divisional officer (27:2–16)—reflects the integration of the military wing of David's government. The duodecimal arrangement, calendrically oriented, is designed to furnish the king with a steady supply of military contingents throughout the year. Just as earlier arrangements organized the Levites, singers, priests, and gatekeepers into shifts at their designated stations in Jerusalem, so this arrangement does the same for the military. The orderly reorganization of the armed forces, part of the Davidic legacy, contributes to the centralization of power in Jerusalem.

"month by month throughout all of the months of the year." There are some parallels between the system of military officers depicted in vv. 2–15 and the system of Solomonic officers and districts depicted in 1 Kgs 4:7–19 and 5:7–8. The Deuteronomist portrays a rotating system of twelve districts supplying Solomon with support during each of the twelve months of the year (MT 1 Kgs 4:7–19; 5:7–8; Knoppers 1993c: 83–84). The various Solomonic districts are headed by "officers" (*śrym;* 1 Kgs 4:2) or "prefects" (*nṣbym;* 1 Kgs 4:19; 5:7). Redistricting provides Solomon with regular tribute from all sectors of his domain (1 Kgs 5:7–8). In this respect, there are some parallels with the system of twelve commanders and divisions depicted here. But there are also differences. Solomon's officials and prefects are responsible for various regions of the country, but David's divisional commanders serve in Jerusalem, at least while they are on duty (27:1; Myers 1965a: 183). The system in Chronicles does not entail any process of redistricting. Moreover, the tribal officers are not part of a larger tribute-bearing system. Nevertheless, in both cases (1 Kgs 4–5; 1 Chr 27), the lists draw attention to the king's administrative abilities (Knoppers 1993c: 84–90).

"each division had 24,000." The appearance of this phrase indicates that the rubric of v. 1 serves as the introduction only to the list of vv. 2–15, and not also to the succeeding list of vv. 16–22. The section dealing with divisional officers is regularly punctuated by the phrase "his division had 24,000" (vv. 2, 4, 5, 7–15). In contrast, the list of vv. 16–22 enumerates a succession of tribal officers and makes no reference to divisions.

27:2. "Jashobeam son of Zabdiel." There are some parallels between the names of the twelve officers in vv. 2–15 and those found in 11:10–47 and 2 Sam 23:8–39. But there are also some variants (see TEXTUAL NOTES). By their very nature, the lists of David's warriors in 2 Sam 23 and 1 Chr 11 are much more comprehensive than the select list of David's twelve divisional leaders (27:2–15). The twelve divisional officers are an elite drawn from the ranks of Israel's ancestral heads, military officers, and officials (v. 1; see COMMENT).

27:3. "Perez." The Judahite phratry of which David was one descendant (2:4–15).

27:4. "Dodai *(dwdy)* the Aḥoḥite." In 11:12, "Eleazar son of Dodai" appears as one of David's most seasoned warriors (see TEXTUAL NOTE).

27:5. "Benaiah." Another of David's most accomplished warriors (11:22–25 [see NOTE]; 18:17).

"the chief priest Jehoiada." See also 11:22, which does not mention, however, that Jehoiada was a priest. In the list of 12:28, Jehoiada appears as the leader for Aaron (הנגיד לאהרן). Priestly lineages and martial service are not mutually exclusive (*pace* Benzinger 1901: 79–80), but the reference is surprising as this "chief priest" is otherwise unattested (COMMENT on 5:27–41).

27:6. "Ammizabad" *(ʿammîzābād)*. Not otherwise attested.

27:7. "Asah-el" *(ʿăśâ-ʾēl)*. This brother of Joab (1 Chr 11:26//2 Sam 23:24) was killed by Abner when David was still ruling from Ḥebron (2 Sam 2:18–23), hence the reference to succession by "Zebadiah his son."

27:8. "Shammoth the Zeraḥite." A "Shammoth the Ḥarodite" is mentioned as one of David's valiant warriors in 11:27 (see TEXTUAL NOTE). See the 2nd TEXTUAL NOTE to 27:8.

27:9. "Ira son of Iqqesh the Teqoaite." So also 11:28.

27:11. "Sibbekai the Ḥushathite." Mentioned as one of David's valiant warriors in 11:29 (1st NOTE; cf. 20:4).

27:12. "Abiezer the Anathothite." The same person appears in the list of 11:28 (see NOTE). On Benjaminite Anathoth, see the 2nd NOTE to 7:8.

27:13. "Mahrai the Neṭophathite, of the Zeraḥites." Another of David's valiant warriors (11:30). The "Zeraḥites" are one of the major Judahite phratries (2nd NOTE to 2:4).

27:14. "Benaiah the Pirathonite, from the sons of Ephraim." See also 11:31. Most of the warriors listed in 27:2–15 hail from Judah and Benjamin, but there are also two Ephraimites named (vv. 10, 14). On the Ephraimite town of Pirathon, see the NOTE to 11:31.

27:15. "Ḥeldai the Neṭophathite, of Othniel." Cf. 11:30 and the TEXTUAL NOTE to v. 15. Because of Othniel's relation to Caleb (Josh 15:17; Judg 1:12–15; 3:9), he was incorporated into Judah.

27:16–22. "in charge of the tribes of Israel." Whereas vv. 2–15 delineate twelve military divisions, which are to rotate monthly in service to the crown, the list of vv. 16–22 delineates thirteen officers, each of whom represents a tribe or a tribal subsection. In Chronicles, the tribal principle is never lost sight of, even with the advent of the monarchy (Willi 1972; Japhet 1989). The system of tribal officers (vv. 16–22) may be compared to the system of tribal chieftains implemented during the wilderness period (COMMENT). In this context, the author does not specify what roles these officers played or to what extent they were integrated into the larger national government. Their presence is presupposed in two later contexts. The "tribal officers" *(śry hšbṭym)* are among those convened by David to support the Solomonic succession (28:1). The "officers of the Israelite tribes" *(śry šbṭy yśrʾl)* contribute generous freewill offerings to the temple project (29:6). The tribal officers are thereafter not mentioned again.

27:16. "The Reubenites" head the list as one might expect, given Reuben's status as firstborn (cf. 1st NOTE to 2:3). Yet the tally (vv. 16–22) does not adhere to any other order of the Israelite tribes found elsewhere in the HB (e.g., Gen 35:23–26; 46:8–27; 49:3–27; 1 Chr 2:1–2). Kallai (1997; 1999) provides a helpful overview of the various tribal systems appearing in the HB. In this case, Leah's six sons appear first by order of birth: Reuben, Simeon, Levi, Judah, Issachar, and Zebulun (Gen 29:31–35; 30:17–20; 35:23). The tribes (or divisions of tribes) associated with Rachel (Gen 35:24) and Bilḥah (Gen 35:25) appear next: Naphtali (Gen 30:8; 35:25), Ephraim, Manasseh, Benjamin (Gen 35:24), Dan (Gen 30:6). As befitting the period depicted (the monarchy), Joseph does not appear (cf. Gen 49:22–26; 1 Chr 2:2). Instead, his sons Ephraim and Manasseh are mentioned (Gen 46:19–20). Gad and Asher, the sons of Leah's maid Zilpah (Gen 30:9–13)—who emerge last in some tribal lists (e.g., Gen 35:26; 1 Chr 2:2)—do not appear at all. To achieve a duodecimal aggregate one would either have to count the two halves of Manasseh together as one tribe or count the leaders of Aaron and Levi as representing one tribe.

"Eliezer son of Zichri." To be distinguished from the Eliezer related to Moses (1st NOTE to 23:17).

"Shephaṭiah" (שְׁפַטְיָהוּ). To be distinguished from the Benjaminite with the same name (12:6; cf. 9:8).

"Maacah" *(mʿkh)*. On the different referents of the PN "Maacah," see the 3rd NOTE to 4:19.

27:17. "Levites." The appearance of the Levites in this list is important. The tribe of Levi, no less than other tribes, has its own tribal representative *(śr)*. Early in David's career 4,600 descendants of Levi were part of a larger tribal muster "who came to David at Ḥebron to turn the kingdom of Saul over to him" (12:24).

"Ḥashabiah." A common Levitical name (1st NOTE to 25:3).

"Qemuel." On the name, see also Gen 22:21 (a son of Naḥor) and Num 34:24 (an Ephraimite leader).

"for Aaron: Zadoq." The author presents Aaron as having his own officer in the larger Israelite federation. Given the tribal nature of the list (vv. 16–22) and the earlier mention of the Levites (v. 17), the appearance of Aaron becomes all the more significant. The formula for Aaron is identical to that used for the other tribes: "for tribe X: PN." The inclusion of Aaron and Zadoq (1st NOTE to 5:34) testifies to the prominence of both in the Chronistic perspective. Elsewhere the descendants of Aaron are genealogically associated with Levi (2nd NOTE to 5:29). An earlier tribal muster in David's reign (12:24–39) also drew some interesting distinctions, mentioning "the descendants of Levi," "Jehoiada the leader of Aaron," and "Zadoq, a valiant young warrior, along with his ancestral house" (12:27–29). In this earlier muster, Jehoiada, Aaron, et al. are all reckoned under a Levitical rubric (12:27). Here the mention of Aaron directly follows the listing for Levi. Because both Levi and Aaron have representatives, the total number of units in vv. 16–22 comes to thirteen.

27:18. "Eliab." The eldest of "the brothers of David" (1 Sam 16:6; 17:13, 28; 1 Chr 2:13; 2 Chr 11:18).

27:19. "Jerimoth." On the name, see the 3rd TEXTUAL NOTE to 23:23.

27:20. "Azaziah" *(ʿzzyhw)* appears elsewhere in Chronicles as a Levitical PN (1 Chr 15:21; 2 Chr 31:13).

27:21. "Iddo" *(yiddô)*. On the name, see also Ezra 10:43 (Kethib). This son of Zechariah is not otherwise attested in Chronicles.

"Jaasiel" *(yaʿăśîʾēl)*. The list in 11:47 also mentions a "Jaasiel," but labels him a Mezobite (see TEXTUAL NOTE).

"Abner." Probably referring to the cousin (Abner *ben* Ner) and army commander of Saul (1 Sam 14:51; 17:55–57; 20:25; 26:5–15; 2 Sam 2:8–4:12; 1 Kgs 2:5–32; 1 Chr 26:28). Given that the text refers to a son of Abner, and not to Abner himself, it seems likely that the author is thinking of the latter part of David's career. Such a conclusion comports with the larger literary context of this material (e.g., 1 Chr 22:5; 23:1).

27:22. "Azarel" *(ʿzrʾl)*. Not an uncommon PN in late texts (1 Chr 12:7; Ezra 10:41; Neh 11:13; 12:36; 1st TEXTUAL NOTE to 25:4).

"Jeroḥam" *(yĕrōḥām)*. The PN appears in a number of different contexts (1 Chr 6:12, 19; 8:27; 9:8, 12; 2 Chr 23:1; Neh 11:12). This Jeroḥam should be distinguished from the Benjaminite Jeroḥam mentioned earlier in David's reign (12:8).

"officers of the tribes of Israel" *(śry šbṭy yśrʾl)*. The list of tribal leaders (vv. 16–22) comprises an independent section within the chapter. The digression on David's census (vv. 23–24) that follows makes no reference to these officials.

27:23. "David did not take a census *(mspr)*." There are two possible referents for this statement: the census of 1 Chr 21 and the census *(mspr)* or roster of 27:1–15. The two options are not mutually exclusive (see SOURCES AND COMPOSITION). The enumeration of twelve military divisions (288,000) may have led the writer to explain why no general census of Israel is included. In any case, the list of tribal officers that immediately precedes this comment (vv. 16–22) does not seem to be in view.

"less than twenty years of age." There is only limited merit to the oft-stated claim (e.g., Curtis and Madsen 1910: 291–92) that the writer portrays the census as conforming to Priestly precedent. In the regulations of the Priestly source (Num 1:3–46), Aaron and the various tribal representatives were to muster only those Israelite males, who were at least twenty years of age. In contrast, David's earlier census (1 Chr 21:1–5), which was never completed (21:6), failed to take divinely mandated legislation into account. But the issue is not so simple. To begin with, the author's explanation alludes to Priestly law, but does not directly quote it. The author justifies the pattern of this census by reference to one of the Abrahamic promises (see below). Second, Priestly legislation mandates a clear distinction between the Levites, who were elected by God to take the place of the firstborn (Num 3:11–13), and the other Israelite tribes. Because of their special status, the Levites were to be excluded from the census (Num 1:47–53; 2:33). Instead, the Levites were to be counted separately after the census for the rest of the Israelites had been completed (Num 3:14–39). The Levites, unlike the rest of the tribes, were to be numbered from the age of one month (Num 3:15, 22, 28, 34, 39). The author makes no mention of this critical distinction, although it is quite possible that he saw no need to because Joab excluded Benjaminites and Levites from his census (1 Chr 21:6) and no Levites are explicitly mentioned in the census of 27:1–15.

"to make Israel as numerous as the stars of the heavens" *(lhrbwt ʾt-yśrʾl kkwkby hšmym)*. One of the Abrahamic promises is numerous progeny (Gen 12:2 [J]; 15:4–5 [J]; 17:2–7, 16–21 [P]; 22:17 [P]). The language used here is close to the formulation of Gen 15:5: "Consider the heavens and the number of stars, if you are able to count them. And he [Yhwh] said, 'Thus shall your offspring be' " *(hbṭ nʾ hšmym wspr kwkbym ʾm twkl lspr ʾtm wyʾmr lw kh yhyh zrʿk)*. But the verbiage is even closer to that of Gen 22:17, "I shall make your offspring as numerous as the stars of the heavens" *(hrbh ʾrbh ʾt-zrʿk kkwkby hšmym)*. The implication seems to be that by counting Israelite males who were less than twenty years of age, David would be casting aspersions on the validity of one of Yhwh's solemn promises to Abraham. The explanation for the pattern of this census constitutes, therefore, an exegetical blend of two distinct Pentateuchal lemmata: the minimum age for military censuses (Num 1:3, 45) and the divine pledge to Abraham (Gen 22:17).

27:24. "but he did not finish." Joab did not complete the census because he found David's order to be abhorrent (21:6).

"wrath *(qṣp)* came upon Israel." See 1 Chr 21:7. Williamson (1982b: 177) helpfully draws attention to the motif of divine wrath *(qṣp)* in Num 1:53, but the outbreak of divine anger spoken of there has to do with the mandate given to the Levites to encamp around the Tabernacle.

"the book of the chronicles of King David" *(sēper dibrê hayyāmîm lammelek dāvîd)*. References to annalistic royal records are found in other biblical books: "the book of the chronicles of the kings of Israel" (*sēper dibrê hayyāmîm lĕmalkê yiśrāʾēl;* 1 Kgs 14:19; cf. 2 Kgs 13:8, 12; 14:15, 28), "the book of the events of the days of the kings of Judah" (*sēper dibrê hayyāmîm lĕmalkê yehûdâ;* 1 Kgs 14:29; 15:7, 23; cf. 2 Kgs 12:19; 14:18), "the book of the events of the days of the kings of Media and Persia" (*sēper dibrê hayyāmîm lĕmalkê māday ûpārās;* Esth 10:2), and "the book of the records, the events of the days" (*sēper hazzikrōnôt dibrê hayyāmîm;* Esth 6:1). The phrase *sēper dibrê hayyāmîm* is also, as we have seen, the standard name given to the book of Chronicles in rabbinic tradition (introduction). But this is the only claim to the existence of royal Davidic chronicles.

# Sources and Composition

Chapter 27 naturally falls into a series of discrete sections (vv. 1, 2–15, 16–22, 23–24, 25–31, 32–34). Given the many parts that together make up the whole, it is appropriate to pay some attention to the composition of each subsection. I shall begin, however, by addressing some general arguments for disunity. According to some commentators (e.g., Rehm 1954: 65; Williamson 1982b: 174; Steins 1995: 335), the opening rubric (v. 1) points toward a secondary stage of composition for part, if not all, of the chapter because the leadership figures mentioned—"the ancestral heads, the officers of thousands and of the hundreds, and the officials"—do not figure in the earlier Davidic convocation and census (23:3–6a). A second argument against originality has to do with the general, if not secular, appointments, which are thought not to reflect the final stage of David's reign (Williamson 1982b: 174). Rather than dealing with secular affairs, this entire chapter is, according to Steins, part of a final, cultically oriented stratum in the book (1 Chr 27; 2 Chr 30–31; etc.) that engages earlier material within the work (e.g., 1 Chr 26:26*, 27f.) and seeks to relate certain practices and figures to ordinances found in Pentateuchal law.

A different but related issue surrounds the composition of the list in vv. 2–15. Some deem vv. 2–15 to be a duplicate of names appearing in 1 Chr 11 and therefore secondary (e.g., Benzinger 1901: 79; Kittel 1902: 98–99). (The relevant comparison is with 1 Chr 11 and not with 2 Sam 23:8–39 because, as the TEXTUAL NOTES make clear, the names in the list of 1 Chr 27:2–15 do not agree with 2 Sam 23:8–39, but with those in 1 Chr 11:11–31.) That there is duplication between the lists of warriors in 1 Chr 11 and 27 is undeniable, as the chart below illustrates.

| *27:2–15* | *11:11–31* |
|---|---|
| Jashobeam son of Zabdiel | Jashobeam |
| Dodai the Aḥoḥite | Eleazar son of Dodai the Aḥoḥite |
| Benaiah son of the chief priest Jehoiada | Benaiah son of Jehoiada |
| Ammizabad his son | — |
| Asah-el brother of Joab | Asah-el brother of Joab |
| Zebadiah his son | — |
| Shammoth the Zeraḥite | Shammoth the Ḥarodite |
| Ira son of Iqqesh the Teqoaite | Ira son of Iqqesh the Teqoaite |
| Ḥelez the Pelonite | Ḥelez the Pelonite |
| Sibbekai the Ḥushathite | Sibbekai the Ḥushathite |
| Abiezer the Anathothite | Abiezer the Anathothite |
| Mahrai the Neṭophathite | Mahrai the Neṭophathite |
| Benaiah the Pirathonite | Benaiah the Pirathonite |
| Ḥeldai the Neṭophathite | Ḥeled son of Benaiah |

There is no compelling reason to see 27:2–15 as dependent on a hypothetical parallel list (*pace* Myers 1965a: 183), given the precise parallels of many names between 1 Chr 11 and 27. On the basis of the evidence presented above, one can go a step further and speak of 1 Chr 11 being the source of the list in 1 Chr 27 (as opposed to the opposite scenario). In a number of instances, the list of 1 Chr 27 evinces a later stage of literary development than the list of 1 Chr 11 does: 27:2 refers to "Jashobeam son of Zabdiel" as opposed to simply "Jashobeam" in 11:11; 27:5 speaks of "Benaiah son of the chief priest Jehoiada," along with "his son Ammizabad" (27:6), while 11:22 speaks only of "Benaiah son of Jehoiada;" 27:7 mentions both "Asah-el brother of Joab," and "Zebadiah his son," while 11:26 speaks simply of "Asah-el brother of Joab." Only in one case could one make the case that 1 Chr 27 has the more primitive text: 27:4 reads "Dodai the Aḥoḥite," while 11:12 (see TEXTUAL NOTE) reads "Eleazar son of Dodai the Aḥoḥite." The preponderance of evidence suggests that the author of 1 Chr 27 borrowed from 1 Chr 11, not vice versa.

But does it follow that the very indebtedness to the earlier list of warriors means that the present list is secondary? Such a conclusion is possible, but not necessary. To begin with, the list is not a straightforward duplication. Because the list of 1 Chr 27 contains some updates, it seems designed to reflect a late stage in David's reign, a generation removed, in some cases, from the time of the earlier tabulation. Indeed, there are references within 1 Chr 23–27 that situate these administrative initiatives within the last years of David's life (2nd NOTE to 26:31). There are also substantial differences between the contextualization and formal characteristics of the two lists. The former comprises a long inventory of warriors who joined David, presumably at Ḥebron, while the latter is a twelvefold enumeration of divisional officers and their troops who provide monthly support for the king in Jerusalem. The latter is by design a select list, drawn in part from the former. Some overlap is to be expected.

Scholars are right to draw a contrast between the leadership depicted in this chapter and that depicted in the limited gathering and census of chapter 23. Nor is the convocation of "the priests," "the Levites," and "the officers of Israel" (*khnym, lwym, śry yśrʾl*; 23:2) the same as the massive national assembly depicted later (28:1). The text of 23:2 does not elaborate as to who the "officers of Israel" are, although David appealed to them earlier (*śry yśrʾl*; 22:17). This raises larger questions about the function and purpose of the earlier convocation ("Excursus: The Composition of 1 Chronicles 23–27"). In my judgment, it seems unreasonable to expect that only those figures mentioned in the limited gathering of 23:2 and the census of 23:3–6 could appear in subsequent events. Much of 1 Chr 23–27 is concerned with the establishment of permanent national institutions headquartered in Jerusalem. Precisely because a variety of new arrangements and personnel are needed to accommodate a centralized state, it would be astonishing, if not anti-climactic, for all of these personnel to be present already at the point of David's initial deliberations. The important question is not whether these groups are all present at the beginning, but whether they are present at the end. If 1 Chr 27:1, 2–15, and 16–22 were later insertions (or part of one large insertion), one would not expect the personnel introduced in these sections to figure in succeeding events. If, however, these personnel do reappear, this lessens the likelihood that the sections within 1 Chr 27 are all later additions.

In this context, the contrast between the limited gathering of 1 Chr 23 and the larger national assemblies of 1 Chr 28 and 29 is telling. The groups David convokes to Jerusalem (28:1) include "Israel's officers" (*śry yśr'l;* 28:1; cf. 23:2), "the tribal officers" (*śry hšbṭym;* 28:1; cf. 27:16–22), "the officers of the divisions, those serving the king" (*śry hmḥlqwt hmšrtym 't hmlk;* 28:1; cf. 27:1–15), "the officers of the thousands" (*śry h'lpym;* 28:1; cf. 26:26; 27:1), "the officers of the hundreds" (*śry hm'wt;* 28:1; cf. 27:1), and "the officers in charge of all the property and livestock for the king and for his sons" (*śry kl-hrkwš wmqnh lmlk wlbnyw;* 28:1; cf. 27:25–31), as well as "the eunuchs, warriors, and every valiant warrior" (*'m-hrsysym whgbwrym wlkl-gbwr ḥyl*); 28:1; cf. 26:6, 31; 27:2–15). In comparing this more exhaustive tabulation of groups with the limited gathering and census depicted earlier (23:2–6), it becomes apparent that many of the new personnel are precisely those who were appointed in the interval (23:6b–27:32).

Nor is the appearance of most of these officials unique. Some make other appearances in the final events of David's reign. Following the royal summons to make freewill offerings for the shrine's construction, "the officers of the ancestral houses" (*śry h'bwt;* 29:6; cf. 27:1), "the officers of the Israelite tribes" (*śry šbṭy yśr'l;* 29:6; cf. 27:16–22), "the officers of the thousands and of the hundreds" (*śry h'lpym whm'wt;* 29:6; cf. 27:1), and "the officers of the royal work" (*śry ml'kt hmlk;* 29:6; cf. 27:25–31) all make donations. The very presence of these officials presupposes their appointment or, at the least, their prior existence. To be sure, "the officers of the Israelite tribes" (*śry šbṭy yśr'l;* 27:16–22) are not a productive concern in the remainder of the coverage devoted to Solomon's reign and the Judahite monarchy. The fact that these tribal officers never appear again (following David's reign) may indicate that this section is a later interpolation.

Finally, the distinction between military and nonmilitary personnel in 1 Chr 23–27 should not be overdrawn. To begin with, as the different categories employed by Williamson (secular) and Steins (cultic) make clear, there is no consensus on how to classify the material in 1 Chr 27. The tabulation of the tribal officers recalls the Priestly system depicted in Numbers 1–4 (Steins), but the tabulation of the divisional commanders recalls the earlier lists of David's warriors (COMMENT). Nor is the census of 27:1–15 the first time soldiers or commanders appear. King David and "the army officers" select the singers—the sons of Asaph, Heman, and Jeduthun—for service (25:1; NOTE). Some of the Israelites chosen as gatekeepers are described in martial terms (COMMENT on 26:1–19). The war spoils taken by "King David, the clan chiefs, the officers of the thousands and of the hundreds, and the officers of the army" are translated into dedicated gifts for the treasuries and the Temple (26:26–27). The divisional method used to organize the military force depicted in 27:2–15 bears similarities to those used elsewhere in 1 Chr 23–27. Like the Levites (23:6–23), priests (24:1–31), singers (25:8–31), and gatekeepers (26:1–12), the military personnel are organized by divisions *(mḥlqwt).* Even if one wished to concede, for the sake of argument, that the author was most concerned about cultic affairs, one could still insist that he would take an interest in the establishment of divisional commanders. Especially in the latter part of his reign, it would be important for David to consolidate the kingdom in preparation for the reign of his son. If Solomon's task was to build the Temple that David himself was forbidden to build, "a well-organized army and trained officials would aid materially in the successful completion of this great undertaking" (Curtis and Madsen 1910: 289).

To be sure, one can still argue that the appearance of the various officials mentioned in 1 Chr 27, in later chapters (1 Chr 28–29), and elsewhere in the discussion of the Judahite monarchy is part of later redaction(s). An editor (or editors) could have interpolated materials into this section of David's reign and then added later references to the personnel mentioned in this chapter. But if so, it must be acknowledged that the editors responsible for such insertions have been careful to integrate them into their new contexts. In what follows, my COMMENT will focus on the present shape of this material within the context of the larger presentation of David's reign.

It remains to discuss the commentary on the census found in 27:23–24. There is no doubt that this short digression is dependent upon the earlier census account (21:1–22:1) because the author directly mentions it. Nevertheless, the passage is abstruse and may be secondary, as many commentators claim. Seebass (1978), followed in part by Williamson (1982b: 176), thinks that the author of this text tones down the criticism of David in 1 Chr 21, presenting the record of David in a more idyllic light. Such a view is understandable. The author seems to place some responsibility upon Joab's shoulders (27:24), although Joab's precise shortcoming is unclear. Was the transgression not finishing the census (v. 24; Wright 1993), or was it numbering children and teenagers (v. 23)?

A related difficulty is determining whether this passage refers only to the national census in 1 Chr 21 (so almost all commentators) or to that census and the one introduced in 27:1 as well. There is no doubt that the earlier census is at least partially in view. This census, alluded to in v. 24, was halted on account of divine wrath (21:7). The census, which resulted in a tabulation of 1,100,000 Israelites and 470,000 Judahites (21:5), was never finished (21:6; 27:24). Nor was it (apparently) entered into the official royal records (27:24). But this standard explanation, focusing only on 1 Chr 21, leaves two major questions unanswered. First, why does the author situate the census digression here? If the text only refers to the first census, why mention it much later? Why discuss it in a setting dealing with divisional and tribal officers? One has to account for the contextualization of this judgment in chapter 27 and not in chapter 21. Second, why does 27:23 speak of David's census as being restricted to those who were at least twenty years of age, while the earlier account of David's census makes no mention of any age limitation at all?

A case could be made that in 27:23–24 both the national census of 1 Chr 21 and an additional census are in view. The author of the digression may have been thinking of the census introduced in 27:1 and tabulated in 27:2–15. The noun *mispār* is used to refer to both the earlier census (21:2) and this limited military census (27:1). The same term is used twice in the digression of vv. 23–24. The list of 27:2–15, although heavily stylized, quantifies military representation from various quarters. The twelve division commanders are in charge of uniformly large divisions of 24,000 each, a total of 288,000 military personnel serving the king in twelve rotas. In neither case, whether in the twelvefold rota of divisions or in the twelvefold system of divisional officers (vv. 2–15), is there anything incomplete or unfinished. The mention of both the census (*mispār*) in v. 1 and the enumeration of twelve divisions in vv. 2–15 may have occasioned the remarks in vv. 23–24. The purpose of the explanation in vv. 23–24 may be not so much to exonerate David as it is to distinguish this complete and successful census from the earlier incomplete and failed census. By observing the minimum age for military musters, this census (27:1–15) conformed to divine legislation (Num 1:3, 45). As such, it may mark another occasion in David's reign in which an initial failure was reversed or followed by a later success (e.g., 13:1–11; cf. 15:1–16:3).

## COMMENT

The figure of David dominates the presentation of the United Monarchy (1 Chr 11–29). In the present text of 1 and 2 Chronicles, nineteen chapters (522 verses; approximately 29 percent) out of a total of sixty-five chapters are devoted to the reign of a single king. One can be even more precise if one counts words and not verses. Using the Andersen-Forbes word analysis of the Leningrad Codex in the Kethib as a base (personal communication), with a margin of error of less than one-tenth of one percent, one can be fairly precise about allocation of coverage. Out of the entire book (24,058 words), 6,618 words appear in 1 Chr 11–29 or 27.5% of the total. This coverage dwarfs the coverage devoted to the nearest competitor, David's successor, Solomon (3,319 words [201 verses] in 2 Chr 1–9; 13.8%). The son receives about half (50.2%) of the attention devoted toward the father. Even when compared to the detailed coverage given to the origins of humanity and the lineages of the various tribes (3,924 words [407 verses] in 1 Chr 1–9; 16.3%), David still comes out ahead. The lineages receive 59.3% of the coverage given to David. If one subtracts the universal genealogy (422 words in 1:1–54) and counts the lineage devoted to David and his royal line (195 words in 3:1–24) as counting toward the coverage awarded to David, the number is even lower. In this revised calculation, the tribal lineages (3,307 words [329 verses] in 1 Chr 2 and 4–9; 13.7%) receive approximately 48.4% of the coverage devoted to David (6,813 words [546 verses] in 1 Chr 3 and 11–29). Even the most auspicious reformer king in the Judahite kingdom, Ḥezeqiah, does not receive anything near the allocation of coverage awarded to King David. The chapters devoted to Ḥezeqiah total 1,853 words, more than the coverage of Ḥezeqiah in 2 Kgs 18–20, but only 28.0% of the coverage devoted to David in 1 Chr 11–29. These data confirm that David is the dominate human figure in the Chronicler's work. Any study of Chronistic theology must take such considerations into account.

The content of the Davidic coverage is also telling. His exploits win Israel the stability, solidarity, and success that were so noticeably lacking under Saul (1 Chr 10). The final chapters of David's reign highlight a different aspect of the Davidic legacy. With his passing clearly in view (22:5; 23:1), the reigning monarch begins to prepare his people for the transition to the reign of his son. If earlier phases of

David's tenure were centered on his person—his military, political, and religious exploits—the final phase of his career depersonalizes his rule. The attention is on creating or reforming national institutions whose very purpose is to serve Israel in posterity. If the chosen heir is to be successful and avoid the chaos that attended Saul's demise, it is important for an aging David to forge an efficient administrative apparatus for Solomon and others to use.

The establishment of permanent new institutions is also an important turning point for the nation, marking a transition to a settled, urban-centered, and temple-focused society. In this respect, the centralization inherent in the system of military divisions advances the cause of Jerusalem in the late Achaemenid era. Israel, as Chronicles redefines it, is Jerusalem-centered. The highly unified and structured nation depicted in the early tenth century sets a standard for generations to follow. Both the establishment of a military system of rotating divisions (vv. 2–15) and the appointment of tribal officers (vv. 16–22) are important steps in a process of national stabilization. During David's tenure, there is a clear shift from a loosely organized polity to a highly organized one. During the time of his rise (11:10–47) David's many troops consolidated his power, but lacked an overall organization. Indeed, some have viewed the references to "the Three" and "the Thirty" in the parallel lists of 1 Chr 11 and 2 Sam 23:8–39 as illustrating that David's troops comprised no more than his personal bodyguard. But it is dangerous to read too much of the context of 1 Chr 11 (and of 2 Sam 23) into the context of 1 Chr 27. The former text details the names and exploits of military personnel who aided David's rise to kingship, while the latter is a structured list of military officers and the divisions they command who are to protect the central government. If the former represents a compendium of individual warriors, the latter represents a national institution centered in Jerusalem.

The presentation in chapter 27 rectifies the impression that Israel's armed forces remained an amorphous assemblage of volunteers. From the ranks of Israel's valiant warriors, twelve are singled out to head units of 24,000 each. In comparison with the force numbering a total of 288,000 here, the *Temple Scroll* from Qumran prescribes a national force of 12,000, drawn equally from each of the Israelite tribes (11QT 57.3–6). Both texts are based on a duodecimal system. Because the constitution of the army rotates evenly, no one division dominates. The size and prestige of individual tribes are of no consequence in this arrangement. The centralized system of divisions (Chronicles) or tribal contingents (the *Temple Scroll*) thus achieves two goals simultaneously. It protects Israel's position in international affairs, while lending stability to the body politic. But the *Temple Scroll*, which explicitly refers to the stipulations of Deut 17:14–20, but not to the system projected in Chronicles, also places a number of restrictions on the king and subjects his leadership to a council of thirty-six leaders drawn from the people, the Levites, and the priests (11QT 57.11–15). Moreover, the pan-Israel force is designed not only to protect the monarch from foreign peoples but also to protect him from lapsing into sinful practices (11QT 57.7–11). In this respect, the twelve-thousand-man contingent called for in the *Temple Scroll* polices against both external threats and internal royal calumny.

In Chronicles no such restrictions are placed on the king in relation to the armed forces stationed in the nation's capital. In any given month, the monarch can count on a sizable military force to protect Israel's vital interests. There are no references to regional operations or to fortified towns. The focus of the list is on the center, rather than on the periphery (contra Junge 1937: 65). The plan for twelve divisions is not intended to replicate the early band of volunteers who rallied to David early in his career, even though it draws on some of its players. The creation of a national security force establishes a standing army in Jerusalem.

To some extent, the system of rotating divisions depicted in Jehoiada's reforms (2 Chr 23:1–21; cf. 2 Kgs 11:4–20) recalls the system portrayed here. Divisions (*mḥlqwt* in 2 Chr 23:8; cf. *ydwt* in 2 Kgs 11:7) along with chiefs of hundreds *(śry hm'wt)* feature in both Chronicles (2 Chr 23:1, 9, 14, 20) and its *Vorlage* (2 Kgs 11:4, 7, 9, 15). On one occasion army officers are mentioned (*pqwdy hḥyl;* 2 Chr 23:14[//2 Kgs 11:15]; cf. *hr'š lkl-śry hṣb'wt* in 1 Chr 27:3). Yet there are also some differences between the system described here and the conspiracy that results in the demise of Queen Athaliah. The shifts depicted in the narrative of 2 Chr 23 (and 2 Kgs 11) are weekly and not monthly. There is also an important variation in the nature and range of participants. In Kings the soldiers comprise the royal guards *(rṣym)* and the Carites *(kry)*, but not the armed forces at large (2 Kgs 11:4). In the Chronicler's version of Jehoiada's reforms, several groups participate in Jehoiada's coup. The conspiracy only occurs after the Levites and ancestral heads have been assembled from Judah's towns to ratify a covenant at a special assembly in Jerusalem (2 Chr 23:2–3). Ancestral heads, priests, Levites, gatekeepers, and singers all play roles in the revolution (2 Chr 23:2, 4, 6–8, 13, 18), even though the "chiefs of the hundreds" *(śry hm'wt)* are also present (2 Chr 23:1, 14, 20). In this way, the Chronicler democratizes Jehoiada's revolution (Williamson 1982b: 213–14; Dillard 1987: 178–79). One might say that Jehoiada's revolt draws on a broad coalition of groups, many of which are mentioned in 1 Chr 23–27.

If the system of twelve divisional commanders (27:1–15) anticipates certain features of Jehoiada's revolt and the pan-Israelite force in the *Temple Scroll,* the system of thirteen tribal officers (vv. 16–22) recalls certain features of the Priestly depiction of Israel's league. In the Priestly writing, ancestral heads are chosen as representatives for each tribe (Num 1:4–16). These officials are assigned to assist Moses and Aaron in conducting a national muster (Num 1:17–46). As in the list of 1 Chr 27:16–22, the Priestly list provides the officer's patronymic and tribal designation (Num 1:5–15). Again, there are differences between the structure and purpose of the two lists. In Numbers the list occurs in the context of a military census and an association is made between Israel as a people and Israel as an armed camp. Hence, the "ancestral tribal chieftains" (*nśy'y mṭwt 'bwtm;* Num 1:16) can also be called the "heads of the thousands of Israel" (*r'šy 'lpy yśr'l;* Num 1:16; cf. 1 Chr 27:1). Because the census counts only Israelite males, those able to bear arms (*kl-yṣ' ṣb' byśr'l;* Num 1:3), the Levites are not included (Num 1:47–53; cf. 1 Chr 27:17). Nevertheless, both arrangements draw on the leadership of Israel's individual tribes for broader purposes.

In the case of Chronicles, the establishment of thirteen tribal officers means that alongside the rationalization involved in reorganizing Israel's national administration, Israel's tribal base is not scuttled. Early in David's rise, representatives from Israel's far-flung tribes registered their enthusiastic support for him in a variety of geographical locales (12:1–39). The thirteen officers, including the Levitical officer and the Aaronide officer (27:17), institutionalize the tribal tradition in Israel's monarchy. This polity develops features that are found in both the Deuteronomistic and the Priestly works. The administration associated with David's reign means that Israel itself is redefined as a highly centralized state, but this monarchy incorporates and honors features of the older tribal league.

# *XXXIV. Royal Overseers and Civil Servants (27:25–34)*

*Twelve Royal Supervisors*

25 In charge of the royal storehouses: Azmaveth son of Adiel;
in charge of the storehouses in the country—in the towns, villages, and towers: Jonathan son of Uzziah;
26 in charge of the country laborers in agricultural work: Ezri son of Chelub;
27 in charge of the vineyards: Shimei the Ramathite;
for the wine cellars: Zabdi the Shiphmite;
28 in charge of the olive trees and the sycamores in the Shephelah: Baal-ḥanan the Gederite;
in charge of the storehouses of oil: Joash;
29 in charge of the cattle pasturing in the Sharon: Shiṭrai the Sharonite;
in charge of the cattle in the valleys: Shephaṭ son of Adlai;
30 in charge of the camels: Obil the Ishmaelite;
in charge of the she-asses: Jeḥdeiah the Meronothite;
31 in charge of the flocks: Jaziz the Hagrite.

All of these were officers of King David's property.

*Royal Advisors and Adjutants*

32 Jonathan, David's uncle, was a counselor, a man of understanding and a scribe. He, along with Jeḥiel the Ḥachmonite, was with the king's sons.
33 Aḥithophel was counselor to the king. Ḥushai the Archite was the friend of the king.
34 And after Aḥithophel was Jehoiada son of Benaiah, counselor to the king, and his priest was Abiathar. The leader of the king's army was Joab.

## TEXTUAL NOTES

27:25. "the royal storehouses" (*ʾṣrwt hmlk*). Thus MT and LXX. In proposing a haplography (*homoioteleuton; bʿyr hmmlkh* [cf. 1 Chr 27:25b; 1 Sam 27:5])

Rudolph (1955: 180) concedes that the final *hê* in *hmmlkh* is an obstacle. If a haplography *(homoioteleuton)* has occurred, it would more likely be *bʿyr hmlk,* "in the royal city," but an urban setting may be inherent in the literary context of the *ʾōṣĕrôt hammelek.*

"Azmaveth" *(ʿazmāwet).* So MT. See also the uncontracted *ḥṣrmwt* in MT 1:20. LXX[BL] *Asmōth;* LXX[AN] *Azmōth.*

27:27. "in charge of the vineyards" *(ʿal hakkĕrāmîm).* So MT. Cf. LXX[B] *epi tōn chōriōn* (LXX[L] *ampelōnōn*); Vg. *vinearumque cultoribus.* On the basis of context, some scholars read *ʿal hakkōrĕmîm,* "in charge of the vinedressers." See also the following TEXTUAL NOTE.

"the Ramathite." MT continues "in charge of that which is in the vineyards" *(ʿal šebakkĕrāmîm).* Cf. LXX *tōn en tois chōriois tou oinou.* In the MT reading, the relative pron. *(š-)* serves as a gen., the obj. of a prep. (Waltke and O'Connor, §19.4b). LXX *kai epi tōn thēsaurōn,* "and in charge of the treasur[i]es." But the phrase *ʿal šebakkĕrāmîm* probably resulted from a dittography of the earlier phrase *ʿal hakkĕrāmîm* in v. 27.

"for the wine cellars." Literally, "for the storehouses of wine" *(lʾṣrwt hyyn).*

"Zabdi" *(zbdy).* Thus MT and LXX[AN] *bb′* (cf. $ye_2$ *Zabdei*). LXX[B] *Zachrei* (= *zkry*).

"the Shiphmite" *(haššipmî).* So MT. LXX[ABN] *ho tou Sephnei;* ce *Sephai;* LXX[L] *Sapham(e)i.*

27:28. "the Gederite" *(haggĕdērî).* LXX[AL] *ho Geddōreitēs* and LXX[B] *ho Gedōreitēs* reflect "the Gedorite."

27:29. "Shiṭrai" *(šṭry).* So Kethib. LXX[AL] *Satrai;* LXX[N*] *Satri;* g *Satre.* Qere, a few Heb. MSS, Tg., and Syr. "Shirṭai." LXX[B] *Asartais.*

"Adlai" *(ʿdly).* So MT. LXX[ABN] *Adai* (= *ʿdyʾ*).

27:30. "Obil" *(ʾôbîl).* So MT. LXX[B] *Abias;* LXX[L] *Ōbia.* An allocutory name. Cf. OSA *ʾbl,* "gather livestock together as booty" (Biella 1982: 2); *ʾbl,* "camels"; Arab. *ʾibil,* "camels"; Akk. *ibilu,* "dromedary."

"Jeḥdeiah" *(yḥdyhw).* Thus MT. LXX[B] *Iadias;* Syr.[A] *yhwdʾ.*

"the Meronothite." The readings of LXX[BL] *ho ek Merathōn,* LXX[AN] *ho ek Marathōn,* and Syr.[A] *mrtwnyʾ* reflect metathesis (*hmrnty* > *hmrtny*).

27:32. "David's uncle" *(dwd-dwyd).* So MT and LXX *(ho patradelphos).* It is also possible to translate MT as "David's beloved." On this meaning of *dôd,* see Isa 5:1; Song 1:13, 16; *passim* (Pope 1977b: 350–51). Cf. Akk. *dādu,* "lovemaking," and Ug. *dd,* "love." Jonathan son of Saul would be the obvious referrent (1 Sam 13:1–14:49; 18:1–20:42; 23:14–18; 31:1–2; 2 Sam 1:1–27; 1 Chr 8:33; 9:39), but Jonathan perished (cf. 1 Chr 10:1–12) before David established his government in Jerusalem.

"a man of understanding and a scribe." Thus MT and LXX[ALN]. The expression "and a scribe" is missing from LXX[B] and $c_2$ due to haplography (*homoioarkton* from *wswpr hwʾ* to *wyḥyʾl*). Alternatively, the haplography could have occurred in the Greek (*homoioteleuton* from *synetos* to *kai grammateus autos*).

"Jeḥiel" *(yḥyʾl).* So MT. LXX[B] and $c_2$ *Ieēl;* LXX[L] *Iaēl.*

"the Ḥachmonite." Cf. LXX[B] and $c_2$ *ho tou Hachamei;* $ye_2$ *ho tou Hachamanei;*

*bb' ho tou Hamachani;* i *ho tou Hachēmani*. MT "son of Ḥachmoni" *(bn ḥkmny)* represents a conflation of two variants: "son of Ḥachmon" *(bn ḥkmn)* and "the Ḥachmonite" *(hḥkmny)*.

27:33. "the Archite" *(h'rky)*. So MT. LXX[AB] read *(ho) prōtos philos*, a title used in the Alexandrian court (Thackeray 1907: 276–78; Gerleman 1946: 18). Cf. $e_2$ *archietairos;* bb' *archieteros* (< *ho Archi hetairos*, "the Archite, friend;" Fernández Marcos and Busto Saiz 1996: 67).

27:34. "Aḥithophel." So MT *(lectio brevior)*. LXX adds *echomenos* ($c_2$ *erchomenos*), "having."

"Jehoiada son of Benaiah." Reading with MT *(lectio difficilior)*. LXX[B] *Iōadae ho tou Banaiou;* LXX[L] *Iōad ho tou Banaiou*. Two Heb. MSS present the (expected) inverse sequence, "Benaiah son of Jehoiada." In so doing, these texts assimilate to "Benaiah son of the chief priest Jehoiada" in 27:5.

"counselor to the king, and his priest was Abiathar" *(ywʿṣ lmlk wkhnw ʾbytr)*. A reconstruction, following Rudolph (1955: 182), which basically presupposes that MT's abstruse *wʾbytr*, "and Abiathar," has suffered haplography (*homoioteleuton* from *bnyhw* to *wkhnw*). As MT stands, Abiathar appears in a list of royal counselors (NOTE). Alternatively, if Rudolph's emendation is too radical, one could posit a briefer haplography, a loss of *(w)khnw*, after *bnyhw (homoioteleuton)*.

"Joab." Thus MT and LXX[AB]. LXX[L] and Arm. add explicating *huios Sarouia*.

# NOTES

27:25–31. This account specifies twelve overseers for David's royal properties. The number matches that of the divisional officers heading the twelve military divisions at the king's service in Jerusalem (27:1–15).

27:25 In the Masoretic counting of verses (פסוקים), this verse marks the halfway point in the text of Chronicles. If the criterion is word count in the Kethib, however, one comes to quite a different conclusion. Using the Andersen-Forbes word analysis of the Leningrad Codex as a base (personal communication), there are 10,746 words in 1 Chronicles, whereas 13,312 words are present in 2 Chronicles. In this calculation, the halfway point in the text of Chronicles appears in the middle of 2 Chr 5.

"In charge of" *(wĕʿal)*. The notice has to be understood against the backdrop of the pattern established in vv. 2, 4, and 16. The chapter begins with a census of the non-Levitical leaders serving in David's time (v.1). This census complements the earlier census taken of the Levites (23:2–5). In the account of David's royal supervisors (27:25–31), the preposition *ʿal* ("in charge of") introduces each royal official.

"Azmaveth." An "Azmaweth the Baḥarumite" served as one of David's valiant warriors (1st NOTE to 11:33; cf. 12:3).

"the storehouses in the country" *(hʾṣrwt bśdh)*. The text lists royal storehouses and country storehouses. The writer is envisioning both kinds of facilities as owned by David and operated under his deputized control (v. 31). In so doing, the author posits some sort of state role in the distribution of wine and oil (see COMMENT).

"villages." In speaking of a village (כָּפָר) as opposed to a town or city (עִיר), the author is probably thinking of an unwalled, small site (1 Sam 6:18; Neh 6:2).

"towers" (מגדלות). By context, the term may refer to isolated citadels or towers in the countryside (Isa 5:2; 2 Chr 26:10; cf. Ps 61:4 [ET 61:3]; Song 7:5 [ET 7:4]) or to fortified towers (2 Chr 14:6; 26:9; cf. Prov 18:10). The fortified towers could be located within a town (Judg 9:51) or be part of a town's fortifications (Jer 31:38; Ezek 26:4; 27:11; Zech 14:10; Neh 12:39; 2 Chr 32:5). In this case, the writer speaks of the citadels as storage facilities. On the different meanings of מגדל, along with a discussion of some archaeological evidence, see Kletter (1991) and Zertal (1995).

27:26. "Chelub" *(klwb)*. This name is otherwise attested only in the genealogies of Judah (4:11; cf. *klwby* in 2:9).

27:27. "the wine cellars." In addition to these storehouses for wine *(l'ṣrwt hyyn)*, the author mentions storehouses *(ʾôṣĕrôt)* for oil (v. 28). As witnessed by their many references in biblical texts and extrabiblical inscriptions, wine and oil were two staples of the ancient Palestinian economy. Winepresses of various types have been found at T. Qasîleh, Gezer, Beth-shemesh, and T. Qiri, while a winery has been found at Gibeon (Borowski 1987: 11–12). Iron Age oil production stations, some of which were quite large, have been found at T. Batash, T. Beit Mirsim, Bethel, Dan, Gezer, Khirbet Jemaʿ, and T. Miqne (Borowski 1987: 117–26).

"the Shiphmite" *(haššipmî)*. Perhaps a resident of Shepham *(špm)* along the eastern edge of the promised land (Num 34:10–11) or, as is less likely philologically, of Siphmoth *(śpmt)* in the Judean Negev (1 Sam 30:28).

27:28. "The Shephelah" ("lowland") refers to the hilly region between the southern coastal plain and the Judean mountains. In biblical historiography, the Shephelah is renowned for its plentiful sycamores (1 Kgs 10:27//2 Chr 1:15; 9:27; cf. Deut 1:7; Josh 9:1; 2 Chr 26:10; Rainey 1983).

"the Gederite." Geder (or Gederah) was a town in southern Judah, probably in the Shephelah (Josh 15:36; 1 Chr 4:23; 12:5). If text originally read Gedor (see TEXTUAL NOTE), Khirbet Jedûr, about 12 km southwest of Bethleḥem in the vicinity of Beth-zur would be a possible referent.

27:29. "Sharon" refers to the coastal plain that extends from the Carmel range in the north to the area of Joppa in the south, an area rich in plant life and pasturage (Isa 33:9; 35:2; 65:10; Song 2:1; *KAI* 14.19).

"Shiṭrai." A hypocoristic PN, not attested elsewhere in the HB.

27:30. "the camels . . . the she-asses." These animals are related directly, not to agriculture, but to trade (Aharoni 1979: 15–16). Because major trade routes of the ancient Near East passed through Palestine, trade was an important sector of the Israelite economy. The author depicts David as having a healthy investment in this commerce.

"Jeḥdeiah." A Levite by this name is mentioned in 24:20 (see NOTE).

"the Meronothite." The precise location of Meronoth is uncertain, although it may have been near Gibeon and Mizpah (Neh 3:7).

27:31. "the Hagrite" *(hhgry)*. See also Bar 3:23 *(ho huios Hagar)*. The Hagrites *(hgrym)* are grouped with the Moabites, Ishmaelites, and Edomites in Ps 83:6, while 1 Chr 5:10 *(hhgrʾym)* and 5:19 *(hhgryʾym)* present the Hagrites as living east of Gilead. The text of 11:38 (see TEXTUAL NOTE) mentions a Mibḥar son of Hagri *(bn hgry)* as one of David's warriors. See further the 1st NOTE to 5:10.

"property" *(rĕkûš)*. Designating goods and possessions, the term *rĕkûš* occurs often in LBH. In Chronicles, *rĕkûš* most often refers to royal holdings (1 Chr 28:1; 2 Chr 21:14, 17; 31:3; 32:29; 35:7). The author thus presents Judah's royal family, somewhat like their royal Canaanite and Mesopotamian counterparts (see COMMENT), as controlling large estates. Such holdings were a significant source of income to the crown. It is in large part because of their accumulation of property, livestock, and cattle that ancient monarchs were able to make freewill offerings to temples and their attendant festivals (e.g., 1 Chr 29:3–5; 2 Chr 31:3; 35:7).

27:32–34. This inventory of seven advisors and officials should be compared with the earlier list of David's cabinet in 18:15–17. There are very interesting differences between the two accounts (see SOURCES AND COMPOSITION).

27:32. "David's uncle" *(dôd-dāwîd)*. According to biblical authors, David placed a number of relatives in significant positions in his government (6th NOTE to this verse). No uncle by the name of Jonathan is attested for David, only a nephew (20:7; R. Braun 1986: 263). It is interesting that in this account David has one of his accomplished uncles, "a counselor, a man of understanding and a scribe," as well as the otherwise unattested "Jeḥiel the Ḥachmonite," present with the royal princes. Oded (in Avishur and Heltzer 2000: 63) calls attention to the fact that the neo-Babylonian rations destined for the five sons of exiled Jehoiachin were delivered into the hands of Qanāma, who seems to have been an official responsible for the king's sons.

"a man of understanding" *(ʾyš mbyn)*. In the sense of being well-informed or well-trained (Dan 8:23; 1 Chr 15:22; 2 Chr 26:5; 34:12).

"scribe." On the importance of scribes in the Chronicler's work, see the 1st NOTE to 2:55.

"Jeḥiel" is a fairly common name in Chronicles and Ezra, especially in Levitical contexts (1 Chr 15:18, 20; 16:5; 23:8; 29:8; 2 Chr 21:2; 29:14; 31:13; 35:8; Ezra 8:9; 10:2, 21, 26). But this Jeḥiel is otherwise unattested.

"Ḥachmonite." See also 11:11(//2 Sam 23:8). Otherwise unattested.

"the king's sons." The reference, presuming the status of the Davidic princes, may allude to their being tutees of David's advisors (De Vries 1989: 214). The earlier cabinet list (18:15–17) mentions that "the first sons of David were at the king's side" (3rd NOTE to 18:17). In ancient Mesopotamian city states, the royal family was one of the king's chief resources. Sons, nephews, uncles, and cousins could be used advantageously to pursue larger administrative and political goals. Descendants of previous kings could be employed effectively in certain governmental posts. Such nepotism was "as much a matter of policy as of charity" (Postgate 1994a: 147). But the usage of the phrase "son of the king" does not seem to be uniform throughout different lands. Judging by ancient texts from a variety of sites (Emar, Ḫattuša, Ugarit), not all of "the king's sons" need have been actually offspring of the reigning king. The terminology sometimes seems to refer to high ranking officials who were dispatched by the monarch to implement specific administrative or political tasks (Beckman 1992: 47).

27:33. "Aḥithophel." For a time, consulting the advice of this royal counselor was tantamount to "consulting the word of God" (2 Sam 16:23). Aḥithophel sided with Absalom (2 Sam 15:31), when Absalom revolted against his father, and fell out of favor with David. When Aḥithophel saw that Absalom's cause was lost, he committed suicide (2 Sam 17:23). Given that Aḥithophel died long before the end of David's life, this list of royal counselors, unlike the list of divisional leaders (27:2–15), cannot reflect the last years of David's reign. This is the only mention of Aḥithophel in Chronicles.

"Ḥushai." Unlike the ill-fated Aḥithophel, Ḥushai remained a loyal advisor to David and became a prominent figure in David's entourage during Absalom's revolt (2 Sam 15:32–37; 16:16–19; 17:5–16; 1 Kgs 4:16). This is the only mention of Ḥushai in Chronicles.

"the Archite" *(hā'arkî)*. Joshua 16:2 situates the Archites, evidently a Canaanite group, near Ataroth.

"the friend (*rʿ*) of the king." A similar title *(rʿh hmlk)* is found in the Deuteronomistic History (1 Kgs 1:8 [cf. LXX$^{L}$, Josephus, *Ant.* 7.346]; 4:5) and is used with reference to Ḥushai (2 Sam 15:37; 16:16). "Friend" and "well-beloved friend" were honorific titles in ancient Egypt (de Vaux 1965: 122–23; Mettinger 1971: 63–69). As mentioned above (see TEXTUAL NOTE), *ho prōtos philos* was a title used in the Alexandrian court. The terms "friend" (*tōn philōn;* 1 Macc 2:18; 3:38; 6:10) and "first friend" (*tōn prōtōn philōn;* 1 Macc 10:65; 11:27; 2 Macc 8:9; Goldstein 1976: 416) are also attested in the Hasmonean period.

27:34. "Jehoiada son of Benaiah." The list of divisional officers mentions the better-known Benaiah son of Jehoiada (27:5). In the earlier list of David's cabinet, Benaiah son of Jehoiada commands "the Cherethites and the Pelethites" (18:17). In Kings, Solomon's cabinet includes "Benaiah son of Jehoiada in charge of the army" (1 Kgs 4:4). Given this evidence, many commentators contend that the present text is in error. This is possible, but I am more inclined to think that the references reflect papponymy, the practice of naming someone after his grandfather (NOTE to 5:36).

"Abiathar" *('ebyātār)*. The reference to Abiathar in this context is initially puzzling (see TEXTUAL NOTE). Is this Abiathar the same Abiathar as the priest who earlier served in David's government? Recourse to the Deuteronomistic History to resolve the issue is not altogether successful because problems of interpretation are not the exclusive province of the Chronicler's work. MT 1 Kings 4:4, for example, mentions both Abiathar and Zadoq as priests in Solomon's government even though Solomon earlier banished Abiathar to Anathoth (1 Kgs 2:26–27, 35; cf. 1 Kgs 1:7, 19, 42; 2:22; 4:2). Moreover, the career and importance of Abiathar in Samuel-Kings differ from that of Chronicles. Abiathar is occasionally mentioned elsewhere in Chronicles as a priest, but the author consistently gives pride of place to Zadoq as fulfilling this role. Zadoq appears twenty-seven times in Samuel-Kings and seventeen times in Chronicles. Samuel-Kings mentions Abiathar some twenty-seven times, but Chronicles only mentions him four times

(1 Chr 15:11; 18:16; 24:6; 27:34). In Samuel-Kings Abiathar is repeatedly spoken of as a priest, along with Zadoq, within David's government (1 Sam 22:20–22; 23:6–9; 30:7; 2 Sam 8:17; 15:24–36; 17:15; 19:11–12; 20:25). But in only one case is Abiathar paired with Zadoq as David's priests in Chronicles (1 Chr 15:11). In four instances his son Aḥimelek (2nd TEXTUAL NOTE to 18:16) serves alongside Zadoq (18:16; 24:3, 6, 31). These latter texts presuppose some sort of succession from Abiathar to his son (2nd NOTE to 18:16). Only in 27:34 does Abiathar appear apart from any reference to Zadoq. At the close of David's reign, when Solomon is anointed, the assembly also anoints Zadoq as high priest (29:22). No mention is made in this context of either Aḥimelek or his father, Abiathar. This strengthens the likelihood that the inventory of vv. 32–34 refers to an earlier portion of David's reign (1st NOTE to v. 33).

"the king's army" (*ṣb' lmlk*). The author may be speaking of David's private army (e.g., 2 Sam 5:6–8; 15:18; 1 Kgs 1:38, 44; de Vaux 1965: 123–24) as opposed to the conscripted national army (*hṣb'*; 1 Chr 18:15). But if so, this list signals a shift from the situation obtaining in 18:15–17. There (18:15) Joab is in charge of the army, while Benaiah son of Jehoiada is in charge of the Cherethites and the Pelethites (18:17).

## SOURCES AND COMPOSITION

Both passages (vv. 25–31 and vv. 32–34) are unparalleled in Samuel-Kings. There is some consensus that at least the first reflects a written source, but its date and origins are unclear. In this register, the duty is listed first, followed by the name of the official and his patronymic or gentilic. Of particular note are the number of non-Israelite names and gentilics included (e.g., "Obil the Ishmaelite," "Jaziz the Hagrite"). The second register (vv. 32–34) usually begins with the official's name and continues with his duty. The placement and content of the second list (vv. 32–34) raise a separate set of issues. It is curious that both Samuel (2 Sam 8:16–18; 20:23–26) and Chronicles (1 Chr 18:15–17; 27:32–34), feature two lists of high officials accountable to the king, separated from one another by several chapters. Whereas the first Chronicles list (18:15–17) is drawn from the author's *Vorlage* of 2 Sam 8:16–18, the second Chronicles list (27:32–34) bears no resemblance to the second Samuel list. Indeed, whereas the two Samuel lists are clearly related to one another, the two Chronicles lists exhibit only partial overlap. The portrayal of Solomon's reign in Kings includes another list of officials (1 Kgs 4:1–6), but that list does not seem to have significantly influenced the composition of 1 Chr 27:32–34. It is interesting that the second Chronicles list includes some personalities who do not figure elsewhere in the Chronistic depiction of David's reign (e.g., Jonathan, Ḥushai) or who belong to an earlier period within his career (e.g., Aḥithophel, Abiathar). Given the partial duplication of lists, although this point should not be pressed too far (see below), and the variation from the Chronicler's own presentation, legitimate doubts may be raised as to whether this material stems from the Chronicler's hand. Even though the names have been mostly drawn from Samuel, they have been put to a different use.

There is some merit to the view expressed by Rudolph (1955: 185), Mettinger (1971: 9), and Roddy Braun (1986: 263) that distinguishes between the character of the two Chronicles lists. The second focuses on those advisors who enjoyed a close personal relationship with David. Similarly, Michaeli (1967: 134) speaks of this list as complementing, rather than contradicting, the earlier list (1 Chr 18:15–17//2 Sam 8:16–18). In this conception, 1 Chr 27:32–34 does not comprise a tally of official governmental positions, but rather a roster of personal confidants and advisors. It may not be altogether helpful to frame the issue in this manner, however. In the ancient Mediterranean world, advisors could have official governmental positions (see below). But the point about the list of 18:15–17 referring to an Israelite cabinet has validity. The list of the highest officials in the neo-Assyrian government, sometimes called the Assyrian cabinet (Parpola 1995), resembles the list of 18:15–17 more than it does the list of 27:32–34. The "great men" (LÚ.GAL.MEŠ) of the Assyrian government included the *masennu* ("treasurer"), the *nāgir ekalli* ("palace herald"), the *rab šāqê* ("chief cupbearer"), *rab ša rēši* ("chief eunuch"), *sartinnu* ("chief judge"), the *sukkallu* ("vizier"), and the *turtānu* ("commander-in-chief"). Parpola (1995: 380) would add the *ummânu* ("scholar") to this list of royal councillors. The military is especially prominent in the Assyrian royal council (Mattila 2000). To the *turtānu* ("commander in chief") may be added the *rab šāqê* ("chief cupbearer," commander of the northern army), the *rab ša rēši* ("chief eunuch," commander of the royal army), and the *nāgir ekalli* ("palace herald," commander of the northeastern army), each possibly representing some martial responsibilities (Mattila 2000: 161–68). There are also some parallels between the Assyrian cabinet and both of the two Chronicles lists. For instance, each has a scribe (1 Chr 18:16; 27:32; cf. 1 Kgs 4:3) or a royal scholar. The military plays a significant role in each set of texts. But while the two biblical lists includes priests (Zadoq and Aḥimelek in 18:16; Abiathar in 1 Chr 27:34), no representative of the sacerdocy appears in the relevant Assyrian materials. No treasurer or chief judge appears in either of the two biblical lists, but treasurers appear, of course, among the other appointments (26:20–28).

Advisory bodies are known from other ancient sources. According to Herodotus (*Hist.* 1.206; 7.8, 53; 8.101), the Achaemenid kings used to convene "the first [or highest rank] among the Persians" to consult their opinions on matters of high importance, such as the planning of military campaigns. But in some settings, the two categories—cabinet officers and royal advisors—do not appear to be mutually exclusive. Note the appearance of Joab and the king's sons in both lists (1 Chr 18:15, 17; 27:32, 34). In Hellenistic states, whose polities were influenced by the structures of the Achaemenid Empire, "the heads of departments, now sometimes described as ministers, . . . together with the most important members of the royal household and court, might meet as a kind of Council of State, a Synhedrion summoned *ad hoc*" (Ehrenberg 1969: 182). This state council, which was not quite the same as an official cabinet, contained a head of imperial finances (with control of the treasury), the first minister or grand vizier, and the supreme bodyguard. Together with other officials, they formed a three-tiered hierarchy of the king's "friends" *(philoi)*, "an official group of dignitaries [whose] advice could be sought on important occasions" (Ehrenberg 1969: 164). In short, the text of 27:32–34 features mostly, but not exclusively, royal advisors. While the first list depicts a royal council, the second mentions royal confidants, a priest, and the commander in chief of David's army. In both cases, the officials participated, whether directly or indirectly, in the governance of Israel. The second log may have been placed in its present literary context by a later editor to complete the earlier inventories of public officials: the supervisors of the treasuries (26:20–28), the regional overseers (26:29–32), the divisional commanders (27:2–15), the tribal officials (27:16–22), and the royal supervisors (27:25–31). As such, the list helps set the scene for what follows as David convokes various dignitaries and high officials for Solomon's coronation (28:1).

## COMMENT

Chronicles presents David as playing an active role in Israelite economic life. The king owns agricultural estates (v. 27), operates storehouses in urban and rural areas for agricultural produce (vv. 25, 27–28), and has an investment in, if not some control over, trade (1st NOTE to v. 30). The king employs a variety of high officials who supervise his estates, fieldworkers, and storage facilities. The king has his own council (18:15–17) and coterie of advisors (27:32–34). Clearly, the monarch is responsible for foreign affairs, but he also has his own estates to manage. The latter duty commanded much more royal attention in ancient Near Eastern societies than some have recognized. The portrayal of Davidic involvement in agriculture, commerce, and trade is largely unparalleled in Samuel-Kings and deserves further study. Comparative study may shed some light on the depiction of a strong king who commands both a sizable bureaucracy and holdings in the countryside. Such a scenario makes sense for the royal estates and palaces of ancient Mesopotamia and Canaan in which kings owned, leased out, and profited from considerable landed properties (Heltzer 1989b; Postgate 1994ab). Some examples will illustrate this important feature of state economies.

During part of its history, the kingdom of Ugarit was held by its native ruler under the authority of the Hittite kings (Boyer 1955: 284–308; Beckman 1992: 41–49). There is substantial evidence to suggest that the Ugaritic kings wielded considerable influence over their domain (Rainey 1975b: 71–107; Heltzer 1979; 1982: 3–48). Ḫattušili III of Ḫatti recognized that his Ugaritic client was the titular owner of all its real estate (RS 17.130.33–34). How much control the Ugaritic king enjoyed over his subordinates is a matter of dispute (Marcus 1981: 53–60; deJong Ellis 1976: 1–8; H. Tadmor 1986). In any case, the palace at Ugarit, as its archives demonstrate, was a great administrative center in which the king held court, dispensing land grants to loyal subjects and taking land from others (Rainey 1962: 13; Heltzer 1982: 141–67; Vargyas 1988). Royal control over certain estates included supervision of those properties by members of the royal family (RS 15.70; 16.139, 140, 148, 206, 353). The king ruled from the palace, but his policies were felt in the countryside.

A second example is the kingdom of Ḫatti. Goetze (1957: 89–122) and others point out that as the Hittite Empire grew, it became increasingly dependent on retainers of the king to whom parcels of land were distributed in exchange for service to the crown. In the texts of the empire period, little is said of the *pankuš* (assembly), which may have partially limited the power of the king during the Old Kingdom. Instead, there are references to the lords *(bēlū)*, the officers (LÚ.DUGUD), and the chiefs (GAL), all of whom were subject to the king. Within this system, the land is thought to have been owned by the gods and, therefore, by the king, the deputy of the gods. The following text, translated by Goetze (1947: 90–91), illustrates this principle well.

> When the king pays homage to the gods, the "anointed" recites as follows: "The tabarnaš, the king is agreeable to the gods. The country belongs to the storm-god; heaven and earth [and] the people belong to the storm-god." Thus he made the labarna, the king, his governor. He gave him the whole country of Ḫattuša. So let the labarna govern the whole country with [his] hand! Whoever comes too near to the person and the domain[?] of the labarna the king [?], let the storm-god destroy him!" (§30.1–8)

Being a pivotal figure in divine-human relations had practical consequences in land tenure. Having been granted property by the divine realm, the king, in turn, bestowed property upon his subjects. Soldiers, priests, and craftsmen entrusted with small parcels of land were obliged to provide support *(šaḫḫan)*, consisting of military service, cultivation, and payment of dues. There is evidence that local authorities held some sway over certain land holdings, but even these were required to render some services to the king (Güterbock 1954: 18–19; Korošec 1974). Estates and large tracts of land were granted to relatives and officials of the king. Priests and high officials who received large royal land grants were given some exemptions from certain duties (Güterbock 1940: 47–55; Riemschneider 1958). Apart from these exemptions, there is little known about what powers and rights such high officials had in the hierarchy of Hittite society. Judging from the Hittite laws, the rights of these officials do not seem to be many (Friedrich 1959: §39–41, 46–47, 50, 52, 54–55).

It would be far too simplistic to suggest that the authors of Chronicles modeled their presentation of David's holdings after a standard ancient Near Eastern prototype. To begin with, a high level of royal involvement in the local economy is not a constant throughout the ancient Near East. In Babylon during the Second Isin Dynasty, for example, there seems to have been significant ownership of land by temples, cities, and private individuals. In this period, if a king wished to make a grant of privately owned land, he first had to purchase it from the individual who owned it (Brinkman 1963: 238–39). Nevertheless, even this era witnessed some significant royal involvement in regional affairs. To sustain a program of public works as well as support the royal household and administration, kings derived income from a variety of sources. These included revenues from crown estates farmed or grazed in his name; taxes on private estates, such as a fixed percentage of a fall crop or of an increase in flocks (BBSt 6.155–157; 8. [top] 21–22); the conscription of men and animals for public-works projects (BBSt 25.7–8; Hinke 3.25–27); the impressment of men and animals into royal service on a more permanent basis (BBSt 24.35–37; 25.9; 9.3–15); the forced provision for royal officials, troops, and animals; the supply of fodder for royal cattle; and the quartering of royal soldiers (Brinkman 1968: 292–96; Marcus 1981: 53–58). These broad powers of taxation were zealously guarded by kings of the Second Isin Dynasty, who only rarely granted exemptions from them.

Within the context of Chronicles, there are further complications. The authors acknowledge the existence of other significant players in the social life and economy of ancient Israel. One important factor was the role played by priests and Levites. Like the authors of Joshua before them, the authors assert that many sites in ancient Israel served as Levitical towns (1 Chr 6:39–66). The authors acknowledge that local families, ancestral houses, and sodalities continued to exercise considerable leverage even after David established his regime in Jerusalem. The authors of Chronicles allege, in fact, significantly more tribal activity and power during the monarchy than the Deuteronomists do. Families and patrilineal clans exercised control over their own properties (Levine 1996). Moreover, the authors do not present a static picture of the relationship between the center and the periphery. Significant contraction in royal power during periods in which Judah's worst monarchs ruled is conceded. The many geographic regions constituting Israel and Judah are another important factor to consider in assessing how much power a Jerusalemite monarch could project into the countryside. The very fact that the authors mention different areas in which royal assets were located, such as the Sharon and the Shephelah, testifies to the fact that they recognized the geographic complexity of the land they attributed to the control of the Davidic monarchy.

Rather than presenting David as a sovereign whose only concern was the center, the authors depict David as a very influential player in the economy, one whose reach extends beyond Jerusalem to other regions within Israel. This emphasis on a kingly role in trade and agriculture is not unique. Royal estates and interests are mentioned in the reigns of several other monarchs. During one of the better periods in his reign, Reḥoboam "strengthened the fortified towns and stationed commanders within them, along with storehouses (*'wṣrwt*) of food, oil, and wine" (2 Chr 11:11). Like his grandfather (1 Chr 18:17; 27:32), Reḥoboam employed his sons in administration, distributing them "among all the lands of Judah and Benjamin, and among all the fortified cities" (2 Chr 11:23). Reḥoboam provisioned much food to the princes and sought (for them) "a throng of wives" (2 Chr 11:23). Centuries later, King Uzziah acquired and administered extensive crown properties to the south and southwest. Uzziah "built towers in the wilderness (מדבר) and hewed out many cisterns, for he had large herds in the Shephelah, farmers on the plain (מישור), and vinedressers in the hills and the Carmel" (2 Chr 26:10). Uzziah, the Chronicler explains, was "a lover of the land" (2 Chr 26:10). The description of Uzziah's royal estates recalls David's patrimony, but his holdings do not match the variety and extent of those ascribed to David. Finally, Ḥezeqiah's reforms include broad economic initiatives. In his prosperity, Ḥezeqiah "made storehouses for himself for silver, gold, precious stones, spices, shields, and every kind of splendid vessel" (2 Chr 32:27). The king built "storehouses *(miskĕnôt)* for the yield of grain, wine, and oil as well as facilities for every kind of cattle" (2 Chr 32:28). Ḥezeqiah also "made cities for himself and [enjoyed] flocks and herds in abundance, because God gave to him vast possessions *(rĕkûš)*" (2 Chr 32:29). All three kings—Reḥoboam, Uzziah, and Ḥezeqiah—are, at least for a time, resourceful builders and energetic administrators. Each amply uses his resources to increase crown estates. In the case of Ḥezeqiah, his total assets rival those of Solomon (Williamson 1982b: 385; Dillard 1987: 252–61; Throntveit 1987: 121–25).

The treatment of various monarchs—David, Reḥoboam, Uzziah, and Ḥezeqiah—reveals that the authors embraced a broader vision of their nation than some have acknowledged. David appears as the founder of several cultic institutions, the major patron of Jerusalem's worship, a well-supported military figure, and a powerful owner of agricultural estates. The writers' perspective both relates to and transcends the world of the Temple. In the context of the late Persian age, a time in which Yehud's residents did not enjoy complete autonomy over their own political affairs, the authors of Chronicles maintain an interest in a secure and independent national state by means of a creative act of writing. This major effort to commemorate the Davidic kingdom's legacy by (re)constructing its past involves, among other things, upholding certain features of the royal state that largely go unmentioned or are altogether ignored in Samuel-Kings. In this context, one may press the matter further. By mentioning a system of twelve centralized military divisions (27:1–15), twelve overseers of the royal estates (27:25–31), and seven royal advisors and officials (27:32–34), the authors ensure that David's patrimony is not thought of merely in spiritual terms. Of the various polities that characterized Israel in earlier literature, the authors of Chronicles uphold the royal. That this regime was also so beneficial for Jerusalem's cult and temple is one of the accomplishments in its favor.

# *XXXV. David Charges the National Assembly (28:1–21)*

*Israel's Leaders Convoked*

1 David assembled all of Israel's officers—the tribal officers, the officers of the divisions, those serving the king, the officers of the thousands, the officers of the hundreds, and the officers in charge of all the property and livestock for the king and for his sons—along with the eunuchs, warriors, and every valiant warrior to Jerusalem.

*David's Speech to the National Convention*

2 Then King David rose to his feet and said:
"Hear me, my kinsmen and my people. I myself had it in mind to build a
house of rest for the Ark of the Covenant of Yhwh and for the footstool of the
feet of our God. So I set out to build. 3 But God said to me, 'You will not build
a house for my name, because you are a man of wars and have shed blood.'
4 And Yhwh the God of Israel chose me out of all of the house of my father to
become king over Israel forever. Indeed, he chose Judah as leader, and
within the house of Judah (he chose) the house of my father, and among the
sons of my father he has been pleased with me to make (me) king over all Israel. 5 And from all of my sons—for Yhwh has granted me many sons—he has
chosen my son Solomon to sit upon the throne of the kingdom of Yhwh over
Israel. 6 So he said to me, 'Solomon your son, he, he will build my house and
my courts, for I have chosen him to be a son to me and I, I shall be a father to
him. 7 And I shall establish his kingdom forever, if he is resolute to perform
my commandments and judgments as is the case today.' 8 Now, in the sight of
all of the assembly of Yhwh, and in the hearing of our God, observe and seek
out the commandments of Yhwh your God so that you may possess the good
land and bequeath it to your children forever after you.

*David's Counsel to Solomon*

9 "As for you, Solomon my son, know the God of your father and serve him
with a whole heart and a willing soul, for Yhwh searches every heart and understands every form of thought. If you seek him, he will let himself be found
by you; but, if you abandon him, he will reject you in perpetuity. 10 Now, take
note that Yhwh has chosen you to build for him a house as the sanctuary. Be
strong and act."

*The Temple Plans Are Handed Over to Solomon*

11 Then David gave to Solomon his son the plan for the entrance hall (of the
Temple) and its buildings, its storerooms, its upper chambers, its rooms, its inner
chambers, and the house of the (ark) cover; 12 and the plan for all that he had by
the spirit: for the courts of the House of Yhwh and for all of the surrounding chambers, for the treasuries of the House of God and the treasuries of the dedicated
gifts, 13 for the divisions of the priests and the Levites, for every work of the service
of the House of Yhwh, and for all of the furnishings of the service of the House of
Yhwh; 14 for all kinds of golden furnishings, by weight, for furnishings of every sort
of service; for all kinds of silver furnishings, by weight, for all furnishings of every
sort of service; 15 and (for) the weight for the golden lampstands and their golden
lamps, by the weight of each lampstand and its lamps; and for the silver lampstands, by weight, for each lampstand and its lamps, according to the service of
each lampstand; 16 and the gold, by weight, for the tables of the row bread, for
each table; and (for) the silver, by weight, for the silver tables; 17 and (for) the flesh
hooks, the basins, and the jars of pure gold; for the golden bowls, by weight, for
each bowl; and for the silver bowls, by weight, for each bowl; 18 and for the altar of
incense, refined gold, by weight; and for the plan of the chariot—the cherubim in
gold spreading out (their) wings and protecting the Ark of the Covenant of Yhwh.

19 "Everything in writing (has come) to me from the hand of Yhwh. He made (me) understand all the pieces of the plan."

*David's Concluding Invocation*

20 Then David said to Solomon his son:

"Be strong, be courageous, and act. Neither fear nor be dismayed, for Yhwh my God is with you. He will neither fail you nor abandon you until every work of the service of the House of Yhwh is completed.
21 Here are the divisions of the priests and the Levites for every kind of service for the House of Yhwh. And with you in all of the work will be all sorts of volunteers, with skill for every kind of service. The officers and all of the people are at your every command."

# Textual Notes

28:1. "the tribal officers" *(śry hšbṭym)*. Thus MT and LXX$^{L}$. Josephus (*Ant.* 7.370) reads similarly, *tous phylarchous*. The reading of LXX$^{AB}$ *archontas tōn kritōn*, "the leaders of the judges" (= *hśry hšpṭym*), may reflect a *bêt/pê* confusion. Allen (1974b: 124) contends that the error was phonetic.

"those serving the king" *(hmšrtym ʾt hmlk)*. Thus MT and LXX$^{L}$. LXX$^{AB}$ *tōn peri to sōma tou basileōs*, "those concerned with the person of the king."

"the officers of the hundreds." Reading with MT (*lectio brevior*). The additions of LXX$^{AB}$ *kai tous gazophylakas*, "treasurers" (cf. 1 Esd 2:11; 8:19, 46), and LXX$^{L}$ *archontas tōn thēsaurōn* (= *śry hʾwṣrwt*) assimilate to 1 Chr 26:20–28.

"the officers in charge of all the property and livestock for the king" *(wśry kl-rkwš-wmqnh lmlk)*. Thus MT. LXX$^{ABL}$ present a different text, *kai tous epi tōn hyparchontōn autou*, "and those in charge of his lieutenants."

"and for his sons" *(wlbnyw)*. The expression is missing from LXX$^{AB}$. LXX$^{L}$ *kai tōn huiōn autou*. Some (e.g., Curtis and Madsen 1910: 296–97; NAB) follow Vg. *filiosque suos* (= *lbnyw*) and connect this expression with what follows ("along with the eunuchs, warriors"), rather than with what precedes ("all the property and livestock for the king"). In this manner, David's sons appear in the national assembly (cf. 29:23–24). Grammatically, however, the expression fits with the preceding construction *(lmlk)*. It is perhaps for this reason that Begrich *(BHK)* reads *wbnyw*, although he does not cite either LXX$^{L}$ or Vg.

"along with the eunuchs" *(ʿim-hassārîsîm)*. Reading with MT and LXX$^{L}$ *syn tois eunouchois* (*lectio difficilior*). The phrase is absent from LXX$^{AB}$. Tg. *rbnʾ* assimilates to the standard term *(śr)* in this verse. On *sārîs*, "eunuch," see 2 Kgs 18:17; 20:18; Isa 56:3; Esth 1:10, 12, 15; 2:3, 14; 4:4; 6:2, 14; 2 Chr 18:8; Sir 30:20 (*HALOT* 769–70). The translation "the eunuchs" *(hassārîsîm)* is maintained even though scholars continue to debate whether there actually were eunuchs in the Jerusalem court (H. Tadmor 1995). Grayson (1995) provides a general discussion of the comparative evidence from Assyria, India, and Persia, while Mattila (2000: 61–76) provides an extensive study of the Neo-Assyrian materials.

"every valiant warrior" (*lĕkol-gibbôr ḥayil*). So MT. Some Heb. MSS have the pl. The *lāmed* is used to introduce the last noun in an enumeration (Joüon §125l). LXX[B] *kai tous machētas*, "and the fighters."

28:2. "to his feet" (*ʿl rglyw*). So MT (*lectio brevior*). LXX (and Arab.) *en mesō tēs ekklēsias*, "in the midst of the assembly." Josephus (*Ant.* 7.370) *stas eph' hypsēlotatou bēmatos*, "standing upon a very high rostrum."

"I myself had it in mind" (*ʾny ʿm lbby*). So MT (maximum differentiation). Some would add *hyh* with LXX, Syr., and 1 Chr 22:7. I am taking the pron. as introducing a *casus pendens* construction, reinforcing the pronominal suf. that follows (GKC §143a, n. 3; Joüon §156b).

"so I set out to build" (*whkynwty lbnwt*). Thus MT (*lectio brevior*). On the construction, compare Gen 37:21; Num 14:40; Jer 37:12. LXX[B] is more expansive, *kai hētoimasa ta eis tēn kataskēnōsin epitēdeia*, "and I provided that which is suitable for the resting place."

28:3. "God." So MT and LXX. Tg., Boh., and Syr. have the tetragrammaton.

"a house for my name" (*byt lšmy*). Thus MT (*lectio brevior*). LXX *emoi oikon tou eponomasai to onoma mou ep autō*, "a house for me, to place my name upon it" (= *byt ly lśwm šmy ʿlyw*).

28:4. "as leader" (*lngyd*). So MT. LXX[AB] *to basileion*, "the royalty."

"among the sons of my father" (*bbny ʾby*). Lacking in LXX[B] due to haplography (*homioteleuton* from *ʾby* to *by*).

"has been pleased" (*rāṣâ*). So MT (maximum differentiation). Tg. reads (again) "chose" (= *bḥr*).

"to make (me) king" (*lhmlyk*). MT is elliptical. On the basis of LXX *tou genesthai me basilea* and Vg. *ut me eligeret regem*, some read *lhmlykny* (e.g., Begrich in *BHK*).

28:5. "the kingdom of Yhwh" (*malkût yhwh*). On the translation, see the 2nd NOTE to 22:10.

28:6. "my house and my courts" (*bêtî waḥăṣērôtî*). On the pair *byt/ḥṣr* and its parallels in Ugaritic and Phoenician texts (e.g., *KAI* 27.5–8; 60.2, 3), see most recently Avishur (2000: 33–34).

"my courts" (*ḥṣrwty*). Thus MT and LXX[AB] (*tēn aulēn mou*). LXX[L] has the sg. *tas aulas mou*.

28:7. "his kingdom" (*ʾt-mlkwtw*). Syr. inserts "throne," hence assimilating this reading to "throne of the kingdom" (*ksʾ mlkwt*) in v. 5.

"if he is resolute." Thus MT and LXX (*ean ischysē*). Syr. *wʾnhw dlʾ nṣbʾ*, "although he is unwilling."

28:8. "all of the assembly." Reading with LXX* (*lectio brevior*). MT features a double reading, "all Israel, (the) assembly of Yhwh" (כל-ישׂראל קהל יהוה).

"and in the hearing of our God, observe" (*wbʾzny ʾlhynw šmrw*). Reading with MT and LXX[AN]. The phrase is lacking in LXX[B], perhaps due to haplography (*homoioarkton* from *wbʾzny ʾlhynw šmrw* to *wdršw*). On the expression "ears of (our) God/Yhwh," see Num 11:1, 18; Ps 10:17. Rudolph (1955: 184) takes a different approach to the textual problems in this verse. Asuming a haplography (in MT) after "our God" (*homoioarkton*), he inserts "hear my words" (*šmʿw ʾt-dbry*).

"seek out the commandments." So LXX[B] and $c_2$. MT and LXX[AN] add explicating *kl* ("seek out all of the commandments").

"commandments of Yhwh." So MT and LXX. Syr. reads the more common "his commandments."

"your God." Thus MT. LXX[B] and Vg. "our God."

28:9. "as for you" *(w'th)*. Reading with MT (maximum differentiation). The lemma of LXX, "and now" (= *w'th*), assimilates to the lemma of v. 8.

"your father" *('byk)*. Thus MT *(lectio difficilior)*. LXX "your fathers" (= *'bwtyk*).

"a willing soul" *(nepeš ḥăpēṣâ)*. LXX *psychē thelousē*. Cf. Deut 4:29; Neh 1:11.

"every form of thought" *(kl yṣr mḥšbwt)*. So MT and LXX[L]. "Form" is lacking in LXX[AB] *pan enthymēma*.

28:10. "build for him." So LXX. MT lacks "for him" *(lw)* due to haplography (*homoioarkton* before *lmqdš*).

28:11. "the entrance hall" *(h'wlm)*. LXX reads here (and in 1 Kgs 6:3; 2 Chr 8:12; 15:8; 29:7) *tou naou*, "of the shrine."

"and its buildings" *(wbtyw)*. Reading with LXX *(kai tōn oikōn autou)*. MT *w't-btyw*. Benzinger (1901: 66) emends to *whbyt*, "and the House" (cf. cursives egim *ton oikon*; Syr. and Vg. *et templi et cellariorum*), while Rudolph (1955: 186) follows Keil (1873: 292) in suggesting *w't tbnyt hbyt*, "plan of the House." The impulse to abandon MT *w't-btyw* is understandable. The suf. would seem to refer to missing *hbyt* and not to the *'ûlām*, which may not have had any buildings attached. But MT may simply be elliptical. In two cases, there seems to be a close association between the *'ûlām (yhwh)* and the Temple (2 Chr 8:12; 15:8), a point also made by Japhet (1993a: 494). In two other instances (2 Chr 29:7, 17), Chronicles employs *'ûlām* ("porch" or "vestibule") as a merism for the Temple.

"inner chambers." Thus MT and LXX. The plus of Syr., "and the outer (chambers)" (= *whḥyṣwnym*), may have been lost by haplography (*homoioteleuton* after *hpnymym*). Cf. 1 Kgs 6:29, 31; Ezek 41:17.

"the house of the (ark) cover" *(bêt hakkappōret)*. Thus MT. LXX *tou oikou tou exilasmou*, "house of the propitiation."

28:12. "by the spirit" *(bārûaḥ)*. So MT. LXX *en pneumati autou*, "in his spirit." Tg. "by the spirit of prophecy."

28:13. "(and) for the divisions *(wlmḥlqwt)* of the priests and the Levites" *(hkhnym whlwym)*. The construct chain with a single construct governing two absolutes is unusual in CH. "The more closely related the genitives are, the more likely they are to form such a phrase" (Waltke and O'Connor §9.3b). Cf. LXX[AB] "of the lodgings" *(kai tōn katalymatōn)*. It is also possible to construe this phrase in MT as a description of one of the uses for "all of the surrounding chambers" (v. 12; Benzinger 1901: 66).

"and for all of the furnishings of the service of the House of Yhwh" *(wlkl-kly 'bwdt byt-yhwh)*. So MT. LXX *kai tōn apothēkōn tōn leitourgēsimōn skeuōn* (LXX[AN] add *tēs latreias oikou Kyriou*), "and of the storehouses of the service of the equipment (of the worship of the House of Yhwh)."

28:14. "for all kinds of golden furnishings, by weight" *(lkl kly hzhb zhb bmšql)*. I am following the reconstruction of Begrich *(BHK)*. The text of MT is disturbed:

"for gold, by weight, for gold" *(lzhb bmšql lzhb)*. Unfortunately, the text of LXX* for v. 14 is only of limited value, *kai tōn stathmon tēs holkēs autōn tōn te chrysōn kai argyrōn*, "and of the weight of their trailing, (both) of the gold and of the silver."

"furnishings." As Samuel Driver (1911) pointed out long ago, the *klym* include a variety of articles and utensils for the sanctuary, hence the traditional translation "vessels" is too narrow.

"for all kinds of silver furnishings" *(lkl kly hksp ksp)*. I am following Rothstein and Hänel (1927) in restoring *ksp* (haplography). MT reads "for silver furnishings" *(lkl kly hksp)*.

"for all furnishings of every sort of service" *(lkl-kly ʿbwdh wʿbwdh)*. Especially in LBH, a noun may be repeated syndectically to indicate diversity (Waltke and O'Connor §7.2.3c).

28:15. "and (for) the weight" *(wmšql)*. Some (e.g., NAB) would delete as a dittography. But it seems better to take *mšql* as the acc. of the object of the verb *ntn* in v. 11. In other words, David prescribes a certain weight for the golden lampstands (cf. 2 Chr 4:7). The same understanding seems to be at work in the much briefer text of LXX* *lychniōn tēn holkēn edōken autō kai tōn lychnōn*, "he gave to him the weight of the lampstands and of the lamps." For a different view, see Dirksen (1996b).

"and their golden lamps" *(wnrtyhm zhb)*. In the phrase, *zhb* is subordinated to *nrtyhm* by apposition (GKC §131d). Waltke and O'Connor (§10.2.2e) prefer to speak of *zhb* as an acc. of specification.

"and for the silver lampstands" *(wlmnrwt hksp)*. So MT. Begrich *(BHK)* and Rudolph (1955) favor adding *ksp*, "silver."

"by the weight for each lampstand and its lamps" *(bmšql lmnwrh wmnwrh wnrtyh)*. The lemma of MT *bmšql lmnwrh wnrtyh* has suffered a haplography *(homoioteleuton)*. Others would simply delete the *lāmed* before *mnrwrh*.

"according to the service" *(kʿbwdt)*. Thus MT. Many Heb. MSS *bʿbwdt*.

28:16. "and the gold, by weight" *(wʾt-hzhb bmšql)*. A restoration based on the supposition of a haplography of *bêt* in MT *ʾt-hzhb mšql*. LXX* *edōken autō homoiōs ton stathmon*, "he likewise gave him the weight (of the tables of setting forth, of each golden table, and in like manner of silver)."

"for the tables of the row bread" *(lšlḥnwt hmʿrkt)*. Thus MT. LXX* for this verse raises a number of issues: *edōken autō homoiōs ton stathmon tōn trapeksōn tēs protheseōs hekastēs trapeksēs chrysēs kai hōsautōs tōn argyrōn*, "he likewise gave him the weight of the tables of setting forth, of each golden table, and in like manner of silver." The translation abridges the repetitive Heb. here and elsewhere in vv. 14–16 (Allen 1974a: 115). Note, for instance, the use of *homoiōs* and *hōsautōs* for repeated nouns in the Heb. The alternative explanation (Benzinger 1901: 67) that MT has been reworked and supplemented in these verses is less compelling.

"and (for) the silver, by weight, for the silver tables" *(wĕkesep bammišqāl lĕšulḥănôt hakkāsep)*. A restoration. MT, *wĕkesep lĕšulḥănôt hakkāsep*, "and the silver for the silver tables."

28:17. "and (for) the flesh hooks" *(whmzlgwt)*. So MT and LXX* *(kai tōn krea-*

*grōn).* Some (e.g., *BHK* and *BHS*) would reconstruct *wlmzlgwt,* "and for the flesh hooks." LXX *kai tōn kreagrōn,* "and of the flesh forks." But in the context of the sequence beginning in v. 12, the Heb. does not have to repeat the prep. in each instance (Kropat, §16).

"the basins" *(hmzrqwt).* So MT. Similarly, LXX *spondeiōn.*

"for each bowl" *(wlkpwr wkpwr).* Rothstein and Hänel (1927), *BHS,* and others add "golden," but by this time in the sequence the point is understood. Note the summarizing of LXX *kai stathmon tōn chrysōn kai tōn argyrōn hekastou stathmou,* "and the weight of the gold and of the silver, of each weight."

"and for the silver bowls." Again, some commentators add "silver" to the following "for each bowl."

28:18. "by weight." So MT. LXX adds "he showed him." To comprehend the clauses in vv. 17–18 the statement in v. 11 must be understood, namely, that these standards were part of the plan that David gave *(wayyittēn dāwîd)* to Solomon. What is implicit in MT, LXX makes explicit by repeating the locution *edōken (autō),* "he gave," in vv. 15 and 16 and providing *hypedeiksen autō,* "he showed him" in v. 18.

"the cherubim in gold" *(hkrwbym zhb).* Construing *zhb* as an attributive acc. of determination (Joüon, §127c). LXX* "of the cherubim."

"spreading out (their) wings" *(lprśym knpym).* So Tg., which presents the standard expression (Exod 25:20; 37:9; Deut 32:11; 1 Kgs 6:27; 8:7; Jer 48:40; 49:22; Job 39:26 [Qere]; 2 Chr 3:13; 5:8). Cf. LXX *tōn diapepetasmenōn tais pteryxin.* MT, which reads *lprśym,* has lost *knpym* by haplography *(homoioteleuton).* Others would read *hprśym whskkym* on the basis of Vg. *extendentium alas et velantium.*

28:19. "everything in writing" *(hakkōl biktāb).* LXX* *panta en graphē,* "all in writing."

"to me" *(ʿly).* Construing the prep. *ʿal* as indicating an indirect object, a construction that becomes common in LBH (Williams §296). Some, with reference to LXX (e.g., Rudolph 1955: 188), would read *ʿlyw,* "to him." But LXX is different, *edōken Daueid Salōmōn,* "David gave to Solomon." In any case, the syntax of this verse is difficult. Reading *ʿly,* Zöckler (1877: 154) translates "from the hand of the Lord upon me." Opting for *ʿlyw,* NAB translates "because the hand of the LORD was upon him." A critical question is whether *ʿly* goes with what precedes *(myd yhwh)* or with what follows *(hiśkîl).* Many (e.g., Benzinger 1901: 67; Japhet 1993a: 498) take *ʿly* with *hśkyl,* hence, "All this, in writing at the LORD's direction, he made clear to me—the plan of all the works" (NRSV). But *ʿly* with *hśkyl* would be an exceedingly rare grammatical construction. The verb *śkl* in the *hipʿil* can stand by istelf (Gen 3:6; Ps 94:8; Dan 9:25), take a direct object (Deut 32:29; Pss 64:10 [ET 64:9]; 106:7; Prov 16:23; Dan 9:22; Neh 9:20; 2 Chr 30:22), or (occasionally) occur with the preps. *min* (Ps 119:99), *bĕ* (Dan 9:13), and *ʾel* (Neh 8:13). But in only one case does the *hipʿil* of *śkl* take the prep. *ʿal:* "he who creates understanding concerning a matter *(mśkyl ʿl-dbr)* will find success" (Prov 16:20). Moreover, in 1 Chr 28:19 the prep. construction *ʿly* occurs before, not after, the verb. This would break the pattern of *śkl* in the *hipʿil* with preps. Hence, there does not seem to be any overriding reason to construe *ʿly* with *hśkyl* in 28:19.

"from the hand of Yhwh" *(myd yhwh)*. So MT. LXX is more ambiguous, *cheiros Kyriou*, "hand of the Lord." For other instances of the expression *myd yhwh/'lhym*, see Josh 22:31; 1 Sam 4:8; Isa 40:2; 51:17; Jer 25:17.

"he made (me) understand" *(hiśkîl)*. So MT. LXX again differs: *kata tēn perigenētheisan autō synesin* (= *ʿal hiśkîl*?), "according to (his) superlative understanding" (Allen 1974b: 74).

"all the pieces of the plan" *(kl ml'kwt htbnyt)*. Reading with MT. LXX *tēs katergasias tou paradeigmatos* (= *ml'kt htbnyt*?), "of the manufacture of the model."

28:20. "Yhwh my God" *(yhwh 'lhy)*. Reading tentatively with LXX, *Kyrios ho theos mou*. MT, "Yhwh God, my God" *(yhwh 'lhym 'lhy)*, seems to have suffered dittography. Alternatively, one could argue that LXX has suffered haplography *(homoioarkton)*.

"the House of Yhwh" *(byt-yhwh)*. There is a long plus in LXX at the end of v. 20, *to paradeigma tou naou kai tou oikou autou kai sakchō autou kai ta hyperōa kai tas apothēkas tas esōteras kai ton oikon tou hilasmou kai to paradeigma oikou Kyriou*. Some scholars, therefore, restore *whnh 't tbnyt h'wlm wbtyw wggzkyw wʿlytyw wḥdryw hpnymym wbyt hkprt wtbnyt byt yhwh*, "and the plan of the entrance hall and its buildings, its storerooms, its upper chambers, its rooms, the inner chambers, and the house of the (ark) cover, and the plan of the House of Yhwh" (cf. vv. 11–12). Torrey (1910: 73) contends that this material was lost by haplography. The material cannot be deemed to be a simple dittography of vv. 11–12 *(pace BHK)* because the plus is only similar to, but not identical to, these earlier verses. Allen (1974b: 143) is skeptical that a haplography occurred, arguing that the mention of rooms and buildings does not fit the later context of vv. 20–21. He contends that the addition reflects an early Heb. gloss on *kl ml'kt htbnyt* in v. 19, which became misplaced in LXX. The material does seem to be an early addition, but I would argue that this material, based on vv. 11–12, was introduced through repetitive resumption (from *byt-yhwh* at the end of v. 20 to *byt yhwh* at the end of the new material). The insertion of this material in LXX creates a parallel to the order of the material in vv. 11–13. In both cases, the description of architectural features (vv. 11–12, 20) leads to the mention of the priestly and Levitical divisions (vv. 13, 21). Hence, the addition reflected in LXX supplies what was perceived to be lacking in the Heb.

28:21. "all sorts of volunteers" *(lkl ndyb)*. So MT. Some read with LXX$^{B}$ *(kai pas prothymos)*, which seems to lack the initial *lāmed*, but there is no need to abandon MT. In LBH the prep. *l-* can introduce a nominative (1 Chr 5:2; 7:1; 26:26; 28:1; 29:6; 2 Chr 7:21; Ezra 7:28; S. Driver 1914: 539). In this case, the *lāmed* introduces the last term of an enumeration (Joüon, §125l).

## Notes

28:1. "assembled" *(wayyaqhēl)*. Assemblies are common in the Chronicler's work (e.g., 1 Chr 13:5; 15:3; 2 Chr 5:2–3; 11:1; 20:26). But this case is exceptional in its breadth of coverage. David convokes all of his nation's dignitaries to Jerusalem to witness his charge to Solomon and to enlist their support for his assignments to Solomon. In contrast with David's earlier select gathering of leaders, priests, and Levites (23:2), this assembly is comprehensive, involving a wide array of officials. Indeed, some of the assembled officials appear as recent appointees, leaders who received their positions as part of the larger central administrative reorganization (23:2–27:34).

"the tribal officers" *(śry hšbṭym)*. See the NOTES to 27:16–22 and the COMMENT on 27:1–24. Indebted to the presentation in Chronicles, Eupolemus also presents the tribal officers as present at the handover of power from David to Solomon (Eusebius, *Praep. ev.* 9.30.8).

"the officers of the divisions" *(śry hmḥlqwt)*. On the position of these military leaders in protecting Israel's central government, see the NOTES to 27:1–15.

"those serving the king" *(hmšrtym ʾt hmlk)*. The use of *mšrtym* for royal officers is common in LBH (1 Chr 27:1; 2 Chr 17:19; 22:8; Esth 1:10; Prov 29:12).

"the officers of the thousands." Along with "the officers of the hundreds" *(śry hmʾwt)*, these military leaders *(śry hʾlpym)* appear elsewhere as participants in the national reorganization (26:26; 27:1). See further the 4th NOTE to 26:26.

"all the property and livestock" *(kol-rĕkûš-ûmiqneh)*. Handled by the officers in charge of the royal estates (27:25–31).

"and for his sons." On the role of royal princes, see the NOTES to 18:17; 27:32.

"warriors, and every valiant warrior" *(hgbwrym wlkl-gbwr ḥyl)*. See also 11:12, 19, 24; 12:4; 26:6, 31; 27:2–15; 29:24.

28:2–10. "King David." His speech to the assembled luminaries falls into two distinct parts. The first (vv. 2–8), addressed to the dignitaries, summarizes David's plans for the succession to the throne and Solomon's mission to build the promised sanctuary. It ends with an appeal for observance of Yhwh's commandments. The second part, addressed more specifically to Solomon (vv. 9–10), instructs the heir in piety and summons him to build the sanctuary. Both parts of the speech are infused with traditional expressions known from older texts. The first part, in particular, explicitly cites Nathan's dynastic oracle (1 Chr 17) and repeats, for the benefit of this large audience, what David had earlier said to Solomon directly (22:7–16).

28:2. "rose to his feet." Probably from his seat. The author has the king assume a proper stance for a public presentation (cf. 1 Kgs 8:22, 54; Knoppers 1995c). It is unlikely that the Chronicler thought of David as sickly or bedridden at this point (*pace* Qimḥi, who refers to 1 Kgs 1:1–4). One must be careful to distinguish between the portrait of David's latter years in Samuel-Kings and the portrait of the same in Chronicles. In the latter, David is a highly active figure in his old age (1 Chr 23:1; 29:28). Japhet (1993a: 486) draws an analogy between Deuteronomy's Moses and the Chronicler's David. Both are still vigorous in their sunset years (Deut 34:7).

"hear me" *(šmʿwny)*. A common beginning to many of the speeches in Chronicles (1 Chr 28:2; 2 Chr 13:4; 15:2; 20:20; 28:11; 29:5).

"my kinsmen" *(ʾḥy)*. That the king is kin to his subjects is an important concept in Deuteronomistic ideology (1 Sam 30:23; 2 Sam 19:12–13) and a condition for kingship in Deuteronomic law (Deut 17:15, 20). The Chronicler expands on this concept by emphasizing the participation of the Israelite populace in royal undertakings.

"a house of rest" (*bêt mĕnûḥâ*). Although this particular phrase is unique within the HB, it and others like it are well attested in the Targums (*Tg. Onq.* Deut 12:9; *Tg. Neof. (M)* Deut 12:9; *Tg. Neb.* Judg 20:43; *Tg. Neb.* Mic 2:10; *Tg. Isa.* 28:12; *Tg. Ket.* Ps 116:7; Hurvitz 1995: 174–77). The Temple is presented as a permanent repository for the roving Ark of the Covenant. In this respect, the Chronicler's ideology has been influenced by both the Deuteronomistic work (1 Kgs 8:1–13) and Ps 132. The author of Kings carefully makes the case that the Temple serves a divinely ordained role as the Ark's permanent home (Knoppers 1995c). Other voices (e.g., 2 Sam 7:4–7) questioned whether such a stationary sanctuary was legitimate, much less necessary. Later, the author of Isa 66:1 has Yhwh question whether anyone could build him a house, or a place, of rest (*mqwm mnwḥty*). This author speaks of heaven as Yhwh's throne and the earth as his footstool. But the authors of Ps 132 present another perspective. The psalm assumes the need for David to find Yhwh an appropriate sanctuary (Ps 132:2–5; cf. 1 Chr 28:10). David avoids his house and abstains from sleep until he finds a domicile for "the Mighty One of Jacob" (Ps 132:3–5). The psalmist celebrates the Ark's ascent to Yhwh's resting place (*mnwḥtk*; Ps 132:6–9), identified as Zion (*mnwḥty*; Ps 132: 13–14). As we have seen in our discussion of the ascent of the Ark into Jerusalem, the Chronicler participates in this older temple theology. His work is especially influenced by Ps 132, even if his own perspective differs from it on some details. That the Chronicler's discussion reflects a polemic against the notion of Ps 132 that David found a place of rest for Yhwh is doubtful because the Chronicler quotes the psalm at the dedication of the Temple (2 Chr 6:41).

"the footstool of the feet of our God." In Ps 132:7 "the footstool of his (Yhwh's) feet" is the Ark (cf. Ps 99:5). But here the expression may refer specifically to the lid (*kprt*; 1 Chr 28:11) upon the Ark (Exod 25:17, 21; 26:34; 30:6; 31:7; 35:12; 37:6–9; Lev 16:2, 13–15; Num 7:89).

"set out to build." In both Samuel (2 Sam 7:1–3) and Chronicles (1 Chr 17:1–2), David desires to build Yhwh a temple and is told initially, at least, that he may do so. Given the context (the divine prohibition against David building the Temple), there is not much justification for seeing a reference here to the materials David gathered for constructing the Temple (contra Keil 1873: 291). Josephus's rewriting of this passage (*Ant.* 7.371) does make mention, however, of David's provision of a great amount of gold and 100,000 talents of silver for the Temple. See further the NOTE to 22:7.

28:3. "but God said to me." Ostensibly, an introduction to a citation of Nathan's dynastic oracle, but the Chronicler's David also cites his earlier explanation to Solomon about the divine prohibition against David's constructing the Temple (22:8). In this respect, the citation is a fascinating combination of one older text and the author's exposition of another related text (see the following NOTES). The connection with Nathan's oracle is made explicit in Josephus (*Ant.* 7.371).

"you will not build." An almost identical phrase occurs in David's earlier speech to Solomon (22:8), which is itself a *traditio* on the *traditum* of 1 Chr 17:4(//2 Sam 7:5).

"a man of wars and have shed blood." The Chronicler extends and modifies the Deuteronomist's explanation for the divine prohibition against David's building a temple (2nd NOTE to 22:8). In Josephus (*Ant.* 7.371) the shedding of blood is explicitly associated with the blood of the enemy.

28:4. "the God of Israel chose (*bḥr*) me." The language directly referring to divine election is striking. Scholars often cite 1 Sam 16:6–13, but the story of how young David was anointed by Samuel does not explicitly refer to David's election. The writer of Ps 132 celebrates David's efforts on behalf of the Ark, but refers (only) to Zion's election (v. 13). For an exact reference to David's election, one has to turn to another psalm, "He chose (*bḥr*) David as his servant" (Ps 78:70). In Chronicles, the Levites (1 Chr 15:2; 2 Chr 29:11), the tribe of Judah, and more specifically David and Solomon are elect of God and occupy a privileged place in the history of Yhwh's relationship with his people. With respect to Solomon, Josephus (*Ant.* 7.338; cf. 7.372) takes matters a step further by referring to Solomon's being elect of God prior to Solomon's birth.

"over Israel forever." The text does not speak of David as simply being king (in Jerusalem) for a time, but of his being king over Israel forever. The Chronicler applies Nathan's dynastic promises (17:14) territorially to all of Israel's tribes and considers these divine pledges to be valid in perpetuity (2 Chr 13:4–12; Knoppers 1990; 1993a).

"chose (*bḥr*) Judah as leader (*ngyd*)." Again, a possible source for this assertion is Ps 78:68, "He chose (*bḥr*) the tribe of Judah." A partial parallel is found within Chronicles itself, "Judah grew mighty among his brothers and a leader (*ngyd*) came from him" (1 Chr 5:2). Josephus (*Ant.* 7.372) refers to Judah as king (*basilea*).

"the house of my father." Referring to the patrimonial house of Jesse (1 Sam 16:1; 1 Chr 2:11–17). David appears not as a renegade upstart, but as one beneficiary among others in a much longer pattern of divine intervention in the life of the Israelite people. The trope is carried further in the programmatic speech of Abijah to Jeroboam and all Israel at the battle of Mount Zemaraim (2 Chr 13:4–12). There Abijah's Davidic pedigree becomes an argument against the legitimacy of Jeroboam's kingship (Knoppers 1993a).

28:5. "many sons." See 1 Chr 3:1–9; 14:3–7.

"he has chosen (*bḥr*) my son Solomon." A fascinating assertion to make in the context of the late Persian and early Hellenistic age. Aside from David, a few other individual figures are divinely elected in the Bible: Abram (Neh 9:7), Aaron (Ps 105:26), and Zerubbabel (Hag 2:23). But Chronicles is the only book that explicitly speaks of Solomon's election (1 Chr 28:5; 29:1). In David's earlier speech to Solomon (22:7–16), David spoke to his son about the succession (22:9–10), but did not provide a discourse about divine election (28:4–5). In this context, David is speaking to a public audience and justifies the choice of Solomon in some detail. The argument for Solomon's admission to the august office is set against the backdrop of a pattern of divine intervention in Israelite history. David's speech to the national assembly provides, in fact, the most detailed public declaration of Solomon's accession, tasks, and goals. David's earlier speech, touching many of the same matters, was addressed to Solomon himself (22:7–16). Only in David's subsequent speech, addressed to "all the officers of Israel," did the king broach the issue of succession. Even then he merely commanded the gathered officials to "help Solomon" (22:17). Most of David's attention in this earlier public oration was focused on rededication and the need to build the Temple. In this context, David explains the rise of Solomon by asserting that Solomon was chosen to succeed David by God himself.

"the throne of the kingdom of Yhwh over Israel." An allusion to Nathan's dynastic promises. The Chronicler repeatedly makes a remarkable association between the Davidic throne and kingdom and Yhwh's throne and kingdom (2nd NOTE to 17:14). Similarly, in the Chronicler's version of the dynastic promises, Yhwh declares, "I shall apppoint him [David's seed] in my house" (17:14; 1st NOTE).

28:6. "Solomon your son, he, he will build my house and my courts." Repeated almost verbatim from 22:10.

"I have chosen him to be a son to me, and I, I shall be a father to him." On the force of these locutions, borrowed from Nathan's dynastic oracle, see the 1st NOTE to 17:13.

28:7. "I shall establish his kingdom forever, if he is resolute to perform my commandments and judgments." In his citation of the dynastic promises, the Chronicler adds a codicil, conditioning the perdurability of the royal throne on Solomon's obedience. Yhwh pledged: "As for him, he will build a house for me, and I shall establish his throne forever" (17:12), but the Chronicler adds that the chosen heir must be "resolute to perform" Yhwh's "commandments and judgments." For similarly worded codicils in the final version of the Deuteronomistic History, see 1 Kgs 2:4; 8:24–25; 9:4 (cf. 1 Kgs 3:14; 8:61). In Chronicles, such obedience centers on Solomon's duty to build the Temple (1 Chr 28:10). See further the COMMENT on 2 Chr 13 in vol. 2 of this commentary.

"as is the case today" *(kayyôm hazzeh)*. This expression, well known from Deuteronomy, Jeremiah, and other writings, is uncommon in Chronicles (2 Chr 6:15//1 Kgs 8:24). Its use in this context conveys harmony in the current relations between Yhwh and David's scion.

28:8. "in the sight of." David finishes this portion of his speech by making a succession of appeals, first to the assembled multitude (v. 8) and second to his son (vv. 9–10). The admonition to the former centers on their duty to follow Yhwh's commandments. Earlier, David had given instructions to Israel's leaders to help Solomon construct the Temple because Israel's time of war and conquest was over. God had given them "rest on every side" (22:17–19). His point in this context is somewhat different. Here an implicit parallel is drawn between the intergenerational relationship of David to his son and the intergenerational relationship of the gathered dignitaries to their own children. Against the backdrop of his ruminations on the place of his heir in the divine economy, David admonishes all of the members of his audience to follow Yhwh's judgments so that they may possess "the good land" and pass it on to their heirs.

"the assembly of Yhwh" *(qĕhāl yhwh)*. The notion of an organized body, a national convocation to deliberate policy issues, is known from a variety of other sources (Num 16:3; 20:4; Deut 23:2–4, 9; Lam 1:10; Mic 2:5; cf. *qĕhāl hā'ĕlōhîm* in Neh 13:1). In this respect David, Solomon, and the gathered dignitaries are not the only parties who have a stake in the decision making. The solemn ceremony is carried out "in the hearing of our God."

"observe" *(šmr)*. Similar exhortations to Torah observance occur in David's speech to Solomon in 22:12–13. Here the addressee is not Solomon, but Israel. Much like the authors of Deuteronomy (4:23–28; 28:58–64; 30:16–18), the Chronicler conditions Israel's possession of the land upon its obedience to Yhwh. Since "the commandments of Yhwh your God" include the mandate for a central sanctuary, once Israel is secure within its own land (Deut 12), it is incumbent upon Israel to support the effort to build the Temple. In this manner, the author integrates both the Davidic covenant and the Mosaic covenant into his larger presentation (Knoppers 1998).

"seek out the commandments *(drš mṣwt)* of Yhwh your God." In Chronicles, one normally seeks *(drš)* God as a matter of worship and religious commitment (4th NOTE to 10:13). Here, as in Ps 119 (Greenberg 1990), the Torah has become in and of itself an object of religious devotion: "I stretch out my hands toward your commandments, which I love; I meditate on your decrees" (Ps 119:48). In both cases, the commandments link Yhwh to his people. In this context, the author's specialized usage of the verb *drš* with a view to the Torah may be compared with his use of *drš* with a view to other objects of religious veneration. As a prime example, one may take David's reference to the disregard for the Ark during the reign of his predecessor: "For we did not seek *(drš)* it in the days of Saul" (13:3; cf. 15:13 [see 3rd NOTE]). Another example occurs in the context of Solomon's reign: "As for the bronze altar, which Bezalel made . . . , Solomon and the assembly sought it" (*wydršhw*; 2 Chr 1:5). In later times, the rabbis envisioned God and the celestial beings studying the Torah in a heavenly academy (*b. B. Meṣiʿa* 86a).

"the good land" *('t-h'rṣ hṭwbh)*. Another cliché borrowed from the Deuteronomistic History (Deut 1:35; 3:25; 4:21, 22; 6:18; 8:10; 9:6; 11:17; Josh 23:13, 15, 16; 1 Kgs 14:15; Weinfeld 1972: 343 [#10]).

"bequeath it [*hipʿil* of *nḥl*] to your children forever after you." The passing of generations brings both opportunities and challenges (Deut 1:38; 3:28; 12:10; 19:1–3; Josh 1:6; 1 Kgs 8:57; Sir 33:24; 44:21–23). In such a time of transition, the danger of apostasy may be apparent (Deut 6:10–15).

28:9–10. "as for you." The second part of David's speech (NOTE to vv. 2–10) is aimed directly at Solomon, encouraging him to follow through and build the promised sanctuary.

28:9. "know the God of your father." The appeal to knowledge finds its home in the world of international diplomacy (treaties, letters, instruction lists) in which the command to "know" someone, usually a superior, denotes legal recognition. In his treaty with his client Ḫuqqana, the Hittite king Šuppiluliuma I declares,

"As for you Ḫuqqana, know only the Sun with respect to lordship; also my son whom I the Sun say, 'This one everyone should know . . . you, Ḫuqqana know him!' " (Friedrich §1.A.i.8–11). A second example stems from the El Amarna letters. Abdi-Ašratu, the besieged king of Amurru, asks his suzerain Amenophis III the king of Egypt for deliverance from the king of Mitanni, "May the king, [m]y lord, know me and put [m]e under the charge of Paḫanate my commissioner" (EA 60.30–32; Huffmon 1966: 32; Moran 1992: 132–33). In this context, Solomon is asked to acknowledge the authority of his father's patron deity as his patron deity (cf. Hos 8:2; 13:4; Jer 24:7; 31:34). Note also David's later declaration that "Yhwh my God is with you" (1 Chr 28:20).

"with a whole heart" *(blb šlm)*. Another favorite expression of the Deuteronomists (e.g., Deut 4:29; 1 Kgs 8:61; 11:4; 15:3, 14) adopted by the Chronicler (1 Chr 12:39; 29:9, 19; 2 Chr 15:17; 19:9; 25:2).

"Yhwh searches *(dôrēš)*." The language of "seeking" is a hallmark of Chronistic diction (Curtis and Madsen 1910: 29 [#23]). The term *drš* usually refers to the need for Israelites to resort to their God in prayer and worship (e.g., v. 9b; 4th NOTE to 10:13) or, less often, to resort to his commandments (v. 8). But the reversal of the pattern occurs here. Yhwh is an active participant in his relations with his people, a deity who is concerned with more than external actions. Yhwh seeks out his people and searches every heart (McConville 1986a).

"every form of thought" *(kl yṣr mḥšbwt)*. The expression is rare. In Gen 6:5 we find *kl yṣr mḥšbwt lbw*, rendered by NJPS as "every plan devised by his mind" (Orlinsky 1969: 72–73). First Chronicles 29:18 is similar, *lyṣr mḥšbwt lbb ʿmk*, "(keep) such forms of thought in the mind of your people."

"if you seek him *(drš)*. he will let himself be found by you *(mṣʾ)*, but, if you abandon him *(ʿzb)*, he will reject you *(znḥ)* in perpetuity." A classic statement of the reciprocity that the Chronicler posits in divine-human relations. The principle is true of the relations between Davidic kings and Yhwh as much as it is of the relationship between the Israelite people and Yhwh. Both relationships are subject to the same core principles. The application of this blessing-and-punishment theme in history is, however, not mechanical or even simply retributive. "There is no balance between blessing, which comes *consistently* whenever Israel 'seeks Yahweh,' and judgment, which can be mitigated or remitted entirely" (B. Kelly 1996: 108). In this case, the Chronicler's understanding of divine justice is applied to Solomon's task of building the Temple.

28:10. "a house *(bayit)* as the sanctuary *(lammiqdāš)*." The influence of the unequivocal call for centralization in Deut 12 is apparent in the Chronicler's view of the Jerusalem Temple. Here the author may be thinking of the Temple as the proper receptacle for the Tabernacle, sometimes called a *miqdāš* in the Priestly writing (Exod 25:8; Lev 16:33; Num 3:38; 18:1; cf. 1 Chr 22:19; 2 Chr 36:17). In the Chronicler's work, the Temple incorporates both the Ark (2 Chr 5:1–6:11, 41) and the Tent of Meeting (2 Chr 5:5).

"be strong and act" *(ḥzq wʿśh)*. The same formulaic expression occurs as the final exhortation in Shecaniah's speech (Ezra 10:4). David repeats the prompt to Solomon later (1 Chr 28:20) to drive home the point (cf. 2 Chr 19:11 [pl.]).

28:11. "plan" *(tabnît)*. The repeated use of *tabnît* is telling (vv. 11, 12, 19). Having established a considerable bureaucracy, David, with divine assistance, draws up a *tabnît* for the Temple and its courts. In this context, David appears as a second Moses, both of whom are associated with the inauguration of a major cultic institution. Like Moses, who was given a plan *(tabnît)* for the Tabernacle (Exod 25:9, 40), David is given a plan for the Temple. The many parallels between the transition from Moses to Joshua and the transition from David to Solomon are developed elsewhere ("Excursus: The Composition of 1 Chronicles 23–27").

"storerooms" *(ggzkyw)*. The term *gagzak*, perhaps a Persian loanword, is a *hapax legomenon*. Cf. *ggzy hmlk*, "royal treasuries" (Esth 3:9; 4:7).

"upper chambers" *(ʿlywt)*. Overlaid (or inlaid) with gold (2 Chr 3:9), these upper parts of the Temple are not referred to in the Deuteronomist's description of the Temple (1 Kgs 6–7). The reference may be to an architectual feature of the Second Temple.

"inner chambers." The term *pĕnîmî* can refer to the innermost part of a house (1 Kgs 6:27) or to an inner court (1 Kgs 6:36; 7:12, 50; Ezek 8:3, 16; 10:3; 40:15–46:1; Esth 4:11; 5:1; 2 Chr 4:22).

"the house of the (ark) cover" *(bêt hakkappōret)*. In speaking of a *kappōret*, the writer is most likely referring to a lid or covering for the Ark. This covering (KJV's "mercy seat") is mentioned quite often in the Priestly writing (Exod 25:17–22; 26:34; 30:6; 31:7; 35:12; 37:6–9; Num 7:89). The phrase *bêt hakkappōret*, although unique in the HB, is common in rabbinic literature (Hurvitz 1995: 172–74). In speaking of "the house of the (ark) cover," the author is alluding to the Holy of Holies, the inner sanctum of the Temple.

28:12. "the plan" *(tabnît)*. The author was probably thinking of a written description, rather than of a blueprint or a drawing (cf. Ezek 8:3; 10:8). If a drawing was meant, it would be hard to imagine how such a sketch would apply to the precise materials (and mixture of materials) from which certain objects were to be made (e.g., gold, pure gold, refined gold). It is also difficult to imagine how a drawing or a model would apply to the divisions of the priests and the Levites (1 Chr 28:13). But an explanation in written form could address issues such as objects, weights, materials, mixtures of materials, location, and dimensions (cf. Exod 25:8–40; Josephus, *Ant.* 7.375). Given this understanding of *tabnît*, there is no compelling need to construe *tabnît* in v. 18 as designating something different from the *tabnît* in earlier verses. For other views, see Rothstein and Hänel (1927: 506), Rudolph (1955: 188), and Dirksen (1996b: 429–31).

"he had by the spirit" *(hāyâ bārûaḥ ʿimmô)*. Some (e.g., Curtis and Madsen 1910: 298) prefer to translate "he had in his mind" (see TEXTUAL NOTE). This is possible, but one wonders why the writer did not write *hāyâ ʿim lĕbābô*, as one might expect (1 Chr 22:7; 28:2; 2 Chr 6:7). David is presented as an inspired figure, a leader privileged to receive revelation. Again, one thinks of the foundational role played by Moses (Exod 35:31; Noordtzij 1937: 226). Although David is not technically depicted as a prophet *(nābîʾ)*, he has a remarkable, divinely authorized place in Israelite history (De Vries 1988; Schniedewind 1995: 202–8).

"the courts *(haḥăṣērôt)* of the House of Yhwh." References to the Temple's (outer) court(s) are found in a variety of biblical sources. Unfortunately, the precise configuration and control of these courts in various Israelite sanctuaries are not entirely clear (Hamp 1986: 131–39). The Priestly source mentions that the Tabernacle had an enclosure or court (*ḥāṣēr;* Exod 27:9–19; 35:17; 38:15–31; 39:40; 40:8, 33). The Deuteronomistic History mentions both a three-tiered great court (*heḥāṣēr haggĕdôlâ;* 1 Kgs 7:9, 12) within the temple complex and a court in front of the temple (1 Kgs 8:64). The latter, at least, seems to be one area within the larger Temple compound to which the public had access, at least on certain occasions (Jer 19:14; 26:2; Ezek 8:7; 9:7; Pss 84:3 [ET 84:2]; 92:14 [ET 92:13]; 96:8; 100:4; 116:19; 135:2). The same is true both for the elaborate Temple envisoned in Ezekiel (42:13–14; 44:19) and for Zerubbabel's temple (Neh 8:16). Ezekiel's temple vision mentions some Levitical activity as taking place in the outer courts. It is within the four enclosures in the outer court that the temple servitors *(mšrty hbyt)* are to boil the people's sacrifices (Ezek 46:21–24; Tuell 1992: 31–33, 66–68). Ezekiel's temple also contains an inner court, which is of restricted access (41:15; 42:7–9; 45:19; 46:1; Zimmerli 1983: 370–500). In Chronicles there is no specific mention of a "great court," but mention is made of "the court of the Temple" (2 Chr 29:16; cf. 33:5) and of a court in front of the Temple (2 Chr 7:7; cf. 20:5). The texts of 1 Chr 28:6, 12 and 2 Chr 23:5 simply refer to the temple courts. Again, the outer court is accessible, at least on certain occasions, to the public (2 Chr 23:5; 24:21). But Chronicles also speaks of Solomon's construction of courts for the priests (2 Chr 4:9). A similar distinction seems to be implied in the account of Ḥezeqiah's reforms. The priests empty the temple hall of unclean things by bringing them to the temple court. From there the Levites take them out of the temple complex (2 Chr 29:16).

"all of the surrounding chambers" *(kol-hallĕšākôt sābîb).* The term *liškâ* can refer generally to a cella, or chamber, of the Temple or more particularly to a storeroom within the Temple (3rd NOTE to 23:28). Although the term does not appear in MT Kings, it does appear in 4QKgs[a] 1 Kgs 7:50–51 (לשכו]ת).

"the treasuries of the House of God." On their importance in the Chronicler's work, see the COMMENT on 26:20–32.

"the treasuries of the dedicated gifts." That is, the Temple storerooms for the holy offerings or donations (3rd NOTE to 26:20).

28:13. "the divisions of the priests and the Levites." The plans David delivers to Solomon pertain to the sanctuary complex, its furnishings, and its sacerdotal organization. In this respect, the Temple plans resonate with the Tabernacle plans in Exodus. Yhwh's provisions cover the Tabernacle, its furnishings, the priesthood of Aaron (Exod 28:1), and its consecration (Exod 29:1–46).

28:14. "all kinds of golden furnishings." David's plan provides, but does not actually list, specific amounts of precious metals to be used in the manufacture of the sacred furnishings. In a few instances, the plan addresses the consistency or preparation of the precious metal: "pure gold" (*zāhāb ṭāhôr;* v. 17) and "refined gold" (*zāhāb mĕzuqqāq;* v. 18). In other cases, the text simply speaks of golden or silver implements.

"silver furnishings." With such references, it becomes clear why David lays aside both gold and silver for the Temple (22:14). The Chronicler's temple, more so than the Priestly Tabernacle and the Temple in Kings, contains many articles of silver.

28:15. "the golden lampstands and their golden lamps." In 2 Chr 13:11 the sanctuary, like the Tabernacle, has one lampstand (Exod 25:31–40; 31:8; Lev 24:1–4; Num 8:2–4; Knoppers 1993a). Elsewhere the Chronicler, in conformity with Kings and Jeremiah, mentions a plurality of lampstands (usually ten) in the Temple (1 Chr 28:15; 2 Chr 4:7; 4:20//1 Kgs 7:49; Jer 52:19; C. Meyers 1997: 405–6). As "a perpetual statute throughout your generations" (Lev 24:3), the candelabrum's lamps were to burn every evening (Exod 25:37; 30:7–8; Lev 24:3; Num 8:2; 2 Chr 13:11).

"the silver lampstands." Unattested elsewhere in biblical sources. A possible exception is the general reference to plunder taken in the Babylonian exile (Jer 52:19), which may intimate their existence. But it is more likely that the reference to silver lampstands reflects the situation of the Second Temple in the late Persian period.

28:16. "the tables" *(šulḥānôt)*. Second Chronicles 4:8 also mentions a plurality of tables, but only one table is mentioned in other contexts (Exod 25:23–30; 37:10; 40:22; 1 Kgs 7:48; 2 Chr 13:11; 29:18).

"the row bread" *(hammaʿăreket)*. The expression "the rows of bread" (*leḥem hammaʿăreket*; 1 Chr 9:32; 23:29; 2 Chr 13:11), or a shortened version of it (*hammaʿăreket*; 1 Chr 28:16; 2 Chr 2:4; 29:18), appears six times in Chronicles and once in Nehemiah (10:33). See further the 1st NOTE to 23:29.

"Silver tables" are unknown from other biblical sources. Second Kings 12:13(//2 Chr 24:14) and 2 Kgs 25:15 mention silver articles in the Jerusalem Temple, but not specifically silver tables. Josephus (*Ant.* 10.145) mentions the deposition of golden tables in the Babylonian exile, but makes no specific reference to silver tables.

28:17. "the flesh hooks." Used for lifting meat (Exod 27:3; 38:3; Num 4:14; 2 Chr 4:16). In Exodus these hooks are made of bronze.

"the basins" *(hmzrqwt)*. A constituent element of both tabernacle (Exod 27:3; Num 4:14; 7:13–85) and temple worship (1 Kgs 7:40, 45, 50; 2 Kgs 25:15; 2 Chr 4:8, 11, 22). The *mizrāqôt* were most likely pouring or serving vessels (Hurowitz 1995: 156–57). Compare the *mzrqyʾ* of the temple at Elephantine (*AP* 30.12; 31.11).

"the jars" *(hqśwt)*. These jars (LXX *spondeia*) were used for libations (Exod 25:29; 37:16; Num 4:7).

"the golden bowls" *(kpwry hzhb)*. These are only mentioned in late sources and probably reflect the Chronicler's own setting in the late Achaemenid era. Sheshbazzar is said to have brought the golden bowls back from Babylon in the time of Cyrus the Great (Ezra 1:10). Ezra brings others with him as a contribution to the Jerusalem Temple (Ezra 8:27).

"the silver bowls" *(kpwry hksp)*. Like the golden bowls, the silver bowls are mentioned only in late writings (Ezra 1:10).

28:18. "the altar of incense" *(mzbḥ hqṭrt)*. A constituent part of both the Priestly tabernacle cultus (Exod 30:1–10, 27; 31:8; 35:15; Lev 4:7) and the Chronistic temple cultus (1 Chr 6:34; 2 Chr 26:16, 19). The altar of incense is not mentioned in the Deuteronomistic History.

"the plan of the chariot" *(tbnyt hmrkbh)*. This reference to the cherubim as a chariot is both unusual and intriguing when compared to the background of Pentateuchal and Deuteronomistic texts referring to the Ark, Tabernacle, and Temple. The chariot seems to serve as a throne for the invisible deity. A number of prophetic sources refer to Yhwh's chariot(s), usually in the context of a theophany or of a march of the divine warrior (Isa 66:15; Hab 3:8; Zech 6:1–8; Hiebert 1986: 97–98). A variety of biblical writers speak of Yhwh as "enthroned upon the cherubim" (e.g., 1 Sam 4:4; 2 Sam 6:2; 2 Kgs 19:15; Isa 37:16; Pss 80:2 [ET 80:1]; 99:1; 1 Chr 13:6; cf. Ps 18:11 [ET 18:10]). In this respect, the author may have been particularly influenced by his understanding of Ezekiel's vision. To be sure, Ezekiel does not explicitly refer to the wheeled object of his vision as a chariot for Yhwh (1:4–24; 10:1–22). Nor does Ezekiel speak of the Ark in this manner. But the book of Ezekiel does refer to the four living creatures who support God's portable throne as "cherubim"(Ezek 10:3–20; 11:22), and Ezekiel's wheeled vehicle was understood as a chariot by generations of later interpreters, as witnessed by writings in the Apocrypha (e.g., Sir 49:8; Marböck 1981), the Qumran Literature (4Q286; 4Q287), Hellenistic synagogal prayers (*AosCon* 7.35.1–10), the Pseudepigrapha (*3 En.* 37:1–2; appendix to *3 En.* 24:1–23; *Apoc. Mos.* 8; 22; 33; 38), and the highly developed *Merkabah* mystical writings of the Middle Ages. Ezekiel also associates the cherubim with Yhwh's throne (10:1–22) and speaks of God's glory as moving from the cherubim (8:2; 10:4, 18, 20; 11:22). Similarly, in the Priestly Code, Yhwh speaks from between the two cherubim (Exod 25:22; Num 7:89). In short, this may be another instance in which the Chronicler fuses images from several sources to create his own distinctive presentation. Indeed, his blend of imagery anticipates the elaborate combination of features seen in later texts.

"the cherubim in gold." So also Exod 25:18–20; 37:7–9; Num 7:89; 1 Kgs 6:23–28; 2 Chr 3:10–13. The cherubim resemble those of the Priestly source in that the cherubim here, as in P, seem to be attached to the lid of the Ark (Exod 25:17–22; Japhet 1993a: 496–97). The cherubim in the Deuteronomist's version of Solomon's temple are structurally independent of the Ark (1 Kgs 6:23–28; 8:6; cf. 2 Chr 3:10–14; 5:7–8). In this manner, the author of our passage conforms the cherubim of the Temple to those of the Tabernacle.

"spreading out *(lpróym)* . . . and protecting *(wskkym)*." One function of the cherubim is to shield the cover of the Ark from above (Exod 25:18–20; 37:7–9; 1 Kgs 8:7; 2 Chr 5:8).

28:19. "everything in writing." The revelation comes to David through writing rather than as a consequence of a vision or a speech. Scholars have drawn a parallel with Moses, who also receives a divine revelation, but there is both continuity and discontinuity with the situation in Exodus. At Mount Sinai there is an emphasis on visual experience. God shows Moses the plan *(tabnît)* of the Tabernacle, which Moses has to commit to memory if he is to be successful in building the sanctuary (Exod 25:9, 40; 26:30; 27:8). Like Moses, David receives a *tabnît*, but this *tabnît* takes the form of a written text. The difference between the two conceptions—one oral and visual, the other written and textual—can only be understood as part of a long development in ancient Israel. The transition from the oral to the written is evident in Ezekiel's temple vision. The prophet is shown "visions of God" (*mrʾwt ʾlhym;* Ezek 40:2) pertaining to a new temple complex, but he is also told to write these instructions down (43:11). The emphasis on the written word is also evident in Ezekiel's call narrative in which the message Ezekiel is to speak takes the form of a scroll (2:1–3:3; Kugel 1986: 18–19). Like Jeremiah (1:9; 15:16), Ezekiel internalizes the word of God. But for Ezekiel the process of internalization is quite literal and the prophet comments that the message tasted "as sweet as honey" (Ezek 3:3). In the case of the prophet Zechariah, the inscripturation of the word of God undergoes a further development. Zechariah (5:1–4) only sees the flying scroll revealed to him; he does not touch it. The revelation "from the hand of Yhwh" given to David should be understood against this broader progression. The divine arrangements for the Temple take the form of a written document, a *kĕtāb* (cf. 2 Chr 35:4).

"made (me) understand all the pieces of the plan." Another remarkable feature of the disclosure given to David. Not only does David receive a document, but Yhwh sees to it that David comprehends it. In this regard, the Chronicler stands firmly within a late Persian period context. Possession of an authoritative text is not enough in and of itself because the text must be properly understood. After Ezra brought the scroll of the teaching of Moses to be recited in the public square, "they read the scroll of the Torah of God, translating *(mĕpōroš)* and establishing the sense *(śôm śekel)* so that they understood the writing" (Neh 8:8). A similar appraisal is applied to the history of divine dealings with Israel in the Levitical address of Neh 9. Israel is held accountable not only for "the laws, commandments, and torah" issued through "Moses your servant" (Neh 9:14) and for "the bread from heaven when they were hungry and the water from a rock when they were thirsty" (Neh 9:15) but also for the fact that "you gave them your good spirit *(rwḥk hṭwbh)* to instruct them *(lhśkylm)*" (Neh 9:20). Attention to the question of interpretation is paramount in Daniel. In his prayer to God, necessitated by his bewilderment over the seventy years of exile decreed for Jerusalem by the prophet Jeremiah (25:11–12; 29:10), Daniel confesses that disaster has struck Israel, just "as is written in the Torah of Moses" (Dan 9:13). Yet it is not clear how long this period will last; the people need to "understand *(lĕhaśkîl)* your truth" (Dan 9:13). To this end, the role of the divinely appointed intermediary Gabriel is critical: "I have come forth to give you understanding" (*lĕkaśkîlĕkā bînâ*; Dan 9:22). Daniel must "know and understand" *(tēdaʿ wĕtaśkēl)* that the Jeremianic prophecy means, in fact, seventy weeks of years (Dan 9:24–25). In the case of David, no heavenly intermediary is necessary. God himself explains the *tabnît* to David.

28:20–21. "David said." The king will deliver other speeches, but this, his final address to Solomon, picks up and extends his earlier admonition (vv. 9–10). As in the earlier speech, David exhorts his son to be courageous in the face of the challenges that await him. Pointing to the continuity of divine leadership ("Yhwh my God is with you") despite the imminent discontinuity in human leadership, David assures his son that God will see him through to the completion of his task. In this respect, David's speech alludes to the plans for the Temple and its courts (vv. 11–19) since Solomon's mission is to build this edifice (v. 20). David's address also involves the assembled dignitaries (v. 1). He assures Solomon that he does not face the future alone. These authorities, as well as others, will assist him in his appointed duties (v. 21). By having David mention the officers, the priests, and the Levites, the writer brings closure to this sequence of events and prepares the reader for the public speeches and installation to follow (29:1–24).

"be strong, be courageous, and act" *(ḥăzaq weʾĕmāṣ waʿăśēh)*. This formula of encouragement is an expanded version of a common Deuteronomistic phrase: *ḥăzaq weʾĕmāṣ* (e.g., Deut 31:6, 7; Josh 1:18; 10:25; Weinfeld 1972a: 343 [#11]). Cf. 1 Chr 22:13; 2 Chr 32:7.

"neither fear nor be dismayed" *(ʾal-tîrāʾ wĕʾal-tēḥat)*. The same expression occurs in David's private speech to Solomon (22:13). As with the previously discussed cliché, this phrase is one that the Chronicler (1 Chr 22:13; 2 Chr 20:15, 17; 32:7) draws from the Deuteronomistic writings (Weinfeld 1972a: 344 [#12]).

"God is with you." A stereotypical formula designating divine support for a privileged individual or group (1st NOTE to 17:8).

"neither fail you nor abandon you." Implementing the plan *(tabnît)* for the Temple of Yhwh is an ambitious and difficult undertaking, but the very God to whom the projected Temple is dedicated will sustain the temple builder in his heavenly appointed task. The point about divine sustenance—the deity's presence with Solomon "until every work of the service of the House of Yhwh is completed"—counsels against a simplistic notion of the Chronicler's understanding of divine justice. The text underscores Yhwh's "covenantal goodness" (B. Kelly 1996: 107).

28:21. "the divisions of the priests and the Levites." These first appear as part of the large administrative reorganization associated with the latter part of David's reign (23:6; 24:1; 26:1, 12, 19; 27:1–15). The orderly partitioning of the priests and Levites into divisions ensures continuous service at the central sanctuary throughout the course of each year. Present at this national assembly (28:1), the priests and Levites are now placed at Solomon's disposal.

"every kind of service for the House of Yhwh." Another allusion to the plan articulated earlier (vv. 13–15).

"all sorts of volunteers" *(lĕkol-nādîb)*. Perhaps an allusion to the artisans mentioned earlier (22:15), but the reference is probably more general.

"with skill *(ḥokmâ)* for every kind of service." The term *ḥokmâ*, normally translated "wisdom," can also denote technical proficiency (Exod 28:3; 31:3, 6; 35:26, 31; 1 Kgs 7:14). David gave Solomon a similar, albeit more detailed, assurance in his earlier speech (22:15).

"the officers and all of the people." The dignitaries, assembled in Jerusalem (v. 1) and charged with obedience (v. 8), are placed under Solomon's command. The words David speaks to Solomon publicly are meant for a greater audience. David is mobilizing popular and elite support for his successor.

## Sources and Composition

Most scholars agree that much of the material in this chapter stems from the Chronicler's own hand. David's speeches are filled with standard Chronistic expressions (S. Driver 1895b; Curtis and Madsen 1910: 295–301). This is not to say that the influence of older biblical texts cannot be found. Quite the contrary, as Samuel Driver (1914: 539) observed long ago, words and expressions known from older biblical poetry come together in a distinctive way to express the Chronicler's theology. Although commentators agree that a substantial portion of this chapter originates with the Chronicler, some consider parts of the work to be later additions. One group of scholars thinks that a good deal of the material dealing with the plan for the Temple (vv. 11–19) is a later interpolation (e.g., Rudolph 1955: 185; Dirksen 1996b), while a second group thinks of scattered additions throughout the text. Roddy Braun (1986: 267–74) considers vv. 1, 4–5, 8, and 13–18 as later interpolations, while Throntveit (1987: 45–47) speaks of the additions as consisting of vv. 1, 4–6a, 8, 12b, 14–18, and 20a. A third group of scholars, most notably Williamson (1982b: 178–83) and Japhet (1993a: 482–500), defends the unity of this chapter.

The textual and exegetical considerations raised by these three groups of scholars are important and do not lend themselves to an easy resolution. In certain parts of the chapter (e.g., vv. 12–18), the text seems troubled. How much these textual and syntactical difficulties may be attributed to textual corruption (see the TEXTUAL NOTES) and how much they may be attributed to the work of different editors is not always clear. Obviously, those who see 1 Chr 23:2–27:34 as a later addition ("Excursus: The Composition of 1 Chronicles 23–27") are more inclined to view this chapter as reflecting several levels of composition than those scholars (such as myself) who view a substantial portion of this material as originating with the Chronicler. Whatever the origin of the difficulties within the text, the following COMMENT will focus on the complete chapter and not a reconstructed subsection thereof.

## Comment

In his speeches to Solomon and the gathered assembly, David publicizes a number of private sentiments. It should therefore come as no surprise that there are parallels between the individually oriented communications of 1 Chr 22 and the public communications of 1 Chr 28. Both contain similar summons to Solomon to build the Temple (22:6, 11; 28:10), similar expressions of support (22:11, 16; 28:20–21), similar explanations of why David was not allowed to build the Temple (22:7–10; 28:2–3), and similarly worded conditional promises (22:11–13; 28:6–7). The parallels show a consistency of kingly purpose.

But there are also notable differences between the two sets of speeches, some of which reflect developments in the course of David's reign and some of which reflect the different audiences to which the speeches are addressed. The first speech to Solomon reassures a youthful and inexperienced son by dwelling on the material resources, bullion, and artisans that David has set aside for sanctuary construction (22:14–16; cf. 22:1–5). The first set of speeches concludes with David issuing a brief command to Israel's leaders to rededicate their lives, build the Temple, and help Solomon (22:17–19). This directive is set against the background of David's impressive string of military victories (14:8–17; 18:1–20:8), summarily presented as Yhwh's subduing the land for his people (22:18). David's later speech to the national assembly justifies the Solomonic accession and explains in much greater detail his major task of building the Temple (28:2–8). In contrast with David's earlier speech to Israel's officers, the king directs the people to observe Yhwh's commands so that they may bequeath the "good land" to later generations (28:8). In contrast with the earlier private speech to Solomon (22:7–16), the speech to the national assembly contains an unparalleled digression on the mystery of divine election, explaining how Solomon was chosen to succeed David and build the Temple (28:4–5). Against the backdrop of this public speech (28:2–8) and David's earlier private speech (22:7–16), David's next speech to Solomon can be brief, summoning his son to seek the God of his father and encouraging him to build the Temple (28:9–10).

The second set of speeches (28:2–8, 9–10, 19, 20–21) reflect additional developments. The king goes beyond furnishing state resources for sanctuary construction by bequeathing to his son a plan for the Temple and its furnishings (28:11–19). Moreover, David takes the collective backing he requested earlier (22:17–19) for granted. He cites this support to encourage Solomon to complete his divinely appointed tasks (28:20–21). He also makes reference to the benefits accrued from the major administrative reorganization that characterizes the latter part of his regnal career. The divisions of the priests and Levites "for every kind of service" are placed at Solomon's command.

Given the developments reflected in the second set of speeches, it will be useful to devote some attention to their unique qualities. Two features are of special note. One is the linkage between the reworked version of the dynastic promises (28:2–3, 6–7) and the assertions of divine election to justify Solomon's succession (28:4–5). The other unique feature is the extended reference to a detailed plan for a temple complex (28:11–19). Both features reveal a heavy engagement with past traditions. The first (28:4–5), part of a larger historical retrospect (28:2–7), is set against the background of David's explanation of why he was forbidden to build the promised sanctuary. The reasons given—David's having gone to war and spilled blood (28:2–3)—echo those given in an earlier private setting (22:7–8). The unparalleled digression that follows has the appearance of an ascending genealogy (28:4–5), but it is more than that. Its coverage is telescopic, tracing a pattern of divine election among the progeny of Israel, Judah, Jesse, and David. In this respect, its force is quite different from the appeal to genealogy found in the Behistun inscription of Darius the Great (in Old Persian). There Darius provides two ascending genealogies for himself. The first is brief, linking him to his father

Hystaspes and his grandfather Arsames (DB I, §1.1.1–3; Kent 1953). The second is more detailed, tracing his lineage five steps back to Achaemenes himself (DB I, §2.1.3–6). In the Behistun inscription the point is clear. Darius hails from impeccable roots: "We are called Achaemenians. From long ago we have been noble" (DB I, §3.1.6–7). Moreover, Darius's claim to the throne is unassailable: "From long ago our family had been kings" (DB I, §3.1.8). In Darius's counting, there were eight in his family who had been king before him. He is, therefore, ninth in a succession (DB I, §4.1.8–11). Given this record, it is not surprising that Ahuramazda bestowed the kingdom upon Darius (DB I, §5.1.11–12).

In David's speech a succession is also traced, a succession in which divine favor may be traced. But this succession is neither predictable nor exclusively royal. That the *apologia* appeals to divine freedom is understandable. David was an upstart who replaced a king from another family. In the period depicted, the early tenth century, the dynastic promises are just that—promises. But the recipient of divine favor comes from a line whose members Yhwh has promoted before. Remarkably, the argument about election also applies to Solomon. The author situates an unfolding divine purpose at work in the United Monarchy, consistent with a larger record of divine dealings with his people. Neither primogeniture nor genealogy are enough to explain such a chain of events. Divine purposes may, in fact, override the rule of primogeniture. Judah was not the firstborn, but he was elect of God as leader (5:1–2; 28:4). The tribe of Judah had many ancestral houses, but it was the house of Jesse that was singled out (28:4). Within the house of Jesse, David had many older siblings, but only he was designated to be "king over Israel forever" (28:4). Given this pattern of divine intervention, the unexpected becomes the expected. Indeed, the pattern works in Solomon's favor. David had many sons, but the status of firstborn was not a major factor in who acceded to the kingship. Of all David's progeny, it was young Solomon who was chosen by Yhwh "to sit upon the throne of the kingdom of Yhwh over Israel" (28:5).

Within the ancient world, the Egyptians and Mesopotamians associated their history as coterminous with cosmogony. Such a view had its many uses, but Israelite writers typically take a different approach. Freedom characterizes Yhwh's history with his people. Within the stories of the Exodus, Israel's marginal status as newcomer is proclaimed as foundational to the people's distinctive status (Machinist 1991; 1994b). That Israel's history is not coterminus with cosmogony is critical to grasping its national identity. The Chronicler carries this trope a step further by applying it to the internal dynamics of Israelite history. The natural course of events is often not Yhwh's way of bringing about his purposes. Direct divine intervention in history becomes a self-authenticating pattern. The success that Judah, David, and Solomon achieve validates the procedure. Chosen tribe and chosen dynasty belong together. That both rise to a position of preeminence through divine election magnifies their importance.

In the setting of a public address, the election motif buttresses the importance of Solomon's calling. What David intended to do but was proscribed from doing (28:2–3), his son is singled out to do (28:6). Yhwh, for his part, confirms one of his pledges to David by providing him with a dynastic succession (1 Chr 17:11–14;

22:8–10; 28:6; cf. 1 Kgs 5:17–18 [ET 5:3–5]; 8:18–21). The realization of this promise lays the groundwork for the realization of another—the construction of the central sanctuary. In this manner, the writer, like the Deuteronomist before him, inextricably links the Davidic promises to the Temple. But in Chronicles, the prospect of temple construction also becomes a rallying point around which to support dynastic succession. Sanctuary construction defines Solomon's purpose, validates David's latter reign, and provides the people with impetus to unite around a most important and timely cause.

If the author appeals to a paradigm of divine intervention to justify the Solomonic succession, his justification of the Temple also appeals to the divine realm. The justification takes, however, a different form. David delivers a pattern *(tabnît)* for the entire temple complex, including the temple courts, chambers, furniture, and utensils (28:11–19) to his son. Much like inspired Moses before him (Exod 25:9, 40), who produces a plan *(tabnît)* for the Tabernacle, David bequeaths a plan for the Temple to his son. The grand architectural design includes plans for "the treasuries of the House of God and of the treasuries of the dedicated gifts" (28:12). Like the *tabnît* of Moses, the *tabnît* of David begins with instructions for the shrine (Exod 25:8–9; 1 Chr 28:11–12), followed by instructions concerning its furnishings (Exod 25:10–39; 1 Chr 28:13–19). In Exodus, the divine command for the sanctuary (Exod 25:8–31:11) is followed (after the intervening golden calf rebellion) by its careful execution (Exod 35:4–40:33). In Chronicles this is impossible because David has been barred from building the sanctuary. This makes the reign of Solomon critical to David's success.

But why produce a plan in such detail? If some of the items mentioned in the descriptions of the First Temple no longer existed, why mention them at all? Granted the sanctuary's urban setting, why draw so many connections to a wilderness shrine? It seems likely that the Chronicler is deliberately drawing parallels between practices at the Tent of Meeting and the Jerusalem Temple because he wishes to associate the observance of the Judean cult in his own time as closely as possible with that of Israel's national beginnings. The establishment of the Davidic dynasty and the construction of the Temple were major developments during the monarchy. The Chronicler, more so than the Deuteronomist, attempts to validate these institutions by positing a direct line between them and the institutions of early Israel. Certain other considerations may buttress the point. The Temple of the Chronicler's day was not the Temple of Solomon, but a temple whose construction was authorized and subsidized by a foreign power (2 Chr 36:22–23; Ezra 1:1–4; 6:1–5; 6:8–12; 1 Esd 2:1–7; 4:47–57, 62–63; 5:71; 6:23–8:24; Fried 2003). In spite of the strong claims put forth by the authors of Chronicles, Ezra, and 1 Esdras, there may have been those who denied a clear link between the two shrines. To these people, the Second Temple may have been seen as an inherently new and different sanctuary from the First Temple. Certainly some of the sacred furnishings of the old establishment were not, and could not be, a part of the new establishment.

To complicate matters further, the Jerusalem Temple was not the only shrine that might attract support in an age in which Judaism had become an international religion. There was for some time a Jewish temple at Elephantine and perhaps a Jewish shrine in the Babylonian diaspora. In the second century B.C.E., Jews would build a temple at Leontopolis in Egypt. (For details, see the INTRODUCTION.) Moreover, even within the southern Levant, Judeans were not the only Yahwists around. There were also, for example, Yahwists in Samaria. While some of the Yahwists in the province of Samaria may have felt a certain allegiance toward the Jerusalem Temple, there were undoubtedly others who did not. These Samarians may have seen Jerusalem in general and the Temple in particular as sources of trouble rather than as symbols of religious unity. The Samarians undoubtedly had their own traditions linking them to the Israel of old. At some point, perhaps already in the Persian period, a temple was built on Mount Gerizim. In the Second Commonwealth, the exclusive authority and privilege of the Temple built under Zerubbabel and Jeshua could not be taken for granted. Its supporters had to argue and promote their case.

In the context of this contested situation, the author makes extraordinary claims for the authority and antiquity of the Davidic-Solomonic sanctuary. The *tabnît* includes a number of features, such as the "inner chambers" (28:11), "the courts *(haḥăṣērôt)* of the House of Yhwh" (28:11), "the surrounding chambers" *(hallĕšākôt sābîb*; 28:12), "the treasuries" (28:12), and the "golden lampstands" (28:15) that recall those of Solomon's temple (NOTES). By making these features and articles part of a divinely authored plan, the writer circumvents the impression left by Kings that these furnishings were merely the creations of Solomon and his craftsman (Japhet 1993a: 494). But the writer goes a few steps further. David's pattern for the Temple also contains items that are elsewhere only attributed to the Tabernacle. Not only the *tabnît* itself but also many of its articles such as "the flesh hooks" (28:17), "the jars" (*hqśwt*; 28:17), and "the altar of incense" (*mzbḥ hqṭrt*; 28:11) explicitly parallel those used in the Tabernacle. The inner shrine is called "the house of the (ark) cover" (28:11), and the Temple itself is called "a house *(bayit)* as the sanctuary" (*lammiqdāš*; 28:10). In one case, the plan of the chariot, the Chronicler's *tabnît* recalls a feature of Ezekiel's visions. When the design for the Temple is understood against the background of these earlier texts, the appearance of new furnishings in the Chronicler's description need not be viewed as baffling. Some of these articles—for example, "the golden bowls" *(kpwry hzhb)*—are only mentioned in late sources. Others—the sanctuary's "storerooms" (*ggzkyw*; 28:11), "upper chambers" (*ʿlywt*; 28:11), "silver lampstands" (28:15), and "silver tables" (28:16)—are unparalleled elsewhere in the Bible. Some of these items may reflect the realities of the Temple in the author's own time, while others may reflect the author's wishes for this Temple. In any case, the combination of features has a variety of benefits.

First, in an age that esteemed things antiquarian, the author establishes a long continuity in cultic affairs from the time of Moses to the time of the monarchy. Second, because David's *tabnît* contains furnishings that are attested in postexilic sources, the work associates the makeup of the postexilic Temple with that of much earlier shrines. The author attempts to establish the very links between the First and Second Temples that some might deny. Third, the Temple appears as the carrier and embodiment of Israel's most sacred institutions. If the Temple contains the major tabernacle artifacts, then the writer can argue, by extension, that the priestly and Levitical arrangements portrayed in his work also supersede those depicted in earlier sources. The very appeal to antiquity bolsters the authority of the author's own literary work. The Davidic-Solomonic period establishes a new orthodoxy and orthopraxis that honor and yet supersede older symbols of national unity. It is, therefore, no accident that the Chronicler presents the Temple as "a house of rest" *(bêt mĕnûḥâ)* for the Ark (28:2). The portable symbols of Israel's wilderness wanderings find a permanent home in the Jerusalem Temple.

Given the communal context in which the *tabnît* of the Tabernacle was implemented at Mount Sinai, it is only appropriate that the formal delivery of the *tabnît* from David to Solomon also occurs in a public setting (1 Chr 28). As conceived in Chronicles, the Temple is never (merely) a royal chapel. The issues David addresses to his "kinsmen" (28:2) have to do with more than succession within a single family. Succession is an issue that could be initially, at least, broached in a private setting (1 Chr 22). But if the Temple was a truly national shrine, its essential features had to be presented, if not approved, in the sight of all Israel (28:8). To be sure, "the assembly of Yhwh" (*qĕhāl yhwh;* vv. 1, 8) is not an active player in the proceedings, but its presence lends gravity to the ceremony. The public recognition given the sanctuary plans in the preexilic period ratifies the Temple's authority in the postexilic period. From the time of the United Monarchy onward, people and temple will be bound together in a common future.

# *XXXVI. David's Last Hurrah (29:1–30)*

*David's Charge to the National Convocation*

1 And King David said to all of the assembly,
"My son Solomon, (the) one whom God chose, is an inexperienced youth
and the work is great because the citadel is not for man, but for Yhwh God.
2 Commensurate with all of my ability, I have set aside for the House of my
God gold for all kinds of gold objects, silver for all kinds of silver objects,
bronze for all kinds of bronze objects, iron for all kinds of iron objects, and
wood for all kinds of wooden objects; onyx stones, stones for setting, stones
of antimony, colorful stones, every kind of precious stone, and marble in
abundance. 3 Moreover, in my solicitude for the House of my God, I have my
own private possession of gold and silver that I have dedicated to the House of
my God, above and beyond all that I set aside for the Holy House: 4 3,000 talents of gold, of the gold from Ophir, 7,000 talents of silver, refined for overlaying the walls of the rooms, 5 for all kinds of gold objects, for all kinds of
silver objects, and for all of the work to be done by the artisans. Who, then,
who is going to make a freewill offering to consecrate himself this day to
Yhwh?"

*Sacred Donations*

6 Then the officers of the ancestral houses, the officers of the Israelite tribes, the
officers of the thousands and of the hundreds, and the officers of the royal work
made freewill offerings. 7 They donated to the service of the House of God 5,000
talents of gold, 10,000 darics, 10,000 talents of silver, 18,000 talents of bronze,
and 100,000 talents of iron. 8 Whoever had (precious) stones donated them to the
treasury of the House of Yhwh under the care of Jeḥiel the Gershonite. 9 And the
people rejoiced about their voluntary giving, because they made freewill offerings
to Yhwh with a whole heart. And King David also rejoiced greatly.

*The Blessing of David*

10 Then King David blessed Yhwh in the presence of all the assembly. And
David said,

"Blessed are you, O Yhwh,
God of our ancestor Israel,
from eternity to eternity.
11 To you, O Yhwh, are the greatness and the power,
the distinction, the glory, and the majesty,
indeed, all that is in the heavens and on the earth.
To you, O Yhwh, belong the kingship
and the exaltation over everything as head.
12 Riches and honor come from before you,
and you rule over everything;
in your hand are strength and power,
and it is in your hand to magnify and to strengthen all.
13 And now, our God, we give thanks to you,
and we praise your glorious name.
14 Indeed, who am I
and who are my people
that we should have the means
to make a freewill offering such as this?
For everything is from you,
and from your hand have we given back to you.
15 Indeed, we are resident aliens before you,
and transients as all of our ancestors were;
like a shadow are our days upon the earth,
and there is no hope.

16 "O Yhwh, our God, all this abundance, which we have set aside to build
you a house for your holy name, stems from your hand, and to you it all belongs. 17 I know, my God, that you test the heart and desire justice. As for me,
with a just heart I have freely offered all these things. Now, your people, those
who are present here, I have seen joyfully make a freewill offering to you.
18 O Yhwh, God of Abraham, Isaac, and Israel our ancestors, keep such forms
of thought in the mind of your people forever and direct their hearts toward
you. 19 And grant to Solomon my son a whole heart to keep your commandments, your decrees, and your statutes, to practice all (of them), and to build
the citadel that I have prepared."

*The Enthronement of Solomon*

20 Then David said to all of the assembly, "Bless Yhwh your God." Then all of the assembly blessed Yhwh the God of their ancestors, bowed down and worshiped before Yhwh and before the king,
21 and sacrificed sacrifices to Yhwh. And they offered up burnt offerings to Yhwh the very next day—1,000 bulls, 1,000 rams, 1,000 lambs, and their libations—sacrifices in abundance for all Israel.
22 They ate and they drank before Yhwh on that day with great joy, and they made Solomon son of David king. They anointed him before Yhwh as ruler and Zadoq as priest.
23 Then Solomon sat on the throne of Yhwh as king instead of David his father. He prospered, and all Israel paid heed to him.
24 The officers, the warriors, and the sons of King David lent their hand in support of Solomon the king.
25 And Yhwh made Solomon exceedingly great in the sight of all Israel and endowed him with a regal majesty that no king over Israel before him ever had.

*Concluding Notices*

26 So David son of Jesse ruled over all Israel.
27 And the time which he ruled over Israel was forty years: in Ḥebron seven years and in Jerusalem thirty-three.
28 He died at a ripe old age, full of days, riches, and honor and Solomon his son reigned in his stead.
29 The acts of King David, former and latter, are written in the records of Samuel the seer, in the records of Nathan the prophet, and in the records of Gad the visionary,
30 together with (the accounts of) all his kingship, his power, and the events that befell him, Israel, and all the kingdoms of the lands.

# Textual Notes

29:1. "(the) one" *(ʾḥd)*. So MT and LXX. The term is missing from one Heb. MS, and Arnold Ehrlich (1914: 352) strikes it here. Curtis and Madsen (1910: 302) emend to *ʿšr*, "that."

"an inexperienced youth." Thus MT and LXX. Syr. "for he is a wise and understanding youth."

"the citadel" *(bîrâ)*. So MT. The term is lacking in LXX$^{B}$. LXX$^{AN}$ *hē oikodomē*, "the edifice"; LXX$^{L}$ *(hē) oikēsis*, "[the] dwelling." The Heb. noun *bîrâ*, which appears only in late literature (Polzin 1976: 130), is often translated figuratively as "palace" or "temple" (so also in v. 19). This impulse is understandable considering the context, but *bîrâ* usually refers to a fortress or citadel (Neh 2:8; 7:2; 2 Chr 17:19; 27:4). In Akk. *birtu(m)* can designate a citadel or a fortified town. Similarly, in Aram. *byrt* (e.g., AP 6.3; 27.5; 30.8) or *b(y)rtʾ* (e.g., AP 6.3, 4, 17; 35.2; *BMAP* 2.2; 3.4; 4.2, 4; 5.2) refers to a fortress, citadel *(DNWSI* 155–56), or occasionally to a fortified administrative capital (Lemaire and Lozachmeur 1987; 1995). The author of Neh 2:8 speaks of "the temple fortress" *(habbîrâ ʿăšer-labbayit)*. Hence, there is reason to believe that *bîrâ* refers here to a complex of buildings, including the Temple (J. Schwartz 1996: 29–49), rather than to a single structure. Note also the tenfold use of *bîrâ* ("fortress of Shushan") in Esth 1:2–9:12, the similar use of *bîrâ* in Dan 8:2, and the use of *byrtʾ* in the Samaria papyri to refer to the citadel of Samaria (e.g., WDSP 4.1).

29:2. "gold for all kinds of gold objects" *(hazzāhāb lazzāhāb)*. So MT and LXX[L]. The Heb. *hazzāhāb lazzāhāb* has a distributive force. Similarly, *hakkesep lakkesep*, "silver and for all kinds of silver objects" (and so forth). In simply listing the precious materials, "gold, silver, brass, iron, wood" here (and in what follows), LXX[AB] may be assimilating to the list of 22:16 or to the tabernacle verbiage of Exod 25:3.

"onyx stones" *(ʾabnê-šōham)*. So MT and LXX[L] *(lithous onychos)*. LXX[B] *lithous soom* transliterates. The translation is based, in part, on *sând/tu* and *sâmtu* ("dark red") stones in Akk. (*AHw* 1019). Josephus (*Ant.* 7.377) *smaragdou*, "emeralds."

"stones for setting" *(millûʾîm)*. Literally, "filled-in (things)" (cf. LXX *plērōseōs*). In context, the term seems to refer to various stones that could be used for mounting (*HALOT* 585).

"stones of antimony" *(ʾabnê-pûk)*. LXX *lithous polyteleis*, "expensive stones." Josephus (*Ant.* 7.378) is similar, *lithous polytelous*. The terminology is obscure. Cf. *bappûk ʾăbānayik* in MT Isa 54:11. In 2 Kgs 9:30 and Jer 4:30 *pûk* seems to refer to a kind of eye makeup, perhaps composed of galena or stibium (W. Holladay 1986: 170), hence "stone of antimony" (NJPS). In this connection, the name of Job's third daughter, *qeren happûk* ("horn of antimony"), is also relevant (Job 42:14). Rashi, followed by some modern commentators (e.g., Kittel 1902: 103; Rudolph 1955: 190), takes *pûk* as a by-form of *nōpek* (cf. Eg. *mfkʾt;* Lambdin 1953: 152), a semiprecious stone whose precise nature cannot be specified—turquoise, garnet, or malachite (*HALOT* 709). For other occurrences, see Exod 28:18; 39:11; Ezek 27:16; 28:13.

"colorful stones." The noun *riqmâ* usually designates embroidery or colored cloth (Judg 5:30; Ezek 16:10, 13, 18; 26:16; 27:7, 16, 24; Ps 45:15 [ET 45:14]; *HALOT* 1291), but the context suggests some sort of colored stones. Rudolph (1955: 190) reads with the previous locution *(ʾabnê-pûk)*, understanding the whole expression to mean colorful stones set into a hard mortar.

"marble *(ʾabnê-šayiš)* in abundance." Alternatively, (chalk) alabaster *(šēš)* stones (Benzinger 1901: 67; *HALOT* 1483).

29:3. "in my solicitude" *(birṣôtî)*. So also NJPS. Traditionally, "in my desire." See further the 1st NOTE to v. 3.

"I have" *(yeš-lî)*. LXX *estin moi*. Assuming a dittography of *yôd*, Rudolph (1955: 190) reads *šelî*. But the Heb. of MT can stand (GKC § 155n).

"private possession" *(sĕgullâ)*. Comparative evidence (Akk. *sikiltu; AHw* 1041) and context indicate that David is referring to what Greenberg (1951), followed by NJPS, calls his own "private hoard" or "trust fund." The traditional rendering might be "privy purse" (cf. Qoh 2:8; *y. B. Bat.* 9.17a; *Num. Rab.* 37b; *Song Rab.* 7.14; *Mek.* 2; *b. B. Bat.* 52a).

"silver." So MT *(lectio brevior)*. LXX adds *kai idou* (= *whnh*).

29:4. "7,000 talents of silver." So MT and LXX. Lacking in Josephus (*Ant.* 7.378).

"refined" *(mĕzuqqāq)*. Thus MT. LXX *en autois*.

"the rooms" *(habbāttîm)*. Thus MT *(lectio difficilior)*. LXX, Syr., Vg., and Arab. have the sg. One possibility is that *qîrôt habbāttîm* is a pl. of a genitival group in which both nouns appear in the pl. (Joüon, §136o), hence "walls of the Temple."

A second, more likely possibility, given the context (vv. 3–4), is that the *bāttîm* refer to parts of a larger compound, the different chambers that make up a larger structure (cf. Amos 3:15; Esth 7:8; Dan 5:10).

29:5. "for all kinds of gold objects . . . for all of the work." So MT and LXX[L]. Lacking in LXX[AB].

"for all kinds of gold objects" *(lazzāhāb lazzāhāb)*. The Heb. has a distributive force (1st TEXTUAL NOTE to v. 2).

"(and) for all kinds of silver objects" *(ûlakkesep lakkesep)*. See the previous TEXTUAL NOTE.

"to consecrate himself." Qere and some Heb. MSS *lĕmallôt (yādô)*; Kethib *lml'wt*. The *qal, nip'al,* and *pi'el* infs. of third *'ālep* verbs occasionally occur on the analogy of third *hê* verbs (GKC §74h). The phrase designates priestly ordination (Exod 28:41; 29:9, 29, 33, 35; Lev 4:5 [LXX]; 8:33; 16:32; 21:10; Num 3:3; Judg 17:5, 12; 1 Kgs 13:33; Ezek 43:26 [LXX]; 2 Chr 13:9; 29:31). A similar expression occurs for ordination in Akk.: *mullû qātam*, "to fill the hand." Because David makes no mention of priests or Levites, some (e.g., A. Ehrlich 1914: 352; Rudolph 1955: 190) would follow the versions and translate "to fill one's hand with (sacred offerings)." Cf. Exod 32:29. But would the author use such an expression in the inf. with this (disputed) meaning immediately after *mitnaddēb?* It seems better to retain the normal trans., recognizing that the writer is employing the expression figuratively (Snijders 1997: 305).

29:6. "(and) the officers of the Israelite tribes" *(wśry šbṭy yśr'l)*. So MT. LXX *kai hoi archontes tōn huiōn israēl* (= *wśry bny yśr'l*).

"and the officers *(ûlĕśārê)* of the royal work." Some would read the expected *wĕśārê* on the basis of LXX *hoi prostatai tōn ergōn*. But the prep. *(l-)* is used in an enumeration before the last noun in a series (Joüon §125l).

"work." So MT. LXX is more expansive, continuing with *kai hoi oikodomoi tou basileōs*, "and the royal builders."

29:7. "10,000 darics." Reading tentatively with MT *'ădarkōnîm ribbô* and Josephus (*Ant.* 7.379) *statēras myrious*, "10,000 staters." LXX[AB] "countless gold" *(chrysous myrious)*; cf. $ye_2$ *drachmas myrias*; bb' *dragmous myrias*. The lemma of Syr., "and good lead for the pipes," probably indicates that the translator was working with a partially illegible *Vorlage* (Weitzman 1999: 115). The reason for the discrepancy between MT and LXX is unclear. It is possible that LXX is leveling toward the verbiage used elsewhere in this verse. The Heb. *'ădarkōnîm* (also appearing in Ezra 8:27) is noteworthy. Traditionally, *'ădarkōnîm* has been translated as "darics," Persian gold coins (cf. Hatra *drykn'*; Gk. *dāreikos*; Syr. *darîk, drykwn'*; *KAI* 60.3 *drknm*; *DNWSI* 261). The term appearing in Ezra 2:69(//Neh 7:70–71) *darkĕmônîm* is taken to refer to "drachmas" (*HALOT* 17,232; Williamson 1977a: 123–26). The drachma was an Attic silver coin worth about six obols (Herodotus, Hist. 7.144; Andocides 4.18). Albright, followed by Cross (1998: 166), argues that the term *'ădarkōnîm* is a corruption (< *darkĕmōnîm*) of Attic *drachmē, drachmai* (cf. *KAI* 60.6 *drkmnm*). Cross contends that "daric(s)" should appear in Heb. as *dryk, drykwn*. The issue is difficult (note the evidence from the versions), but contextually "darics" makes more sense than "drachmas." A gold daric would be worth approximately twenty silver drachmas. Hence, the relatively small amount of drachmas would not comport well with the immense quantities of gold and silver listed elsewhere in this verse.

"talents of bronze." Thus MT and LXX. The explication of Syr., "Corinthian bronze," reveals something of the context in which its translators worked (Weitzman 1994: 157). Cf. Josephus (*J.W.* 5.201), Cicero (*Verr.* 2.2.34), and Pliny the Elder (*Nat.* 34.1, 3; 37.12).

29:10. "King David blessed." So LXX. MT's "David blessed" reflects a haplography (*homoioteleuton* from *wybrk hmlk dwyd* to *wybrk dwyd*).

29:11. "indeed, all" *(kî-kol)*. Bertheau (1873) proposes emending to "indeed, to you *(lk)* all," as elsewhere in this verse.

"and on the earth" *(wbʾrṣ)*. LXX adds "you are master (of)" *(despozeis)*.

"to you, O Yhwh, belong the kingship and the exaltation over everything as head" *(lk yhwh hmmlkh whmtnśʾ lkl lrʾš)*. LXX *apō prosopou sou tarassetai pas basileus kai ethnos*, "before your presence, every king and nation are confounded." See also the TEXTUAL NOTE to v. 12.

"to you." To restore *lāk* before *lĕkā* (e.g., Kittel 1902: 104) is unnecessary if one reads the previous *kî* as asseverative (Williams, §449).

"as head" *(lĕrōʾš)*. A few Heb. MSS and Vg. simply have *rōʾš*. It is possible that MT (the *lectio difficilior*) reflects a dittography of *lāmed* after *lĕkōl*, but it is more likely that the Heb. MSS and Vg. reflect a haplography.

29:12. "over everything." LXX explicates, *Kyrie ho archōn pasēs archēs*, "Lord, the ruler of every dominion."

29:14. "who are my people." So MT and LXX In what follows Syr. reads "For from all of my teachers I have learned. Indeed, it is your way of life that aided me and you are our hope, O Lord our God." This translation, indebted to Ps 119:99, has David quoting from one of the Psalms at the end of his life. Aphrahat's citation of Ps 119:99, according to the form of this lemma, shows his familiarity with the Peshiṭta of Chronicles (Weitzman 1999: 115). The Peshiṭta of Psalm 119 reads somewhat differently.

29:15. "resident aliens before you." Syr. explicates "insignificant in the world."

"there is no hope" *(ʾên miqveh)*. LXX* may reflect the same *Vorlage*, *ouk estin hypomonē* ("there is no abiding"). Syr. is entirely different, "so that they might live."

29:16. "O Yhwh . . . to you it all belongs." Thus MT. The markedly different text of Syr. may have resulted from a faulty *Vorlage* (Weitzman 1994: 151; 1999: 208). See also the previous TEXTUAL NOTE.

29:17. "my God." Thus MT. LXX "LORD."

"desire justice." So MT and LXX. Syr. "take delight in faith."

"have freely offered all these things." Syr. again differs from MT, "have uttered all this praise" (Weitzman 1999: 215).

29:18. "keep such forms of thought (in) the mind of your people forever" *(šmrh-zʾt lʿwlm lyṣr mḥšbwt lbb ʿmk)*. The *Vorlage* of LXX may have been slightly briefer, "keep these (things) in the thoughts of the heart of your people forever" *(phylaxon tauta en dianoia kardias laou sou eis aiōna)*. See also the 4th NOTE to 28:9.

29:19. "to practice all (of them) *(lʿśwt hkl)*, and to build the citadel that I have prepared." LXX is again somewhat different, "and to the end of accomplishing the preparation of your house" *(kai tou epi telos agagein tēn kataskeuēn tou oikou sou)*.

"that I have prepared" *(ʾšr-hkynwty)*. At the end of David's prayer Syr. differs completely from the MT, "that your great name may be consecrated and praised in the world, which you created before those that fear you." As Weitzman (1999: 43, 212–13) points out, David's words in Syr. draw upon the opening of the Qaddish prayer *(ytgdl wytqdš šmyh rbʾ bʿlmʾ dy brʾ krʿwtyh)*. Evidently, the Peshiṭta translator found his Hebrew version of Chronicles to be faulty or illegible and quoted the Qaddish, recited by Jews at the end of a discourse (*b. Sot.* 49a), in its place.

29:20. "your God." Thus MT. LXX* and Vg. have "our God."

29:21. "and sacrificed" *(wayyizbĕḥû)*. LXX has a different subject, *kai ethysen Daueid*.

"and they offered up" *(wayyaʿălû)*. Consistent with its earlier reading, LXX has the sg.

"the very next day." Literally, "on the morrow of that day" *(lmḥrt hywm hhwʾ)*. LXX *tē epaurion tēs prōtēs hēmeras*, "on the morrow of the first day."

29:22. "great joy." LXX$^{B}$ *charas*, "gratitude."

"made . . . king" *(wymlykw)*. MT and LXX$^{ALN}$ add "second (time)" *(šēnît)*. Lacking in LXX$^{B}$, $c_2$, Syr., and Arab. MT's lemma is probably an early addition prompted by 23:1 and 28:1–10 (Benzinger 1901: 68; Kittel 1902: 104). Less likely is the influence of 1 Kgs 1 (*pace* Williamson 1982b: 187).

"(and) they anointed him" *(wayyimšĕḥû)*. Given the testimony of LXX *(kai echrisan auton)*, Tg., and Vg., MT seems to have suffered parablepsis (from **wayyimšĕḥûhû* to *wayyimšĕḥû*).

"as ruler" *(lngyd)*. So MT *(lectio difficilior)*. LXX "as king" *(eis basilea)*.

"as priest" *(lĕkōhēn)*. The syntax in this verse creates problems for interpretation. Both NRSV and NAB translate *wayyimšĕḥû lyhwh lĕnāgîd ûlĕṣādôq lĕkōhēn* as "they anointed him as the LORD's prince, and Zadok as priest." Hence, the prep. *l-* in *lyhwh* is construed as a possessive, but the prep. *l-* in the parallel *lĕkōhēn* is not. One could just as easily translate this section as "they anointed (him) before Yhwh as ruler and before Zadoq as priest." But this would suggest that Solomon was anointed as both ruler and priest. Sense dictates differently. My translation largely follows NJPS: "they anointed him as ruler before the LORD, and Zadok as high priest."

29:24. "the officers." So LXX *(lectio brevior)*. MT expands to "all of the officers."

"the sons." So LXX. MT expands to "even all of the sons" *(gm kl-bny)*.

"King David." So MT *(lectio brevior)*. LXX adds "his father."

"lent their hand in support" *(ntnw yd tḥt)*. So MT. A similar expression occurs in 2 Chr 30:8 *(tnw yd l-)*. LXX$^{ABL}$ *hypetagēsan autō*, "subjected (themselves to) him."

29:25. "over Israel." Reading with MT and LXX$^{L}$ *(tou Israēl)*. Lacking in LXX$^{AB}$. The LXX omission makes Solomon a universally incomparable monarch.

29:26. "over all Israel." So MT. LXX "over Israel" (= *ʿl yśrʾl*) has lost *kl* by haplography *(homoioteleuton)*.

29:27. "and the time which he ruled over [LXX[L] + all] Israel" *(whymym ʾšr mlk ʿl-yśrʾl)*. So MT and LXX[L]. Lacking in LXX[ABN] due to haplography (*homoioteleuton* or *homoioarkton* from *ʿl-kl-yśrʾl* (v. 26) to *ʿl yśrʿl* [v. 27]). See also the source text of 1 Kgs 2:11, *whymym ʿšr mlk dwd ʿl-yśrʾl,* "and the time which David ruled over Israel (was forty years)."

"in Ḥebron seven years, and in Jerusalem, thirty-three." So LXX* *(lectio brevior)*. MT expands toward 1 Kgs 2:11: "in Ḥebron he reigned seven years and in Jerusalem he reigned thirty-three."

29:29. "and the acts of King David" *(wdbry dwyd hmlk)*. So MT *(lectio brevior)*. LXX expands toward the standard formula, "the rest of the acts of King David" *(hoi de loipoi logoi tou basileōs Daueid)*.

"and latter" *(wĕhāʾaḥrōnîm)*. So many Heb. MSS. MT *wĕhāʾăḥrōnîm.*

"in the records of Nathan the prophet." So MT and LXX. Lacking in Syr.[A].

"Gad the visionary" *(gād haḥōzeh)*. Thus MT (maximum differentiation). LXX[AB] (*blepontos*, "seer") and LXX[L] (*horōntos*, "seer") employ the same title as with Samuel (MT *hārōʾeh*).

29:30. "all the kingdoms of the lands" *(kol-mamlĕkôt hāʾărṣôt)*. Another example of a pl. of a genitival group in which both nouns appear in the pl. (Joüon, §136o).

"the lands." In LXX*, 2 Chr 1:1 (MT) is appended to the end of this verse. LXX[B] $bcc_2$ add a subscript identifying this section of the book, *paraleipomenōn a′* (see "Introduction"). The Peshiṭta comments that "David did right before the Lord, departing not from all that he commanded him, all the days of his life." See further Weitzman (1999: 234) and the references there.

# Notes

29:1–5. David's speech, addressed to the national assembly, should be viewed against the background of his earlier public statements and actions. Having convoked his nation's leadership to a major public convention in Jerusalem (28:1), the king delivered a series of addresses to these dignitaries (28:2–8) and to his designated heir (28:9–10, 19, 20–21). Most of the earlier orations focused on Solomon. To the assembled leaders, David presented a program for the succession and a rationale for the construction of the Temple in the next royal generation (28:2–8). David gave young Solomon a command to be faithful and to build the future Temple (28:9–10), provided his son with a plan for the Temple (28:11–19), encouraged him with assurances of divine presence (28:20), and bequeathed to him the priestly and Levitical divisions (28:21). David now turns his attention back to the assembled authorities. He will not speak directly to Solomon again. Israel's reverend king cites his own personal donations to make an effective appeal for broader material support.

29:1. "whom God chose." The Chronicler consistently depicts Solomon as elect of God (COMMENT on 28:1–21).

"an inexperienced youth." Literally, "a youth and weak" *(naʿar wārak)*. The term *naʿar* can connote immaturity (2nd NOTE to 22:5). To account for his own copious preparations, David contrasts young Solomon's vulnerability with the tremendous task that lies ahead.

"the citadel" *(habbîrâ)*. The size and location of the (postexilic) *bîrâ* is unclear. In the light of his excavations in the old city of Jerusalem, Benjamin Mazar (1975: 193) thinks of the *bîrâ* (of Nehemiah's time) as a fortress located on the northwestern angle of the temple mount. Many scholars think of this fortress as a single building, perhaps the forerunner of the Antonia fortress of Herod the Great on the northern side of his temple (1 Macc 13:52; Josephus, *Ant.* 15.403). But archaeological data and later (rabbinic) material suggest that the citadel was actually a complex of buildings, including the Temple itself (J. Schwartz 1996). The temple fortress is also thought by some to have included the Tower of Hananel and the Tower of the Hundred (Neh 3:1). In employing the term "the citadel" instead of the more narrowly defined "temple," the author may be stressing the enormity of the task that awaits Solomon. See also the 2nd TEXTUAL NOTE to v. 1.

"not for man." In the ancient Mediterranean world, temples were built to function as residences for gods or goddesses. The various services and rituals associated with the shrine were performed on the deity's behalf. In this context, the whole cluster of buildings of which the Temple is one part has acquired an aura of holiness. That the citadel belongs to Yhwh lends gravity to the preparations for construction. The author of MT Neh 11:1 further develops this concept of holiness by describing Jerusalem itself as "the holy city" *(ʿîr haqqōdeš)*. In this late text (not present in LXX), the entire city of Jerusalem has acquired a sacred aura. See also the *Temple Scroll* (11QT), which carries the notion of sanctity to an even higher level.

29:2. "commensurate with all of my ability." David expresses a similar sentiment in his earlier speech, "in my humility, I have provided" (22:14).

"gold for all kinds of the gold objects." In Exodus (25:1–7), Yhwh informs Moses of the gifts that he will accept from the Israelites for the Tabernacle. After the passage of some time, the people make such donations (and more) for the construction of this portable shrine (Exod 35:4–9, 20–29). There are a number of parallels between the materials listed in Exodus and those listed here, including gold, silver, bronze, and wood (for other parallels, see the following NOTES). Similarly, in Chronicles those assembled volunteer a variety of donations to the Temple (vv. 6–8). In this manner, the writer establishes a series of typologies: between the two sanctuaries, between their two human patrons (Moses and David), and between the Israel of Mount Sinai and the Israel of the United Monarchy. Yet there are also a few interesting differences. In Chronicles, for example, it is David who takes the lead in donating to the Temple (vv. 2–5) and it is David who summons the leadership of Israel to contribute to the building project (v. 5).

"onyx stones." Also one of the gifts for the tabernacle arrangements (Exod 25:7; 35:9, 27).

"stones for setting" *(millûʾîm)*. See also Exod 25:7; 28:17; 35:9, 27; 39:13.

29:3. "in my solicitude" *(birṣôtî)*. In a late legal context, the locution can denote free volition. Many Murabbaʿat conveyances of property begin with the clause

אני מרצוני, "I, of my own free will" (Benoît, Milik, and de Vaux 1961: 105; Muffs 1992: 127). The first-person declaration is important because David presents his own choices as unemcumbered and uncoerced. The Aramaic papyri from Elephantine are also illuminating in this regard because they occur in the first person and stress the affection and thoughts of the donor to the donee (Muffs 1969: 133–35). The giver declares his total willingness to part with the property, thereby precluding later claims against the legal act, including those brought by the donor himself. Such challenges could seek to invalidate the gift by declaring that the donor made it with reservations. David's absolute pledge, couched in the first-person, underscores the perpetuity of his gift, thereby linking him indelibly to the Temple built by Solomon.

"private possession" *(sĕgullâ)*. The royal estates and possessions were sketched earlier (27:25–31; 3rd TEXTUAL NOTE to v. 3). David's contributions to "the Holy House" in his official capacity as king were announced in one of his earlier speeches (22:14). The private contributions outlined in this context go "above and beyond" the earlier state endowments.

"the Holy House" *(bêt haqqōdeš)*. The use of this interesting locution fits well in a late context. Within the HB, the phrase *byt (h)qdš* appears only here and in Isa 64:10, *bêt qodšēnû wĕtip'artēnû*, "our holy and beautiful house." In both cases, the referent is the Jerusalem Temple. The phrase becomes much more common in later Jewish literature (1QS 8.4–6; 9.5–6; *Tg. Neof.* Exod 29:6; *Tg. Neof.* Lev 10:18; *Tg. Neof.* Num 7:85; *Tg. Ps.-J.* Num 7:85; *Tg. Neof.* Gen 31:47; *Tg. Ps.-J.* Gen 31:47; Hurvitz 1995: 168–70).

29:4. "3,000 talents of gold." A talent (ככר), a round disk, weighed approximately 28–30 kg. and was equivalent to about 3,000 shekels (cf. Exod 38:25–26). Although incredible, the amounts of bullion donated from David's private holdings are much smaller than those he donated on behalf of the state. For example, in contrast with the 3,000 gold talents listed here, 100,000 talents of gold were donated earlier (22:14). On the typically round and gargantuan numbers involved, see the NOTE to 12:38.

"gold from Ophir" *(mizzĕhāb 'ôpîr)*. A similar expression occurs on the eighth-century B.C.E. ostracon (#2) from T. Qasile: "Gold of Ophir for the Temple of Ḥoron [or Beth-ḥoron]—30 shekels" (*zhb. 'pr.lbyt.ḥrn.*[ ] *š 30;* Davies, §11.002.1–2). On the location of Ophir in southwestern Arabia, see the 1st NOTE to 1:23.

"refined" *(mĕzuqqāq)*. The same term is used of precious metals in 1 Chr 28:18 and Ps 12:7 [ET 12:6], and of settled wines in Isa 25:6 (Curtis and Madsen 1910: 29 [# 32]).

"overlaying the walls of the rooms." A task carried out by Solomon using gold leaf (2 Chr 3:4–9). A variety of chambers are part of the *tabnît* given to Solomon by David (1 Chr 28:11).

29:5. "the artisans" *(ḥārāšîm)*. Appointed by David for Solomon's use (1 Chr 22:15; cf. 2 Chr 24:12; Ezra 3:7; Neh 11:35).

"who." Having narrated his own private contributions to the sanctuary project, David now tenders a broader appeal and asks the notables for their own direct contributions.

"make a freewill offering" *(mitnaddēb)*. The freewill offering (*nĕdābâ;* Lev

22:18, 23; 23:38; Num 29:39) denotes a sacrifice or a gift to a sanctuary that normally did not involve a prior obligation or vow (Tigay 1996: 121; Weinberg 1995). As such, the freewill offering is a voluntary expression of thanksgiving and devotion. Often connected with times of rejoicing (Exod 36:3–7; Lev 7:16; Deut 12:6–7, 17–18; Ezra 1:4; 2:68–69; 3:5), freewill offerings are brought forward by the people in conjunction with the construction of the Tabernacle (Exod 35:21–29). As a sacrifice, the freewill offering could take the form of a burnt offering or an offering of well-being.

"to consecrate himself." By making freewill offerings to the cause of the Temple, the Israelites would be ordaining themselves to the service of Yhwh (see TEXTUAL NOTE).

29:6. "the officers of the ancestral houses" *(hāʾābôt)*. In Chronicles, the leaders or, more commonly, heads of ancestral houses represent large kinship (or quasi-kinship) groups. These authorities were mentioned earlier as part of David's administrative reorganization (27:1).

"the officers of the Israelite tribes." These traditional authorities were also mentioned earlier as part of the larger administrative reorganization (27:16–22; 28:1). Josephus (*Ant.* 7.378) mentions the specific involvement of the priests and the Levites, but this reference is lacking in MT and LXX.

"the officers of the thousands and of the hundreds." See the 4th NOTE to 26:26.

"the officers of the royal work" *(śārê mĕleʾket hammelek)*. These are not explictly mentioned earlier. The reference is clearly not to those Levites and priests who were in charge of the Temple work (23:4, 24; 28:13, 20–21). Given the context, these officials may have been in charge of the royal household.

29:7. "5,000 talents of gold." Given that a talent weighed about 3,000 shekels (Exod 38:25–26), the text projects Israel's leaders as donating a fantastic amount of gold bullion. By way of contrast, Ḥezeqiah pays tribute of thirty talents of gold and three hundred talents of silver to Sennacherib (2 Kgs 18:14). The tribute claimed by Sennacherib was higher (thirty talents of gold and eight hundred talents of silver), but either of these figures pale in comparison with the fantastic numbers in Chronicles (NOTE to 12:38).

"10,000 darics." The daric was a Persian gold coin, thought to weigh approximately 8.4 grams, minted sometime after 515 B.C.E. (Ezra 8:27). See further the 1st TEXTUAL NOTE to v. 7.

29:8. "Jeḥiel the Gershonite." Head of the descendants of Laadan (23:8). See also the 3rd NOTE to 26:21.

29:9. "the people rejoiced." In his use of the verb *sāmaḥ*, the author emphasizes free and cheerful giving (2 Chr 15:12–14; 24:5–10; Muffs 1992: 183–85). The point is underscored by the remark that "they made freewill offerings to Yhwh with a whole heart" *(lēb šālēm)*. In his stress on volition, the Chronicler anticipates the rabbinic tradition in which the good intentions of the donor, although not critical from a legal standpoint, are accorded substantial religious consideration (Muffs 1992: 166). The emphasis on free and spontaneous giving is also found in early Christian literature (e.g., Rom 12:6–8; 2 Cor 8:3–5; 9:5, 7–8; cf. Acts 5:1–11).

29:10–19. "King David blessed Yhwh." The sequence of events narrated by the author is extraordinary. The outpouring of giving from the assembled leadership does not lead to a round of self-congratulations. Instead, it leads to an address to Yhwh by David. David's blessing (or prayer) in Chronicles may be compared with the blessings uttered by Solomon at the temple dedication in Kings. Unlike the first Solomonic blessing, which praises Yhwh for realizing certain Davidic promises (1 Kgs 8:14–21), and the second Solomonic blessing, which requests divine sustenance for Israel and divine consideration for Solomon's prayer (1 Kgs 8:55–61; Knoppers 1995c), this blessing highlights divine majesty and sovereignty. The prayer begins with a doxology (1 Chr 29:10–12), continues with a thanksgiving (v. 13) and a confession (vv. 14–17), and concludes with two petitions (vv. 18–19). The significance of this public prayer is discussed further in the COMMENT.

29:10. "blessed are you, O Yhwh" (ברוך אתה יהוה). Most biblical blessings appear either in the third person, hence ויברך את כל-קהל ישׂראל, "and he [Solomon] blessed all the assembly of Israel" (1 Kgs 8:55) or switch to the third person after אשׁר or כי, hence ויאמר ברוך יהוה אלהי ישׂראל אשׁר . . ., "and he [Solomon] said, 'Blessed be Yhwh, the God of Israel, who . . .' " (1 Kgs 8:15). The formulation of this blessing, maintaining the second-person address while using the personal pron. אתה, represents a shift in the postexilic age (see also Ps 119:12) that anticipates the direct address of synagogal prayers and blessings. Note especially the use of the formula ברוך אתה יהוה in the *ḥătîmôt* (epilogues) of the Eighteen Benedictions. The change in address may indicate, as Towner points out (1968: 397–99), that Jewish liturgical customs of the synagogues standardized the direct style of blessing that was prevalent in Jewish worship during the Persian and Hellenistic periods.

"our ancestor Israel." In his references to the ancestors, the author privileges the progenitor of the twelve tribes. Although Chronicles contains few direct references to Abraham (e.g., v. 18), the Ancestral period is highly important in the Chronicler's view of the past, because it represents the formative age of his people's beginnings. In the genealogies (2:3–8:40) each of the tribes is traced to one of Israel's sons.

29:11. "to you, O Yhwh, belong the kingship." A consistent theme in the prayers of David (17:14; 29:11–12) and in the psalm medley included in the Chronicler's work (16:22–33).

29:12. "you rule over everything." Consistent with the tenor of his age, the author depicts Yhwh as a universal deity, sovereign over the nations. David's acclamation resonates with the sentiments expressed in the psalm anthology sung by the Levites at the ascension of the Ark (16:24–26) and in the prayer David offered following Nathan's dynastic oracle (COMMENT on 17:16–27). David's words of acclamation become, in turn, a model for later kings on important public occasions (Pratt 1987: 183–96; Throntveit 1987: 94–95). The emphasis on divine sovereignty, in particular, is echoed in the Judahite monarchy during international crises (Balentine 1993: 97–100). Confronting an immense Cushite invasion, Asa acclaims: "O Yhwh, for you there is no difference between helping the many and helping the powerless; help us, O Yhwh our God, for we rely on you" (2 Chr 14:10 [ET 14:11]). Similarly, when Jehoshaphaṭ is faced with a foreign invasion, he declares to Yhwh, "You rule over all the kingdoms of the nations, and in your hand are strength and power; there is none with you who can withstand you" (2 Chr 20:6).

29:14. "who am I and who are my people." A similar expression of humility appears in David's earlier prayer: "Who am I, O Yhwh God, and what is my house that you have brought me so far?" (17:16).

"everything is from you." The piety expressed posits a relationship between divine sustenance and human praise. In a Babylonian prayer, the petitioner proclaims, "Marduk, O Great Lord, grant me life, and I shall be satisfied to walk before you in light [*maḫarka namriš atalluka*]" (Ebeling 1953: 64). From David's point of view, everything that he and the people donate to Yhwh belongs, in fact, to Yhwh: "from your hand have we given back to you." Because "all the goods in the world belong to the Divine, the only real contribution man can offer is the willingness with which he gives his contributions, and the alacrity with which he performs the act" (Muffs 1992: 166).

29:15. "resident aliens." In many texts a *gēr* is someone without inherited rights—originally at least—a newcomer or outsider (Kellermann 1975: 439–40; van Houten 1991). In Chronicles such *gērîm* have a mediate status (3rd NOTE to 22:2). Earlier, the Israelite ancestors were presented as sojourning *(gārîm)* in Canaan (1 Chr 16:19//Ps 105:12). Here the Israelites themselves are presented as resident aliens before God "as all of our ancestors were." The metaphorical application of *gēr* status to those gathered in the national assembly underscores the transiency of life before God (cf. Pss 39:12; 144:3–4; Job 8:8–9; 14:1–2; Estes 1991). The use of the metaphor is no doubt connected to David's own situation. The transition to Solomon's reign (1 Chr 29:1, 20–25) and the imminent end of David's life (vv. 26–30) become the occasion to reflect on human mortality (see COMMENT).

29:17. "you test the heart *(ʾattāh bōḥēn lēbāb)*. For similar expressions, see 1 Chr 28:9; 1 Sam 16:7; Jer 11:20; Pss 7:10 [ET 7:9]; 139.

"desire justice" *(mēšārîm tirṣeh)*. An echo of a prophetic theme. Offering sacrifices is not enough; Yhwh also wants justice (1 Sam 15:22–23; Jer 7:5–6; Mic 6:6–8).

29:18–19. David's prayer contains two petitions, one focused on the people and the other focused on his son.

29:18. "direct their hearts toward you." The linkage between divine involvement and human obedience is also a constituent feature of Solomon's second blessing at the temple dedication. There, the king asks that Yhwh "might incline our hearts toward him, to follow in all of his ways, to observe his commandments and statutes, which he commmanded our fathers" (1 Kgs 8:58; Knoppers 1995c). A similar concept is attested at Qumran. There petitioners (e.g., 1QS 11:15–17; 1QH[a] 16:12–13; 4Q427) request the deity to deepen and complete the favor that the deity himself has freely given (Knohl 1996: 29–30).

29:19. "grant to Solomon." David prays that Solomon might have the same resolve and dedication that the leaders are manifesting during this assembly (v. 9).

"to keep your commandments." Summons to obey Yhwh's statutes and judgments are ubiquitous in Deuteronomy (e.g., 7:11; 11:32) and the Deuteronomistic History (Weinfeld 1972a: 332–39). Loyalty to Yhwh's statutes is a major theme Moses stresses to Joshua (Deut 31:5; Josh 1:7–8). As we have seen ("Excursus: The Composition of 1 Chronicles 23–27"), the transition from David to Solomon is partially based on the Moses-Joshua transition. Hence, it is not surprising that David summons Solomon to obey divine law (1 Chr 22:11–13; 28:9–10, 20). Solomon repeats the same theme in the context of his own reign (2 Chr 6:15–17; 7:17–18). Such adherence to Yhwh's statutes is consistently linked to temple construction (R. Braun 1976).

29:20–25. "said to all of the assembly." Having concluded his prayer, David leads all those assembled in a ceremonial sacrificial feast. Part of the celebrations involves publicly anointing Solomon and Zadoq and installing Solomon as king. In the context of this official coronation, the officers, warriors, and other princes all pledge loyalty to the new king. Rather than being a summary of 1 Kgs 1 (Beecher 1885: 75), the author presents an alternative version of events.

29:20. "bowed down and worshiped before Yhwh and before the king." Cf. 1 Kgs 1:31, 53.

29:21. "and sacrificed" *(wayyizbĕḥû)*. The text of vv. 21–22 refers not to two pairs of sacrificial ceremonies in one day, but to one ceremony that extends over two days. Hence, v. 21 goes on to refer to thousands of burnt offerings "the very next day."

"sacrifices." As part of his drive for kingship, Adonijah also offers sacrifices in a public setting (1 Kgs 1:9–10, 25–26). As much as the Chronicler's presentation of the David-Solomon succession departs from the picture of chaos and court intrigues in Samuel-Kings, there are a few formal parallels, such as designation by the ruling monarch, public anointing, sacrifices, and public feasting.

29:22. "they ate and they drank before Yhwh." A feast also attends Adonijah's ill-fated campaign for kingship (1 Kgs 1:9, 25). But the best parallels to this sacred repast celebrating Solomon's investiture may be found in the feast at Mount Sinai, during which "they saw God and ate and drank" (Exod 24:1–11), and the pan-Israel feast celebrating the national acclamation of David as Israel's new king (1 Chr 12:39–41). Within the Chronicler's work, there is a parallel between the coronation of David and the coronation of his son. At the coronation feast of David, there too "was joy in Israel" (12:41).

"they made Solomon." Whereas David earlier made Solomon king over Israel (23:1), all of Israel's leaders now choose to do the same in a public ceremony. The presumably private, royal designation of succession is eventually followed by a public designation of succession by Israel's officers. Whether one should think of an actual coregency between David and Solomon (Baltzer 1971) is open to dispute. Solomon does not exercise any regal role; he is a completely passive figure in the last portion of David's tenure (23:2–29:23). David initiates and oversees the administrative appointments even though these appointments are made with a view to Solomon's reign. In this respect, the presentation differs markedly from that of Kings. The succession in Chronicles is a methodical, deliberate, and well-organized operation, a careful mixture of private and public events. In Kings the decision to make Solomon king is only rendered after Adonijah publicly launched his own campaign for the throne (1 Kgs 1:11–31). Set against the background of factionalism within David's own government, the public spectacle is reactionary, designed to contest and void the threat posed by Adonijah's rise (1 Kgs 1:5–10). In Chronicles David acts proactively. The public ceremony ratifying and celebrating Solomon's ascent takes place after David has created the necessary conditions to ensure Solomon's acclamation.

"they anointed him." In Kings, this anointing involves a select few—Nathan, Benaiah, and Zadoq (1 Kgs 1:34, 39, 44).

"ruler" *(nāgîd)*. The term is also used in 1 Kgs 1:35 by David to designate Solomon as his successor. On the frequent use and various connotations of *nāgîd* in Chronicles, see the 4th NOTE to 26:24.

"Zadoq." Chronicles, unlike Kings (1 Kgs 2:35), presents Zadoq's rise to (exclusive) power as transpiring already in David's reign (NOTES to 15:11; 18:16). In Kings the banishment of Abiathar, occurring after Solomon consolidates power, punishes Abiathar for supporting Adonijah's attempted coup (1 Kgs 1:7, 50–53; 2:35). In Chronicles the anointing of Zadoq during the last period of David's reign authorizes his exclusive standing during Solomon's reign. Eupolemus erroneously presents Eli as high priest at the time of the transfer of power from David to Solomon (Eusebius, *Praep. ev.* 9.30.8).

29:23. "then Solomon sat *(wayyēšeb)*." Chronicles anomalously presents Solomon's accession formulas before David's death formulas. The son sits on the throne instead of his father. The effect of this is to draw the two reigns more closely together (Williamson 1982b).

"the throne of Yhwh." The Chronicler consistently associates the kingship and kingdom of David and Solomon with that of Yhwh (2nd NOTE to 17:14).

"he prospered" *(wayyaṣlaḥ)*. Thus fulfilling one of David's hopes for his successor, articulated in his private speech to Solomon (22:13).

"all Israel paid heed to him." David's efforts to ensure a smooth succession achieve success. Again, the contrast with Samuel-Kings is startling. There Solomon does not win widespread assent to his rule until after a bloody and somewhat prolonged power struggle (1 Kgs 1:1–2:12). Even then, Solomon finds it necessary to suppress or eliminate what he deems to be further internal threats to his rule (1 Kgs 2:13–46; Knoppers 1993c: 57–77).

29:24. "the officers *(śārîm)*, the warriors *(gibbōrîm)*." The acclamation of Solomon is unanimous. Israel's civil and military officials join forces in endorsing David's chosen successor. On the role of the military in David's administration, see also 26:1–19 and 27:1–15.

"the sons of King David." In Samuel-Kings not only do two sons (Absalom and Adonijah) actively campaign for kingship, but each commands considerable support. In the former case, David and his entourage have to flee Jerusalem (2 Sam 15:1–16:14). In the latter case, Adonijah is backed by Abiathar, Joab, some army officers, and the *vox populi* (1 Kgs 1:9–10, 25–26; 2:15). All of the other sons of the king, except Solomon, are invited to Adonijah's feast (1 Kgs 1:9, 25). In contrast, no princes are mentioned as taking part in the public anointing of Solomon (1 Kgs 1:38–40). But in Chronicles, the sons of David, who were earlier given various roles in the national administration (NOTES to 18:17; 27:32; 28:1), all support Solomon. Influenced by the Chronicler's presentation, Josephus underscores David's wish that the other princes support Solomon (*Ant.* 7.372–373).

29:25. "exceedingly great *(wygdl . . . lmʿlh)* in the sight of all Israel." This theme reappears at the beginning of the narration of Solomon's reign (2 Chr 1:1): "Yhwh was with him and made him exceedingly great" *(wygdlhw lmʿlh)*. The author is drawing another parallel between the leadership transition from Moses to Joshua and the transition from David to Solomon (see "Excursus: The Composition of 1 Chronicles 23–27"). The exaltation of Joshua by Yhwh (Josh 3:7; 4:14) contributes to the consolidation of his rule over Israel in the wake of Moses' death.

"a regal majesty *(hôd malkût)* that no king over Israel before him ever had." This notice establishes Solomon's reign as unparalleled by all those who went before him. Admittedly, this list comprises only Saul and David. The Chronicler's Solomon fulfills the petition of David's courtiers in Kings: "May God make his name more famous than your name and his throne greater than your throne" (1 Kgs 1:47; Knoppers 1993c: 68). A similar wish is expressed by Benaiah (1 Kgs 1:37; Plöger 1957: 40–42). The Deuteronomist depicts Solomon's reign as unrivaled, but on more specific grounds: wealth, wisdom, and glory (Knoppers 1992b: 414–17). In the dream theophany at Gibeon, Solomon is informed, "I have given you a wise and understanding mind unlike any which has ever preceded you; nor will anyone like you arise again" (1 Kgs 3:12). This incomparability statement is also found in the Chronicler's version of the Gibeon incubation (2 Chr 1:12). But in Kings, incomparability formulas are also applied to Ḥezeqiah (unparalleled trust) and to Josiah (unparalleled reforms; Knoppers 1992b: 418–30). In Chronicles, incomparability formulas are applied neither to Ḥezeqiah nor to Josiah, but two incomparability formulas are applied to Solomon. This has the effect of individuating Solomon's reign. Instead of there being three matchless kings, there is one. In the context of the monarchy, the two incomparability formulas (regal majesty; wisdom, wealth, and glory) distinguish Solomon's reign as the highpoint in Israelite history.

29:26–30. The concluding formulas to David's tenure are an expanded version of the formulas appearing in 1 Kgs 2:11–12. The burial notice of 1 Kgs 2:10 does not appear, however, in Chronicles. Most of the additions contributed by the Chronicler resemble the concluding formulas used for later monarchs, especially Solomon (2 Chr 9:29–31). In Chronicles regnal formulae play an important historiographic role in configuring a monarch's reign (Japhet 1993a; Glatt 2001). To be sure, the author borrows relevant materials from Samuel-Kings, but his additions to introductory notices, source citations, summations, evaluation formulas, and death and burial notices reveal his own theological perspectives.

29:27. "Ḥebron seven years." In his depiction of the inception of David's reign, the Chronicler creates the impression that all Israel supported David from the outset (11:1–3) and that David's first major task as king was to take Jerusalem (11:4–9). But in tracing the evolution of pan-Israel support for David, the author admits that David's rise to power was a much longer process (11:10–12:41). So too in the concluding regnal formulas to David's reign (cf. 1 Kgs 2:11–12), the writer volunteers that David ruled in Ḥebron before he came to rule in Jerusalem. But the Chronicler avoids stating that David ruled over only Judah in Ḥebron (2 Sam 2:4) before he came to rule there over all twelve tribes (2 Sam 5:1–3). In Chronicles David "ruled over all Israel" (1 Chr 29:26).

29:28. "a ripe old age." Security and longevity are marks of divine blessing (2 Chr 24:15; Deut 4:40; 5:16; Isa 52:10; 65:17–19; Job 42:17; Mason 1990: 224–25). The notation rectifies the impression left by Kings (e.g., 1 Kgs 1:1–4) that David no longer had possession of his full powers during his declining years. In Chronicles not only does David authorize the Solomonic succession in advance of his own death, but he also does so with his full wits (NOTES to 23:1; 28:2). That the king dies full of "riches and honor" confirms David's blessed state.

29:29. "the acts of King David, former and latter." A typical regnal formulation in Chronicles (e.g., 2 Chr 9:29; 12:15; 16:11), but lacking in Kings for David.

"records of Samuel *(dibrê šĕmûʾēl)* the seer." For almost two centuries scholars have debated the import of this extended citation (Peltonen 1996). The reference is not unique. Prophetic compositions are cited elsewhere (2 Chr 9:29; 12:15; 13:22; 20:34; 26:22; 32:32; 33:19). Do these citations refer to prophetic, annalistic, midrashic, or biblical traditions? Or are the prophetic-source citations merely a literary convention? Of the various possibilities, the prophetic stories of Samuel-Kings are the most likely source because almost all of the prophets who appear in the Chronicler's citations are found within these books. Two of those who do not—Iddo and Ḥozai—may be derived from source material within Samuel-Kings (Schniedewind 1995: 227). Moreover, the Chronicler's accounts of these prophets do not contain any additional material to that which appears in Samuel-Kings. The prophetic-source citations found in the concluding formulas of 1 Chr. 29:29 resemble the editorial superscriptions of two prophetic books—Jeremiah *(dibrê yirmĕyāhû)* and Amos *(dibrê ʿāmôs)*. This may suggest that the author drew upon the editorial superscriptions of these books in composing his prophetic source citations (Schniedewind 1995: 218; cf. Freedman 1987).

We have been discussing the origins of the prophetic-source citations. An interesting and related question involves what the prophetic citations say about the author's attitude toward the prophetic figures and the larger literary work of which their stories are a part. To begin with, the very fact that David has three prophetic figures commenting upon his reign is itself a compliment to his kingship (Glatt 2001). Each one of the prophetic figures who plays a role in David's reign is also a compiler of events in his reign, a writer concerned with recording traditions for posterity. In the Chronicler's depiction, Samuel, Nathan, and Gad appear as literati, scribes who take a consistent interest in writing about the times in which they lived. Moreover, the interest of these seers is in more than national events; their writings comprehend David's "kingship" and "power," as well as "the kingdoms of the lands" (v. 30). The Chronicler stands, therefore, within a tradition of interpretation, preserved in the divisions of the HB, that views the historical books of Joshua through Kings as prophetic in character (the Former Prophets). As such, the Deuteronomistic work carries a certain prestige for the Chronicler. Indeed, one can make the case that the Former Prophets have more authority for the Chronicler than whatever extra-biblical source material may have been available to him.

29:30. "the kingdoms of the lands." A common Chronistic expression, referring to neighboring nations (2 Chr 12:8; 17:10; 20:29). The concluding formulas to David's tenure stress his international stature and accomplishments.

## SOURCES AND COMPOSITION

Most scholars regard 1 Chr 29 as integral to the Chronicler's work, but there are exceptions. Consistent with his dual redaction theory, Galling (1954: 69–70, 76–78) attributes vv. 20, 22*, 23–30 to an author different from and earlier than the author of vv. 1–19, 21, and 22. More recently, Mosis (1973: 105–7) and Throntveit (1987: 89–96) have renewed and extended arguments for disunity. Mosis defines the secondary interpolation as encompassing all of vv. 1–19, while Throntveit limits it to vv. 1–9, 14b, 16, 17, and 19. These scholars point to peculiarities in the vocabulary, content, and placement of vv. 1–9: the use of *bîrâ* in v. 1 and the verb *twḥ* in v. 4; repetition in content between 22:2–11, 28:2–12a, 20–21, and 29:1–9; exaggeration in numbers in 22:14–19 and 29:1–5 compared with 22:1–5 and 2 Chr 3:3–4:22.; and stylistic surprises, such as the use of *wy'mr dwyd hmlk* (29:1) instead of the expected *wy'mr dwyd* (13:2; 22:7; 28:20; 29:20). As for the prayer (vv. 10–19), all (Mosis) or part (Throntveit) of it is deemed secondary because of references within vv. 14b, 16, and 17 to vv. 1–9, the conditionalization of the Davidic promises in v. 19 (Mosis), and the reappearance of *bîrâ* in v. 19. Mosis also considers vv. 21b–22 (the second day of offerings) to be a redactional seam necessitated by the insertion of vv. 1–19.

Some of the aforementioned arguments, based on minor issues of grammar and philology, do not seem to be overly significant. The presence of *bîrâ* in vv. 1 and 19, for example, is not so odd considering that this word only appears in the Persian and Hellenistic periods (Esth 1:2, 5; 2:3, 5, 8; 3:15; 8:14; 9:6, 11, 12; Dan 8:2; Neh 1:1; 2:8; 7:2; cf. *bîrānîyôt* in 2 Chr 17:12; 27:4). There are a few unusual stylistic traits in 1 Chr 29:1–19, but these traits do not seem to be sufficiently jarring to justify assigning this material to the work of a later redactor or interpolator.

Moving on to larger arguments, the predication of the dynastic promises upon Solomonic obedience is a consistent trait of the Chronicler's presentation of the United Monarchy (1 Chr 22:12–13; 28:7–10; 29:19; 2 Chr 6:15–17; 7:17–18; Knoppers 1998). There seems to be no compelling reason to excise this material as the work of a later glossator. These passages form an integral part of the Chronicler's treatment of David and Solomon. Drawing upon his version of Kings (Knoppers 1993c: 99–103), the Chronicler takes conditional passages from Solomon's reign (1 Kgs 2:3–4; 8:25–26; 9:4–5), modifies them, and integrates them into his treatment of David and Solomon. In this manner, he unifies these two reigns within his larger presentation (Williamson 1977a; 1983b).

It is true that the account of Solomon's building campaign (2 Chr 3:3–4:22) does not contain the inflated numbers of 1 Chr 22:14–19 and 29:1–5, but this also holds true for the account of 22:3–4, which speaks of "iron in abundance," "bronze in abundance beyond weighing," and "innumerable cedar logs." Exegesis, rather than redaction, may well be the reason for the conflict between the inordinate numbers of 1 Chr 22, 28, and 29 and the lack thereof in 2 Chr 3–4. In his presentation of Solomon's reign, the Chronicler depends heavily upon the presentation of Kings. In most of the passages where he draws from his *Vorlage*, the author does not exaggerate numbers. He may creatively omit, supplement, and recontextualize the text before him, but his actual quotation of material from Kings is conservative (see Introduction). Discrepancies between the numbers he includes from Kings and the numbers he creates within his own work are to be expected.

The assumption that repetition in the speeches of David signals redactional diversity fails to take into account literary considerations of audience, thematic development, and setting. David's earlier speech (22:6–16) is a private pronouncement to Solomon. Later speeches to Solomon occur, however, in the context of a national assembly (28:9–10, 19, 20–21). The speech of 22:17–19 is delivered to Israel's officers, while the later speeches (28:2–8; 29:1–5) are delivered to the leaders gathered at the national convocation in Jerusalem. That there is some duplication between the speeches, even in phraseology, should not occasion great surprise. One can assume, given the Chronicler's laudable presentation of David, that David's private counsel to Solomon and his public counsel to Solomon will overlap significantly. Similarly, one expects some consonance between what David tells Solomon about his program and what he tells Israel's leaders about his program. Finally, in the aftermath of David's speaking to the national assembly about the succession (28:2–8) and of his delivering a temple plan to Solomon, it is not surprising that David offers Solomon words of encouragement (28:9–10, 20–21).

The more important question is not whether there is repetition between David's orations, but whether there is, in spite of the repetition, some movement from one speech to another and whether there is some coherence to the group of speeches as a whole. As the NOTES and the COMMENTS to the relevant chapters make clear, there is a progression from David's supply of materials as head of state (22:2–5) to his supply of materials as a private citizen (29:1–5), from his request to Israel's officers to help build the sanctuary of Yhwh (22:18–19) to his request to the national assembly to make donations to the temple project (29:5), from his detailed speech to Solomon (22:6–16) to his shorter exhortations to Solomon at the national assembly (28:9–10, 20–21). The sequence of speeches, delivered in different contexts and given to a variety of audiences, both before and after the administrative appointments (23:6–27:34*), gives the impression of a deliberative and carefully orchestrated process. For some scholars the repetition inherent in this sequence of events suggests the work of several authors, but to other scholars the repetition is one means by which a single author makes a larger point.

# COMMENT

In biblical literature, great leaders, such as Jacob (Gen 49:1–28), Moses (Deut 32:1–43, 45–47; 33:1–29), Joshua (Josh 23:1–16; 24:1–28), Samuel (1 Sam 12:1–25), and David (1 Kgs 2:1–9), deliver parting addresses to their successors or followers. The speeches vary in their content and differ in their form—historical reviews, admonitions, pleas, rebukes, predictions, exordiums, complaints, accusations, and appeals. Some appear in poetry, while others appear in prose. Coming near the end of a leader's career, such discourses signal the passing of one era and the beginning of another. They may rehearse the past, address the present, predict the future, or do all three. In reflecting upon the past and in engaging the present, the speeches shape a leader's legacy. In forecasting the future or in providing instruction to the leader's followers, the orations set an agenda for the next generation. Precisely because such addresses are employed to define a legacy, they are a significant tool through which authors communicate to their audiences.

In Chronicles David delivers a series of speeches that mark the transition to a new era. Writing late in the biblical period, the author presents David as one of Israel's most important authorities, a leader whose actions and public declarations draw upon older models. But if the Chronicler follows a standard practice in having David deliver a final address, the form of this address departs from earlier prototypes. The larger biblical setting provides, therefore, one context in which the king's final statements and actions may be read. But there are others. The story of the preparations for the Temple and the rule of Solomon may be read in at least two additional contexts: the context of the writer's presentation of the monarchy and the context of the Chronicler's own time, the postexilic age. Rather than comparing, for example, the latter years of Moses and David, the second approach deals with David's dotage within the setting of the Chronicler's larger depiction of Saul, David, and Solomon. The third approach deals with the text's possible meanings in Persian period Yehud. The three contexts are inevitably related because no writer ever composes a work in a historical or social vacuum. Moreover, one's apprehension of the late Achaemenid period is inevitably affected by the testimony of those biblical texts that scholars think were written during this era. Nevertheless, it will be useful to pursue the first two interests—the biblical context and the Chronicles context—before addressing the third—how the internal world of the text addresses the external world of the writer.

The Chronicler's version of David's last years presents a striking contrast to the stories of adultery, rape, deception, chaos, betrayal, and murder found in Samuel-Kings. The Chronicler does not simply contest the version of Samuel-Kings; he creates a comprehensive alternative to it. The writer employs Nathan's dynastic oracle (17:1–15) as a cipher by which to organize much of David's reign. Nathan's prophecy about Yhwh's subduing all of David's enemies (17:10) is fulfilled by David's victories over surrounding nations (18:1–20:8). The basis for the fulfillment of a second promise—the construction of a house for Yhwh (17:12)—is adumbrated by the selection of a site for the Temple (21:1–22:1). The promise of a son, divinely designated to be his successor (17:11–12), is fulfilled in Solomon's acclamation and coronation (22:7–10; 28:4–7; 29:22–25). In responding to Nathan's prophecy, David is not passive. In his prayer (17:16–27), the king acknowledges that much of what Nathan spoke about pertains to the future and not to the present. Nevertheless, the king shows no hesitation or complacency. To avoid the fate of his predecessor, David makes elaborate plans to ensure a peaceful transition to his appointed heir (17:9–11, 13). The founding father initiates a series of strategic steps to prepare for a future that he will not and cannot see (17:16–17). Much like Moses, who labors on despite being denied access to the promised land, David labors to see Israel succeed in a new generation. The king seizes upon the fulfillment of some of Nathan's promises, such as security in the land (17:9–10; 22:17–18) and the gift of an heir (17:11–12; 22:7–10; 28:4–7), to press for the fulfillment of other promises. David bequeaths to Solomon the pattern for the sanctuary and its furnishings that David receives from God (28:11–19). It is no wonder, then, that the final stage in David's reign is marked by a series of state appointments (23:6–27:34) that will bridge the gap between the two reigns and set the stage for building the Temple (17:12).

With the end of his life in view, the founding father prepares his heir for his accession. In this respect, the model for the transition from David to Solomon is not David and Solomon in Samuel-Kings, but Moses and Joshua in Numbers-Deuteronomy-Joshua (see "Excursus: The Composition of 1 Chronicles 23–27"). Just as a series of speeches prepare Moses' designated successor for the travails that lie ahead (Num 32:28–30; Deut 1:37–38; 3:21–22, 28; 31:7–8, 14–15, 23; 32:44; Josh 1:1–9), so a series of speeches prepare Solomon for the future (1 Chr 22:7–16; 28:9–10, 20–21). Since the legacy of the reigning monarch is very much at stake in the career of his heir, it is in the father's best interests to set an agenda for his son. In this manner, David may directly influence the tenure of his heir for years, if not decades, to come. By the same token, it is in the best interests of the reigning king to allocate state resources to aid and abet the agenda he sets for the crown prince (22:1–5, 14–16). To this end, David makes his own generous personal contribution (29:3–5). The decision to publicize his intentions at this point is strategic. In a communal setting, David's gifts induce popular generosity (29:5–9). The unsparing contributions of the people explicitly recall the people's gifts to the Tabernacle in the time of Moses (NOTES). The quality and quantity of endowments legitimate the Temple and ease the burden of Solomon's task (Josephus, *Ant.* 7.377–378).

If the transition to the reign of the heir apparent is to be orderly, it should be well-planned and carefully managed. Such diligent preparation requires concerted action in both the private world of the royal family and the public world of civic policy. To this end, David prepares his courtiers, officers, governmental officials, and sacerdocy for the royal succession (22:17–19; 28:1–8). To be sure, as royal servitors, state officials may actually have little public voice in the larger issues of the transition, but it is nevertheless useful to inform them and secure their support. As part of the official preparations, it is no less important that the heir apparent receive public backing from other princes within the royal family and from state bureaucrats (29:23–24). In this respect, the grooming of the heir apparent in public serves a variety of complementary purposes. Communal ceremonies instruct the crown prince, secure his position among the elite, and enlist public backing for the proposed succession. Indeed, in the final round of official ceremonies (29:1–24), David does not speak to Solomon at all. Instead, David focuses his energies on the body politic (29:1–9, 20). Public displays of support may establish a momentum that will be difficult to arrest, much less reverse.

But even all of these provisions, however prudent, may not be enough. The days of the elderly potentate are numbered and his death could unleash forces beyond his control. The bureaucracy, established to provide continuity and security, could become unwieldy or, worse, resistant to the new monarch's rule. The new king, "young and inexperienced," could prove to be unequal to the task. In Chronicles, Reḥoboam is a parade example (Knoppers 1990). Taking office after Solomon's death, a weak and inexperienced (נער ורך-לבב) Reḥoboam could not withstand (התחזק) those much stronger than him (2 Chr 13:4–7; cf. 1 Chr 29:1). Even supposing that the heir apparent could secure the kingdom, the new monarch, having been freed from the control of his father, might wish to pursue a new and different course.

David's final prayer (29:10–19) should be set against this background. Unlike the farewell discourse of Jacob (Gen 49:1–28) and the Blessing of Moses (Deut 33:1–29), both of which concentrate on predicting the future of individual tribes, David's farewell address opens with a doxology (1 Chr 29:10–13), continues with a thanksgiving and confession (29:14–17), and concludes with petitions (29:18–19). Unlike the Song of Moses, which lists divine benefactions, a history of Israelite disloyalty, divine punishments, and a future divine deliverance (Deut 32:1–43), the prayer of David does not forecast the future. To be sure, David's earlier speeches, as well as the petitions (1 Chr 29:18–19), establish his understanding of what remains to be done. But as in his earlier dynastic prayer (17:16–27), David acknowledges that the future is ultimately out of his control. In this respect, the tone and tenor of David's final speech could not differ more from his final speech in Kings. There David commands Solomon to obey Yhwh's commands and employ his wisdom to wreak vengeance on a series of remaining foes (1 Kgs 2:1–9). Here, however, David ends his public career with self-abnegation. Tributes to Yhwh's majesty, greatness, and power amount to more than perfunctory praise. In this respect, there are parallels between David's final prayer and the psalm anthology he had the Asaphite Levites sing at the ascent of the Ark (16:8–36). Prayerful acclamations of divine sovereignty (29:11–12) are appropriate at critical moments in the life of cult and kingdom (NOTES to v. 12) because the future belongs to God. Yhwh's own involvement in the life of Solomon will be crucial to determining David's legacy and establishing Solomon's success.

The thanksgiving and confession (29:13–17) following the opening address (vv. 10–12) situate the events of the moment in a larger theological perspective, contrasting divine power, everlasting rule, and benevolence with human weakness, transience, and dependence. David's poignant remarks about the transience of life (v. 15) befit someone about to end his life's work. Israel's accomplishments under David do not affect the fundamental fact that "even within their secure boundaries the people are still sojourners" (Williamson 1982b: 185–86). Taken by themselves, David's efforts are not and cannot be enough. Whatever his accomplishments might be, they represent the work of one generation and pale in comparison with Yhwh's eternal and universal power (v. 14). Indeed, what David and the people offer to God is itself indicative of Yhwh's beneficence to them (vv. 13–14, 16). David can only point to the devotion and joy with which he and the people have brought their offerings (v. 17).

Ascriptions and confessions contrasting divine majesty and constancy with human vulnerability and helplessness lay the foundation for two petitions (vv. 18–19). David and the people he commands are resident aliens before Yhwh (v. 15), but the deity whom David worships is the God of the Ancestors (vv. 10, 15), the "God of Abraham, Isaac, and Israel" (29:18). The founding father asks that God, who is not limited by the passing of generations, take charge of future generations, directing the hearts of his people (v. 18) and granting Solomon a "whole heart" to practice Yhwh's commandments and build the citadel (v. 19). In this manner, David's final prayer reinforces and augments the sentiments he proclaimed in his earlier prayer (17:16–27). There, in response to Nathan's dynastic oracle, David praised Yhwh's incomparability, his election of Israel, and his control over the past and the future to petition for the realization of Yhwh's pledge to establish David's house (17:23–26). With dynastic continuity for one generation all but assured (23:1; 29:22–24), David petitions for the realization of another divine promise: the construction of the Temple.

If David's prayer can be read in the context of the Chronicler's work and, more broadly, in the context of earlier biblical writings, it can also be read in the context of the late Persian and early Hellenistic periods. The use of late terminology (e.g., *bîrâ*) blurs the distinction between the First and Second Temples. In seeing such terminology, the Chronicler's readers would be more likely to associate David's temple complex with their own. That the preparations resemble those for the Tabernacle only reinforces the authority of the Second Temple. If readers recognized the allusions to Moses' preparations for the construction of the Tabernacle and the people's generous response to these efforts (see NOTES), they might also discern a line of continuity from the central cultic institution of the Sinaitic era to the central cultic institution of their own era.

The repeated stress on the voluntary and generous giving is also noteworthy in a late setting. David's provisions for the Temple were "commensurate with all of [his] ability" (29:2). Out of solicitude for "the house of my God," David gave abundantly out of his own private holdings (vv. 3–5). The Israelite leaders responded to David's request for freewill offerings by making all sorts of gifts to the treasury of the House of Yhwh (29:6–8). One cannot help but wonder whether the presentation of boundless kindness, the donation of "freewill offerings to Yhwh with a whole heart" (29:9), is geared toward addressing the needs of the author's own time. Constructing a temple along with its attendant buildings was an expensive proposition in the ancient Mediterranean world and the maintenance and staffing of these buildings required a continuing investment of considerable resources (Oppenheim 1961: 165–68; Whitelam 1986; 1992). These costs could be offset, however, by the income that temples and palaces received or generated through offerings, endowments, conscription, gifts, taxes, booty, and tribute (Heltzer 1979: 459–96; Larsen 1979: 79–86; Liverani 1979). But the Jerusalem Temple, unlike most other temples in the Achaemenid Empire, does not seem to have had its own extensive lands to support it (Dandamaev and Lukonin 1989: 360–66). This meant that the Jerusalem Temple depended on the goodwill of supporters for its maintenance.

To complicate matters further, Persian period writers do not speak with one voice on the subject of the shrine in Jerusalem. The author of Isa 66:1 distances the Second Temple from God's heavenly residence, questioning whether the transcendent Yhwh really needed this earthly abode:

The heavens are my throne,
and the earth is my footstool.
Where is this house that you would build for me?
And where is this place for my rest?

In the early Persian period, the prophet Ḥaggai was told by the people that the time had not yet come to rebuild Yhwh's sanctuary (1:2). Ḥaggai complains that Yehud's residents were more anxious to build their own houses than they were to build the House of Yhwh (1:2–4). The people reside in "paneled houses," while the House of Yhwh lies "in desolation" (1:4). Living at a time in which the Temple had already been built, the author of Mal 3:6–9 protests that Judeans were not always generous in either the quantity or the quality of their temple offerings.

One wonders whether the high view of the central sanctuary in Chronicles is designed to counter such positions. Over against the author of Isa 66:1, David refuses to drive a wedge between Yhwh's heavenly and earthly residences. The Temple is "the Holy House," "the House of my God" (1 Chr 29:3). The king, in fact, distances the Temple as a house of worship for Israelites from the Temple as a house of God when he asserts that "the citadel is not for man, but for Yhwh God" (29:1). Similarly, one wonders whether the enthusiasm and wholehearted support with which all of the people greeted David's plans for endowing the Temple is meant to address concerns similar to those raised by Ḥaggai and Malachi. The king prays for the kind of devotion toward the sanctuary that the people do not manifest in the books of Ḥaggai and Malachi. Israel's reverend king does his utmost to prepare for the Temple even though he himself is expressly forbidden from building it. That "the time has not come" to build the sanctuary does not dissuade a conscientious ruler from doing all in his power to make the promised shrine a reality. The priorities reflected in the distinction between the people's living in paneled houses and the House of God lying in desolation are the reverse of those expressed by David and Israel's leadership. Knowing that God "tests the heart" *(bōḥēn lēbāb)* and "desires justice" *(mêšārîm tirṣeh)*, David generously donated, "with a just heart" *(bĕyōšer lĕbābî)*, a wealth of materials for temple construction and watched with joy as the people of Israel did likewise (29:17).

It would seem that the Chronicler exhorts his audience to exhibit the unanimity and devotion that attended the preparations for the First Temple. The Israel of the United Monarchy acted without hesitation or complaint. In this respect, the first petition is especially relevant, because it is more open-ended than the second. The second petition centers on one person in one generation: Solomon. David prays that Yhwh might grant his son "a whole heart" *(lēbāb šālēm)* to follow Yhwh's commands and build the citadel for which David made provision (29:19). But the first petition, aimed at the people, is explicitly intergenerational. David asks that the God of the Ancestors "keep such forms of thought in the mind of your people forever *(lĕʿôlām)* and direct their hearts *(hākēn lĕbābām)* toward you" (29:18). David's final request for his people is that they might always manifest such enthusiasm and commitment toward Yhwh. The use of prayer to end David's reign turns out to be an effective means through which the author communicates central concerns to his audience. Inherent in David's blessing is a recognition of Yhwh's ability to take care of his people throughout the generations. Inherent in David's confession is a candid acknowledgment that Israel is ultimately dependent on God for its very existence. Inherent in both petitions is an expression of trust in God's willingness to involve himself in the life of his people. What David asks of his subjects is that they respond to Yhwh in accordance with their God-given talents and abilities. In portraying the unanimity and generosity of Israel in David's final days, the Chronicler provides his readers with an ideal of such devotion.

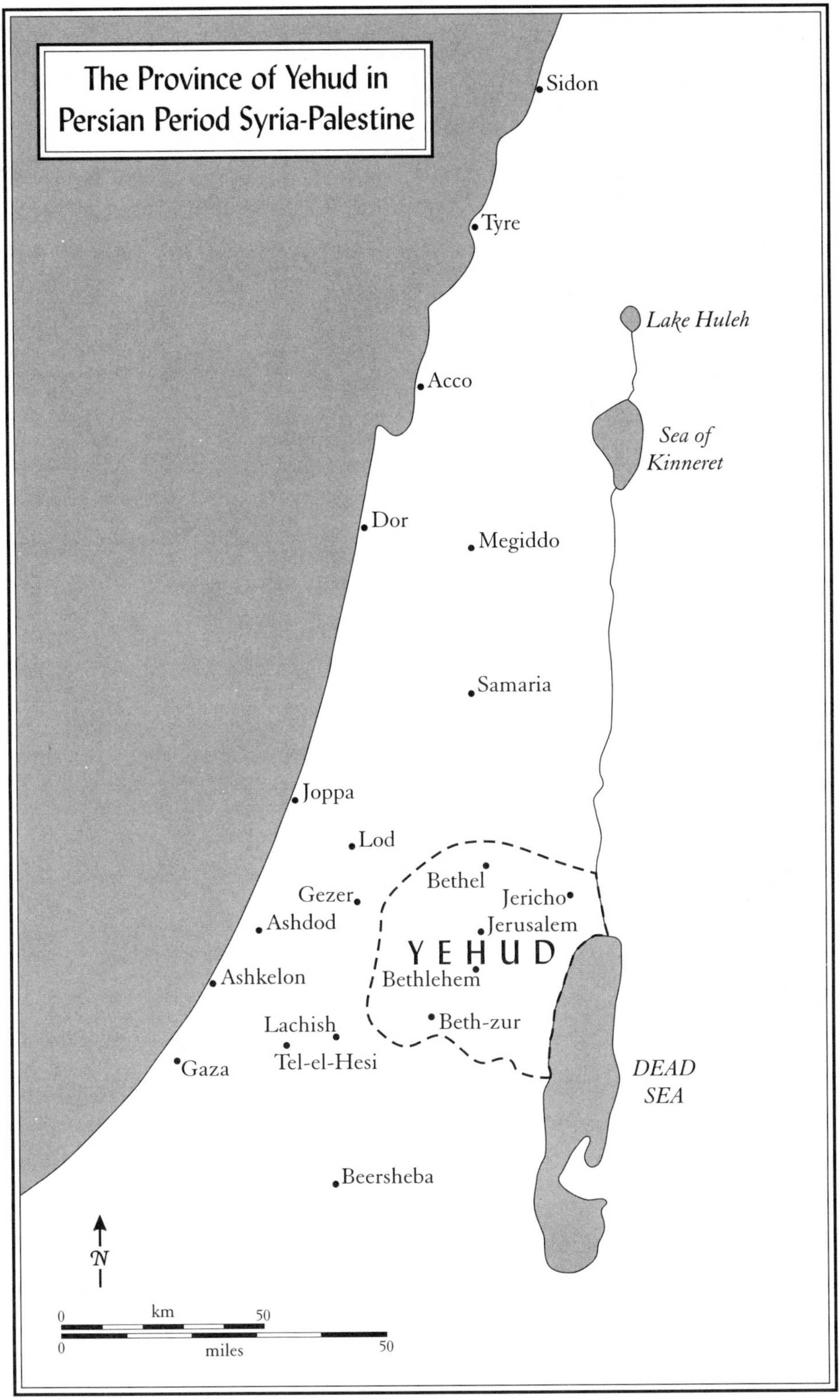
The Province of Yehud in Persian Period Syria-Palestine
Sidon
Tyre
Lake Huleh
Acco
Sea of Kinneret
Dor
Megiddo
Samaria
Joppa
Lod
Bethel
Gezer
Jericho
Ashdod
Jerusalem
YEHUD
Ashkelon
Bethlehem
Lachish
Beth-zur
Gaza
Tel-el-Hesi
DEAD SEA
Beersheba
N
0
km
50
0
miles
50

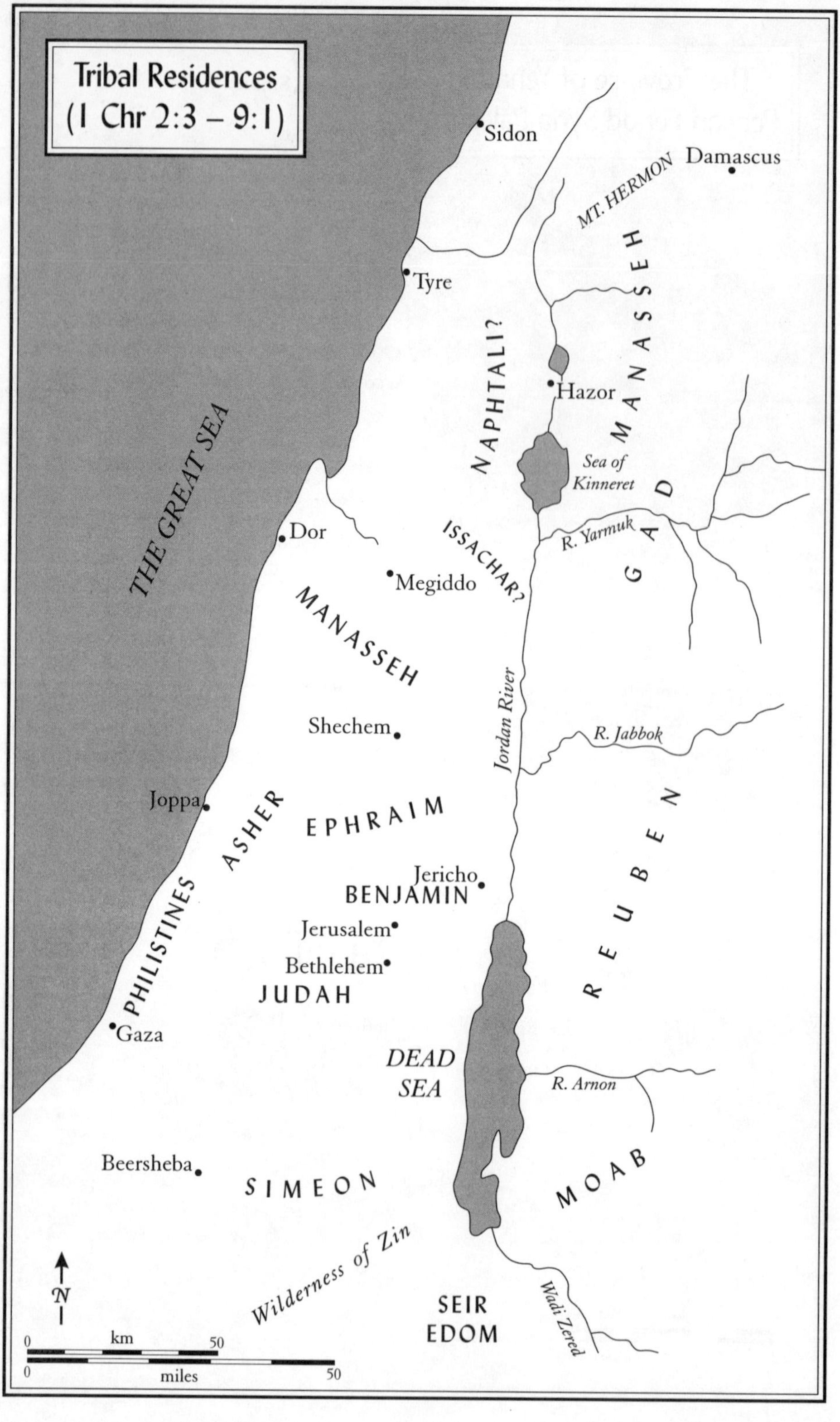

Tribal Residences
(1 Chr 2:3 – 9:1)
Sidon
Damascus
MT. HERMON
Tyre
MANASSEH
NAPHTALI?
Hazor
Sea of Kinneret
GAD
THE GREAT SEA
Dor
ISSACHAR?
R. Yarmuk
Megiddo
MANASSEH
Jordan River
Shechem
R. Jabbok
Joppa
ASHER
EPHRAIM
REUBEN
Jericho
BENJAMIN
PHILISTINES
Jerusalem
Bethlehem
JUDAH
Gaza
DEAD SEA
R. Arnon
Beersheba
SIMEON
MOAB
Wilderness of Zin
N
SEIR
EDOM
Wadi Zered
0 km 50
0 miles 50

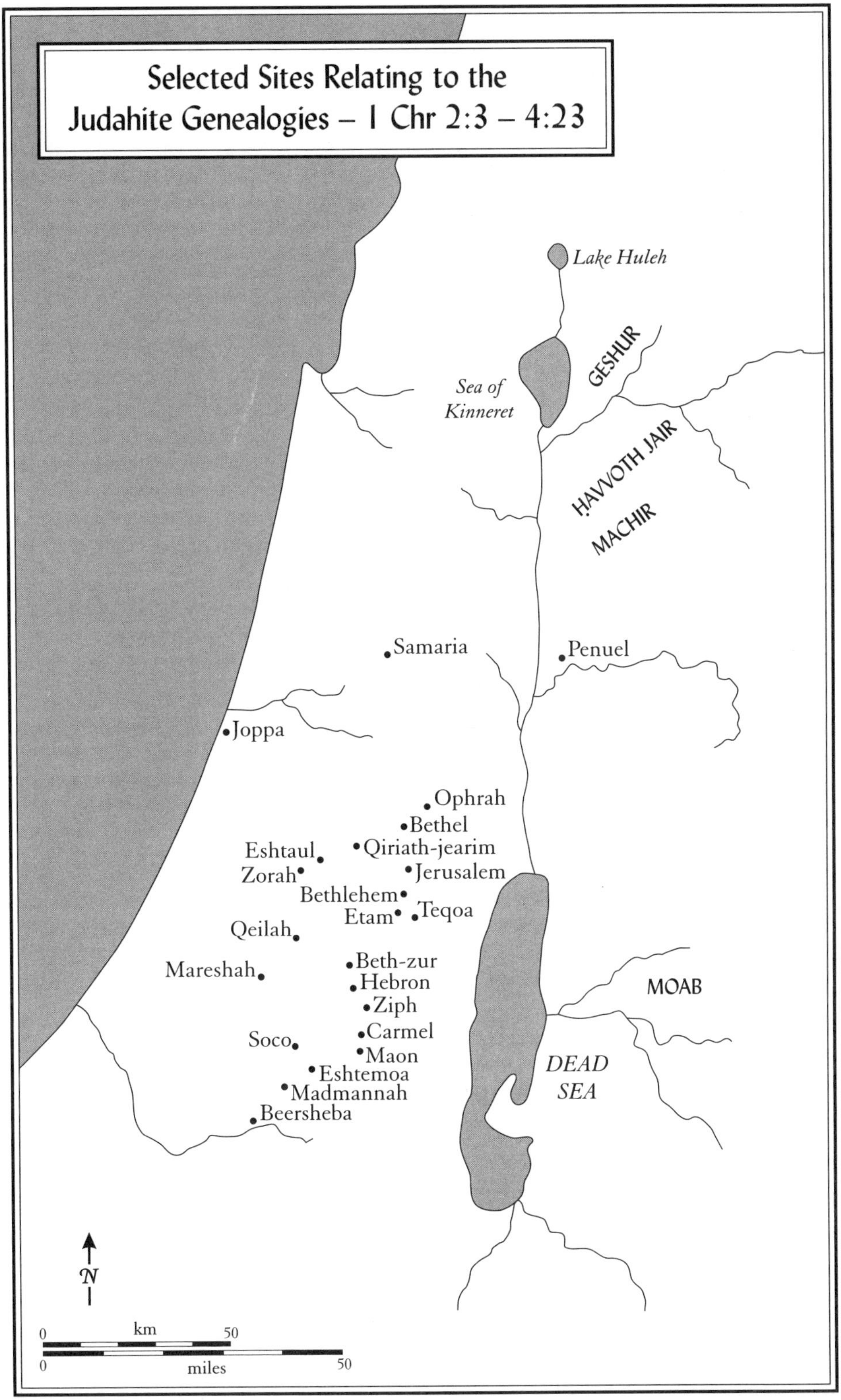
Selected Sites Relating to the
Judahite Genealogies – 1 Chr 2:3 – 4:23
Lake Huleh
GESHUR
Sea of
Kinneret
ḤAVVOTH JAIR
MACHIR
Samaria
Penuel
Joppa
Ophrah
Bethel
Eshtaul
Qiriath-jearim
Zorah
Jerusalem
Bethlehem
Etam
Teqoa
Qeilah
Mareshah
Beth-zur
Hebron
Ziph
MOAB
Carmel
Soco
Maon
Eshtemoa
DEAD
SEA
Madmannah
Beersheba
N
0
km
50
0
miles
50

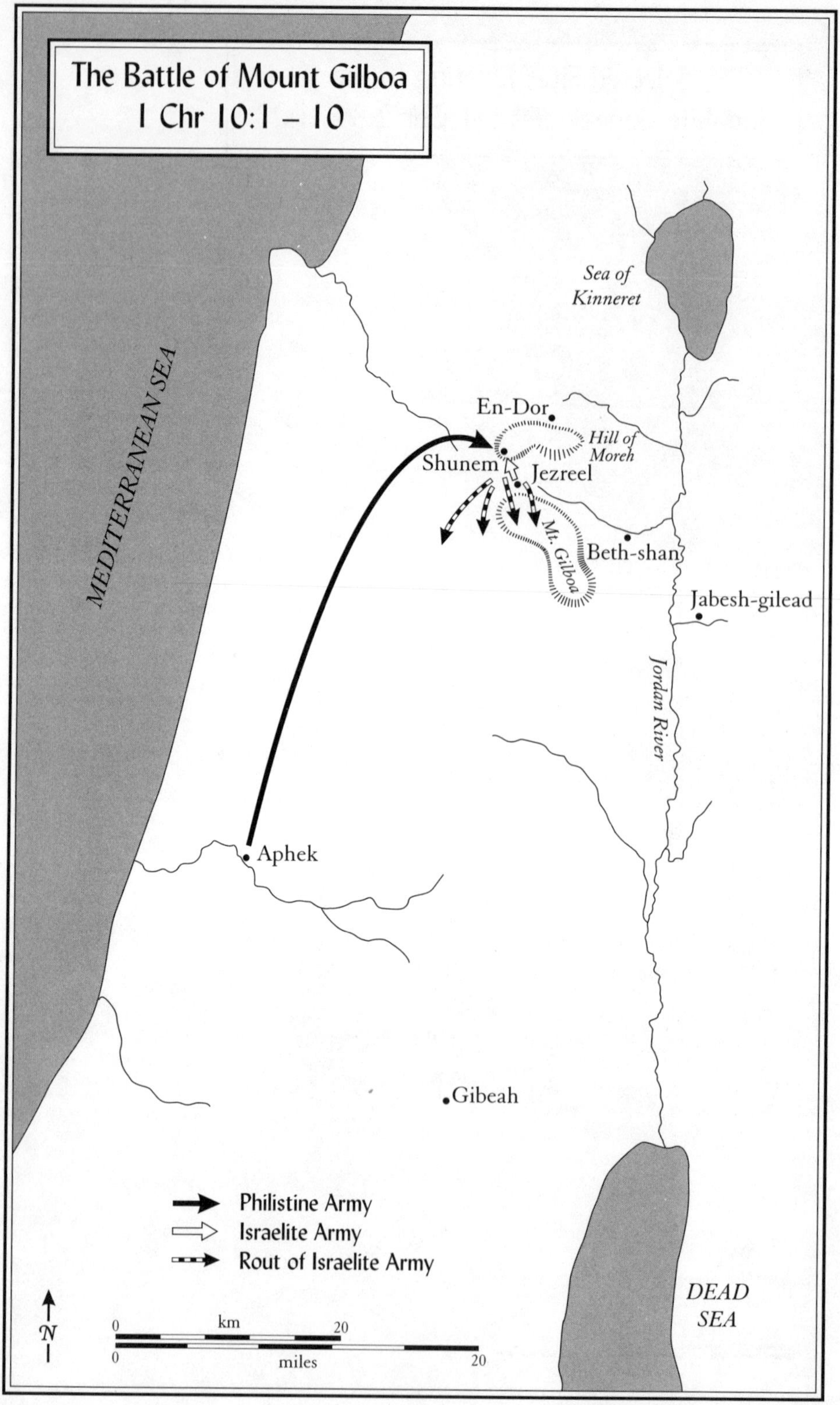
The Battle of Mount Gilboa
1 Chr 10:1 – 10
MEDITERRANEAN SEA
Sea of Kinneret
En-Dor
Hill of Moreh
Shunem
Jezreel
Mt. Gilboa
Beth-shan
Jabesh-gilead
Jordan River
Aphek
Gibeah
DEAD SEA
Philistine Army
Israelite Army
Rout of Israelite Army
N
0
km
20
0
miles
20

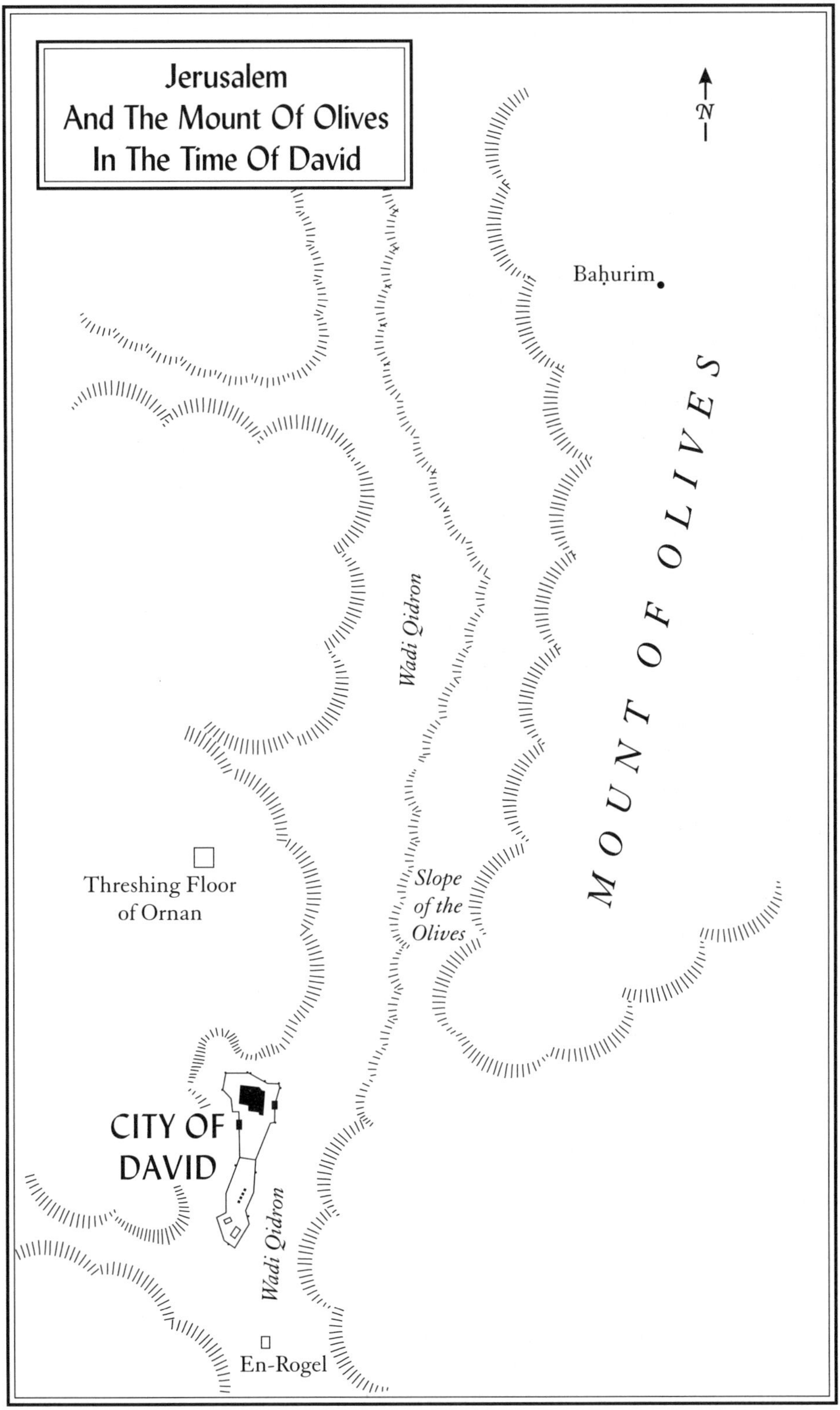
Jerusalem
And The Mount Of Olives
In The Time Of David
N
Baḥurim
MOUNT OF OLIVES
Wadi Qidron
Slope of the Olives
Threshing Floor of Ornan
CITY OF DAVID
Wadi Qidron
En-Rogel

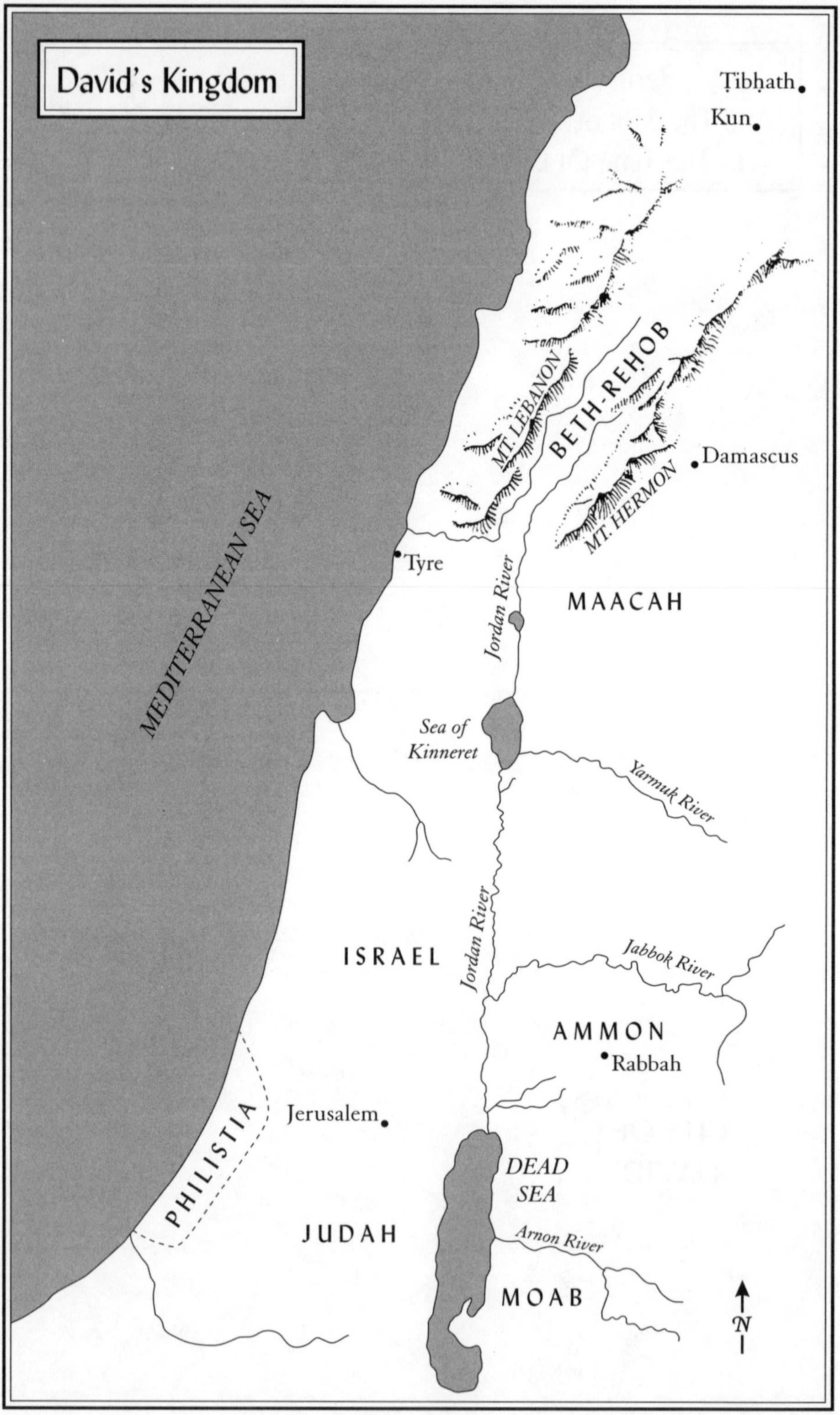
David's Kingdom
Ṭibḥath
Kun
MT. LEBANON
BETH-REḤOB
Damascus
MT. HERMON
MEDITERRANEAN SEA
Tyre
Jordan River
MAACAH
Sea of Kinneret
Yarmuk River
Jordan River
ISRAEL
Jabbok River
AMMON
Rabbah
PHILISTIA
Jerusalem
DEAD SEA
Arnon River
JUDAH
MOAB
N

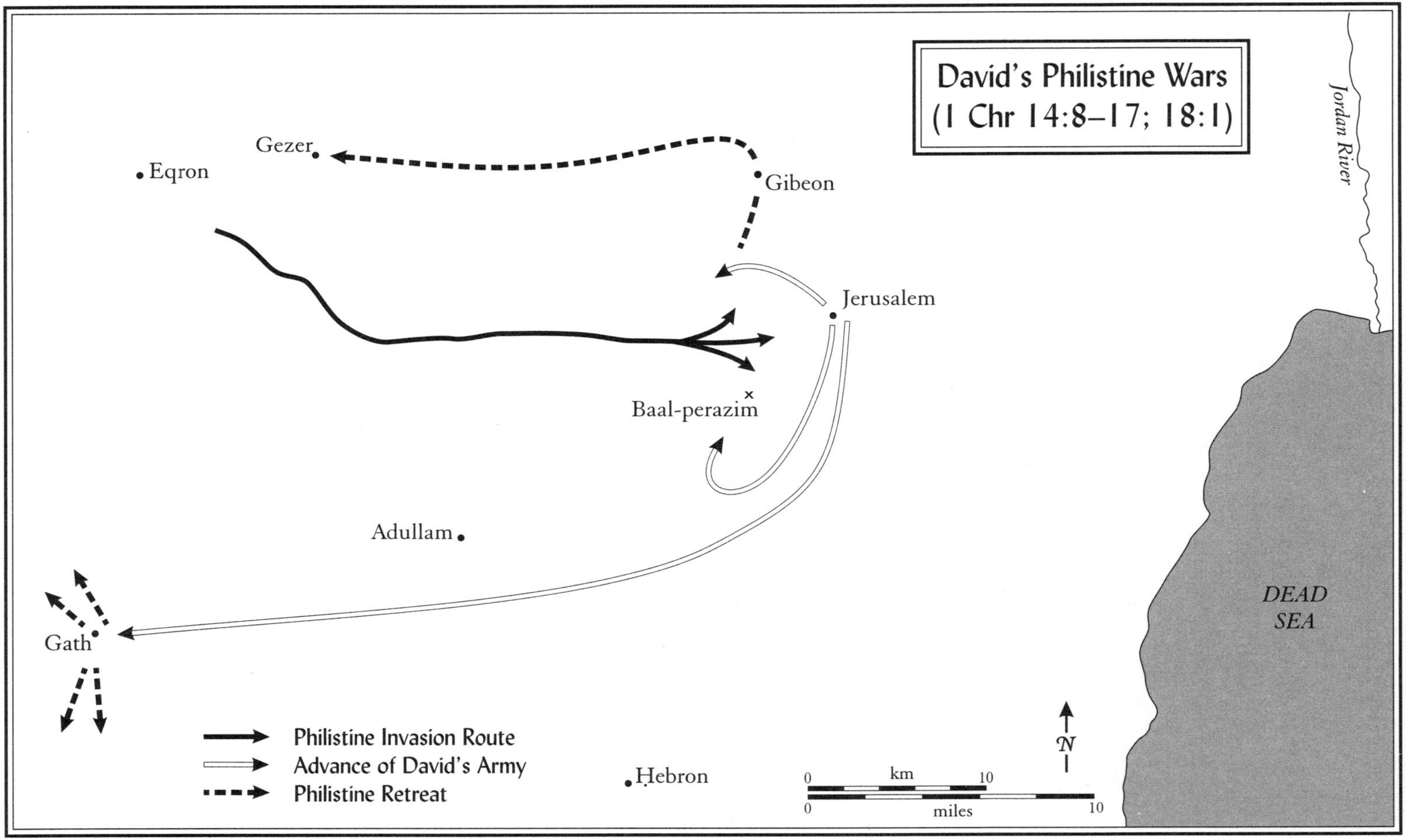
David's Philistine Wars
(1 Chr 14:8–17; 18:1)
Jordan River
Gezer
Eqron
Gibeon
Jerusalem
Baal-perazim
Adullam
Gath
DEAD SEA
Hebron
Philistine Invasion Route
Advance of David's Army
Philistine Retreat
N
0
km
10
0
miles
10

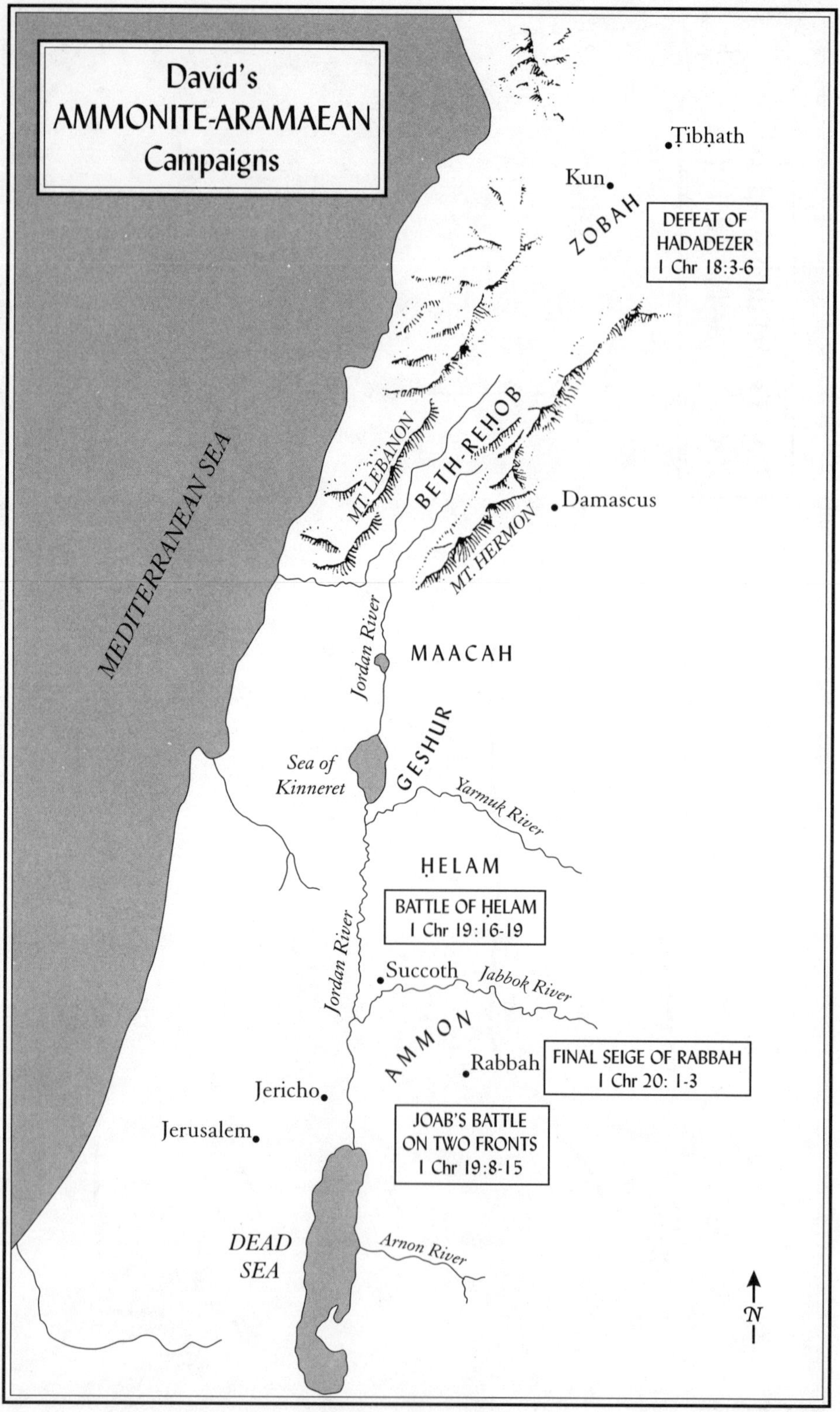
David's
AMMONITE-ARAMAEAN
Campaigns
Ṭibḥath
Kun
ZOBAH
DEFEAT OF
HADADEZER
I Chr 18:3-6
MEDITERRANEAN SEA
MT. LEBANON
BETH-REḤOB
Damascus
MT. HERMON
Jordan River
MAACAH
GESHUR
Sea of
Kinneret
Yarmuk River
ḤELAM
BATTLE OF ḤELAM
I Chr 19:16-19
Jordan River
Succoth
Jabbok River
AMMON
Rabbah
FINAL SEIGE OF RABBAH
I Chr 20: 1-3
Jericho
Jerusalem
JOAB'S BATTLE
ON TWO FRONTS
I Chr 19:8-15
DEAD
SEA
Arnon River
N

# Index of Biblical References

◆

# Index of Ancient Text References

# INDEX OF MODERN AUTHORS

◆

# INDEX OF SUBJECTS

C

D

H

I

Q



R